JUVENILE
DELINQUENCY

Sara Miller McCune founded SAGE Publishing in 1965 to support the dissemination of usable knowledge and educate a global community. SAGE publishes more than 1000 journals and over 800 new books each year, spanning a wide range of subject areas. Our growing selection of library products includes archives, data, case studies and video. SAGE remains majority owned by our founder and after her lifetime will become owned by a charitable trust that secures the company's continued independence.

Los Angeles | London | New Delhi | Singapore | Washington DC | Melbourne

JUVENILE
DELINQUENCY

PATHWAYS AND PREVENTION

CHRISTOPHER A. MALLETT

Cleveland State University

MIYUKI FUKUSHIMA TEDOR

Cleveland State University

Los Angeles | London | New Delhi
Singapore | Washington DC | Melbourne

FOR INFORMATION:

SAGE Publications, Inc.
2455 Teller Road
Thousand Oaks, California 91320
E-mail: order@sagepub.com

SAGE Publications Ltd.
1 Oliver's Yard
55 City Road
London EC1Y 1SP
United Kingdom

SAGE Publications India Pvt. Ltd.
B 1/I 1 Mohan Cooperative Industrial Area
Mathura Road, New Delhi 110 044
India

SAGE Publications Asia-Pacific Pte. Ltd.
3 Church Street
#10–04 Samsung Hub
Singapore 049483

Acquisitions Editor: Jessica Miller

Content Development Editor: Adeline Wilson

Editorial Assistant: Rebecca Lee

Marketing Manager: Jillian Ragusa

Production Editor: Veronica Stapleton Hooper

Copy Editor: Sheree Van Vreede

Typesetter: C&M Digitals (P) Ltd.

Proofreader: Dennis W. Webb

Indexer: Beth Nauman-Montana

Cover Designer: Gail Buschman

Printed in the United States of America

Library of Congress Cataloging-in-Publication Data

Names: Mallett, Christopher A., author. | Tedor, Miyuki Fukushima, author.

Title: Juvenile delinquency : pathways and prevention / Christopher A. Mallett, Cleveland State University, Miyuki Fukushima Tedor, Cleveland State University.

Description: Thousand Oaks : Sage, [2019] | Includes bibliographical references and index.

Identifiers: LCCN 2018008353 | ISBN 9781506361024 (pbk. : alk. paper)

Subjects: LCSH: Juvenile delinquency—United States. | Juvenile justice, Administration of—United States. | Juvenile delinquents—United States.

Classification: LCC HV9104 .M238 2019 | DDC 364.360973—dc23
LC record available at https://lccn.loc.gov/2018008353

This book is printed on acid-free paper.

18 19 20 21 22 10 9 8 7 6 5 4 3 2 1

BRIEF CONTENTS

©iStockphoto.com/imaginima

DETAILED CONTENTS

Chapter 2. The History of Juvenile Justice and Today's Juvenile Courts   26

Chapter 3. The Measurement of Juvenile Crime   44

©iStockphoto.com/South_agency

PART II: THEORIES OF DELINQUENCY

©iStockphoto.com/BrandyTaylor

PART III: PROBLEMS THAT LEAD TO DELINQUENCY

©iStockphoto.com/powerofforever

©iStockphoto.com/DGLimages

©iStockphoto.com/Daisy-Daisy

©iStockphoto.com/omgimages

PART IV: SOLUTIONS TO DELINQUENCY

©iStockphoto.com/Rawpixel

©iStockphoto.com/Ralph125

©iStockphoto.com/Magaiza

©iStockphoto.com/shironosov

PREFACE

*J*uvenile Delinquency: Pathways and Prevention explores the major themes and causes of delinquency, with a specific focus on young people most at risk for involvement with the criminal justice system. With a practitioner-oriented perspective, this textbook provides the full story of juvenile delinquency—one that emphasizes the pivotal role that family, trauma, mental health difficulties, and schools play, while exploring evidence-based prevention and intervention programs. Recognizing the many aspects that affect childhood and adolescent delinquency, this text offers students a framework and foundation for understanding juvenile delinquency that covers the traditional background needed (functioning and history of the courts, the measurement of delinquency, and theoretical explanations of crime) but goes much further in detailing the nature and diverse pathways of delinquency and what can be done to deter offending and criminal behavior.

The objective of this stand-alone textbook is to provide a comprehensive assessment of delinquency and the juvenile justice system that is focused on children and adolescents who are most at risk for involvement with the juvenile courts. In so doing, a broad paradigm is used, supported by and encompassing several theoretical views—social disorganization, life course (developmental), strain, and social learning—that integrate the individual, family, school, and community risks for delinquency. This textbook encapsulates the major explanations for why young people become formally involved with the juvenile courts, but it also shows how the recent punishment era has harmed adolescents and young adults. In addition, an extensive review is included of what evidence-based practice and policy recommendations should be pursued by juvenile justice and related stakeholders.

This textbook is organized into 4 distinct sections and 14 chapters. Each chapter includes many interactive and critical thinking sections, as well as special interest boxed features on (a) practice—"What can I do?"; (b) policy—"What's being done?"; and (c) research—"What works?." The **first** section (***Juvenile Justice System***) is an overview of the juvenile justice system—functions, processes, history, juvenile court structure, and measurements of delinquency and youthful offending.

Chapter 1 reviews how the juvenile justice system operates. From the initial police contact, diversion, and arrest decision-making, to youthful offender risk assessment, juvenile court referral, delinquency adjudication, and use of detention/incarceration facilities. This chapter presents this overview and highlights the purpose of the juvenile justice system, interrelationship with the adult criminal courts, and rights of the arrested and accused. In addition, the functioning of the child welfare system is included, as well as examining how it interacts with the juvenile courts.

Chapter 2 reviews the history and formation of the juvenile justice system. This includes an analysis of juvenile justice's ongoing historical shifts from a rehabilitative to a punitive focus (almshouses, houses of refuge, the Child-Saving Movement, and the institutionalization of youthful offenders), along with the establishment of the juvenile courts around the turn of the 20th century. Also included is an analysis of the establishment of youthful offender Constitutional rights, recent U.S. Supreme Court decisions on youthful offender sentencing, and today's state trends moving away from a "tough-on-crime" paradigm and the utilization of evidence-based juvenile court practice.

Chapter 3 provides up-to-date information from key national data sources on arrests, status offenses, police contact, detention, and deeper penetration by young people into the juvenile justice system including incarceration and transfers to adult criminal court. This includes reporting on the following: Uniform Crime Reports; National Incident-Based Reporting System; National Crime Victimization Survey; National Longitudinal Survey of Youth; National Youth Survey-Family Study; Monitoring the Future; Youth Risk Behavior Surveillance System; and national (Office of Juvenile Justice and Delinquency Prevention) juvenile court reports.

The **second** section (***Theories of Delinquency***) is an in-depth overview of the many historical and current theories of delinquency and crime, highlighting how these have changed over time and what empirical evidence there is across these paradigms. These two comprehensive theory chapters provide frameworks to understand the substantial issues related to delinquency and the juvenile justice system discussed throughout the textbook.

Chapter 4 begins with a discussion of theoretical issues and concepts of delinquency and crime, including the definition of crime, the conflict versus consensus models of law, the stance on human nature, the unit of analysis, the nature versus nurture debate, free will versus determinism, internal or external factors, change or static factors, distal or proximate explanations, and specific versus general explanations. Next reviewed are important theories—the preclassical and classical, early biological, early social structural, modern biological, and modern psychological—while keeping the chronological order of the theory development and highlighting some of the historical backdrops wherein these theories of crime were developed.

Chapter 5 reviews the theories of crime that emerged post-1930, including sociological theories and the biosocial approach. The differences among the major sociological paradigms of crime and delinquency are compared and contrasted, including the following: strain/anomie theories; social disorganization theory; learning theories; subcultural theories; control/neoclassical theories; modern classical theories; social reaction, critical, and feminist theories; and life-course theories.

The **third** section (***Problems That Lead to Delinquency***) is a comprehensive assessment of the struggles experienced by many vulnerable children and adolescents in the United States. A developmental perspective is used to review childhood and family delinquency risks and difficulties—poverty, maltreatment, unsafe neighborhoods, trauma, and mental health—and later adolescent challenges—offending behaviors, special education disabilities, academic failure, drug use, and bullying, among others. In so doing, it is explained how and why certain numbers of these young people end up involved in harsh school and/or juvenile justice discipline systems and who are disproportionately impacted, what traumas they experience, who have poor school outcomes, and what delinquency pathways they follow.

Chapter 6 reviews the disproportionate impact punitive juvenile justice and school policies have on certain child and adolescent populations, including racial/ethnic minorities, victims of abuse or neglect and those who have witnessed violence; those with special education disabilities; and those who identify as lesbian, gay, bisexual, or transgender (LGBT).

Chapter 7 examines how adolescents are developmentally different from young adults and the numerous pathways youthful offenders take to harsh discipline outcomes. The most difficult and harmful are juvenile and adult criminal justice incarcerations, placements that preclude successful reentry for many of the young people returning back to their community. These punishment pathways make it difficult for youthful offenders to divert from poor outcomes and are reinforced by zero-tolerance-focused school policies and punishment-focused juvenile courts. The risk for traumatic experiences and suicide greatly increases the further a young person penetrates the juvenile justice system and, in particular, when incarcerated.

Chapter 8 traces the historical development of discipline in schools, with a focus on the most recent zero tolerance movement that significantly shifted and increased school discipline in the 1990s. These discipline measures brought increased student exclusion through school suspensions and expulsions, decreasing the chances for these students to succeed in school and increasing their risk for juvenile court involvement. These changes were brought about because of several factors—school shootings, fear of adolescent "super-predators," and the juvenile justice system's shift toward punishment and away from rehabilitation. Because of these changes, most schools greatly increased security measures within their buildings and the use of police officers on campus. These changes lead to what many have come to identify as a "school-to-prison" pipeline.

Chapters 9 and 10 use the social disorganization and life-course (developmental) theoretical frameworks to review the impact of trauma and related difficulties (including maltreatment), mental health disorders, and special education disabilities on delinquency outcomes. With most youthful offenders formally involved with juvenile courts suffering from at least one, if not more than one, of these difficulties or disabilities, evidence is clear that these problems are significant risks for delinquency. These two chapters cover specific discussions of the types, impact, and prevalence of these problems for children and adolescents, gender-identified differences, and how the juvenile courts have become the inappropriate referral of last choice for many of these young people.

The **fourth** section (***Solutions to Delinquency***) reviews the empirical evidence on what stakeholders in the juvenile justice, youth-caring, and schools systems can do to improve child and adolescent outcomes. These chapters focus on minimizing childhood and adolescent risks and traumas through early assessment and prevention, treatment of the risks and problems identified, school inclusion efforts, diverting and rehabilitating most of these young people away from punishment and the juvenile justice system, and identifying what works for those adolescents formally involved (low level and serious offending) with the juvenile courts.

Chapter 11 discusses how many of the factors linked with later juvenile court involvement are rooted in childhood, making it critical to investigate this developmental time period, and it is divided into two sections—primary- and secondary-school-aged young people. The earlier a difficulty or problem is identified in children, the better the chance that harm can be minimized and outcomes improved; hence, striving to understand onset and occurrence of these matters is important. If the etiology and scope of the problems are identified and understood, more effective steps can be taken by policy makers and stakeholders in delinquency prevention. Programs that focus on the primary risk factors for delinquency are included in prevention and intervention/programming for trauma, maltreatment, and mental health/substance abuse problems.

Chapter 12 provides evidence of how to move from punitive to rehabilitative policies and practices in schools and school districts. In some states and jurisdictions, there have been successful changes, modifications to policies, and much improved outcomes for most students. To do so, schools have moved away from zero tolerance policies and have incorporated reformations as well as inclusive (keeping students in school) programming—positive behavioral protocols, conflict resolution, truancy prevention, and increased family and student engagement, among others. In addition, improved screening and identification of risks and difficulties can lead to significantly improved outcomes and fewer referrals to police and juvenile courts.

Chapter 13 focuses on the rehabilitation and diversion of low-level offenders from the juvenile courts. Most young people who have an initial contact with law enforcement and the juvenile courts do not have a second contact. These initial contacts are most often misdemeanors or status offenses. Nonetheless, contact with the juvenile justice system provides an important opportunity for the juvenile courts and related youth-caring systems to identify and assist adolescents with difficulties, as well as to desist behaviors or decisions that lead to initial contact. Thus, there is a focus on these effective interventions and diversions, used in the juvenile justice system and through community-based efforts.

And finally, *Chapter 14* focuses on the rehabilitation of serious and chronic offenders involved with the juvenile courts. Most of these young people have committed felonies or have become habitual low-level offenders. Hence, examples, discussions, and highlights are provided of how juvenile courts use their supervision and programming, probation departments, and detention and incarceration facilities to improve serious youthful offender outcomes. There are effective ways to reduce recidivism, have youthful offenders complete school, and improve transitions to young adulthood.

DIGITAL RESOURCES

SAGE edge offers a robust online environment featuring an impressive array of tools and resources for review, study, and further exploration, keeping both instructors and students on the cutting edge of teaching and learning. SAGE edge content is open access and available on demand. Learning and teaching has never been easier!

SAGE edge for Instructors supports teaching by making it easy to integrate quality content and create a rich learning environment for students.

- **Test banks** provide a diverse range of pre-written options as well as the opportunity to edit any question and/or insert personalized questions to assess students' progress and understanding.
- Editable, chapter-specific **PowerPoint® slides** offer complete flexibility for creating a multimedia presentation for the course.
- EXCLUSIVE! Access to full-text **SAGE journal articles** have been carefully selected to support and expand on the concepts presented in each chapter to encourage students to think critically.
- **Video and multimedia links** that appeal to students with different learning styles
- **Lecture notes** summarize key concepts by chapter to ease preparation for lectures and class discussions.
- **Sample course syllabi** for semester and quarter courses provide suggested models for structuring one's course.
- A **list of today's key theorists** related to juvenile delinquency with links to their webpages and photographs
- A set of all the **graphics from the text**, including all of the maps, tables, and figures, in PowerPoint, .pdf, and .jpg formats for class presentations
- SAGE's **course cartridges** provide you with flexible, editable content in formats that import easily into your learning management system. Course cartridges include test banks, PowerPoint® slides, and links to multimedia assets to help you build an engaging, comprehensive course. SAGE's course cartridges are compatible with many popular learning management systems.

SAGE edge for Students provides a personalized approach to help students accomplish their coursework goals in an easy-to-use learning environment.

- Mobile-friendly **eFlashcards** strengthen understanding of key terms and concepts.
- Mobile-friendly practice **quizzes** allow for independent assessment by students of their mastery of course material.
- **Video and multimedia links** that appeal to students with different learning styles

- <u>EXCLUSIVE!</u> Access to full-text **SAGE journal articles** that have been carefully selected to support and expand on the concepts presented in each chapter

ACKNOWLEDGMENTS

This textbook could not have gotten off the ground without the keen professional work and perspective of SAGE's former publisher, Jerry Westby. Through early text draft proposals and consultations, Jerry saw that the broad and inclusive early outlines had the potential to bring a unique review of delinquency to students. Jerry's efforts set the stage for SAGE's subsequent publisher, Jessica Miller, and her top content development editors, Neda Dallal and Adeline Wilson, to take this project through the important and vital review stages, significant revisions, and final production. Jessica and her team worked tirelessly to keep the project on track and to creatively and professionally improve the text organization and every chapter. The textbook would not be nearly what it is without them. The SAGE Team is an impressive industry-leading group.

Publisher's Acknowledgments

SAGE wishes to acknowledge the valuable contributions of the following reviewers:

Kenneth Colburn, Butler University

Verna R. Jones, PhD, Jackson State University

Soraya (Kris) Kawucha, University of North Texas, Department of Criminal Justice

William E. Kelly, PhD, Auburn University

Victor Shaw, California State University—Northridge

Tia Stevens Andersen, University of South Carolina

Riane M. Bolin, Radford University

Kadee L. Brinser, Sam Houston State University

Mary E. Pyle, MSCJ, MSHE, Tyler Junior College

Michael Pittaro, PhD, East Stroudsburg University, East Stroudsburg, Pennsylvania

Shelley Grant, Jacksonville University

Angela Wartel, Lewis-Clark State College

Melissa Harrell, Bainbridge State College

Prof./Atty. Daniel Hebert, Springfield Technical Community College

Robbin Day Brooks, MSW, CPP—Arizona State University's School of Criminology & Criminal Justice

Dr. S. Kawucha, Sam Houston State University

Dr. Dorinda L. Dowis, Professor, Columbus State University

Dr. J.W. Carter II, Mount St. Joseph University

Karin Tusinski Miofsky, PhD,.

Michael D. Brooks, Associate Professor of Criminal Justice, Dyersburg State Community College

ABOUT THE AUTHORS

 **Christopher A. Mallett**, Professor of Social Work, teaches delinquency, trauma, mental health policy, research methods, and statistics graduate and undergraduate courses at Cleveland State University. Dr. Mallett is licensed in Ohio as a social worker and attorney, and he has a 20-year history of clinically working with, advocating for, and representing vulnerable children, adolescents, and their families. His research is focused on disability law, juvenile delinquency, and young people with certain difficulties and their involvement with the juvenile justice system and school discipline protocols, specifically the impact of mental health disorders, substance abuse, special education disabilities, and trauma victimizations. As a consultant whose expertise is nationally tapped by juvenile courts, school districts, and children's service agencies, Dr. Mallett has published more than 55 research papers, book chapters, and technical assistance training briefs, as well as three books on these topics.

Miyuki Fukushima Tedor is an associate professor in the Department of Criminology, Anthropology, and Sociology at Cleveland State University. She received BA degrees in philosophy, psychology, and sociology and MA and PhD degrees in sociology. Her research is focused on cross-national testing of theories of crime and delinquency, gender and crime, juvenile delinquency, and drug and alcohol use and crime. She has taught in these areas for many years. Professor Tedor is originally from Japan and enjoys talking to her students about what it was like growing up there.

JUVENILE JUSTICE SYSTEM

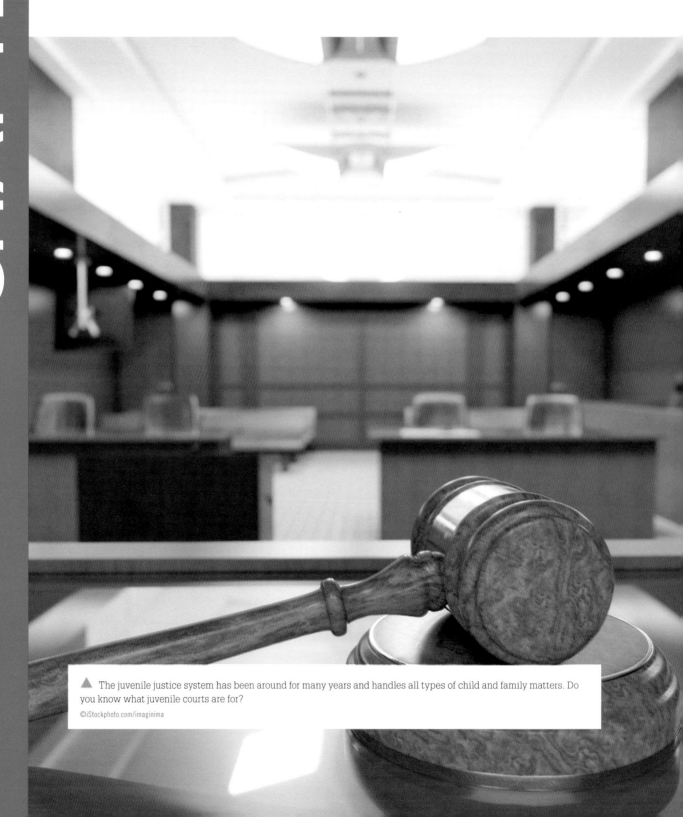

CHAPTER 1

THE FUNCTIONING OF THE JUVENILE JUSTICE SYSTEM

▲ The juvenile justice system has been around for many years and handles all types of child and family matters. Do you know what juvenile courts are for?

©iStockphoto.com/imaginima

INTRODUCTION

The juvenile justice system handles legal matters involving a *juvenile*, defined for jurisdictional purposes in most states as a person who is younger than 18 years of age, although there are exceptions. A separate legal system for juveniles was established in the United States more than 100 years ago based on the belief that children are different than adults, and thus, they should be treated differently. The juvenile justice system in the United States is not a cohesive framework, and although there are similarities across state laws, policies, and procedures, each state has its unique system. Even though it is common to focus on the court, the juvenile justice system encompasses several subsystems, such as the police, probation, and corrections, all of which work together to bring about the process that is referred to as *juvenile justice*. Ancillary systems also exist that are unique to the juvenile justice system, including the child welfare system, schools, and behavioral health (mental health and substance abuse) systems. These ancillary systems are intricately involved with the juvenile justice because of the myriad difficulties and troubles that young people and their families face before and during involvement with the juvenile justice system. Although not considered to be part of the juvenile justice system, ancillary systems have a significant impact on the juvenile justice process and outcomes of those involved.

JUVENILE COURTS

Juvenile courts are controlled by local jurisdictions and exist in every state throughout the country as part of 50 different and separate state court systems. Federal courts also exist, where a small but significant number of young people end up, as well as tribal courts on Native American territories. In some states, courts with juvenile jurisdiction are referred to as district, superior, circuit, county, family, or probate courts. Regardless of the name used, each state has a court that has specific jurisdiction to hear cases involving a juvenile. In addition, many courts with jurisdiction over juveniles also hear other family-related cases, including child support parentage and custody issues between unmarried individuals, adoption, and guardianship, as well as some criminal cases involving a child victim (Sickmund & Puzzanchera, 2014).

Juvenile courts were established based on the doctrine of "parent of the nation" (*parens patrie*); as such, it acts "in the place of a parent" (*in loco parentis*) for the best interest of children who are in need of help and guidance. Juvenile court, therefore, differs from adult court in with a focus on individual, rather than on offense, and an emphasis on treatment and rehabilitation rather than on punishment. Juvenile court is considered civil, not criminal, and the juvenile is charged with engaging in a delinquent act, rather than in a crime. Civil courts handle most matters that do not involve criminal acts; criminal courts handle personal and property crimes (Platt, 2009; Sickmund & Puzzanchera, 2014).

When a jurist (judge or magistrate) determines that a juvenile has committed a delinquent act, he or she does not find the juvenile guilty of a crime because the word "guilt" implies criminal intent; rather, he or she adjudges the juvenile to be delinquent. Once adjudicated as delinquent, the jurist does not impose the juvenile a sentence because a "sentence" implies punishment for a crime; rather, he or she renders his disposition. This distinction in most

Juvenile (Juvenile Offenders): Term used commonly in the juvenile justice system for adolescents (persons younger than 18 years of age) involved with the courts.

Parens patriae: Philosophical and legal doctrine ("parent of the country") that becomes a guiding juvenile justice principal with the state acting as benevolent legal parent to a child.

In loco parentis: A philosophical and legal doctrine that is part of the juvenile justice framework and means "in place of the parents."

Civil Courts: Courts dealing with noncriminal cases.

Criminal Courts: Courts dealing with personal and property criminal cases.

 Juvenile court proceedings include a judge (magistrate), prosecuting attorney, defense attorney, the young person, and depending on the situation, family members. How would you have handled a situation like this as a teenager?

instances means that a juvenile who is found delinquent has not been "convicted" of a crime, which relieves the jurist of any duty to report his or her delinquency finding. When a young person who has been found delinquent seeks education, employment, or housing, and is asked whether he or she has a criminal conviction, in most cases, as long as the case was handled in juvenile court, the young person can truthfully answer "no" to that question. Not having to report a finding of delinquency as a crime helps reduce some of the stigma and supports the rehabilitative philosophy that began the juvenile justice system (Sickmund & Puzzanchera, 2014).

The rehabilitative framework in juvenile justice, however, has shifted numerous times over the past few generations. A rehabilitative philosophy today no longer extends to all matters related to delinquency, and many states have increasingly passed more punitive laws that are focused on punishing juvenile offenders. Different states today allow for findings of delinquency to extend into adulthood, and several additional consequences can negatively impact juveniles who have been found delinquent. These "collateral consequences" vary between states, but some can be severe and include enhancements to adult sentences based on findings of delinquency (Burrell & Stacy, 2011; Griffin, 2008; Snyder & Sickmund, 2006). The consequences that a youth offender and his or her family might be subjected to include lifelong registration on a public offender list if convicted of a sexual offending crime; significant hurdles to attaining education; barriers to employment, professional licensing, subsidized housing, military service, and college entrance; assessment of fines, penalties, and restitution; publically available court records; risk to immigration status; termination of the right to vote or to serve on a jury; loss of driving privileges; and possible future prosecution.

JUVENILE COURT PURPOSE

Each state's juvenile code begins with a purpose statement that provides a framework for decision-making in cases involving juveniles charged with delinquent acts and provides an understanding of the state's philosophy on juvenile justice (Table 1.1). State juvenile code purpose statements fall into five distinct groups, with numerous states incorporating more than one of these philosophies of purpose. First, the purpose clauses in at least 20 states and the District of Columbia are modeled after the Balanced and Restorative Justice (BARJ) philosophy that provides for a balance between public safety, individual accountability to the victim and community, and the development of skills to help offenders become law-abiding and productive citizens. Second, 20 states model their purpose clauses after the **Standard Juvenile Court Act** (originally issued in 1925 and revised in 1959), which provides that, "[E]ach child coming within the jurisdiction of the court, shall receive. … the care, guidance and control that will conduce to his welfare and the best interest of the state, and that when he is removed from the control of his parents the court shall secure for him as nearly as possible equivalent to that which they should have given him" (Office of Juvenile Justice and Delinquency Prevention, 2013). Third, 11 states model their purpose clauses after the *Legislative Guide for Drafting Family and Juvenile Court Acts* (Sheridan, 1969) that is concerned with the care and protection of children's mental and physical development, incorporating supervision and rehabilitation, removing a child from their home only when necessary to the child or public safety, and guaranteeing constitutional rights. Fourth, the purpose clauses in at least five states have a child welfare focus, with the "best interest of the juvenile" as the sole or primary purpose of the juvenile justice system. And fifth, those in at least six states are considered "tough on

Adjudges: Jurist makes a decision; also, adjudicates.

Disposition (Hearing): A legally binding decision by a judge or magistrate.

Standard Juvenile Court Act: A federal act that was originally issued in 1925 concerning the handling of children under the care of the court.

ADOLESCENTS ARE NOT YOUNG ADULTS

The recent development in brain science, through different imaging technologies, allows professionals to see the differences in adult and adolescent brains and has confirmed the long-held view that children are different than adults. Today, there is an increased understanding that children are developmentally immature compared to adults neurologically, cognitively, intellectually, and psychosocially. This affects how adolescents think and behave, which is different from the way adults think and behave. The brain section that controls "executive functioning" does not stop developing until well into early-to-mid-20s. This brain area, called the *prefrontal cortex*, is associated with numerous important cognitive functions, such as long-term thinking,

weighing consequences of one's decisions and behaviors, and delaying impulsive reactions, all of which are found to be significantly associated with the engagement in risky behaviors, including delinquency and crime (Gottfredson & Hirschi, 1990; Larson & Grisso, 2011).

1. **Why do you think that the threat of long-term imprisonment is often an ineffective deterrent for young people?**

2. **How should juvenile court judges approach teenagers, knowing they are so different from adults?**

---

crime," resembling the purpose of the adult criminal court, in that they emphasize offender accountability and punishment, deterrence, and community protection (Office of Juvenile Justice and Delinquency Prevention, 2013).

JUVENILE COURT JURISDICTION

In most states, the juvenile court has the original jurisdiction over cases that involve delinquency committed by those who were younger than age 18 at the time of an offense, arrest for an offense, or referral to the juvenile court for an offense. There are exceptions to this general rule and significant variations by state in terms of the definition of delinquency and status offense, the age of jurisdiction, and waiver to other court jurisdictions.

AP Photo/Jake May | MLive.com

▲ Young people who are formally involved with the juvenile courts experience hearings and procedures that are similar in many ways to adult criminal courts. Do you think this is the best practice?

Delinquency and Status Offenses

Though **delinquency** is an act committed by a juvenile that would be considered a crime if committed by an adult, a **status offense** is a violation only when it is committed by a person younger than the age of 18 because of his or her status as a juvenile (Development Services Group, Inc., 2015). The definition of both delinquency and status offense varies depending on each state's definition, much like the definition of crime (e.g., the recreational use of marijuana is legal in some states but illegal in others). Delinquency offenses include murder, rape, assault, burglary, robbery, larceny-theft, motor vehicle theft, drug sales, illegal possession of firearms, and arson, among others. Status offenses include alcohol law violation, running away from home, curfew violation, disobeying parents, and truancy, among others. The term used to classify a status offender varies by state and includes "a child in need of supervision," "a child in need of services," "a child in need of aid, assistance or care," and "unruly child" (Office of Juvenile Justice and Delinquency Prevention, 2014b).

Delinquency (Delinquent): Ongoing committing of criminal acts or offenses by a young person, normally younger than 18 years of age.

Purpose Clauses for Juvenile Courts, 2012

Statistical Briefing Bok > Juvenile Justice System Structure & Process

Organization & Administration of Delinquency Services

Q: How do states define the purpose of their juvenile courts?

A: There is considerable variation in the way states define the purposes of their juvenile courts. Some declare their goals and objectives in exhaustive detail; others mention only the broadest of aims. Often more than one philosophy influences a single state's purpose clause.

Purpose Clauses for Juvenile Courts, 2012

State	Balanced and restorative justice	Standard Juvenile Court Act	Legislative guide	Emphasis on punishment, deterrence, accountability, and/or public safety	Emphasis on Child welfare
Number of states	21	20	11	6	5
Alabama	X				
Alaska	X				
Arizona					X
Arkansas		X	X		
California	X	X			
Colorado	X				
Connecticut				X	
Delaware		X			
District of Columbia	X				
Florida	X	X			
Georgia		X			
Hawaii				X	
Idaho	X				
Illinois	X	X			
Indiana	X				
Iowa		X			
Kansas	X				
Kentucky					X
Louisiana		X			
Maine		X	X		
Maryland	X				
Massachusetts		X			
Michigan		X			
Minnesota	X	X			
Mississippi		X			

State	Balanced and restorative justice	Standard Juvenile Court Act	Legislative guide	Emphasis on punishment, deterrence, accountability, and/or public safety	Emphasis on Child welfare
Missouri		X			
Montana	X		X		
Nebraska	X				
Nevada		X			
New Hampshire			X		
New Jersey	X	X	X		
New Mexico			X		
New York		X			
North Carolina				X	
North Dakota					X
Ohio			X		
Oklahoma	X				
Oregon	X				
Pennsylvania	X				
Rhode Island		X			
South Carolina		X			
South Dakota		X			
Tennessee			X		
Texas			X	X	
Utah				X	
Vermont	X				
Virginia			X		
Washington	X				
West Virginia					X
Wisconsin	X				
Wyoming			X	X	

- The juvenile court purpose clause in at least 20 states and the District of Columbia incorporates the language of the Balanced and Restorative Justice movement, which advocates that juvenile courts give balanced attention to three primary interests: public safety, individual accountability to victims and the community, and the development in offenders of those skills necessary to live law-abiding and productive lives.

- The purpose clauses in at least 20 states appear to be influenced by the Standard Juvenile Court Act. The purpose of this Act, originally issued in 1925 and subsequently revised numerous times, was that "each child coming within the jurisdiction of the court shall receive . . . the care, guidance, and control of his parents the court shall secure for him care as nearly as possible equivalent to that which they should have given him."

- Other states use all or most of a more elaborate, multi-part purpose clause contained in the Legislative Guide for Drafting Family and Juvenile Courts Acts, a publication issued by the Children's Bureau in the late 1960s. The Legislative Guide's opening section declares four purposes: (a) to provide for the care, protection, and wholesome mental and physical development of children involved with the juvenile court; (b) to remove from children committing delinquent acts the consequences of criminal behavior, and to substitute therefore a program of supervision, care, and rehabilitation; (c) to remove a child from the home only when necessary for his welfare or in the interests of public safety; (d) to assure all parties their constitutional and other legal rights.

- Purpose clauses in 6 states can be loosely characterized as "tough," in that they stress community protection, offender accountability, crime reduction through deterrence, or outright punishment, either predominantly or exclusively.

- Statutory language in 5 states emphasizes the promotion of the welfare and best interests of the juvenile as the sole or primary purpose of the juvenile court system.

Source: OJJDP Statistical Briefing Book 2012.

In most states, the same court handles both delinquency and status offense cases. The process of handling status offenders in the juvenile justice system, however, differs from the process of handling delinquent offenders. The Juvenile Justice and Delinquency Prevention Act, for instance, mandates that the state not incarcerate juveniles who are involved in status offenses or abuse and neglect cases. In particular, the Act cites neglect as one of the areas over which juvenile courts also have jurisdiction, and child welfare cases where a child's needs are not being met (Office of Juvenile Justice and Delinquency Prevention, 2014b).

The U.S. Congress passed the Juvenile Justice and Delinquency Prevention Act in 1974 (revised in 1980, 1992, 1996, and 2002), the first comprehensive federal law for the prevention of delinquency. The Act is overseen by the Office of Juvenile Justice and Delinquency Prevention (OJJDP), part of the U.S. Department of Justice (DOJ). The Act provides funding to states that comply with four "core requirements" (Table 1.2). In 2015, all states, except Wyoming, and the U.S. territories participated in the program, and almost all of them met the first three requirements, but many are trying to address the disproportionately higher involvements of minority offenders at every stages of the juvenile justice system, also known as racial and ethnic disparities (Office of Juvenile Justice and Delinquency Prevention, 2015a).

Age of Jurisdiction

State laws vary concerning who falls under the jurisdiction of the juvenile court and the minimum ages at which juvenile offenders can be transferred to the adult court (Table 1.3). Nine states have the upper age for original juvenile court jurisdiction over delinquency cases younger than 17 (age 15 in NY and NC and age 16 in GA, LA, MI, MS, SC, TX, and WI as of 2015). In most states, there are statutory exceptions to the age of juvenile court jurisdiction, depending on the offender's age, the offense, and the prior juvenile court record of the offender, which may place some cases involving juvenile offenders under the jurisdiction of criminal (adult) court or under the jurisdiction of both juvenile court and criminal court. All but two states have the upper age of juvenile court jurisdiction over status offense cases at age 17 (age 16 in SC and TX as of 2015; Office of Juvenile Justice and Delinquency Prevention, 2015b).

Most states do not specify the lower age for juvenile court jurisdiction for delinquency cases. This means that these states can formally prosecute children at any age, except for 18 states that have the lower age of original juvenile court jurisdiction over delinquency

▼ TABLE 1.2

OJJDP Act Core Requirements

Deinstitutionalization of status offenders and nonoffenders	This requirement mandates that the liberty of youth offenders not be taken away through detention or placement in a secured facility if they did not commit a "crime," unless it is for a violation of a court order.
Sight and sound separation	This requirement mandates juvenile offenders be separated from adult offenders when they are being detained, such that detained juveniles should not be able to see, hear, or have any interactions with adult criminals.
Jail and lockup removal	This requirement mandates that juveniles not be detained in adult jails. Exceptions can be allowed as long as the "sight and sound separation" requirement can be met, such as in rural areas where there may be only one jail.
Disproportionate minority confinement	This mandates an effort to reduce the disproportionately higher minority youth involvement, relative to their proportion in the population, at every stage of the juvenile justice system.

Source: OJJDP Statistical Briefing Book.

Upper and Lower Age of Juvenile Court Delinquency and Status Offense Jurisdiction, 2016

Statistical Briefing Book > Juvenile Justice System Structure & Process

Jurisdictional Boundaries

Q: What are the upper and lower ages of delinquency and status offense jurisdiction?

A: **In the majority of states, the upper age is 17 and the lower age is not specified for delinquency and status jurisdiction.**

Upper and Lower Age of Juvenile Court Delinquency and Status Offense Jurisdiction, 2016

State	Delinquency lower age	Delinquency upper age	Status lower age	Status upper age
Alabama	NS	17	NS	17
Alaska	NS	17	NS	17
Arizona	8	17	8	17
Arkansas	10	17	NS	17
California	NS	17	NS	17
Colorado	10	17	NS	17
Connecticut	7	17	7	17
Delaware	NS	17	NS	17
District of Columbia	NS	17	NS	17
Florida	NS	17	NS	17
Georgia	NS	16	NS	17
Hawaii	NS	17	NS	17
Idaho	NS	17	NS	17
Illinois	NS	17	NS	17
Indiana	NS	17	NS	17
Iowa	NS	17	NS	17
Kansas	10	17	NS	17
Kentucky	NS	17	NS	17
Louisiana	10	16	NS	17
Maine	NS	17	NS	17
Maryland	7	17	NS	17
Massachusetts	7	17	6	17
Michigan	NS	16	NS	17
Minnesota	10	17	NS	17
Mississippi	10	17	7	17
Missouri	NS	16	NS	17
Montana	NS	17	NS	17
Nebraska	NS	17	NS	17
Nevada	NS	17	NS	17

(Continued)

State	Delinquency lower age	Delinquency upper age	Status lower age	Status upper age
New Hampshire	NS	17	NS	17
New Jersey	NS	17	NS	17
New Mexico	NS	17	NS	17
New York	7	15	NS	17
North Carolina	6	15	6	17
North Dakota	NS	17	NS	17
Ohio	NS	17	NS	17
Oklahoma	NS	17	NS	17
Oregon	NS	17	NS	17
Pennsylvania	10	17	NS	17
Rhode Island	NS	17	NS	17
South Carolina	NS	16	NS	16
South Dakota	10	17	NS	17
Tennessee	NS	17	NS	17
Texas	10	16	NS	17
Utah	NS	17	NS	17
Vermont	10	17	NS	17
Virginia	NS	17	NS	17
Washington*	NS	17	NS	17
West Virginia	NS	17	NS	17
Wisconsin	10	16	NS	17
Wyoming	NS	17	NS	17

Note: Table information is as of the end of the 2016 legislative session. *NS:* lower age not specified. *In Washington the lower age of delinquency jurisdiction is applied through a state juvenile court rule, which references a criminal code provision establishing the age youth are presumed to be incapable of committing crime.

- The upper age of jurisdiction is the oldest age at which a juvenile court has original jurisdiction over an individual for law violating behavior. An upper age of 15 means that the juvenile court loses jurisdiction over a child when they turn 16; an upper age of 16 means that a juvenile court loses jurisdiction when a child turns 17; and a upper age of 17 means that a juvenile court loses jurisdiction over a child when they turn 18.

- State statutes define which youth are under the original jurisdiction of the juvenile court. These definitions are based primarily on age criteria. In most states, the juvenile court has original jurisdiction over all youth charged with a criminal law violation who were below the age of 18 at the time of the offense, arrest, or referral to court. Some states have higher upper ages of juvenile court jurisdiction in status offense, abuse, neglect, or dependency matters—often through age 20.

- Many states have statutory exceptions to basic age criteria. The exceptions, related to the youth's age, alleged offense, and/or prior court history, place certain youth under the original jurisdiction of the criminal court. This is known as *statutory exclusion.*

- In some states, a combination of the youth's age, offense, and prior record places the youth under the original jurisdiction of both the juvenile and criminal courts. In these situations where the courts have concurrent jurisdiction, the prosecutor is given the authority to decide which court will initially handle the case. This is known as *concurrent jurisdiction, prosecutor discretion, or direct filing.*

- Since 1975 eight states have changed their age criteria. Alabama raised its upper age from 15 to 16 in 1976 and from 16 to 17 in 1977; Wyoming lowered its upper age from 18 to 17 in 1993; New Hampshire and Wisconsin lowered their upper age from 17 to 16 in 1996; Rhode island lowered its upper age from 17 to 16 and then raised it back to 17 again 4 months later in 2007; Connecticut passed a law in 2007 to raise its upper age from 15 to 17 gradually from 2010 to 2012; Illinois raised its upper age for misdemeanors from 16 to 17 in 2010; Massachusetts raised its upper age from 16 to 17 in 2013; Illinois raised its upper age for most felonies from 16 to 17 in 20147; and New Hampshire raised its upper age from 16 back to 17 in 2015.

Source: OJJDP Statistical Briefing Book 2016.

matters (age 6 in NC; age 7 in CT, MD, MA, NY, and ND; age 8 in AZ; and age 10 in AR, CO, KS, LA, MN, MS, PA, SD, TX, VT, and WI as of 2015). In these states, children who are younger than the specified age cannot be adjudicated delinquent and, thus, are not subjected to the formal prosecution. Additionally, six states had the lower age of original juvenile court jurisdiction over status offense matters (age 0 in AR, age 6 in MA and NC, age 7 in CT and MS, and age 10 in TX as of 2015; Office of Juvenile Justice and Delinquency Prevention, 2015b).

Waiver to Adult Court

Waiver to an adult court occurs when the jurisdiction of a case involving a juvenile offender is transferred from the juvenile justice system to the criminal justice system (also called a certification, transfer, or remand). Waiver is also used in federal cases involving juveniles who are at least 15 years of age and have violated federal criminal law. The waiver can occur at any stage of the juvenile justice system and, although jurisdictions vary in specific procedures, usually occurs in one of three ways (Sickmund & Puzzanchera, 2014).

First, in many jurisdictions, a serious violent offense, such as capital crime or murder, is automatically in the jurisdiction of the criminal justice system by statutory law and results in the automatic waiver or transfer of the youth offender to the adult court (also known as legislative waiver or statutory exclusion). Second, in some jurisdictions, certain offenses are in the jurisdiction of both the juvenile justice system and the criminal justice system (concurrent jurisdiction), and prosecutors have the discretion to decide whether to transfer such cases to the criminal justice system (also known as prosecutorial waiver or direct file). One issue considered by the prosecutor is the amenability of the juvenile offender to the intervention offered through juvenile court, which may be determined based on the juvenile's history of involvement in delinquency. Third, the most common waiver is judicial waiver, which gives the discretion to the judge to determine whether to transfer a case to the criminal justice system. During the 1980s, many states reformed laws to make it easier to try juveniles as adults in the criminal court by lowering the minimum age when juveniles can be transferred and expanding the eligible offense and prosecutorial discretion (Hockenberry & Puzzanchera, 2014a; Redding, 2010).

Some states have a "once an adult, always an adult" provision that requires a juvenile be tried as an adult for all subsequent offenses once he or she has been tried as an adult for an offense. Although some states have reverse waiver laws, which provide the criminal court judge the discretion to transfer a juvenile offender back to the juvenile court or to treat a defendant as a juvenile during sentencing (Sickmund, 2003), as of 2011, 14 states (AK, AR, CO, CT, IL, KS, MA, MI, MN, MT, NM, OH, RI, and TX) had juvenile court blended sentencing laws that allow juvenile courts to render a criminal sentence or both a juvenile disposition and a criminal sentence on certain offenses, usually serious offenses. In effect, blended sentencing laws allow for juvenile courts to render the same punishment to juveniles that adults receive on certain offenses. Also, 17 states (AR, CA, CO, FL, ID, IL, KY, MA, MI, MS, NE, NM, OK, VT, VA, WV, and WI) had criminal court blended sentencing laws that allow criminal courts to determine a juvenile disposition to juveniles who are transferred to the criminal court and found guilty of a crime. Both criminal court blended sentencing and reverse waiver are "fail-safe mechanisms" against mandatory statutory waivers, allowing the criminal court judge to reverse the decision and move the youth offender back to juvenile court jurisdiction. Nevertheless, of the 44 states with some type of mandatory waiver laws moving youth offenders to criminal court jurisdiction, only 33 of these states had a way to transfer the young person back to juvenile court jurisdiction (Sickmund & Puzzanchera, 2014).

Federal Courts and Jurisdiction

The **Federal Juvenile Delinquency Act** (implemented in 1938 and amended in 1948, 1974, and 1984) defines delinquency as "the violation of a law of the United States committed by a person prior to his eighteenth birthday which would have been a crime if committed by an adult" (Scalia, 1997, p. 1). Although small in number (less than 500 arrests per year), some juveniles

Federal Juvenile Delinquency Act: The first federal law established to handle those younger than the age of 18 who committed federal offenses.

who are apprehended by federal law enforcement agencies may be prosecuted in federal courts, (known as U.S. District Courts) and placed in the federal prisons, through the Federal Bureau of Prisons (Sickmund & Puzzanchera, 2014).

Juvenile offenders are most likely to encounter the following federal law enforcement agencies: Border Patrol, Drug Enforcement Agency, U.S. Marshals Service, and Federal Bureau of Investigation. In most cases, juveniles who are determined to have broken a federal criminal law are turned over to state or other local agencies if they are willing to accept the jurisdiction over the cases. A small number of delinquency cases, however, may be certified by the Attorney General for prosecution in U.S. District Courts, especially those involving a serious offense, such as a violent felony, an offense involving a firearm, or drug trafficking, and cases that are of interest to federal agencies (Sickmund, Sladky, & Wang, 2014).

THE PROCESS OF THE JUVENILE JUSTICE SYSTEM

With 50 state laws and the District of Columbia, having both philosophical and, in some areas, fiscal and regulatory impact on their local juvenile court jurisdictions, differences do exist across the juvenile justice system even within states. Although some procedures differ across juvenile court jurisdictions, most follow similar stages across case and delinquency processing (Figure 1.1).

Law Enforcement

Even though most juveniles in the United States admit to breaking law at some point, only a small number of juveniles end up being processed through the juvenile justice system. For these youthful offenders, the first contact with the juvenile justice system most likely occurs when they are apprehended by a law enforcement officer. The remaining cases are referred to the juvenile court by others, including parents, victims, school personal, and probation officers. A much smaller percentage of cases involving status offenses is referred to the juvenile court by law enforcement agencies because status offense cases are more likely to be referred by a child welfare agency (Sickmund & Puzzanchera, 2014).

The law enforcement agencies have a unique and important role within the juvenile justice system because of their involvement with noncrime matters, such as missing children, curfew violation, runaways, truancy, and neglect and abuse. One of the important functions of the law enforcement officer is the protection of children and the prevention of delinquency (Sanborn & Salerno, 2005). Most local police departments (90%) have special units dedicated to cases involving juveniles and family issues, and many (42%) employ sworn officers at schools, often known as school resource officers (Sickmund & Puzzanchera, 2014; U.S. Department of Education, 2016a).

After an apprehension, the law enforcement officer talks to the juvenile offender, the victim, and parents; reviews the offender's court record; and determines whether the offender should be referred to a juvenile court or diverted out to alternative programs. Of the cases where the juvenile justice system is the original jurisdiction, more than two thirds of cases are referred to juvenile court, whereas the remaining cases are either referred to criminal court or handled within law enforcement agencies. Alternatives to apprehension or referral to a juvenile court include questioning and warning, issuing a citation, or referral to a diversion program or service (Sickmund & Puzzanchera, 2014).

In case the temporary detention of a juvenile is required while contacting parents or a guardian or arranging the transportation to a juvenile detention facility, law enforcement agency personnel are required by federal regulations to detain the juvenile in a secure environment for no more than six hours. In addition, the Juvenile Justice and Delinquency Prevention Act mandates separation of juvenile offenders from adult offenders when they are being detained

Attorney General: Principal legal officer who represents a country or a state in legal proceedings and provides legal advice to the government.

School (Police) Resource Officers: Police officers that work on school campuses.

Flowchart of the Juvenile Justice Process

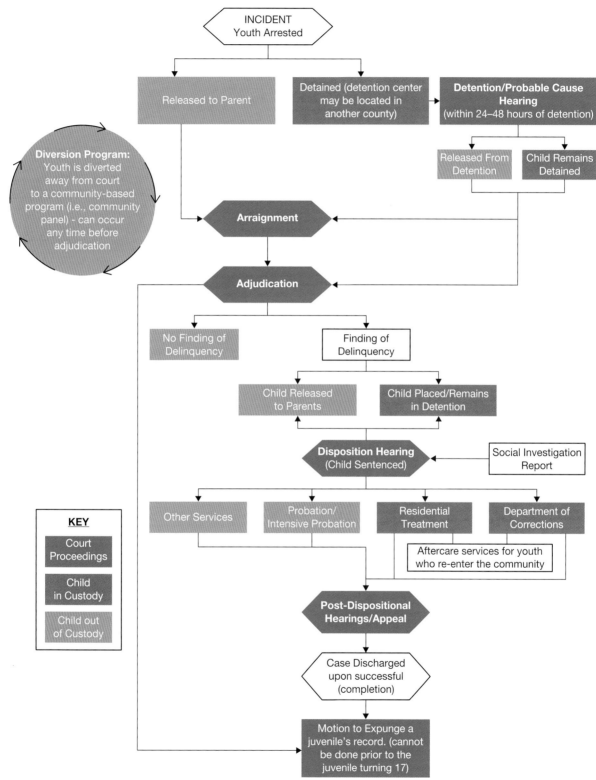

Source: Reprinted with permission from the National Juvenile Defender Center.

DUE PROCESS RIGHTS

A due process clause is included in the Fifth and Fourteenth amendments to the U.S. Constitution, which protects against unfair treatment and arbitrary administration of justice by the government. A series of landmark Supreme Court rulings in the 1960s have extended the following due process rights to youthful offenders in the juvenile courts, which traditionally were not subject to providing these rights because of their fundamental differences in philosophy with the criminal court:

- The Fourth Amendment guarantee against search and seizure.

- The Fifth Amendment guarantee against double jeopardy and self-incrimination.

- The Sixth Amendment guarantee for a speedy trial, knowing the charge, confronting and cross-examining the witness, calling witnesses at trial, and attorney representation.

- The Eighth Amendment guarantee against cruel and unusual punishment.

- The Fourteenth Amendment guarantee for equal protection (regardless of race, creed, color, or status).

1. **Do you think that providing these due process protections for youthful offenders was the right decision for the juvenile courts?**

2. **Do you think youthful and adult offenders should be afforded the same due process protections?**

▲ Police officers are at the front lines of community policing and are responsible for a majority of youth referrals to the juvenile courts. What have been your experiences with police officers?

Miranda Warning: A right-to-silence warning given by police to criminal suspects in police custody before they are interrogated.

(Office of Juvenile Justice and Delinquency Prevention, n.d.).

Advisement of Rights

Before questioning an individual in a criminal case, law enforcement officers are required to give a Miranda warning to inform the individual in custody of the right to remain silent and protection against self-incrimination and the right to an attorney. An individual is considered "in custody" if he or she does not reasonably feel free to leave in the presence of law enforcement. This is a complicated issue with juveniles because they may not understand Miranda rights as well nor feel as free to leave in the presence of law enforcement as adults do (Grisso & Schwartz, 2000; Rogers, Blackwood, Fiduccia, Steadham, & Drogin, 2012). In addition, because the juvenile court is expected to act in the best interest of the children, it originally was not subject to the procedural due process protections afforded to adult suspects, whose liberties were at stake. This began to change in the 1960s with a series of U.S. Supreme Court rulings that amended the procedures of the juvenile justice system, which today resembles the criminal justice system, and has increasingly afforded the same due process rights to juvenile offenders.

One issue that the U.S. Supreme Court has ruled on numerous times is the use of interrogation and the confession of juvenile suspects, which is a leading cause of wrongful conviction among youthful offenders, who are much more likely than adults to falsely confess (Malloy, Shulman, & Cauffman, 2013). The Court ruled more than 60 years ago for the first time on this issue arguing for law enforcement to interrogate juveniles with

MIRANDA RIGHTS, PROTECTION OF THE CONSTITUTION'S FIFTH AMENDMENT

A popularly used Miranda warning (see first quote below) requires a tenth-grade level of comprehension (Rogers, Hazelwood, Sewell, Harrison, & Shuman, 2008), which researchers in published empirical reviews (Grisso, 1980) indicate many juveniles may lack. When a law enforcement officer is dealing with a juvenile offender, the International Association of Chiefs of Police (2012, p. 7) in conjunction with the OJJDP, therefore, recommends a simplified version of Miranda warning (see second quote below) that requires a third-grade level of comprehension. In addition, the American Bar Association also called for the simplified Miranda warning to be used (in 2010) with juveniles (Rogers et al., 2012). Along with the simplified Miranda warning, the Association recommends that law enforcement also inform juvenile suspects before questioning that speaking may result in being tried as an adult.

"You have the right to remain silent. Anything you say can and will be used against you in a court of law. You have the right to an attorney. If you cannot afford an attorney, one will be provided for you. Do you understand the rights I have just read to you? With these rights in mind, do you wish to speak to me?"

"You have the right to remain silent. That means you do not have to say anything. Anything you say can be used against you in court. You have the right to get help from a lawyer right now. If you cannot pay a lawyer, we will get you one here for free. You have the right to stop this interview at any time. Do you want to talk to me? Do you want to have a lawyer with you while you talk to me?"

1. **Why do you think the revised Miranda warning version may be beneficial to youthful offenders?**

2. **Do you have other suggestions or changes that you think would help young people understand these rights?**

special care due to their immature age. The Court's position on this issue changed during the nation's "get tough on crime" period. In *J.D.B. v. North Carolina* (2011), however, the Court returned to its original position arguing that the suspect's youthful age should be taken into account when a law enforcement officer is determining whether the suspect is entitled to a Miranda warning.

Because juveniles who are questioned by a law enforcement officer at school often do not feel free to leave, they should be given a proper Miranda warning before being questioned. In addition, in *N.C. v. Commonwealth* (2013), the Kentucky Supreme Court ruled that a Miranda warning is required before students are questioned by school officials who are working in conjunction with law enforcement on a delinquency matter. Juveniles, like adults, can waive Miranda rights, but the prosecution must establish, before the evidence from the police questioning is admitted to the court, that the juvenile understood his or her rights and freely waived them before being questioned—the same standard used with an adult Miranda waiver (Feld, 2013).

Contrary to the depiction on TV police dramas, only a few states require a presence of a parent or a guardian during the questioning of a juvenile by law enforcement. Many states, however, require that a parent or a guardian be notified (or at least attempted to be notified) before a juvenile is being questioned. The presence of a parent during questioning by law enforcement can, however, be detrimental to a juvenile who is suspected of a delinquency because parents often pressure their child into a confession (Farber, 2004). Unfortunately, even with the high false confession and wrongful conviction rates, most law enforcement officers are not trained to interrogate youthful offenders (International Association of Chiefs of Police, 2012).

Diversion

Diversion occurs when a case is handled informally outside of juvenile courts and can occur at any stage of the juvenile justice system, from apprehension to postadjudication. Diversion to an

> **Diversion:** Definitions include nonarrest and release of a youthful offender back to the community, addressing the identified problems through rehabilitative means, and any attempt to divert from the juvenile justice system.

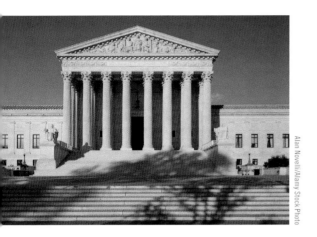

Alan Novelli/Alamy Stock Photo

▲ The United States Supreme Court has become increasingly involved in decisions on youthful offending sentencing, including the death penalty and life sentences without the possibility of parole. What do you think should be the most extreme sentence available for youthful offenders who commit a homicide? Does age make a difference? How about mitigating circumstances of the crime?

alternative program and service minimizes the negative consequences associated with being formally processed through the juvenile court (e.g., stigma, missing school, having a juvenile court record, and the school being notified). Diversion is also less costly and reduces the burden on the juvenile court that can then focus its limited resources on more serious and chronic offenders (including gang membership and activity).

An admission to the engagement in an alleged offense is required in most jurisdictions for a case to be processed informally. In what is considered formal diversion (differs from immediate diversion by law enforcement), the juvenile must also agree to specific conditions for a specified time period, spelled out in a written agreement, called a **consent decree**, and a probation officer is usually assigned to monitor the juvenile's compliance with the consent decree. If the juvenile successfully complies to all conditions, the case may be dismissed, although the case may be returned to the juvenile court and the formal processing of the case may resume if the juvenile fails to comply with the conditions (Sickmund & Puzzanchera, 2014). Diversion conditions may include victim restitution, fine, community service, school attendance, attendance in a drug and alcohol treatment program, and probation supervision. Various community, school, and private services and programs are offered through diversion, such as drug court, mental health court, teen court, victim–offender medication programs, mentoring programs, treatment programs, intervention programs, and parent training programs (Development Services Group, Inc., 2010).

The Prosecutor's Office

Once referred to the juvenile court, a juvenile offender goes through an intake screening, which is usually handled by probation departments or the prosecutor's office. After reviewing the case, including the age of offender, the seriousness of the offense, the juvenile court record, school record, and family information, an intake officer assigned to the case decides to request a formal intervention by juvenile court, proceed to informally handle the case, or dismiss the case altogether. Only half of all cases referred to juvenile court result in a formal intervention by juvenile court, whereas the other half are handled informally, and many informally handled cases are eventually dismissed often due to lack of evidence. For some serious offenses, the intake officer has no choice but to request a formal intervention by juvenile court, as dictated by law (Sickmund & Puzzanchera, 2014).

Once the intake officer decides to formally process a case in juvenile court, one of two petitions must be filed: a delinquency petition requesting an adjudicatory hearing or a waiver petition requesting a waiver hearing. The delinquency petition explains the allegations of the offense and requests that the juvenile be adjudicated a delinquent and made a ward of juvenile court. The waiver petition requests transferring of a case from juvenile court to criminal (adult) court.

Shelter Care Hearing and Pretrial Detention

After an apprehension by law enforcement, many juveniles are immediately released to a parent or a guardian. After the case is reviewed by an intake officer, some juveniles are held in a secure juvenile detention facility, pending a hearing before the judge. The decision for this detention is made by an intake officer based on seriousness of the alleged offense, the risk for flight or the likelihood of the juvenile appearing for the hearing, and the safety of the juvenile and the community. This is known as pre-adjudication detention, whereby youthful offenders are detained before adjudicated delinquent, which was held by the U.S. Supreme Court to be constitutional in *Schall v. Martin* (1984) to protect the juvenile and the community.

Juveniles may be placed in a secure detention facility at any stage of the juvenile justice system. Some juveniles may go in and out of a detention facility throughout the process until a dispositional hearing, and detention may sometimes extend beyond adjudicatory and dispositional hearings until a residential placement bed (e.g., shelter home or foster home) becomes available.

Consent Decree: An agreement or settlement that resolves a dispute between two parties without admission of guilt (in a criminal case) or liability (in a civil case).

In most states, juvenile offenders do not have the **right to bail** while awaiting the hearing, unlike adult offenders. In all states, a detention hearing in front of a judge must be held within a few days, usually within 24 hours, to determine whether the pre-adjudication detention of a juvenile is in the best interest of the community and the juvenile. If a juvenile is held in pre-adjudication detention, most states also require that an adjudication hearing take place within a specified time period, usually between 10 and 180 days (Sickmund & Puzzanchera, 2014).

Plea Bargaining

A **plea bargain** occurs when an offender admits to committing an offense in exchange for a lesser charge and a possibility of lesser sentence/disposition. Plea bargains are common; of all convictions in state and federal cases in both adult and juvenile courts, more than 95% are the result of plea bargaining (Redlick, 2010). Plea bargaining may occur at any stage of the juvenile justice system, but most likely it will occur prior to the adjudication hearing. States vary in terms of the use of plea bargain; some states with a heavy juvenile caseload may more frequently resort to plea bargains to free up the court load to focus on a smaller number of serious cases (Sickmund & Puzzanchera, 2014).

A plea bargain likely results in a lesser disposition for an offender, but the offender then relinquishes the right to a trial. The American Bar Association (ABA) warns juveniles against pleading guilty because of the extralegal "collateral consequences" discussed earlier in the chapter that are associated with this outcome. Like the use of interrogation and the higher risk for false confession, and thus, wrongful conviction among juveniles, there is also a higher risk among juveniles than adults for falsely pleading guilty to a "crime" they did not commit (Redlick, 2010; Shepherd, 2008).

Trial

Most juvenile courts have bifurcated hearings (trials) with a separate **adjudicatory hearing** and a **disposition hearing**. At the adjudicatory hearing, the facts of the case are presented in front of a judge who determines whether a juvenile is responsible for an alleged offense and, thus, should be adjudicated a delinquent. In two thirds of cases presented before a judge in juvenile court, juvenile offenders are adjudicated delinquent for the alleged offense. Only in some states do juveniles have the right to a **jury trial**. Juveniles today are afforded many other due process rights and the same rules as adults at the hearings (Sickmund & Puzzanchera, 2014).

Once a juvenile is adjudicated delinquent, a probation officer prepares a disposition plan based on his or her assessment of the juvenile, support systems, and available programs and services. The juvenile court may order psychological evaluations and diagnostic tests so that the probation officer can provide appropriate recommendations to a judge at the dispositional hearing. In addition to the probation officer, a prosecutor as well as a youthful offender may provide dispositional recommendations. After considering all the dispositional recommendations, the judge renders a disposition in the case (Sickmund & Puzzanchera, 2014).

Competency

To have a fair trial, a defendant must be competent to stand trial to be prosecuted for his or her alleged offense. Legal **competency** requires that a defendant understand the charges brought against him or her and their seriousness and possible penalties. Additionally, a defendant must be able to follow proceedings and defend himself or herself during the trial. At any point during the proceedings in the criminal court, if the competence of the defendant is questioned, the court may order an evaluation. Anyone who is deemed mentally incompetent due to mental health problems or disabilities cannot be convicted of a crime (Larson & Grisso, 2012).

Because of the developmental immaturity, which varies widely among adolescents, the question of competency is even more relevant when dealing with youthful offenders, but it was not an issue in the juvenile courts until the 1990s. Today, most states do have separate guidelines for the use of competency in juvenile courts and do not as often have to apply the criminal court guidelines. Nevertheless, as more juveniles have been transferred

Right to Bail: Release of an arrested or imprisoned accused person when a specified amount of security is deposited or pledged (as cash or property) to ensure the accused's appearance in court.

Plea Bargain: Arrangement between a prosecutor and a defendant whereby the defendant pleads guilty to a lesser charge in the expectation of leniency.

Adjudicatory Hearing: Hearing in which the purpose is making a judicial ruling such as a judgment or decree. It is sometimes used in juvenile criminal cases as another term for a trial.

Disposition (Hearing): A legally binding decision by a judge or magistrate.

Jury Trial: Legal proceeding in which a jury makes a decision or findings of fact, which then directs the actions of a judge.

Competency: Mental capacity of an individual to participate in legal proceedings or transactions, and the mental condition a person must have to be responsible for his or her decisions or acts.

U.S. SUPREME COURT DECISIONS ON MIRANDA AND RELATED RIGHTS

In *J.D.B. v. North Carolina* (2011), a police officer, who interrogated a 13-year-old suspect of two burglaries, did not give a Miranda warning prior to the interrogation because the officer believed that since the juvenile was interrogated at school, he or she was not "in police custody" and was, therefore, free to stop the interrogation at any time. Citing findings from brain science studies that show that juveniles are less likely than adults to feel free to leave in the presence of a police officer, more vulnerable to the fear and stress during interrogation, and therefore more at risk of confessing to a "crime" they did not commit (Drizin & Leo, 2004; Tepfer, Nirider, & Tricarico, 2010), the Court ruled that when a law enforcement officer is determining whether an individual is in police custody, and therefore, entitled to a Miranda warning, the suspect's age should be taken into account.

....

1. What is your reaction to interacting with police officers? What has influenced your perspective?

2. What do you think it means to be "in police custody?"

to the adult court and tried in recent years, the criminal court has had the difficult task of determining the competency of juveniles to stand trial in criminal court (Larson & Grisso, 2012).

Decision-Making in Juvenile Court

Although the criminal and juvenile justice systems have become more similar in recent years, one major difference between the two courts is focus. To serve the best interest of the juvenile, the juvenile court has traditionally focused on the *individual* offender to determine an individualized intervention program that emphasizes *rehabilitation* and *treatment*. This is in contrast to the criminal courts that have traditionally focused on the *offense* to determine an appropriate *punishment,* especially since the "get tough on crime" period of the 1980s and 1990s with an increased application of the mandatory sentences throughout the nation that has significantly decreased judicial discretion. In summary, mandatory sentences make sure that the same offense results in the same punishment, no matter who committed the offense or any circumstantial differences.

On the other hand, throughout the juvenile justice system, from the apprehension to the disposition, all those who are involved, including the law enforcement officer, the intake officer, the probation personnel, the prosecutor, and the judge, are expected to take into account both extralegal and legal factors in deciding what is best for the juvenile. Extralegal factors are factors that are not directly related to the legal issues at hand, including family information, school record, available support system, the history of drug and alcohol use, and work record. On the other hand, legal factors include the history of delinquency, juvenile justice system involvement, and the type and seriousness of an alleged offense (Sickmund & Puzzanchera, 2014).

Disposition

Several disposition options are available for the judge in the juvenile justice system, including a warning, restitution to the victim, community service, attendance in counseling service or program, probation, and confinement in a secured residential facility. Most dispositions rendered in juvenile court include some supervised probation but also other requirements, such as restitution

CASE STUDY

A SIX-YEAR-OLD MURDERER

In the year 2000, a six-year-old girl, Kayla Rolland, was shot by her six-year-old friend, Dedrick Darnell Owens, at Buell Elementary School in Mount Morris, Michigan. At that time, Kayla was the youngest victim of a school shooting in the United States until the Sandy Hook Elementary School shooting in Connecticut in 2012. Dedrick, however, is still considered the youngest perpetrator of a school shooting in U.S. history. Dedrick, a first grader, had been living in a "crack house" with a drug-addict mother and his eight-year-old brother when he found a loaded .32-calliber handgun in the house, brought it along with a knife to school, and shot his friend in front of a teacher and 22 other students. Prior to that, Dedrick had been in trouble at school numerous times because of behavioral problems, including for stabbing another girl with a pencil. Because of his age, Dedrick was not legally charged with murder.

1. Should this boy have been prosecuted for murder?

2. What would you do as the prosecutor or judge in a case like this?

to the victim, included as a part of probation order. The probation term may be open-ended or a specific duration of time, and during that time, review hearings monitor the progress of the offender. Once a juvenile offender successfully completes the term of probation, the judge or magistrate terminates the case (Sickmund & Puzzanchera, 2014).

Less than a third of adjudicated youthful offenders are ordered to be placed in a residential facility, which include numerous options, from large public facilities that resemble adult prison to small private shelter homes, varying in the level of security. In many states, it is the responsibility of the state department of juvenile corrections to decide which facility the juvenile offender is placed in and when he or she will be released. In other states, the judge determines the length of placement through review hearings that assess the progress of each juvenile offender. In 2011, 27 states required parents to pay at least part of the costs of the juvenile residential placement (Office of Juvenile Justice and Delinquency Prevention, 2013). After release from a residential facility, the juvenile offender is often ordered to be under supervision of the court or the juvenile correction department, much like adult parole. If the juvenile fails to follow the conditions of the supervision, the judge may order the juvenile to be recommitted to the same or a different facility (Sickmund & Puzzanchera, 2014). The disposition options available to federal judges are similar to ones listed already for the judges in the state juvenile courts (Figure 1.2).

Confidentiality

The juvenile courts have shifted their view on the confidentiality of court proceedings and juvenile court records over the years. In general, making the court proceedings open to the public allows scrutiny and increases government accountability, and it is in accordance with the First and Fourteenth amendments to the U.S. Constitution, which guarantee the presumption of innocence and freedom of the press. After adoption of the Standard Juvenile Court Act in 1952, however, many states instituted laws that prohibited the public, and often the press, from attending juvenile court proceedings to protect the privacy of the youthful offenders involved. This was especially pertinent to the "family court" matters that involve sensitive private matters of family.

In 1977, the U.S. Supreme Court ruled in *Oklahoma Publishing Company v. District Court in and for Oklahoma City* that the court order prohibiting the publication of a legally obtained name or photograph of a youthful offender involved in the juvenile court proceeding to be unconstitutional because of its infringement on the freedom of the press. Similarly in *Smith*

Confidentiality: Process of keeping juvenile court records and proceedings private.

Case Processing Overview: Juvenile Court Processing for a Typical 1,000 Delinquency Cases, 2014

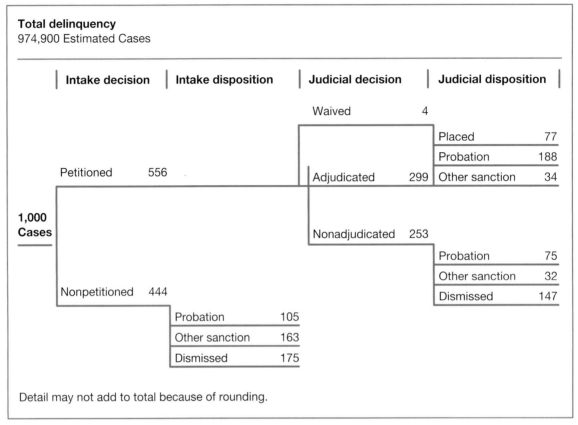

Total delinquency
974,900 Estimated Cases

Intake decision	Intake disposition	Judicial decision	Judicial disposition

Waived   4

Petitioned   556

Adjudicated   299

Placed	77
Probation	188
Other sanction	34

1,000 Cases

Nonadjudicated   253

Probation	75
Other sanction	32
Dismissed	147

Nonpetitioned   444

Probation	105
Other sanction	163
Dismissed	175

Detail may not add to total because of rounding.

Source: OJJDP Statistical Briefing Book 2014

v. *Daily Mail* (1979), the Court ruled that the state cannot punish the press from publishing a legally obtained alleged juvenile delinquent's name. Beginning in the 1980s, most states modified or removed confidentiality provisions and made the juvenile justice proceedings more open. In 2011, only 13 states had statutes making delinquency hearings closed to the public, except for compelling reasons, for example, public safety (Office of Juvenile Justice and Delinquency Prevention, 2013).

In 2009, all states, except for RI, had procedures in place for the sealing or expungement of juvenile court records. States vary in terms of how they expunge or seal the juvenile record, from physically destroying the record to storing away the record that may be accessed only in limited circumstances (Sickmund, 2010). Most states, moreover, have procedures for unsealing the juvenile court records under certain circumstances, such as following a subsequent offense or a court order (Office of Juvenile Justice and Delinquency Prevention, 2013).

All states have laws that govern the circumstances under which youthful offenders are fingerprinted for alleged or adjudicated delinquent offenses. In 2009, only 10 states (HI, IN, NV, NJ, NM, NY, NC, ND, UT, and WI) limited the age (from 10 to 14 years) that youthful offenders could be fingerprinted, whereas other states had no age restriction. In addition, as of 2008, all but six states had school notification laws that require a school to be notified when students are involved in the juvenile justice system for delinquent activities. States vary, however, as to when in the juvenile justice process a school should be notified (charge, adjudication, etc.) and regarding what type of offense (Sickmund & Puzzanchera, 2014).

THE CHILD WELFARE SYSTEM

Although the juvenile court and other subsystems play formal roles within the juvenile justice system, there is significant involvement of ancillary systems that are unique to children, including child protective services, schools, and behavioral health providers. Ancillary systems are not considered formal parts of the juvenile justice system, but they are intertwined because youthful offenders are often involved in these youth-caring systems prior to their involvement in the courts. These ancillary systems also play critical roles in supporting youthful offenders and their families while they are being processed through the juvenile justice system.

▲ The child welfare system protects young people from abuse and neglect by investigating cases and providing family supervision. Do you know of anyone who has had experiences with their local child welfare system?

Federal Policy

As one of the important ancillary systems, the child welfare system (child protective services) focuses on ensuring the safety of children from maltreatment protecting and promoting stable and permanent family relationships, and caring for the well-being of children who experienced maltreatment. The Child Abuse and Prevention Act (CAPTA) of 1974 defines child maltreatment as serious harm to children caused by parents or primary caregivers, including babysitters and extended family members. Harm includes all types of abuse, such as physical, sexual, and emotional, as well as neglect. As will be discussed in later chapters, because many youthful offenders who get into trouble with the law often are victims of abuse and neglect and because the two systems are intertwined, it is important to understand how the child welfare system operates (Child Welfare Information Gateway, 2011).

Although specific child welfare policies vary by state, the federal government plays an important role in providing support through funding and legislative initiatives, which are implemented by the Children's Bureau, U.S. Department of Health and Human Services (HHS). The Children's Bureau is also responsible for the publication of *Child Maltreatment*, an annual count of national child and abuse reports. Figure 1.3 highlights important federal child welfare laws that have a significant impact on how child welfare services and programs are delivered at the state and local levels (Child Welfare Information Gateway, 2013).

State Policy

Like the juvenile justice system, each state manages its own child welfare system. These child protective systems, therefore, vary from state to state and include both public and private services and programs offered at the federal, state, and local levels. Although the child welfare system is complex and specific procedures vary across states, most child welfare cases go through a similar investigatory and supervision process (Child Welfare Information Gateway, 2011; see Figure 1.4).

Most families become involved with the child welfare system because of a report of suspected child maltreatment by parents or primary caregivers; cases involving harm to a child caused by acquaintances or strangers are referred directly to law enforcement instead of to a child welfare agency. Any concerned person can report suspected child abuse or neglect to a local child welfare agency; most reports, however, are made by those who are required to report a suspicion of child abuse and neglect, including social workers, teachers, healthcare workers, mental health professionals, childcare providers, law enforcement officers, and medical examiners. Fewer than 20 states require all persons, regardless of profession, to report a suspected child abuse and neglect (Child Welfare Information Center, 2015).

Timeline of Federal Child Welfare Acts

1900

1978: Indian Child Welfare Act
(ICWA) governs the jurisdiction of maltreated American Indian/Alaskan Native children and prioritizes the role of the tribal governments in decision-making.

1974: The Child Abuse and Prevention Act
(CAPTA) was the first federal law concerning child maltreatment and today provides states funding for the prevention, assessment, investigation, prosecution, and treatment for abuse and neglect, as well as leadership around data collection and technical assistance training.

1997: The Adoption and Safe Families Act
(ASFA) marked a fundamental change to child welfare and shifted the emphasis towards children's health and safety concerns and away from a policy of reuniting children with their birth parents without regard to prior abusiveness. This law requires annual permanency hearings for children placed out of their home and a permanent family plan (reunification or adoption) within two years for most children in care.

1994: Multi Ethnic Placement Act
(MEPA) prohibits the discrimination of the foster care/adoption placement based on the race, color, or national origin of parent(s) or child.

1999: Foster Care Independence Act
(John H. Chafee Independent Living Law) provides programming and other funding opportunities to help older youth who are aging out of foster care (ages 18 to 21) achieve independent living skills.

2000

2008: Fostering Connections to Success and Increasing Adoptions Act covers many areas, including proving support for relative caregivers and tribal foster care and adoption, improving the successful outcomes of children in foster care, and increasing incentives for adoption.

Stages of Child Maltreatment Case Processing

What are the stages of child maltreatment case processing in the child protective services and juvenile/family court systems?

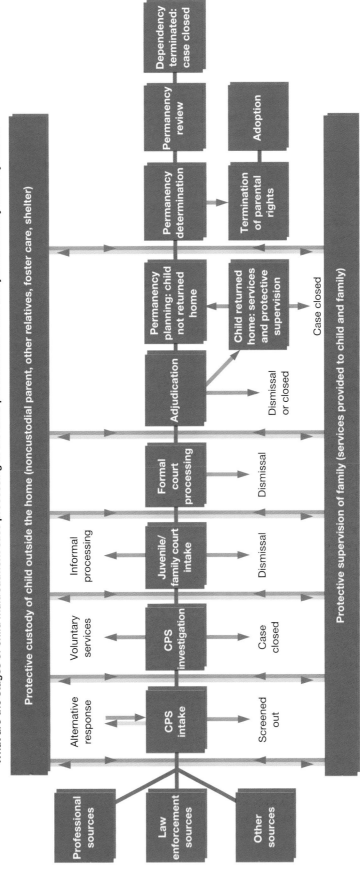

Source: Sickmund & Puzzanchera (2014). *Juvenile Offenders and Victims: 2014 National Report.* National Center for Juvenile Justice.

Child protective service (CPS) agencies receive reports of suspected abuse and neglect and screen them for further investigation. If CPS determines that there is not enough information to warrant a further investigation or the case does not meet the state's definition of maltreatment, it may refer the person who reported the incident to other services or to law enforcement. Once a case is determined to warrant a further investigation (approximately 40% of cases), CPS caseworkers speak with the parents, the child involved in the case, and other people who are in contact with the child, such as healthcare workers, teachers, and child-care providers, within a time period required by state law (typically one to three days). If CPS caseworkers determine that the child is in immediate danger, the child may be removed from the home during the investigation pending the proceedings in some states. A court order is required in other states before removing a child from their home, and in the case of emergency removal of a child, a preliminary protective hearing (or shelter care hearing) is required in these states (Sickmund & Puzzanchera, 2014). Families are often directed to local services and resources during this time after caseworkers assess the specific family needs and difficulties (Child Welfare Information Center, 2015).

At the completion of an investigation, the CPS caseworkers determine whether the findings of abuse or neglect are substantiated (founded) or unsubstantiated (unfounded). When findings are determined unsubstantiated, and for other "low-risk" child maltreatment cases, CPS may offer services to children and families to help reduce the risk of future potential problems. The range of possible actions available when findings are substantiated varies from state to state and depends on the severity of maltreatment, the history of the CPS involvement, the immediate danger to child safety, and the available services and programs for the family. If findings are substantiated and CPS determines that the juvenile court needs to be involved through a child protection or dependency proceeding to keep the child safe, a juvenile court action is filed.

Once a court action is filed, the juvenile court may order the child to be temporarily removed from the home and placed in a safe alternative (e.g., shelter, respite home, or with a related family member), provide or direct services for the child and family, or restrict certain individuals who are suspected in the abuse or neglect to have no contact with the child. At the adjudicatory hearing, the juvenile court hears the evidence provided by the CPS and determines whether child maltreatment occurred and if the child should be removed from the home and remain in the custody of the court. At the dispositional hearing (some states combine the two hearings into one), the juvenile court may order parents to comply with services and programs and determine the provisions on visitation between parents and the child. In most child maltreatment cases, the juvenile court assumes jurisdiction over the cases to monitor the child welfare agencies' effort to reunite the family, as stipulated by the Federal Adoption Assistance and Child Welfare Act. In cases involving severe child maltreatment or death, law enforcement may be notified and a charge may be filed in criminal court against those who are responsible for the child maltreatment. In many states, certain types of abuse, such as sexual abuse and serious physical abuse, are automatically reported to law enforcement (Child Welfare Information Center, 2015; Sickmund & Puzzanchera, 2014).

Most families of children who are removed receive services to reduce the risk of maltreatment in the future and to reunite with the child, which is usually part of the permanency plan for child maltreatment cases. The juvenile court is required by federal law to hold a permanency hearing within 12 months after the child is removed from home and placed in foster care. The juvenile court often reviews each case every 12 months thereafter, or more frequently, to ensure that the child welfare system is protecting and promoting stable and permanent family relationships for each child who enters the system. Unlike the juvenile justice system whose age of jurisdiction typically ends at age 18 or younger, many allow for supervision of young people who are in CPS custody up to ages 20 or 21. These young people receive support in forming permanent family relationships and in developing independent living skills until they leave care or age out (Child Welfare Information Center, 2015).

CHAPTER REVIEW

CHAPTER SUMMARY

This chapter provided an overview of the juvenile justice system, its jurisdiction, purposes, and functions, as well as a framework of important concepts and concerns that are developed and discussed in later chapters. Specifically, the issues addressed included the purpose and jurisdiction of the juvenile court, the case processing of how young people become involved in the juvenile justice system (from police contact to delinquency adjudication to lock up), unique juvenile court concerns including delinquency and status offenses, issues related to confidentiality, and how the child welfare system operates and how it intersects with the juvenile courts. Adolescents are different from adults, and the juvenile courts were established for this and other related reasons. Hence, juvenile courts have certain discretions in deciding when to involve youthful offenders formally, to charge them, and to prosecute.

KEY TERMS

adjudges **3**

adjudicatory hearing **17**

Attorney General **12**

civil courts **3**

competency **17**

confidentiality **19**

consent decree **16**

criminal courts **3**

delinquency **5**

delinquent **3**

disposition **3**

disposition hearing **17**

diversion **15**

Federal Juvenile Delinquency Act **11**

in loco parentis **3**

jury trial **17**

juvenile **3**

Juvenile Justice and Delinquency Prevention Act **8**

Miranda warning **14**

Office of Juvenile Justice and Delinquency Prevention (OJJDP) **8**

parens patriae **3**

plea bargain **17**

racial and ethnic disparities **8**

right to bail **17**

school resource officers **12**

Standard Juvenile Court Act **4**

status offense **5**

DISCUSSION QUESTIONS

1. Do you think a separate justice system is necessary for young people? Explain.

2. Discern and highlight the steps from informal involvement to delinquency adjudication in the juvenile justice system. In other words, how does a young person go from committing an offense to lockup?

3. What role does the federal government or federal law have in the operation of local juvenile courts? Identify the impact and policies.

4. Do you think that juveniles are different than adults and, thus, should be treated differently when they commit the same offense as adults? Explain.

5. Should we punish a juvenile offender who commits homicide the same as adults, no matter how young the person? What if the person was 17 with a history of violence? What if the person was 15 with a history of violence?

6. Explain how a youthful offender could avoid formal juvenile court involvement; where are possible diversion points?

7. What are some of the potential consequences for young people who are adjudicated delinquent and supervised by the juvenile court? What are potential outcomes for youthful offenders who continue to commit delinquent acts?

8. How does the child welfare system typically interact with the juvenile court process and structure? In other words, what cases are handled by the juvenile courts and what cases remain part of the child welfare system?

9. What are the possible outcomes of a child welfare agency investigation? How do federal laws impact child protective service decision-making for maltreatment children and adolescents?

10. Argue the pros and cons of keeping juvenile delinquency proceedings confidential. What is your opinion about whether these matters; should they remain private?

https://edge.sagepub.com/mallett

$SAGE edge™ **Sharpen your skills with SAGE edge!**

SAGE edge for students provides a personalized approach to help you accomplish your coursework in an easy-to-use learning environment. You'll find mobile-friendly eFlashcards and quizzes, as well as videos, web resources, and links to SAGE journal articles to support and expand on the concepts presented in this chapter.

CHAPTER 2

THE HISTORY OF JUVENILE JUSTICE AND TODAY'S JUVENILE COURTS

▲ The history of the juvenile justice system has many changing approaches to working with delinquent young people. Why do you think this is the case?

INTRODUCTION

The juvenile justice system has a long history of shifting paradigms from rehabilitating to punishing those considered wayward, troubled, or delinquent children. In the early days, most juvenile justice efforts were punitive as evidenced by the use of dangerous and ineffective warehouse types of institutions: almshouses, houses of refuge, and similar alternatives. The first shift away from punishment and toward a rehabilitative paradigm was during the later 18th and early 19th centuries, a progressive era across parts of the nation, leading to the establishment of the juvenile courts as they are recognized today. These efforts at formalizing a juvenile court system, though, often ended up expanding the juvenile justice system and imprisoning more children and adolescents for noncriminal activities. Since the 1950s, and in response to the large numbers of institutional placements, due process rights were established for youthful offenders. The reach of the juvenile courts, however, expanded significantly once again during the 1980s and 1990s "tough-on-crime" approach to juvenile justice and the schools implemented similar zero tolerance discipline and school exclusion policies, forming what many have called the "school-to-prison pipeline." Looking back, the early approaches to juvenile justice were far different from today's juvenile court structure.

LEARNING OBJECTIVES

1 Identify how the history of juvenile justice in the United States has been a series of distinct stages, some emphasizing reform and others focusing on punishment of young people

2 Discuss how the distinct historical shifts set the stage for the more recent "tough-on-crime" approach to juvenile justice and today's reform-focused efforts

3 Identify the major state-level reforms occurring across the juvenile justice system today, and describe how and why today's juvenile courts are at distinct and different stages of reform across the country

4 Explain how recent juvenile justice system changes have been impacted by federal policies

JUVENILE JUSTICE: CYCLES OF REHABILITATION AND PUNISHMENT

1750–1850: From Almshouses to Houses of Refuge

Prior to the establishment of today's juvenile justice system, troubled children were offered intervention efforts focused on family control, in addition to use of the **almshouses**—locked, one-room buildings that housed many types of people with many different problems. During the later 1700s, the family was responsible for control of children, with the most common response by the community being to remove children and place them with other families (a philosophy and legal doctrine that came to be known as *in loco parentis*); typically, this happened because of poverty. Many times, these children were "bound out," becoming indentured servants for the new family as a form of social control of troubled children. If there was no suitable placement with a family, however, an almshouse was one of the few community alternatives (Bremner, Barnard, Hareven, & Mennel, 1970; Grob, 1994; Rothman, 1971).

> "The almshouse in Boston," observed a committee in 1790, "is, perhaps, the only instance known where persons of every description and disease are lodged under the same roof and in some instances in the same contagious apartments, by which means the sick are disturbed by the noises of the healthy, and the infirm rendered liable to the vices and diseases of the diseased, and profligate." (Grob, 2008, p. 14)

By the 1800s, with the impact of increased poverty across many regions of the country, urban growth particularly in the Northeast, economic downturns, and immigrant influxes

Almshouses: Colonial-era, locked, one-room buildings that housed many types of people with many different problems, including troubled or orphaned children.

Liszt Collection/Newscom

▲ Almhouses existed in most Colonial communities and were a place of last resort for many troubled adults and orphaned children. Do we have any institutions like this today?

(in particular, from Ireland), new facilities were established in major cities to help control troubled, wayward, or orphaned children—the **houses of refuge**. There was a movement to discontinue the use of adult jails or almshouses for these children and to establish separate facilities. Many reformers supporting the establishment and expansion of these houses during this time period were wealthy conservatives, concerned about the impact of a growing poverty class and fear of social unrest, as well as about its influence and impact on children. This effort was not as noble as it may sound, for there were worries by these reformers that efforts would not solve the pauperism problem, threatening the social order of the time and the wealthier class positions in society (Cohen & Ratner, 1970; Krisberg, 2005; Mennel, 1973).

The philosophical doctrine of *parens patriae* ("parent of the country") was established through numerous legal decisions and supported the houses of refuge's efforts in the belief that the state should act as a benevolent legal parent when the family was no longer willing or able to serve the best interests of the child; this included parental inability to control or discipline their child. Houses of refuge were the first institutions to provide separate facilities for children, apart from adult criminals and workhouses, and incorporated education along with reform efforts. Some of the earliest houses were established in New York in 1825, Boston in 1826, and Philadelphia in 1828; later houses also were established in larger urban areas (Chicago, Rochester [NY], Pittsburgh, Providence, St. Louis, and Cincinnati). These individual facilities housed a many young people (as many as 1,000) including those who were delinquent, orphaned, neglected, or dependent. The structure was often fortress-like and used punitive environments, corporal punishments, and solitary confinement, with many reports of neglect and abuse. The early facilities either excluded black children and adolescents or housed them separately. For example, the city of Philadelphia established the separate House of Refuge for Colored Juvenile Delinquents in 1849, alongside its original house or refuge for whites only, with significantly longer lengths of stay for black children compared with white children (Mennel, 1973; Platt, 1969, 2009; Ward, 2012). The following is a description of the early days of the New York House of Refuge.

The *parens patriae* philosophy continued to guide the reformers from the houses of refuge to the Child-Saving Movement and the eventual establishment of the juvenile courts. The juvenile courts would represent the first time a separate criminal code would be written in the United States that would not be universally applied to all citizens (Krisberg, 2005; Lawrence & Hemmens, 2008).

1850–1890: The Child-Saving Movement

The beginning of a new era (1850 to 1890), called the **Child-Saving Movement**, was focused on the urban poor, trying to keep children sheltered, fed, and when possible and old enough, employed. Early organizations included the Children's Aid Society (1853) and the New York Juvenile Asylum (1851). In addition to these specific organizational efforts, reformers consisted of a diverse collection of public and private community programs and institutions. These organizations helped to provide some unique programs for young people, including probation supervision for status offenders and minor delinquents. One of the newer approaches started by the Children's Aid Society was a "**placing out**" system for impoverished and troubled children whereby more than 50,000 were rounded up from mostly urban East Coast cities, boarded on trains, and sent to western states. The train stopped along the way for families to inspect the

Houses of Refuge: Facilities built in the 1800s and established in major cities to help control troubled, wayward, or orphaned children.

Child-Saving Movement: A 19th century movement that influenced the development of the juvenile courts and focused on the prevention of delinquency through education and training of young people.

Placing Out: Failed 19th century practice for impoverished, troubled, or orphaned children whereby more than 50,000 children from mostly urban East Coast cities boarded trains and were sent to western states to be adopted by farm families.

NEW YORK HOUSE OF REFUGE

The reformatory opened January 1, 1825, with six boys and three girls. Within a decade, 1,678 inmates were admitted. Two features distinguished the New York institution from its British antecedents. First, children were committed for vagrancy in addition to petty crimes. Second, children were sentenced or committed indefinitely; the New York House of Refuge exercised authority over inmates throughout their minority years. During the 19th century, most inmates were committed for vagrancy or petty theft. Originally, the institution accepted inmates from across the state, but after the establishment of the Western House of Refuge in 1849, inmates came only from the first, second, and third judicial districts (Ch. 24, Laws of 1850).

A large part of an inmate's daily schedule was devoted to supervised labor, which was regarded as beneficial to education and discipline. Inmate labor also supported operating expenses for the reformatory. Typically, male inmates produced brushes, cane chairs, brass nails, and shoes. The female inmates made uniforms, worked in the laundry, and performed other domestic work. A badge system was used to segregate inmates according to their behavior. Students were instructed in basic literacy skills. There was also great emphasis on evangelical religious instruction, although non-Protestant clergy were excluded. The reformatory had the authority to bind out inmates through indenture agreements by which employers agreed to supervise them during their employment. Although initially several inmates were sent to sea, most male and female inmates were sent to work as farm and domestic laborers, respectively (New York State Archives, 1989, p. 4–5).

1. Do you think these institutions were helpful for the young people?

2. How do they compare with today's youth-caring institutions?

children and decide whether to accept them. Preference was given to farm families, with the philosophy that these families offered the best hope for rescuing these children from city streets and neglectful or deceased parents. This program often did not find placements for many of the children (Mennel, 1973).

Although these efforts tried to improve conditions for wayward children, all legal matters for children continued to be handled by adult civil courts, achieving haphazard outcomes in decreasing delinquency or offending behaviors across communities. This was because civil courts handled primarily adult issues—divorce, torts, and contracts—and had no specialization or training to handle children's issues. Because of these civil court failings and an ineffective approach across other public and private community provider programs, including the failed "placing out" of children from the cities to Midwest farms, reform schools were established (Hawes, 1971; Lawrence & Hemmens, 2008).

In contrast to the large and controlling houses of refuge, **reform schools** were designed as small, rural, cottage-like homes run by parental figures who worked to educate and care for the children and adolescents. These were first established in Massachusetts in 1886 (Lyman School for Boys) with 51 schools established nationwide by 1896. They were less common in southern and western states, however. Most facilities were operated by state or local governments, which was a significant shift in policy from charity and philanthropic support in earlier eras, and they offered separate facilities for boys and girls. These homes, though, rarely included adolescents convicted of serious crimes, who were still imprisoned with adults. Reform schools were criticized for lacking proactive efforts to change the behavior of troubled children and adolescents, the long-term housing of this population (typically 18 years of age for girls and 21 for boys), and the exploitation of those housed in the facilities under indentured or contract labor systems, similar to the houses of refuge.

Reform Schools: 19th century movement and reaction to ineffective houses of refuge consisting of homes designed as small, rural, cottage-like facilities run by parental figures who educated and cared for the children and adolescents.

HOUSE OF REFUGE, RANDALL'S ISLAND, NEW YORK.

▲ A house of refuge was a large institution, often overcrowded, that housed many different types of people with troubles. How have these type of institutions changed over time?

The reform schools proved to be of little improvement over earlier attempts to manage or rehabilitate this population; both the houses or refuge and reform schools ended up being punitive in design and oppressive for those sheltered (Hawes, 1971; Liazos, 1974). Consistent with the racial biases of the era, these facilities were used primarily by white children and adolescents. Black children and adolescents (along with other minority groups—Native Americans and Mexican Americans, depending on location across the country) were considered unamenable to rehabilitation; they typically remained in adult jails and prisons. When blacks were infrequently placed in reform schools, they were segregated from whites and rarely participated in the education or training components, but they were required to work and help maintain the school campus (Lawrence & Hemmens, 2008; Nellis, 2016).

1899–1920: Establishment of the Juvenile Courts

As the Child-Saving Movement's influence expanded, it included philanthropists (leaders included Julia Lathrop, a social reformer for education and child welfare; Jane Addams, established the profession of social work; and Lucy Flower, children's advocate and major contributor to establishment of the juvenile courts), middle-class citizens, and professionals focused on motivating state legislatures to extend government interventions to save troubled children and adolescents. The movement was formally recognized through the establishment of the nation's first juvenile court in Cook County (Chicago), Illinois, in 1899, an institution that was to act *in loco parentis* (in place of the parents).

In addition to the establishment of the juvenile courts, this era represented other advancements across social services, schools, and how children were viewed, including the recognition of adolescence as a distinct life stage; establishment of child labor laws that limited work and promoted mandatory school attendance; emergence of the social work and related professions; epidemiological tracking of poverty and delinquency, allowing for the first time an ability to identify and track social problems; and the legal recognition of delinquency that allowed the states to take a proactive and protective role in children's lives. Thus, the establishment of juvenile courts and having distinct juvenile (children's) judges began proliferating. By 1920, 30 states, and by 1925, 46 of the existing 48 states had established juvenile or specialized courts for children and adolescents (Coalition for Juvenile Justice, 1998; Feld, 1999; Krisberg, 2005; Platt, 2009).

The juvenile courts were different from any prior court that handled children's issues. The guiding principles included optimism that the young person could be reformed, a focus on how to best accomplish this, and a separation and distinction from the adult court system that did not keep hearings and information confidential. Most juvenile courts also handled minor offenses and status offenses. Court proceedings were held in private and did not include jury trials, indictments, or other adult system formalities, treating these cases as civil, not as criminal. In addition, the juvenile courts took on child supervision roles in determining what came to be known as "the best interests of the child's welfare" (Platt, 2009; Redding, 1997). For the first time, state laws began to define delinquency. For example, in Oregon, it was identified by state law that truant, idle, and disorderly children would be considered in need of state supervision:

The words "a delinquent child" shall include any child under the age of 16 . . . years who violates any law of this State or any city or village ordinance, or is incorrigible, or who is a persistent truant from school, or who associates with criminals or reputed criminals, or vicious or immoral persons, or who is growing up in idleness or crime, or who frequents, visits or is found in any disorderly house, bawdy house or house of ill-fame, or any house or place where fornication is enacted or in any saloon, bar-room, or drinking shop or place . . . or in any place where any gaming device is or shall be operated. (Nellis, 2016, p. 13)

Jacob A. Riis/Museum of the City of New York/Getty Images

▲ The Child-saving Movement focused on orphaned and delinquent children, offering housing and education. How did these efforts shape some of today's juvenile justice system?

Juvenile courts handled most matters as civil cases, viewing the child as in need of rehabilitation and supervision and treating delinquency as a social problem instead of as a crime. The courts often employed **probation officers**, social workers, and psychologists to work with the child and family, as well as to guide the decision-making of juvenile courts. These professionals were to act in the best interests of the child, which was a significant change from earlier benevolent or controlling philosophies. Over subsequent decades, however, the juvenile courts moved away from these initial reformative and informal supervision plans. This happened because of the significantly large numbers of young people who became involved with the juvenile courts requiring an expansion of rules and processes to hear many types of child and adolescent cases. Many of these situations could have been handled without state intervention or supervision, but nonetheless they came to the juvenile courts' jurisdiction.

As with earlier eras in juvenile justice, most children and adolescents involved with the juvenile courts were from poor families and many immigrant neighborhoods, and segregation across racial lines was common in the court staff who supervised the young people (Liazos, 1974; Ward, 2012). This differential treatment of black children and adolescents, however, extended beyond limited access to the earlier era reform schools (or other possible rehabilitative alternatives) and the newly established juvenile courts. Although many black youthful offenders were simply prosecuted in adult courts and placed into adult prisons, they were also involved in the convict-lease system (the southern states' provision of prisoner labor to private parties, such as plantations and corporations), longer periods in detention, and higher rates of corporal punishment and execution (Ward, 2012).

An early assessment of the juvenile courts was skeptical of the impact. "It was the evident purpose of the founders of the first juvenile courts to save, to redeem, and to protect every delinquent child . . . After two decades this exalted conception . . . has not been realized in its fullness. . . . Children . . . are but little different from those of the last century" (U.S. Department of Labor, Children's Bureau, 1922, pp. 14–15). Criticism grew after World War II with many finding that the expansion of rules, processes, and supervision within the courts had eliminated constitutional and due process protections for the youthful offenders. The early goals of the juvenile courts were difficult to achieve, and the *parens patriae* doctrine and expanded supervision of many young people led to harsher discipline and punishment for low-level delinquency and status offenders (Allen, 1964; Caldwell, 1961).

1920–1960: Institutionalization of Youthful Offenders

The significant expansion and commitment of many youthful offenders to juvenile court detention and **incarceration facilities** was far from the juvenile court's original rehabilitative philosophy. Like the houses of refuge and reform school eras, institutionalization became

Probation Officers: Juvenile court employees that supervise youthful offenders who have been adjudicated delinquent.

Incarceration Facilities: State-run correctional facilities that house youthful offenders, typically for longer periods of time.

▲ Chicago, Cook County, established the country's first juvenile court in 1899. How did this change the treatment of youthful offenders?

the primary determination and outcome for those involved with the juvenile courts. Most young people who were brought before the juvenile courts were adjudicated delinquent and placed within a locked facility. Correctional facility placement of delinquent youthful offenders across the country expanded from 100,000 in the 1940s to 400,000 in the 1960s.

Most of these facilities were substandard and overcrowded, did not include rehabilitative services or medical care, and employed a controlling and punitive environment. Although varying interventions were tried within the institutions—therapy, group treatment, and environmental management techniques, among others—outcomes remained poor, both inside the facilities and for those who left (Lerman, 2002; President's Commission on Law Enforcement and Administration of Justice, 1967; Roberts, 2004). The juvenile courts continued to predominantly involve low-income and "other people's children," although some alternatives to incarceration of youthful offenders were introduced as community-based corrections. These included group homes, partial release supervision, and halfway houses, but these types of programming were not widely implemented across the country (Krisberg, 2005; Nellis, 2016). The next phase of the juvenile justice system brought a short-lived shift away from institutionalized placement of youthful offenders toward more community-based alternatives, as well as the expansion of due process rights for young people formally involved with the juvenile courts.

1960–1980: Juvenile Justice and Individual Rights

Although juvenile courts were established as part of a reform effort to more humanely provide for the best interest of neglected, abused, and delinquent children, their reformation and delinquency prevention impact continued to be limited. Even though local city and county juvenile courts processed youthful offender cases and referred many to probation supervision and residential placement, juvenile court dockets expanded to include more minor offenses, truancy issues, and child welfare concerns, along with criminal activity. Beginning in the 1960s through the 1970s, significant changes were made within the juvenile justice system, driven by three primary forces: (a) a stronger federal government role, (b) state reformation and depopulating the overcrowded juvenile incarceration facilities, and (c) **U.S. Supreme Court** decisions establishing youthful offender rights in juvenile proceedings (Binder, Geis, & Bruce, 1988; Krisberg, 2005; Nellis, 2016).

The 1950s were a time of increasing youthful offender crime and delinquency, causing stakeholders to begin to address the problems beyond just local and state efforts in the 1960s. An early federal initiative emanated from a 1961 juvenile delinquency committee was appointed during the Kennedy Administration. Recommendations from this committee, many that were pursued, included a preventative focus for those children and adolescents most at risk; identification that delinquency was linked to urban decay, poverty, school failure, and family instability; and establishing diversion alternatives away from delinquency adjudication for adolescents (President's Commission on Law Enforcement and Administration of Justice, 1967). Although federal funding was made available during the 1960s for delinquency prevention and diversion programs, the first established federal grant-making law was the Juvenile Justice and Delinquency Prevention Act of 1974. This law did fund certain programs for juvenile courts, but it also required youthful offenders to be separated from

Truancy: Act of staying away from school without good cause.

U.S. Supreme Court: Highest federal court in the United States that decides cases on Constitutional issues and has jurisdiction over all other courts.

adults in local jails, that status offenders be removed from juvenile institutions (youthful offenders locked up often in training schools or prisons where their only "crime" was disobeying parents, school truancy, or running away), and the removal of adolescents from the adult criminal justice system unless they are charged and transferred as adults (Public Law No. 93–415, 1974).

Some states also pursued shifting their large-scale and often poorly maintained correctional facilities toward smaller, community, home-type environments. This movement was influenced by the broader deinstitutionalization of state psychiatric facilities, driven by federal court decisions that focused on due process protections. These state efforts were led by Massachusetts, Missouri, Vermont, and Utah, decreasing their youthful offender incarceration populations in some cases by 90%. Such progress was difficult for many states to achieve, however, and most continued to house large numbers of youthful offenders throughout the 1970s and 1980s as they had for decades (Mechanic, 2008; Nellis, 2016).

The continued poor treatment of many juvenile justice system-involved youthful offenders, particularly those in confinement, and the perception that a social welfare approach was doing little to curb expanding juvenile crime, resulted in an increased focus on due process protection rights. Critics at the time argued that the juvenile courts could no longer justify their broad disposition powers and invasion of personal rights on humanitarian grounds. Delinquent offenders were often treated like adult criminals, yet they had none of the legal protections granted to adults (Scott & Grisso, 1997). Eventually, due process concerns came to the forefront of juvenile justice in the Supreme Court's *Gault* decision (*In re Gault*, 387 U.S. 1, 1967).

The intent of *Gault*, and these other due process decisions, was to balance the broad powers of the juvenile court by providing legal protections to youthful offenders. The *Gault* decision also focused attention on similarities between the juvenile and adult courts and on the differences in intent underlying the two systems. Although, in theory, still oriented toward rehabilitation, the new focus on due process resulted in the juvenile system orienting toward retribution as a means to address delinquency—the hallmark of the adult criminal justice system. This shift toward treating adolescents as adults in prosecution was combined with the influential but misunderstood message of "nothing works" in rehabilitating youthful offenders that impacted stakeholders throughout the 1970s (Martinson, 1974; Schwartz, 2001). This belief that nothing works to help rehabilitate youthful offenders involved with the juvenile courts was simply not correct, for various prevention programming—from probation supervision to community-based case management to therapeutic programs—showed significant decreases in adolescent crime and recidivism (Scarpitti & Stephenson, 1968). The lack of acknowledgment and dissemination of these programs' effectiveness and shifts in other policy areas set the stage for the tsunami movement toward punishment and retribution within juvenile justice.

The 1990s: "Tough on Crime"

As federal initiatives and Supreme Court decisions drove changes in the juvenile justice system and to juvenile court proceedings, the pendulum started to swing toward a law-and-order approach to dealing with youthful offenders. The 1980s and early 1990s marked an aggressive shift toward public safety and accountability as the primary goal in developing responses to crime, in both the juvenile and adult courts. Punitive legal reforms increased juvenile detainment and incarceration as well as the wholesale transfer of many youthful offenders into the adult criminal justice system. The dismantling of the *parens patriae* approach within the juvenile courts accelerated, and in some areas expanded, the extensive use of institutional control. At its peak, between 1992 and 1997, 47 of the 50 states moved toward "get tough" and "adult crime, adult time" type policies and passed laws accordingly;

JERRY GAULT AND DUE PROCESS PROTECTIONS

Gerald (Jerry) Gault was 15 years old when he was arrested in Arizona for making a prank phone call. He was detained, his parents were never notified, the prosecution included no witnesses or transcripts, and he was sentenced to six years in a secured state facility. Upon appeal and consideration, the U.S. Supreme Court stated that if the defendant had been 18 years of age, procedural rights would have been afforded automatically because of existing Constitutional protections. But because of Jerry Gault's age, no Constitutional rights were available. In reversing the lower court's decision, the Supreme Court found that youthful offenders facing delinquency adjudication and incarceration are entitled to certain procedural safeguards under due process protections of the Fourteenth Amendment. What was missing in this case included the following: a notice of charges, a detention hearing, a complaint at the hearing, sworn testimony, records of proceedings, and a right to appeal the judicial decision (387, U.S. 1, S.Ct. 1428, 1967). The Supreme Court followed up over the next decade in three more decisions, expanding and guaranteeing additional due process rights to youthful delinquent offenders: the need for proof beyond a reasonable doubt standard for conviction, whereby lower evidentiary thresholds like a preponderance of the evidence was no longer Constitutional (*In re Winshop*, 397 U.S. 358, 1970); the right to a jury trial (*McKeiver v. U.S.*, 403 U.S. 528, 1971); and no prosecution in adult criminal court on the same offense a youthful offender had already been prosecuted for in a juvenile court (this is known as the double jeopardy protection; *Breed v. Jones*, 421 U.S. 529, 1975).

1. Why do you think the U.S. Supreme Court decided at this time and in this way on the Gault case?

2. What would have happened if these youthful offender due process rights were delayed another few decades?

Gerald (Jerry) Gault: Fifteen-year-old from Arizona who was prosecuted and incarcerated for six years for prank phone calls. Upon consideration, this landmark U.S. Supreme Court established Constitutional due process rights for youthful offenders in 1967 including notice of charges, a detention hearing, a complaint at the hearing, sworn testimony, records of proceedings, and a right to appeal the judicial decision.

45 state legislatures increased transfers of youthful offenders to the criminal courts; 31 state legislatures expanded juvenile court mandatory minimum sentencing options; 47 state legislatures made juvenile records and court proceedings less confidential; 26 states changed their juvenile justice state codes to endorse the use of punishment, accountability, and protection of public safety; and 22 state legislatures increased the role victims had in juvenile court proceedings, expanding prosecutions and lengthening conviction sentences (Bishop, Lanza-Kaduce, & Frazier, 1998; Griffin, 2008; Scott & Grisso, 1997; Scott & Steinberg, 2008a, 2008b; Snyder & Sickmund, 2006).

Numerous reasons are often cited to explain this change from rehabilitative to a retributive philosophy during this time: opinions across both liberal and conservative stakeholders and policy makers, along with the general public, that believed juvenile offender crime was out of control; concern about a largely fictional new class of juvenile super-predators; and a growing belief that juvenile courts were soft on crime and ineffective, and that preventative or intervention programs do not work with delinquent adolescents, particularly those considered serious and chronic offenders (Butts, 2000; Howell, 2009; Shepherd, 1999; Sherman, 1994). The explanations for this punitive paradigm shift, however, were both more nuanced and complicated.

Beginning in 1985, there was a growing crime problem in the youthful offender population across many states, although it was short lived. The number of adolescents arrested for robbery, forcible rape, aggravated assault, and murder rose 64% over an eight-year time period (1985–1993). In particular, juvenile homicide arrests increased by more than 200%, with urban, inner-city neighborhoods experiencing the greatest increases in violent crime. From 1986 to 1993, arrests for homicide increased 40% for white youthful offenders but 278% for black youthful offenders. Most violent crime was perpetrated by black adolescents using handguns, with victims being primarily other black males living in urban neighborhoods (Blumstein, 1995; Fagan & Wilkinson,

1998; Nellis, 2016). The combination of an increase in handgun access and usage alongside an expanding drug trade, due primarily to the crack cocaine epidemic, in many of the nation's cities fueled much of this increase in youthful offender crime. Significant amounts of this crime activity took place in communities that were already impoverished and provided few opportunities to those who lived there, in particular, to male adolescents and young adults. Many young people lived in fear of the increase in violence, and a growing number joined gangs for security and a sense of protection (Baumer, Lauritsen, Rosenfeld, & Wright, 1998; Ousey & Augustine, 2001).

▲ The use of incarceration facilities exponentially expanded during the 1980s and 1990s "tough-on-crime" approach to youthful offending. What do you think was the impact of incarceration on the adolescents?

The public reaction, media coverage, and many policy makers' responses to these violent offenders were disproportionate to what was happening in these communities. The portrayals of youthful offenders shifted from one in need of interventions and supports toward retribution and harsh accountability. The recommendations coming from stakeholders were to apply severe punishments and sanctions on youthful offenders, both for deterrence and to incarcerate many adolescents. These public perceptions about juvenile crime, its causes, and victimization risk were often wrong—many believed that crime would continue to expand and not abate, when in fact this short-lived increase in violent adolescent offenses had already peaked by 1993 (Zimring, 1998).

From this crescendo of reactions to youthful offender crime rates, the story of an emerging **superpredator** class of adolescents was portrayed by the media and a limited number of academics. These stories often exaggerated the violence, focusing only on serious crimes that accounted for a minority of adolescent crimes, and disproportionately portrayed minority youthful offenders as the culprits (Bennett, DiIulio, & Walters, 1996; Nellis, 2016). This prediction of a growing class (some estimates in the hundreds of thousands) of impulsive, brutal, and remorseless adolescents who committed serious violent crimes never materialized, but it was used by many legislatures to justify a move toward punishment and away from rehabilitation in juvenile justice. In fact, after 1993, violent youthful offender crime decreased by 67% in the subsequent decade (Butts & Travis, 2002; Fox, 1996; Zimring, 2005).

Even so, the story or concern held true in the halls of Congress where U.S. House Representative Bill McCollum testified before the House Subcommittee on Early Childhood, Youthful, and Families:

In recent years, overall crime rates have seen a modest decline—nevertheless, this general decline masks an unprecedented surge of youthful violence that has only begun to gather momentum. Today's drop in crime is only the calm before the coming storm. . . . It is important to keep in mind that [the current] dramatic increase in youthful crime over the past decade occurred while the youthful population was declining. Now here is the really bad news: This nation will soon have more teenagers than it has had in decades. . . .This is ominous news, given that most [sic] violent crime is committed by older juveniles (those fifteen to nineteen years of age) than by any other age group. More of these youthfuls will come from fatherless homes than ever before, at the same time that youthful drug use is taking a sharp turn for the worse. Put these demographic facts together and brace yourself for the coming generation of "super-predators." (Zimring, 2005, pp. 1–3)

Superpredator: 1990s phrase used to describe a fictional class of impulsive, brutal, and remorseless adolescents who committed serious violent crimes.

RESEARCH: WHAT WORKS?

YOUTHFUL OFFENDER MYTHS

Throughout the history of the juvenile justice system, from the early institutions to the Child-Savers Movement, and during the establishment of today's juvenile court systems, myths concerning child and adolescent crime have often driven policy. Early myths about juvenile crime were really proxies for fear about this population, racial bias, anxiety about immigrants, and dislike of the poor. Although more recent public opinion, particularly during the later 1980s and 1990s "tough-on-crime' era, was simply wrong about juvenile crime, with most Americans believing that youthful offenders commit much more violent crime than they actually do and that school-based violence is much more common than it really ever has been. During this time of punitive and retributive responses by stakeholders across the country, these misperceptions and myths created additional support to transfer increasing numbers of adolescents to adult courts and to incarcerate them with adult offenders (Krisberg, 2005; Wolfgang, Thornberry, & Figlio, 1987).

A related myth, also exaggerated, was that juvenile courts could not handle nor respond to a growing class of violent youthful offenders labeled super-predators or serious and chronic offenders and, in tandem, that preventative programming and interventions were ineffective. The juvenile courts were viewed as too lenient and their rehabilitative focus useless for serious offenders who were often portrayed as impulsive, remorseless, and irredeemable (Jones & Krisberg, 1994; Redding, 1997). In response, the incarceration of youthful offenders in juvenile facilities expanded significantly with the belief that longer mandatory sentences would reduce crime because serious juvenile crime was being committed by this group. As it turned out, no class of super-predators ever emerged and incarceration for longer periods of time did nothing but increase the risk of offender recidivism—a retributive policy that made the problems worse (Howell, 2009; Loughran et al., 2009; Winokur, Smith, Bontrager, & Blankenship, 2008).

1. Why do you think some of these myths formed and are still believed by some today?

2. How would you address or fix this problem in others believing these types of myths?

In 1994, one of the most sweeping crime bills—the **Violent Crime Control and Law Enforcement Act**—was passed by Congress and signed into law by President Bill Clinton. A second crime-related bill—the **Gun-Free Schools Act**—was also enacted in 1994, and its impact, both intended and unintended, will be discussed in the upcoming school discipline sections. The Violent Crime Control and Law Enforcement law had several important consequences for youthful offenders: It lowered the age for adult prosecution from 15 to 13 for certain federal offenses; funded military-style boot camps (although there was no evidence that they were effective); made the penalties for drug distribution near schools, playgrounds, and youthful centers (covering almost all areas in most urban communities) three times more harsh; and made firearm possession a federal offense (P.L. 103–322, 1994).

Violent Crime Control and Law Enforcement Act: Passed in 1994, the largest crime bill in federal history that focused on punishment for crimes and a "tough on crime" approach to adult and juvenile justice.

Gun-Free Schools Act: Passed in 1994, a federal law that encouraged states to take a tough on crime approach to their schools by introducing "zero tolerance policies."

TODAY'S JUVENILE COURT REFORM

The punitively focused fortress built within the juvenile justice system began to be dismantled for several reasons in some parts of the country toward the end of the 1990s. Although this change and reformation has been intermittent and local and state government driven, a tide has turned in recognition that the myths that took hold during the tough-on-crime era were by and large not true and that the responses taken by policy makers were causing more harm than good across communities. With large expenses for punitive juvenile justice discipline straining many state budgets, an increased recognition that most juvenile offenders are not serious or chronic and that they do respond to preventative and diversionary interventions, and significant advances in the development of effective and evidence-based treatments and protocols, harsh punishments of youthful offenders have decreased and correspondingly improved public safety (Bonnie, Johnson, Chemers, & Schuck, 2013; Howell et al., 2013; Scott & Steinberg, 2008a, 2008b). In fact, from 2000 to 2012, nationwide arrests of juvenile offenders decreased 31%, offender cases decreased 34%, delinquency adjudications dropped 38%, commitments to juvenile court facilities decreased by 44%, and judicially waived cases to the adult courts decreased 34% (Sickmund, Sladky, & Wang, 2014).

State Trends

Correspondingly, several reformative trends have been happening across various states and, consequently, local juvenile courts. The first trend is for states to recognize some of these problems and to complete reviews of their juvenile justice system effectiveness, leading often to legislative reform. These broader reforms have focused on improving public safety, diverting first-time and low-level youthful offenders away from the courts, and investing in the use of effective prevention and treatment alternatives. Key states that have more fully pursued these reforms include Arkansas, Georgia, Hawaii, Indiana, Kansas, Kentucky, Nebraska, New Hampshire, South Dakota, Utah, and West Virginia (National Conference of State Legislatures, 2015).

A second state trend is the reformation of some laws returning or maintaining more adolescents within the juvenile court jurisdiction. Between 2011 and 2013, several states limited their **transfer and waiver criteria laws** for transfers of juvenile offenders to the adult criminal courts—Arizona, Indiana, Nevada, Missouri, Ohio, Vermont, and Wisconsin. In addition, some states raised their minimum age of juvenile court jurisdiction. By 2015, 41 states had set the maximum age at 17 years and 9 states set had this age at 16 and 15 (New York and North Carolina at age 15). Recently, the trend has been to increase the minimum age and keep these adolescents under the jurisdiction of the juvenile courts: Since 2011, Connecticut, Massachusetts, and New Hampshire moved their age of jurisdiction from 16 to 17, and numerous other states have been moving in this direction (National Conference of State Legislatures, 2015).

> **Transfer and Waiver Criteria Laws:** State laws that allow the transfer of youthful offenders to adult criminal courts based on certain age and offense criteria.

CASE STUDY

PETER A.

At the time of his crime, Peter A. was a 15-year-old sophomore in high school, living at home in Chicago, Illinois, with his mother, her fiancé, and his younger brother. He was seven years old when his parents divorced, and he was then raised by his mother, who supported the family through welfare and other public assistance. According to Peter, he was not particularly interested in school, although he enjoyed and did well in his earth science class, which involved a lot of "lab work with my hands." His probation officer reported him to be an "average student."

Peter spent much of his time with his older brother, who had his own apartment. Peter said: "[My brother] tried to keep me out of trouble . . . my sophomore year— homecoming—he said, 'there's gonna be trouble, they're gonna be shooting at the school. You can't go.' . . . and

they were shooting at the school, he was right. He wouldn't let me go to house parties or nothing. He was trying to keep me out of trouble, but at the same time, he had me along." Peter's older brother was involved in drug dealing, mostly cocaine. Peter said he would sometimes act as a courier for his brother, delivering drugs to customers. He also learned how to steal cars at an early age and had a juvenile adjudication for possession of a stolen vehicle when he was 13. He was placed on one year of probation and completed it to the satisfaction of his probation officer. He had no record of violent crime and no felony convictions. He experimented with both alcohol and marijuana, but he says he stopped using any drugs or alcohol when he was placed on probation.

After a theft of "drugs and money" from his brother's apartment, Peter said that he went with an 18-year-old to steal a van to help get the stolen goods back. Peter says he acted on his brother's instructions, and he has always admitted his involvement in stealing the van. Peter says he sat in the back seat of the stolen van with another young man, age 21, and the 18-year-old driver, both of whom had guns. They drove to the home of the men they were told had robbed Peter's brother. No one sat in the front passenger's seat because "there was glass on the seat" from the window Peter had broken during the theft.

According to Peter, when the three arrived at the victims' home, Peter stayed in the stolen van while the other two went inside. Peter heard shots, and a few seconds later, one of the co-defendants came running out of the house, without having recovered the drugs or the money. The two sped away from the home, leaving the other young man behind. Peter said that he learned on return to his brother's apartment that two people had been shot to death in the botched robbery. A few days later, he found out that one victim was a close high school friend of his, a young man who had no involvement in the original robbery of Peter's brother. This friend, as Peter put it, was "completely innocent . . . just in the wrong place at the wrong time." Peter was arrested approximately one week after the crime, after his two co-defendants were already in custody.

Peter was questioned for a total of eight hours at the police station, without his mother or an attorney present. During this time, he readily admitted to his role in stealing the van. His admission, "which the assistant State's Attorney wrote down, did not state whether defendant intended to kill the victims." Peter explained, "Although I was present at the scene, I never shot or killed anyone." There was no physical evidence indicating that Peter had entered the victims' home, and one of his co-defendants was proven at trial to have been the triggerman in the crime, for which he was convicted. Peter

was convicted of felony murder (two counts), which carries a mandatory sentence of life without parole. He was held accountable for the double murder because it was proved he had stolen the van used to drive to the victims' house.

The judge in Peter's case found that Peter, without a father at home, had fallen under the influence of his older brother. The judge called Peter "a bright lad" with "rehabilitative potential" and stated that he had qualms about sentencing Peter to life without parole. In his decision, he wrote: "[T]hat is the sentence that I am mandated by law to impose. If I had my discretion, I would impose another sentence, but that is mandated by law." Peter's defense attorney told a researcher for this report that one of the other perpetrators of the crime "was subsequently acquitted. So, now you have a fifteen-year-old who was waiting outside with a stolen car doing life without parole and a murderer on the streets." Peter, who has already spent nearly half his life behind bars, was 29 years old when he was interviewed for this report in 2005. In prison, has obtained his G.E.D. and completed a correspondence paralegal course, from which he graduated with very good grades. He works as a law clerk in the prison law library and has received one disciplinary ticket in the past six years of his incarceration for possessing an extra pillow and extra cereal in his cell (Human Rights Watch, 2005, p. 12).

1. If you were the judge, and had no sentencing guidelines or restrictions, what would you have decided?

2. Can Peter ever be released from prison? If so, how; if not, is it the right outcome?

Source: Human Rights Watch (2005). *The rest of their lives: Life without parole for child offenders in the United States.* New York, NY: Human Rights Watch.

Evidence-Based Interventions: Research-based (empirical) programs that have been found effective at their stated goals (for example, delinquency prevention and truancy reduction).

Evidence-Based Practices: Research-based (empirical) programs that have been found effective at their stated goals (for example, delinquency prevention and truancy reduction).

MacArthur Foundation (Models for Change Initiative): Leading national organization that has led juvenile justice reform from punishment toward a rehabilitative approach.

A third state trend is detention and incarceration reform and a corresponding focus on prevention, diversion of juvenile offenders from ongoing juvenile court involvement, and the use of **evidence-based interventions** within juvenile courts. Ohio and Texas have shifted dollars from institutional commitments to community-based alternatives, whereas Arkansas, Idaho, Mississippi, South Dakota, and West Virginia have increased state dollars to improve existing programs and expand community-based alternatives. **Evidence-based practices**, requiring rigorous evaluation methods, have been employed by these state stakeholders, as well as many other local and county jurisdictions (National Conference of State Legislatures, 2015; Soler, Schoenberg, & Schindler, 2009). Specifically, by 2016, 18 state statutes committed to the use of research-based practices in their juvenile justice system, with some states (Florida, North Carolina, Pennsylvania, and Washington) requiring thorough program evaluations to determine effectiveness. Washington state leads the way in evaluative research and evidence-based prevention and intervention programming for juvenile-justice–involved adolescents, as well as for those needing mental health and/or children's services supports (Nellis, 2016).

These reform efforts are also led by independent foundations, with the two most involved being the **MacArthur Foundation (Models for Change Initiative)** and **The Annie E. Casey Foundation** (Juvenile Detention Alternatives Initiative, JDAI). Later,

U.S. SUPREME COURT JUVENILE SENTENCING DECISIONS: 2002–2016

The Constitution's Eighth Amendment requires punishment to be proportioned to the offense (*Roper v. Simmons*, 543 U.S. 551 at 560, 2005). A key factor in this proportionality determination is the culpability of the offender. Since 2002, the Court in *Atkins v. Virginia, Roper v. Simmons, Graham v. Florida, Miller v. Alabama*, and *Montgomery v. Louisiana* narrowed the available use of the most severe criminal punishments for four categories of youthful offenders, finding these sentences violated the Amendment's Cruel and Unusual Punishment Clause.

Prior to the *Atkins v. Virginia* case, juvenile and adult offenders who were developmentally delayed (although in earlier years the descriptive term used was "mental retardation"—a term still commonly used in criminal law) could be sentenced by a jury to death row, in other words, a death sentence. If the individual committing a crime meets state statutory requirements, this sentence was allowed and the developmental and intellectual deficits were not mitigating or an excusable factor. In 1995, 18-year-old Daryl Atkins, along with an older accomplice, robbed a man, drove him to an ATM to withdraw more money, and took him to an isolated location where they shot him eight times. At trial, school records and the results of an intelligence quotient test confirmed that Atkins had an IQ of 59. As a result, the defense proposed that he was mildly mentally retarded; nonetheless, Atkins was sentenced to death. Upon appeal, in the Supreme Court's *Atkins* decision (2002), it was found that juvenile and adult offenders with lower intellectual functioning could not be sentenced to death because their disabilities limited impulse control and judgment abilities. "[T]hey do not act with the level of moral culpability that characterizes the most serious adult criminal conduct" (Atkins, 536 U.S., 304, p. 305). The Court further reasoned that the use of this severe punishment neither afforded retribution for the offender's act nor deterrence. This decision was important in providing serious juvenile and adult offenders with significant developmental disabilities respite from the death penalty.

From 1976 to 2005, those younger than 18 years of age could be sentenced to death for certain serious crimes (almost always homicide). If the crime was proven committed and the youthful offender guilty, this sentence was allowed across many states. In 1993, Christopher Simmons, at the age of 17, planned to murder Shirley Crook, bringing along two younger friends. The plan was to commit burglary and murder by breaking and entering, tying up the victim, and tossing the victim off a bridge. The three met in the middle of the night; however, one accomplice dropped out. Nonetheless, Simmons and the remaining accomplice broke into Mrs. Crook's home, bound her hands and covered her eyes, then drove her to a state park, and threw her off a bridge. At trial, Simmons confessed to the murder, performed a videotaped reenactment at the crime scene, and there was testimony that showed premeditation. Simmons was sentenced to death. Upon appeal, in the *Roper* decision (2005), the Supreme Court found juvenile offenders less culpable for

similar impulse control reasons cited in *Atkins*, among others, but went further to find adolescence itself a mitigating factor. The Court found differences between those younger than 18 years of age and adults so consequential as to not classify adolescents among the worst offenders. These differences include an underdeveloped sense of responsibility leading to impetuous actions as well as a lack of maturity, lessened character development, and vulnerability to negative influences and outside peer pressure. For these reasons, "almost every State prohibits those under 18 years of age from voting, serving on juries, or marrying without parental consent" (Roper, 543 U.S. 551, p. 557). The juvenile death penalty was thus abolished, and these individuals were resentenced to life without the possibility of parole (LWOP; Mallett, 2009).

Once the death penalty was found unconstitutional for juvenile offenders younger than the age of eighteen, the most severe sentence available was a life sentence without the possibility of parole (LWOP). It was argued that this life sentence to prison was little different from a sentence of death. This sentence, however, was available across many states for crimes that were nonhomicide, for example, rape or armed robbery. In 2003, Terrance Graham, along with two accomplices, attempted to rob a restaurant in Jacksonville, Florida. Aged 16 at the time, Graham was arrested for the robbery attempt and was charged as an adult for armed burglary and attempted armed robbery. After a guilty plea, county jail time, and a community-based probation sentence, Graham was arrested again six months after jail release for home invasion robbery. Although Graham denied involvement, he acknowledged that he was in violation of his plea agreement, and he was charged with probation violation, with the trial court sentencing him to life in prison. Because the Florida legislature had abolished their system of parole, this became a life sentence without parole. Upon appeal, in the *Graham* decision (2010), the Court found that sentencing nonhomicide youthful offenders to this life term was unconstitutional. In so holding, the Court reinforced and relied on its *Roper* decision in reiterating that youthful offenders are different from adult offenders, and that the differences in characteristics mean that "[i]t is difficult even for expert psychologists to differentiate between the juvenile offender whose crime reflects unfortunate yet transient immaturity, and the rare juvenile offender whose crime reflects irreparable corruption" and that "developments in psychology and brain science continue to show fundamental differences between juvenile and adult minds" (Graham 560 U.S. 48, p. 122). The Court decision, however, did not extend this constitutional protection to juvenile offenders sentenced to LWOP for homicide crimes. It did so next, although only for those states that had mandatory LWOP sentences for homicide crimes.

Numerous states had allowed life sentences for juvenile offenders convicted of murder; and under some state

(Continued)

(Continued)

laws, this sentence was mandatory. In 2003, Evan Miller, a 14-year-old from Alabama, was convicted in juvenile court, transferred to criminal court, and sentenced after he and another teenager committed robbery, arson, and murder. Miller committed the homicide in the act of robbing his neighbor after all three of them (Miller, accomplice, and neighbor) had spent an afternoon drinking and smoking marijuana. While attempting to rob the neighbor, a fight ensued and the neighbor was beaten unconscious. Miller and the accomplice later returned to destroy the evidence of what they had done by setting fire to the neighbor's trailer, killing him. Once found guilty, Alabama state law mandated an LWOP sentence for Miller. Upon appeal, in the *Miller* decision, the Supreme Court found these LWOP mandatory state laws to be unconstitutional. The Court furthered the reasoning from *Roper* and, more significantly from *Graham*, in finding that these laws "run afoul of our cases' requirement of individualized sentencing for defendants facing the most serious penalties" (Miller, 567 U.S. slip op

at 2). And most recently, in the 2016 *Montgomery* decision, the Supreme Court found that the decision in *Miller* must be retroactively applied to all juvenile offenders so sentenced (approximately 3,000 at the time), allowing a resentencing hearing or for immediate parole eligibility (577 U.S.___ 2016). Advocates are next pursuing cases to appeal to the Supreme Court that address any LWOP sentence for someone so convicted and younger than 18 years of age at the time of the crime.

1. **Why do you think the U.S. Supreme Court has made these decisions, all providing more Constitutional protections for youthful offenders?**

2. **Where do you think the next logical steps would be for state and local policies based on these court decisions?**

The Annie E. Casey Foundation: Leading national organization that has led juvenile justice reform since the 1980s from punishment toward a rehabilitative approach, including the Juvenile Detention Alternatives Initiative.

Developmentally Delayed (Developmental Disability): Description of individuals who are cognitively impaired or limited in some related ways; term used in earlier times was "mentally retarded."

Juvenile Death Penalty: Practice of sentencing to death those who committed their crime (homicide in all cases) when younger than 18 years of age. This was allowed from 1976 until 2005 when the U.S. Supreme Court found in *Roper v. Simmons* the juvenile sentence to violate the Constitutions' Eighth Amendment forbidding cruel and unusual punishment.

Life Sentence Without the Possibility of Parole (LWOP): Sentence that requires the offender to serve the rest of his or her life in prison (state or federal) without the chance of being released.

in Part III of the text, significant reviews will be presented about these foundation efforts, for their leadership has been important in showing stakeholders how juvenile courts can move from punitive to rehabilitative paradigms. For example, the JDAI program works to decrease the use of detention through collaboration across adolescent caring systems (including child welfare, mental health, schools, and other social service agencies), builds community-based rehabilitative alternatives, and uses standardized assessment instruments and data collection within juvenile courts to direct decision-making. Results, depending on length of implementation, have been positive in the more than 150 jurisdictions in 35 states in which the Initiative has been involved. These results include the lowering of detention populations and reoffending rates, sometimes by greater than 40%, and state incarceration placements by more than 34%, thus, often freeing up limited juvenile justice system resources to be used for more productive and cost-effective programming (Mendel, 2014).

A fourth state trend is the expansion in due process protections for juvenile offenders, with many states limiting the ability to waive counsel, improving the provision of quality attorney representation, and increasing attention to whether the adolescent is competent—having the cognitive ability to comprehend and participate in legal proceedings. By 2015, 23 states had expanded definitions of competence for juvenile offenders to include the review of mental health problems, intellectual disabilities, and/or developmental immaturity, with 12 states having done so since 2010—Arkansas, California, Idaho, Louisiana, Maine, Maryland, Michigan, New Hampshire, Nevada, Ohio, Oklahoma, and South Dakota (National Conference of State Legislatures, 2015).

Federal Trends

At the federal level, the Juvenile Justice and Delinquency Prevention Act has moved forward on numerous priorities and reforms since the 1990s, thus helping to direct and incentivize states to follow. These initiatives have helped to shift states toward a rehabilitative paradigm as well as to identify what efforts are significantly problematic at the state and local level. The Act requires states to determine the existence and extent of their disproportionate contact and confinement of minority youthful offenders and highlights the difficulties and challenges of having juvenile offenders in adult jail and prison facilities. The Office of Juvenile Justice and Delinquency Prevention continues to support the rehabilitation of most youthful offenders and to have them remain in the juvenile justice system, with attention on the involvement of girls and delinquency, mental health collaboration across juvenile courts, the impact of trauma on the system, and funding evidence-based programs (Lawrence & Hemmens, 2008; Office of Juvenile Delinquency and Prevention, 2014a, 2014b). Although funding for this federal law has not been a priority for Congress, its grant dollars have been decreased by 80% from 2007 to 2015. On a different federal front, in 2016, the Obama Administration banned the use of solitary confinement for juvenile offenders being held in adult federal prisons (Shear, 2016), a practice that has lasting harmful impacts on most incarcerated prisoners and is a topic explored more fully later in the text.

These initiatives and priorities, along with supportive developmental and brain science research, have increasingly recognized that youthful offenders are different from adult offenders (Bonnie et al., 2013). Of significant impact, the Supreme Court has established a new paradigm on youthful offender sentencing since 2002, relying on the developmental and brain science evidence that adolescents are not adult offenders and have capacities to change, as well as on social and behavioral science evidence that distinguishes youthful from adult offenders. Some of the findings of this research reveal that adolescent brains do not fully develop until the mid-20s, and this age group is found to be emotional and impulsive and, thus, susceptible to external coercion (Steinberg, 2014a).

CHAPTER REVIEW

CHAPTER SUMMARY

This chapter reviewed the history of the juvenile justice system, its ongoing shifts from a rehabilitative to punitive focus, and today's challenges, along with progress, moving away from a "tough-on-crime" paradigm. The history of juvenile justice has delineated stages: from 1750 to 1850 and the almshouses and houses of refuge; from 1850 to 1890, an era characterized by the Child-Saving Movement; from 1899 to 1920 and the establishment of the juvenile courts; from 1920 to 1960, whereby the institutionalization of youthful offenders greatly increased; from 1960 to 1980 and the introduction of individual rights for youthful offenders; the 1990's "tough-on-crime" approach; and today's reform efforts and movement toward rehabilitative justice.

Reform today includes legislative changes that require numerous states to use evidence-based efforts, keep more youthful offenders out of the adult criminal justice system, minimize the use of detention and incarceration facilities, improve due process and attorney representation for those young people involved with the juvenile courts, and address the disproportionate minority involvement problem across the juvenile justice system. Much of this reform and paradigm shift has been seen in U.S. Supreme Court decisions since 2005, where it has been repeatedly found that adolescents are developmentally different from adults and they should not be held to the same legal standards or consequences.

KEY TERMS

almshouses 27

Child-Saving Movement 28

developmentally delayed 39

evidence-based interventions 38

evidence-based practices 38

Gun-Free Schools Act 36

houses of refuge 28

incarceration facilities 31

juvenile death penalty 39

life sentence without the possibility of parole (LWOP) 39

MacArthur Foundation (Models for Change Initiative) 38

placing out 28

probation officers 31

reform schools 29

superpredator 35

The Annie E. Casey Foundation 38

transfer and waiver criteria laws 37

truancy 32

U.S. Supreme Court 32

Violent Crime Control Act and Law Enforcement Act 36

DISCUSSION QUESTIONS

1. How has the juvenile justice system changed over time; are there themes or cycles to these changes?

2. What are the outcomes and implications for the tough-on-crime approach in juvenile justice?

3. What factors are leading to today's juvenile court reformation?

4. What are the more important changes that juvenile justice reformers have accomplished over the past few decades?

5. What does the early history of the juvenile courts tell us about later shifts in juvenile justice philosophy?

6. What policies have been ineffective in the history of the juvenile courts? Why were these policies supported and implemented?

7. What race and gender issues have been identified in the history of juvenile justice?

8. What do you think are the best public policies for the juvenile courts to pursue?

9. What are the themes of the most recent Supreme Court juvenile offender sentencing decisions? Do you agree or disagree with these Court decisions?

10. If you could predict the future, what would the juvenile justice system be like in 10, 20, or 30 years? What do you think it should look like or be, and why?

11. What are the most pressing problems facing today's juvenile courts? Justify your answers

---

https://edge.sagepub.com/mallett

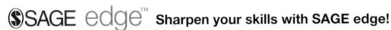 **Sharpen your skills with SAGE edge!**

SAGE edge for students provides a personalized approach to help you accomplish your coursework in an easy-to-use learning environment. You'll find mobile-friendly eFlashcards and quizzes, as well as videos, web resources, and links to SAGE journal articles to support and expand on the concepts presented in this chapter.

CHAPTER 3

THE MEASUREMENT OF JUVENILE CRIME

1,733.00	20,796.00	3,445.00	34,557.00	34,
2,315.00	2,315.00	45,534.00	7,566.00	42,45
3,207.00	38,484.00	38,484.00	38,484.00	5,34!
1,347.00	16,164.00	16,164.00	16,164.00	16,16
2,621.00	15,726.00	15,256.00	33,245.00	3,42:
2,276.00	2,276.00	25,412.00	54,322.00	2,342
3,029.00	18,174.00	3,654.00	23,312.00	3,42:
4,610.00	55,320.00	55,320.00	9,220.00	234,42:
2,619.00	31,428.00	31,428.00	31,428.00	31,428
1,231.00	14,772.00	14,772.00	14,772.00	14,772
		16,392.00	16,392.00	16,392
1,264.00	15,168.00	15,168.00	15,168.00	15,168
4,890.00	58,680.00	58,680.00	58,680.00	58,
1,142.00	13,704.00	13,704.00	13,704.00	13,7(
1,327.00	15,924.00	15,924.00	15,924.00	15,924
4,250.00	51,000.00	51,000.00	51,000.00	51,000
3,907.00	46,884.00	46,884.00	46,884.00	46,884
3,156.00	37,872.00	37,872.00	37,872.00	37,872
	480,091.00	512,600.00	550,009.00	3,955,090

▲ Data is your friend, and the only way to really understand delinquency and crime trends.
©iStockphoto.com/echoevg

INTRODUCTION

During the U.S. presidential election in 2016, Hillary Clinton's remark on President Bill Clinton's 1994 Violent Crime Control and Law Enforcement Act was criticized repeatedly by her opponents. During Bill Clinton's reelection campaign in 1996, Hillary Clinton said in support of the Act (C-Span, January 28, 1996):

> We also have to have an organized effort against gangs, just as in a previous generation we had an organized effort against the mob. We need to take these people on, they are often connected to big drug cartels. They are not just gangs of kids anymore. They are often the kind of kids called "super-predators": no conscience, no empathy. We can talk about why they ended up that way, but first we have got to bring them to heel.

Every generation views children as becoming more violent and dangerous (i.e., "super-predators") than the children in the previous generations (Bernard & Kurlychek, 2010). Such views have propelled dramatic changes in the juvenile justice system over the past generation that have increasingly treated juvenile offenders like adult criminals.

But are children really becoming more violent and dangerous? Numerous data sources on youthful offending and juvenile crime are used by researchers to try to find an answer to this question. These data sources are largely of three types: official data, victim data, and self-report data. As will be discussed in this chapter, all three types of data sources have strengths and limitations in trying to present the actual delinquency offending and victimization across the country. The best way to find an answer to the question "are children getting more violent and dangerous today?" is to refer to more than one type of data source that complement each other's limitations.

OFFICIAL DATA

Official data on juvenile delinquency include data collected from government agencies that handle delinquency cases, such as law enforcement agencies, juvenile courts, and correctional institutions. Official data, therefore, include only those juveniles who have gone through the juvenile justice system. Because not all juveniles who engage in delinquency end up in the juvenile justice system, official data may not reflect the actual number of delinquencies in any given year, even for the most serious offenses like murder and aggravated assault. This is sometimes referred to as the "dark figure of crime" (Gibbons, 1979) or the number of crime and delinquency acts that do not come to the attention of law enforcement. What the official data reflect, instead, may be the juvenile justice system's handling of youthful offenders. An increase in the number of arrests of suspected gang members in one year, for instance, may not reflect an actual increase in gang activity that year but may reflect a change in law enforcement handling of the gang. Such change may be driven by the perception that gang activity is increasing and becoming more violent. The increase in gang arrests, then, provides support for the negative perception, resulting in a self-fulfilling prophecy. Nonetheless, official data provide valuable information regarding law enforcement agencies and the juvenile justice system's handling of delinquency and status offense. Three major types of official data exist: Uniform Crime Reports' Summary Reporting

▲ The FBI is a leading national organization that gathers data on crime and delinquency.

System, National Incident-Based Reporting System, and juvenile court data.

Uniform Crime Reports

When there is a news report on an increase or decrease in the U.S. crime rate, it is most likely based on the Uniform Crime Reporting (UCR) data. The Federal Bureau of Investigation (FBI) began the UCR program in 1930 to collect, report, and archive national crime data, which today covers more than 18,000 law enforcement agencies at the city, university/college, county, state, tribal, and federal levels. No reliable national crime data existed in the United States until the UCR program. The participation in the UCR program is voluntary, and the percentage of the total population covered in the UCR program has been increasing and reached almost 98% of the total population in 2015 (Federal Bureau of Investigation, 2016b). The UCR program does not cover 100% of the U.S. population because some agencies, especially smaller agencies, might fail to report their crime data for whatever reasons, such as lack of budget or a computer tracking mistake.

Because states vary in the statutory definition of crime and delinquency, the FBI provides a uniform definition on 28 offenses (see Table 3.1) and a handbook to explain how to classify and count these offenses. The UCR program today encompasses four subprograms: Summary Reporting System (SRS) program, National Incident-Based Reporting System (NIBRS) program, Law Enforcement Officers Killed and Assaulted (LEOKA) program, and Hate Crime Statistics Program, all of which produce an annual report.

Summary Reporting System

The traditional SRS program (often referred to as the "UCR") collects two major types of data: "offenses known to law enforcement" and "persons arrested." The data on "offenses known to law enforcement" are collected on eight offenses, which are divided into **violent offenses**, including murder, rape, robbery, and aggravated assault, and **property offenses**, including burglary, larceny-theft, motor-vehicle theft, and arson. By its nature, no information on offenders is available for the data on "offenses known to law enforcement," but the SRS program collects supplementary information on each offense, such as the time of day when a burglary occurred. The data on "persons arrested" are collected on 20 additional offenses, including other assaults, forgery and counterfeiting, fraud, embezzlement, stolen property (buying, receiving, and possessing), vandalism, weapons (carrying, possessing, etc.), prostitution and commercialized vice, sex offenses (except rape and prostitution), drug abuse violations, gambling, offenses against family and children, driving under the influence, liquor law violations, drunkenness, disorderly conduct, vagrancy, all other offenses, suspicion, and curfew and loitering law violations. Until 2010, the SRS program collected data on one additional offense: runaways. The SRS also collects the clearance rate for the eight offenses from "offenses known to law enforcement."

Unlike "offenses known to law enforcement" where offenders are unknown, the data on "persons arrested" include some information about individuals who are arrested, including gender, age, and race/ethnicity. Thus, delinquency data can be gathered only from the data on "persons arrested." The SRS program considers all children who are younger than 18 years of age as juveniles, irrespective of the state's definition of juvenile. The SRS arrest data exclude the contacts with police where no offense was committed and the juvenile detentions for abuse and neglect. In 2014, 1,024,000 arrests were made involving adolescents who were younger than 18 (Office of Juvenile Justice and Delinquency Prevention, 2017). This does not mean that 1 million juveniles were arrested in 2015 because some juveniles

Violent Offenses (Crimes): Crimes that are often against persons and felonies (homicide, rape, robbery).

Property Offenses (Crimes): Offenses that are committed only on property, not against persons, for example, burglary or motor vehicle theft.

UCR Offense Definitions

Criminal homicide	a.) Murder and nonnegligent manslaughter: the willful (nonnegligent) killing of one human being by another. Deaths caused by negligence, attempts to kill, assaults to kill, suicides, and accidental deaths are excluded. The program classifies justifiable homicides separately and limits the definition to: (1) the killing of a felon by a law enforcement officer in the line of duty; or (2) the killing of a felon, during the commission of a felony, by a private citizen. b.) Manslaughter by negligence: the killing of another person through gross negligence. Deaths of persons due to their own negligence, accidental deaths not resulting from gross negligence, and traffic fatalities are not included in the category Manslaughter by Negligence.
Forcible rape/legacy rape	The carnal knowledge of a female forcibly and against her will. Rapes by force and attempts or assaults to rape, regardless of the age of the victim, are included. Statutory offenses (no force used—victim under age of consent) are excluded.
Revised rape	Penetration, no matter how slight, of the vagina or anus with any body part or object, or oral penetration by a sex organ of another person, without the consent of the victim. Attempts or assaults to commit rape are also included; however, statutory rape and incest are excluded. In December 2011, the UCR program changed its definition of SRS rape to this revised definition. This change can be seen in the UCR data starting in 2013. Any data reported under the older definition of rape will be called "legacy rape."*
Robbery	The taking or attempting to take anything of value from the care, custody, or control of a person or persons by force or threat of force or violence and/or by putting the victim in fear.
Aggravated assault	An unlawful attack by one person upon another for the purpose of inflicting severe or aggravated bodily injury. This type of assault usually is accompanied by the use of a weapon or by means likely to produce death or great bodily harm. Simple assaults are excluded.
Burglary (breaking or entering)	The unlawful entry of a structure to commit a felony or a theft. Attempted forcible entry is included.
Larceny-theft (except motor vehicle theft)	The unlawful taking, carrying, leading, or riding away of property from the possession or constructive possession of another. Examples are thefts of bicycles, motor vehicle parts and accessories, shoplifting, pocketpicking, or the stealing of any property or article that is not taken by force and violence or by fraud. Attempted larcenies are included. Embezzlement, confidence games, forgery, check fraud, etc., are excluded.
Motor vehicle theft	The theft or attempted theft of a motor vehicle. A motor vehicle is self-propelled and runs on land surface and not on rails. Motorboats, construction equipment, airplanes, and farming equipment are specifically excluded from this category.
Arson	Any willful or malicious burning or attempt to burn, with or without intent to defraud, a dwelling house, public building, motor vehicle or aircraft, personal property of another, etc. Arson statistics are not included in this table-building tool.

Notes: In December 2011, the UCR Program changed its SRS definition of rape: "Penetration, no matter how slight, of the vagina or anus with any body part or object, or oral penetration by a sex organ of another person, without the consent of the victim." Starting in 2013, rape data may be reported under either the historical definition, known as "legacy rape," or the updated definition, referred to as "revised." For more information, see the FBI's New Rape Definition Frequently Asked Questions at https://ucr.fbi.gov/recent-program-updates/new-rape-definition-frequently-asked-questions/view

Source: Uniform Crime Report, 2016. U.S. Department of Justice, Federal Bureau of Investigation.

are arrested more than once in a year and each arrest is counted toward the total arrests for that year.

The SRS data have several major strengths. First, the SRS program has amassed almost nine decades worth of U.S. crime data. No other sources, other than the juvenile court data discussed later, have collected crime data for such a long time period. Although there have been some methodological changes over time in how data are collected and in the definition of some offenses (e.g., the older definition of rape did not consider that males can be a victim of rape), the SRS data can describe a trend (or change) over time in the number of "offenses known to law enforcement" and "persons arrested." The SRS data could, therefore, provide an answer for the question, "are children getting more violent and dangerous today?" Second, although the SRS program does not cover 100% of the U.S. population, it is the only program that attempts to collect **census data** on all offenses known to law enforcement

Census Data: Data collected from everyone in the population of interest (e.g., all juveniles who are incarcerated).

CLEARANCE RATE

In the UCR program, an offense can be cleared by law enforcement agencies when the following three conditions are met: (1) at least one offender is arrested for the offense, (2) at least one offender is charged with the offense, and (3) at least one offender is handed over to a criminal or juvenile court for prosecution. A clearance rate of an offense is calculated based on the number of offenses that are cleared and not based on the number of arrests. One person who committed multiple offenses can clear more than one offense in one arrest, whereas multiple arrests may result in only one offense clearance if those who are arrested committed a single offense as a group. It should be noted that many offenses are not cleared within a year; thus, some clearances in any given year may pertain to offenses from preceding years.

1. How does this situation make tracking crime easier or more difficult?

2. Do you have suggestions on a better way to do this?

and persons arrested. The likelihood of an offense being reported to law enforcement and the clearance rate vary greatly by offense, but especially for serious offenses like murder, the SRS data can provide a good estimate of the extent (or level and prevalence) of crime in the United States.

Some limitations of the SRS data need to be considered. First, the SRS delinquency data rely on arrest data because the age of offender is unknown for the data on "offenses known to law enforcement." One major limitation of arrest data is that they underestimate the number of actual offending because only a small number of individuals who break a law are ever arrested, especially when it comes to minor offenses. Second, even the data on "offenses known to law enforcement" underestimate actual offending because only a small number of offenses come to the attention of law enforcement ("the dark figure of crime"), particularly with **victimless crimes**, such as prostitution, liquor law violation, and drug abuse violation. Third, even for the offenses involving a victim, such as rape and domestic violence, many victims do not report the victimization, thus, escaping the attention of law enforcement. Fourth, the FBI uses a hierarchy rule when determining arrest data and counts only the most serious offense committed by a person who is arrested for multiple offenses. If a person is arrested for a murder that he or she committed during a burglary, only the murder is counted toward the SRS data. The SRS arrest data count the arrests of more than one persons, all of whom may be arrested for a single offense, another reason why arrest data do not necessarily reflect the actual offending, and this is a pertinent issue with youthful offenders because children are more likely than adults to engage in law-breaking behaviors in groups. Finally, the SRS may include inaccurate data reported by the participating law enforcement agencies, some of which are mistakes and others are possibly intentional by downgrading crimes to less serious offenses, classifying offending to gang-related (to get federal funding), and "unsubstantiating" or discouraging crime reports to law enforcement (Eterno & Silverman, 2012).

National Incident-Based Reporting System

The National Incident-Based Reporting System (NIBRS) was developed in 1988 to address the limitations of the traditional SRS data and to improve the detail, amount, and quality of national crime data. The FBI is working currently to make the NIBRS program an exclusive national crime data collection program to replace the SRS program by 2021. Several major differences exist between the SRS and the NIBRS programs. First, the NIBRS program collects data on

Victimless Crimes:
Crimes that do not involve a victim because everyone who is involved consents to the law-breaking behavior.

CRIME RATE

Because the population size varies (year to year and group to group), and more importantly, the proportion of persons who are in the delinquency/crime-prone years (late teens to early twenties) in a population varies, it is important to compare crime rates instead of raw numbers of offenses or arrests when examining the trend in crime over time or the extent of crime across different groups. A rate for murder in one year is calculated, for example, by dividing the number of murders in the year by a total number of the population in the same year, estimated from the U.S. Census. The UCR program multiplies all rates by 100,000 to calculate rates per 100,000 population. According to the SRS data, the violent crime rate (based on murder, rape, robbery, and aggravated assault) was 372.6 per 100,000 in 2015, which means that for every 100,000 people in the United States, there were 372.6 violent crimes in 2015 (Federal Bureau of Investigation, 2016b).

1. How best would you present this to policy makers who may not understand crime rate comparisons?

2. Why do you think the public at times believes violent crime rates are increasing in their communities when it is not true?

32 offenses: 22 Group A offenses and 10 Group B offenses (see Table 3.2). The offense definitions used in the NIBRS program are based on common-law definitions, as well as on the definitions used in the traditional SRS program. These 32 offenses are classified into three types of crime: those against persons, property, and society. Second, the NIBRS program is based on incident, rather than on offense, arrest, or offense clearance, and it reports a greater amount of detail for each incident that comes to the attention of law enforcement. Only the arrest data for each incident are available for Group B offenses. The NIBRS program captures up to 57 data elements that consist of information on the following six segments: incident, offense, property, victim, offender, and arrestee (see Table 3.3). Third, unlike the traditional SRS program, in which the hierarchy rule is used, the NIBRS program counts multiple offenses (up to ten) for each incident. Fourth, the NIBRS program distinguishes attempted and completed offenses for Group A offenses. Fifth, whereas the SRS program collects information on the victim–offender relationship on murder only, the NIBRS program collects the victim–offender relationship information on all "crime against person" offenses and robbery. Sixth, the NIBRS program collects data on the suspected drug use during or prior to an engagement in another crime on which arrest occurred. Additionally, the NIBRS program collects information on the weapon use for all violent offenses. Finally, the NIBRS collects the basic demographic information, including age, sex, and race, of all those who are involved in the incident, including victims, offenders, and arrestees.

The NIBRS program is a significant improvement to the traditional SRS program through the use of automation and standardization. Nevertheless, given the changes in the data collection methodology, a caution is in order when comparing the crime data over time, especially when combining the data from the SRS and the NIBRS programs. In addition, the participation rate in the NIBRS program by law enforcement agencies is still low with less than 40% (6,648 out of more than 18,000) of law enforcement agencies that participated in the SRS contributed data in 2015 (Federal Bureau of Investigation, 2016a). Yet, some of the same limitations of the SRS program apply to the NIBRS program because it also suffers from "the dark figure of crime" problem. Even if the quantity, detail, and quality of data collected from law enforcement agencies are improved, the NIBRS data are still based only on those offenses known to law enforcement, whereas many offenses, especially minor offenses,

NIBRS Group A and Group B Offenses

Group offenses and NIBRS Group B offenses		
Group A offenses		
Offense category	Offense types	Crime against
Arson	Arson	Property
Assault offenses	Aggravated assault	Person
	Simple assault	Person
	Intimidation	Person
Bribery	Bribery	Property
Burglary/breaking and entering	Burglary/breaking and entering	Property
Counterfeiting/forgery	Counterfeiting/forgery	Property
Destruction/damage/ vandalism of property	Destruction/damage/vandalism of property	Property
Drug/narcotic offenses	Drug/narcotic violations	Society
	Drug equipment violations	Society
Embezzlement	Embezzlement	Property
Extortion/blackmail	Extortion/blackmail	Property
Fraud offenses	False pretenses/swindle/confidence game	Property
	Credit card/automated teller machine fraud	Property
	Impersonation	Property
	Welfare fraud	Property
	Wire fraud	Property
Gambling offenses	Betting/wagering	Society
	Operating/promoting/assisting gambling	Society
	Gambling equipment violations	Society
	Sports tampering	Society
Homicide offenses	Murder and nonnegligent manslaughter	Person
	Negligent manslaughter	Person
	Justifiable homicide	Person/not a crime
Kidnapping/abduction	Kidnapping/abduction	Person
Larceny/theft offenses	Pocket-picking	Property
	Purse-snatching	Property
	Shoplifting	Property
	Theft from building	Property

Group offenses and NIBRS Group B offenses		
Group A offenses		
Offense category	**Offense types**	**Crime against**
	Theft from coin-operated machine or device	Property
	Theft from motor vehicle	Property
	Theft of motor vehicle parts or accessories	Property
	All other larceny	Property
Motor vehicle theft	Motor vehicle theft	Property
Pornography/obscene material	Pornography/obscene material	Society
Prostitution offenses	Prostitution	Society
	Assisting or promoting prostitution	Society
Robbery	Robbery	Property
Sex offenses, forcible	Forcible rape	Person
	Forcible sodomy	Person
	Sexual assault with an object	Person
	Forcible fondling	Person
Sex offenses, nonforcible	Incest	Person
	Statutory rape	Person
Stolen property offenses	Stolen property offenses	Property
Weapon law violations	Weapon law violations	Society
Group B offenses		
Offense category	**Offense type**	**Crime against**
Bad checks	Bad checks	Property
Curfew/loitering/vagrancy violations	Curfew/loitering/vagrancy violations	Society
Disorderly conduct	Disorderly conduct	Society
Driving under the influence	Driving under the influence	Society
Drunkenness	Drunkenness	Society
Family offenses, nonviolent	Family offenses, nonviolent	Society
Liquor law violations	Liquor law violations	Society
Peeping tom	Peeping tom	Society
Runaway[a]	Runaway	Not a crime
Trespass of real property	Trespass of real property	Society
All other offenses	All other offenses	Person, property, or society

[a]In January 2011, the FBI discontinued the collection of arrest data for runaways. Agencies may continue to collect data on runaways, but the FBI will no longer use or publish that data.

Source: A Guide to Understanding NIBRS. Uniform Crime Reporting Program, National Incident-Based Reporting System. U.S. Department of Justice, Federal Bureau of Investigation.

NIBRS Segments

NIBRS segments	
• Incident Information 　○ Incident Date 　○ Incident Hour 　○ Exceptional Clearance 　○ Exceptional Clearance Date • Offense Information 　○ Offense Codes 　○ Attempted vs. Completed 　○ Offender Suspected Use (of alcohol, drug, or computers) 　○ Location 　○ Type and Number of Premises Entered 　○ Type of Criminal Activity/Gang Information 　○ Weapon/Force Used 　○ Bias Motivation • Property Information 　○ Loss Type 　○ Property Description 　○ Value of Property 　○ Date Recovered 　○ Number of Motor Vehicles Stolen/Recovered 　○ Drug Types and Amounts • Victim Information 　○ Connection to Offenses 　○ Type of Victim 　○ Age/Sex/Race/Ethnicity/Resident Status of Victim 　○ Assault and Homicide Circumstances 　○ Injury Types 　○ Relationships of Offenders	• Offender Information 　○ Age/Sex/Race of Offender • Arrestee Information 　○ Arrest Date 　○ Type of Arrest 　○ Arrest Offense Code 　○ Arrestee Weapons 　○ Age/Sex/Race/Ethnicity/Resident Status of Arrestee 　○ Disposition of Minors • Group B Arrest Information 　○ Type of Arrest 　○ Arrestee Weapons 　○ Age/Sex/Race/Ethnicity of Arrestee 　○ Disposition of Minor	

Source: A Guide to Understanding NIBRS. Uniform Crime Reporting Program, National Incident-Based Reporting System. U.S. Department of Justice, Federal Bureau of Investigation.

victimless offenses, and offenses of rape and domestic violence, go unreported and escape the attention of law enforcement and several of those who engage in delinquency never go through the juvenile justice system.

Juvenile Court Data

The Children's Bureau of the U.S. Department of Labor began collecting information on cases that are processed by juvenile courts in 1926 and started publishing *Juvenile Court Statistics* reports. The data collection effort was taken over by the Office of Juvenile Justice and Delinquency Prevention (OJJDP) of the U.S. Department of Justice in the 1970s, and the National Center for Juvenile Justice (NCJJ), a division of the National Council of Juvenile and Family Court Judges, was funded by OJJDP in 1975 to collect both aggregated and individual case data. Unlike the UCR, the information on the juvenile court data collected on individual cases from each state is not uniform; however, all cases include basic demographic information of the juvenile (including age at referral, gender, and race), the offense(s) charged, the referral date, the characteristics of processing (e.g., detention), and the disposition. The National Juvenile Court Data Archive (NJCDA), which was established by the OJJDP, holds more than 15 million cases that have been handled by juvenile courts and continues producing *Juvenile Court Statistics* reports. The unit of the count of cases used in these reports is the number of cases that resulted in disposition, and the offense categories examined are similar to the UCR offense categories.

The strengths and limitations of the juvenile court data are similar to those of the UCR data. Like the SRS, the NJCDA has amassed more than nine decades worth of data totaling 15 million cases handled by juvenile courts, which allows for the examination of the trend over time in the cases being processed by juvenile courts. Given the changes in the methodology in collecting data and in the type of data collected over time, however, caution is in order when comparing the juvenile court data year to year. Like the SRS program, the NCJJ attempts to collect the census data on all cases processed by juvenile courts, but the percentage of the juvenile population covered by this data collection effort is much smaller than the comparable number for the SRS. The *Juvenile Court Statistics 2013*, the most current report, for instance, was based on data collected from approximately 2,400 juvenile courts, which covered only 84% of the juvenile population (Hockenberry & Puzzanchera, 2015). Finally, the same major limitation of the UCR data applies to the juvenile court data because only a few juveniles who engage in delinquency and status offense are arrested; of those who are arrested, only a few are referred and end up being handled by juvenile courts; and out of those, a rare few get a disposition. Noting this, Thorsten Sellin (1931, p. 337) cautioned many years ago that "the value of a crime rate for index purposes decreases as the distance from the crime itself in terms of procedure increases." In other words, the further away from the actual criminal offending that the data collection takes place, from offenders to victims to law enforcement to juvenile courts to correctional institutions, the less reliable the data become in terms of representing the crime. Nevertheless, juvenile court data offer valuable information at both the national and local levels for researchers, policy makers, and other stakeholders to identify problems and improve the juvenile justice system and society's handling of the youthful offender population.

NATIONAL CRIME VICTIMIZATION SURVEY

The National Crime Victimization Survey (NCVS, formally known as the National Crime Survey until 1992), sponsored by the Bureau of Justice Statistics (BJS) of the U.S. Department of Justice, is a national survey on victimization of crime, collected annually by the U.S. Census Bureau since 1972. The NCVS is a nationally representative household survey; in 2015, it involved 163,880 individuals age 12 or older residing in 95,760 households or group quarters like dormitories (Truman & Morgan, 2016). All individuals residing in selected households are eligible for an interview every six months for a three-year period about their criminal victimization experiences during the six months prior to each interview. The NCVS collects individual victimization data on personal crimes, including rape, sexual assault, robbery, aggravated assault, simple assault, and purse snatching/pocket-picking, and household victimization data on property crimes, including household burglary, motor vehicle theft, and property theft (see Table 3.4). The NCVS does not collect data on murder (because murdered victims cannot take the survey), kidnapping, arson, and victimless crimes (including prostitution, gambling, and drug use). For each victimization incident, the NCVS collects information on the type of crime, whether it is attempted or completed; type of victimization (monetary loss or physical injury); characteristics of the victim and perpetrator (including age, sex, race, and victim–offender relationship); and whether victimization incidents were reported to law enforcement.

The NCVS was created with four specific purposes, which distinguish the NCVS from the UCR: "(1) to develop detailed information about the victims and consequences of crime,

Crime Classification Taxonomy

Personal crime	Violent crime	Rape/sexual assault	Rape	Completed
				Attempted
			Sexual Assault	Completed
				Attempted
		Robbery	With injury	Completed
				Attempted
			Without injury	Completed
				Attempted
		Assault	Aggravated	Completed with injury
				Attempted/threatened with weapon
			Simple	Completed with injury
				Attempted/threatened without weapon
		Purse snatching/pocket picking		Completed
				Attempted
	Property crime	Burglary	Forcible entry	Completed
				Attempted
			Unlawful entry without force	Completed
				Attempted
		Motor vehicle theft		Completed
				Attempted
		Theft	Less than $50	Completed
				Attempted
			$50–$249	Completed
				Attempted
			$250 or more	Completed
				Attempted
			Amount not available	Completed
				Attempted

Source: Bureau of Justice Statistics, National Crime Victimization Survey, 2013.

(2) to estimate the number and types of crimes not reported to the police, (3) to provide uniform measures of selected types of crimes, and (4) to permit year-to-year comparisons" (Bureau of Justice Statistics, 2014b, p. 1). One key strength of the NCVS, especially when compared with the UCR program, is that the NCVS attempts to shed light on the unreported crimes ("dark figure of crime") that do not come to the attention of law enforcement by collecting information from victims of crime rather than from law enforcement agencies. The NCVS also collects more detailed information on each incident of crime than does the traditional SRS program. Although the methodology of data collection has changed over time, the NCVS, like the UCR program, allows for the examination of the trend in

REPRESENTATIVE SAMPLING

How do representative samples work? When a population of interest is large (e.g., an entire population of juveniles in a country, or even a state), it is not feasible to collect self-report data from everyone in the population. Self-report data can, instead, be collected from a small subset of the population, called a *sample*. When carefully and randomly selected from a population, a sample, although small, can represent the population well, and such a sample is called a *representative sample* of whatever the population of interest. A nationally representative sample of a population, for instance, refers to a sample that is representative of, or identical to, the entire population of the United States, except for the size.

. . . .

1. So why are representative samples important in research on crime?

2. What if we just used nonrandom sampling techniques? What's the problem?

victimization over a long time period (almost five decades). Finally, although the NCVS does not collect census data, or the victimization experiences from the entire population of the United States, because it carefully selects a nationally representative sample of the population, the NCVS allows for the estimation of the extent of criminal victimization in any given year for the population as a whole and for subgroups based on sex, age, race, and the location of residence.

The NCVS has several limitations. First, like any other self-report data, there are concerns over the validly and reliability of the survey questions in measuring consistently what they are supposed to measure. Because the statutory definition of crime and delinquency varies by state and the definition of crime likely varies from individual to individual (e.g., do you count fist-fighting with your brother as an assault?), the NCVS collects characteristics of each victimization incident through a series of questions, instead of asking which criminal victimization respondents experienced. Based on the characteristics of an incident that are collected, an algorithm, and a classification taxonomy, the NCVS then determines which specific crime victimization (e.g., "completed assault") to classify each incident. This method allows for a standardization of coding each criminal victimization, minimizing the variations from individual to individual and across states in the definition of crime. Another difficulty with a self-report survey like the NCVS is the telescoping effect, which refers to the tendency to incorrectly perceive the timeline of past events. To minimize the telescoping effect and other recall bias, the NCVS interviews respondents every six months for three years for a total of seven times, thus, providing a clearer and shorter time frame for past events and prevents duplicate counting or memory loss. Finally, there is a question of honesty in answering interview questions, especially on sensitive victimization experiences like rape and domestic violence, particularly if the victim knows the perpetrator and a family member is the perpetrator.

Second, the NCVS has limited use when it comes to examining delinquency offending because victims often do not know the exact age of the perpetrator to determine whether they were victimized by children younger than 18 years of age. The NCVS is also limited with respect to victimization among juveniles because children who are younger than 12 years of age are excluded from the survey. Third, the NCVS excludes individuals who are homeless or institutionalized in correctional institutions and the following: shelters for abused women, mental hospitals, soup kitchens, "regularly scheduled mobile food vans," "targeted no sheltered outdoor

▲ Measurement is a science; there are rules to follow that allow findings to be reliable and valid.

locations," and "group quarters for victims of natural disasters" (Bureau of Justice Statistics, 2014b, p. 7). Although small in number, some households that are on the Census Bureau's Dangerous Address Database may also be excluded from the NCVS survey because of the concern over safety of field representatives. In other words, the NCVS excludes vulnerable members of the society with a possibly higher chance of criminal victimization, such as homeless persons, women and children in shelters, individuals in mental institutions, inmates in correctional facilities, and individuals who reside in a dangerous neighborhood, all of which inevitably include some youthful offenders.

Self-Report Data

Self-report data on delinquency offending are obtained by asking juveniles to report on their delinquency offending through interview or questionnaire; thus, it is "the nearest data source to the actual behavior" (Thornberry & Krohn, 2000, p. 34). Since the first self-report survey of delinquency was conducted in the 1950s (Short & Nye, 1958), the self-report survey has been a popular source of delinquency data among researchers and policy makers because it allows for the inclusion of questions that are not about delinquency that the other data sources do not include. This is important for explaining the **etiology** of delinquency (e.g., information on education, socioeconomic status of parents, relationships with parents, and friends' delinquency). In addition, self-report surveys on delinquency, like the NCVS, attempt to shed light on the "dark figure of crime" or on the unreported crimes that do not come to the attention of law enforcement by collecting information from juveniles themselves. There are no census data on delinquency offending, unlike the UCR; however, all self-report surveys discussed in this chapter are based on a nationally representative sample of juveniles. There are numerous self-report surveys of delinquency, but this chapter is focused on four of the most well-known surveys: National Longitudinal Survey of Youth, National Youth Survey-Family Study, Monitoring the Future, and Youth Risk Behavior Surveillance System. Because these self-report surveys share similar strengths and limitations, they are discussed together after describing each survey.

National Longitudinal Survey of Youth. The National Longitudinal Survey of Youth (NLSY) is part of a larger study called the *National Longitudinal Surveys (NLS)* sponsored by the U.S. Bureau of Labor Statistics (BLS) and conducted by the Center for Human Resource Research (CHRR) at the Ohio State University. The NLS began in the 1960s to collect labor-market experiences among nationally representative samples of four cohorts—older men, mature women, young men, and young women. The longitudinal studies of these four original cohorts have ended, but the NLS has added four additional longitudinal studies, funded by numerous different agencies, and has continued to collect data. First, the National Longitudinal Survey of Youth (NLSY79) study has been collecting data since 1979, annually until 1994 and biennially since then, from a nationally representative sample of 12,686 men and women who were between the ages of 14 to 22 at the initial interview. Second, the "NLSY79 children" (ages 0–14) and the "NLSY79 young adults" (ages 15 and older) studies have been collecting data since 1986 from 11,512 children born to women who participated in the NLSY79. Finally, the NLSY97 study has been collecting data annually since 1997 from a nationally representative sample of 8,984 children who were between the ages of 12 and 18 at the initial interview. The sample sizes at the initial interview have changed over time due to some dropping out of the study or relocating without notice (Bureau of Labor Statistics, n.d.).

Etiology: Cause, or set of causes, for a certain outcome.

MEASUREMENT VALIDITY AND RELIABILITY

The accuracy of criminal offending/victimization data obtained by a survey can be assessed in terms of validity and reliability of survey questions used to collect the data. Measurement validity refers to the accuracy of survey questions in measuring what they are supposed to measure, and measurement reliability refers to the consistency with survey questions in measuring what they are measuring. Let's assume that we want to find out the age when juveniles drank alcohol for the first time. The question "how old were you when you drank alcohol for more than a taste for the first time?" is probably a valid measure of the first age of drinking alcohol. The same question, however, is not a valid measure of the first age of buying alcohol or using drugs. The question can also be reliable if the same answer (e.g., age 13) is obtained from a respondent consistently, unless a young person who has never drank alcohol at the first survey drank alcohol before the next survey. Another question "how many days in the past year have you drank alcohol?" may not be a reliable measure of the number of drinking days in a year (ranging from 0 to 365 days) with young people who drink frequency if they have to guess their answer every time. In most self-report social science surveys, concepts such as "delinquency" are measured using more than one question.

1. In research, why are we concerned about measurement reliability and validity?

2. What happens if a measurement is not valid?

Let's ask the question, how do cross-sectional and longitudinal designs work? Cross-sectional data are collected from a group at one point in time, whereas longitudinal data are collected from the same group more than once over an extended period. Longitudinal surveys of delinquency that follow the same juveniles over an extended period are rare because of the difficulty in collecting such data. Longitudinal data are, however, valuable in determining a time order of events and in establishing a causal relationship between theoretical variables—for example, association with delinquent peers, experience of abuse, and dropping out of school—and delinquency.

Although the core questions of the NLSY are related to labor-market experiences, supplemental questions include alcohol and drug use, delinquency and criminal behaviors, and arrest and incarceration record (see Table 3.5). The data collected for the NLSY studies are massive, the specific data collected vary from study to study, and listing them all is beyond the scope of this chapter, for the data collection goes beyond a series of interviews to include standardized test scores, school transcripts, cognitive, socio-emotional, and physiological assessments, among many other sources. The NLSY97 study, for instance, collects information on employment, education, parents and family-process information, dating and marriage, sexual activity and pregnancy, income, health, various attitudes (e.g., on justice systems), and crime and substance use. The NLSY97 collects information on delinquency offending using a delinquency index, arrest and incarceration history, and the use and abuse of alcohol, tobacco, and various different illicit drugs and legal drugs. The delinquency index includes the following behaviors: running away from home, carrying a gun, belonging to a gang, damaging a property, stealing something worth less than or more than $50, attacking or assaulting someone, and selling drugs. Although the number and the detail of delinquency data collected by the NLSY studies are small, the NLSY studies allow for the longitudinal examination of delinquency of four different cohorts and the intergenerational transmission of delinquency over two generations. Because data on various aspects of life are collected, the NLSY also allows for the examination of the etiology of delinquency. Finally, the NLSY studies oversample minority groups, including blacks and Hispanics or Latinos, allowing for the focused examination of trend and extent in delinquency across these groups (Bureau of Labor Statistics, n.d.).

NLS: Survey Groups, Sample Sizes, Interview Years, and Survey Status

Survey group	Age cohort	Birth year cohort	Original sample	Initial year/ latest year	Number of surveys	Number at last interview	Status
Older men	45–59	4/1/06–3/3/21	5,020	1966/1990	13	[a]2,092	Ended
Mature women	30–44	4/1/22–3/31/37	5,083	1967/2003	21	2,237	Ended
Young men	14–24	4/1/41–3/31/52	5,225	1966/1981	12	3,398	Ended
Young women	14–24	1943–1953	5,159	1968/2003	22	2,859	Ended
NLSY79	14–21	1957–1964	[b]12,686	1979/2004	21	[c]7,724	Continuing
NLSY79 children	birth–14	—	[d]—	1986/2004	10	[c]3,190	Continuing
NLSY79 young adults	[e]15 and older	—	[d]—	1994/2004	6	[c]4,238	Continuing
NLSY97	12–16	1980–1984		1997/2004	8	[c]7,756	Continuing

[a]Interviews in 1990 also were conducted with 2,206 widows or other family members of deceased respondents.

[b]After dropping the military (in 1985) and economically disadvantaged nonblack/non-Hispanic oversamples (in 1991), the sample contains 9,964 respondents eligible for interview.

[c]The latest sample size available is from the 2002 survey.

[d]The size of the NLSY79 child sample depends on the number of children born to female NLSY79 respondents, attrition over time, and the gradual aging of the children into the young adult sample. The size of the young adult sample depends on the number of children who reach age 15 in each survey year. Information about the number interviewed in each survey is available in Chapter 4.

[e]In 1998 only, the young adults eligible for interview were limited to those ages 15 to 20.

Note: The latest sample size available is from round 7.

Source: Bureau of Labor Statistics. (n.d.) *National longitudinal surveys: A program of the U.S. Bureau of Labor Statistics.* National Longitudinal Surveys, Bureau of Labor Statistics, Washington DC.

National Youth Survey-Family Study. The National Youth Survey-Family Study (NYSFS, formally known as the National Youth Survey until 2000) began in 1976 by the Institute of Behavioral Science at the University of Colorado (Elliott, Huizinga, & Ageton, 1985). The NYSFS, funded by the Department of Health and Human Services of the National Institutes of Health (NIH) and the National Institute of Mental Health, collected data from a nationally representative sample of 1,725 adolescents between the ages of 11 and 17 and of 1,683 of at least one of their parents. The NYSFS is a longitudinal survey that followed the original respondents into their forties until 2004, and 12 waves of data (i.e., data are collected in 12 different time periods) have been collected for the 27-year time period. The NYSFS examines changes in attitudes, beliefs, and behaviors related to delinquency and drug use. In 2003 and 2004, the NYSFS added data collected from the original respondents' partner and children and now includes three-generational data that allow for the examination of the intergenerational transmission of delinquency attitudes, beliefs, and behaviors. The index of delinquent behaviors used by the NYSF (see Table 3.6) has been replicated and used in subsequent self-report studies.

Monitoring the Future. The University of Michigan Survey Research Center, with grants from the National Institute on Drug Abuse (NIDA) of the NIH, has been conducting the Monitoring the Future (MTF) project annually since 1975 to collect data on drug use among young people (Johnston, O'Malley, & Backman, 1996). The original project included 12th-grade students only, and 8th-grade and 10th-grade students were added to the project starting in 1991; the project surveys approximately 50,000 students in ~420 public and private middle and high schools each year. The MTF project has been expanded to include college students and young adults. In addition to the cross-sectional data collected from these age groups, the MTF has also been collecting longitudinal data biennially from a representative sample of each of the 12th-grade samples of students since 1976 until they turn age 55. The

MTF is a school-based survey given in students' classrooms, although the longitudinal data are collected via questionnaire sent by mail. The MTF data are limited to just one type of delinquent behavior, drug use, but detailed and extensive data on the following four issues are collected on each drug examined: (1) lifetime, past 12 month, and last 30 days use; (2) perceived risk of using; (3) the level of disapproval of the use; and (4) perceived availability. Both legal and illicit drugs are examined by the MTF survey, including marijuana/hashish, inhalants, hallucinogens, LSD, ecstasy, cocaine, crack, other cocaine, heroin (with a needle and without a needle), narcotics other than heroin, amphetamines, methamphetamines, crystal methamphetamine, sedatives, tranquilizers, any prescription drug (without a prescription), Rophypnol, alcohol, cigarettes, smokeless tobacco, electronic vaporizers, steroids, nitrites, PCP, and methaqualone.

Youth Risk Behavior Surveillance System. The Youth Risk Behavior Surveillance System (YRBSS) has been conducted biennially since 1990 to track health risk behaviors and their consequences, such as death and disability, among young people. Health risk behaviors examined include law-breaking behaviors in terms of both victimization and offending, drinking and driving, texting and driving, drug, tobacco, and alcohol use; carrying a weapon to school; getting into a physical fight, rape; and other inappropriate sexual behaviors. The YRBSS is a school-based survey that encompasses both national and local surveys involving representative samples of 9th- through 12th-grade students, and since its inception more than 3.8 million students have participated (Centers for Disease Control and Prevention, n.d.). The national survey is conducted by the Centers for Disease Control and Prevention (CDC) among a nationally representative sample of students in both public and private schools, and local surveys are conducted by the Departments of Health and Education using the representative sample of students at each local level. Although the YRBSS is a limited data source on delinquency, compared with other self-report surveys, because its focus is on health behaviors among young people, it can be used to confirm the results of other self-report surveys of delinquency. Additionally, the YRBSS includes other various health-related measures that may be related to delinquent behaviors and the etiology of delinquency, such as basic health information, sexually transmitted diseases, HIV and AIDS, mental health, suicide ideation and attempt, bullying, sexual behaviors, and physical activity.

Methodological Strengths and Limitations. Two of the most significant limitations of the earlier self-report surveys (MTF and YRBSS) have been their tendencies to focus on minor delinquency and status offenses and the potential exclusion of at-risk young people because self-report surveys are often given at school (Hindelang, Hirschi, & Weis, 1981). This excludes those who skipped, dropped out, or were expelled from school and those who are in mental health/substance abuse residential facilities or correctional institutions. Even with those not given at school, earlier self-report surveys are criticized for their absence of serious offenders, thereby undermining both the prevalence and the degree of delinquency offending. Critiques of earlier self-report studies also include the way questions were asked (e.g., the use of the set of response categories such as "never," "once or twice," "several times," and "often") that resulted in the masking of a small number of repeated offenders who may engage in a significantly high number of delinquency.

▼ TABLE 3.6

Specific Delinquency and Drug Use Scales

Drug use		General delinquency	
1.	Hallucinogens	1.	Stole motor vehicle
2.	Amphetamines	2.	Stole something GT$50
3.	Barbiturates	3.	Bought stolen goods
4.	Heroin	4.	Runaway
5.	Cocaine	5.	Carried hidden weapon
Minor delinquency		6.	Stole something LT$5
1.	Hit teacher	7.	Aggravated assault
2.	Hit parent	8.	Prostitution
3.	Theft LT$5	9.	Sexual intercourse
4.	Joyriding	10.	Gang fights
5.	Disorderly conduct	11.	Sold marijuana
6.	Panhandled	12.	Hit teacher
7.	Runaway	13.	Hit parent
Index offenses		14.	Hit students
1.	Aggravated assault	15.	Disorderly conduct
2.	Sexual assault	16.	Sold hard drugs
3.	Gang fights	17.	Joyriding
4.	Stole motor vehicle	18.	Sexual assault
5.	Stole something GT$50	19.	Strong armed students
6.	Broke into bldg./vehicle	20.	Strong armed teachers
7.	Strong armed students	21.	Strong armed others
8.	Strong armed teachers	22.	Stole something $5–50
9.	Strong armed others	23.	Broke into bldg./vehicle
		24.	Panhandled

Source: *Explaining Delinquency and Drug Use* by D.S. Elliott, David Huizinga & Suzanne S. Ageton. Reprinted with permission from SAGE Publications, Inc.

In addition to the continued improvements in the sampling and administration of the survey, the self-report surveys underwent significant changes over time, including a focus on serious and chronic offenders (Elliott & Ageton, 1980; Wolfgang, Figlio, & Sellin, 1972). Although there are limitations of the self-report survey, it is considered to offer a more accurate estimate of actual delinquency offending than the UCR data addressing and uncovering information on the "dark figure of crime" (Thornberry & Krohn, 2000).

JUVENILE DELINQUENCY

In considering the strengths and limitations of each of the major sources of delinquency—official data, victim data, and self-report data—similarities and differences in what the data indicate about both the extent (or level and prevalence) and the trend (or change) in delinquency are examined. Specifically, data related to delinquency and the juvenile justice system are examined, including the following: arrest data, court data on delinquency, court data on status offense (public order), youthful offender commitments, juvenile detention, and state correctional facilities. Additionally, what some of the available data indicate about the gender and race/ethnicity differences are also discussed.

Youthful offending and delinquency have been on the decline since the mid-1990s. Why do you think this has happened?

Arrest Data

The trials and tribulations of juvenile justice policy, as it has changed historically and as it is now shifting away from a tough-on-crime approach, still impacts many young people today. In 2014, 1,024,000 arrests were made involving adolescents who were younger than 18 years of age. This represents only 9% of all arrests nationwide and is a decrease of 50% since 2005 for **youthful offenders**. Half of these juvenile arrests were for drug abuse violations, simple assault, larceny-theft, and disorderly conduct (Office of Juvenile Justice and Delinquency Prevention, 2017).

Arrest rates for those younger than 18 are at historic lows (see Figure 3.1), including arrests for violent crimes (down 44% since 2005) and all other offenses reported in the UCR. The juvenile arrest rate peaked at approximately 8,500 per 100,000 in 1996 and has been decreasing rapidly ever since, down to almost one third of the peak in 2014. Assuming that the arrest data represent some aspects of delinquency offending, they indeed indicate the increase in offending among young people at the time Hillary Clinton made the infamous remark in 1996 (in fact, it was at the peak), but her argument that young people are becoming "super-predators" does not seem to be accurate because the arrest rate, even just for violent crime, among juveniles has not stopped its downward trend since 1994.

Youthful Offenders: Those under the age of majority (typically 18 years of age) who come under juvenile court supervision.

Delinquency Adjudication: Juvenile court order that finds the minor delinquent and places the young person under state (and typically probation) supervision.

Court Data—Delinquency

Juvenile courts handled almost one million delinquency cases in 2014, which was a decrease of 46% since 1997 across all delinquent offense categories (person, property, drug, and public order). More than 80% of the cases were referred to the juvenile court by law enforcement. Most (83%) cases involved high-school–aged adolescents (14 years of age and older), with 16- and 17-year-olds accounting for nearly half of all cases (48%).

Juvenile Arrest Rate Trends: Arrests per 100,000 Juveniles Ages 10–17, 1980–2016

All Crimes
Arrests per 100,000 persons ages 10—17

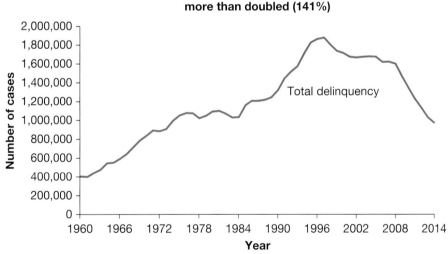

Source: OJJDP Statistical Briefing Book & Bureau of Justice Statistics.

▼ FIGURE 3.2

Juvenile Court Delinquency Caseloads, 1960–2014

Between 1960 and 2014, juvenile court delinquency caseloads more than doubled (141%)

Total delinquency

Source: Furdello & Puzzanchera (2015). *Delinquency cases in juvenile court, 2013.* OJJDP.

Since 1997, **delinquency adjudications** decreased as follows: person offenses—decreased 34%; property offenses—decreased 42% (larceny theft and vandalism decreased 19% and burglary and trespassing decreased 21%); drug law violations—decreased 23%; and public order offenses—decreased 38%. The person offenses include violent crimes, down overall 9% since 2001, such as **criminal homicide** (decreased 23%), **forcible rape** (decreased 15%), and aggravated assault (decreased 21%). Robbery is an exception for there was a 22% increase in the number of cases handled by juvenile courts since 1997. Although

Criminal Homicide: Killing of one person by another; often, first degree homicide is the most serious, requiring preplanning of the murder.

Forcible Rape: Sexual assault of another person against his or her will.

Number of Cases Handled by Juvenile Courts, 2005–2014

Most serious offense	Number of cases 2014	Percent change		
		10 year, 2005–2014	5 year, 2010–2014	1 year, 2013–2014
Total delinquency	974,900	–42%	–27%	–5%
Total person	262,800	–40%	–23%	–3%
Violent Crime Index[a]	57,100	–36%	–22%	0%
Criminal homicide	900	–31%	–7%	14%
Forcible rape	8,600	–23%	–4%	–1%
Robbery	20,900	–22%	–21%	–2%
Aggravated assault	26,700	–46%	–27%	2%
Simple assault	173,400	–39%	–23%	–4%
Other violent sex offenses	7,700	–34%	–13%	–5%
Other person offenses	24,600	–51%	–31%	–3%
Total property	333,500	–46%	–33%	–6%
Property Crime Index[b]	242,200	–42%	–31%	–6%
Burglary	59,500	–42%	–31%	–6%
Larceny-theft	166,800	–40%	–31%	–6%
Motor vehicle theft	12,000	–63%	–23%	5%
Arson	4,000	–51%	–25%	–7%
Vandalism	48,400	–53%	–38%	–8%
Trespassing	26,500	–50%	–38%	–8%
Stolen property offenses	9,700	–51%	–30%	–3%
Other property offenses	6,700	–62%	–29%	–6%
Drug law violations	128,900	–30%	–20%	–6%
Public order offenses	249,700	–44%	–27%	–7%
Obstruction of justice	128,200	–36%	–21%	–2%
Disorderly conduct	65,000	–51%	–35%	–11%
Weapons offenses	20,200	–52%	–29%	–13%
Liquor law violations	5,900	–62%	–58%	–16%
Nonviolent sex offenses	10,800	–22%	–6%	3%
Other public order offenses	19,700	–51%	–28%	–12%

[a]Includes criminal homicide, forcible rape, robbery, and aggravated assault.

[b]Includes burglary, larceny-theft, motor vehicle theft, and arson.

Note: Detail may not add to totals because of rounding. Percent change calculations are based on unrounded numbers.

Source: Furdello & Puzzanchera (2015). *Delinquency cases in juvenile court,* 2013. OJJDP

the declines in delinquency adjudication rates have been consistent across the juvenile justice system nationwide, the juvenile courts still handle more than three times as many cases as they did in the 1960s (Furdella & Puzzanchera, 2015; Sickmund & Puzzanchera, 2014).

The decrease in the overall arrest and juvenile court caseload rates over the past decade has had little impact on the disproportionate involvement of adolescents of color in the juvenile justice system (Puzzanchera & Robson, 2014). In 2010, black youthful offenders were more likely to be processed through juvenile court for person offenses, whereas whites and other minority group youths were more likely to be processed through juvenile court for property offenses, although the disparity between white and black youthful drug offenders has narrowed over the past decade (see Figures 3.3 and 3.4; Sickmund & Puzzanchera, 2014; U.S. Census Bureau, 2014).

Girls made up 26% of delinquency cases handled by juvenile courts in 2013, which was an increase from 19% in 1985 (see Table 3.8). The recent declines in all delinquency adjudications and offenses is similar across gender in person offenses (decreased 29% for females and 37% for males), property offense (decreased 42% for both), drug law violations (decreased 23% for both), and public order offenses (decreased 38% for females and 37% for males). Females have a high level of involvement in some delinquency offenses, according to the juvenile court data: larceny theft (45%), simple assault (30%), liquor law cases (32%), and disorderly conduct (35%). There is also similar disproportionate involvement in the juvenile justice system among black girls, with 41% of juveniles who were being processed through the juvenile court for person offenses being in this group (Furdella & Puzzanchera, 2015; Sickmund & Puzzanchera, 2014).

Court Data—Status Offenses (Public Order)

In addition to delinquencies, the juvenile courts nationally processed nearly 150,000 status offense cases in 2013, those acts that are only illicit for those younger than 18 (see

▼ FIGURE 3.3

Juvenile Court Delinquency Caseloads by Race

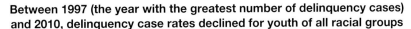

Between 1997 (the year with the greatest number of delinquency cases) and 2010, delinquency case rates declined for youth of all racial groups

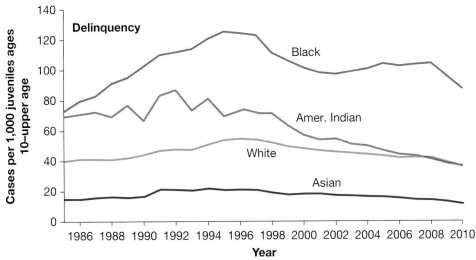

Source: Sickmund & Puzzanchera (2014). Juvenile Offenders and Victims: 2014 National Report. National Center for Juvenile Justice.

Juvenile Court Caseloads by Race per Offense

Case rate trends varied across race and offense but, in all offense categories and in nearly all years from 1985 through 2010, the rates for black youth were substantially higher than the rates for other youth

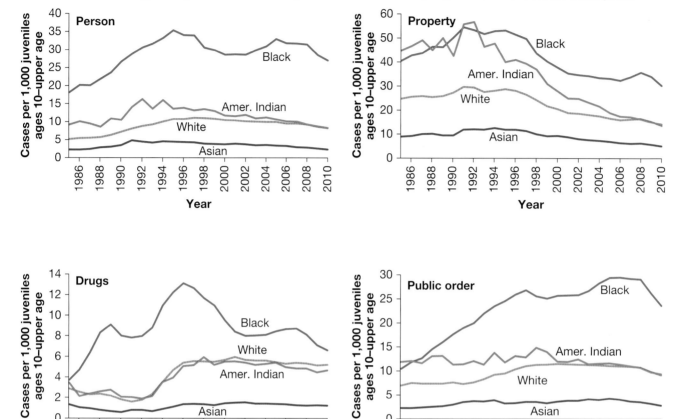

Source: Sickmund & Puzzanchera (2014). *Juvenile Offenders and Victims: 2014 National Report*. National Center for Juvenile Justice.

Figures 3.5 and 3.6). This represented a small increase since the mid-1990s and a 6% increase since 2001. Law enforcement agencies were responsible for 60% of status offense referrals, an increase of 6% since 2001, with violations for truancy being most common (36%), followed by liquor law violations (22%), **ungovernability** (12%), running away (11%), curfew violations (10%), and other violations (9%). Females make up 43% of status offenses cases processed by juvenile courts (runaways, 58%; truancy, 46%; curfew violations, 33%; ungovernability, 42%; and liquor law violations, 39%). In 8% of status offense cases handled by juvenile courts, the adolescent was placed outside the home into locked juvenile court facilities (Levin & Cohen, 2014; Puzzanchera & Hockenberry, 2010; Salsich & Trone, 2013; Sickmund & Puzzanchera, 2014).

Youthful Offender Commitments

Most delinquency adjudications result in formal probation supervision and, for some, **out-of-home placement**. In 2013, person and public order cases were more likely ordered to some type of **residential placement**, whereas property and drug offenses cases were more likely ordered to formal probation supervision. From this juvenile offender population, 70,000 are

Percentage Change in Cases Handled by Juvenile Courts by Gender, 1985–2010

	Percent change			
	1985–2010		2001–2010	
Most serious offense	Male	Female	Male	Female
Total delinquency	5%	69%	−21%	−13%
Person offense	62%	190%	−18%	−8%
Violent Crime Index	3%	58%	−8%	−13%
Criminal homicide	−18%	−17%	−21%	−38%
Forcible rape	15%	85%	−15%	−18%
Robbery	0%	58%	21%	32%
Aggravated assault	6%	59%	−22%	−20%
Simple assault	102%	222%	−21%	−8%
Other violent sex offenses	51%	118%	−4%	50%
Other person offenses	102%	359%	−24%	−3%
Property offense	−39%	12%	−28%	−15%
Property Crime Index	−44%	14%	−28%	−12%
Burglary	−40%	−15%	−21%	−21%
Larceny-theft	−44%	21%	−27%	−7%
Motor vehicle theft	−61%	−41%	−57%	−61%
Arson	−21%	8%	−42%	−29%
Vandalism	−14%	41%	−20%	−16%
Trespassing	−24%	−3%	−22%	−21%
Stolen property offenses	−52%	−30%	−42%	−42%
Other property offenses	−43%	−28%	−53%	−59%
Drug law violations	110%	117%	−15%	−11%
Public order offenses	68%	126%	−16%	−14%
Obstruction of justice	147%	158%	−18%	−25%
Disorderly conduct	89%	236%	−11%	2%
Weapons offenses	43%	115%	−11%	−17%
Liquor law violations	−26%	19%	−1%	12%
Nonviolent sex offenses	−15%	1%	−26%	5%
Other public order offenses	−10%	−1%	−26%	−27%

Notes: Between 1985 and 2010, the overall delinquency caseload for females increased 69%, compared with a 5% increase for males. Among females, the number of aggravated assault cases rose substantially (up 59%) from 1985 to 2010. In comparison, among males, aggravated assault cases were up 6%. Between 2001 and 2010, the number of aggravated assault cases dropped for both males and females, but the decline for males (22%) was slightly greater than the decline for females (20%). Detail may not add to totals because of rounding. Calculations are based on unrounded numbers.

Source: Adapted from Puzzanchera and Hockenberry's *Juvenile Court Statistics 2010.*

Source: Sickmund & Puzzanchera (2014). *Juvenile Offenders and Victims: 2014 National Report.* National Center for Juvenile Justice.

Petitioned Status Offense Cases Over Time, 1995–2002

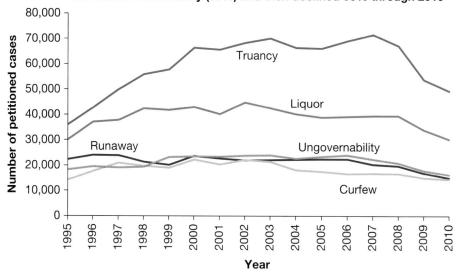

Between 1995 and 2002, the formally handled status offense caseload increased considerably (59%) and then declined 33% through 2010

Source: Sickmund & Puzzanchera (2014). *Juvenile Offenders and Victims: 2014 National Report.* National Center for Juvenile Justice.

FIGURE 3.6

Petitioned Status Offense Case Rates by Race, 1995–2010

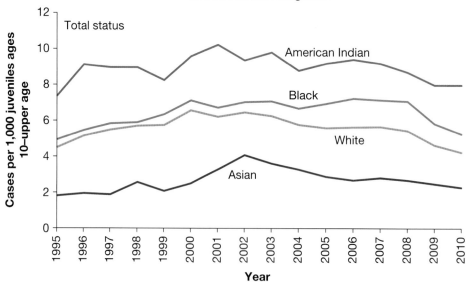

For all years between 1995 and 2010, the total petitioned status offense case rate for American Indian youth was higher than that for juveniles of all other racial categories

Source: Sickmund & Puzzanchera (2014). *Juvenile Offenders and Victims: 2014 National Report.* National Center for Juvenile Justice.

confined on any given day to detention centers, residential facilities, or state correctional facilities, with two thirds of these placements in public facilities, and one third in private facilities. The placement numbers involving juvenile offenders have declined by half since 1999 and across all major delinquency offense types that preceded placement. Of those confined in 2010,

Delinquency Outcomes, 2010

Most serious offense	Adjudicated cases			
	Number ordered to placement	Percent ordered to placement	Number ordered to probation	Percent ordered to probation
Total delinquency	112,600	26%	260,300	61%
Person offense	31,300	29%	68,300	63%
Violent Crime Index	12,400	38%	19,100	58%
Criminal homicide	200	53%	100	42%
Forcible rape	600	37%	1,000	57%
Robbery	6,500	45%	7,500	52%
Aggravated assault	5,100	31%	10,400	63%
Simple assault	15,400	25%	40,500	64%
Other violent sex offenses	1,700	29%	3,900	65%
Other person offenses	1,700	23%	4,800	66%
Property offense	36,800	25%	93,000	63%
Property Crime Index	27,500	26%	66,000	63%
Burglary	13,800	33%	25,800	61%
Larceny-theft	10,200	19%	35,000	65%
Motor vehicle theft	3,100	40%	4,000	52%
Arson	400	24%	1,200	69%
Vandalism	4,600	20%	15,300	68%
Trespassing	1,600	18%	5,700	62%
Stolen property offenses	1,900	33%	3,400	57%
Other property offenses	1,100	27%	2,600	62%
Drug law violations	9,200	19%	33,700	69%
Public order offenses	35,300	29%	65,400	53%
Obstruction of justice	26,200	34%	37,300	49%
Disorderly conduct	3,400	15%	13,700	60%
Weapons offenses	3,100	31%	6,400	63%
Liquor law violations	400	13%	2,100	69%
Nonviolent sex offenses	900	26%	2,200	65%
Other public order offenses	1,400	19%	3,800	55%

Notes: Cases involving youth adjudicated for serious person offenses, such as homicide or robbery, were the most likely cases to result in residential placement. Probation was the most restrictive disposition used in 260,300 cases adjudicated delinquent in 2010—61% of all such cases handled by juvenile courts. Obstruction of justice cases had a high residential placement rate, stemming from the inclusion in the category of certain offenses (e.g., escapes from confinement and violations of probation or parole) that have a high likelihood of placement. Detail may not add to totals because of rounding. Calculations are based on unrounded numbers.

Source: Sickmund & Puzzanchera (2014). *Juvenile Offenders and Victims: 2014 National Report*. National Center for Juvenile Justice.

Case Processing Overview

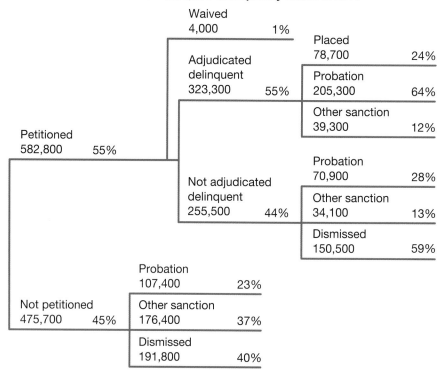

Case flow for 1,058,500 delinquency cases in 2013

Source: Furdello & Puzzanchera (2015). *Delinquency cases in juvenile court, 2013.* OJJDP.

89% had a prior conviction and were adjudicated delinquent prior to the current court order for placement; of these, 33% were for person offenses (24% for violent offenses) and 4% for status offenses (see Table 3.9 and Figure 3.7). These offense percentages have changed little over the past two decades (Office of Juvenile Justice and Delinquency Prevention, 2017; Sickmund & Puzzanchera, 2014).

Juvenile Detention

Detention is ideally used by law enforcement for safety reasons only, to protect the youthful offenders and/or the community, and it is used for either **pretrial holding** (adjudication determination) and/or post-trial sentencing purposes for both low-level and more serious offenses (as explained in Chapter 1). In many jurisdictions, detention centers also serve as the point of intake and initial detention after adolescents are arrested by law enforcement. Although still serving these purposes, the use of the detention centers has shifted since the mid-1990s to include the holding of more nonviolent offenders. Of those youthful offenders adjudicated delinquent, 18,000 are held nationally in detention centers on any given day, a rate that has, however, declined 20% since 2001. Lengths of stay can vary from less than a day for minor offenses to months for complicated and more serious person offenses, though the average is fewer than 60 days with higher averages for those placed in public facilities and for males.

It should be noted that some states report their detention center placement numbers to include group homes, shelter care facilities, and other similar options; however, these other

Pretrial Holding:
Placement of a youthful offender in a detention center prior to adjudication or judicial decision.

placements often make up less than 5% of the detained population. Of those youthful offenders who were held in detention, the following was the offense that led to this outcome: person offenses account for 32%, property cases 30%, status (public order) offenses 29%, drug offenses 9%, and technical violations (e.g., violations of court orders) 14%. Males are 150% more likely than females and black youth 140% more likely than white youth to be detained (see Figure 3.8; Office of Juvenile Justice and Delinquency Prevention, 2017; Sickmund & Puzzanchera, 2014; The Council of State Governments Justice Center, 2015).

State Correctional Facilities

From the adjudicated delinquent juvenile offender population, 38,000 are confined on any given day to state correctional facilities, averaging 3 to 12 months of confinement. This represents a decrease of 51% since 1999 for youthful offenders placed after delinquency adjudication, which corresponds with a closure of one third of the juvenile incarceration facilities nationwide. In total, approximately 400,000 adolescents were in some form of out-of-home placement ordered by a juvenile court every year, with between 120,000 and 200,000 adolescents younger than 18 transferred to and tried in adult courts nationwide. Exact figures on youthful offender transfers are not available because most states do not report this information

▼ FIGURE 3.8

Gender, Race, and Detention

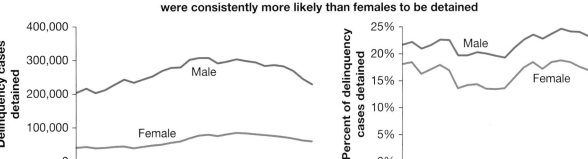

Males accounted for most delinquency cases involving detention and were consistently more likely than females to be detained

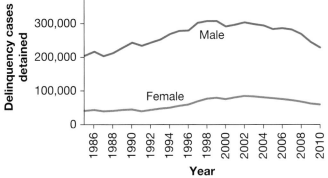
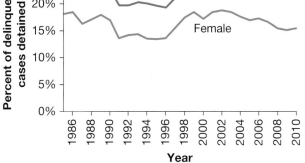

White youth accounted for the largest number of delinquency cases involving detention, although they were the least likely to be detained

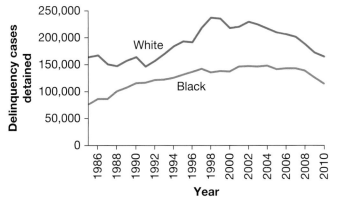
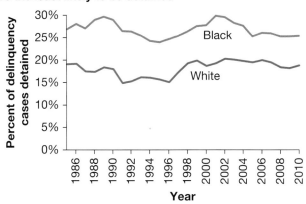

Source: Sickmund & Puzzanchera (2014). *Juvenile Offenders and Victims: 2014 National Report.* National Center for Juvenile Justice.

JUVENILE COURT POPULATIONS—COMORBIDITY OF DIFFICULTIES

Many of the young people, of all races and gender, involved with the juvenile courts struggle with individual, school, or family difficulties, even prior to the involvement in juvenile courts. Trauma, maltreatment, mental health problems, and school problems are associated with profound challenges for many of these juveniles. These experiences and disabilities are often linked to later or subsequent offending and delinquent behaviors, which for some becomes a cycle of offending (recidivism). The link from these childhood difficulties to delinquency is most evident in the juvenile detention and incarceration population. Most youthful offenders in the incarceration facilities have been identified with at least one mental health disorder or maltreatment, although many of these youthful offenders have combinations of these problems before, during, and after release from being incarcerated (Garland et al., 2001; Mallett, 2009; Rosenblatt, Rosenblatt, & Biggs, 2000). The prevalence rates of youthful offenders within correctional facilities with these difficulties are significantly higher when compared with the prevalence of these problems among adolescents in the general population (see Table 3.10).

In the United States, only a small percentage of children are diagnosed with a mental health disorder before they are 18 years of age (9% to 18%), have an active substance abuse problem (4% to 5%), are a victim of maltreatment (less than 1%), or have a special education disability (6% to 9%), the latter of which a majority of these school-related difficulties are learning disabilities or emotional disturbances (President's New Freedom Commission on Mental Health, 2003; Substance Abuse and Mental Health Services Administration, 2014a; U.S. Department of Health and Human Services, 2014a). Nevertheless, reviews of detained and incarcerated youthful offenders have found a significantly higher prevalence of these problems within this population compared with the general population of youth:

▼ TABLE 3.10

Rates of Comorbid Mental Illnesses

Problem type	Detained/incarcerated youthful offender population (%)	General adolescent population (%)
Maltreatment victimization	26–60	1
Special education disabilities (learning disabilities and emotional disturbances)	28–45	4–9
Mental health disorders	35–80	9–18
Substance abuse	30–70	4–5

Two to four times more for mental health disorders and certain special education disabilities to as many as 60 times more for maltreatment victimizations and related traumas (Abram et al., 2013; Chassin, 2008; Grisso, 2008; Leone & Weinberg, 2010; Mears & Aron, 2003; Teplin et al., 2006).

1. Why do you think so many youthful offenders have these myriad of difficulties?

2. What do you think is the link from mental health, trauma, or maltreatment to incarceration?

Trauma: Acute trauma is considered a single traumatic event that is time limited, for example, a dog bite, accident, or natural disaster such as an earthquake or tornado.

Mental Health Disorder (Psychiatric Disorder): Diagnosis by a mental health professional of a behavioral or mental pattern that may cause suffering or a poor ability to function in life. In the United States, diagnosis is through the use of the Diagnostic and Statistical Manual of Mental Disorders (DSM).

and because of the multitude of ways that adolescents are transferred through various state laws (Hockenberry, 2014; Mendel, 2012; National Juvenile Justice and Delinquency Prevention Coalition, 2013; Nellis, 2016; Office of Juvenile Justice and Delinquency Prevention, 2017; The Sentencing Project, 2015).

Race and Gender Issues

As noted, there are race and gender impacts and concerns within juvenile court populations. Race is a significant predictor of detention placement and incarceration outcomes, although it is not fully understood why. A black youthful offender is six times more likely to be detained, and a Hispanic youthful offender three times more likely, than a white youthful offender, even when accounting for many of the important legal factors that influence these detention decisions such as number of offenses and offense type. It is also more likely that a minority youthful offender will further penetrate the juvenile justice system when compared with similarly offending and charged white youthful offenders. The phenomenon, called **disproportionate minority contact** or **confinement (DMC)**, is a major focus of attention for national, state, and local stakeholders (Bishop, 2006; Kempf-Leonard, 2007; National Council on Crime and Delinquency, 2007; Piquero, 2008; The Sentencing Project, 2015).

These race disparities are even more profound within state juvenile incarceration facilities, institutions that hold youthful offenders in confinement for much longer periods than detention centers. Nationwide, youthful offender commitments to incarceration facilities, as noted earlier, have decreased significantly since 1999: Whites fell by 51%, blacks by 43%, Hispanics by 52%, and American Indian by 28%. With these decreases, though, the racial gap between incarcerated white and black youthful offenders has actually increased by 15%. Today, black youthful offenders are more than four times likely to be incarcerated as white youthful offenders; American Indian youthful offenders more than three times as likely; and Hispanic youthful offenders more than twice as likely, although there are distinct differences across the states (The Sentencing Project, 2016).

The number of adolescent females involved with the juvenile courts has increased over the past two decades, which has led to more female offenders being adjudicated delinquent and held in detention, even more likely than male offenders for certain offenses such as assault and running away (Chesney-Lind & Irwin, 2008; Office of Juvenile Justice and Delinquency Prevention, 2017; Tracy, Kempf-Leonard, & Abramoske-James, 2009; Zahn, Hawkins, Chiancone, & Whitworth, 2008). Rather than adolescent females today becoming more violent than adolescent females in prior decades, this increased involvement with the juvenile justice system by adolescent females may reflect differential treatment, mandatory arrest polices for domestic violence, other changes in law enforcement policies (e.g., releasing status offenders from detention centers), or a decrease in public tolerance for juvenile crime overall (Feld, 2009; Pasko & Chesney-Lind, 2010).

Disproportionate Minority Contact (Racial and Ethnic Disparities): Phrase that represents the disproportionate number of youthful offenders of color who come into contact with the juvenile justice (and adult) system.

CHAPTER REVIEW

CHAPTER SUMMARY

This chapter presented the multiple sources of data on juvenile crime, offending, and victimization. Over the past few decades, a movement toward harsher penalties and a punitive approach more than doubled the number of adolescents adjudicated delinquent and brought under juvenile court supervision, although delinquency adjudications and incarcerations have been decreasing since 2000, and even precipitously since 2010. Nevertheless, it remains a policy challenge when low-level, first-time, and truant offenders enter the juvenile courts, and this group comprises most delinquency cases. The youthful offenders who are adjudicated delinquent have a high chance of spending time in detention or incarceration facilities, due in large part to how the juvenile justice system operates and less so because they pose safety risks to their communities. The impact is greatest on youthful offenders of color and those with mental health problems or school-related disabilities.

KEY TERMS

census data **47**

criminal homicide **61**

delinquency adjudications **60**

disproportionate minority contact or confinement (DMC) **71**

etiology **56**

forcible rape **61**

mental health disorder **70**

out-of-home placement **64**

pretrial holding **68**

property offenses **46**

residential placement **64**

trauma **70**

ungovernability **64**

victimless crimes **48**

violent offenses **46**

youthful offenders **60**

DISCUSSION QUESTIONS

1. Does the juvenile justice system have an accurate count of youthful offender crime and victimization rates? Justify your position through an analysis of current data-gathering methods.

2. What is the difference among personal crimes, property crimes, and status offenses?

3. Why do you think so many low-level and first-time offending adolescents become involved with the juvenile courts and/or adjudicated delinquent?

4. What race and gender differences are there in youthful offender populations? In other words, what is disproportionate minority contact and disproportionate minority confinement?

5. Why do you think that the adolescents who end up in detention and incarceration facilities have so many other problems or difficulties?

6. Are the detention and incarceration facility youthful offender populations similar to their non–juvenile-court-involved peers? If not, how do they differ? Be thorough, respond via race, gender, and disability.

7. Why are status offenses different from other youthful offender crimes?

8. What are the primary data sources for tracking youthful offender crime nationwide? What are the methodological strengths and limitations of these sources?

9. If you could design the perfect juvenile court data reporting system, what would it include and how would you improve current data-gathering methods?

10. Why do you think juvenile crime and victimization rates have been decreasing over the past few decades?

---

https://edge.sagepub.com/mallett

 **Sharpen your skills with SAGE edge!**

SAGE edge for students provides a personalized approach to help you accomplish your coursework in an easy-to-use learning environment. You'll find mobile-friendly eFlashcards and quizzes, as well as videos, web resources, and links to SAGE journal articles to support and expand on the concepts presented in this chapter.

PART II

THEORIES OF DELINQUENCY

CHAPTER 4

CLASSICAL, BIOLOGICAL, AND PSYCHOLOGICAL THEORIES OF CRIME

▲ Theories on delinquency and crime outcomes have proliferated over the past century. Why do you think delinquency happens?

Roy Scott/Science Source

INTRODUCTION

Why do some juveniles engage in delinquency? Do you have a "theory" to explain this phenomenon? Terms like "theory" and "hypothesis" are used often in everyday conversations to refer to an idea that explains the world around us. To be scientific, however, a theory must be more than just a hunch, an opinion, or even an educated guess. A scientific theory consists of logically consistent propositions that explain a certain phenomenon, and a hypothesis is an empirically testable proposition that is derived from a theory. Unlike an opinion, a scientific theory must go through rigorous scrutiny and be open to change in light of opposing empirical evidence. Logical consistency and empirical validity are the two pillars of science (science is often called logico-empiricism) that make its theory more trustworthy and valuable than a mere opinion. Additionally, in science, more value is placed on theories with a larger scope of application and that are simple. For instance, a theory that explains law-breaking behaviors of both males and females using a few simple propositions is valued more than a theory that explains law-breaking behaviors of only males using ten complex propositions. In social science, moreover, a greater value is placed on a theory with a policy implication. Thus, it is not just an accumulation of knowledge and an increased understanding of a social phenomenon but the utility of the knowledge in making the world better that is also valued in social science (Akers & Sellers, 2009).

Theoretical Issues and Classification

Humans have long attempted to explain why some people engage in crime. Many theories of crime are discussed in this chapter and the next. Before discussing each theory, several important theoretical issues that form the basis for classifying criminology theories into paradigms are discussed. Many of these issues are not specific to criminology but also apply to other social science fields. They include the definition of crime, the conflict versus consensus models of law, the stance on human nature, the unit of analysis, the nature versus nurture debate, free will versus determinism, internal or external factors, change or static factors, distal or proximate explanations, and specific versus general explanations. Three major paradigms of criminology include the classical school perspective, the positive school perspective, and the conflict/critical perspective (Tibbetts & Hemmens, 2010). Although many criminology theories are better suited to explaining law-breaking behaviors of children than of adults, criminology theories for the most part do not distinguish crime and delinquency because they are the same behaviors that are explained by the theories. Because of this, the two terms—crime and delinquency—are not distinguished and used interchangeably.

Definition of Crime

Before explaining a certain phenomenon, a theory should define the phenomenon that it is trying to explain. Raffaele Garofalo (1885) coined the term "criminology" to refer to the scientific study of crime. Edwin Sutherland, considered a contemporary father of criminology, defined criminology further as "the body of knowledge regarding crime as a social phenomenon. It includes within its scope the processes of making laws, of breaking laws, and of reacting toward the breaking of laws"

Empirical Validity: Describes how closely an idea corresponds to empirical data (what we observe).

Paradigm: A distinct set of thoughts; a school of thoughts.

(Sutherland & Cressey, 1966, p. 3). Most theories discussed in this textbook attempt to explain "breaking of laws," and this is considered a legalistic approach because the definition of criminology, and of crime, is based on laws. The reliance on laws to define crime may be problematic, however, because specific behaviors that are prohibited by law often vary across time and space (e.g., prostitution, drinking alcohol, and recreational use of marijuana). Defined legally, a criminology theory used to explain a criminal behavior in one jurisdiction may, therefore, not be applicable in explaining the same behavior in another jurisdiction if the behavior is not a crime in the latter jurisdiction. A scientific theory should, however, be universal, and the subject matter of criminology should also be universal and be defined in an abstract way rather than legally, according to Michael Gottfredson and Travis Hirschi (1990, p. 15), who went on to define the subject matter of criminology as "acts of force and fraud committed by individuals in their self interest." Defined this way, the subject matter of criminology can include deviant behaviors, which are atypical behaviors that are usually the violation of societal norms, if not of laws, including lying and infidelity.

Consensus Versus Conflict Perspectives

The conflict/critical perspective that has shifted the focus of inquiry away from "breaking of laws" emerged in the 1960s and 1970s when people, including those in academia, became critical of the status quo and what was going on in society. The conflict/critical perspective assumes that a society consists of groups with competing interests and values that do not always agree on what behaviors should be regulated and punished by law. The conflict/critical perspective argues that a group with power uses the law to control the behaviors of other groups. Instead of focusing on the question "why do some individuals break laws?" therefore, this perspective focuses on examining why and how some laws were created and the society's reaction to behaviors that are considered criminal. More specifically, the conflict/critical perspective asks questions like "why can't 18-year-olds drink alcohol even though they can enlist to serve in the military?" or "why is the punishment for a child killing a parent harsher than the punishment for a parent killing a child?"

An alternative to the conflict/critical perspective is the consensus perspective that assumes that there is societal consensus on behaviors that should be regulated and punished by law. The consensus perspective may have support when it comes to the behaviors of *mala in se* or behaviors that are "evil in itself" that are serious and violent and are prohibited almost universally, including homicide, assault, and rape. There are, however, many behaviors of *mala prohibita*, or behaviors that are "evil because prohibited," that, like the conflict/critical perspective posits, not everyone agrees should be controlled and punished, including the recreational use of drugs, prostitution, and gambling. Troy Duster (1970) went on to argue that laws are often used to "legislate morality" or to reinforce one moral ideology over another, as seen in sodomy laws that make gay sexual intercourse a crime.

Human Nature

Our belief in human nature as inherently good or inherently bad impacts the explanation for why people commit crime. There are three major stances on human nature. Thomas Hobbes (1588–1679) assumed in the "doctrine of original sin" the idea that humans are inherently selfish and hedonistic. Like a depiction in the novel *Lord of Flies* by William Golding (1959), Hobbes believed that when left to our own devices, humans would engage in "war of all against all." Jean Jacques Rousseau (1712–1778), on the other hand, assumed in "innate purity," the idea that humans are born essentially pure and good. It is, therefore, the environment that corrupts some individuals into engaging in law-breaking behaviors. Finally, John Locke (1632–1704) assumed that humans are born with *tabula rasa* or "a blank state," neither inherently good nor inherently bad. It is our experiences that turn us into good or bad persons.

The classical school perspective takes the Hobbesian notion of human nature as inherently selfish and hedonistic and sees humans as capable of committing criminal acts unless somehow restrained from doing so. The classical perspective thus asks the question, "what prevents crime?" The Hobbesian notion of human nature was abandoned after the emergence of the positivist school of criminology in the 19th century and was replaced with the search for causations of crime, characterized by their essential question, "what causes crime?" The positivist perspective takes either the "innate purity" assumption of human nature, like strain theories that focus on factors that push/motivate people to commit crime, or the *tabula rasa* assumption of human nature, like learning theories that argue that everyone can learn to commit crimes. It is not just the explanation for criminal behavior, but the type of government, the law, the criminal justice system, the school, and even how to raise a child may all be impacted by the stance on human nature one assumes.

Free Will Versus Determinism

Criminology theories differ in terms of the extent to which our free will accounts for our own behaviors, including criminal behaviors. The classical perspective assumes that humans have free will and thus views individual playing an active role in choosing their own behaviors. Combined with the Hobbesian assumption on human nature, the classical perspective assumes that humans rationally choose to commit crime after weighing the cost and benefit of the behavior. Based on Charles Darwin's theory of evolution, the positivist perspective, on the other hand, assumes that human behaviors are governed by the law of nature, the mechanism of the cause and effect, rather than by free will. The positivist perspective, therefore, abandons the notion of human free will in favor of determinism. The positivist perspective instead assumes that human behaviors are determined by factors such as biology, intelligence, and peer influences. In more recent years, the positivist perspective has adopted the position of soft determinism, emphasizing the interaction between determinism and free will, by giving weight to human agency in the decision-making process.

Unit of Analysis

Some theories explain group phenomenon, some theories explain individual phenomenon, and other theories explain both group and individual phenomenon. In general, micro-level theories focus on the individual-level behaviors and characteristics and on the personal-level processes, such as with friends and family. On the other hand, macro-level theories focus on group-level characteristics and processes, such as a social change. Micro-level theories are also called "social process theories," emphasizing the individual-level processes, whereas macro-level theories are also called "social structural theories," emphasizing the criminogenic (crime-causing) social structures. At the heart of this distinction is the unit of analysis, which is usually used in the context of empirical research. The unit of analysis is the level of a population on which a theory/research focuses, such as juveniles, adult males, families, racial/ethnic groups, neighborhoods, states, or countries. It is important to clearly identify the population that each theory attempts to provide an explanation for because an invalid conclusion may result if individual-level data are used to draw a group-level conclusion, called the "reductionist fallacy," or if group-level data are used to draw an individual-level conclusion, called the "ecological fallacy."

Nature Versus Nurture

The nature versus nurture debate refers to the debate concerning the relative importance of our heredity (nature) and environment (nurture) on our developmental outcomes. The predominant idea during much of the 19th century and the first half of the 20th century was that people are born criminal. The heinous act of violent crime is, therefore, committed by people who are born somehow different from the rest of us. Darwin's theory of evolution and natural selection reinforced this idea and set the stage for the scientific research of human behaviors and the development of theories of crime that attempt to explain how criminality was passed down through generations (nature). On the other hand, Edwin Sutherland (1947), in advancing differential association theory, assumed that people were born with a blank slate and argued that everyone could learn to commit crime

Free Will: Acting on one's own discretion, not believing in fate.

through interactions with criminals (nurture). Like that of Sutherland, many of the theories of crime developed in the field of sociology focus on environmental factors, although there are a small number of biological explanations of crime, which are also discussed in this chapter. With the revival of biological research on criminal behaviors following the advance in science and the emergence of the biosocial perspective of crime, which looks at the interaction between heredity and environment, the nature versus nurture debate has continued to be important in criminology.

Internal Versus External

Some theories focus on the internal factors or the characteristics of individuals to explain why they engage in crime, whereas other theories focus on external factors that are external to the individuals or the interactions between the individual and the external factors. Since the sociological positivism, which has dominated the field of criminology, moved away from biological or psychological explanations of crime that focus exclusively on internal factors as explanations of crime, it has tended to focus on social factors that are external to individuals, including social structures and cultures for the explanation of crime, while holding individual, internal, factors constant.

Change Versus Static

Some theories focus on the process of change on the criminal offending, whereas other theories focus on the static characteristics to explain criminal offending. For instance, Terrie Moffitt's (1993) developmental theory focuses on the developmental processes and changes that explain why some continue and others stop engaging in crime. Michael Gottfredson and Travis Hirschi (1990, p. 144), on the other hand, proposed the invariance thesis of age on crime, represented by their claim that "crime everywhere declines with age while differences in 'crime' tendency across individuals remain relatively stable over the life course" by focusing on an enduring characteristic, self-control, to explain criminality. Criminality is thought of as the individual's tendency to commit crime, whereas crime is the law-breaking behavior. An individual with high criminality may not engage in crime because of a lack of opportunity to engage in crime. Rather than focusing on criminality and criminals, one of the theories in the next chapter focuses on the opportunity for crime and explains situations that make crime/victimization more likely. The failure to distinguish crime and criminality and the fact that individual factors are held constant are given as reasons for positivistic sociology's failure in explaining the maturation effect on crime, or the tendency of crime engagement to decline as an individual gets older, as shown in the age-crime curve discussed in Chapter 5 (Gottfredson & Hirschi, 1990).

Distal Versus Proximate

The issue of distal versus proximate explanations of delinquency has to do with the temporal distance of the explanation of crime to the crime that it is trying to explain. An explanation as to why an individual engages in binge drinking could focus on factors that happened immediately preceding the behavior (proximate explanation), such as drinking with friends or drinking at a bar, or on factors that happened a while ago (distal explanation), such as the first age of drinking alcohol. Some theories, including Gottfredson and Hirschi's (1990) self-control theory, focus on factors that are distal or distant temporally from the engagement in crime, whereas other theories, such as Lawrence Cohen and Marcus Felson's (1979) routine activities theory, focus on factors that are more proximate or close temporally to the engagement in crime.

General Versus Specific

Some theories attempt to be general or universal, explaining all law-breaking behaviors and applying to everyone, whereas others may explain only specific types of criminal behaviors engaged by a specific group of people, thinking that not all criminals or criminal behaviors are the same. The positivist perspective replaced rationalism, or deductive reasoning and the construction of a theory derived from relationships among abstract concepts, which are the basis of the classical perspective. The positivist perspective, instead, relies on a scientific method, explaining cause and effect through the analysis of the empirical data. The positivist perspective thereby also abandons an effort to construct a general theory, which is central to the classical perspective. Instead, the methodology of analytical induction inevitably leads to the construction of specific theories for specific types of behaviors (Gottfredson & Hirschi, 1990). This is also related to the issue of the definition of crime. The problem of the heterogeneity in behaviors of crime arises for most theories of crime because they define crime legally. Therefore, a single theory may not be able to explain white-collar crime, hate crime, rape, substance use, domestic violence, and serial killing, but each of these behaviors may require a different theoretical explanation. Some theories also offer a specific context under which the theory may apply; for instance, a theory may be applicable only for explaining crimes committed by males or juveniles. Most sociological theories of crime reviewed in the next chapter offer a nomothetic explanation, focusing on commonalities that apply to a group of individuals, rather than on an idiographic explanation, which focuses on differences and explains a single case. Robert Merton's (1938) anomie theory may be an exception because of its unique focus on explaining the high crime rate in the United States by focusing on unique characteristics of the United States (e.g., American Dream).

This chapter and the next one cover criminological theories that have emerged in Europe and in the last century mostly in the United States. Theories are organized chronologically based on when the major ideas within each theoretical perspective emerged. Figure 4.1 summarizes the timeline of the development of each perspective along with important historical events and backdrops of the western countries. Theories are not born in a vacuum; thus, it is important to understand the larger historical and intellectual context within which each of the theoretical perspectives emerged and became popular. Organizing theories chronologically also helps us see the intellectual development of the field of criminology over the past 250 years since the publication of Cesare Beccaria's *On Crimes and Punishments* in 1764, the first theory of crime, that is reviewed next.

PRECLASSICAL AND CLASSICAL THEORIES OF CRIME

For most of human history, crime was believed to be caused by supernatural evil forces. During the Middle Ages, criminals were thought to possess unique physical features, like ugliness, that distinguished them from noncriminals. The idea that criminals are somehow different from noncriminals is a popular idea even today, providing some comfort to understanding why some individuals commit heinous violent crimes (e.g., Charles Manson or Adam Lanza and the Sandy Hook Elementary School shooting). During the 18th century, the views about crime and punishment in Europe were based on the spiritual view of St. Thomas Aquinas, which equated crime with sin, and the divine right of the monarchy, which gave the power to the king to rule the people. During this time, it was believed that humans were inherently good, criminals were thought of as being controlled by the devil, punishment was thus ruthless and often seen as an entertainment, and torture was frequently used to get a confession. Laws were not **codified** (nor were people literate), and thus, people were frequently accused of an offense that they did not know was a crime. There were no **rules of laws**, and judges rather than laws determined, often arbitrarily, the punishment. Society consisted of a small group of nobilities who controlled everything and often got away with a serious crime, whereas people from a lower class, who had no individual rights or any voice within the government, were often punished for a minor crime or for no reason.

Age of Reason

The Middle Ages has come to be known as one of the most inhumane periods in human history with the invention of many torture techniques and devices. The Enlightenment era, also called

Codified: Arranging laws or rules into a systematic code; for example, state laws are codified.

Rules of Law: Restriction of the arbitrary use of power by established laws.

Timeline of Criminological Theories

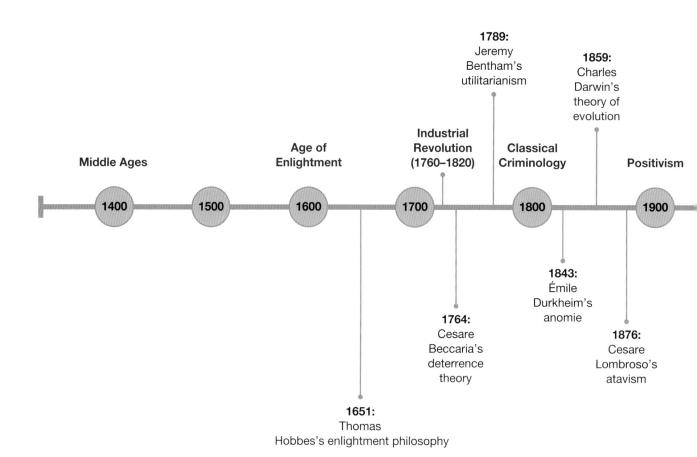

the Age of Reason, and the use of reason as a way of knowing (in contrast to the use of religion or tradition as a way of knowing) emerged in the 17th century against the backdrop of this period. The Enlightenment scholars were critical of tradition, especially those of the church and the monarchy, and its divine right, arguing that everyone was created equally. One of the Enlightenment scholars of the time, Thomas Hobbes (1651/1982) in *Leviathan*, argued that humans are inherently hedonistic and self-seeking but are rational. Thus, to avoid the "war of all against all," people would come to an agreement, called a "social contract," to give up the self-interest pursuit, which has to be enforced by the government. Unlike Thomas Aquinas, Hobbes believed that crime was natural (instead of a result of supernatural forces) because it is a reflection of our innate characteristics. Hobbes also argued that the right to rule people was given to the government by the people and not by God. Other Enlightenment scholars such as Jean Jacques Rousseau and John Locke further emphasized the importance of social contract, democracy, and equality and individual rights. Enlightenment scholars believed that for the social contract to work and for people to abide by the laws, they must have a voice in government and be treated fairly. The classical perspective of criminology emerged in the 18th century as a part of the Enlightenment movement. The classical perspective assumed that humans are rational and hedonistic and have free will and applied Enlightenment ideas, including social contract, democracy, and individual rights.

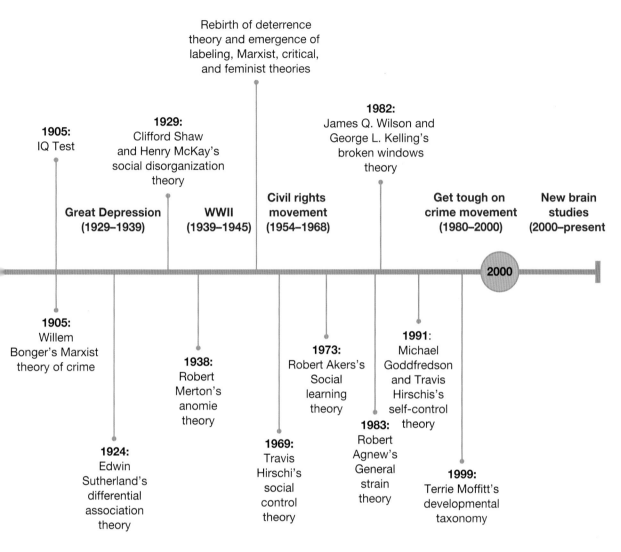

Cesare Beccaria (1738–1794)

Cesare Beccaria, who is considered the father of the classical perspective and of criminal justice, laid out deterrence theory in *On Crimes and Punishments* (1764/1986). Like other Enlightenment scholars, Beccaria was critical of how criminal justice was carried out in the Middle Ages and argued that the purpose of punishment should be **deterrence** but not revenge or entertainment for nobility, and it should be meted out fairly and equally. Beccaria also argued that the punishment should be in proportion to the offense for which it intends to deter and should cause just enough pain to offset the "pleasure" from the offense. Beccaria was among the first scholars to argue for the application of punishment based solely on *actus reus* (offense), rather than on offender, without the consideration for *mens rea* (mental state or intent). Beccaria also believed that judges should not interpret the law but instead prescribe punishment according to the law, so that there is no room for discretion and arbitrary application of the law.

According to Beccaria, for a punishment to be deterrent, it has to be swift, certain, and severe. The swiftness has to do with how quickly after a crime a punishment follows. Beccaria argued that the more quickly the punishment is applied after a crime, the stronger the association in the minds of people between the crime and the punishment. The certainty

Deterrence: Act of discouraging an action by instilling doubt or fear of the consequences.

▲ Cesare Beccaria
(1738–1794)

has to do with the certainty with which a punishment follows a crime, and the severity has to do with the severity of the punishment. The U.S. criminal justice system is based on the philosophy of deterrence, and although it has mainly attempted to deter crime by increasing the severity of punishment, Beccaria argued that the certainty of punishment is the most important of these three elements of punishment. This is understandable. Consider when you were in middle school and having a curfew. Your parents could have made the punishment for breaking a curfew as severe as they wanted (high severity), but if they rarely caught you breaking curfew (low certainty), such severe punishment would have no deterrent effect. Beccaria, moreover, believed that punishments that are too severe are inhumane and may lead to more crime, rather than deter crime. Beccaria thus argued that torture and the death penalty should be abolished because he believed that torture was barbaric and useless in getting the truth in confession and the death penalty violated social contract.

True to the idea of democracy, Beccaria believed that crime and punishment should be defined by legislatures who represent the people and not by kings and nobilities. The process of the criminal justice, moreover, should be open to the public for general deterrent effect. General deterrence targets a population of people, who are not being punished but are observing offenders being punished, from engaging in crime, whereas specific deterrence targets the offender, who is being punished, from engaging in crime. Beccaria, thus, believed that the punishment deters not just the offenders but also other would-be offenders from engaging in crime. Finally, Beccaria argued that people would accept the legitimacy of the law if a society developed a system of justice that reflected the interests of people and people are educated about its importance. Beccaria, therefore, advocated for the importance of public education for everyone. Beccaria's work had significant influences on the Bill of Rights in the U.S. Constitution, the U.S. criminal justice system, and the legal systems and laws in many European countries.

Jeremy Bentham (1784–1832)

Another important scholar in the classical perspective of criminology is Jeremy Bentham (1789), who elaborated on the idea of utilitarianism based on hedonism and rationality, basically the idea of maximizing benefits while minimizing costs. Bentham proposed the idea of "felicific calculus," which considered humans like calculators figuring in costs and benefits in deciding on the best course of action. In addition, he argued that the ideal society is one that maximizes overall pleasure and minimizes overall pain in society. Bentham is also known for a prison design called *panopticon*, which looks like a wheel with a guard post in the center that overlooks the prison and extends outward 360 degrees like spokes in a wheel.

Neoclassical School of Criminology

The neoclassical school of criminology takes into account one of the major criticisms of the classical perspective. Beccaria argued that the application of punishment should be based solely on offense (*actus reus*) instead of on offender and without a consideration for the intent (*mens rea*). This was a noble idea because at the time he was writing, the status of the individual had a considerable impact on the punishment. Beyond merely considering the offense, the neoclassical school of criminology, however, takes into account both the **mitigating circumstances** and the **aggravating circumstances** in determining the appropriate punishment. Most current criminal justice systems agree with neoclassical criminology. For instance, a juvenile who committed a crime for a first time is usually not punished as severely as an adult who committed the same crime numerous times. In most criminal justice systems, moreover, *mens rea* is important in determining the extent of responsibility and the severity of punishment, especially for murder (e.g., homicide compared to manslaughter; Tibbetts & Hemmens, 2010).

▲ Jeremy Bentham (1784–1832)

National Portrait Gallery

EARLY BIOLOGICAL THEORIES OF CRIME

With the publication of Beccaria's *On the Crime and Punishment* (1764/1986), the classical perspective dominated criminology for almost a century, giving the foundation to the current legal and criminal justice systems of many western countries, including the United States. The classical perspective, however, lost its dominance in criminology theorizing after the publication of Darwin's *On the Origin of Species* (1895/1998). The idea that reason was a way of knowing was replaced by the positive school of criminology that emphasized empiricism as a way of knowing, and Darwin's theory paved the way for the use of the scientific method to understand human behaviors. Indeed, the works of classical criminologists, like Beccaria and Bentham, are philosophical instead of scientific because they were not based on empirical data. Only in the 1960s was the classical perspective revived when scholars began collecting empirical data to test Beccaria's deterrence theory.

The classical criminology based on the Enlightenment ideas considered humans to be equal, whereas the positivist criminology based on Darwin's theory of evolution considered humans to be different. Because people differ in terms of the extent to which they engage in crime, the positivist criminologists began the quest to find the causes of this difference using the scientific method. Given Darwin's focus on biology, the early positivist criminology also focused on biological variations as the causes of the variation in crime, and until the advance in science, the positive school focused on crude measures of biological variations that can be easily observed, such as physical features and appearances.

Pre-Darwin Perspectives

One of the first theories to focus on biological variations to explain crime is craniometry. Craniometrists measured skulls of people and the brains of the deceased and determined

Mitigating Circumstances: Situations and factors that lead to an event. For example, bullying that preceded a student from hitting another student.

Aggravating Circumstances: Factors that increase the severity or culpability of a criminal act, including, but not limited to, heinousness of the crime, lack of remorse, and prior conviction of another crime.

▲ Charles Darwin
(1809–1882)

that the people of white, European descent were superior than people of other racial/ethnic groups because of their larger skull and brain size. Craniometry, like other early positivist criminology theories, had an agenda of advancing the idea of the superiority and inferiority of one group over others. Craniometry became unpopular because subsequent empirical studies could not substantiate such a blatantly racist idea. The second early positivist theory that followed was phrenology, which was the study of the shape and abnormalities of the skull to determine the personality or abnormalities in the personality, including criminality. Although most ideas of the phrenology, like craniometry, have been discredited, studies have supported the idea that different areas of the brain are responsible for different functions (e.g., specific areas of brain for sight and hearing). Finally, physiognomy is the study of facial and bodily features to determine individual characters including criminality. The early studies of physiognomy focused on establishing racial and ethnic superiority and inferiority of a group over others by focusing on the variations on facial and bodily features among different racial/ethnic groups, and the differences in facial and bodily features were used as evidence to advance, once again, the racist idea.

Charles Darwin (1809–1882)

Charles Darwin published *On the Origin of Species* in 1859 and introduced the theory of evolution and natural selection. The theory of evolution explained the increased biological diversity over generations through the process of natural selection and suggested the evolution of human species from more primitive ancestors. Darwin's theory ushered in the development of social science and had a profound impact on the use of the scientific method to study human behaviors. Darwin, however, strongly rejected the application of the theory of evolution to understanding intra-specie evolution, such as the variations among human species, as well as to understanding the "evolution" of society by Herbert Spencer (1820–1903), who introduced the idea of social Darwinism. The early positive school perspective unfortunately took Darwin's theory literally, applying it to explain the intra-specie variations across racial and ethnic groups. The early positive school perspective is, therefore, strongly associated with the Eugenics Movement and was welcomed by the wealthy and powerful ruling class.

Cesare Lombroso (1835–1909)

Cesare Lombroso is often considered the father of criminology as well as the father of the positive school of criminology because he was the first scholar to apply the scientific method to study crime. Applying Darwin's theory of evolution and natural selection, Lombroso (1876/2006) in *Criminal Man* argued that criminals are evolutional throwbacks and that some individuals are born criminals. Lombroso called this "atavism." After studying criminals and noncriminals, Lombroso noted that those who are evolutional throwbacks can be identified by their unique physical features called "stigmata," which mostly consisted of

THE EUGENICS MOVEMENT

The Eugenics Movement incorporated the philosophy of improving the quality of the human race thorough reproduction. Eugenics became popular during the 19th century at the time when slavery was common and there was a backlash against Western imperialism around the world. The scientific studies that examined why people differ and why some individuals and groups were inferior to others were used to justify the mistreatment of certain groups of people. Eugenics was used by Nazi Germany to justify its policies and programs that resulted in the Holocaust and other travesties. The early positivist perspective is, therefore, a dark history of criminology. It is, however, important to understand this historical backdrop because the idea of trying to establish superiority and inferiority of a certain group over others to explain crime and criminality did not go away and has resurfaced over time.

1. Why do you think the Eugenics Movement had such "scientific" support during the 19th century?

2. Is there any connection from the Eugenics Movement and more recent biological determinism explanations for crime (or other outcomes)?

abnormal apelike facial and physical features. Lombroso changed his view later and took into account environmental factors (e.g., poverty, migration, and urban conditions) in explaining why people commit crime. Like Lombroso, Ernest Hooton (1887–1954) also argued that criminals differ from noncriminals in terms of physical features, including nose shape, ear length, skull size, height, and weight, and that traits that are prevalent among criminals are inferior to those prevalent among noncriminals. Charles Goring (1870–1919), who was critical of biological determinism, compared more than 3,000 prisoners and an equally large number of noncriminals that included college students and found that there was no significant difference in physical characteristics between the two groups. Many studies that followed Goring's suggested that biological determinism of criminality based on mere appearances was too simplistic and incorrect.

William Sheldon (1898–1977)

William Sheldon borrowed the idea of somatotyping, or a body type theory, from the German psychiatrist Ernst Kretschmer. After examining nude photographs of boys, Sheldon identified three major body types: mesomorphs (muscular, strong, firm, and heavy-boned), ectomorphs (fragile, thin, and delicate), and endomorphs (round and soft). Sheldon believed that specific psychological characteristics like personalities and temperament were associated with each of these body types, which are largely hereditary,

▲ Cesare Lombroso (1835–1909)

and concluded that mesomorphs were associated with risk taking, self-centeredness, and aggression and are overrepresented among the delinquent population. Subsequent empirical studies, however, discredited the association between body type and criminality.

Henry Goddard (1866–1957)

The Binet test, modified versions of which later come to be known as the intelligence quotient (IQ) test, was developed at the beginning of the 20th century by a French psychologist named Alfred Binet (1857–1911). The test was originally developed to determine special education needs for French public schools, and Binet strongly insisted that the test was not a measure of intelligence and that the score can be improved over time. Henry Goddard brought the IQ test to the United States and applied it as a measure of intelligence to explain why some people commit crime. Goddard (1915) argued in *The Criminal Imbecile* that although those with mental ages younger than 8 years old (an IQ of less than 50) are not a problem to society because they lack the intelligence to commit crime, those who are feebleminded with mental ages between 8 and 10 years old (an IQ between 50 and 75) are a threat because of their engagements in crime. Goddard believed that the feebleminded are intelligent enough to hold jobs but are not intelligent enough to stay out of trouble. Goddard believed that intelligence, as measured using the IQ test, is innate and inherited, passed down through generations, and cannot be changed over time. Goddard, thus, recommended the deportation (of immigrants), institutionalization, and **forced sterilization** of people with low IQ scores.

Henry Goddard
(1866–1957)

EARLY SOCIAL STRUCTURAL THEORIES

As the biological explanations of crime were emerging, replacing the classical perspective in criminology, sociological explanations of crime that focused on social structure were also being developed in the 19th century. Darwin's ideas had a profound impact on not only the way human behaviors are studied but also on the way societies and its "evolution" are studied. August Comte (1798–1857), a contemporary of Darwin who is considered to be the father of sociology (credited with coining the term "sociology"), argued in *A System of Positive Polity* (1851/2001) that the scientific method can be used to study regularities and variations (such as of crime rate) across societies. Additionally, many countries, especially in Europe where early social structural theories emerged, were experiencing rapid social changes during the Industrial Revolution, which began in the mid-18th century and lasted until the mid-19th century. The changes in the economic structure and the increased urbanization and population size in many cities, resulting from the Industrial Revolution, produced social problems, including crime and delinquency. Therefore, the field of sociology emerged during this time to explain the urbanization and modernization that was transforming many societies, and some began to focus on social structure for the explanation of crime. These social structural theories are considered sociological positivism because they applied scientific method to study social structure and held the deterministic view on crime. These sociological explanations were, however, largely ignored until the 20th century because it is much easier to put the

Forced Sterilization:
Programs or government policies that mandated the surgical sterilization, preventing individuals the ability to have children.

FORCED STERILIZATION

The United States was one of the first countries to institute the forced sterilization of undesirable populations for the purpose of eugenics. These forced sterilizations targeted females who were deaf, blind, disabled, or with low intelligence, epilepsy, physical deformity, parents who had lower IQ, and criminals. The U.S. policy of forced sterilization lasted almost 100 years, between 1897 and 1981, and approximately 65,000 individuals were sterilized (most prior to the 1970s) across 33 states (Bruinius, 2006). Many believe this was a dark era of this country's human rights history.

1. Why do you think this policy was upheld, or not ended, for so many years?

2. What do you think were the motivations around this policy?

blame on the individuals, and their characteristics, and to institutionalize them than to put the blame on the societal conditions and to change those conditions that produce crime.

Adolphe Quetelet (1796–1874)

Quetelet, who is considered the first statistician and sociological criminologist, thought that if the classical perspective is correct and humans have free will to choose their own behaviors, all places should have the same level of crime. After comparing crime data in Belgium, Holland, and France, Quetelet, however, found that the level of crime varies across places, and thus he concluded that something about places must affect crime. More specifically, Quetelet found that the places with more males, more young people, and higher inequality all had higher levels of crime, whereas places with more unemployment and poverty had lower levels of property crime (because there are less opportunities for property crime compared to in wealthier places). Quetelet also found that the areas with a greater relative deprivation, or a greater difference in wealth, had a higher level of crime. Finally, Quetelet found that places that are going through rapid economic changes have a high level of crime and stated that "the crimes which are annually committed seem to be necessary result of our social organization. . . . Society prepares the crime, and the guilty are only the instruments by which it is executed" (Vold, Bernard, & Snipes, 1998, p. 31). Similarly, André-Michel Guerry (1802–1866) analyzed the crime data of France (one of the first countries to begin collecting national crime data) and reported higher violent crime in poor areas and higher property crime in wealthier areas in the *Essay on the Moral Statistics of France* published in 1833.

This image is available from the United States Library of Congress's Prints and Photographs division under the digital ID cph.3b11632

▲ Adolphe Quetelet (1796–1874)

Émile Durkheim (1858–1917)

Durkheim, who is also considered one of the "fathers" of sociology, proposed one of the first social structural theories of crime. Durkheim (1893/2014) noted in *The Division of Labor in Society* that primitive societies are characterized by mechanical solidarity with strong

▲ Émile Durkheim
(1858–1917)

Wikimedia Commons/PD-1923

influences of norms and a shared collective conscience (a set of moral beliefs in society), whereas modern societies, like many countries in Europe and in the United States, are characterized by organic solidarity with weakening of the sense of belonging and the influence of societal norms. The weakening of norms, or anomie (referred to as "normlessness"), becomes especially profound during the period of rapid social changes, whether the change is better or worse, and crime increases during the period of anomie. In support of this idea, Durkheim (1897/1966) reported that suicide is higher during both the economic growth and the decline. Durkheim argued that modern societies with weak collective conscience and weakening of the influence of social norms must regulate the behaviors and interactions of the people through law. In the period of rapid social changes, however, societies often fail to function as a regulatory mechanism to enforce the law; thus, crime increases.

Moreover, Durkheim was a functionalist who considered crime to be functional for society because it sets boundaries between what is right and wrong, reaffirming the collective conscience, and it increases the solidarity among law-abiding people who are reaffirmed that they are different from criminals. Durkheim went so far as to argue that societies with low levels of crime would "create" crime (by changing laws) to turn some individuals into criminals, as the following famous quote by Durkheim depicts: "Imagine a community of saints in an exemplary and perfect monastery. In it crime as such will be unknown, but faults that appear venial to the ordinary person will arouse the same scandal as does normal crime in ordinary consciences. If therefore that community has power to judge and punish, it will term such acts criminal and deal with them as such" (Durkheim, 1895/1982, p. 100). Durkheim's ideas influenced almost all sociological theories of crime that came after him, which will be discussed in the next chapter.

Willem Bonger (1876–1940)

Bonger is considered to be the first scholar to introduce the ideas of Karl Marx (1818–1883) and Fredrick Engles (1820–1895) to criminology because Karl Marx did not talk about crime in his writing; thus, he is considered to be the first Marxist theorist of criminology. In *Criminality and Economic Conditions,* Bonger (1905/1970) developed a theory of crime based on class relationships, arguing that precapitalist, primitive "communist" societies were characterized by altruism, whereas modern capitalist societies were characterized by egoism or greed. Bonger argued that capitalism emphasizes accumulation of wealth and production for the purpose of exchange; thus, instead of cooperation for a common good, it encourages competition, ambition, and greed among people. According to Bonger, the egoism of the poor is made criminal and controlled, whereas the egoism of the wealthy is not made criminal and is encouraged in capitalist societies. Bonger's Marxist theory was revived in the early 1970s and will be discussed in the next chapter along with the conflict and critical perspective.

MODERN BIOLOGICAL PERSPECTIVES

The advance in science in the 20th century was followed by more sophisticated ways, than merely looking at appearances, of examining biological factors to explain why people commit crime. The studies in the early 20th century examined the extent to which criminal tendency is passed down from parents to their offspring using family studies, twin studies, adoption studies, and studies examining twins separated at birth. This line of research investigated the nature versus nurture debate and overall supported the influence of genetics on criminal tendency. These earlier studies were, however, criticized for not separating out the effects of environmental impact and genetics. As will be seen, the progression from family studies to studies of twins separated at birth represents the progression in the way studies attempted to take into account the environmental influences in thinking about the heredity of criminality.

Family Studies

Richard Dugdale (1841–1883) traced the family tree of the "Jukes" family for 200 years and found a high degree of criminal offending in the family and attributed this to their "degenerate nature" that was passed down through generations. Similarly, Henry Goddard (1866–1957) traced the family tree of Martin Kallikak, a Revolutionary War soldier, who had a legitimate son through a "fine Mormon woman" and an illegitimate son with a "disreputable woman." Goddard (1912) found a high degree of criminal offending among the descendants of the illegitimate son and attributed this to the "moral degeneracy" that had been passed down through generations. These family studies indicate that crime is more common in some families, but neither of the studies properly separated out the environmental influences from biological influences because family members tend to share similar environments. It is possible that, rather than the gene for "degenerate nature," the degenerate environment that increases criminal offending was passed down through generations in these families.

Twin Studies

Twin studies compared the concordance (similarity) rates in criminality between monozygotic twins (MZ) and dizygotic twins (DZ). Although MZ twins (or identical twins) share 100% of their genes, DZ twins (or fraternal twins) share only 50%, much like other nontwin siblings. If criminality is inherited, then there should be a higher concordance rate in criminality among MZ twins than there is among DZ twins. Studies usually support this expectation based on the genetic inheritance of criminality, showing sometimes twice the higher concordance rates among MZ twins compared with DZ twins in criminal propensity. These studies have, however, been criticized for the assumption that the environmental influences between MZ and DZ twins are the same because MZ twins are often treated more similarly than DZ twins are because they look alike and thus may share much more similar environments while growing up than do DZ twins. Thus, the higher concordance rate found among MZ twins compared with DZ twins may not be explained solely by the greater genetic similarities among MZ twins compared with among DZ twins (Barnes et al., 2014).

Adoption Studies

Adoption studies compared the influences of biological parents (nature) and adopted parents (nurture) on their offspring's criminal offending. In most adoption research, children were adopted prior to the age of six months; thus, the biological parents had almost no influence on the children's lives. Adoption studies overall suggest that although biology may be more important in explaining criminality than environment because they indicate a stronger influence of biological parents than of adoptive parents on their offspring's criminal propensity, both biology and environment are important in explaining criminal propensity. This was so because children who had both a biological parent and an adoptive parent with a criminal record were more likely to engage in crime than any other children. One major criticism of the adoption studies is the selective placement based on demographic characteristics that adoption agencies often used to place children into homes that are similar to biological homes. It is, therefore, difficult to conclude that similarities between biological parents and their offspring are explained solely by the genetic inheritance because they may also share a similar environment because of the selective placement (Joseph, 2001).

Studies of Twins Separated at Birth

In more recent years, studies began examining twins who were separated at birth, which took into account the criticism of the earlier twin studies of not separating out fully the environmental and genetic influences. In most cases, these twins did not even know that they had a twin sibling. One study conducted at the University of Minnesota found a significantly higher concordance rate of criminal propensity among twin pairs who were separated at birth and were raised (in many cases) in significantly different environments, even more so than among identical twins who were raised in the same family (Bouchard, Lykken, McGue, Segal, & Tellegen, 1990). One explanation offered for the higher concordance among twins separated at birth compared with among twins who grew up together, as an alternative to the genetic inheritance of criminality explanation, is that twins who grow up together may try really hard to be different from each other (although this is contradictory to the criticism of the twin studies that argued that MZ twins share a much more similar environment than do DZ twins).

These twin and adoption studies ultimately have shown that there is some genetic basis to criminality that could not be explained by environmental factors. More recently in the 21st century, behavioral genetics studies that have focused on the interplay between the genetics and the environment have shown a significantly high percentage of heritability of many of the human behaviors, including criminal and delinquent behaviors (Burt & Simons, 2014). Other biological studies since the last half of the 20th century have focused on physiological features, including cytogenetic studies examining XYY chromosome abnormality, hormones and neurotransmitters, brain injuries, and central and autonomic nervous systems. Finally, a recent addition to the field of criminology called "biosocial approaches," which criticizes sociology's exclusive emphasis on social environmental factors, focuses on the intersection of biology and environment in explaining criminal tendency.

Cytogenetic Studies Examining XYY Chromosome Abnormality

Cytogenetic studies focus on the genetic makeup and chromosome abnormalities. One of the most studied chromosome abnormalities related to criminality is the XYY chromosome abnormality (often called "super males"), which produces an extra Y chromosome in males. A study by Herman, Goodenough, and Hirschorn (1977) found that the percentage of criminal conviction among XYY males was much higher than in the general population. The crimes that XYY males were convicted of were, however, not always violent crimes, and when only the violent crime conviction rate was compared, there was no significant difference between XYY males and XY males. This is a common criticism with the biological theories of crime. Although most biological theories attempt to explain the biological basis of aggression and violence, the most common crimes are property crimes. The findings from a series of cytogenetic studies like the one by Witkin nevertheless suggest a relationship between chromosome abnormality and criminality (Walsh, 1995).

Hormones

Hormones not only shape our physical appearance but also have profound influences on our behaviors because they influence our perceptions and thoughts. A high level of testosterone (male hormone), for instance, is associated with risk-taking, greater tolerance for pain, and preference for sensory stimuli. Studies that examined the link between testosterone and crime first appeared in the 1970s and found an increased level of aggression related to an increase in the level of testosterone. A study by Booth and Osgood (1993), who examined 4,462 Vietnam veterans, however, found that only ~1% of the variations in criminality among adults are explained by testosterone level. This is understandable given that aggression does not always have to lead to violence but can be used productively in law-abiding ways, including playing sports and working in the armed forces. Other studies found that a high number of females commit crimes while their estrogen (female hormone) level was at its lowest (during the

ARE YOU BORN TO COMMIT CRIME?

By all accounts, Stephen Anthony Mobley had a pretty normal life. He came from an affluent, white, middle-class American family, and he was not abused or mistreated as a child. He did not have difficulties in school, had friends and peer support, and functioned well during his adolescent years. As he grew up, however, he became increasingly violent, and at the age of 25, he walked into a pizza store and casually shot the 25-year old manager in the neck after robbing the cash box and joking that he would apply for the job vacancy when the man was dead. He was sentenced to death and subsequently executed in 2005. This is one of the first cases to use genetic predisposition as a defense in which the lawyer argued that Mobley had "a variant of a gene linked to violent behavior: the MAO-A or so-called warrior gene." (Szalavitz, 2012, para. 5).

1. Was Stephen Mobley born to commit this violent act?

2. Are some young people destined to commit violent acts? Justify your position.

menstrual cycle), thus, suggesting the influence of hormones on engagement in crime among females (see for a review, Easteal, 1991). It is possible, however, that the menstrual cycle and premenstrual syndrome just make women more likely to get caught rather than increasing criminality, and this area of research is still not inconclusive.

Neurotransmitters

Neurotransmitters are chemicals that carry electric impulses/signals that the brain uses to communicate. There are many types of neurotransmitters, but the two that have been studied most often in relation to criminal offending are dopamine and serotonin because these two chemicals are related to the feelings of pleasure that are associated with eating food and sex but also drug use such as cocaine, heroin, and methamphetamine. Research findings are somewhat inconclusive in terms of the relationship between the levels of dopamine and crime, but the results of some studies suggest that a lower level of this chemical is associated with a higher crime. Low levels of serotonin, on the other hand, have been found consistently to be related to criminal offending (see, for a review, Berman & Coccaro, 1998).

Neurophysiology—The Central Nervous System (CNS)

The central nervous system includes the brain and the spinal cord. New technologies like magnetic resonance imaging (MRI) and electroencephalographs (EEG) make it possible to learn more in detail what is going on with our brain. This is a significant improvement from the debunked theory of craniometry, which only looked at the size and shape of the skull and brain. The findings from more recent research indicate that brain damage and irregularities, especially to the frontal and temporal lobes, which are related to emotions and regulations of our impulses, significantly increase the likelihood of criminal offending (Pillmann et al., 1999). There have been hundreds of studies that have examined brain wave patterns using EEG of violent offenders, and these studies have identified a link between violent crime and abnormal (slower) brain wave patterns. There is some evidence that irregular brain wave patterns may be inherited, but irregular patterns can also occur because of brain damage (Raine, 1993).

The autonomic nervous system (ANS) controls involuntary functions like heart rate and is controlled by the limbic system in the brain. The ANS is active in the "fight or flight" situations

DOES LEAD-POISONING CAUSE DELINQUENCY?

The Flint, Michigan, water crisis began in 2014 when the drinking water source for the city of Flint was switched from the treated water from Detroit to the untreated Flint River without necessary corrosion inhibitors. This resulted in more than 10,000 Flint residents, many of them poor black children, being exposed to high levels of lead through drinking water. Studies have shown a significant link among lead poisoning, premature birth, and low birth weight (if a mother is exposed to lead poisoning during pregnancy) and permanent intellectual and learning disabilities along with behavioral problems among other physical alignments. There have been numerous studies completed that examined the relationship between lead poisoning and delinquency, finding significant correlations (Stretesky & Lynch, 2004).

1. With many of the less prosperous urban areas in the United States having numerous older houses with serious lead levels, what would you do as mayor of one of these cities?

2. What should have been done differently with the water crisis in Flint, Michigan?

by increasing heart rate and respiratory rate, causing the state of "anxiety" that many of us are familiar with. This is the basic function of a lie detector test, which examines the signs of anxiety upon lying. Children are conditioned to feel this anxiety in anticipation of punishment in situations when they face the opportunity to do something bad that they know they should not do, and they are rewarded for not engaging in the behavior because the anxiety disappears upon disengagement. Research that examined the ANS produced two key findings that are relevant to criminology. First, people vary in terms of the level and the speed at which the ANS activates the feeling of anxiety in the "fight or flight" situations. Children who experience a low level of anxiety at the slow speed may be more likely to do things they are not supposed to do because they are less likely to experience the anxiety from punishment. Such children are thus difficult to socialize because they feel no anxiety or fear from possibility of punishment. This is one reason why a lie detector test may be unreliable because those who are more likely to commit crime are less likely to show the signs of anxiety for lying because of their low ANS function. Second, research, however, has also found that the low ANS functioning does not necessarily lead to criminal behaviors because some low-ANS-functioning individuals may become professional athletes, law enforcement officers, or military soldiers where it is functional and even effective to experience low anxiety and stay calm in the "fight or flight" situations (Raine, 1993).

MODERN PSYCHOLOGICAL THEORIES

It has been increasingly difficult to differentiate academic disciplines because of the increase in interdisciplinary studies and crossover of areas of study. Psychology has expanded from social science and has become a part of biological science because it now often examines the biological basis to psychological issues, obscuring the line between psychology and biology. Psychology and sociological criminology also share theories of criminality, especially as they are related to attachment, self-control, and learning theories. What might set the psychological theories and sociological theories apart is that most of the following psychological theories discussed in this chapter are general theories that are not developed specifically to explain criminality or criminal offending. On the other hand, the sociological theories of crime discussed in the next chapter are developed specifically for explaining criminality and crime. Some psychological theories include intelligence (following the work of Goddard and IQ), psychoanalytic, moral development, attachment, personality, and psychopathology theories. Because sociological learning theories will be discussed extensively in the next chapter, psychological theories on learning are included there.

Intelligence

Following the work of Goddard and IQ, William Shockley, a physicist who won the 1956 Nobel Prize in Physics, argued that the IQ test measured "social capacity," or the ability to be successful in society, which was inherited and the differences in IQ scores explained the higher prevalence of poverty and crime experienced among African Americans in the United States. In support of Shockley, after analyzing data, Arthur Jensen (1969) argued that 80% of the variation in intelligence was due to inheritance. Similarly, Richard Herrnstein and Charles Murray (1994), in their controversial book called *The Bell Curve*, argued that social class and race are related to criminality through intelligence, meaning that lower class people and blacks are more likely to commit crime because of their inherited lower intelligence. There have been numerous empirical studies that have examined the relationships between social class and race and IQ, and IQ and crime, as well as numerous alternative explanations given for these relationships. Although the argument that lower intelligence causes crime is somewhat tenuous, Farrington and West (1981) found that the IQ measured at an early age is a pretty good predictor of engagement in future delinquency.

Psychoanalytic Theories

There are several versions of psychoanalytic theory, but the most famous version was developed by Sigmund Freud (1856–1939), who, however, did not offer a theory specifically to explain criminality. Freud developed theories on three psychic phenomena that included id (primitive impulses that include sexual and aggressive drives), ego (a mediator between id and superego), and superego (moral conscience) and defense mechanisms, such as displacement and reaction formation. According to Freud, everyone feels the presence of the id, the natural impulses, but when people develop a healthy superego, they can use defense mechanisms to channel the natural impulses to acceptable behaviors instead of engaging in crime or deviant behavior. The most important contributors to applying psychoanalysis to understanding crime and delinquency are August Aichorn (1925/1984) in his book *Wayward Youth* and Kate Fredlanger (1947) in her book *The Psychoanalytic Approach to Juvenile Delinquency*. According to psychiatric theories of crime, the cause of crime lies in the superego that is underdeveloped, which makes people unable to control the natural id impulses to commit crime.

Theory of Moral Development

Lawrence Kohlberg (1927–1987) argued that people go through a normal course of moral development, much like physical development, which includes largely three levels. At the preconventional level, children up to age 10 years old decide what is right and wrong based on the rewards and punishments. At this level, there are no wrong behaviors but only behaviors that are bad because they lead to punishment. At the conventional level, children up to teenage years begin to care what other people think of them and accept the rules and norms of society. At the postconventional level, people begin forming their own set of moral principles and think independently for themselves, and such a moral principal may not entirely coincide with society's norms. According to this theory, people who engage in crime are those who are stuck at the preconventional stage who thus do not understand right from wrong unless punishments follow the behavior that are costly to them.

Attachment Theory

John Bowlby (1907–1990) developed attachment theory, which emphasized the importance of attachment or bond between mother and infant during the first nine months after the infant's birth. According to Bowlby, the attachment formed during this period of the infant's life impacts adulthood relationships and attachment. Bowlby argued that criminals are those who failed to form healthy attachment during infancy, and thus, they failed to form healthy attachment during subsequent childhood, adolescent, and adulthood. Criminality is thus explained by the lack of caring and warm relationships.

ABNORMAL PSYCHOLOGY

Issac Ray (1807–1881) in the United States and Henry Maudsley (1835–1918) in England are considered to be the forbearers of the insanity defense. They argued that some people should not be held responsible for their crime because of their mental difficulties or problems. In recent years in the United States, as the evidence for the connection between mental disorders and mass shootings has surfaced (e.g., Sandy Hook Elementary School shooting in 2012), there has been a debate on the restriction of gun access to those who have a history of mental health problems. The idea that criminals, especially those who commit a senseless stranger homicide, have mental disorders or abnormal personalities is popular, depicted frequently in television shows and movies. The field of abnormal psychology emerged in the early 20th century and focuses on abnormal behaviors, thought processes, and emotions often, but not always, related to mental health disorders. Sociological theories of crime, which dominate criminology today, have been criticized for their focus on minor forms of crime and delinquency. Unlike abnormal psychology, these sociological theories, which will be discussed in the next chapter, do not explain very well crimes such as mass shootings, sadistic killings, and serial killings that are rare, and may be associated with mental health disorders.

1. **What do you think should be the role of an insanity defense for heinous crimes?**

2. **Do you agree that abnormal psychology helps to explain some of these heinous crimes? Why or why not?**

Personality Theories

There are several different personality inventory tests. First, the Minnesota Multiphasic Personality Inventory (MMPI) was developed in 1940 to detect psychological issues and abnormalities. One scale of the MMPI that is relevant to criminality is the Psychopathic Deviation (PD) scale, which measures aggression, irresponsiveness, and immaturity. When comparing the PD scales between criminals and noncriminals, studies found that criminals score significantly higher on this scale. Nevertheless, the scale from the MMPI that was found to be related most strongly to criminality is the F scale, which is a scale that measures the validity and reliability of respondents' answers. The higher value of the F scale indicates more inconsistencies and inaccuracy in answering the questions on the test, which may be related to the level of analytic skills. Second, unlike the MMPI, the California Personality Inventory (CPI) measures the personality profiles of the general population and not just the population of individuals with psychological issues. The CPI claims to measure 18 unique personality traits, such as dominance, tolerance, and flexibility. Research has found that criminals score lower than the general population on three traits, including socialization (following rules), self-control (self-regulation), and responsibility (conscientiousness and dependability). Finally, Hans Jurgen Eysenck (1916–1997) and Sybil B.G. Eysenck (1927–) developed the personality theory of criminality. According to Eysenck (1964), criminals score high on all three of the following personality dimensions: neuroticism, extraversion, and psychoticism. Research on both the MMPS and the CPI has been criticized because most of the empirical studies compared the incarcerated population and the general population. Because not everyone who engages in crime has been incarcerated, the incarcerated population does not represent the entire population of those who have engaged in crime or who have high criminality tendencies (only those who have been caught). Another critique is that both inventories use questions on criminal and delinquent behaviors; thus, it is tautological because their inventories merely indicate that those who are incarcerated engaged in more crime than did the general population.

Psychopathology (Mental Disorders)

Deinstitutionalization of the state psychiatric patients occurred during the 1950s to the early 1970s because of the overcrowding and safety concern of psychiatric hospitals, a movement toward disability rights, and a desire to care for those with mental health problems in community-based settings. It should be noted, however, that there were never enough community-based supports put in place nationwide. This deinstitutionalization movement followed an increase in the arrest and incarceration of mental health patients for violent crimes. A closer examination of the data, however, revealed that the higher rates of arrest and incarceration among mental health patients were found only among those with criminal records and not among those without any criminal record prior to the institutionalization. Monahan and Steadman (1983) thus concluded that there was no direct relationship between mental illness and criminality (in other words, mental illness does not cause crime). The results of empirical studies, however, indicate that certain psychiatric diagnoses are more prevalent among violent offenders, including psychopath (or sociopath or anti-social personality). Psychopaths are people who do not feel shame or guilt and are incapable of forming attachment to others.

CHAPTER REVIEW

CHAPTER SUMMARY

This chapter introduced the theories of crime and important issues related to criminology theorizing, including the definition of crime, the conflict versus consensus models of law, the stance on human nature, the unit of analysis, the nature versus nurture debate, free will versus determinism, internal or external factors, change or static factors, distal or proximate explanations, and specific versus general explanations. In so doing, a chronology of crime paradigms was reviewed, including the intellectual development of theories of criminology from religious explanation to the classical perspective based on the Enlightenment philosophy. The classical perspective dominated criminology theorizing for a century and had profound influences on the legal and criminal justice systems of the United States and other western countries. The classical perspective was replaced by the positivist perspective after the introduction of Darwin's theory of evolution and natural selection. Since then, until the 1930s, the biological determinism within the positivist perspective dominated criminology theorizing, claiming that criminals were somehow born different from noncriminals. Modern biological and psychological theories were then reviewed, which offered more sophisticated explanations for criminality than did the early biological theories.

KEY TERMS

aggravating circumstances **83**	empirical validity **75**	mitigating circumstances **83**
codified **79**	forced sterilization **86**	paradigms **75**
deterrence **8**1	free will **77**	rules of laws **79**

DISCUSSION QUESTIONS

1. Think of examples of "theories" of crime you have heard on TV or from someone you know. How do these "theories" differ from scientific theories of crime?

2. Should "crime" and the subject matter of criminology (i.e., what theories of crime should explain) be defined legally? Can you think of a universal definition of the subject matter of criminology that is not based on law?

3. Which of the three major stances on human nature do you agree with the most? Why?

4. Do you think humans have a free will to decide their own behaviors like the classical perspective assumes, or do you think humans have no free will like the positivist perspective assumes?

5. Do you think our biology determines our personalities, emotions, and behaviors?

6. Can you think of examples where societies low on crime would "create" crime (by changing laws) to turn some individuals into criminals?

7. What alternative explanations can you think of that explain the racial/ethnic differences in IQ scores?

8. Why do you think the racist explanations of crime (e.g., crack use and violence among African Americans) that

are reminiscent of early biological theories of crime based on the eugenics philosophy keep reappearing?

9. Can you develop a perfect study involving twins and adoptions that could separate out the environmental and hereditary influences?

10. Even if there is some biological basis to aggression, why do you think some individuals use the aggression for violence while others use it in a more productive way?

---

https://edge.sagepub.com/mallett

(\$)SAGE edge™ **Sharpen your skills with SAGE edge!**

SAGE edge for students provides a personalized approach to help you accomplish your coursework in an easy-to-use learning environment. You'll find mobile-friendly eFlashcards and quizzes, as well as videos, web resources, and links to SAGE journal articles to support and expand on the concepts presented in this chapter.

CHAPTER 5

MODERN SOCIOLOGICAL THEORIES OF CRIME

▲ Theories on delinquency and crime outcomes have proliferated over the past century. Why do you think delinquency happens?

©iStockphoto.com/RichLegg

INTRODUCTION

After replacing the classical school of criminology in the 19th century, biological positivism dominated criminology theorizing until the Great Depression in the 1930s which affected so many people in the United States, irrespective of their social class, education, or race/ethnicity. Biological positivism had a serious problem in explaining spatial and temporal variations in crime because it is difficult for biological characteristics alone to account for geographic variations and historical changes in crime rates. Therefore, criminologists once again looked to the sociological explanations, and three prominent sociological perspectives that are all rooted in Émile Durkheim's (1893/2014) work and remain important today emerged in the 1930s: the strain perspective, the social disorganization perspective, and the learning perspective. Biological positivism, as it was associated with the eugenics movement, continued to lose its popularity in the 1950s because of the atrocities caused by the Nazi Germany that used the eugenics philosophy to slaughter the people of Jewish descent during World War II. The control perspective, another sociological perspective rooted in Durkheim's work, emerged during this time and has remained important today. The shift toward sociological explanations of crime in the middle of the 20th century was followed by the increased use of self-reported survey that allowed empirical testing and development of theories of crime, which also led to a revival of Cesare Beccaria's (1764/1986) deterrence theory and the emergence of the modern classical perspective in the 1960s. Almost all of these sociological theories noted thus far in history had been developed by white male scholars. It is no surprise then that the critical, conflict, and feminist perspectives that are critical of the status quo and the traditional criminology theorizing emerged in the 1960s and 1970s, reflecting the fervor of social movements of that time. With the addition of the life-course perspective that emerged in the 1970s, these sociological explanations have dominated criminology for the past 60 years, with an increased interest in recent years in the biosocial approach that combines both biological and sociological explanations of crime and delinquency.

STRAIN/ANOMIE THEORIES

The Great Depression the United States experienced in the 1930s showed that nobody was immune to the effects of the economic disaster. It was not easy to blame people for their dire condition when so many people became poor and needed the help of government interventions and programs. Crime rates, both violent and property crime, increased during this time, suggesting the possibility that economic condition, rather than individual characteristics (suggested by the biological perspective), may be to blame for crime. It is no surprise that the strain perspective that focused on the economic structure of society, rather than on individual characteristics, emerged during this time period. Today more than one variation of the strain perspective is focused on strain, or stress, as the primary cause of crime with differences in what they consider the primary source of strain.

Robert K. Merton (1910–2003)

Merton's (1938) version of strain theory is often called "anomie theory" because he borrowed the term "anomie" from Durkheim's (1893/2014) work to refer to the disjuncture between culturally accepted goals and the means that the society provides to achieve those goals. The means include normative rules of society (such as working hard, delaying gratification, being honest, and being studious) and opportunities that the social structure provides. Merton's anomie theory is primarily about the United States, where he believed that the culture places too much emphasis on material success to the detriment of the importance of following societal rules to achieve the goal. Individuals who follow the rules of society, therefore, often do not get any satisfaction without material success. Furthermore, although the culturally accepted goal of material success and normative rules of society are the same for everyone, the opportunity to achieve the goal is not equally available to everyone in the United States, especially for the people in the lower class. This is contrary to the fundamental idea of the "American Dream" that everyone who follows the rules of society and works hard can achieve material success. In other words, Merton argued, anomie, or the disjuncture between goals and the means, is the largest for the people in the lower class, and only a very small proportion of people in the lower classes may achieve material success by following societal rules.

According to Merton (1938), this disjuncture between goals and means, or wanting something and not being able to get them, creates strain, which then sometimes leads to crime. Merton argued that crime occurs when an individual accepts the goal of material success but rejects the normative or legitimate means of achieving it, and uses instead an innovative or criminal way (such as stealing, cheating, and lying) of achieving the goal. Merton, however, believed that when faced with this anomie, crime is not the only outcome but is just one of five possible outcomes or "modes of adaptation" (see Table 5.1). The adaptation of conformity occurs when an individual accepts both the culturally accepted goals and the legitimate means of achieving them, even if he or she may not achieve the goals. The adaptation of innovation occurs when an individual commits a crime to achieve the culturally accepted goals by rejecting legitimate means and instead using illegitimate means of achieving them. The adaptation of ritualism occurs when an individual gives up on culturally accepted goals but still follows the normative rules of society to avoid getting into trouble. The adaptation of retreatism occurs when an individual rejects both culturally accepted goals and legitimate means of achieving them and becomes a social "dropout." Merton believed that drug addicts are examples of dropouts of society. Finally, the adaptation of rebellion occurs when an individual rejects both culturally accepted goals and legitimate means and replaces them with new ones (such as political or religious ideologies).

Merton's (1938) anomie theory formed the basis of the War on Poverty during the 1964 Johnson Administration to combat the high national poverty rates (that were near 20%); the Nixon Administration later dismantled and shifted some of the funding for these programs. The War on Poverty had attempted to reduce poverty by creating a "level playing field" for everyone by providing those in the lower class skills they needed to achieve material success. Merton's theory also formed the basis for one of the major theoretical perspectives in criminology that focuses on strain or stress as the cause of crime. Merton's version of the strain theory may be thought of as a class-based theory because of its focus on the varying opportunity structure across social class that presumably explains why people in the lower class are more

▼ TABLE 5.1

Merton's Modes of Adaptation

Modes of adaptation	Culturally accepted goals	Legitimate means
Conformity	+	+
Innovation	+	−
Ritualism	−	+
Retreatism	−	−
Rebellion	*	*

likely to engage in crime. Because the Uniform Crime Reports (UCR) Program does not collect information on the offenders' social class, only after the emergence of the self-reported data in the 1960s was there the examination of the relationship between social class and crime at the individual level. These studies, however, have not always found the expected relationship between social class and crime. When a relationship was found between social class and crime, moreover, it was not always for the property crime, even though Merton's anomie theory would suggest that the strain resulting from not being able to achieve material success leads to property crime (through innovation). For the most part, empirical studies support the relationship between social class and crime/delinquency only when aggregate (group-level) and official data (UCR) are examined but not when individual-level self-report data are examined (Tibbetts & Hemmens, 2010).

Robert Agnew (1953–)

For more than 30 years, Agnew has been developing and refining general strain theory (Agnew, 1985, 1992, 2001, 2007), which is considered one of the leading theories in criminology today. In response to mounting criticisms and empirical evidence against social class as an explanation for crime and delinquency, Agnew (2012, p. 34) has expanded sources of strain beyond the inability to achieve material success. General strain theory, instead, focuses on the negative emotions resulting from "the inability to escape from painful or aversive conditions," which sometimes lead to crime.

According to Agnew, there are three major sources of strain (see Figure 5.1). The first source, with three subtypes, is the failure to achieve positively valued goals. The first subtype of this source is concerned with the disjuncture between aspirations for achieving certain goals and expectations for actually achieving those goals. This subtype most closely resembles Merton's (1938) concept of strain. Agnew (1985), however, expanded goals beyond those related to material success to include immediate goals that may be important for adolescents, such as popularity among peers, getting a good grade in class, and graduating from high school. Additionally, instead of assuming that "goal commitment" is constant for everyone, Agnew (1985) considered it to vary by individual, such that people in the lower class may have a lower aspiration for achieving a certain goal (like graduating from high school) than people in the middle class. The second subtype is concerned if the actual outcomes of achieving certain goals fail to meet one's expectations, creating a disjuncture between expectations of achieving goals and actual outcomes. The third subtype is concerned with the disjuncture between perceived just or fair outcomes of achieving certain goals and actual outcomes of achieving them. Furthermore, Agnew (1992, pp. 57–58) added two additional sources of strain, not directly tied to achievement of goals, but may nonetheless cause strain: One occurs when "positively valued stimuli are removed" (e.g., the death of loved one), and the other occurs when "negative stimuli are presented" (e.g., abuse and neglect at home, living in an unsafe neighborhood, and racial/ethnic discrimination). Unlike Merton's anomie theory, Agnew believed anyone, not just those in the lower class, could experience strain and thus negative emotions.

According to Agnew (1992), these three sources of strain increase the likelihood that individuals experience negative emotions, such as anger and frustrations. Although most people who experience strain, and thus negative emotions, rely on legitimate coping methods to deal with such negative emotions (such as talking to friends, exercising, etc.), others may resort to a deviant and even a delinquent or criminal coping if they have exhausted their resources, especially under repeated severe strain (Agnew, 2007). Much like Merton's (1938) anomie theory, general strain theory considers deviance and crime a possible adaptation mechanism to cope with the negative emotion. Although empirical studies often support general strain theory and find that strain is related to crime, it is usually not the most important variable in explaining crime.

Agnew's General Strain Theory

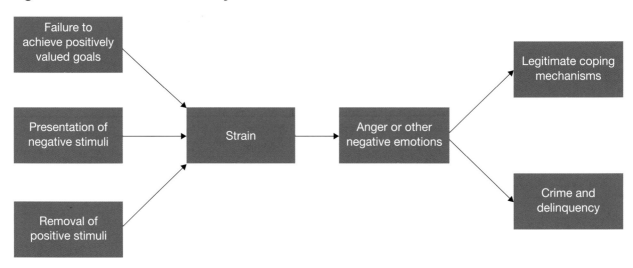

Stephen F. Messner (1951–) and Richard Rosenfeld (1948–)

In *Crime in the American Dream*, Messner and Rosenfeld (1994) proposed a modified version of Merton's (1938) anomie theory, called "institutional anomie theory," that focuses on the institutional power imbalance in society, which results in a high crime rate. Institutions that Messner and Rosenfeld considered include economy, education, religion, polity, and family. Family, for instance, places a value on providing loving support, education places a value on knowledge, and economy places a value on material success. Messner and Rosenfeld argued that when these institutions provide checks and balances of each other, one institution does not dominate at the expense of other institutions, and society will have a lower crime rate. The United States, however, experiences institutional power imbalance, thus a high crime rate, because the institution of economy dominates all institutions of society. This is seen in parents being too busy with work and having no time to have a dinner or to be patient with their children, or religious organizations, instead of focusing on faith, becoming profit-oriented mega churches. Examples of policy changes suggested by Messner and Rosenfeld to strengthen the institution of family, and decreasing the crime rate, include offering flexible work hours, family leave, and childcare by the employer.

SOCIAL DISORGANIZATION PERSPECTIVE

Another prominent sociological perspective that emerged in the 1930s is the social disorganization perspective, developed by criminologists at the University of Chicago; thus, it is also called the Chicago School of Criminology. Like other major cities in the United States at the beginning of the early 20th century, Chicago was experiencing rapid urbanization, population growth from an increase in immigration, and increased social problems like delinquency and crime. During the early 20th century, more than half of the population in Chicago was foreign born and spoke different languages and brought with them different cultural norms and values. Chicago was experiencing in many respects, what Durkheim (1893/2014) called "anomie," or the normlessness, resulting from rapid social changes (Vold, Bernard, & Snipes, 1998). The social disorganization perspective differs from other theories of crime because of its focus on characteristics of environments (and not on individuals) that are associated with high crime rates.

The social disorganization theory is rooted in two studies from the 1920s that were also conducted at the University of Chicago. First, W. I. Thomas and Florian Znaniechi (1927) examined Polish families who immigrated to the urban, industrial society, the United States, and how their traditional social norms and values influenced the adjustment. Like Durkheim (1893/2014), Thomas and Znaniechi believed that the weakening of the solidarity, especially of the family, explained the "social disorganization" of Polish communities in the United States. Second, Robert Park and Ernest Burgess (1925) applied the principles of ecology, through the process of invasion, dominance, and succession of new species (e.g., plants, trees, and fish) in an environment, to understand how a city grows over time (as seen in urban sprawl). According to the concentric zone model (see Figure 5.2), proposed by Park and Burgess, when a new immigrant group without skills or money moves into a city, he or she usually lives in the least desirable part of the city, called the "zone of transition," which surrounds the central business district. The zone of transition tends to be multicultural with other immigrant groups already living in the zone. Over time, individuals who live in the zone of transition make economic progress and move to more desirable areas of the city, like the "zone for working class" or even further out to the "residential zone" and the "commuter zone."

Clifford Shaw (1896–1957) and Henry D. McKay (1899–1980)

Combining the works of the two earlier studies, Shaw and McKay developed the theory of social disorganization that they presented over several books, including *Delinquency Areas,*

▼ FIGURE 5.2

Robert Park and Ernest Burgess's Theory of Concentric Zone Model

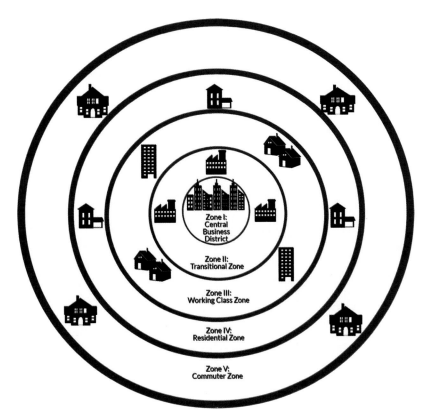

Zone I:
Central
Business
District

Zone II:
Transitional Zone

Zone III:
Working Class Zone

Zone IV:
Residential Zone

Zone V:
Commuter Zone

Source: Adapted from Rubenstein (2016). Graphic created via Piktochart.

© iStockphoto.com/DenisTangneyJr

▲ Theories on delinquency and crime outcomes have proliferated over the past century. Why do you think delinquency happens?

published in 1929 (written by Shaw); *Social Factors in Juvenile Delinquency,* published in 1931; and *Juvenile Delinquency and Urban Areas,* published in 1942 (the latter two were written by both Shaw and McKay). After analyzing a massive amount of police data in Chicago from the years 1900–1933 at the census-track level, Shaw and McKay found that the areas with a high crime rate remained the same over time, even though the racial and ethnic group that resided in the area changed over that period and no racial or ethnic group escaped the high crime rate when they resided in the high crime area. Shaw and McKay, therefore, concluded that the high crime rate found among blacks and foreign born today can be explained by the concentration in the areas of the city with a high crime rate that these groups tended to occupy. Shaw and McKay further argued that it is not the ethnic groups or the nationality, or their unique characteristics, that are related to crime but something about the areas with a high crime rate that are related to crime.

That something, according to Shaw and McKay (1942), is the social disorganization, which refers to the inability of an area or a neighborhood to control and regulate the behaviors of its residents, especially of youth. Shaw and McKay believed that social disorganization in the high crime area or the zone of transition is the result of its poor economy, residential instability, and ethnic heterogeneity. As the name suggests, residents in the zone of transition tend to be transients who do not develop relationships and networks among themselves, and the ethnic heterogeneity, the mixture of many racial and ethnic groups with different cultures and languages, makes interactions among residents further unlikely. In an area with a low informal social network, residents may not watch out for each other, report misbehaviors of children, or share information with each other. This lack of an informal social network and informal social control leads to social disorganization, according to Shaw and McKay, and to the inability to prevent crime or the genesis of delinquent groups like gangs. Additionally, the high residential instability and ethnic heterogeneity are more likely to produce conflicts among residents and further increase the formation gangs and their activities around different ethnic/racial groups. By the 1980s, numerous empirical studies came out in support of social disorganization theory, finding overall that the inner-city neighborhoods with high residential instability and ethnic heterogeneity tended to have high crime rates (e.g., Bursik, 1988; Laub, 1983; Sampson, 1985).

William J. Wilson (1935–)

In *The Truly Disadvantaged: The Inner City, the Underclass, and Public Policy* (1987) and *When Work Disappears: The World of New Urban Poor* (1997), Wilson discussed how the postindustrialization era in the United States beginning around 1965–1970 and resulted in a decline in unskilled and low-skilled manufacturing jobs from the central cities that created a "truly disadvantaged" or "underclass" in many urban U.S. cities. Park and Burgess noted that when a new immigrant group without skills or money moves into a city, it lives in the least desirable part of the city around the central business district with a high crime rate, but with economic progress over time, every group historically makes a move to more desirable areas of the city. Wilson argued that making economic progress was possible before the postindustrialization era when the central business district offered a stable blue-collar job to uneducated, low skill workers. Since the disappearance of manufacturing jobs from the city center, however, which were then replaced with low-paying, service jobs, blacks, who had been making the Great Migration to the urban cities from rural southern states since the early 20th century, and now recent immigrants, such as Hispanic and Southeast Asian immigrants, are stuck in the undesirable, high crime areas, unable to obtain a decent job or make economic

THE SURVEILLANCE STATE

In a book titled *On the Run: Fugitive Life in American City*, Goffman (2014) described her six years of research observing people who reside in one of the disadvantaged neighborhoods in Philadelphia, much like the one Shaw and McKay (1942) called "socially disorganized." Although social disorganization theory focused on the characteristics of the neighborhood that explain its high crime rate, Goffman focused on the punitive criminal justice policy, which began with the "war on drugs" in the 1980s, and the creation of the "surveillance state" that disproportionately targets the disadvantaged neighborhoods as the causes for the deterioration of these neighborhoods and the worsening in crime. Goffman showed that the creation of the "surveillance state" devastates all fabrics of life (including family, friendships, romantic relationships, education, and employment) in the neighborhood that is under constant police supervision, which leads to a vicious cycle of involvement in the criminal justice system among its residents and further prevents its residents from making any economic progress or even from becoming a productive member of the society.

1. What does Goffman mean by "surveillance state?"

2. Have you ever experienced this phenomenon called a "surveillance state?"

progress. Wilson, thus, provided a refinement to the social disorganization theory and an explanation why blacks and other recent immigrants today live disproportionately in high-crime, inner-city neighborhoods.

Robert J. Sampson (1963–)

Sampson and his colleagues (1997) offered a revision to Shaw and McKay's (1942) social disorganization theory by adding a concept, "collective efficacy," which refers to the cohesion among residents and their ability to act for the common good for the neighborhood. The level of collective efficacy of neighborhood depends on the level of residential instability and poverty; therefore, poverty is related to crime because poverty, combined with residential instability and family disruption, lowers the collective efficacy of the neighborhood to control crime in the neighborhood. The presence of a crime patrol or crime watcher group represents a high collective efficacy, and according to Sampson, that type of neighborhood tends to have a low crime rate, whereas, ironically, a neighborhood with a high crime rate, thus in need of a crime-control group, often lacks the collective efficacy to tackle crime problems in its neighborhood.

LEARNING THEORIES

Another prominent sociological perspective that emerged in the 1930s is the learning perspective. Learning occurs through association, and children, including newborn babies, learn through association. There are three major theories on the process of learning. First is the classical conditioning, depicted in the Pavlov's dog experiment conducted by Ivan Pavlov (1849–1936), whereby a dog begins to salivate upon hearing a sound of bell after a repeated association of the sound of bell and the presentation of food (see photo on page 106). Second is operant conditioning, developed by B. F. Skinner (1904–1990), whereby rewards and punishments are used to reinforce behaviors. Third is social learning that incorporates cognition in the learning process by considering both actual and expected rewards and punishments in reinforcing behaviors. In addition, Albert Bandura (1925–), who developed social learning theory/social cognitive theory, is known for his Bobo-doll experiment (see photo on page 107), which showed learning of aggressive behaviors among children through modeling and imitation. Bandura argued that children learn aggression and violence through observing and modeling behaviors of others, especially on television. Social learning occurs when

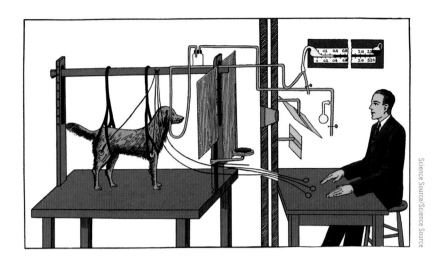

individuals learn through observation the expectations of punishments and rewards associated with a certain behavior (Vold. Bernard, & Snipes, 1998). These psychological theories of learning provided a foundation to the sociological learning theories of crime.

The learning perspective of criminology is rooted in the work of Edwin H. Sutherland (1947) and his differential association theory, although Gabriel Tard (1843–1904) was the first scholar to propose the idea that criminal behavior is learned like any other behaviors. The idea that "criminal behavior is learned" was revolutionary at the time Sutherland was developing his theory in the 1930s because the predominant idea of criminality, based on biological determinism, was that some people are born criminal. Sutherland instead argued that anyone can become criminal because criminal behaviors can be learned like any other behaviors and anyone can learn to commit a crime. There are different versions of the learning theory, but they all assume that criminal behaviors are learned behaviors rather than instinctive behaviors present at birth.

▲ Behaviorist psychology is often remembered with the Pavlov dog experiment. Does this help to explain delinquency and crime outcomes?

Edwin H. Sutherland (1883–1950)

Sutherland was influenced by the work of a prominent psychologist named George Herbert Mead (1863–1932), who was responsible for the development of symbolic interactionism. Mead stated that our behavior in a situation depends on our "definition" of the situation, which is based on the "meanings" we attach to similar situations from our past experiences. For instance, based on your past experiences, you might come to define people cutting you off while driving as being disrespectful, and thus while driving, if someone cuts you off, you would not hesitate to yell and give them a middle finger. According to Mead, we develop "definitions" and "meanings" through interactions with intimate groups, such as family and friends. If your parents always define situations in a negative way and are quick to assume that people are always disrespecting them, like when people cut them off while driving, then you will come to define those situations similarly.

Sutherland developed the theory of differential association over time: *Criminology*, published in 1924, and later *Principles of Criminology*, the first edition of which was published in 1934. Differential association theory is the first contemporary theory of crime to focus on the process of becoming delinquent rather than on the genesis of crime or criminal subcultures. Not all children who grow up in a disadvantaged neighborhood join a gang and live a life of crime; some children who grow up in a disadvantaged neighborhood instead go on to attend college and live a productive life. The difference between these two types of children is not the disadvantaged condition in which they grew up, rather, according to Sutherland, the difference is the "definitions" they come to attach to situations/conditions they encounter. Sutherland, Cressey, and Luckenbill's (1992) theory is summarized in the following nine statements:

1. Criminal behavior is learned.

2. Criminal behavior is learned in interaction with other persons in the process of communication.

3. The principal part of the learning of criminal behavior occurs within intimate personal groups (i.e., "associations" with people).

4. When criminal behavior is learned, the learning includes

   a. Techniques of committing the crime, which can be simple or complex

   b. Specific directions or motives, drives, rationalizations, and attitudes.

5. The specific direction of motives and drives is learned from definitions of the legal codes as favorable or unfavorable.

Creative Commons Attribution-Share Alike 4.0 International

6. A person becomes delinquent because of an excess of definitions favorable to violation of law over definitions unfavorable to violation of the law.

7. Differential associations may vary in frequency, duration, priority, and intensity.

8. The process of learning criminal behavior by association with criminal and anti-criminal patterns involves all of the mechanisms that are involved in any other learning.

9. Although criminal behavior is an expression of general needs and values, it is not explained by those general needs and values because noncriminal behavior is an expression of the same needs and values.

▲ Albert Bandura's Bobo Doll experiment showed that children learn through observing aggressive behaviors of adults. The finding resulted in a huge debate concerning the influence that violent media have on children's behaviors. Do you think watching a violent movie, playing a violent game, or listening to violent music causes children to engage in violence?

Differential association theory consists of the explanations of the "content" and the "process" of learning, such as specific techniques, motives, drivers, rationalizations, and attitudes toward certain crimes, as well as general definitions of laws as favorable or unfavorable, and of the process of learning, which includes the interactions in intimate groups (Vold et al., 1998).

There have been several revisions to Sutherland's differential association theory. For instance, in a series of articles published in the 1950s and 1960s, Daniel Glaser argued that intimate personal interaction was not necessary for the learning of delinquent behaviors to occur and that identifying with delinquent roles and role models is more important than merely associating with delinquents. Glaser also believed that expectations of consequences of a certain criminal behavior are more important than the definitions of the behavior. C. Ray Jeffrey (1965, 1971) developed differential reinforcement theory by incorporating the principle of the operant conditioning. This theory is reminiscent of classical criminology, especially the rational choice theory, which will be discussed later in this chapter. According to Jeffrey, individuals have different experiences with crimes; those who have more rewarding experiences with a certain criminal behavior are more likely to engage in the behavior than are those who have less rewarding experiences with the behavior.

Ronald L. Akers (1939–)

The most sophisticated revision of Sutherland's differential association theory is Akers's social learning theory. Akers has been presenting social learning theory for 50 years in a series of articles and a book titled *Deviant Behavior: A Social Learning Approach,* published in 1973. Some key concepts in Akers's social learning theory include differential association, definitions, differential reinforcement, imitation, feedback, and social structure. "Differential association" refers to the process of being exposed to definitions that are favorable or unfavorable to delinquency. "Definitions" refers to the attitudes and meanings an individual attaches to a specific delinquent behavior or law breaking in general. These two concepts are similar to the concepts in differential association theory.

What is unique in Akers's social learning theory is the idea of "differential reinforcement," which refers to the rewards and punishments that are associated with a behavior. Akers considered social reinforcers, in the forms of praise, condemnation, status, and reputation in a peer group, to be much more important than the material reinforcers, especially for young people. According to Akers, an individual who engages in a delinquent behavior depends on his or her anticipated and actual rewards and punishments of the behavior, especially by the peer group. Borrowing the idea of "modeling" from Albert Bandura's (1977) social learning theory, Akers argued that imitation or modeling can result in an initial act of delinquency. For the behavior to continue, however, Akers argued, reinforcement is more important than imitation. Akers also introduced the idea of "feedback," which refers to the vicious cycle in which once an individual engages in a delinquent behavior, the behavior can influence the differential association, and thus, the differential reinforcement and the definition of the behavior, which then increases the likelihood of engagement in the delinquency behavior. In his later work, Akers added social structure to his theory, such that an individual's location in the social structure (e.g., type of neighborhood one resides or one's social class, gender, and race/ethnicity), influences his or her differential associations and differential reinforcements.

Akers's social learning theory, more specifically the variable measuring association with delinquent friends, has consistently been found to have one of the strongest relationships with delinquency when examined with other individual-level theories of crime (e.g., Warr, 2002; see also Akers and Jensen, 2008, for a review of the current state of this theory). Differential association is especially relevant for the study of delinquency because children often engage in unlawful behaviors in group, much more so than adults, who tend to engage in crime alone. Furthermore, for some delinquent behaviors, such as smoking marijuana, researchers have found that learning the techniques of smoking and even learning how to perceive pleasure from smoking marijuana is necessary for an individual to continue engaging in the behavior (Becker, 1963), in support of social learning theory. Along with Agnew's general strain theory, Akers's social learning theory is considered today one of the most important theories in criminology.

SUBCULTURAL THEORIES

Shaw and McKay's (1942) theory of social disorganization described the formation of delinquent groups, like gangs, in a socially disorganized neighborhood with a weak informal social network and social control and inability to prevent the genesis of crime and criminal subcultures. The learning perspective focused on the "process" of becoming delinquent and how criminal definitions were transmitted in delinquent groups. Rather than merely claiming that delinquent subcultures have definitions favorable for breaking laws, some theories, termed "subcultural theories of crime," explain the "content," or the norms and values, of such delinquent subcultures.

Albert K. Cohen (1918–2014)

In *Delinquent Boys: The Culture of the Gang*, Cohen (1955) introduced a theory of blocked opportunity/gang formation based on Merton's (1938) anomie theory. Cohen argued that lower class young people experience a blocked opportunity to achieve status and gain respect in the conventional society because status and respect are earned by meeting middle-class standards. Lower class young people are disadvantaged because although middle-class values (such as ambition, responsibility, industry and thrift, and controlling aggression) are necessary to achieve the middle-class standards, lower class parents are

ASSOCIATION WITH DELINQUENT PEERS

Children often misbehave in group, much more so than adults who tend to engage in crime alone. A study based on a nationally representative sample of adolescents found that 73% of all delinquent offenses were committed in a group, including 91% of all burglaries, 71% of all assaults, and 44% of all thefts (Warr, 1996). Indeed, the association with delinquent peers often has one of the strongest relationships with delinquency, indicating that children with delinquent friends are more likely to engage in delinquency than are those without a delinquent friend. Differential association's influence on delinquency is not limited to friends; however, researchers have also found that individuals with a delinquent romantic partner are more likely to engage in delinquency themselves (Haynie, Giordano, Manning, & Longmore, 2005). As a result, Warr argued that

social learning theory might be a key to explaining the gender difference in criminality—the fact that boys are overall more delinquent than girls. In an article, cleverly titled, "Girl friends are better: Gender, friends, and crime among school and street youth," McCarthy, Felmlee, and Hagan (2004), indeed, found that irrespective of gender of the youth, those who have friends who are boys are more delinquent than those who have friends who are girls.

1. **Why do you think that adolescents are more likely to commit crimes within groups?**

2. **How might you address this problem if you were a police officer, school principal, or juvenile court judge?**

less adequate in teaching those values to their children, as compared with middle-class parents who grew up with the middle-class values. Because of the blocked opportunity to achieve status and gain respect, lower class youth experience frustration and, what Sigmund Freud (1856–1939) termed, "reaction formation," or the intensely adverse reaction to the middle-class standards and values. Cohen argued that lower class youth then turn to the opposite standards and values present in the delinquent subculture. According to Cohen, not all lower class children turn to a delinquent subculture; some become "corner boys" who accept their lower class status and engage in nondelinquent activities, whereas others became "college boys" who, despite the odds, manage to achieve some success in conventional society.

Walter B. Miller (1920–2004)

Miller (1958) developed a theory of focal concerns and believed that it is the lower class values, not the reaction against middle-class values, like Cohen argued, that are the cause of high delinquency involvements among young people. According to Miller, although the people in the middle class share "middle-class values" (such as working hard), the people in the lower class share lower class values called "focal concerns." These concerns include trouble (children who get into trouble often gain status among peers), toughness, street smart, excitement and thrills, fatalism (the belief that what happens is outside one's control), and autonomy (or strong resistance of authority, control, and rules). Miller argued that lower class children are often raised in a family without a father figure or any other male role models because lower class fathers are often in prison or absent in the family. As a result, young, lower class males look to those in the street in a same-sex peer group for role models who reinforce the lower class focal concerns. According to Miller, the focal concerns are responsible for the cycle of delinquency and crime among the people of the lower class because such negative values keep producing males who would abandon their family and thus children who would look to the street for male role models.

Richard A. Cloward (1926–2001) and Lloyd E. Ohlin (1918–2008)

Cloward (1959) offered some revisions to Merton's (1938) anomie theory and argued that the legitimate means but also the illegitimate means of achieving the goal of material success

⚠ Youth gangs have been a concern and problem in many neighborhoods. Why do you think young people join gangs?

are distributed unequally. People in the lower class are often surrounded by criminal opportunities in the neighborhood (such as gangs, drugs, prostitutions, pawn shops, and gambling); thus, it is much easier for them to engage in crime by taking advantage of those available opportunities. Cloward also argued that individuals need to learn to take advantage of the opportunities for achieving goals, be it legally or illegally; thus, even if a legitimate opportunity is available to everyone equally, not everyone could take advantage of it. In a book titled, *Delinquency and Opportunity: A Theory of Delinquent Gangs*, Cloward (1960) with Ohlin further elaborated on the unequal distribution of illegitimate means. Accordingly, the blocked opportunity may lead to different types of delinquent subcultures organized around different types of crime because the opportunity for illegal means of achieving material success is distributed unequally. Cloward and Ohlin specifically noted three types of delinquent subcultures that may develop in lower class neighborhoods. First, the criminal subculture, organized around illegitimate means of achieving material success (e.g., theft, extortion, fraud, and drug dealing), develops in a stable lower class neighborhood with established adult criminal activities around those illegitimate means. Second, in a less stable lower class neighborhood with fewer illegitimate means of achieving material success, the delinquent subculture may develop around violence and fighting to achieve status in the neighborhood. Third, the retreatist delinquent subculture is organized around the use of alcohol and drugs, and Cloward and Ohlin considered those juveniles who are involved in the retreatist subculture as "double failures" who failed in both the dominant culture and the criminal and conflict subculture.

Mervin Eugene Wolfgang (1924–1998) and Franco Ferracuti (1927–1996)

In *The Subculture of Violence: Toward an Integrated Theory in Criminology*, Wolfgang and Ferracuti (1967) argued that there is a subculture among the lower class in the United States that has conduct norms (expected behaviors in certain situations) that promote the use of violence. After studying homicides in Philadelphia, Wolfgang found that many of the homicides committed among people of the lower class, especially among lower class blacks, resulted from trivial reasons. Wolfgang and Ferracuti argued that there are class and race differences in attitudes toward violence, such that lower class black males view violence as a response to a conflict more favorably than other groups. Howard Erlanger's (1974) nationally representative study, however, found no such class or race differences in attitudes toward the use of violence, contrary to Wolfgang and Ferracuti's argument. The subculture of violence thesis has been studied extensively, especially with respect to the violence in the South (to explain its historically high violent crime rate) and among blacks across the United States (Vold et al., 1998).

Elijah Anderson (1943–)

In *Streetwise: Race, Class, and Change in an Urban Community* (1990) and *Code of the Street: Decency, Violence, and the Moral Life of the Inner City* (2000), Anderson explored the street subculture of black urban communities with a "code of the street" that promotes the use of violence. The code of the street emphasizes the importance of respect, and because respect is scarce in poor inner-city communities, violence is accepted as a way to stand up against someone who is disrespectful. Anderson argued that this subculture emerged out of a lack of trust in the criminal justice system (thus, residents began taking matters into their own hands) and the frustration with chronic poverty. Anderson found two kinds of families in poor inner-city communities; "street families" encourage children to abide by the code of the street, whereas "decent families" try to keep children off the street and away from the street subculture, often unsuccessfully.

John Hagan (1946–)

Hagan (1993) borrowed the idea of "social embeddedness" from economist Mark Granovetter and applied it to criminology. According to Granovetter, regular employment involves being embedded in a conventional social network of people the employed individual interacts with on a regular basis. Similarly, Hagan argued that an individual can be socially embedded in a criminal network, especially if his or her parents and peers are also socially embedded in the networks of crime and criminal markets (such as drug dealing). Furthermore, once an individual is involved in delinquency, Hagan argued, he or she tends to isolate further from the conventional social networks, such as the network of legitimate employment, which then strengthens his or her social embeddedness in the criminal network.

CONTROL THEORIES/NEOCLASSICAL CRIMINOLOGY

Control theories are rooted in the classical school of criminology; thus, this perspective is often called the "neoclassical school of criminology." Like Hobbes, and early classical criminologists like Beccaria and Bentham, control theories assume that people are inherently hedonistic, seeking pleasure and avoiding pain, and have free will to decide their own behaviors. Furthermore, control theories assume that the motivation for crime is universal, equally available to everyone, because crime is the most efficient and effective way of satisfying one's desires (e.g., stealing versus working to save money to buy a pair of jeans). Because control theories assume that we are all equally motivated to commit crime, the question then becomes, "what prevents (controls) people from engaging in crime?" instead of "what causes people to engage in crime?"

Early control theories laid out important concepts that have formed the basis of contemporary control theories. Albert J. Reiss (1951), who is considered one of the first contemporary control theorists, distinguished between "internal controls," internalization of the norms of society, and "external controls," relationships with parents, parenting practices the parents used, and the type of neighborhood. Reiss found that although both types of controls are important, internal controls were more important overall than external controls in preventing delinquency.

In explaining why some children in a socially disorganized neighborhood do not engage in delinquency, Jackson Toby (1957) devised the concept, "stake in conformity," which is considered one of the most profound concepts in control theories today. Toby argued that even though everyone is motivated to engage in crime, individuals who have a higher stake in conformity, or individuals who have more to lose by engaging in crime, are less likely to engage in crime. Imagine two individuals: one is a high school dropout without employment or a family, and another is a married college graduate with employment and children. Which individual has more to lose by engaging in crime and getting caught for it (thus having a high stake in conformity) and, therefore, is less likely to engage in crime? Although learning theories tend to focus on peers as the most important reinforcers of delinquency, control theories tend to focus on family as the most important control agent against delinquency.

As one of the first criminologists to focus on family in crime theorizing, F. Ivan Nye (1958) distinguished three ways that the family controls delinquency: direct control, indirect control, and internal control. Direct control occurs when parents punish a misbehavior and reward a good behavior of children. Indirect control occurs when children refrain from engaging in misbehavior out of concern for their parents (e.g., not wanting to make them disappointed). Finally, internal control occurs when parents instill in children the rules of society. Similarly, Scott Briar and Irving Pilliavin (1965) tried to determine what gave an individual a high stake in conformity to rules and society expectations; they found that individuals with the following characteristics did so: affectionate ties to parents and peers (who are not delinquent), motivation to do well in school, aspiration for employment, belief in God, and fear of arrest and punishment.

Gresham M. Sykes (1922–2010) and David Matza (1930–)

The findings of empirical studies indicated that there did not seem to be a difference in values between delinquents and nondelinquents, contrary to the expectation based on subcultural theories. In *Delinquency and Drift,* David Matza (1964) furthered this notion that delinquency is a "matter of drift" in that delinquents are not always being delinquents but instead constantly moving back and forth between being delinquents and nondelinquents. Matza then asked, "how do delinquents free themselves from the conventional values they hold to sometimes engage in delinquency?" The answer lies in the "subterranean" (under the surface) values, which are different from the dominant values and promote hedonism, seeking pleasure, and excitement. Additionally, according to Sykes and Matza (1957), the reason why delinquents so easily move into the subterranean values that encourage delinquency is because of the five "techniques of neutralization" that they use to justify their delinquency engagement. First, "the denial of responsibility" occurs when an individual claims that the delinquency was caused by a force outside of their control (e.g., delinquent peers, bad parents, or disadvantaged neighborhood), and therefore, they are not responsible for the action. Second, "the denial of injury" occurs when an individual claims that even if the behavior may be against the law, there was nobody who was being injured by his act (e.g., "borrowing" a car instead of stealing it). Third, "the denial of the victim" occurs when an individual, who admits to the involvement in delinquency that may have caused injury, claims that there was no victim of the act because the victim somehow deserved the injury (e.g., vandalism at school, attacks on homosexuals, homeless men, etc.). Fourth, "the condemnation of the condemners" occurs when an individual shifts the attention to those who condemn the delinquent acts (e.g., police, teachers, etc.) who are, in the individual's mind, "hypocrites, deviants in disguise, or impelled by personal spite" (Sykes & Matza, 1957, p. 668). Fifth, "the appeal to higher loyalties" occurs when, despite upholding the dominant values, an individual may engage in delinquency because of the loyalties toward his social groups, such as a gang, friends, and siblings, among others.

Walter C. Reckless (1899–1988)

In *The Crime Problem* (1967), Reckless proposed containment theory, which includes explanations for both what motivates and what prevents (or controls) crime. Reckless considered that both the motivation (also called "push factors") and control (also called "pull factors") are important in explaining delinquency involvement. Push factors include both external (e.g., poverty and blocked opportunity) and internal (e.g., hostility and boredom) factors, and pull factors also include both external (e.g., belonging to a nondelinquent group and school and family informal social control) and internal (e.g., a sense of responsibility or a positive self-concept) factors. Self-concept, an internal pull factor, refers to the perception of oneself as being a good or a bad person, which, according to Reckless, develops by age 12. Like Reiss, Reckless in the end considered the internal control, in particular self-concept, to be the most important factor that explains delinquency.

Travis Hirschi (1935–2017)

One of the most influential control theories was proposed by Hirschi (*The Causes of Delinquency,* 1969). Hirschi (1979) strongly believed that combining both motivations and controls in criminology theories is illogical because they are derived from different assumptions of human nature. If one, for instance, takes the Hobbesian stance on human nature as inherently hedonistic and self-seeking and that crime is the most efficient and effective way of satisfying one's desires, then the motivation for crime should be constant and requires no explanation. With this assumption of the control perspective, Hirschi (1969, p. 16) proposed that "delinquent acts result when an individual's bond to society is weak or broken." Bonds to society consist of four elements, all of which are interrelated with one another: attachment, commitment, belief, and involvement. Attachment refers to the emotional ties

▲ Adolescents are most concerned about their friends and peers. How do you think peers influence youthful offending and delinquency?

an individual develops with parents, peers, and teachers/school. Hirschi further elaborated on "attachment to parents" as comprising three components: affectional identification (the feeling of love and respect), intimacy of communication (sharing of intimate personal concerns and problems), and supervision ("the psychological presence" of parents in our thoughts when contemplating delinquency). Commitment, like Toby's (1957) "stake in conformity," is the extent of investment one makes in the conventional society. Belief refers to individuals' belief in law and society's rules. Finally, involvement refers to the participation in conventional activities. Hirschi (1979) found that attachment, especially attachment to parents, is the most important element explaining delinquency, followed by belief.

Michael R. Gottfredson (1951–) and Travis Hirschi (1935–2017)

In *A General Theory of Crime,* Gottfredson and Hirschi (1990) proposed a different version of control theory, called "self-control theory." Self-control, or one's ability to control and regulate desires and impulses, had been extensively studied in psychology. For instance, one of the most famous studies related to self-control is the Stanford marshmallow experiment conducted in the 1960s and 1970s that examined children's ability to delay gratification. A follow-up study to the original experiment found that the self-control measured at an early age had a significant association with later outcomes, such as drug use, obesity, employment, and education (Mischel, Shoda, & Rodriguez, 1989). Likewise, Gottfredson and Hirschi argued that an individual's level of self-control is fixed at age five and remains stable throughout the life course. As a control theory, self-control theory also assumes that humans are born hedonistic, seeking pleasure and avoiding pain; thus, it is assumed that humans are inherently born with a low self-control. According to Gottfredson and Hirschi, it is the parents or guardians who instill self-control in their children by monitoring behaviors, recognizing misbehaviors, and punishing misbehaviors as they are recognized.

Gottfredson and Hirschi (1990) identified six characteristics of low self-control, including impulsivity, risk seeking, preference for a physical over a mental activity, preference for a simple over a complex activity, selfishness, and a bad temper. Given opportunities to commit "crime" (which Gottfredson and Hirschi defined as "acts of force or fraud in pursuit of one's self-interest"), individuals with a low self-control would do it, whereas others with a high self-control refrained from doing it. Gottfredson and Hirschi considered that low self-control would explain not just law-breaking behaviors but also other deviant behaviors, such as not wearing a seat belt, getting into accidents, and unprotected sexual intercourse. This idea is

THE STUDY OF GANG PREVENTION

Shaw and McKay's (1942) social disorganization theory noted the link at the macro-level between the inability of a neighborhood to control its residents' behaviors, especially of young people, and the genesis of delinquency and delinquent subculture in the neighborhood. Hirschi (1969), however, believed that delinquents, by definition, lack social bonds and do not have close relationships with their peers. Instead, delinquents form "cold and brittle" relationships with one another and are socially isolated and lack bonds to society. Hirschi believed that delinquent subculture is, therefore, not an important cause of delinquency, and instead the weak social bonds explain delinquency and the involvement in a delinquent group. Some empirical studies on gangs seem to support Hirschi's claim. For instance, studies by Chesney-Lind (1999) and Esbensen and Huizinga (1993) found that youth gang groups tend not to be cohesive, and that most of these gang members do not intend to stay in the gang for a long time. Another study by Maxson and Klein (1995) also found that street gangs naturally lack cohesiveness—they tend to loosely connect to one another, and memberships tend to be ephemeral for most of the members—unless outside forces (e.g., gang war) enforce cohesiveness among group members. Other studies, on the other hand, indicate the negative influence of gang membership on delinquency engagement. For instance, the results of a longitudinal study by Esbensen and Huisinga (1993) show evidence for both control theory and subcultural theory, in that gang members tend to have a higher level of individual delinquency involvement prior to joining a gang compared with nongang members. Nevertheless there are increases in delinquent activities, as well as in rates of involvement in delinquency, after becoming a gang member compared with nongang members.

1. Why do you think gang members tend to have "cold and brittle" relationships with one another?

2. How does knowledge about the relationships among gang members inform gang prevention efforts?

called "generality of deviance" (Osgood, Johnston, O'Malley, & Bachman, 1988) in that the same underlying factor, such as low self-control, explains the persistent and frequent engagement in reckless behaviors, including deviance and crime.

MODERN CLASSICAL PERSPECTIVE

The classical perspective dominated criminology theorizing for almost a century beginning with the publication of Cesare Beccaria's *On Crimes and Punishments* in 1764. Although Beccaria's ideas still form the foundation of the U.S. criminal justice system, the classical perspective was replaced by positivism when Darwin's *The Origin of Species* was published in 1859, popularizing the theory of evolution and propelling the use of the scientific method to understand human behaviors. The classical perspective remained dormant for 100 years in criminology theorizing until the 1960s when scholars began testing Beccaria's theory of deterrence using empirical data.

Rational Choice Theory

Rational choice theory was adopted from the field of economics to explain law-breaking behaviors. Like the Enlightenment philosophy and the classical perspective of criminology, rational choice theory assumes that humans are rational and hedonistic and weigh the costs and benefits. Unlike deterrence theory, which focuses solely on the costs of punishment, however, rational choice theory takes into account all factors (formal and informal and costs and benefits) that could go into the decision-making process. Rational choice theory came to the forefront of criminology theorizing with the publication of D. Cornish and Ron Clarke's (1986) *The Reasoning Criminal: Rational Choice Perspectives on Offending* and Jack Katz's (1988) *Seductions of Crime*. These authors were the first to emphasize the importance of the benefit of crime in offending. Rational choice theory today also takes into account informal sanctions such as loss of self-esteem, social disapproval, and self-sanctions (feelings of shame and embarrassment) that affect decisions to engage in criminal and delinquent behaviors. Deterrence theory and rational choice theory have had profound impacts on the U.S. criminal justice system, which has increasingly recognized the importance of family, employment, and community in rehabilitative efforts to reduce recidivism among offenders.

Routine Activities Theory/Lifestyle Theory

Routine activities theory was developed by Lawrence Cohen and Marcus Felson (1979) who argued that the convergence of three factors—motivated offenders, suitable target, and lack of guardianship for the target—makes crime more likely. Unlike most other theories of crime, routine activities theory does not explain the reasons for offending because the theory considers the motivation for crime to be constant (i.e., everyone is motivated to engage in crime, much like the classical school perspective). The theory instead focuses on explaining the suitable target and the lack of guardianship, or the opportunity for crime. Locations that have a high convergence of the three factors are often referred to as "hot spots." In recent years, geographic profiling is used in policing tactics that target high crime areas for, for instance, prostitution, drug dealing, or gang activities. Unlike other theories, routine activities theory has strong empirical support, finding that crime occurs during certain days and times. For instance, the highest frequency of delinquency occurs between 3:00 p.m. and 6:00 p.m. when young people are unsupervised after school and before many parents get home and occurs along the routes taken by young people to and from school. An extension of the routine activities theory is called the "lifestyle theory," which posits that a person who lives a riskier lifestyle (e.g., spends a lot of time in places that have a high crime rate) will be at a greater risk for involvement in crime, both as offender and as victim, because of his or her high frequent encountering with crime-prone opportunities. This explains the reason why offenders and victims of violent crimes tend to share similar characteristics (Truman & Langton, 2015).

Modern Classical Perspective

The tough-on-crime approaches, such as "three strikes and you're out" and felony murder doctrine, are based on the assumption that punishment deters crime. Unfortunately, however, researchers consistently find that the severity of punishment is not as important as the certainty of punishment in deterring crime, especially when the certainty of punishment is low like in the United States. Consistent with Beccaria's (1764/1986) argument, some studies even found an increase in violence as a result of such severe punishments, indicating that individuals who already have two strikes might do whatever they can, including killing the victims, witnesses, and police officers, even for a minor offense, to escape getting caught the third time. Another application of the deterrence idea is the use of shaming as a form of punishment. A judge might order as a punishment an individual who is convicted of shoplifting to wear a sign that says "I am a shoplifter" in front of the store that he or she shoplifted. Other examples of shaming as punishment include the special license plate that those convicted of drunk driving are ordered to place on their cars or a billboard sign for the pictures of convicted sex offenders. The policy applications of the routine activities theory range from police tactics that target "hot spots" to change in individual behaviors that could prevent being the victims of crimes, including adding more street lights, clearing the windows of convenience stores from fliers so that the inside of the store is easily visible from outside, having a dog at home, and the way neighborhoods are structured.

SOCIAL REACTION, CRITICAL, AND FEMINIST THEORIES

Although Bonger introduced Marxist theory of criminology in the early 20th century, it was not until the 1960s and 1970s when the social reaction, conflict, and critical perspective of

EMPIRICAL STUDIES ON DETERRENCE THEORY

There are three phases of research on deterrence theory that emerged in the last half of the 20th century. The first phase consisted of aggregate studies testing the state-level data on deterrence, examining for instance, the deterrent effect of capital punishment on crime rate. The criticisms of the aggregate level of testing deterrence theory, such as the lack of the examination of the perceptions of the certainty, swiftness, and severity of punishment on offending, lead to the second phase of research on deterrence. The second phase consisted of the cross-sectional, individual-level studies using survey data that focused on examining the perceptions of deterrence on offending. These cross-sectional studies were also criticized subsequently because all variables were measured at the same time and it was not clear whether the perception of the cost of the punishment preceded the behavior or the other way around. The third phase of deterrence research thus addressed this limitation using longitudinal studies that followed the same individuals over time to examine how the perception of punishment and the behavior influence each other. These longitudinal studies found that it was the behaviors that influence perceptions of the certainty and severity of punishment, rather than the perceptions of the punishment influencing behavior. This is called an "experiential effect" and is contrary to what deterrence theory would predict (Paternoster, 1987). After these series of empirical studies, scenario studies using vignette designs emerged that provided respondents hypothetical situations and measured contemporaneous responses on both perceptions of the certainty and severity of punishment and the likelihood of offending. The scenario studies were also criticized later, however, because they use hypothetical examples and may not reflect what people actually do in a real situation (Miller & Anderson, 1986).

Overall, these deterrence studies produced four important findings. First, the deterrent effect of the increased severity of punishment on crime is mixed, especially with capital punishment. Some studies even found what is called the "brutalization effect," whereby the use of capital punishment led to an increase in violent crime (Cochran, Chamlin, & Seth, 1994). This is consistent with Beccaria's argument more than 250 years ago that punishments that are too severe may encourage crime instead of reducing it. Second, the deterrent effect of punishment is not the same for everyone, and the individuals who have more to lose by the punishment (i.e., the individuals with a higher stake in conformity) are more likely to be deterred by punishments and, thus, are less likely to engage in crime (Sherman, Smith, Schmidt, & Rogan, 1992). Third, and related to the second finding, is that the individuals who should be deterred the most are the least deterrable because they often have a lower stake in conformity, having nothing to lose, and therefore, do not fear punishment. Finally, informal punishment by family, friends, employers, and the community is often more important than formal punishment by the criminal justice system in deterring people from offending (Grasmick & Green, 1980). Deterrence theory had a profound impact on the U.S. criminal justice system, with the theory forming the basis of how we punish criminals in the United States.

1. What is your opinion on how best to deter youthful offending and delinquency?

2. If adolescents are focused on immediate future and are not influenced by long-term and harsh lock-up laws, what might be more effective deterrence policies?

---

criminology, including Marxist criminology, became popular. This occurred during the period of mass social movements and protests against the government and status quo, including the civil rights movement, women's rights movement, antiwar (Vietnam) movement, Hispanic and Chicano movement, and gay rights movement. Although most theories of crime attempt to explain "breaking of laws," by focusing on the offenders, the social reaction, conflict, and critical perspective attempts to explain the other two aspects of criminology noted by Sutherland (1947), "making laws" and "reacting toward the breaking of laws," by shifting the focus away from the offenders to the government, the law, and the police.

Labeling/Social Reaction Theory

Labeling theory focuses on how an individual's self-image and behavior are influenced by the reactions of the society, especially through labeling. Labeling theory is based on the work of symbolic interactionists, including George Herbert Mead (1863–1931) and Charles Cooley (1864–1929). Symbolic interactionism posits that we develop our self-image based on our perception of what others think of us, and our behavior is based on the meaning we assign to the situation that develops through social interactions. Social reaction theory focuses on the societal reaction to the law breaking or how a label is being applied to some groups of individuals. For instance, a police department labels a neighborhood as a high crime neighborhood and conducts targeted policing in the neighborhood, a teacher labels a student as not smart and does not bother spending any more time with him, or a parent labels a girl from her daughter's school as promiscuous and delinquent and tells her daughter not to hang out with her. Labeling theory recognizes the negative effect such labeling has on those who are being labeled. Individuals who are being labeled often begin behaving in the way that confirms the label applied to them, thereby resulting in a self-fulfilling prophecy. The residents in the neighborhood that was labeled as a high crime neighborhood get arrested more and may commit more crime as a result, the student who was labeled as not smart gets behind with school work and eventually stops showing up to school, and the girl who was labeled as promiscuous and delinquent cannot make any friends with children who are not delinquent and thus starts hanging out with other kids who are also labeled delinquents.

Labeling theories argue that negative labels are often not applied equally but one's sociodemographic characteristics, such as social class, gender, and race, often affect society's reaction toward crime, offenders, and how labels are applied. As one of the most influential statements in criminology, Howard Becker said (1963, emphasis original), "*social groups create deviance by making rules whose infraction creates deviance,* and by applying those roles to particular people and labeling them as outsiders. From this point of view, deviance is *not* a quality of the act the person commits, but rather a consequence of the application by other of rules and sanctions to an 'offender.' The deviant is one to whom that label has been successfully applied; deviant behavior is behavior that people so label" (p. 240). Given the negative effects of labeling, some social labeling scholars have gone so far to argue for the end of the criminal justice response to delinquency and have advocated for the hands-off approach to dealing with delinquency. Labeling theories, therefore, have been responsible for the increased use of diversion, decriminalization, and deinstitutionalization during this time (Tibbetts & Hemmens, 2010). The various terms for status offenders used today, such "a child in need of supervision," "a child in need of services," "a child in need of aid, assistance or care," and "unruly child," also emerged around this time to prevent the negative stigma associated with labeling minor status offenders as delinquents.

Based on the writings of Mead and Cooley, three scholars offered important insights into the labeling theory of crime. In *Crime and the Community*, Frank Tannenbaum (1938) argued that society can eliminate the negative consequences of labeling by ending the dramatization of evil, which occurs when a society overreacts (dramatizes) to a minor form of misbehavior. In *Human Deviance, Social Problems, and Social Control,* Edwin M. Lemert (1972) distinguished between primary deviance, which is often not serious and less frequent, and secondary deviance, which is usually more serious and frequent. According to Lemert, children move on to engaging in more serious secondary deviance because they happened to get caught for primary deviance, negatively labeled as delinquent, incorporate the label into their self-image, and start behaving according to the self-image. Lemert believed that if society ignores the less serious primary deviance, children will not go on to engage in the secondary deviance. Although labeling and social reaction theory have had a profound influence on the criminal justice policy, strong empirical evidence does not exist for labeling theory. In more recent years, scholars have begun examining the effects of informal labeling by primary social groups rather than the effects of formal labeling by the criminal justice system (Zhang, 1997).

Marxist Theories

Marxist criminology is based on the work of Karl Marx and was first proposed by Willem Bonger (1905/1970) via class structure, as discussed in the previous chapter. Marxist

theories, overall, posit that the ruling class of the society, the bourgeoisie, uses its power, including the law and the criminal justice system, to keep the poor, the proletariat, in its place in society. Recent 1970s developments in Marxist criminology are called "neo-Marxist criminology." Richard Quinney (1974) argued that crimes committed by both lower class and ruling class are caused by the way the economy is structured or, more specifically, by greed-promoting capitalism. Quinney (1974) argued that the crimes committed by the ruling class are crimes of domination and repression that are committed to keep the lower class poor and the ruling class rich and more powerful in society.

Conflict Theories

The conflict perspective is contrasted with the consensual perspective of the **functionalism**, discussed in the previous chapter. Conflict theories assume that a society consists of groups with competing values and needs. These groups also vary in the amount of power and resources, and a powerful group tends to dominate in making the laws and rules of society for their benefit to maintain their status and power in society. Like Marxist theories, conflict theories see that laws and the criminal justice system are used, not to enforce justice, but to maintain the status quo and to ensure the powerful stay powerful in society. According to conflict theories, the injustice, unfairness, and oppression felt by those who have less power are the primary cause of crime.

Several different types of conflict theories have been offered over the years. Thorsten Sellin (1938), for instance, argued that cultural heterogeneity in industrialized societies produces separate cultures in a society with separate norms and values that divert themselves from the dominant culture. Laws that are based on the dominant culture, thus, create a "border culture conflict" of values and norms within less powerful cultures. Another conflict theorist, George Vold (1958), in *Theoretical Criminology*, argued that people form groups based on shared needs, values, and interests, and groups compete for power to create and enforce laws. Finally, Austin Turk (1969) also believed that the primary cause of crime is the competition among various groups in society for power. Turk, like Durkheim (1893/2014), believed that some conflicts and competitions among groups are beneficial, especially if they promote social change and progress. Turk also pointed out the conflict that occurs among various groups within the criminal justice system (the courts, the police, the lawyers, etc.).

Feminist Theories

Feminist theories of crime emerged in the 1970s in response to the lack of attention paid to women and girls who were involved in the criminal justice system and the lack of policies, programs, and studies that were developed for females. Feminist criminology shifts the attention to women and questions the legitimacy of traditional theories of crime that were developed, specifically, to explain male criminality. To this end, feminist criminologists have raised two important questions: Can criminological theory explain equally well delinquency of males and females, and can criminological theory account for the differences in the level of delinquency between males and females? The first question is referred to as a generalizability problem, and the second question is referred to as a gender ratio problem (Daly & Chesney-Lind, 2004, pp. 25–24). Liberal feminism, one of the first feminist theories of crime, tackled the gender ratio problem and argued that females engage in a lower level of crime than males do because of the lack of opportunity for women in society; thus, with an increase in gender equality over time, there should be a decrease in the gender difference in crime involvement (Adler, 1975; Simons, 1975).

▲ Girls have become increasingly involved with the juvenile justice system. Why do you think this is the case?

©iStockphoto.com/Vicheslav

Functionalism: An idea that things that exist in society (e.g., crime, as argued by Durkheim in the previous chapter) exist because they serve a function in society.

CASE STUDY

FEMALE LIBERATION OR LACK THEREOF?

The national trend of the female liberation movement led many to believe that the increased opportunity and equity resulting from the women's movement resulted in a subsequent increase in female incarceration rates in the United States (Chesney-Lind & Rodriguez, 1983). Nevertheless it was found that the typical female inmate in the United States is young, poor, of a racial/ethnic minority, lacks education (i.e., tends to be a high school dropout), is single, and has dependent children. Additionally, most female inmates are victims of child abuse, from broken homes, held low-wage "dead-end" employment or did not have any job at the time of arrest, were dependent on drugs, had engaged in prostituting, and tended to have a more traditional view of gender and gender roles than what conventional feminists assume liberated women would have. In other words, incarcerated women seem to represent the group of women who benefited least from the women's liberation movement, contrary to the assumptions of Adler's (1975) female liberation hypothesis. Indeed, the findings of Chesney-Lind and Rodriguez (1983) suggest that it is not liberation, but lack thereof, or the lack of opportunities within a nondeviant world, which underlies the female inmates' continued participation in the deviant behaviors.

1. Why do you think the female liberation movement was found to not have little impact on incarcerated women?

2. Why do incarcerated women have the common background struggles described above?

Over the years, feminist criminology proposed three major approaches when considering the theoretical issues of women and crime. The first approach is what was termed by Chesney-Lind (1986, p. 81) as the "add women and stir," the mainstream approach favored in traditional criminology theorizing that treats gender as a mere **control variable** in the statistical analysis testing male-oriented criminological theories. Using this approach, women are not only marginalized statistically, because fewer women commit crimes compared with men, but also more importantly, because traditional theories are usually developed based on male-only samples for male criminality (Flavin, 2001). For this reason, Sharp and Hefley (2004) stated that, although gender was found to have one of the strongest relationships with crime, the mainstream approach adds no new insights into the issue of women and crime other than merely confirming that males commit more crime than females. With the second approach in theorizing women and crime, the feminist theory emerged as the second wave of feminist criminology that treats women as the focal point of explanation and analysis and challenges the traditional criminological theories. Such feminist theories may focus on female-specific issues, such as rape, running away from home, sexual and domestic violence, and sexual harassment as females being the victims of these offenses and the relationships of these victimizations to their later offending (Chesney-Lind, 2006). Chesney-Lind (2006, p. 8) called this approach the "theorizing gender" approach. Overall, feminist criminology as a perspective does not necessarily advocate the generation of separate female-specific and male-specific theories of crime. Feminist criminological theorists instead advocate the expansion of knowledge through examining females in addition to males (Sharp & Hefley, 2004). An example of this second approach is Meda Chesney-Lind's feminist pathway model.

Meda Chesney-Lind (1947–)

One of the most prominent feminist criminologists, Chesney-Lind (2006), proposed a feminist pathway model, which attempts to generate a female-specific theory by taking into account the unique social, structural, and cultural context (e.g., **patriarchy**) of female experience in society. Females are often the victims of physical and sexual violence because, Chesney-Lind argued, our culture of patriarchy, which affects every aspects of our life and social interactions, tends to view

Control Variable:
A characteristic (e.g., gender) that is held constant in statistical analysis to examine a relationship between two main variables (the independent and dependent variables).

Patriarchy:
A cultural context where men hold power over every aspect of society.

females as sexual property (as seen in how females are often depicted in the media). Chesney-Lind also argued that although the self-reported survey responses indicate that boys are more likely than girls to run away from home, the overwhelming majority of those who are picked up by the police for running away from home are girls, and these girls are often returned to their home to abusive parents, usually against their wishes. Such criminal justice practices reflect paternalism and treating girls, and often women, as helpless and who are thus in need of protection.

Lastly, the most recent approach advanced by the third wave of feminist criminology is intersectionality. The main concern of this approach is the intersection of "systems of power" that results in differentiation and inequality, including gender, but also race, ethnicity, age, religion, class, and sexuality (Burgess-Proctor, 2006). This perspective borrows ideas from the critical analysis of gender and crime, including radical feminism that focuses on male domination, Marxist feminism that focuses on subordinate class position of females, and socialist feminism that focuses on the intersection of gender and class within a system of power. Furthermore, intersectionality affords strong support from minority feminist criminology, such as black feminist criminology, which specifically draws attention to black women's "multiple marginalized and dominated position in society, culture, community, and families" related to their victimization and criminality (Potter, 2006, p. 107). The postmodern perspective taken by the intersectionality approach, for instance, the deconstruction of existing values and meanings established through the patriarchal domination, probably affected the overall way feminist criminology analyzes the issues of gender. This perspective focuses on the underlining process and maintenance of differentiation and the resulting inequality, rather than focusing on each system of stratification separately. Therefore, feminist scholars might focus on the root of our socialization processes whereby we internalize our values and meanings (e.g., why do victims of rape often feel like they did something wrong?), by employing critical thinking, empathy, and standpoints that purport to set us apart from preexisting values and help us question our assumptions and values. This perspective might be used to analyze, for instance, the crime of rape and to bring attention to the continued sexual victimization that victims of rape often feel when going through the criminal justice system process (Naffine, 1996).

LIFE-COURSE PERSPECTIVE

For the most part, traditional, individual-level theories of crime (such as strain, learning, and control theories) focus on characteristics at one point in time, usually during adolescence. These theories are called "static theories," whereas in recent years, dynamic theories have focused on the developmental process from birth onward on engagement in delinquency and crime in later years (Tibbetts & Hemmens, 2010). The emergence of the developmental focus followed the increase in the availability of longitudinal data on delinquency and crime based on life-course factors. The findings from these studies strongly suggest that involvement in crime is a dynamic, developmental process, with strong signs of antisocial tendency appearing during early childhood (e.g., conduct problems at school). Indeed, evidence indicates that one of the best predictors of criminal involvement is the early onset of delinquency.

Robert J. Sampson (1963–) and John H. Laub (1953–)

Sampson and Laub proposed the age-graded theory or life-course theory (*Crime in the Making: Pathways and Turning Points through Life,* Sampson & Laub, 1993, and *Shared Beginnings, Divergent Lives,* Laub & Sampson, 2003). In longitudinal reviews, Sampson and Laub found that although many of the former delinquents continued to engage in crime into adulthood, some had changed their antisocial trajectory after experiencing "turning points" or "transitions," which are significant life events. Among the sample of delinquent men in their study, turning points that are important include marriage, employment, and military service. Applying Hirschi's (1969) idea of social bond, Sampson and Laub (1993) argued that the desistance in crime was explained by the increased social bonds to conventional society formed during adulthood as a result of these important turning points in their life. On the other hand, a decrease in social bonds during adulthood, through divorce, for instance, can also increase crime, according to Sampson and Laub, even among men who had formed strong social bonds during childhood.

Terrie Moffitt (1955–)

Moffitt (1993) proposed a developmental taxonomy, in which she distinguished two groups of delinquent offenders. According to Moffitt, most people engage in antisocial behaviors (such as drinking alcohol or smoking marijuana) but only temporarily, limited to during adolescence through young adulthood. This group of offenders makes up most of the general population, and its members are called "adolescence-limited offenders." A tiny number of offenders, called "life-course-persistent offenders," however, engage in chronic violent offenses and contribute to most of the serious violent offenses in society. The identification of this serious offender group led to the call for attention on more serious chronic offenders and their offenses in criminology. Because many self-reported studies of delinquency thus far have been conducted at school and because only a small percentage of the general population is considered to be serious offenders, most such studies on delinquency have tended to focus on minor forms of delinquency (e.g., most of these studies omitted a question about murder). Even though Moffitt focused on sociological factors, such as association with friends, to explain the surge in antisocial behaviors during adolescence among adolescence-limited offenders, she applied the biosocial perspective as an explanation for the engagement in chronic offending among life-course-persistent offenders, focusing on both neurological problems and the criminogenic environment in which they are raised. Moffitt's developmental taxonomy offers an explanation for the age–crime curve (see Figure 5.3), the universal finding that shows that crime peaks during late teens to early 20s and then declines over time. According to Moffitt, the increase in crime during adolescence can be explained by the engagement in crime by adolescence-limited offenders.

James C. Howell (1942–)

Howell (2009) presented a theory of juvenile delinquency based on the risk-protection framework (popularly used in public health to determine the risk for a certain illness), which identifies risks and protections against delinquency involvement as the young person relates and interacts

▼FIGURE 5.3

Age–Crime Curve

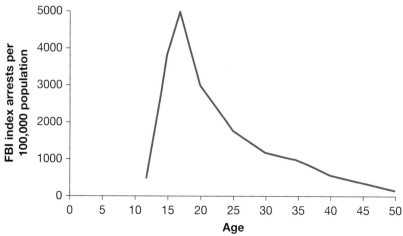

Source: Adapted from "Criminal Career Research: Its Value for Criminology," by A. Blumstein, J. Cohen, and D.P. Farrington, 1988, *Criminology*, 26, p. 11.

with family, peers, school, and community/neighborhood. The model combines developmental theory and Terrence Thornberry's (1987) interactional theory of risk and protective factors across developmental stages. The interactional theory, which is considered an integrated theory of crime, focuses on the reciprocal relationships among some key variables from both social learning theory and social control theory (including attachment, belief, commitment, association with delinquent friends, and delinquent values). This model recognizes that delinquency risks are intertwined with other problems (e.g., academic performance, friendship, family relationship, etc.), and that they vary over the developmental life course, depending on the age of risk onset. In other words, this approach to understanding delinquency and serious offending allows researchers to focus on juvenile justice populations to determine which young people are most at risk and how these risks may change over time to develop effective, individualized, intervention programs.

CHAPTER REVIEW

CHAPTER SUMMARY

This chapter covered the theoretical development within criminology that emphasizes sociological factors and the development of sociological theories of crime that began in the 1930s. Three prominent sociological perspectives emerged during that time in response to the increase in crime rates after the Great Depression: the strain, the social disorganization, and the learning perspectives. With the development of the control perspective in the 1950s, three of the most prominent individual-level theories of crime were established. The development of sociological theories of crime was strengthened by the increased use of the self-reported survey in criminology since the 1950s. The use of self-reported survey in criminology also revived classical criminology, in particular Beccaria's (1764/1986) deterrence theory, which has been extensively tested using empirical data since the 1960s. Modern classical criminology also emerged around this time, of which routine activities theory had profound impacts

on the crime prevention as well as on the programs used by the criminal justice system. One of the most recent additions to criminology are developmental theories, which followed the increased availability of longitudinal data in criminology to examine the developmental changes over time. In particular, Moffitt's (1993) developmental taxonomy and the identification of life-course-persistent offenders led to a shift in attention to more serious, chronic offenders as well as to the emergence of the biosocial perspective in criminology theorizing. The dominant theories in criminology have been developed for the most part by white male criminologists in the United States, and since the 1960s along the various social movements of the time, a critical perspective that questions how the traditional theorizing in criminology emerged. The critical perspective shifted the focus away from offenders to the government, the law, and the criminal justice system's treatment of offenders.

KEY TERMS

functionalism **118**

control variable **119**

patriarchy **119**

DISCUSSION QUESTIONS

1. Can you think of ways to explain geographic variations and historical changes in crime rates using biological theories?

2. Explain how three perspectives that emerged in the 1930s (including the strain, the social disorganization, and the learning perspectives) account for the historical changes (such as the Great Depression) in crime rate.

3. What are the policy implications of the three major individual theories of criminology: strain theories, learning theories, and control theories?

4. While thinking back on your own experiences growing up, which sociological theory discussed in this chapter best describes your delinquency involvement (or noninvolvement)?

5. Thinking about the inner-city neighborhoods in your state that best fit Shaw and McKay's (1942) definition of social disorganization, what are some of the common characteristics of these neighborhoods besides the ones given by Shaw and McKay?

6. Thinking back to when you first engaged in (drinking alcohol, smoking cigarettes, smoking marijuana, shoplifting, etc.), what was the situation like? Were you with someone? Did your friends pressure you to engage in the behavior? Did you "learn" how to engage in the behavior?

7. Why do you think formal punishment (e.g., threat of incarceration) is not an effective deterrent against crime?

8. The classical perspective assumes that humans are rational, weighing the cost and benefit, in deciding our own behaviors. Do you think people rationally calculate the cost and benefit before committing crimes? Explain your position.

9. What characteristics are common in "hot spots" where motivated offender, suitable target, and lack of guardian tend to converge?

10. Besides the "turning points" identified by Sampson and Laub (1993), can you think of any other "turning points" in your life that have altered your antisocial trajectory?

11. Do you think criminal behaviors are best described using the biosocial perspective that examines both biological and sociological factors? Are there any behaviors that are more suited to the explanation by the biosocial perspective versus others that are more suited to the explanation by sociological factors alone?

PROBLEMS THAT LEAD TO DELINQUENCY

PART III

CHAPTER 6

DELINQUENCY RISKS AND DISPROPORTIONATE IMPACT

▲ There are many reasons young people get into trouble with the court systems. What do you think are the most important explanations for delinquency?

©iStockphoto.com/BrandyTaylor

INTRODUCTION

Punitive juvenile justice (and school) policies have a disproportionate impact on certain populations of young people. Those caught in school's exclusionary policies and/or in the juvenile courts share several common preexisting vulnerabilities. This chapter discusses the common experiences or traits that make some children and adolescents more vulnerable to delinquency.

The two upcoming examples touch on many of the concerns addressed in this text, including the impact of zero tolerance policies, subsequent school inflexibility in taking into account mitigating circumstances to determine student discipline, police decision-making and involvement, and how this involves certain groups of young people disproportionately. The first story is about a black male student from a poor family; the second story is about a middle-class female student who identifies as lesbian, gay, bisexual, and transgender (LGBT). Their backgrounds differ, but they experienced similar difficult outcomes. These initial experiences could lead to ongoing poor outcomes, a process that is further explored in Chapter 7:

> By most accounts, Marlon Morgan is a great kid. The soft-spoken junior plays basketball for Saguaro High School. He was nominated for Youth of the Year last year by a branch of the Boys and Girls Clubs of Scottsdale. So why were his classmates wearing "Free Marlon" t-shirts last week? The 17-year-old had just been arrested on campus during lunch for wearing his baseball cap sideways instead of to the front and refusing to turn it the other way. Morgan, who is Black, believes he was singled out. Other teens in the same room were wearing their hats that way . . . Morgan was having lunch when Saguaro security guards approached him about his hat. It is against school policy to wear hats sideways because it can be a sign of disrespect for authority, the police report said, but Morgan said that the rule is enforced selectively. According to a police report, he pointed to several white students whose hats were on sideways. (Kupchik, 2010, p. 159)

An LGBT youth of color faced constant bullying from peers (and) did not report the abuse to school staff because, as she put it, "No one (was) going to do anything." "After months and months of harassment she blew up and really hurt another student. She ended up getting extended suspension so, you know, she just dropped out. She was sixteen at the time and just didn't see the point of that anymore. And she felt like she wasn't going to be supported in the school." In this case "extended suspension" amounted to 45 days, as opposed to the 10 days of suspension her bully received. This lack of protection from harassment and bullying, exposure to violence, along with differential and harsh discipline ultimately resulted in the student's departure from school altogether. Although seemingly a choice, such a departure is part of a larger pattern of school push-out (Burdge, Licona, & Hyemingway, 2014, p. 11).

These two students were disciplined for noncompliance to rigid rules and/or for fighting, and without consideration for mitigating circumstances that may help explain why the incidents occurred. Application of zero tolerance policies and rigid discipline protocols within school systems, and the arrest and referral to the juvenile courts, have an inequitable impact on certain students, including minorities, LGBT adolescents, and those with education disabilities. Once arrested or adjudicated delinquent, these young people have a higher risk of staying involved with the juvenile justice system through reoffending and recidivating. Many of these

LEARNING OBJECTIVES

1 Describe the common risk factors that increase the likelihood for receiving school discipline, engaging in delinquency, and involvement with the juvenile court

2 Identify the countervailing protective factors that impede young people from juvenile justice system involvement

3 Understand the differences and commonalities across delinquency and school discipline risk factors

4 Discern how this myriad of risk and protective factors do not tell the whole story of why young people become involved in delinquent activities

5 Recognize the young people who are disproportionately impacted by school exclusions policies and involvement with the juvenile courts

6 Explain why some young people are disproportionately involved with the juvenile justice system

children and adolescents are already vulnerable, even prior to getting into trouble, because of their individual, family, peer, and/or community-based experiences. These experiences are often called "delinquency risk factors."

© iStockphoto.com/gilaxia

▲ Some high school students are identified as "trouble makers" and may be targeted by school personnel. Do you think this is justified?

Risk Factors: Experiences, traits, or issues that make an outcome (delinquency or mental health problems, for example) more likely.

Static Risk Factors: Risk factors for individuals that are difficult to change.

Dynamic Risk Factors: Risk factors for individuals that are changeable, for example, parenting quality, school issues, adolescent skills deficits, and peer associations.

Protective Factors: Protective factors may be the absence of certain delinquency risk factors. Or, protective factors may be an external or internal influence that decreases the impact of risk factors or influences a more positive outcome.

FACTORS THAT INFLUENCE DELINQUENCY

Risk factors are experiences, traits, or issues that make an outcome (delinquency or mental health problems, for example) more likely. Some risk factors are associative (correlated or associated) with these outcomes, whereas others are causative (related directly) to outcomes. The more risk factors experienced by a young person, or his or her family, the greater the chance of delinquency and juvenile court involvement. Risk factors are considered either static or dynamic. **Static risk factors** cannot or are difficult to change and include things like demographic variables (age, race, and sex, among others) and socioeconomic status. **Dynamic risk factors** can be modified and include things such as substance use, peer choices, academic effort, school connectedness, and some mental health problems, among others (Heilbrun, 1997; Thornberry, 2005).

It is important to note the difference when it comes to predicting delinquency (or other nefarious outcomes) between associative and causative factors. By definition, all relationships between two variables are associative, which means that when the score on one variable changes, the score on the other variable also changes. For instance, there is a relationship between hours per week students study and their test scores. This means that the test score increases or decreases when a student studies longer or shorter. The two variables ("hours per week studied" and "test score") have no association if the test score remained unchanged after a change in the hours per week students study. Just because two variables are related does not mean that such a relationship is a causal relationship. Only some of the associative relationships are also causative, which means that a variable has a causal effect on the other variable. Establishing a causal relationship in research is not easy because it requires the use of a rigorous experimental design.

Protective factors are experiences that decrease the likelihood of harmful outcomes. As with risk factors, the more protective factors are present in a young person's life, the less likely he or she is to experience these outcomes. Protective factors are more difficult to both identify and measure. Protective factors may just be the absence of risk factors, may reduce the likelihood of harmful outcomes, may decrease the impact of risk factors, or may promote positive outcomes (e.g., academic success). Protective factors may reduce the likelihood of experiencing harmful outcomes by either moderating the impact of risk factors or exerting an independent influence on the negative outcome, whether the risk factors are present or not. For example, having a strong and stable parent who keeps involved with his or her child's life is often a strong protective factor to avoiding delinquency (DeMatteo & Marczyk, 2005; Loeber, Farrington, Stouthamer-Loeber, & White, 2008).

ECOLOGICAL/PSYCHOSOCIAL MODEL

Several delinquency risk prediction models have been developed, including the following: the categorization of risk factors into demographic or historical categories; identifying criminological

and clinical (mental health) factors; and an eco-
logical/psychosocial approach (Heilbrun,
1997; Monahan et al., 2001; U.S. Department
of Health and Human Services, 2001). The
ecological/psychosocial model is used in this
chapter as a framework to understanding delinquency through its focus on the etiology and
interrelations of the risk factors, while recognizing
the ongoing impact of adolescent development.

The ecological/psychosocial model uses
a multidimensional classification approach,
identifying risks as the young person relates
and interacts with family, peers, school, and community/neighborhood. Based on **longitudinal studies**, the Howell model combines developmental theory and interactional theory of
risk and protective factors across stages within this framework (Loeber & Farrington, 2001;
Thornberry, 2005). This model recognizes that delinquency risks are intertwined, yet with
other problems, and that they vary over the developmental life course, depending on the age of
risk onset. In other words, this approach to understanding delinquency and serious offending
allows researchers to look at juvenile justice populations to determine which young people are
most at risk and how these risks change over time (DeMatteo & Marczyk, 2005; Hawkens
et al., 2000).

What follows is a review of the literature that supports this theoretical approach to understanding delinquency and related outcomes. This overview includes school-related factors
(bullying, truancy, and suspension/expulsion, among others), individual issues (mental
health and substance use), key family problems (maltreatment and trauma), and neighborhood impacts (peers and poverty, among others). These experiences and risks are often
cumulative, both over time, as well as in the number of issues (**comorbidity**) with which
a child or adolescent has to contend and disproportionately impact certain young people.
Some of these most important and influential factors that impact delinquency and juvenile
court involvement are expanded on in later chapters—school problems and exclusion in
Chapter 8, trauma in Chapter 9, and mental health, developmental, and learning problems
in Chapter 10.

▲ Many students are
disciplined in school,
including classroom
removal and in-school
suspensions. Do you think
these experiences help the
student?

**Ecological/Psychosocial
Model:** Multidimensional
classification approach,
identifying risks as the
young person relates and
interacts with family, peers,
school, and community/
neighborhood.

Longitudinal Studies:
Cohort studies that follow
over time a group of similar
individuals who differ with
respect to certain factors
under study, to determine
how these factors affect rates
of a certain outcome.

**Comorbid
(Comorbidity):**
Simultaneous presence of
two problems (difficulties,
diseases) in one person—for
example, post-traumatic
stress disorder (PTSD) and
physical abuse for a child.

SCHOOL DISCIPLINE RISK FACTORS

The students involved in school discipline protocols and those who are excluded from attending
share commonalities that place them at higher risk for poor outcomes. Most school discipline and
suspension/expulsion risks are also factors for involvement with the juvenile courts. Two areas
are highlighted here, however—**poverty** and maltreatment/trauma—because of their particular
harmful impact on education across primary and secondary school as well as increasing the risk
for school discipline problems.

Poverty-Related Risk Factor

More than one in five children grows up in poverty. Those who grow up in poverty are, both
minority and white, less likely to graduate from high school and more likely to be poor as adults
(Holzer, Schanzenbach, Duncan, & Ludwig, 2007). The southern states have the highest number of the nation's poor children (42%) and the highest child poverty rate (24%), although there
are significant state-by-state variations. Children of color are disproportionately more likely
to grow up poor, with the youngest children most at risk, and nearly one in three children of
color was poor in 2013. Black children were the poorest (40%), followed by American Indian/
Native Alaskan children (37%), and Hispanic children (34%). More than two thirds of minority

SPOTLIGHT

HOWELL'S DELINQUENCY MODEL

Researchers have applied the ecological/psychosocial model across a developmental timeline, which is important when trying to understand adolescence. Adolescence is a time period that is marked by change, immaturity, impulsiveness, and ongoing development for preteens and teens alike. An example that incorporates parts of the ecological/psychosocial approach along a developmental timeline can be seen in Howell's (2009) model for delinquency and gang involvement (see Figure 6.1).

▼ FIGURE 6.1

Howell's Delinquency Model

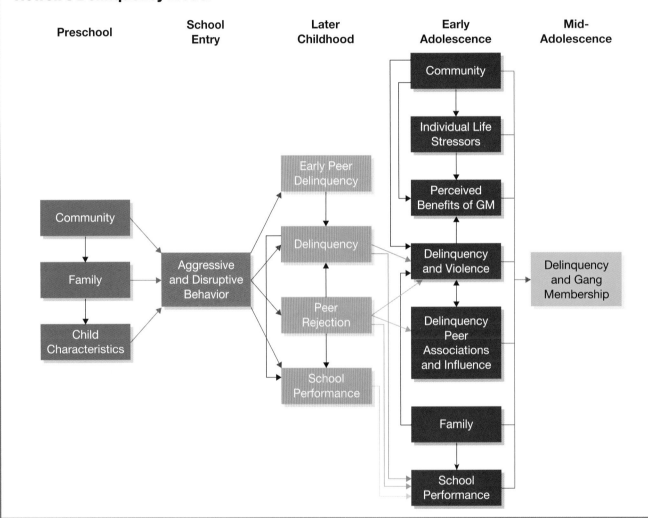

Source: *Preventing and Reducing Juvenile Delinquency* by James C. Howell. Reprinted with permission from SAGE Publications, Inc.

Poverty: U.S. Government considers a person to be living in poverty if household income is below a certain income threshold. These poverty guidelines are available through the Department of Health and Human Services and are revised annually.

children who are born into poverty will be persistently poor for at least half of their childhoods. Sixty-six percent of black children born between 1985 and 2000 were raised in neighborhoods with a poverty rate of at least 20%, compared with only 6% of white children. The families of these children have more difficulty finding and accessing safe housing and, when needed, in securing mental health care (Children's Defense Fund, 2014; U.S. Department of Health and Human Services, 2014b).

Poverty impacts education outcomes for children, and students of color fare worse than poor white children. Nearly three quarters of lower income fourth-and eighth-grade students cannot read or compute basic mathematics at grade level, compared with only half of higher income (middle and upper) students. Seventy-eight percent of public school students graduated high school in four years in 2010, with percentages much lower for Hispanic students (70%) and black students (66%). More difficult is that young children in poor families, compared with those in nonpoor families, are two times more likely to have behavioral, developmental, or social delays (Children's Defense Fund, 2014). Many families living in poverty, or near poverty, also experience homelessness, with 1.2 million public school students experiencing homelessness during the 2011–2012 school year. If a child experiences homelessness, he or she is twice as likely to have moderate-to-severe health problems, to repeat a school grade, to be suspended or expelled, and to drop out of high school (National Low Income Housing Coalition, 2013).

Maltreatment/Trauma-Related Risk Factor

Students living in poverty are disproportionately involved in school discipline protocols. Poor families are also disproportionately more likely to be involved in the **child welfare system** because of abuse or neglect. In other words, poverty and minority status are factors contributing to a greater chance of a family being involved with a children's protective services (CPS) agency (Piquero, 2008; The Center for Civil Rights Remedies, 2013).

The greater involvement of poor families with CPS agencies, however, cannot be explained by the difference in the number of abuse and neglect incidents by social class. Instead, a child or family's ethnicity significantly influences the decisions at almost every investigative stage that the child welfare professionals make. Black and non-Hispanic Indian families are twice as likely to be involved, compared with white families, in the child welfare system. In addition, of those children who are formally supervised by a CPS agency, fewer services and rehabilitative programs are offered to minority families, compared with white families; this is particularly true for **kincare placements**. The lack of services and programs children and families receive contributes to poorer reunification outcomes and, for many children, being moved from one home to another and, thus, one school to another. Changing schools often during formative periods of adolescence can increase the risk for poor peer choices, absenteeism, and school discipline (Drake & Zuravin, 1998; Hill, 2005; Lu et al., 2004; U.S. Government Accountability Office, 2007).

Students with child maltreatment histories have significant educational risks and learning issues, including lower academic performance and grades, falling behind in grade level, lower standardized testing and proficiency scores, and increase in the identification of learning disabilities and emotional disturbances. For some abused or neglected children, a foster home is their only safe alternative. In 2000, black children represented 38% of the foster care population while comprising only 16% of the child and adolescent population; although through concerted federal and state efforts, this disparity has lessened since 2004. Nevertheless, it is still twice as likely today that a black or non-Hispanic Indian child, compared with a white child, will be placed into a foster care home and not remain with their biological family (Summers, Wood, & Donovan, 2013). These foster care placements are typically nine months longer for minority children—22 months for whites compared with 31 months for minorities. In addition, more than 23,000 teenagers aged out of foster care in 2012 because they turned 18 and had not been returned home, adopted, or placed with a legal guardian. This group of young people, also disproportionately minority, are at increased risk for not graduating from high school, becoming homeless, and/or becoming involved with the criminal justice system (Children's Defense Fund, 2014; U.S. Government Accountability Office, 2007).

DELINQUENCY RISK FACTORS

Young people typically experience increased risk of involvement with delinquent behaviors and the juvenile courts as a result of a combination of risk factors, rather than any single experience.

Child Welfare System: U.S. government agency responsible for investigating child abuse and neglect allegations; also known as children's protective services (CPS).

Kincare Placements: When a child is removed from a parent's or guardian's home because of maltreatment concerns and placed with a related family member.

© iStockphoto.com/Daxus

▲ Arrests on school campuses have exponentially increased with police now working in many schools. What do you think the role of police should be in schools?

Individual risk factors rarely act alone but interact with the individual's environment in influencing young people toward delinquency. These risks impact both childhood/primary school-age groups (ages infancy to 11) and adolescent/secondary school-age groups (ages 12 to 17; Howell, 2009; Lipsey & Derzon, 1998).

Individual-Related Delinquency Risk Factors

Children. Delinquency risk factors during early childhood include a difficult temperament, impulsive behavior, aggressiveness, and an inattentive personality. Physical aggression in childhood and violence in adolescence are strongly linked, and part of the explanation is that aggressive children are often unsuccessful in having prosocial and positive peer relationships. In other words, aggressive children attract other aggressive children as friends and companions. The earlier the onset of these behavior difficulties, the greater chance there is for adolescent delinquency. Other factors for children include indicators of psychological difficulties or mental health problems (hyperactivity and behavior disorders, among others), limited social relationships or ties to peers, exposure to or victimization of violence, and substance use (Howell, 2009; Thornberry & Krohn, 2000; Warr, 2002).

Adolescents. Adolescents who are less connected to their schools or peers are at greater risk for delinquency, exacerbated by poorly functioning families and any early onset of offending behaviors. Being a perpetrator or a victim of violence predicts ongoing delinquent activities, other life stressors (living conditions and poverty, among others), and mental health problems. The mental health concerns include a history of early oppositional or conduct problems, hyperactivity, and substance use or dependence. Other individual factors include risk-taking, high impulsivity, and poor behavioral controls (Chassin, 2008; Grisso, 2008; Hawkens et al., 1998).

Juvenile justice involvement across numerous metrics is also predictive or influential of ongoing delinquency. These include the following: An earlier onset of delinquency adjudication predicts ongoing offending behaviors; the greater number of prior arrests increases later arrest risk; and out-of-home placement greatly increases the chance for formal and ongoing juvenile court involvement. In a related matter, substance abuse or use, itself an illicit activity, is a risk for ongoing delinquency, although the direction of the influence with delinquency is unclear (DeMateo & Marczyk, 2005; Hawkens et al., 2000).

Students with special education disabilities and those who are victims of maltreatment are at greater risk for delinquency adjudication, detention, and incarceration. Factors that increase the likelihood that an individual will develop a special education disability, in particular learning disabilities, include living in poverty, family dysfunction, being adopted, male gender, and low parent education levels. The risk factors related to special education disabilities are also, not surprisingly, related to the delinquency engagement (Altarac & Saroha, 2007; Sum, Khatiwada, McLaughlin, & Palma, 2009). Students with learning disabilities are two to three times more at risk than their peers to be involved with offending both on and off school grounds, to be arrested while in school, and to have higher delinquency recidivism rates (Matta-Oshima, Huang, Johnson-Reid, & Drake, 2010).

Maltreatment victimization increases risk for further problems in the juvenile courts. Adolescents who have been victims of physical abuse and neglect have a higher risk for engaging in delinquency. Researchers, however, are still trying to determine the etiology and differential impact abuse or neglect have on specific delinquent activities (Wiebush, Freitag, &

Baird, 2001; Wiggins, Fenichel, & Mann, 2007; Yun, Ball, & Lim, 2011). The cumulative impact of maltreatment, in addition to other risks associated with maltreatment, such as substance abuse and school difficulties, may affect females more negatively than males. Repeat maltreatment victimization predicts the earlier initiation and often greater severity of delinquent activity. When other risk factors are accounted for, repeat maltreatment victimization seems to be the strongest predictor of serious or chronic youthful offending (Lemmon, 2006; National Center for Child Traumatic Stress, 2009; Smith, Ireland, & Thornberry, 2005; Stewart, Livingston, & Dennison, 2008).

Family-Related Risk Factors

Children. Family exerts a significant influence during children's early years. Families with the following traits or characteristics increase the chance for their children to commit delinquent acts, as well as some school-related problems: lower parental education levels; families that move often or provide different caregivers for the child (e.g., early loss of a parent); families with parents who have poor parenting skills; families who experience domestic violence; families with members who are involved in criminal activities, including substance abuse; younger mother families; and families with the history of abuse or neglect (Loeber et al., 2003; Pogarsky, Lizotte, & Thornberry, 2003; U.S. Department of Health and Human Services, 2001).

As highlighted earlier, poverty has a powerful impact and is a risk factor for many family difficulties. Families living in poverty often remain in poverty; they have little upward socioeconomic mobility. Growing up in poverty, or experiencing it as an older child or adolescent, makes school achievement more difficult, increases exposure to more unstable neighborhoods, and causes interfamilial stress. Family dysfunction and instability, often resulting from poverty, are risk factors for delinquency (Dembo et al., 2000; Felitta et al., 2008).

Adolescents. Specific age-related risks have been identified, including poor parent–child relationships, parent–child separation (family disruption, foster care, and kincare placement, among others), poor living conditions, a family history of crime or problematic behavior, poor parenting skills, and maltreatment. Of these, one of the strongest risks for adolescent delinquency is intrafamilial violence—domestic violence, spousal/partner abuse, and other related problems. These experiences have been linked to individual adolescent aggressive behaviors whereby adolescents learn this behavior from family members (Dembo et al., 2000; Dong et al., 2004; Hawkins et al., 1998).

Peer-Related Risk Factors

As children become adolescents, their relationship focus shifts from parents or guardians to peers. Proper adolescent development is important for young people to manage this challenging transition, and several factors have been identified that impede this transition and increase the risk for delinquency. Peer rejection during early school years increases susceptibility to the influence of negative and more deviant peers. Aggressive and more anti-social peers tend to associate with each other during primary school and may continue into middle and high school years. Associations with delinquent peers, as well as associations with delinquent siblings, increase the chances for offending behaviors and violence. In particular, deviant peers and the use of drugs are risks for ongoing and more serious and chronic youthful offending, including gang involvement (Coie & Miller-Johnson, 2001; Farrington, 1997; Howell, 2009).

School-Related Risk Factors

As discussed throughout the text, there are clear links from school difficulties, academic failure, truancy, and bullying to school exclusion policies that lead to formal juvenile court involvement. When reviewing specific risk factors for students and delinquency, the following experiences have been identified: low academic achievement, poor academic performance in elementary school, failure to complete school, failing an academic grade, low commitment to school (academics and attendance), frequent absences, changing schools (particularly at important developmental stages), and having delinquent peers. In addition, schools that are poorly organized, function below minimal safety standards, and do not promote safe learning environments are additional risk factors for students to be involved with the juvenile courts (Hawkins et al., 2000; Howell, 2009).

Community/Neighborhood-Related Risk Factors

In addition to the impact of poverty and growing up in a lower socioeconomic neighborhood, there are other impacts that communities have on the risk for youthful offending and delinquency. The more unstable a neighborhood is, the greater the risk for poor child and adolescent outcomes, including juvenile court involvement. The high prevalence of crime, including drug-selling, and low-income housing are linked to a high rate of delinquency in a community, as is the high exposure to violence. Witnessing violence is associated with aggressive behavior and trauma, which also are linked to adolescent delinquent activities. These more violent communities are often disproportionately poor communities of color (Kracke & Hahn, 2008; Margolin & Gordis, 2000; Schwartz & Gorman, 2003).

PROTECTIVE FACTORS

Protective factors for delinquent activities and formal juvenile court involvement have been less widely researched than risk factors. Although, as noted earlier, the absence of some or all risk factors may act as protective factors for many young people as they move through different developmental stages, research has identified some important protective factors for this age group, including a positive parent/caregiver–child relationship; strong child self-efficacy; and social support from peers, teachers, and family members (Durlak, 1998). Research on delinquency prevention also found several additional protective factors for children and teens, including strong educational curriculum, such as positive reinforcement from school teachers and administrators; involvement in extracurricular school and nonschool structured activities (sports and academic clubs, for example); an attitude of intolerance toward deviant behavior; strong acceptance of social norms and peers; individuals with more flexible coping styles; improved problem-solving, anger management, and critical thinking skills; families that provide nonaggressive role models as well as clear and consistent norms; the establishment of at least one close relationship with a supportive adult (parent, family member, teacher, volunteer, or other); and a community with strong cohesion and structure (DeMatteo & Marczyk, 2005; Howell, 2009).

RESILIENCY

Children react to individual, family, peer, school, and community difficulties in various ways. Some are resilient to the challenges and can avoid harmful long-term outcomes. **Resiliency** with young people is seen in two ways: the ability to thrive despite difficulties and the ability to adapt despite difficulties. In other words, some do not let trauma, negative peers, poverty, difficult family situations, or other challenges impact their lives in a consequential way, whereas others are harmed by the difficulties but find ways to cope and move past these problems toward positive young adult lives. The presence or accumulation of protective factors, or the presence of numerous protective factors and their interaction with the risks, helps some young people become resilient (Fergus & Zimmerman, 2004).

Resiliency: Measured and defined in several ways: the capacity for children and adolescents to thrive in the face of risks and difficulties, and a capacity for successful adaption despite the circumstances.

DISPROPORTIONATE IMPACT

Children and adolescents who experience these delinquency risk factors, and particularly those who have comorbid experiences, are more likely to be involved with the juvenile courts. These delinquency, and school exclusion outcomes, however, disproportionately impact certain groups, including those who grow up in poverty; those of color; students who have special education

MARGARET'S STORY

It is hard to reconcile Margaret Samuel's electric, infectious smile with her story of abuse, violence, and juvenile detention. Margaret Samuel's life was marked by trauma that sent her reeling into the juvenile justice system. In this case, it was not the lack of love from a mother but physical and sexual abuse and other incidents she euphemistically refers to as "unfortunate events" at the hands of her father that left her a broken person.

She was the only daughter of seven children. "Growing up I felt lonely, isolated and often had to fight to be heard. I grew up in a household with an abusive father, school and friends as an outlet of escape," she said to a rapt audience. "Yet the instability at home caused me to have behavior issues at school." Those issues led to a physical fight at school that led to criminal charges, indefinite probation, time in a juvenile detention center, and frequent appearances in court. "I had probation violations from missing curfew, running away from home for weeks at a time," she said. "I felt the court system was another entity which tried to control me and not help me."

Samuel said her life was saved by a group of counselors, advocates, and probation officers she described as her "A-Team." It was an inside joke for all the people who helped her work through her trauma and turn her life around. They, like all the probation professionals gathered in the ballroom, were there to "weather life's storms," she said. And she was grateful they were there for her. When she was sent to Foundations, a probation facility for girls in Fairfax, Virginia, she was able to see life differently, she said.

"When I wanted to give up they reminded me of the light at the end of the tunnel," Samuel said. "I knew that I needed help. The safe environment allowed me to put down my mask and carefully tear down the brick walls that I spent years putting up. For the first time in my life I was in a space where I could learn about myself and grow. I saw the possibility of living a different life so I decided to work toward it." Now she is studying psychology at Northern Virginia Community College, working as an artist and making plans to build a therapeutic youth center in her home country of Sudan. (Kahn, 2016, p. 2)

1. Do you think that Margaret's positive life outcome is the norm for these types of childhood trauma experiences?

2. What do you think are the outcomes for most youthful offenders like Margaret who come under juvenile court supervision?

Source: "Troubled No More, Youths Bring Stories of Their Resilience to Probation Professionals," D. Kahn, April 26, 2016. Reprinted with permission from the Juvenile Justice Information Exchange.

---

disabilities; maltreatment victims; and those who identify as LGBT. These impacts are reviewed next and, when possible, are separated into school and juvenile justice categories.

Impoverished Children and Adolescents

Schools. Poor and lower income students are more likely than nonpoor students to be punished in school and with harsher discipline, and to be referred to the juvenile courts. Although students who grow up in poverty are overrepresented in populations that experience more school discipline, poverty is not an explanatory or a correlative reason for these outcomes. The relationship between poverty and school disruption or behavioral disorders is quite small (Fabelo et al., 2011; Noltemeyer & Mcloughlin, 2010; Skiba & Williams, 2014). Schools are the safest environment for children and teens, built on the relationships and trust among students and faculty. Safe schools are found across poor and nonpoor communities, and it is this environment that keeps students in school and academically successful (Carter, Fine, & Russell, 2014; U.S. Department of Education, 2014b, 2014d).

Students who are most impacted by punitive policies—in both schools and the juvenile courts—are low-income males of color. In school settings, it is particularly true that minority students are treated more harshly in underresourced urban schools. Specifically, schools with a greater proportion of black students have increased zero tolerance policies and use harsher, compared with diversion or in-school, discipline measures. In these strict discipline-focused school environments, the chance of school exclusion is greatest for poor black male students (Payne, 2012; Payne, Gottfredson, & Gottfredson, 2008; Welch & Payne, 2010).

Juvenile Justice. Poverty and living in more unstable communities, where there are higher crime rates, greatly increases the risk for young people to become delinquent. Part of the explanation for higher delinquency risks is that poorer and more unstable neighborhoods have weaker social controls, increasing residents' isolation, which is related to high neighborhood turnover (Hawkens et al., 2000). Although this link has been established, a limited number of analyses remains to determine how many of the youthful offenders involved in the juvenile courts come from poor families, or what proportion of adjudicated or detained youthful offenders are from poor families. Even though the risk from poverty to delinquent activities is established, national or longitudinal studies of the courts are limited by different reporting expectations and lack of local courts' data collection or sharing (Puzzanchera & Robson, 2014).

Children and Adolescents of Color

Schools. During the past three decades, reviews have found students of color to be significantly more at risk than white students for school discipline and involvement with the school-to-prison pipeline (Advancement Project et al., 2011). Black students have been identified as most at risk although possibly because historical investigations are less complete for other minority groups, including Hispanic and Native American students. Nonetheless, since 1975, black students have been suspended from school at two to three times the rates of white students, with some finding even higher disparities (Children's Defense Fund, 1975; Gregory, Skiba, & Noguera, 2010; Losen & Martinez, 2013; Morgan, Salomon, Plotkin, & Cohen, 2014; Rausch & Skiba, 2004; U.S. Department of Education, 2000).

These disparities are found across different school locations and school districts, and in all regions of the country. Today, nationwide, black students constitute 18% of students but represent 39% of expulsions and 42% of referrals to law enforcement while in school; and in more disparate contrast, black and Hispanic students constitute 42% of students but account for 72%

of those arrested for school-related offenses. These disparities are also found, although to lesser degrees, for Native American students as well as for English language learning students, depending on the location of the school district (Losen, Hewitt, & Toldson, 2014; The Center for Civil Rights Remedies, 2013). More specifically, black students are 3.5 times more likely to be suspended or expelled than their peers, with one in five black male students being suspended out of school for at least one day during the 2011–2012 and 2013–2014 school years. As noted, these race disparities cannot be explained by student misbehavior or the difficulties of living in poverty (Carter et al., 2014; Nicholson-Crotty, Birchmeier, & Valentine, 2009; Skiba, Shure, & Williams, 2012; U.S. Department of Education, 2014b, 2016a).

▲ Why do you think there are racial and ethnic disparities in school discipline? In other words, why are more minority students than white students suspended or expelled from school?

Juvenile Justice. Adolescents of color are overrepresented at each decision-making point within the juvenile justice system, from arrest to charges to disposition, with the greatest race and ethnic disparities the further a youthful offender penetrates the system. Nationwide, black youthful offenders are referred to the juvenile courts for delinquency at a rate 140% greater than white youthful offenders. If adjudicated and supervised youthful offenders continue through the juvenile justice system to out-of-home placement, moreover, the disparity becomes even more stark: Blacks

RACIAL AND ETHNIC DISPARITIES

A review of 364 elementary and middle schools in the 2005–2006 school year found black students were more than twice as likely as their white peers in elementary school and nearly four times more likely than their white peers in middle school to be referred to the office for problem behaviors. In addition, black and Hispanic students were more likely than their white peers to be suspended out of school or expelled for the same or a similar infraction of school discipline policies. A 2012 longitudinal study of Florida schools found that 39% of black students had experienced suspension, 26% of Hispanic students, and 22% of white students, with black students having longer suspension time frames even after controlling for the impact of poverty. Gender has also been found to have an impact on these disparate discipline outcomes. Although males were significantly more likely than females to be suspended or expelled, generally around twice the risk, black males were most at risk for school-based arrest and suspension, and black females were at higher risk than Hispanic or white females for these same discipline outcomes

(Balfanz, Byrnes, & Fox, 2015; Darensbourg, Perez, & Blake, 2010; Skiba & Williams, 2014).

Where racial and ethnic disparities exist, black and other minority students, compared with white students, are more often disciplined for more subjective infractions or misbehaviors—disrespect, loitering, and excessive noise, among others. This is important when investigating race and ethnic disparities because a significant majority of suspensions and expulsions are because of nonserious behaviors, with disobedience—defiance and/or disruptive behavior—being the most common reason (The Equity Project at Indiana University, 2014; Wald, 2014).

1. Why do you think racial and ethnic disparities exist in most school discipline outcomes?

2. How might schools address this problem?

and Hispanics represent one third of this country's adolescent population, but more than two thirds of those are held in juvenile incarceration facilities (Hockenberry & Puzzanchera, 2014a, 2014b; National Council on Crime and Delinquency, 2007; Puzzanchera & Robson, 2014). Of the youthful offenders incarcerated who are minorities, approximately 60% are black, 33% are Hispanic, and depending on the jurisdiction, between 1% and 4% are American Indian or Asian. These disparities are found in nearly all states with a greater impact on minority males than on minority females (Office of Juvenile Justice and Delinquency Prevention, 2014b; Piquero, 2008).

Students With Special Education Disabilities

School Districts. Students with special education disabilities represent a larger percentage of the suspended and expelled student population—20% to 25% compared with the typical 11% to 14% of the population that students with special education disabilities represent within their school districts. Compounding this problem is that the risk for students of color to be diagnosed with learning disabilities is significantly greater than white students: Hispanics are almost 20% more likely, blacks are over 40% more likely, and American-Indians are 80% more likely (Mallett, 2011; U.S. Department of Education, 2014b, 2016a).

Of all students with a special education disability, students with an emotional disturbance have been found to be most at risk for school discipline. Some researchers have found that almost three fourths of this group were suspended or expelled during their high school years, and school exclusion was between 7 and 12 times more likely for students with emotional disturbances compared with students without this special education identification. In some jurisdictions (the state of Texas and the city of Los Angeles), black students with emotional disturbance disabilities were most at risk, with significantly higher numbers being suspended or expelled than white students with disabilities (Fabelo et al., 2011; Losen & Gillespie, 2012; Wagner, Kutash, Duchnowski, Epstein, & Sumi, 2005). Students with an emotional disturbance are more likely to be placed in restrictive settings and have significantly elevated school dropout rates, while 50% have at least one arrest during or soon after high school (American Psychological

Racial and Ethnic Disparities (Disproportionate Minority Contact): Phrase that represents the disproportionate number of youthful offenders of color who come into contact with the juvenile justice (and adult) system.

©iStockphoto.com/LSOphoto

▲ Trauma impacts many children and adolescents and to varying degrees. What types of trauma experiences do you think are most harmful to young people?

Association, 2006; Harry & Klingner, 2006; Losen & Gillespie, 2012; Losen & Martinez, 2013; Merrell & Walker, 2004).

Juvenile Justice Institutions. Significantly large numbers of adolescents involved with the juvenile courts have special education disabilities, particularly those in detention and incarceration facilities—between 28% and 43%. Among incarcerated youthful offenders with special education disabilities, 48% have been identified with an emotional disturbance, 39% with a specific learning disability, 10% with developmental disabilities, and 3% with other health impairments. Of concern, between 5% and 10% of the adolescent population with identified emotional problems and diagnoses develop serious emotional disturbances that cause substantial impairment in functioning at home, at school, and/or in the community. This group, which accounts for significantly less than 1% of all adolescents, has long histories of multiple mental health disorders that will normally persist into adulthood but makes up between 15% and 20% of the juvenile justice incarceration facility populations (Quinn, Rutherford, Leone, Osher, & Poirier, 2005; Rozalski, Deignan, & Engel, 2008; Substance Abuse and Mental Health Services Administration, 2013b; Wang, Blomberg, & Li, 2005; White & Loeber, 2008).

MALTREATMENT AND TRAUMA VICTIMS

The connection across child maltreatment, school performance and exclusion, and juvenile delinquency is significant although underinvestigated. Research is gradually revealing how victimization experiences may contribute to the child and adolescent's pathways into delinquency. Yet, this remains a complex issue because of the hidden and unidentified victims, differential impact of maltreatment types, diverse harmful outcomes, cumulative impact of trauma experiences, and comorbidity of problems for maltreatment victims. The issue is further complicated by the fact that several maltreatment outcomes are themselves delinquency risk factors.

CASE STUDY

TONEY J.

" Toney Jennings was illiterate when he was arrested at age 16. In the six months he spent at the Lowndes County Jail in Eastern Mississippi, he says he played basketball, watched TV and "basically just stayed to myself." A special education student, Jennings qualified for extra help in school. Those services should have carried over to the justice system, but Jennings said he never even attended class while in jail. Now 20, he is still unable to read or write.

After several months at Lowndes, Jennings was sent to the Walnut Grove Youth Correctional Facility. At the time, the prison, a privately run facility an hour northeast of Jackson, was the only place for youths age 13 to 22 who had been tried as adults. Although the facility did have a school, a 2010 lawsuit by the Southern Poverty Law Center alleged that, among other things, fewer than half of the 1,200 inmates there attended classes.

Jennings, who is currently out of prison on appeal, unemployed, and living with his grandmother, said he took GED classes at Walnut Grove, but he did not get the extra help he needed. Before going to prison, he read at a kindergartener's level, according to his IEP. His math skills were that of a first grader. But he'd been making progress at the alternative school, where teachers gave him more individual help (Butrymowicz & Mader, 2014, pp. 1–3).

1. **Why do you think the institution did not provide special education services for Toney?**

2. **What do you think his transition was like going back to public (alternative) school?**

Source: "Pipeline to Prison: How the juvenile justice system fails special education students," Sarah Butrymowicz & Jackie Mader, *The Hechinger Report,* October 26, 2014. http://hechingerreport.org/pipeline-prison-juvenile-justice-system-fails-special-education-students/

As reviewed later in the text, maltreatment and related traumas have profound impacts on the educational outcomes of some children, including making the transition from primary to secondary school more difficult; poorer academic grades; increased risk of school grade failure and cognitive and language delays; higher absenteeism rates; lower standardized testing scores; and lower high school graduation rates (Boden, Horwood, & Fergusson, 2007; Smithgall, Gladden, Howard, Goerge, & Courtney, 2004; Wiggins et al., 2007). In addition, the more serious, earlier in life, or pervasive the maltreatment victimization, the greater the risk of special education disabilities, and having special education disabilities then is related to a higher risk for involvement in school discipline and exclusion. In particular, those in foster care, a group that is disproportionately black and non-Hispanic Indian, are at an elevated risk for special education disabilities, high school dropout, homelessness, juvenile and/or criminal court involvement, among others (Children's Defense Fund, 2014; National Council of Juvenile and Family Court Judges, 2016a; Scarborough & McCrae, 2009).

The links from maltreatment, particularly for younger victims, to school difficulties is clear. Thus, maltreatment may be a strong, and for many students a direct, link to disproportionate school discipline. In addition, it is speculated by many child welfare experts that the identified and substantiated cases of child maltreatment is significantly undercounted–with the actual number of maltreatment being many times greater than the annual count of about 800,000 (Finkelhor, Turner, Shattuck, & Hamby, 2013; U.S. Department of Health and Human Services, 2013a). If so, maltreatment and its subsequent impact on students' school outcomes may be a larger explanatory link to students' eventual involvement in the school discipline protocols and, for some, the juvenile courts. This explains why the juvenile court populations include such a disproportionate number of youthful offenders with a history of maltreatment—between 26% and 60%, with the higher percentages being of populations that are detained and incarcerated (Bender, 2009; Ford, Chapman, Hawke, & Albert, 2012; Sedlak & McPherson, 2010).

LESBIAN, GAY, BISEXUAL, AND TRANSGENDER STUDENTS

Students who identify as LGBT have been found to be at greater risk for involvement in school discipline, delinquent activities, and the juvenile courts. The increased attention to the disproportionate risks that LGBT students experience in recent years may be due to an ease at which students can identify themselves as LGBT today, and thus, researchers can more readily access this population. It is also possible that the disproportionate involvement of LGBT youth in the punishment protocol and the juvenile justice system has always been a problem (Losen et al., 2014):

> Asante Colman, a seventeen-year-old junior at Charles City High School in Charles City County, Virginia, was suspended for three days after refusing an order from a school official to take off a pair of high heels he was wearing. "I'm not advertising. I'm being myself," said Colman. "I want to be able to be a regular student. A gay regular student that attends CCHS." (Mitchum & Moodie-Mills, 2014, p. 11)

LGBT students experience exclusionary discipline—suspensions and expulsion—and hostile school environments more often than their peers, increasing the risk for arrests and juvenile court involvement. School environments have been found to be hostile and unsafe for many LGBT students, leading some to become confrontational and aggressive to maintain safety (Himmelstein & Bruckner, 2011; Kosciw, Greytak Diaz, & Bartkiewicz, 2010; Savage & Schanding, 2013; Skiba, Arredondo, & Rausch, 2014).

Many LGBT students avoid school suspensions/expulsions or juvenile court involvement but feel unsafe in school, leading to increased absenteeism, poorer academic outcomes, and decreased school engagement as a result of these and related problems. Almost three out of four LGBT students report experiencing harassment (e.g., threatened, called names), half were threatened online because of their sexual orientation or gender identity, and almost one of every five reported being physically attacked. LGBT students of color were more likely targeted than white LGBT students. A majority of LGBT students did not report these incidents to school authorities, nearly one in three of them missed at least one day of school, and one in ten missed more than ten days of school over a prior month (Kosciw, Greytak, Palmer, & Boesen, 2014; Murdock & Bolch, 2005; Russell, Kostroski, Horn, & Saewyc, 2010). In-school victimizations of LGBT students has been associated with harmful psychological effects, including depression and other mental health difficulties, and high rates of suicide compared to their non-LGBT peers (Himmelstein & Bruckner, 2011; Human Rights Watch, 2009; Toomey, Ryan, Diaz, & Russell, 2011).

The difficulties may also begin for many of these young people at home, where there is a significantly increased risk for family violence once an adolescent tells family members he or she is LGBT. LGBT adolescents are also nearly three times more likely to report being a victim of childhood physical or sexual abuse, with boys more at risk than girls (Wilson, Cooper, Kastanis, & Nezhad, 2014). In addition, a disproportionate number of LGBT adolescents run away from home, and homelessness is a significant predictor juvenile justice system involvement; up to 40% of homeless adolescents are LGBT (Burwick, Oddo, Durso, Friend, & Gates, 2014; Estrada & Marksamer, 2006; Majd, Marksamer, & Reyes, 2009).

> My mom (told the judge that I was gay). She told him I wouldn't go to school and I got kicked out. (But the problem was) I was getting harassed at school. My probation officer lied and said it wasn't as bad (at school) as it was. (Mitchum & Moodie-Mills, 2014, p. 8)

Historical myths that LGBT adolescents are rare or nonexistent in the juvenile courts have given way to more reliable studies of this adolescent population. Emerging evidence has found that LGBT adolescents are twice as likely to be arrested and detained for status and other nonviolent offenses (typically truancy, running away, and prostitution), and that between 13% and 15% of youthful offenders formally processed in the juvenile courts and being held in the detention centers are LGBT (Beck, Cantor, Hartge, & Smith, 2013; Irvine, 2010). Surveys conducted in Louisiana and California found that a youthful offender who identified as LGBT is three times more likely to be held in detention for running away or nonviolent offenses, and upward of 50% of girls in the California juvenile justice system identified as LGBT (Irvine, Wilber, & Canfield, 2017; Wilson, 2014). A disproportionate number, up to 60%, of these arrested and detained LGBT adolescents nationwide are black or Hispanic, mirroring or expanding the racial and ethnic disparities within the juvenile courts (Center for American Progress, 2017; Hunt & Moodie-Mills, 2012).

WHY THE DISPROPORTIONATE IMPACT?

The question remains, why are the children and adolescents who are troubled and vulnerable disproportionately involved with the juvenile justice system and school discipline protocols? Several possible explanations should be included in any inquiry by a juvenile court or school district: implicit and explicit bias, the impact of comorbid difficulties, inequitable distribution of school resources, and racial and class segregation.

Inherent Bias and Targeting

Implicit and explicit bias and stereotyping are not explanations that make juvenile court or school personnel comfortable. Nevertheless, most individuals have stereotypes that may unknowingly affect their perceptions of others. Research continues to show that cultural stereotypes impact perceptions and reactions to minority groups, and those with whom the majority

INEQUITABLE DISTRIBUTION OF SCHOOL RESOURCES

Not all school districts or school discipline protocols are alike, differentiated via location, student population, family income levels, and community resources, among others reasons. Inequitable and resource-driven differences across school districts have led to several troubling outcomes, including the following: Low-income students are more likely to be punished within schools; large school districts with greater minority populations have increased security measures and discipline outcomes; the No Child Left Behind Act had a significantly more harmful impact on low-performing, often poorly resourced, school districts; and more poorly performing schools have trouble hiring and retaining qualified teachers (Heitzeg, 2014; Kupchik, 2010; McCurdy, 2014; McNulty-Eitle & Eitle, 2004). The multifaceted impact that

policies and subsequent rules and regulations that accompany school funding decisions at the local, state, and federal level should be taken into account when discerning these complex explanations for the rise of the school-to-prison pipeline, as well as how to appropriately correct these problems in the schools and the juvenile courts.

1. Why do you think school funding is disparate across districts and states?

2. What was your experience in middle and high schools? In other words, thinking back, did you attend a poorly or well-funded school?

---

is different (Graham & Lowry, 2004; Hunt & Moodie-Mills, 2012; Kirwan Institute, 2014; Levinson, 2007). Decisions to invoke school discipline, knowing that a significant majority of the infractions are for disobedience, and the fact that a majority of youthful offender arrests are for misdemeanor or status offenses, involve the ideology, perceptions, values, and potential biases of those making the decisions. Most studies find that the students who are disproportionately involved with school discipline and the juvenile courts do not misbehave more nor are they more prone to causing school- or community-based problems. Instead, unfair targeting by school and police personnel may explain such disparity, a practice that runs counter to the principles of quality education and appropriate socialization toward young adulthood (Carter et al., 2014; Devine, 1996; Kupchik, 2010).

Comorbid Difficulties

With the myriad of difficulties experienced by the groups that are disproportionately involved in the juvenile courts and in school exclusion, explanations should also entail a review of the combination of risks over time. Rarely is it a singular experience that leads to students' involvement in the school-to-prison pipeline or other pathways to the juvenile courts. Researching and investigating the impact of cumulative risks factors and its impact on these child and adolescent populations should continue. In addition, juvenile justice and school personnel should diligently investigate mitigating history and circumstances when possible before invoking arrests or school exclusion policies. This includes the impact of family functioning, neighborhoods, poverty, trauma, and related difficulties on the child or adolescent (Summers et al., 2013; U.S. Department of Education, 2012).

Segregation by Race and Class

A common narrative for many students caught within school discipline protocols and those adolescents formally involved with the juvenile courts is that there is subtle, or not-so-subtle, **racial profiling** leading to disproportionate outcomes for those of color. As discussed, racial and ethnic disparities are also found within the following subgroups: impoverished students (minorities are more often poor than whites), those with special education disabilities (certain minority groups disproportionately identified), and those who identify as LGBT (disproportionately involved in school exclusion and held in detention centers). Inherent bias may impact teachers

Racial Profiling: The use of race or ethnicity as grounds for suspecting someone of having committed an offense.

and other school personnel and has generated concerns about teacher and student ethnicities in school settings. Furthermore, there may be an alternative paradigm or explanation: Many schools are **segregated** by class and race, and most low-income students of color attend different schools from most middle-class and Caucasian students; thus, the problem may be structural (NAACP, 2005).

Consequently, when administrator and educators at many of the more segregated schools see the potential for greater safety concerns, they may develop school discipline procedures that rely more heavily on out-of-school alternatives for students identified as risky or troublesome. These punitive responses to students, primarily low-income students and/or those of color and concentrated in larger urban school districts, may emanate from teachers of any ethnic group. Thus, the response may be related to the race and class differential and less so to teacher/administrator/school resource officer perceptions or bias. In other words, it may be less about the cultural insensitivity of those working with young people who are different (race, disability, and socioeconomic class, among others) and more about the school district and neighborhood structural explanations that need to be accounted for (Addington, 2014; Ferguson, 2000; Hirschfield, 2010). Nevertheless, this narrative is incomplete and any investigation into race and class segregation must be completed at the local school district and juvenile court level (McLoughlin & Noltemeyer, 2010; Roch, Pitts, & Navarro, 2010; Rocha & Hawes, 2009).

Segregated (Segregation): To separate or divide (people, activities, or institutions) along racial, sexual, or religious lines.

CHAPTER REVIEW

CHAPTER SUMMARY

This chapter reviews the myriad of risk and protective factors that increase the chances for a young person to be involved with delinquent activities and/or school discipline and removal. These risk factors increase the chances for involvement with the juvenile courts, but they can be counter-balanced by protective situations or individual and family resiliency. These protections notwithstanding, the following young people are disproportionately impacted and involved with the juvenile courts and excluded from their schools: those living in poverty, those of color, maltreatment victims, students with special education disabilities, and those who identify as LGBT. This disproportionate impact has possible explanations, some including inherent and explicit bias, as well as stereotyping.

KEY TERMS

Child Welfare System   **131**

dynamic risk factors   **128**

ecological/psychosocial model   **129**

explicit bias   **140**

implicit bias   **140**

kincare placements   **131**

longitudinal studies   **129**

poverty   **129**

protective factors   **128**

racial and ethnic disparities   **137**

racial profiling   **141**

resiliency   **134**

risk factors   **128**

segregated   **142**

static risk factors   **128**

stereotyping   **140**

DISCUSSION QUESTIONS

1. Why are certain groups of young people more at risk for juvenile court involvement or school suspensions or expulsions? Who are these young people, and what pathways can you identify that may explain why some groups are disproportionately involved?

2. Why is maltreatment difficult to accurately identify and prevent? What implications may this have for juvenile court judges and school administrators?

3. What does it mean if a young person is resilient? Why do you think some children and teens are more resilient to

difficult lives than others? What protective factors may help build resiliency?

4. What are the key risk factors for juvenile delinquency and for school suspensions, expulsions, and drop out? How do these risk (and protective) factors impact outcomes?

5. What is the potential impact of comorbid risk factors over time for children and teens?

6. How does poverty impact children and teens and their involvement in the "school-to-prison pipeline"?

7. Why do you think there is disproportionate involvement of certain groups of young people who get excluded from school and/or formally involved with the juvenile courts?

8. What are the strengths and limitations of the ecological/psychosocial model in explaining delinquency, serious offending, and gang involvement? How does the developmental (life-course) model apply to children and teens?

9. If you were designing a delinquency prevention program, what would it look like? Justify these program recommendations based on risk and protective factor research evidence to date.

https://edge.sagepub.com/mallett

$SAGE edge™ **Sharpen your skills with SAGE edge!**

SAGE edge for students provides a personalized approach to help you accomplish your coursework in an easy-to-use learning environment. You'll find mobile-friendly eFlashcards and quizzes, as well as videos, web resources, and links to SAGE journal articles to support and expand on the concepts presented in this chapter.

CHAPTER 7

PUNITIVE JUVENILE JUSTICE POLICIES

▲ Many policies in the juvenile justice system are focused on punishment and control, though it is known that this approach is fairly ineffective for most youthful offenders. If so, why do you think these policies are continued?

©iStockphoto.com/powerofforever

INTRODUCTION

The juvenile justice's tough-on-crime approach that began in the 1980s and the parallel movement of the school's zero tolerance policies have drawn millions of at-risk children in the United States into punishment pathways. Punitive policies and punishment pathways, as discussed in this chapter, are policies and procedures that make it much easier for young people to be excluded from school and/or become involved with the juvenile courts. The term "pathway" is used because once placed in this direction, it is difficult for many young people to deviate from ongoing troubles or difficulties. These difficulties are often reinforced or exacerbated by juvenile justice system policies.

The "tough-on-crime" policy approaches were pursued with good intent, even though they were disproportionate reactions to school shootings, drug use, and youthful offender crime; however, this resulted in many unintended consequences (Howell, 2009). The population of young people captured within these increasingly punitive systems often included children who were already facing difficulties at home, in classrooms, or in their neighborhoods. Once they become formally involved with the punishment pathways, their academics, school problems, or offending outcomes normally do not improve. Rather, punitively focused punishments and disciplines make their transitions into young adulthood significantly more difficult and less successful (Petrosino, Turpin-Petrosino, & Guckenburg, 2010; Sickmund & Puzzanchera, 2014).

ADOLESCENTS ARE DIFFERENT THAN YOUNG ADULTS

Adolescent Development and Brain Neuroscience

Adolescents develop as a result of interactions across many factors, including family and environmental influence, brain development, and emotional, cognitive, and psychological developments and their capacities. **Adolescence** is a formative developmental stage that accompanies rapid and dramatic changes within individual and in important social contexts, such as the family, peer groups, and school. This stage is marked by gradual increases in logical reasoning abilities (in particular, deductive reasoning), emotional intensity produced by puberty, a shift from parental to peer orientation, an increase in autonomy, and a desire for independence from authority figures. Although these changes do not occur uniformly, the emotional instability and risk taking that increase during earlier adolescence are followed a few years later by the development of logical reasoning and increased ability to control impulsive behaviors (Steinberg, 2014b).

Ongoing research has delineated that adolescents are different from young adults across most developmental areas–biological, cognitive, emotional, social, and interpersonal. Adolescents' decision-making ability is limited in scope and is impacted by immaturity, impulsivity, and an under-developed ability to appreciate consequences, especially the long-term

> **Adolescence:** Formative developmental stage that changes the young person rapidly and dramatically, but also in major social contexts, including within the family, in peer groups, and at school.

consequences. These developmental immaturities are intertwined, reinforced, and at times dictated by the adolescent brain that is still developing neurologically into young adulthood (early to mid-20s). During adolescence, therefore, the young person's brain is quite malleable. Neuroscientists have documented age-related changes in brain structure and functioning, including in the prefrontal cortex that is in charge of self-control and planning. This brain area dictates executive functioning, the ability for advanced thinking processes around planning, controlling impulses, and weighing risks and rewards; whereas the ability to understand and develop social and emotional typically happens later. Because adolescents are still developing in so many different ways, they are quite vulnerable to negative and traumatic experiences (MacArthur Foundation, 2015; Steinberg, 2014).

Although older adolescents have adult cognitive capacities, their ability to use decision-making steps is not fully employable due to lack of life experiences. In addition to the limited experiences, another inhibiting factor is adolescents' focus on the present and a diminished ability to delay gratification or have a future orientation, which explains why most adolescents have a lower appreciation of long-term consequences or outcomes in their decision-making. Adolescents don't put facts together and draw conclusions in the same way as adults and are less likely to recognize the risks in the choices they make. When it comes to the juvenile justice system and offending behaviors, many adolescents will not respond as adults to concerns about long-term punishment or other future consequences. The more immediate concern for adolescents often is whether they will get caught breaking the law. In addition, when adolescents do become involved with the juvenile courts, they often do not understand their legal rights, are less capable of making reasoned decisions, and are highly susceptible to coercion primarily because of their developmental immaturities (Giedd, 2004; Somerville & Casey, 2010; Steinberg, Dahl, Keating, Kupfer, & Masten, 2006).

In addition to these developmental issues, adolescents are vulnerable to external peer pressure (and coercion), particularly during the middle school years, due to their **unformed character development**. These peer influences typically peak at age 14 and decline into young adulthood, and are particularly influential in group situations. A significant percentage of youthful offending happens in groups, whereas most adults commit crime alone. This peer influence, along with adolescents' increased preference for risk taking, based on the minimizing of the risk and the overinflation of rewards, leads many to make poor decisions in schools and elsewhere. The young person is often in a quandary, for resisting peer pressure can have negative and ostracizing outcomes including being shunned, bullied, or isolated (Fagan, 2000; Moffitt, 1993). Scott and Steinberg discussed the case of Timothy Kane:

> Consider the case of Timothy Kane, a fourteen-year-old junior high school student who never had any contact with the justice system until one Sunday afternoon in January 1992. Tim was hanging out with a group of friends when a couple of older youths suggested that they break into a neighbor's house; Tim agreed to go along. On entering the house, the boys were surprised to find the elderly neighbor and her son at home—whereupon the two older boys killed them while Tim watched from under the dining room table. Interviewed years later as he served a life sentence under Florida's draconian felony murder law, Tim explained that he went along because he didn't want to stay behind alone—and he didn't want to be called a 'fraidy-cat.' Tim's fatal decision to get involved in the break-in appears to be, more than anything else, the conduct of a fourteen year-old worried about peer approval. (Scott & Steinberg, 2008a, p. 21)

Recognizing Adolescent Differences

In many ways, juvenile justice and school policies that are focused on strict punishment and discipline procedures, including, for example, school suspension for truancy problems and the detention of low-level youthful offenders, may have little-to-no deterrent effect of these behavers

Unformed Character Development: Trait of adolescence whereby ongoing social, cognitive, and psychological development continues.

on adolescents. Of note, most adolescents involved in school discipline problems or delinquent activities eventually grow out of these antisocial tendencies as their learning continues, experiences accumulate, and the brain develops. These adolescent activities are part of identify formation, a process that includes experimentation and, many times, risk-taking decisions and behaviors. This experimental phase ends when identify formation completes itself (Scott & Steinberg, 2008b).

For these reasons, by age 16, most adolescents discontinue criminal activity (referred to as **adolescence-limited offenders**), with only fewer than 5% of adjudicated delinquent young people continuing offending into young adulthood (referred to as **life-course-persistent offenders**; Moffitt, 1993). A significant difference between these two adolescent groups is that those who do not continue committing adult offending behaviors have developed **psychosocial maturity**. Such maturity requires three important components: the involvement of at least one caring and committed adult in the adolescent's life; a peer group that values academics and pro-social behavior; and the development of independent and critical thinking skills (Mulvey, 2011; Piquero, Farrington, & Blumstein, 2003).

The diminished capacities of the young people have been recognized in numerous Supreme Court decisions since 2002 (discussed earlier in the text), finding adolescence, or its age, itself a mitigating factor in harsh sentencing decisions. These Court decisions have ended some of the most extreme sentences for juvenile offenders in recent years, including the death penalty and mandatory life imprisonment without parole (*Roper v. Simmons* in 2005, *Graham v. Florida* in 2010, and *Miller v. Alabama* in 2012). One of the more recent cases had Justice Kagan speak to how adolescents are different from adults.

FROM THE CLASSROOM TO THE COURTS

Discipline problems at school often start as minor incidents or infractions. Almost all school suspensions or expulsions begin as disobedient behavior or disruptions of the classroom or school. The following are examples of inflexible policies with a focus on control or punishment:

A 17-year-old high school junior shot a paper clip with a rubber band at a classmate, missed, and broke the skin of a cafeteria worker. The student was expelled from school. (Heitzeg, 2014, p. 21)

A 14-year-old girl was arrested and charged with battery for pouring a carton of chocolate milk on the head of a classmate. The girl explained that she heard that the victim was "talking about her." Local police state that they believed "the quickest way to resolve it was to charge her." (Advancement Project, 2005, p. 13)

A 14-year-old girl was arrested in school in Wauwatosa, Wisconsin, after refusing to stop texting on her cell phone in class. A school resource officer's report says that student refused to stop texting during class after a teacher told her to stop and the student told the resource officer she didn't have a phone after she was pulled out of the classroom . . . The officer noted that the student is "known to me and the administration based on prior negative contacts" . . . after the arrest, the student was suspended for a week. (McCurdy, 2014, p. 93–94)

An 11-year-old girl in Orlando, Florida, was Tasered by a police officer, arrested, and faced charges of battery on a security resource officer, disrupting a school function, and resisting with violence. She had pushed another student. (Heitzeg, 2014, p. 22)

A 16-year-old transgender student attending Hercules High School in California, who claimed that fellow students bullied her for years, was charged with misdemeanour battery after getting into a schoolyard fight. Despite video footage capturing the altercation

Adolescence-Limited Offenders: Phenomenon that most adolescents will discontinue delinquent and criminal activity on their own by age 16.

Life-Course-Persistent Offenders: Name category for adolescents (fewer than 5% of all youthful offenders) who continue criminal activity into adulthood.

Psychosocial Maturity: Ability to respond appropriately to the environment. For adolescents, this refers to peers, family, school, and other environments.

MILLER V. ALABAMA

In 2003, Evan Miller, a 14-year-old from Alabama, was convicted in juvenile court, transferred to criminal court, and sentenced after he and another teenager committed robbery, arson, and murder. Miller committed the homicide in the act of robbing his neighbor after all three of them (Miller, accomplice, and neighbor) had spent an afternoon drinking and smoking marijuana. Although attempting to rob the neighbor, a fight ensued and the neighbor was beat unconscious. Miller and the accomplice later returned to destroy the evidence of what they had done by setting fire to the neighbor's trailer, killing him. Once found guilty, Alabama state law mandated a life sentence without the possibility of parole (LWOP) for Miller. Upon appeal, in the *Miller* decision, the Supreme Court found these LWOP mandatory state laws to be unconstitutional (Miller, 567 U.S. slip op at 2).

Justice Kagan found in her *Miller* decision that "(m)andatory life without parole for a juvenile precludes consideration of his chronological age and its hallmark features—among them, immaturity, impetuosity, and failure to appreciate risks and consequences. It prevents taking into account the family and home environment that surrounds him—and from which he cannot usually extricate himself—no matter how brutal or dysfunctional. It neglects the circumstances of the homicide offense, including the extent of his participation in the conduct and the way familial and peer pressures may have affected him. Indeed, it ignores that he might have been charged and convicted of a lesser offense if not for incompetencies associated with youth—for example, his inability to deal with police officers or prosecutors . . . . And finally, this mandatory punishment disregards the possibility of rehabilitation even when the circumstances most suggest it" (United States Supreme Court Justice Kagan, *Miller v. Alabama*, 132 S. Ct. 2455, at p. 2461, 2012).

1. Do you think the *Miller v. Alabama* decision was the right one?

2. Do you believe that someone deserves a second chance if they commit murder? Does your opinion differ if it is a teenager or a young adult?

---

between the girl and three other teenagers, she was the only student to be criminally charged. The other three students only received out-of-school suspensions. (Mitchum & Moodie-Mills, 2014, p. 18)

A high school student was arrested and charged with second degree breach of peace for a shouting argument with his girlfriend. Bridgeport students and parents protested the over-reliance on law enforcement in schools after 140 students were arrested during the first six weeks of the 2004–2005 school year. (Advancement Project, 2005, p. 13)

These student outcomes, being arrested by school police (resource) officers or suspended or expelled from school, are problematic because the young people did not pose serious risks to others or the school. Nevertheless, zero tolerance policies do not allow mitigating circumstances to be considered by school administrators when applying punishments. The combination of strict punitive policies, along with the presence of school resource officers, increases the risk that the removal and arrest outcomes will continue across many schools nationwide. Students disciplined through zero tolerance policies are often first-time offenders, for minor, nonviolent incidents. Nonetheless, these students are placed at higher risk of receiving continued disciplines because their risk for juvenile court involvement is also high (Kang-Brown, Trone, Fratello, & Daftary-Kapur, 2013).

Counterintuitively, some students who misbehave and are the targets of zero tolerance policies are doing well academically before punishments; therefore, the policy prescriptions and impact on the school environment themselves may lead to school disengagement by the student, thus, increasing the risk of academic failure. Being disengaged and removed from school are significant risks for making poor peer choices and, for some, delinquent offending behaviors (Hoffman, Erickson, & Spence, 2013; Skiba, Arredondo, & Rausch, 2014; Skiba et al., 2006).

Punitive school-exclusion policies (suspension and expulsion) can have a cascading impact on students. Just one school suspension in the ninth grade has been found to double the risk for the failure of subsequent academic courses in high school and to raise the risk of dropping out by 20% (Balfanz, Byrnes, & Fox, 2015; Marchblanks et al., 2014). Being retained in grade level significantly increases the risk of dropping out of high school. The risk of dropping out of high school is also doubled if a young person is arrested on or off schools grounds and is four times greater if the young person is formally involved with the juvenile courts (Kang-Brown et al., 2013; Sweeten, 2006).

▲ Police officers who work in schools have become common place today. What do you think about having police on school grounds?

School Failure

High school dropout rates declined from 14% to 7% from 1967 to 2014 (see Figure 7.1). Although the dropout rate continues to disproportionately impact minority and foreign-born students, students who identify as LGBT (up to one third of this group drops out of school, by some estimates), and males (5% for white males, 7% for black males, and 11% for Hispanic males). These dropout estimates do not include individuals who are incarcerated (disproportionately minority), partially explaining why the gap between white and minority dropout rates is not as wide as expected. These counts also do not reflect the lower graduation rates (less than 70%), as measured by four years in high school, that are disproportionately found in lower income, minority, and urban public schools (Child Trends, 2015a).

The high school dropout rate is explained in many different ways. Some of the more influential reasons include high rates of absenteeism or truancy, low parental education, low grades and academic performance, grade level retention, school disengagement, moving to a new school in the ninth grade, work or family responsibilities, and delinquent behaviors (American Psychological Association, 2012; Balfanz & Letgers, 2004; Suh & Suh, 2007).

School suspensions and expulsions increase the chances for school failure or dropout, poor peer choices, and offending behaviors. Suspension or expulsion due to a discretionary school violation makes juvenile court involvement almost three times more likely. Being suspended as a freshman in high school doubles the risk for school dropout, with more than one third of males who are suspended for more than ten days also sentenced to a juvenile correctional facility. Placement into a juvenile correctional facility makes completing high school difficult for most youthful offenders (Fabelo et al., 2011; Shollenberg, 2015).

Findings from recent studies continue to show the impact of harsh discipline on students, translated in terms of the financial impact. Researchers from **The Civil Rights Project in Los Angeles** followed a national cohort of tenth graders and found that the out-of-school suspensions for this group lead to 67,000 dropouts from high schools. Using economic loss data, it was determined that for each student dropout, $163,000 was lost in lifetime tax revenue and $364,000 was spent on additional social, medical, or criminal justice costs. This meant that the total cost of the 67,000 additional dropouts caused by school suspensions nationally exceeded $35 billion (Rumberger & Losen, 2016).

Alternative Education

School exclusion may also entail removal from school and placement into an **alternative education program** within the school or in a separate facility. Alternative education schools are often used as placements for students most at risk for school failure and/or disciplinary concerns, even though they are not positive solutions for many students and may exacerbate the problems. Racial

The Civil Rights Project in Los Angeles: Organization with a mission to create a new generation of research in social science and law on the critical issues of civil rights and equal opportunity for racial and ethnic groups in the United States.

Alternative Education Program: Separate school, or part of a school building, where students are removed to because they were unsuccessful academically or behaviorally in their original classroom.

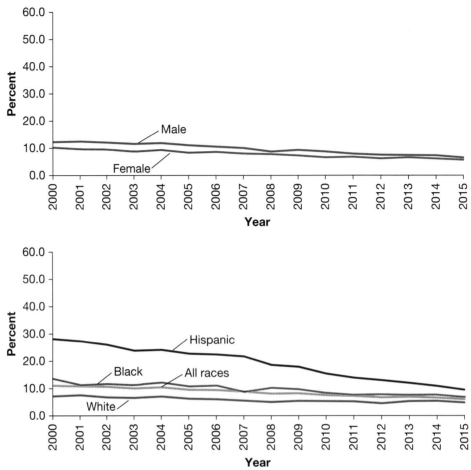

▼ FIGURE 7.1

Status Dropout Rates of 16- to 24-Year-Olds by Sex and by Race/Ethnicity, 1960–2015

Source: U.S. Department of Education, National Center for Education Statistics. (2017). *The Condition of Education 2017* (NCES 2017-144), Status Dropout Rates.

disparities are found across many alternative schools, and their suspended student populations mirror the disparity by race within the juvenile court referrals (Nicholson-Crotty, Birchmeier, & Valentine, 2009; Vanderhaar, Petrosko, & Munoz, 2014).

School Dropout Consequences. Dropping out of school does not just limit educational and vocational options, it also increases the chances for living in poverty and receiving public assistance in young adulthood (such as TANF, Temporary Assistance for Needy Families; subsidized housing; and food stamps). In addition, when a student drops out of high school, the risk of lifetime incarceration increases more than threefold (Martin & Halperin, 2006). Formal juvenile delinquency adjudication, even without an adult incarceration experience, may impede young adults from accessing student loans, being accepted for military service, or receiving public or subsidized housing (Pinard, 2006).

THE POLICE AND ADOLESCENTS

The pathway an adolescent takes to the juvenile court begins with the commission of an offense and subsequent interaction with a law enforcement officer. Options for law enforcement when making a decision on a youthful offender include questioning, warning, and community release; taking the young person to the police station and recording the offense; a referral to a diversion program; issuing a citation and making a formal referral to the juvenile court; or, depending on the circumstances, concerns, or any safety issues, taking the adolescent to a **detention center** or group/shelter home. Many factors influence the decision of law enforcement at this point, including the young person's profile, the law enforcement officer's perspectives, organizational policies, specific offense and circumstances, available community alternatives or programming, and any community pressures (Lawrence & Hemmens, 2008).

This first point of contact can be a pivotal time for youthful offenders with mental health problems, trauma, or other difficulties. A decision by the law enforcement officer to release the adolescent or to make a referral for diversion or treatment services may provide far greater opportunities for assistance and rehabilitation, compared with a formal juvenile court referral or detainment. In fact, most youthful offenders who are arrested one time are likely never arrested a second time. So, generally, either inaction or informal actions by the police and juvenile court (if involved) seem to be appropriate for first-time offenders in that there is such a low recidivism rate. Nevertheless, keeping the community safe weighs most heavily for law enforcement officers who are making the decision about a formal juvenile court referral. In addition, most police officers are not trained to identify mental health difficulties, trauma risks, or school-related problems, limiting their assessment abilities (Mulvey, 2011; Rosado, 2005).

DELINQUENCY ADJUDICATION

Juvenile courts across the country receive many referrals for criminal behaviors, status offenses, family problems, and child abuse or neglect, among other reasons. From the one million arrests of young people annually, nearly half become formally involved and thus adjudicated delinquent and end up being supervised by a juvenile court judge or magistrate (Puzzanchera & Robson, 2014). As discussed earlier in the text, delinquency adjudication is an official judicial decision

Detention Center: County-run facility that houses low-level, status, or other youthful offenders, typically for short periods of time.

providing legal control over the juvenile to the court and the assignment of a probation officer and ongoing supervision. Most school referrals and arrests that are brought to the juvenile courts are for minor misdemeanors, such as disobedience (talking back to teachers or administrators), disturbing the peace, or fighting (aggravated battery), thus, resulting in adolescent misbehaviors and disruptions to be criminally prosecuted (Advancement Project, 2005).

The zero tolerance policy movement still continues to impact students in punitive ways. For example, 13 states have laws that criminalize "disturbing schools." This vague term, found in school's student codes of conduct, allows for the prosecution of many forms of misbehavior and disobedience that may occur in the classroom, hallways, or at school events, among other campus-related gatherings. The "disturbing schools"

Jamie Pham/Alamy Stock Photo

▲ Being arrested is the most common first step into the juvenile justice system. What happens next? Were you or your friends ever arrested, and if so, what happened?

language, therefore, casts a wide net over students who, prior to strict zero tolerance policies, would not have been at risk of school exclusion for their minor indiscretions (Fuentes, 2014; Majd, 2011).

Once young people are adjudicated delinquent and come under formal supervision, depending on their offense, they are court ordered to perform certain activities, refrain from

PRACTICE: WHAT CAN I DO?

TRUANCY AND PARENTS

The judge peered down at Ashley Derrick from the bench and scolded her for being late to a 9 a.m. hearing in his Garland, Texas, courtroom. Derrick, 26, explained that she'd hit traffic coming from one of her two jobs as a phlebotomist. Her alleged crime: contributing to her child's nonattendance at school, a misdemeanor punishable by a fine of up to $500 and community service for each unexcused absence.

"Your son has six lates to school and two leaving early," Judge John Sholden declared. "How do you plead?"

"Not guilty," answered Derrick. The judge set a pretrial hearing for June 27.

Outside the courtroom, Derrick, who was dressed in brightly printed scrubs, looked weary but resigned. Her son Marcus, 7, had indeed missed class time, but it was for medical appointments.

"My son has chronic asthma and also ADHD," she said, "and he panics a little when he has breathing problems. So we have him seeing a counselor."

Marcus's doctor had been tardy herself in providing mandatory excuse notes to his school, prompting the principal to file a truancy case in the Texas court.

"There's no flexibility," Derrick said. "But I know I will have the doctor's notes, so I pled not guilty."

The harried African American single mom was among the hundreds of parents and students who attended truancy court on that single May day in Dallas County. Unlike Derrick, most pled guilty or no contest and were given a fine of at least $195, due in 30 days. Students risked losing their drivers licenses, too, and those who failed to appear in court for one reason or another risked arrest warrants. (Fuentes 2012, para. 1–5)

• •

1. Do you think these types of laws focused on truancy and parent responsibility are effective?

2. Are there different ways to handle cases like this?

Source: Excerpt from "The Truancy Trap," Annette Fuentes, *The Atlantic*, September 5, 2012.

---

other activities or continue making negative choices, and/or change certain outcomes. Although many youthful offenders are successful in meeting their probation and court-order expectations, others are set up for failure because of resistance to supervision, the inability to meet the court order expectations, or other intervening or confounding problems (Sulok, 2007).

For example, if a student has a **truancy** history, which triggers the school disciplinary system, and is referred to the local juvenile court because of too many absences, then he or she is usually court ordered to attend school. If there are no intervening alternatives, such as interventions with the family or investigations as to why he or she is truant in the first place, such a court order does little to address the underlying or mitigating reasons why he is not attending school. A court order that, without changes in circumstances or addressing the reasons why, simply orders the student to follow the probation plan and attend school inevitably leads the young student to violate it. The student may be truant because he or she is a target of severe bullying at school because of sexual orientation, or because the parents or caregivers in the home are substance users, thus, providing little-to-no structure or incentive to attend school regularly. Whatever the reason is for truancy, there are many difficulties once these matters are referred to the juvenile courts, including the impact on parents, and formally handled by the juvenile justice system.

The juvenile court personnel may or may not discover the reasons for the school attendance problems, only the fact that the outcome is truancy. If the probation plan for those under supervision is not followed or met, the juvenile court judge has few options at his or her disposal, leading many times to the finding of a court-order violation and increased punitive responses. Under current federal and many state laws, juvenile courts are allowed to detain or incarcerate youthful offenders solely for **violations of a court order**—a technical violation for not adhering to a judge's order, not a criminal violation or a new offense. A juvenile court judge decision that a youthful offender has violated a court order is the reason that more than

Truancy: Act of staying away from school without good cause.

Violations of a Court Order: Technical violation for not adhering to a judge's order, not a criminal violation or a new offense.

35% of offenders are held in detention centers and 16% are incarcerated in juvenile facilities nationwide (National Center for Youth Law, 2008; Puzzanchera, 2011; Sickmund & Puzzanchera, 2014).

DETAINED AND INCARCERATED YOUTHFUL OFFENDERS

Most young people who end up in the juvenile justice system's detention and incarceration facilities have troubled lives before their offending behaviors began. These difficulties are across a range of life experiences that occur within their families, neighborhoods, communities, and schools (Hawkens et al., 2000). These experiences place many of the children and adolescents at such a significant risk that they end up in a detention or an incarceration facility, although this is not preordained, nor is it destiny. Nevertheless, the profile of youthful offenders in these facilities tells much about how they ended up there: disproportionately those from poorer neighborhoods, those with traumatic and maltreated childhoods, those involved with school discipline protocols and academically behind in school, and those with mental health and related difficulties. Most juvenile justice systems are not equipped or designed to be able to identify these difficulties or mitigating factors that impact and influence many youthful offending activities.

Failure of Early Screening and Assessment

The correctional institutions have become the placement of last resort across most of the youth-caring systems, used by schools, mental health providers, and law enforcement because too few alternative or rehabilitative options exist when these young people run into trouble. Often, at the front end of these outcomes is the failure to correctly or accurately identify risks factors, traumas, mental health problems, or underlying school-related difficulties based on appropriate or empirically sound assessment tools (Baird et al., 2013; National Council on Crime and Delinquency, 2014). If you do not know what the young person may be struggling with or what impairments he or she may have, you cannot effectively intervene or plan appropriately. Knowing that most of the young people caught within school exclusion discipline policies and those who end up in juvenile justice institutions have multiple risks and disabilities, it would be important for the juvenile justice system to improve early identification and prevention efforts to minimize further involvement in the system (Washington State Institute for Public Policy, 2007).

Although empirically supported screening and assessment instruments are available that can help inform decisions by school (teachers, counselors, and administrators) and juvenile court personnel (intake workers, probation officers, magistrates, and judges), a less coherent and haphazard decision-making process is all too often the norm in determining the balance of a young person's dangerousness, blameworthiness, and likely future behavior. School systems and juvenile courts too often make uniformed decisions based on zero tolerance policies and traditions, without gathering relevant and important information or the use of actuarial or screening instruments for needs and risk assessment (National Council on Crime and Delinquency, 2014; Mulvey & Iselin, 2008).

Rehabilitative Alternatives Are Not the Norm

Most juvenile justice detention and incarceration facilities use punitive approaches. There is an increased recognition, however, that a rehabilitative environment better achieves important public policy goals of decreasing youthful offender recidivism and, subsequently, increasing community safety (U.S. Department of Justice, 2014). There is evidence that incarceration facilities that identify youthful offender problems and provide treatment services and quality education programs can have a significant impact on decreasing recidivism. Nevertheless, most serious youthful offenders who are incarcerated across the nation are still in large training schools, facilities with low-quality education, and rehabilitative alternatives that resemble adult prison. Such facilities generally provide little-to-no rehabilitative care for those adolescents with disabilities, traumas, or mental health problems; often they do not meet the education or special education needs of the youthful offender; and can be overcrowded and unsafe (Garrido & Morales, 2007; Hockenberry & Puzzanchera, 2014b; Sedlak & McPherson, 2010).

Many of the tens of thousands of adolescents who remain every day in detention and incarceration facilities have become the most difficult to rehabilitate because their problems remain complex and often worsened. Although many juvenile court jurisdictions have not made significant progress moving away from a punitive approach in their decision-making and expanding intervention alternatives, for approximately two thirds of the young men and women still confined, most have histories of multiple mental health disorders and related difficulties, often substance abuse and trauma, which continue into young adulthood. For these adolescents, detention and incarceration outcomes are life changing and harmful (MacArthur Foundation, 2012).

Impact of Incarceration

The outcome of incarceration among youthful offenders is poor. Incarceration does not decrease future adolescent crime whereas the experience of incarceration itself is part of the problem. More specifically, placement into these facilities has either no correlation with offender rearrest or recidivism rates or is associated with an increased risk for offender rearrest (Loughran et al., 2009; Winokur, Smith, Bontrger, & Blankenship, 2008). Placement in locked incarceration facilities and longer lengths of stay increase the risk for reoffending after release for most youthful offenders, typically within 18 to 30 months. This increased risk is particularly acute for low-level offenders, which is the profile of most incarcerated youthful offenders in many states (Bhati & Piquero, 2007; Petrosino et al., 2010). Although incarcerated, many of these adolescents do not receive services that may assist in mitigating the prior offending behavior. In other words, they are not provided with rehabilitative programming (for mental health, education, or trauma, among others) that may be needed. Most incarceration facilities are not equipped to meet the rehabilitative needs of the adolescents placed within the institution, let alone the needs of the youthful offenders with serious comorbid problems and educational deficits (The Council of State Governments Justice Center, 2015).

©iStockphoto.com/Bastiaan Slabbers

Time spent in these facilities harms adolescent development and decreases cognitive and social functioning, decision-making abilities, and character formation. The longer a young person is incarcerated, the greater the immediate and longer term risk to both physical and mental health (Barnert et al., 2017). In addition, incarceration lessens an adolescent's ability to function independently because of the rigid expectations of the justice facility, and social and coping skills are diminished for similar reasons. Many education systems within state incarceration facilities receive failing grades, do not address gaps in the adolescents' school abilities, and do not provide appropriate services for those with learning disabilities. Incarceration facilities lack necessary rehabilitation services, separate the adolescents from their families, and are many times dangerous and violent environments—all factors in exacerbating poor outcomes (Dmitrieva, Monahan, Cauffman, & Steinberg, 2012; Hockenberry, 2014).

▲ Most youthful offenders who are involved with the juvenile justice system do not end up in locked facilities. But for those that do, what do you think the impact is of incarceration?

JUVENILE CONFINEMENT COSTS

Policy makers are increasingly concluding that, except for the smaller number of youthful offenders who pose a serious community risk, detaining and incarcerating large numbers of youthful offenders, whether in juvenile or adult facilities, is not a sound fiscal public policy. The costs of these incarcerations are substantial, with more than $5 billion spent annually incarcerating young people in juvenile institutions. On average, it costs $240.00 per day (greater than $88,000 per year) to detain or incarcerate a youthful offender in a juvenile justice facility. In comparison, the costs of all other juvenile court administrative, programming, and supervision efforts are estimated to be half as much as these facility placement costs (Council of Juvenile Correctional Administrators, 2009; Florida Department of Juvenile Justice, 2010). Younger adolescents who become involved early on with the juvenile courts and commit numerous offenses over time typically cost upward of $220,000 by age 17; if this adolescent progresses to serious offending, the cost rises to greater $800,000 in total. Some estimates have identified that if one serious offending adolescent is diverted away from delinquency early on, between $2 and $5 million could be saved over the person's lifetime (Cohen & Piquero, 2009; Welsh et al., 2008).

1. **Do you think these costs are reasonable for youthful offender incarceration?**

2. **What are the possible alternatives to youthful offender incarceration and the use of some of these dollars?**

Adult Criminal Activity

These difficulties do not end for the adolescent after leaving the juvenile justice system, for most adult criminals begin their careers as youthful offenders. Several factors predict involvement with the adult criminal courts, mostly related to the onset and persistence of youthful offending behaviors. These include adolescents whose offending behaviors start early and continue through later teen years; who commit more offenses (primarily person and violent types); are more frequently adjudicated delinquent; and whose offenses escalate over time (Aizer & Doyle, 2013; Loeber & Farrington, 2008). In some jurisdictions, both serious and low-level youthful offenders who were incarcerated in juvenile facilities, compared with those who received nonincarcerated sentences, were three times more likely to be incarcerated in adult facilities. For low-level youthful offenders, it is the incarceration experience itself that is precipitating future crimes, often more serious in nature. If more serious youthful offenders do not desist these negative patterns, but continue their involvement with the criminal courts as adults, their prospects are often bleak (Pew Center on the States, 2011; Trulson, Haerle, DeLisi, & Marquart, 2011).

Solitary Confinement

"Being in a room for 21 hours a day is like a waking nightmare, like you want to scream but you can't. You want to stretch your legs, walk for more than a few feet. You feel trapped" (American Civil Liberties Union, 2014, p. 4). Solitary confinement is the holding of an incarcerated young person in an isolated locked room with no contact with other offenders and, most of the time, with little-to-no staff contact. This physical and social isolation may be for 22 to 24 hours per day and could last for days, weeks, or months. Isolation cells are typically windowless, and those confined are deprived of any institutional programming (exercise, education, and rehabilitative options, among others). These solitary confinements are used as interventions throughout the juvenile justice system and are referred to by various names, depending on the length of the practice—segregation, separation, seclusion, room confinement, and exclusion (Human Rights Watch & American Civil Liberties Union 2012).

The use of solitary confinement does not make facilities safer or deter dangerous behavior, it is widespread, and it is applied unevenly across juvenile populations and facilities. It also has

Solitary Confinement: Holding of an incarcerated young person (from hours to months) in an isolated locked room with no contact with other offenders, and most of the time with little-to-no staff contact.

debilitating and permanent harmful impact on youthful offenders, including serious developmental harm, significant trauma, severe mental health problems (psychosis, depression, and anxiety), uncontrollable anger or rage, and self-harm and suicide (Feieman, Lindell, & Eaddy, 2017). "I cut myself. I started doing it because it is the only release of my pain. . . . I wanted the staff to talk to me. I wanted them to understand what was happening to me" (Human Rights Watch & American Civil Liberties Union, 2012, p. 29–30). Half of all suicides in juvenile incarceration facilities have occurred while young people were held in solitary confinement; and 60% of those young people who committed suicide in these facilities had a history of isolation. Many experts note that this practice is dangerous and constitutes cruel and unusual punishment. Adolescents who are confined in this way are at risk of harm more than adults because of their ongoing development, and those with trauma and maltreatment histories are particularly vulnerable (American Civil Liberties Union, 2014; National Council on Disability, 2003). Kalief Browder spent three years incarcerated at Riker's Island in New York, where he spent time in solitary confinement:

> Browder's 16-year-old son, Kalief, was accused of stealing a backpack. But he refused to plead guilty to something he said he didn't do. Instead, he spent years in detention, waiting for a trial that never happened. "He was a child being locked up for 23 hours a day for nearly two years," Browder said. "That's enough to destroy a man's mind, let alone a child's."
>
> . . .
>
> Browder said her son tried to hang himself at Rikers. When corrections officers found him, he got a beating—and more time in isolation. Eventually, authorities dropped the prosecution. Kalief came home, got a GED and took classes at community college. But Browder said her son was struggling. "The look on his face—physically he was here, but mentally he wasn't," she said. "And it was too many days like that. It just overpowered him." Kalief Browder took his own life last year. Criminal justice researchers said that story is all too common. (Johnson, 2016, para. 5 & 7)

▲ Solitary confinement is used in many juvenile incarceration facilities. What do you think about its use and impact?

mavrixphoto/Newscom

For these and other reasons, in 2016, the Obama Administration banned the practice of holding juveniles in solitary confinement in federal prisons. Approximately 10% of all inmates held in this country are in federal prisons, although a small number of these inmates comprised juvenile offenders when they were transferred to the adult federal judicial system (The White House, 2016). This same decision to eliminate or lessen the use of solitary confinement for youthful offenders in juvenile justice facilities has also occurred across state incarceration facilities, although these modifications have been a recent phenomenon. Many states have passed legislation accordingly, so that as of 2015, 20 states and the District of Columbia prohibit the use of solitary confinement. Nevertheless, three of these states still allow for confinement up to four hours per day (Illinois, Maine, and Missouri), whereas the other 17 states and the District of Columbia allow confinement for safety purposes. Twenty more states impose other time limits ranging from 6 to 90 days, with the most common time limit being 3 to 5 days. And ten states still allow confinement with no time limits (Alabama, Georgia, Kansas, Kentucky, Louisiana, Michigan, Oregon, Tennessee, Texas, and Wyoming; Kraner, Barrowclough, Wang, Weiss, & Fisch, 2015). So although some limitations on juvenile solitary confinement have been pursued across the states in recent years, most still allow the practice in some form (see Figure 7.2).

Suicide in Detention and Incarceration Facilities

The comorbid impact of youthful offenders' childhood maltreatment, school difficulties, bullying, and/or mental health problems, and a juvenile justice system that is not designed to handle many of these adolescent difficulties, has resulted in ineffective detention and incarceration facilities. In particular, the incarceration experience itself increases youthful offenders' risk for suicide during and after release from the institutions. Researchers have begun to analyze how facility characteristics may be related to suicide attempts and death, with some finding that facilities that house larger populations of youthful offenders and facilities that have locked sleeping room doors have the highest risk of suicide (Gallagher & Dobrin, 2006; Thompson, Ho, & Kingree, 2007). In addition to incarceration, there are other suicide risk factors these adolescents may experience before or during their juvenile justice system involvement: a family or individual history of suicide, a history of depression, serious alcohol or drug abuse, loss (trauma), and easy access to lethal methods

▼ FIGURE 7.2

States That Limit or Prohibit Juvenile Shackling and Solitary Confinement

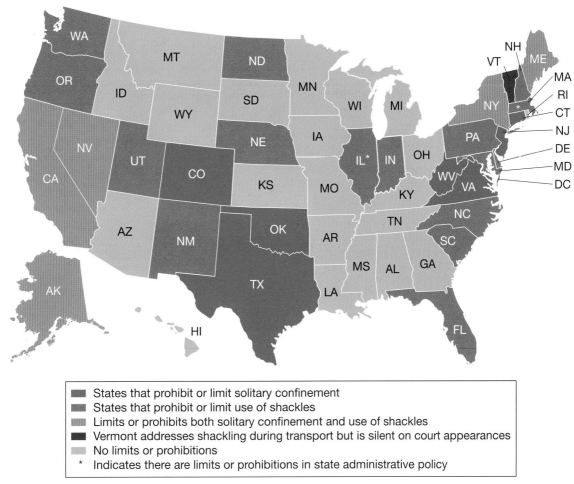

Legend:
- States that prohibit or limit solitary confinement
- States that prohibit or limit use of shackles
- Limits or prohibits both solitary confinement and use of shackles
- Vermont addresses shackling during transport but is silent on court appearances
- No limits or prohibitions
- * Indicates there are limits or prohibitions in state administrative policy

Source: States that Limit or Prohibit Juvenile Shackling and Solitary Confinement, National Conference of State Legislatures (2016).

©iStockphoto.com/ljubaphoto

▲ Suicidal thoughts and acts are more common for young people in locked facilities. Why do you think this is the case?

(Centers for Disease Control and Prevention, 2009; U.S. Department of Justice, 2012).

In comprehensive reviews of youthful offenders in custody, between 11% and 22% reported that they tried to kill themselves during their lifetime, which a significantly higher risk than that reported for nonoffending adolescents (Abram et al., 2014; Memory, 1989; Sedlak & McPherson, 2010). A national study of court-ordered juvenile offenders in placement found that 110 completed suicides occurred between 1995 and 1999. Of the 79 cases with complete information, it was found that 42% of the suicides took place in secure juvenile court facilities and training schools, 37% in detention centers, 15% in residential treatment centers, and 6% in reception or diagnostic centers (Hayes, 2009). In addition, even though institutionalized, thoughts of suicide have ranged from 15% to 50% of adolescents in long-term institutions (Abram et al., 2014) and between 25% and 30% for those in detention facilities (Cauffman, 2004; Putnins, 2005; Sedlak & McPherson, 2010).

Because the detained and incarcerated population of youthful offenders is disproportionately minority and male, it is important to note that adolescent males are more likely to die from suicide attempts, as well as to use more violent means. Adolescent females are more likely to report attempting suicide. Native American/Alaskan Native and Hispanic adolescents have been found to have the highest rate of suicide deaths and suicidal ideation, whereas white adolescent females reported more incidents of suicide or self-injury than did their black counterparts (Centers for Disease Control and Prevention, 2013; Graham & Corcoran, 2003; Holsinger & Holsinger, 2005).

Predicting suicide risk is difficult, however, for risk factors vary in their impact and intensity, although involvement in the juvenile justice system is a contributing cause. Even when other risk factors—age, ethnicity, gender, alcohol or drug problems, depression, and impulsivity—are accounted for, delinquency was still related to suicidal ideation and attempts up to one year after adjudication, and to suicidal ideation up to seven years after adjudication. Youthful offenders with an arrest history are more likely to report a suicide attempt than are those without an arrest history (Thompson et al., 2007; Tolou-Shams, Brown, Gordon, & Fernandez, 2007). In addition, demonstrating the impact of comorbid problems, young people in juvenile justice facilities who have experienced maltreatment as a child are more than twice as likely to have attempted suicide as their peers who had experienced maltreatment but were not in these facilities. Those who committed suicide had experienced rates of maltreatment two to ten times greater than the general child and adolescent population (Croysdale, Drerup, Bewsey, & Hoffman, 2008; Gray et al., 2002; Hayes, 2009).

Transfers to Criminal Court

Transfer Laws: State laws that allow the transfer of youthful offenders to adult criminal courts based on certain age and offense criteria.

All 50 states have **transfer laws** that allow or require the criminal prosecution of some youthful offenders by mandating the transfer of these adolescents from the juvenile courts to the adult criminal courts (see Figure 7.3). Most states place the responsibility on the prosecution to show that the youthful offender should be transferred and tried in adult criminal court, with many taking into account the nature of the alleged crime and the individual adolescent's history, age, maturity, and other rehabilitative concerns. In 29 states, however, transfers to criminal court are "automatic" if the youthful offender commits a certain type of offense not permitted in juvenile court and is a certain minimum age. For example, in New York State, a 17-year-old may be transferred automatically for certain weapon-possession crimes, whereas murder is the offense most common for automatic transfer in all 29 states (Griffin, Addie, Adams, & Firestine, 2011; Neelum, 2011).

JUVENILE OFFENDER TRANSFERS TO CRIMINAL COURT

The handling of youthful offenders is not limited to the juvenile courts for upward of 100,000–125,000 adolescents are transferred to adult criminal courts every year. Reports from several states have found that 9 out of every 1,000 delinquency cases are transferred automatically without any judicial or prosecutorial review, although this is difficult to determine nationally because of disparate state reporting practices. This, however, is not a recent phenomenon. In 1966, in *Kent v. U.S.*, the U.S. Supreme Court determined that transferring juvenile offenders to adult criminal courts was permissible, even though certain procedures and reviews of circumstances were necessary, including the seriousness and type of offense, prosecutorial merit of the complaint, adolescent maturity, home environment, and

previous court history. From the 1970s to the 2000s, as the movement to be "tough on crime" shifted the juvenile and adult courts away from rehabilitation, state legislatures made automatic and prosecutorial-determined youthful offender transfers easier (Griffin et al., 2011; Mulvey & Schubert, 2012; Nellis, 2016).

1. **Do you think that transferring youthful offenders to adult criminal courts is an effective policy?**

2. **What alternatives might be available for this group of young people if they were not transferred to adult court?**

Transfers of adolescents to the adult criminal justice system are controversial because they divide the youthful offender population into two categories: those worthy of rehabilitation and those subject to retributive punishment. The concern about bifurcating this population is that youthful offenders' rights to due process might be violated, that significant mitigating circumstances around adolescent development and related problems may not be reviewed prior to transfer, and that public policy goals of increased public safety and youthful offender accountability are not met. There is little evidence that these state transfer laws have reduced arrest or crime rates or recidivism. In fact, transferred youthful offenders appear more likely to reoffend after release from an adult jail or prison (Fagan, 2008; Marrus & Rosenberg, 2005; Redding, 2010). For these and other reasons, from 2011 to 2015, 14 states limited their transfer and waiver criteria or focused more on offender risk potential, and 30 states now prohibit transfer for first-time misdemeanor offenders. Also, 12 states have expanded the use of reverse transfer, allowing the movement of a youthful offender case from the adult system back to the juvenile court (Campaign for Youth Justice, 2017; MacArthur Foundation, 2015).

Adult Imprisonment

Imprisonment of youthful offenders with adult offenders attempts to address several public policy goals, including community safety, personal retribution, and discouragement of reoffending. Unfortunately, this last goal is most often not met. Recidivism is very high, with a recent survey of more than 80% of the states, representing almost 90% of all released state inmates, finding that 44% of inmates were returned to prison within three years and youthful offender recidivism rates to adult prisons even higher. Such high recidivism rates to adult incarceration facilities have been found across many jurisdictions and have remained fairly stable over the past two decades (Nellis, 2016; Pew Center on the States, 2011; Trulson et al., 2011). In one study of prisons in 30 states from 2005 to 2010 (see Figure 7.4), higher recidivism rates were found when following released prisoners longer than three years: 68% of the 404,638 released prisoners were arrested within three years of release and 77% were arrested within five years of release, resulting in 55% being returned to prison (Durose, Cooper, & Snyder, 2014).

There are also problems within the adult incarceration facilities. Over the past two decades, as the punitive approach expanded the number of adult jails and prisons, many education or rehabilitative programs were eliminated. Jails and prisons are also violent and traumatizing

Complaint: First document filed with the court (actually with the County Clerk or Clerk of the Court) by a person or entity claiming legal rights against another. The party filing the complaint is usually called the "plaintiff" and the party against whom the complaint is filed is called the "defendant."

Recidivism: Repeating of criminal behavior, including offending, detention, or incarceration placement.

(a) Automatic Transfer Laws Proliferated in the Decades After 1970 as Did (b) Prosecutorial Discretion Laws

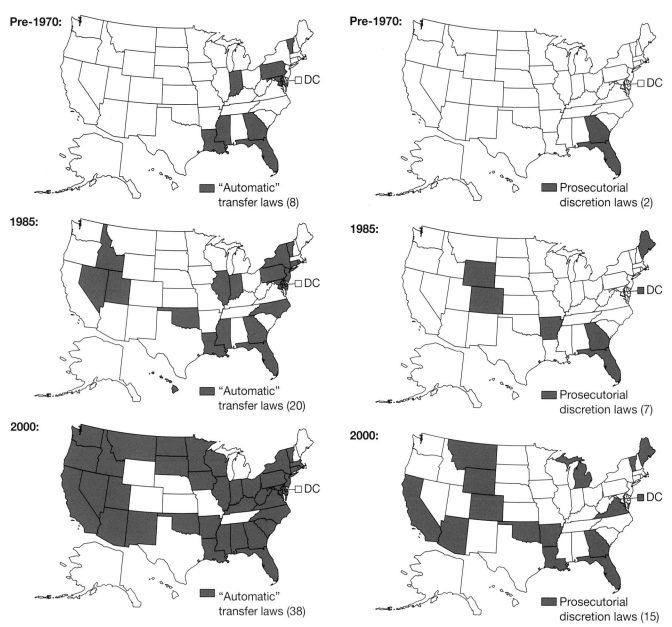

Source: Griffin, Addie, Adams, & Firestine (2011). *Trying juveniles as adults: An analysis of state transfer laws and reporting.* OJJDP, Office of Justice Programs, U.S. Department of Justice, Washington DC.

places for most inmates, even for adult inmates, with high levels of physical and sexual assaults and suicide attempts. Difficulties encountered while incarcerated may impose new learned behaviors, increasing antisocial activities. In addition, the racial and ethnic disparities problem found within juvenile detention and incarceration facilities is also profound in adult incarceration facilities. Minorities are significantly overrepresented in jails and prisons, up to three times the number than might be expected from their community populations (Golinelli & Minton, 2014; Petteruti & Walsh, 2008; Wolff, Blitz, Shi, Siegel, & Bachman, 2007).

Ex-prisoners face significant and substantial barriers to reintegration and successful **re-entry** to their communities after release from adult incarceration facilities. Incarceration may perpetuate criminal activities because of the socioeconomic harm caused by the imprisonment

Re-Entry: Process of returning from an incarceration facility back to a home community.

Recidivism of Prisoners Released in 30 States in 2005

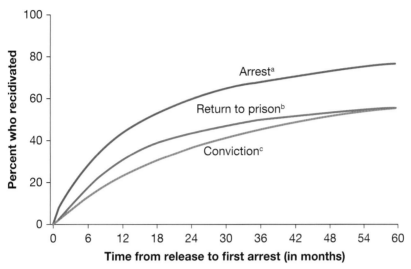

Source: Durose, Cooper, & Snyder (2014). *Recidivism of prisoners released in 30 states in 2005: Patterns from 2005 to 2010.* Bureau of Justice Statistics, Office of Justice Programs, U.S. Department of Justice.

on offenders, their families, and communities. This socioeconomic harm is seen in that employment is necessary for the ex-prisoners to successfully re-enter into the community, yet there is a mismatch within the communities to which the offenders return between employment opportunities and the ex-prisoners' vocational skill set. There are not typically enough low-skill jobs in the communities where the ex-prisoners return, leaving few if any alternatives to crime or black market economies (Bellair & Kowalski, 2011; Hirschfield & Piquero, 2010; The Annie E. Casey Foundation, 2016).

Some of these barriers explain the significant risk for and high levels of homelessness among ex-offenders released from jails and prisons. Although the data are not complete, some city's ex-offender populations have a 30% to 50% rate of experiencing homelessness within one year of release from the prisons (National Healthcare for the Homeless Council, 2012). Beyond work and employment difficulties, other well-established risks impact ex-prisoners' likelihood of reoffending and recidivism, including being a younger adult offender, male, and single; having low educational attainment and/or school failure; having an increased number of convictions; and having an earlier age of onset for offending behaviors (Dodge, Dishion, & Landsford, 2006; Loeber & Farrington, 2008; Piquero, Farrington, & Blumstein, 2003; Uggen, 2000).

CASE STUDY

MAYRA (SERVING A LIFE SENTENCE IN A WOMEN'S PRISON)

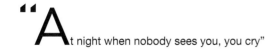

"**A**t night when nobody sees you, you cry"

Were you ever into school?

I dropped out of school when I was 13, seventh grade. Because my family didn't have enough money and the rest of the girls, I used to see them every day with different

kinds of clothes. I used to be with the same clothes almost every day you know. It used to hurt me seeing them have everything. So that's when I dropped out.

Did your parents try to discipline you?

I had a lot of discipline, 'cuz my dad is coming from Mexico. You know the whips for the horses, he would hit us with those. With anything he could find he hit us with until my back would be bloody. When I was in Mexico, he hang me from a tree and hang me there for one hour 'cuz I think I stole a candy. He was abusive to my mother. My dad used to leave black eyes on her, and when the cops came and she would cover it with her hair. That's one thing, it didn't work. 'Cuz that makes you angrier. After he used to hit me or whip me, he would tell me don't cry, why you crying, I'm gonna hit you harder, I ain't hitting you hard. I had to hold it in, I couldn't cry because he'd hit me more. So I had to hold my tears in and it built up you know.

What do you think your parents could have done that would have helped?

I would have liked for my mother when my dad was hitting me to tell him something. My dad hitting me and she wouldn't do nothing. I would like for my mom to stick up for me. If I did something wrong instead of hitting me, it would be better if they would have told me that's wrong.

What was it like when you first came to Juvenile Hall?

The first time when I got arrested my friend told me, they're gonna ask you where you're from, they're gonna rape you. So get in there and put a front and start walking like you're crazy. So I was walking like this (she swaggers with her arms raised to her chest). When I first came all the girls started laughing at me and one said, what are you doing? I said I don't know, I'm scared. And she said, it shows.

How does it feel to lose your freedom?

It hurts. It hurts being here 'cuz every time they see their mother on Sunday, they see them cry and that's what breaks your heart in here. You miss your family. You don't want people to see you cry so at night when nobody sees you, you cry.

What do you need to help you get through this?

I need my mother. I need when I go to sleep to have her next to me and tell me everything's gonna be okay. I need my son. I was pregnant here and I had him here. He's six months old. His name is James.

How are you preparing for adult prison?

I'm kind of scared. Just the thought of being with all those old people. I'm not prepared. I'm just scared. Rapes, guards, getting raped by women. I'm not ready, I'm scared. If I do go over there, I have a good friend. But I'm still not ready, I don't think I'll ever be ready. But if I have to go, I have to go. (Williams, 2018, Section "At night when nobody sees you cry, you cry")

1. What can Mayra expect while being incarcerated?

2. Are her fears justified?

3. Why do you think she ended up imprisoned for life?

Source: © 1998–2013. L.A. Youth, a publication of Youth News Service (YNS). http://www.layouth.com/behind-bars-four-teens-in-prison-tell-their-stories/

CHAPTER REVIEW

CHAPTER SUMMARY

This chapter examined the pathways youthful offenders take to harsh discipline outcomes. The most difficult and harmful being juvenile and adult criminal justice incarceration, placements that preclude successful re-entry for many of the young people returning back to their community. These punishment pathways make it difficult for youthful offenders to divert from poor outcomes and are reinforced by zero tolerance-focused school policies and punishment-focused juvenile courts. In particular, the risk for traumatic experiences and suicide greatly increase the further a young person penetrates the juvenile justice system, and in particular when incarcerated. Rehabilitative juvenile courts are still not the norm across the country, although the trend is shifting away from a "tough-on-crime" approach.

KEY TERMS

adolescence **145**

adolescence-limited offenders **147**

alternative education program **149**

complaint **159**

detention center **151**

life-course-persistent offenders **147**

psychosocial maturity **147**

recidivism **159**

re-entry **160**

solitary confinement **155**

The Civil Rights Project in Los Angeles **149**

transfer laws **158**

truancy **152**

unformed character development **146**

violations of a court order **152**

DISCUSSION QUESTIONS

1. What options do police have when responding to youthful offending behaviors? If you were a police officer, what approach would you take to your daily work with adolescents?

2. How do students get referred from schools to the juvenile courts? Why does this happen?

3. How do school exclusion policies lead to juvenile court involvement?

4. What is the impact of incarceration on youthful offenders? When are detention centers and incarceration facilities best used within the juvenile justice system?

5. How are adolescents developmentally different from young adults? What does this mean for police officers, probation officers, and juvenile court judges?

6. Do you think the juvenile justice system should account for adolescent developmental differences? Justify your position. If you believe so, how might this be accomplished?

7. Who is most at risk for dropping out of school, and why is this the case?

8. Is solitary confinement an effective option for juvenile detention and incarceration facilities? Justify your position.

9. What are the risk factors for suicide? What does it mean if you have experienced some of these risk factors?

10. Why does suicide risk increase when young people are detained or incarcerated? Which groups of youthful offenders are most at risk for suicide attempts and/or completions?

11. What are the ways youthful offenders can be transferred to adult criminal courts? Does transferring youthful offenders out of juvenile courts meet policy agendas? Justify your position through empirical evidence.

12. What is re-entry, and what challenges does it pose for youthful offenders leaving juvenile or adult prisons? How would you as a juvenile court judge or probation officer handle the re-entry of a youthful offender from a 60-day placement in the local detention center facility?

---

https://edge.sagepub.com/mallett

**SAGE** edge™ **Sharpen your skills with SAGE edge!**

SAGE edge for students provides a personalized approach to help you accomplish your coursework in an easy-to-use learning environment. You'll find mobile-friendly eFlashcards and quizzes, as well as videos, web resources, and links to SAGE journal articles to support and expand on the concepts presented in this chapter.

CHAPTER 8

SCHOOL VIOLENCE, ZERO TOLERANCE, AND SCHOOL EXCLUSION

▲ Some students have troubles in their classrooms and schools. Why do you think this happens?

©iStockphoto.com/DGLimages

INTRODUCTION

This chapter reviews some of the history of establishing public schools through compulsory attendance laws for children, as well as the use of school discipline over time. The primary focus is on more recent times whereby the public schools across the country followed the juvenile justice system's "tough-on-crime" pathway since the 1990s. Although there was crossover impact between juvenile justice and school policies, the punitive movements were both independent and interdependent. The increased use of zero tolerance policies and police (safety resource officers) in the schools has exponentially increased school-based arrests and referrals to the juvenile courts. In the school systems, and particularly in those that are overburdened and underfinanced, many students have also been increasingly suspended and expelled due to criminalizing both typical adolescent developmental behaviors as well as low-level type misdemeanors: acting out in class, truancy, fighting, and other similar offenses. Despite impacting many, these changes disproportionately ensnared a smaller group of at-risk and already disadvantaged students (and

their families), including certain minorities, those with special education disabilities, and those who identify as lesbian, gay, bisexual, or transgender (LGBT).

COMPULSORY EDUCATION AND STUDENT DISCIPLINE

Schools and education were not part of most children's lives during the nation's early colonial and postcolonial years as families worked together at trades or farming. Nevertheless, as children's rights were recognized in the mid-to-late 1800s and as adolescence was identified as distinctly developmental, and at times troubling, stage, schools became increasingly responsible for not just the education of students but for managing and disciplining them as well.

Formal Schooling and Compulsory Education

During the colonial and early years of the United States, schools were voluntary enterprises. Most children did not attend school for they were needed to work in the trades or on the farm to support the family and the community. The wealthier class, though, did establish numerous private schools throughout the states (primarily in the northeastern part of the country), and these schools outnumbered public schools until the mid-1800s. As the century progressed, and in particular during the later 1800s, however, several factors made schooling for all children more important: the Industrial Revolution and its accompanying urbanization of the population, a significant wave of immigration to the cities, and child labor laws. This influx of immigrants and their children, fears of families being unable to live in urban poverty, and concerns about these children being sent to factories to work were significant influences driving a wave of compulsory education. By 1890, 27 states had passed compulsory public school attendance laws for most children younger than 14 years of age; by 1918, all 48 states had such laws enacted (Graham, 1974). This time period also represented an expanded and more centralized role for the federal government, including citizen rights for more Americans, a military draft, and a federal taxation system. This movement toward increased federal involvement in what were traditionally state and

▲ Early progressive schools introduced standard curriculum and grade levels for students. How do you think discipline problems were handled during this era?

local issues included schooling, with the establishment of a cabinet-level, and later a bureau- and a department-level, education agency (Perkinson, 1968).

Public schools introduced several novel features as they expanded across the country: placing children in grade levels based on age, using examinations to test skill and knowledge development, and using uniform courses of study that included mathematics, grammar, and spelling, among other topics. As student enrollment exponentially grew, schools were concerned about control and were structured through strict organization, regularity, and discipline in preparation for students' training for vocational and indus- trial trades. In addition, a progressive era of education dominated reforms from the 1900s to the 1930s and provided additional educational opportunities for students, expansion of the curriculum that traditionally focused only on trades and vocations, the use of developmental textbooks and other instructional material, and the improvement of teacher education and school designs.

As school populations continued to expand and diversify, there were worries about school and student management. These concerns included children of immigrants and their ability to assimilate, middle-class families and worries about their own children, and the impact of more diverse urban neighborhoods on children's character development. These issues influenced reform and the establishment of the "child savers" movement. The child-saving movement, as discussed earlier in the book, focused on an underclass of delinquent children brought into the emerging juvenile justice system and juvenile courts. Nevertheless, the worries were also across many middle-class families that were under increasing stressors as fathers spent most hours of the day at factories or offices working and, often, much supervision of the children shifted to the schools. As children spent more hours at school, the local districts developed management and control protocols to handle the growing student populations (Katz, 1975; Urban & Wagoner, 2009).

School Discipline Before Zero Tolerance

Schools have not historically been mired in the discipline dispensation techniques in use today, but there was always a focus on control of students, particularly those difficult or troubling to manage. This balance among education, discipline, and school management has had chal- lenges over time. As schools developed in the northeastern part of the country during the later parts of the 1800s, their discipline organization and operations were influenced by the only similar institution being used as a human service institution—the psychiatric asylum. In other words, the schools developed with a focus on control and custodial care, as well as to prepare future workers for U.S. industries. These early schools also were called on to assume greater responsibil- ity for rearing certain at-risk groups: urban child populations, neglected children, and immigrant children. With the growth in school enrollments due to changing expectations that children attend and the influx of immigrant families during from the 1880s to 1920s, the schools were overrun with difficulties, leading to significant discipline protocols (Cremin, 1988; Insley, 2001). These protocols were uniform in nature and controlling in practice. A daily morning set of instructions recited by students describes the daily expectations of students quite well: "[S]tand in line, per- fectly motionless, bodies erect, knees and feet together, the tips of shoes touching the edge of a board in the floor" (Rice, 1893, p. 98).

School Management: Philosophy or framework that guides school policies on conduct and discipline.

Psychiatric Asylum: Hospital for mentally incompetent people; the use of the term asylum comes from the earlier 20th century.

Over the course of the 1900s, many school administrations incorporated corporal punishment including threats of discipline or harm, physical beatings, and isolation practices within classrooms and the school buildings. Many remnants of these discipline techniques were still used as regular classroom and school management practices into the 1960s and 1970s. Although as school populations again expanded significantly during this time period, violence among students increased, and corporal punishment became less acceptable and effective. Other techniques at student management and discipline were employed including school suspensions and expulsions of disruptive and difficult students. Because of legal challenges, however, in particular the *Goss v. Lopez* Supreme Court decision in 1975 (419 U.S. 565), which found due process violations in the suspension and expulsion of students without hearings, schools altered their policies to include in-school suspensions. In the *Goss* case, nine students at two high schools and one middle school in the Columbus Public School District were given ten-day suspensions for destroying school property and for disrupting the learning environment by their principals without any hearings or parent meetings, and Ohio law did not require them to do so.

▲ Student discipline begins in the classroom. What do you think most often leads to school suspensions or expulsions?

After this court decision, due process protocols were put in place across school districts, although in-school and out-of-school suspensions were increasingly used. These alternative in-school suspensions removed disruptive students from the classroom but kept them inside the school to complete their work. More inclusive and rehabilitative efforts were favored by most school administrators through the 1980s until the growth of mandatory disciplinary protocols and zero tolerance policies for disruptive students became the norm. Zero tolerance policies means that there are predetermined, and often severe, consequences for identified student transgressions or misbehaviors while on school grounds. These consequences are automatic, and there is little investigation as to any mitigating or historical reasons for the student problems (Hyman & McDowell, 1979; Jones, 1996).

SCHOOL DISCIPLINE IN THE ZERO TOLERANCE ERA

Policy makers do not set forth to harm children or adolescents in schools (or juvenile justice settings, for that matter). School personnel have the best interests of young people as a focus, trying to teach each student effectively, guide him or her accordingly, and reach academic and graduation goals. Nevertheless, almost all social policies have unintended consequences, as was the case with the policies that established a punitive regime within most public school systems since the mid-1990s (Marx, 1981). During this tough-on-crime juvenile justice era movement, schools were impacted by federal laws, state policies, and tragic school events that unduly moved the schools toward criminalizing student behaviors and, for some groups of students, their educational experience. These movements toward control and punishment in schools differed according to school size, location, and demographic makeup of the student body. In larger schools, however, more anti-violence and punitive policies were established; urban schools established the largest proportion of punitive policies; and anti-violence polices were practiced more frequently both in the southern and western states, in schools with larger minority student populations, and in schools with higher enrollments in free or reduced price lunch programs. Much of these disparate impacts and outcomes are still true today (Arum, 2003; Kupchik & Monahan, 2006; Muschert & Peguero, 2010).

The expansion of school anti-violence policies across school districts nationwide has created an environment of social control that is more prison-like in efforts to maintain safety. Historically, there have been eras when student school violence was perceived as problematic, including the 1960s and 1970s where safety concerns were often interrelated with civil rights

Corporal Punishment: Disciplinary action that is physical in nature and delivered by teachers or school administrators as punishment for some type of student misbehavior.

Goss v. Lopez: 1975 Supreme Court decision that found a public school must conduct a hearing before subjecting a student to suspension. Also, a suspension without a hearing was found to violate the Due Process Clause of the U.S. Constitution's Fourteenth Amendment.

Zero Tolerance Policies: School district policies that mandate predetermined consequences or punishments for specific offenses that are intended to be applied regardless of the seriousness of the behavior, mitigating circumstances, or situational context.

and school population shifts; this led to harsher impacts on minority students in school exclusionary policies (Children's Defense Fund, 1975). Nevertheless, the more recent shift toward discipline policies in the 1990s was exceptionally broader in the impact on schools and student populations (Hirschfield, 2008; Kang-Brown, Trone, Fratello, & Daftary-Kapur, 2013).

The 1980s and 1990s spawned fears and media reports of young people, often minorities, committing horrific crimes, gang violence, and concern for the emergence of the "juvenile super-predator" that were wholly disproportionate to the reality of youth violence. Although crime has decreased across the country since 1994 for youthful offenders, state and federal legislation was enacted throughout the 1990s that increased punitive outcomes for many adolescents (Griffin, 2008; Puzzanchera & Hockenberry, 2010; Walker, Spohn, & DeLone, 2012). These policy changes and perception problems set the stage for the movement toward control and discipline within the schools and, in particular, within urban schools. When this punitive paradigm was impacted by the fallout from school shooting incidents, however, movements toward school lockdowns and more security-focused environments progressed across the country (Cornell, 2006).

School Shootings

The 1999 Columbine High School Shooting in Colorado that resulted in several deaths significantly impacted the public nationwide. The breadth of the incident caused by two students—Dylan Klebold and Eric Harris—shocked the country with the deaths of 12 students and a teacher, and the wounding of 23 others, before Klebold and Harris both committed suicide. This remains one of the deadliest mass shootings in the United States and the deadliest high school shooting.

The Columbine High School incident was not the first school shooting of this era, but it was the most deadly of the tragedies at the time, had the greatest impact on public perceptions, was covered more extensively by the media, and reinforced and spurred on the security environment movement within schools. In the decade before the Columbine tragedy there were other school shooting incidents with far less media coverage. These included Bethel Regional High School in Alaska, Pearl High School in Mississippi, Health High School in Kentucky, Frontier Middle School in Washington, and Thurston High School in Oregon. Most of these shootings occurred in what many families considered to be "safe" school districts—white, suburban, and middle class, leading to the increased fear that these tragic incidents could happen anywhere. Although explanations of the killers' motivations were difficult to identify, a new brand of adolescent violence or predator was now feared at hand, a transition that also reinforced and reignited the idea of a juvenile super-predator, one that now could reside in poorer urban as well as in wealthier suburban schools (Fuentes, 2014; Hirschfield, 2010; Kupchik & Bracy, 2009). Despite being unfounded, media attention and public discourse greatly expanded the impact of the Columbine shootings, leading to widespread changes in security practices across many primary and most secondary schools (Muschert, 2009).

Nevertheless, as tragic as shoot shootings are, they are uncommon events across the nation's schools. Since 1992, from a school population of 49 million students, the number of children or adolescents killed by homicide on school grounds remains between 11 and 34 annually, with an additional one to ten students, depending on the year, who have committed suicide on school grounds. Similarly, violent victimizations, student drug use, and student-related delinquency activities on school grounds have low prevalence rates and have been declining since 2000. These trends are highlighted by the significantly larger risks that children and adolescents have of being victims of violent crime outside of school, in

▲ The drug free gun free zones were established by federal law in 1994. What do you think was the outcome of this new policy?

philipus/Alamy Stock Photo

Columbine High School Shooting: 1999 school shooting at Columbine High School in Colorado that remains one of the deadliest mass shootings in the United States and the deadliest high school shooting.

their neighborhoods, and for some, in their homes (Justice Policy Institute, 2011; U.S. Department of Education, 2014b, 2014e).

Although school shooting incidents are tragic, cause the deaths of innocents, and strike fear in parents, schools remain the safest place for children and adolescents. With very low rates of violent crime that occur on school grounds, and the positive impact that a nurturing and well-structured school setting provides, most students have opportunities that should allow for strong learning outcomes and social supports. When positive structures and supports are lacking or when security measures and distrust increase throughout schools, however, many students

▲ The Columbine High School shootings galvanized the nation around school safety concerns. How do you remember this 1999 tragedy?

are impacted negatively, including poorer academic outcomes, strained social bonds with teachers and administrators, and increased risk for school failure (Carter, Fine, & Russell, 2014; Robers, Zhang, & Truman, 2012; Sojoyner, 2014; Steeves & Marx, 2014).

School Environments

The expanded punitive environment within the juvenile courts, fears of school shootings and violence, the crack cocaine epidemic that had a devastating impact on many poor communities, and worries about adolescent gangs were all factors that led Congress to enact the Gun-Free Schools Act in 1994 (20 U.S.C. § 8921(b)). This federal legislation promoted zero tolerance policies in school districts. Even though the law itself only made states' receipt of federal funding for K–12 education contingent on imposing a one-year expulsion for a student found in possession of a gun on school grounds and a mandatory referral to the juvenile or adult justice system, the march toward school security and immediate discipline had begun. Within two years of the law's passage, all states had enacted compliant legislation (Brady, 2002).

Subsequent amendments to the Gun-Free Schools Act and state laws have broadened the focus from firearms to other types of weapons, as well as to nonweapon possession problems—use of alcohol/drugs and tobacco, fighting, and disobedience of school rules. Since 1996, the percentage of schools that subsequently enacted strict and punitive discipline policies has never fallen below 75%, with some estimates as high as 90%. These policies established mandatory suspensions or expulsions for an expansive range of student incidents, including violent behavior, fighting, assault, harassment, indecent exposure, vandalism, and destruction of school property, among others. Nevertheless, these policies also included nonviolent student behaviors, such as verbal harassment, disobedience, obscene language, and truancy (Birkland & Lawrence, 2009; Kupchik & Monahan, 2006; Muschert & Peguero, 2010; U.S. Department of Education, 2013c).

In many schools these policies are supported and reinforced through the use of security guards, metal detectors, police officers working in the building, and surveillance by cameras. Security practices are not new to schools, but they have changed over time from a focus on property crime and thefts, to a concern about individual victimizations, toward today's broad security operations. During the rise of zero tolerance policies, the use of security guards, police officers on campus, and cameras significantly rose, with higher utilization rates in urban, inner-city areas. Today's school security measures have become common: Nearly 6% of all public schools use random use metal detectors (10% for middle schools, 13% for high schools, although disproportionately impacting black students), impacting 11% of all students; mandatory walkthrough metal detectors are used in 2% of middle schools and 4% of high schools; 36% of schools use security cameras (42% of middle schools and 64% of high schools), impacting

Crack Cocaine Epidemic: 1980s surge in the use of crack cocaine nationwide, but with the greatest impact in urban environments. This lead to increases in large city crime rates and influenced the shift toward a "tough-on-crime" approach.

SANDY HOOK ELEMENTARY SHOOTINGS

After the 2012 Sandy Hook Elementary School Shooting in Connecticut where Adam Lanza shot and killed 20 children and 6 adult staff members, the national reaction was an outpouring of grief and increased school security measures. In 2013, and because of this horrific shooting event, the Texas legislature passed a law requiring all schools to annually conduct at least one evacuation drill, one lockdown, and one shelter-in-place exercise. The new law also created a school safety task force that has studied emergency operations and makes recommendations for further security planning. The Austin, Texas, city school district went further by installing more safety measures, including security cameras (able to be viewed by police and school administrators), door buzzers, panic buttons across all schools, and hired six more school police officers for the elementary schools.

I. **What do you think is the right balance of security and safety for schools?**

2. **How did the Sandy Hook Elementary School shootings impact you?**

58% of all students; and 42% of schools employ security guards, impacting almost 65% of all students. These control measures often, and in particular in low-income and inner-city public schools, create prison-like environments (Addington, 2014; Lawrence, 2007; Ruddy et al., 2010; U.S. Department of Education, 2014b).

These environments, even when designed in security-friendly architecture typically found in newer suburban schools, have unintended consequences for many students by making learning more difficult because of the increased monitoring. In lower income neighborhoods with more poorly funded schools, the impact of these security personnel and measures can be harsher on students. These secure environments, for any student, can produce negative reactions, fears, or worries about their school; however, in some schools, students may feel resentment and negative feelings toward the surveillance and oversight itself. In fact, schools with more disruptions and disorder within the buildings and classrooms use more security measures, but as will be an emergent theme, it may be these security measures themselves that are contributing to the disorder (Addington, 2009; Kupchik, 2010; Mayer & Leone, 1999; Sipe, 2012). These reactions to the safety measures may interfere with an effective learning environment, even though additional and ongoing evaluation of these environments is necessary to determine whether an improved balance between the policy objectives and student learning is possible (Addington, 2014; Bracy, 2010).

Zero Tolerance Policies

The term "zero tolerance" was nationally recognized and used during the Reagan Administration's war on drugs in the mid-1980s, referencing both a violent drug trade occurring across many U.S. cities and foreign policy affairs in drug-importing countries (Fuentes, 2014). This war on drugs initiative and policy focus was imported to the public schools in 1986 with the passage of the Drug Free Schools Act, requiring a strict prohibition against drugs or alcohol possession (20 U.S.C. § 3181(a)).

In 1989, school districts in Louisville, Kentucky, and Orange County, California, enacted zero tolerance policies calling for student expulsion for drug- and gang-related activity, as well as in Yonkers, New York, for school disruption. These strict response discipline and punishment ideas became popular in education policy-making circles as well as with the general public, and by 1993, many schools began to use the term "zero tolerance" as a philosophy that mandated the application of severe predetermined consequences for unsafe or unacceptable student behaviors (American Psychological Association, 2008). In conjunction with the Gun-Free Schools Act of 1994 and its weapons prohibitions, the foundation was set for zero tolerance policies to become the norm in school management and discipline dispensation.

Sandy Hook Elementary School Shooting:
2012 school shooting in Connecticut where Adam Lanza shot and killed 20 children and 6 adult staff members. This remains the most deadly school shooting in U.S. history.

These policies have often eliminated the consideration by school administrators for why events occur, what motivated the students' involvement, and any mitigating history that impacted the event and led to the involvement of school or law enforcement personnel and, for some students, removal from school. Many of these school discipline protocols are for first-time offenses and lead to suspension or expulsion of students (Kang-Brown et al., 2013). Although these procedural outcomes are common across many school districts, no single definition of zero tolerance exists across the country's schools. Nevertheless, there are common goals of zero tolerance policies, including maintaining a safe school climate for students and teachers that is conducive to learning, predicated on the philosophy that removing students who engage in illicit or disruptive behavior will both deter others and improve the education climate (Skiba et al., 2006):

▲ Zero tolerance policies have been adopted by school districts since the 1990s. How were you or your friends impacted by these increased school safety and discipline measures?

> Zero tolerance is a philosophy or policy that mandates the application of predetermined consequences, most often severe and punitive in nature, that are intended to be applied regardless of the apparent severity of the behavior, mitigating circumstances, or situational context. Such an approach is intended to deter future transgressions, by sending a message that no form of a given unacceptable behavior will be tolerated under any circumstances. (Skiba et al., 2006, p. 26)

These promoted school discipline policy outcomes are far from achieved, and the policies themselves look to be part of the problem. These policies were put in place often through state laws, for many states passed legislation during the 1990s and 2000s mandating zero tolerance policies in their school districts. For example, from 1999 to 2017, Ohio law directed the school districts to adopt a zero tolerance policy "for violent, disruptive, or inappropriate behavior and excessive truancy, and establish strategies to address such behavior that range from prevention to intervention" (Ohio Revised Code 3313.534(A)). This law had supported harsh discipline rules that led to large numbers of students being removed from Ohio schools through suspensions, expulsions, or alternative placements for inappropriate behaviors and truancy. Ohio laws and Colorado laws had taken a punitive approach to school discipline, although they have changed more recently toward a more inclusive approach.

Strict state laws and policies were established across most states, making school discipline a one-size-fits-all approach across most school districts, regardless of the number of student troubles or misbehaviors or history to the events. Thus, school district policies require adherence to strict guidelines, do not review mitigating circumstances, and are automatic responses to students' infractions. For example, the 2009–2010 School District of Philadelphia's Student Code of Conduct stated its purpose was to "support the creation of a safe learning environment for all members of the school community, to provide clear and explicit expectations for social behaviors … and to describe explicit methods of corrective instruction and consequences for responding to behavior offenses" (The School District of Philadelphia, 2010, p. 2). This School Code of Conduct, a document that spells out the rules and consequences for students and families, includes what is typical of zero tolerance policies: the option of school

School Code of Conduct: Document that spells out school policies, rules, and consequences for students and families.

OHIO AND COLORADO TRUANCY LAWS

From the 2002–2003 to the 2017–2018 school years, Ohio law defined habitual truants as students who missed five or more consecutive school days, seven or more days in one month, or 12 or more days in a year. Chronic truants were students who missed seven or more consecutive school days, ten or more days in one month, or 15 or more days in a year. Under this Ohio law (ORC § 3321.191), when a student was truant from school, education officials *may* have taken the following steps: (a) require the parent/guardian attend an educational program to encourage parental involvement in compelling the attendance of the child at school; (b) shall "examine into" any truancy within the district and warn the child, if found truant, and the child's parent, guardian, or other person having care of the child, in writing, of the legal consequences of truancy and require the youth's attendance (if the child did not attend, the superintendent *may* direct the parent or other person to attend the educational program and may file a complaint in the juvenile court); or (c) for habitual truants, the board of education of the school district or the governing board of the educational service center *must* do either or both of the following: Take actions described in Ohio law, or file a complaint in the juvenile court. For chronic truants, the complaint was to be filed in juvenile court. Under this law, the juvenile court could have intervened by requiring the child to attend an alternative school, participation in an academic or community service program, drug or alcohol treatment, medical or mental health counseling, or any other order. The court was also allowed to start criminal charges against the parents. In addition, Ohio's truancy law required some offenses, those defined as "chronic" or "double habitual" truants, to be considered adjudicated delinquent with the local juvenile court automatically. Because this law led to a large number of truant students entering the juvenile justice system, the Ohio legislature made the following changes (House Bill 480) for the 2017–2018 school year: a model school discipline code focused on prevention and alternatives to suspension and expulsion for all school districts; after parental/guardian notification, the school may provide truancy interventions for students who miss school; for ongoing truancy, an absence intervention team is put in place for 60 days to help address the truancy problems, and if this is unsuccessful, then a referral may be made to the juvenile court for a diversion program (not adjudication); formal filing with the court is the last option; and

does not allow school suspension or expulsion for students whose only infraction is missing school.

Colorado had a similar strict truancy law to Ohio's earlier law but amended their regulations to help decrease the number of students being referred to the juvenile courts. In Colorado's initial laws (CRC § 22–33–107(3)), no filing of truancy was to happen with a juvenile court until a coordination and treatment plan was attempted by school personnel, parents, and community service providers. This assessment stage, though, was not mandated, only encouraged, and many truant students were referred for juvenile court supervision, adjudication, and for some, incarceration. A significant move toward rehabilitation of students dealing with truancy problems was accomplished in the 2013 Colorado state legislature through the addition of procedural requirements for school districts to demonstrate interventions attempted before resorting to juvenile court filings. Since 2014, to establish a petition to compel attendance, a school district must submit the following evidence to the juvenile court: (a) the student's attendance record before and after the point at which the student was identified as habitually truant; (b) whether the student was identified as chronically absent and, if so, the strategies the school district used to improve the student's attendance; (c) the interventions and strategies used to improve the student's attendance before school or school district personnel created the student's plan; and (d) the student's plan and the efforts of the student, the student's parent, and school or school district personnel to implement the plan (CRC § 22–33–107(3)(4p)). This change greatly reduces the chance that a student will be referred to juvenile court for truancy problems. Even in a state that has addressed a strict approach to truancy, current Colorado law still allows a detention center placement for up to five days for chronically truant students after these intervention efforts have been tried and failed.

. . . .

1. **Why do you think these two states, as well as numerous others, have modified their truancy laws?**

2. **Do you think truancy should be against the law (as a status offense); why or why not?**

removal for minor infractions or school disruptions. The following could lead to a one- to three-day suspension from school in the Philadelphia School District if the student does not respond to certain in-school interventions: failure to follow classroom rules; disrespect for authority figures; using profane/obscene language or gestures; and public display of affection; among others. It is easy to see how misbehaving and related student actions, that prior to zero tolerance policies were handled inside the classroom or principal's office, can lead to school removal:

In the words of one student, Sadiq, these truancy/tardy policies or rules had little to no impact. "I always came to school with a lot of stuff on my mind. I came to school at times where we had no electricity for weeks. I did not care about talking to any of my teachers about it, because I really didn't have a connection to any of them. There were times when I would have to wake up early and iron my clothes with a large pot (by putting hot water in it and running it across my clothes) so that I wouldn't have to wear wrinkled clothes to school. I was embarrassed about my circumstances and didn't want anyone to know what I was going through." For Sadiq, being disciplined for coming to school late under such circumstances made him feel as though the school did not really care about him or what he was facing, which eventually led to him becoming disengaged from the learning environment at school. (Levy-Pounds, 2014, p. 138)

These types of strict zero tolerance policies have a disproportionate impact on schools with more minority students and schools located in poorer communities. In particular, inflexible punitive policies have greater impact on inner-city and low-income school districts. Despite past efforts at school integration, re-segregation of public schools has been occurring across many districts, further separating students and neighborhoods by race and class (Addington, 2014; Fry & Taylor, 2012; Orfield, 2009). Students in low-income school districts have fewer educational opportunities, are less likely to enroll in four-year colleges, and are more likely to attend schools where most of the population includes students of color. Nationwide, the average black student attends a school where nearly two of every three classmates are low-income, double the comparative white student rate. School districts that are disproportionately poor and minority are more likely to use security measures and to have police officers in their schools (Children's Defense Fund, 2012; Hirschfield, 2010; Orfield, Kucsera, & Siegel-Hawley, 2012).

No Child Left Behind Act

There is legitimate concern that the enactment of the No Child Left Behind (NCLB) Law in 2001, juxtaposed with zero tolerance policies, unintentionally, at least in the initial rollout of the law, exacerbated the school discipline problems. The NCLB law set standards across the nation's public schools that required all students to be tested across primary and secondary grades. School districts were required to take disciplinary and administrative actions based on these testing results. The NCLB law was implemented to hold schools accountable for student performance, with concerns for students who traditionally have performed poorly—those with special education disabilities, certain minority groups, students living in lower socio-economic class, and those whose first language is not English (Fuentes, 2014; Nolan, 2011). Nevertheless, the prescriptive NCLB policies that focused on those schools with low standardized proficiency scores narrowed educational instruction, thus, teaching to the test. For some, this encouraged the removal of low-performing students by referring these students to alternative schools and General Education Development (GED) programs, eliminating them from attendance roles, or using zero tolerance policies to expand school removals through suspensions and expulsions. Once students are removed from school, it is many times more difficult to overcome the barriers to re-entry and successful high school completion. One ongoing difficulty was that the NCLB Act failed to provide the necessary funding to address the resource disparities among the nation's schools. It did, however, provide funding for school-based law enforcement officers and encouraged the officers' involvement in problem or disruptive student discipline (Advancement Project et al., 2011; Klehr, 2009; Ryan, 2004). Although the NCLB law and requirements ended in 2015, replaced by the federal Every Student Succeeds Act, its impact was significant in direction, and seemingly harming, many school environments and students.

No Child Left Behind (NCLB) Law: 2001 law (expired in 2016) that set standards across the nation's public schools that required all students to be tested across certain academic areas in all primary and secondary grades. School districts were required to take disciplinary and administrative actions based on results.

School Police (Resource) Officers

Reinforcing the shifts toward discipline, the Safe Schools Act of 1994 (and the 1998 Amendment Act) promoted and funded partnerships for in-school police forces, also known as **school resource officers**, in primary and secondary schools (42 U.S.C. § 3711). These Acts were initiated by the Clinton Administration's reaction to the school shootings and killings at Westside Middle School in Arkansas and had two policy objectives: to help build school and police force collaborations and to improve school and student safety (Rich-Shea & Fox, 2014). Before these Acts, the following was unlikely to have occurred:

> A student was asked (by a school staff member) to remove his 'do-rag" upon arriving at school prior to the start of the day. He resisted at first, but then removed it (unhappily). He then cussed out the assistant principal, who wrote him a referral for doing so. Then he was sent to the office, and he wanted to leave, but Mr. Majors (another assistant principal) stood in his way and wouldn't let him leave. The student tried to push Mr. Majors aside, and as a result he was handcuffed by the school resource office and arrested for pushing a staff member. (Kupchik, 2010, p. 79)

> In a hallway between classes, a police officer asked a student to stop, believing that an administrator was looking for her. She ignored him and started to walk up a flight of stairs. He pursued her, at which point she allegedly swore, refused to go with him, stated that she was going to her next class, and continued to walk away. The officer attempted to grab her by the arms so that he could handcuff her. She tried to pull away, striking him in the face. They continued to struggle and stumbled backwards down the stairs into a crowd of students. The student was charged with assault and battery on a police officer, disturbing a lawful assembly and resisting arrest. (Dahlberg, 2012, p. 24)

> A boy was found with a cell phone in his book bag in violation of school policy. School administrators confiscated the phone and told the student that his mother would have to come to the school to retrieve it. The student then started "walking around the office" and stated that he needed his "f-cking phone." The student was warned that he was becoming disruptive, but continued to swear and state that he needed his phone. He was advised that he was going to be arrested, stated that he did not care, and was then handcuffed and told to sit down. He was charged with disturbing a lawful assembly. (Dahlberg, 2012, p. 24)

With the expansion of police officers in schools and subsequent amendments and funding from federal laws, police in schools became the norm, with nearly $1 billion spent from 1994 to 2012 and employing more than 17,000 officers annually. Forty-two percent of high schools across the country have school resource officers (with 51% of high schools that have a majority black or Hispanic student population) as well as 24% elementary schools. For example, the Los Angeles Unified School District employs 126 officers in most high schools and middle schools. These school resource officers' responsibilities vary, although most of their day (more than 50%) is dedicated to law enforcement activities, followed by advising, mentoring, and teaching students (Morgan, Salomon, Plotkin, & Cohen, 2014; Petteruti, 2011; U.S. Department of Education, 2016b).

School resource officers are well thought of by stakeholders and generally provide a feeling of safety for many inside the school leading to some increases in crime reporting by students and some school personnel and students reporting decreases in fighting and bullying. In addition, school police have duties beyond just security issues, including advisement and mentoring of students, curriculum instruction such as **A.L.I.C.E. (Action, Lockdown, Inform, Counter, Evacuate)** training (proactive training for active shooter incidents), and often are a consistent presence for students and faculty within the school buildings (Bazemore, Leip, & Stinchcomb, 2004; Martinez, 2009).

School Resource Officers: Police officers who work on school campuses.

A.L.I.C.E. (Action, Lockdown, Inform, Counter, Evacuate): Series of trainings for students on what to do during an active shooter situation.

Nevertheless, the impact that police officers in schools have in reinforcing zero tolerance policies and the utilization of more formal methods of discipline is a concern in reinforcing the school-to-prison pipeline. The pipeline is often a term used to describe the increasing connections and referrals from student school problems to the juvenile courts—for example, school-based arrests and reporting truant students to the courts. The presence of police officers has increased student arrests on school grounds between 300% and 500% annually since 2000, most of the time for nonserious offenses—unruly behaviors, disobedience, or status offenses. This may in part be because most officers are trained to address criminal adult behavior, and have a limited understanding of issues related to child development, education, or adolescent psychology. Many school-based officers find that they have to unlearn many past trainings and experiences to work effectively in middle and high schools. Some critics argue that the only schools that need a police officer present are those with serious and persistent crime problems (Kupchik, 2010; Na & Gottfredson, 2011; Thurae & Wald, 2010). Here is an example from Wauwatosa, Wisconsin:

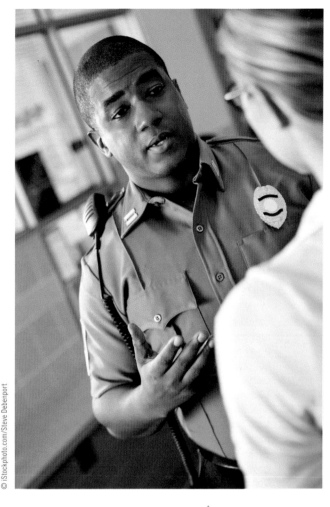

A 14-year-old girl was arrested in Wauwatosa, Wisconsin, after refusing to stop texting on her cell phone in class. A school resource officer's report says the student refused to stop texting during class after a teacher told her to stop and the student told the resource officer she didn't have a phone after she was pulled out of the classroom. She continued denying she had a phone, forcing the resource officer to return to the classroom twice and find other students who saw her with it, according to the report. The male school resource officer called for a female officer to conduct a search, the report says. The student laughed as the female officer explained that she found the Samsung phone in the student's clothes, hidden near her buttocks. The officer notes that the student "is known to me and the administrations based on prior negative contacts." The officer gave the student a $298 ticket for disorderly conduct and kept her Samsung phone. A police spokesperson said that she was arrested more for her behavior than for the texting; "all she had to do was put the phone away and that would have been that." After the arrest, the student was suspended (from school) for a week. (McCurdy, 2014, pp. 93–94)

▲ Police officers in schools have become the norm across many school districts. What do you think the impact is for having police in school?

There has been limited input from the courts on zero tolerance policies, its impact on students' due process and other Constitutional rights, or disparate outcomes of these punitive school policies. Nevertheless, in 2011, the U.S. Supreme Court (in *J.D.B. v. North Carolina;* 131 S.Ct. 2394) decided a case involving a middle school student and school resource officers. The student was called out of his eighth grade class and questioned for more than 30 minutes by two law enforcement officers and two school administrators without contacting his legal guardian, his grandfather. The investigation issue was questioning about some home break-ins, although the student (J.D.B.) did not receive any *Miranda* warnings nor did the officers let him know he was free to leave the room. After encouragement by the officers for the student to help his situation, juvenile detention was threatened. This lead J.D.B. to confess to his involvement in the break-ins, and the young man was convicted of the crimes. Upon review, the Supreme Court reversed the decision and found that police must factor in the age of young suspects whom they intend to question into their decisions about whether to give *Miranda* warnings. The Court stressed that children are more vulnerable to pressure than are adults and to use common sense in such situations; no further guidelines were provided by the Court, however.

CASE STUDY

THE IMPACT OF ZERO TOLERANCE POLICIES

JAZMIN (RECENT GRADUATE FROM A SOUTH L.A. HIGH SCHOOL, HISPANIC)

I just didn't like school. There were a lot of things going on in my life. I had a lot of family issues, my parents were breaking up. So I would ditch and go to different places, and one of those times I got my first citation. I was 2 blocks away from school in front of my friend's house. They handcuffed me and searched me and my friend's parents came out and said, "What is going on?" They said, "You're supposed to be at school." They patted me down, they searched me, put me in the police car and drove me back to my middle school. When we got to school, they made me walk through the halls in handcuffs to the dean's office, which was really embarrassing. At the dean's office they gave me a citation. The second time I got a ticket, I was at Venice Beach and they took us to a school gym set up like a detention center with all the students they had rounded up. After they searched you and went through the whole process of confiscating your stuff, you had to go up and sit there in the gym stands—all these seats and all these students, you just had to sit there and wait for your parents to come. And when my mom came, the officer told my mom "You know most of the students that ditch do drugs and you should really have her drug tested because her eyes look really dilated right now." It made me really upset. Nobody ever asked what was going on, how was I really doing. I was just being put in a box: if I was ditching then I must be doing drugs. After that, things got worse with my mom. And when I see police, even to this day, I'll get nervous, even if they're just next to me in the car. If I have to talk to them I get nervous and feel like I did something wrong.

Lydia (Grade 12, Hispanic)

When I was in middle school, I got a ticket for being tardy. I was in 7th grade and, at the time, I didn't even realize there were police on campus. One day I was walking in and an officer stopped me and said I was late and took me to the principal's office. The principal told everyone to get out of the office, even though everyone could see through the glass what was happening inside. That year I had been getting into trouble at school, so he told me that I'd better straighten up: "If you keep acting like this you'll get sent to another school and then you'll see. If you were at another school and you acted like this you'd get jumped." Then the officer came in and wrote me a ticket for ditching. While at school since then, I have been stopped by police, questioned by police, yelled at by police, had my bag searched, been patted down, put in a police car and taken home by police. I have friends who have been ticketed or arrested for skipping class, fighting, having cigarettes or marijuana on them, tagging, being on school grounds when they say you're not supposed to, and stealing. Even for minor things, it seems like police are always involved in our lives at school. When you get treated like this it is demeaning and it's a big part of how we get pushed out of school. A lot of people I know just stop caring about school. They just don't care anymore. And it fits with how police treat us in South L.A. at school and in the neighborhood, the message is: "You are nothing." What we need is for schools and police to stop this treatment, stop ticketing and arresting and harassing students of color. We need positive alternatives at school like counseling, rehabilitation programs, and therapists.

James (Grade 11, black)

I got bullied and harassed starting in middle school. It affected me a lot inside but I still managed to do alright in school. When I was in 10th grade, a couple of boys took it to another level. One day in second period, they started throwing paper at me, calling me names and saying they were going to kick my ass. When school ended they found me walking with my girlfriend and started following us and saying they were going to hurt me. But when we got to the front, they saw my mom's car and pulled back, telling me to be ready tomorrow. The next day I started bringing a knife in my bag for self-defense. A couple of days later in my 3rd period English class, the dean came in with three security guards for a random bag search. The teacher told us all to make it go easy by taking out anything we had, so I took out my knife and put it on my desk. I told them why I brought it but they took me to the school police office on campus and told me they had no choice but to arrest me because that was the law if it was longer than your palm, and mine was an inch too long. They took me to the police station and booked me, then took me to another station where I was questioned and kept in a holding cell for four hours until my mom could come pick me up. This was a shock to me since it was my first time getting into any kind of trouble. I'd never been suspended, expelled, ticketed or arrested before. When I went to the court referee, they gave me community service and an essay to write. My mom eventually got my record expunged. It gets to me that I was treated like that for trying to protect myself in the first place. There was no one at the school I felt I could talk to or trust, especially since it would be easy to get labeled a "rat" for telling. It just felt like school staff were there to catch me doing something wrong rather than preventing the bullying or helping me. (Community Strategy Center, 2013, pp. 17–20)

I. How did zero tolerance policies impact these students?

2. What alternatives would you like to have had available if you were a school principal or school police officer in handling these situations?

3. How could the students or families have been helped in preventing these outcomes?

Source: Labor/Community Strategy Center (2013). *Black, brown and over-policed in LA schools.* Community Rights Campaign of the Labor/Community Strategy Center. Los Angeles, CA.

SCHOOL DISCIPLINE

Suspensions and Expulsions

School discipline involves millions of children and adolescents across the country (see Figure 8.1). There have been many regional reviews of school districts discipline data as well as national studies of the 2011–2012 and 2013–2014 academic years by the U.S. Department of Education's Civil Rights Division of more than 99% of the country's public school districts and their 50 million+ students. Of the students enrolled in the 2011–2012 academic year, 3.5 million students experienced in-school suspension (whereby the school maintains a supervised school-based room and students are expected to do academic work), 1.9 million students were suspended from school (out-of-school suspension) for at least one day (with an average suspension being 3.5 days), 1.6 million students were suspended from school more than one time for at least one day, and 130,000 students received an expulsion from school for the remainder of that academic year. Comparatively, in 2012, only 40% more students (3.2 million) graduated from high school than were involved with in- or out-of-school suspension. Some states had disproportionately high suspension rates of their students, including Arkansas, Florida, Illinois, Indiana, Louisiana, Michigan, Missouri, Nebraska, Nevada, Ohio, Pennsylvania, Tennessee, Wisconsin, and the District of Columbia.

The extent of these problems is possibly underestimated because the Department of Education surveys comprised samples of fewer than 3,000 of the more than 95,000 schools nationwide, making the findings projections. Even so, this represents 2.2% to 2.4% of all elementary school-aged students and 11.0% to 11.3% of all secondary school-aged students who were out-of-school suspended during the 2011–2012 and 2013–2014 academic years. There were some declines in overall suspension rates, up to 20%, reported across school districts during this two-year reporting period, for the total number of out-of-school suspensions decreased from 3.5 million to 2.8 million students.

Racial Disparity

Nevertheless, these school exclusions were racially disparate (see Figures 8.2 and 8.3): Although 6% of all primary and secondary-aged students received one or more out-of-school suspensions, the percentage is 18% for black male students, 10% for black female students, 5% for white male students, and only 2% for white female students. These disparities are greater in secondary school student populations (Fuentes, 2014; U.S. Department of Education, 2013b, 2014c, 2016b).

These annual out-of-school suspension rates are more than double the number of out-of-school suspensions from the mid-1970s. This increase in suspension rates, however, is fully accounted for by increases in suspensions for minority students (blacks, Hispanics, American

In-School Suspension: Suspension (typically 1 to 3 days) from the regular classroom whereby the student is to remain and complete academic work in a supervised school room.

Out-of-School Suspension: Suspension from school where the student is not allowed back on the campus until the suspension ends.

Expulsion: Decision by the school that the student is removed for a period of time and not allowed back on campus.

Rate of Suspension and Expulsion by Gender

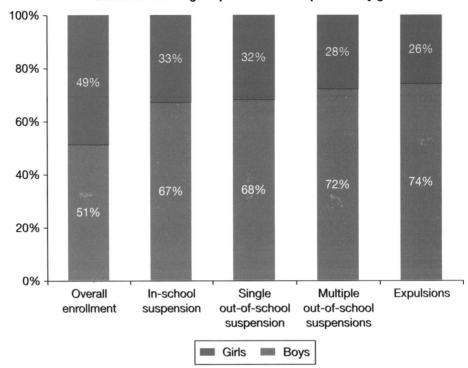

Students receiving suspensions and expulsions by gender

Source: U.S. Department of Education (2014). *Civil rights data collection, data snapshot: School discipline, Issue brief* No. 1. Office of Civil Rights, Washington, DC.

Indian, and multiracial), not for white students, thus, making it three times more likely today that a minority student is suspended compared with a white student and four times more likely for black girls than for white students (Losen, 2012; Losen & Martinez, 2013; Losen & Skiba, 2010; U.S. Department of Education, 2014c). When reviewed longitudinally, it is estimated that between 30% and 50% of students experience suspension between kindergarten and 12th grade, with reports as high as 60% in some middle and high schools, and, dependent on location, 70% for certain students of color. To be poignant, every two seconds a student is suspended from school: black students every four seconds, white students every five seconds, Hispanic students every seven seconds, and Asian/Pacific Islander students every two minutes.

These disparities are also seen for students who are expelled: Black male students represent 8% of all students but 19% of those expelled without educational services; multiracial male students represent 2% of all students but 4% of those expelled without educational services; and white male students represent 26% of all students but only 35% of those expelled without educational services. It should be noted that Hispanic and Asian American students, as well as white female students, are not disproportionately expelled from their schools (Children's Defense Fund, 2014; U.S. Department of Education, 2016b). There are wide suspension and expulsion disparities across school districts, as well as a disproportionate impact on other student populations.

Students With Disabilities

Students with **special education** disabilities are also disproportionately involved with school discipline protocols (see Figure 8.4). A student with any special education disability is more than two times more likely to receive one or more out-of-school suspensions (11% to 13%) compared with those without a disability (5% to 6%), with the most common disability types for suspended students being **learning disabilities** and severe emotional disturbances. Students of color with

Special Education: Form of learning provided to students with exceptional needs, such as students with learning disabilities or behavioral challenges. These disability categories are set forth by the Individuals with Disabilities in Education Act (IDEA).

Learning Disability: Disorder in one or more of the basic psychological processes involved in understanding or in using language, spoken or written, that may manifest itself in an imperfect ability to listen, think, speak, read, write, spell, or do mathematical calculations.

Rate of Suspension and Expulsion by Race/Ethnicity

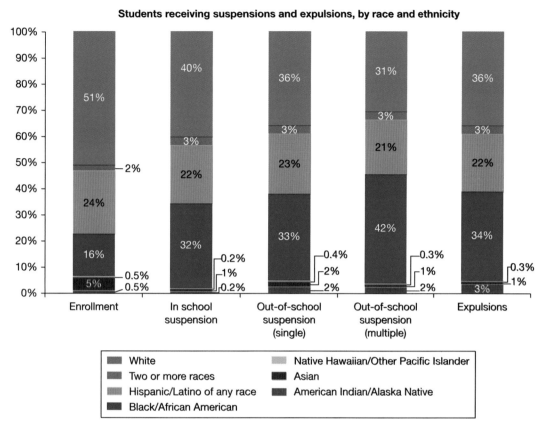

Students receiving suspensions and expulsions, by race and ethnicity

Legend:
- White
- Two or more races
- Hispanic/Latino of any race
- Black/African American
- Native Hawaiian/Other Pacific Islander
- Asian
- American Indian/Alaska Native

Source: U.S. Department of Education (2014). *Civil rights data collection, data snapshot: School discipline, Issue brief No. 1.* Office of Civil Rights, Washington, DC.

▼ FIGURE 8.3

Rate of Out-of-School Suspension by Race and Gender

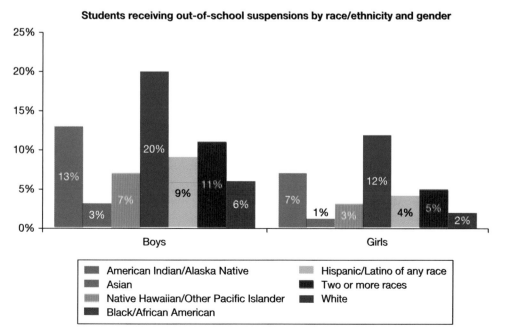

Students receiving out-of-school suspensions by race/ethnicity and gender

Legend:
- American Indian/Alaska Native
- Asian
- Native Hawaiian/Other Pacific Islander
- Black/African American
- Hispanic/Latino of any race
- Two or more races
- White

Source: U.S. Department of Education (2014). *Civil rights data collection, data snapshot: School discipline, Issue brief No. 1.* Office of Civil Rights, Washington, DC.

Rate of Out-of-School Suspension for Disabled Students by Race and Gender

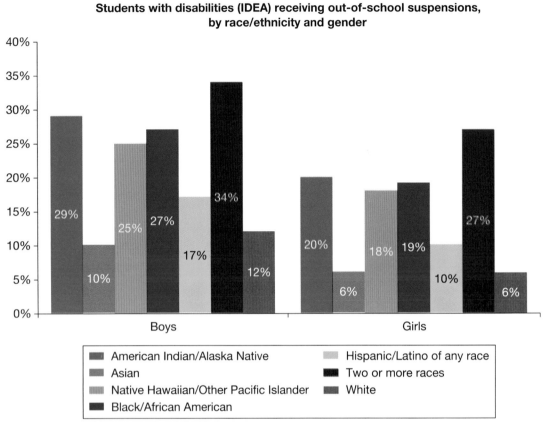

Students with disabilities (IDEA) receiving out-of-school suspensions, by race/ethnicity and gender

Legend:
- American Indian/Alaska Native
- Asian
- Native Hawaiian/Other Pacific Islander
- Black/African American
- Hispanic/Latino of any race
- Two or more races
- White

Source: U.S. Department of Education (2014). *Civil rights data collection, data snapshot: School discipline, Issue brief No. 1.* Office of Civil Rights, Washington, DC.

special education disabilities (black, Hispanic, and multiracial), although not Asian American students, experienced much higher suspension rates—from 22% to 25% for males and 20% for females (Fabelo et al., 2011; Kang-Brown et al., 2013; U.S. Department of Education, 2014c, 2016b). Racial disparities also exist across the special education student population as well; students of color have been found disproportionately to be identified with severe emotional disturbances and developmental delay. Some have concluded that referral bias from school personnel and related reasons explain these disparities, which is a topic that was explored in more detail in Chapter 6 (Harry & Klingner, 2006).

Punishment Disparity—Schools to Juvenile Courts

In the 2009–2010 academic year, 96,000 students nationwide were arrested while on school grounds and 242,000 were referred to the juvenile courts by school officials (see Figure 8.5). These arrests and referrals are not equitably distributed across most schools because low-income students and those of color are significantly more likely to be involved in harsh discipline protocols (McCurdy, 2014; McNulty-Eitle & Eitle, 2004; Skiba, Michael, Nardo, & Peterson, 2002). The U.S. Department of Education identified in 2012 that in school districts with more than 50,000 students, black students represented 24% of enrollment but 35% of on-campus arrests, with lower, but still disparate rates for Hispanic students. For all schools nationwide, blacks represent 16% of students but account for 27% of students referred to law enforcement and 31% of school-based arrests. These findings were also replicated in the Department of Education's review of the 2013–2014 academic year, with black students more than twice as likely as white students to be referred to law enforcement or to be subject to a school-related arrest.

Students Subjected to Referrals to Law Enforcement by Race/Ethnicity

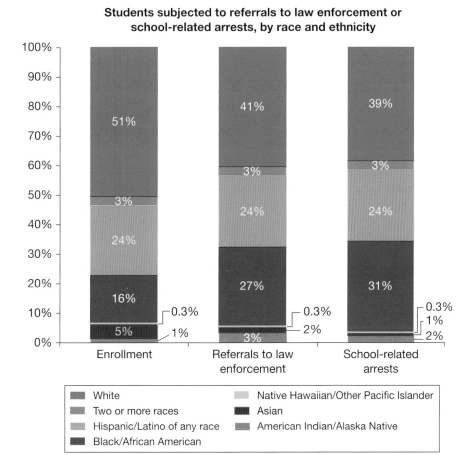

Students subjected to referrals to law enforcement or school-related arrests, by race and ethnicity

Legend:
- White
- Two or more races
- Hispanic/Latino of any race
- Black/African American
- Native Hawaiian/Other Pacific Islander
- Asian
- American Indian/Alaska Native

Source: U.S. Department of Education (2014). *Civil rights data collection, data snapshot: School discipline, Issue brief No. 1.* Office of Civil Rights, Washington, DC.

Similarly, students with special education disabilities represented only 12% of students but accounted for 25% of school-based arrests (see Figure 8.6; U.S. Department of Education, 2014c, 2016b). Of the largest school districts nationwide in 2012, those with the most per-capita student arrests were Los Angeles; Chicago; Philadelphia; Orange County, FL; Grinnett County, GA; Hillsborough County, FL; San Diego; Broward County, FL; Palm Beach County, FL; Duval County, FL; Hawaii Department of Education; Cobb County, GA; New York City; Miami-Dade County, FL; and Montgomery County, MD. To highlight, over a two-year period (2010–2012), black students were on average 31% of the Oakland Public Schools student population but accounted for 73% of all school-based arrests (Black Organizing Project, 2013; Community Strategy Center, 2013).

Even after controlling for other possible explanations—misbehavior, academic performance, student attitudes, parental attention, school characteristics and location, and socioeconomic status—it has been found that these disparities are most likely a result of unfair targeting of the students (Kupchik, 2010; Payne & Welch, 2010; The Equity Project at Indiana University, 2014). Students of color in schools that have larger proportions of black students are more likely to receive punitive and not rehabilitative discipline responses by school personnel, again, identified after controlling for other possible explanations (Addington, 2014; Majd, 2011; Skiba & Williams, 2014). These disparity arrest and punishment rates correlate to the increased police presence in schools, thus, criminalizing more student problems that were earlier seen and handled by school teachers and administrators. Since most students

▼ FIGURE 8.6

Students Subjected to Referrals to Law Enforcement by Disability Status

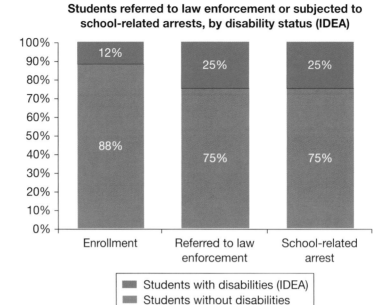

Students referred to law enforcement or subjected to school-related arrests, by disability status (IDEA)

■ Students with disabilities (IDEA)
■ Students without disabilities

Source: U.S. Department of Education (2014). *Civil rights data collection, data snapshot: School discipline, Issue brief No. 1.* Office of Civil Rights, Washington, DC.

punished under harsh discipline protocols and policies are because of discretionary offenses, negative perceptions by school and police personnel increase their risk for trouble through minor misbehaviors. This often exacerbates the disadvantages faced by impoverished students and students of color, entangling them within discipline regimes (Kupchik, 2010; Payne & Welch, 2010; Stinchcomb, Bazemore, & Riestenberg, 2006). In addition, longitudinal reviews have found that suspension from school tends to precede serious delinquency for black and Hispanic students and that delinquent behaviors are often triggered by academic disengagement (The Center for Civil Rights Remedies, 2013).

Texas has led the research investigation into these school and discipline problems. In a six-year (2000–2006) longitudinal review of all students in Texas schools, as well as of these students' state juvenile justice involvement and outcome data, concerning results were found. These include the following: 54% of students were suspended or expelled between their 7th-and 12th-grade school years; of those removed from their classrooms, black students and those with special education disabilities were disproportionally included; students suspended or expelled were held back one grade 31% of the time compared with only 5% for all students; 10% of suspended or expelled students dropped out of school; students suspended or expelled for discretionary reasons (which accounted for 97% of all disciplinary actions) were three times more likely to be involved with the juvenile courts the following year even after controlling for other possible explanations. The results did vary across schools, depending on the diversity of student populations (Fabelo et al., 2011).

These punitive school discipline policies have also, based on more recent data collection, directly or indirectly targeted a disproportionate number of LGBT students. LGBT students are up to three times more likely to experience harsh disciplinary treatment than are non-LGBT peers, even though misbehavior and disobedience to school rules among these two groups is not significantly different. Some LGBT students report being pushed out of the classroom environment because of a hostile school climate, which includes bullying, verbal abuse, and threats, among others (Himmelstein & Bruckner, 2011; Majd, Marksamer, & Reyes, 2009; Mitchum & Moodie-Mills, 2014).

RACIAL AND ETHNIC DISPARITIES IN SCHOOL DISCIPLINE

In the Boston (Massachusetts) Public School District, during the 2007 to 2009 academic school years, black students made up one third of the student population but accounted for two thirds of the school-based arrests. Seventy percent of these arrests were for public order offenses: "[A] 14-year-old boy at the Kennedy Middle School in Springfield, Massachusetts, was arrested after he refused to walk with a teacher to her office and instead returned to his classroom. According to the police report, he yelled at the teacher, bounced a basketball in a school hallway, failed to respond to a police officer's request to go with the teacher and slammed his classroom door shut. He was subsequently taken into police custody, handcuffed, transported to the police station and charged with "disturbing a lawful assembly" (Dahlberg, 2012, p. 5).

Los Angeles, California, had a daytime curfew law that was only recently amended. For years, students in the LA School District (the country's second largest) were ticketed and referred to the LA Juvenile Court for being absent, tardy, or late to school. More than 10,000 students were ticketed every year; greater than 90% of these students were black or Hispanic.

Most of the families who received these $250.00 tickets could not afford to pay them and the $1,000 court costs, with the unpaid fines staying on the students' records. Progress, and the city law being changed, has been swift since 2013 whereby there have been 80% reductions in ticketing of students for truancy, and school police ticketing of all offenses is down 50%. Nevertheless, the racial and ethnic disparity in ticketing has worsened: Hispanic students are twice as likely as white students; a black student is now six times (compared with only four) more likely to be ticketed and arrested at school than a white student; and black and Hispanic students are 6 to 29 times more likely than white students to be ticketed for the same behaviors or infractions (Community Strategy Center, 2013).

. . . .

1. Why do you think the racial and ethnic disparities worsened in the LA School District after reform efforts?

2. Do you have alternative ideas or ways to handle daytime curfews on and around school campuses?

More poignantly for all students caught in school exclusion policies, just one suspension in the ninth grade has been found to double the risk for failing subsequent academic courses in high school and raises the risk of dropping out by 20% (Balfanz, Byrnes, & Fox, 2015; Kang-Brown et al., 2013; Marchblanks et al., 2014). The risk of dropping out of high school is doubled if a student is arrested on or off schools grounds, and it is four times greater if the student is formally involved with the juvenile courts (Gagnon & Leone, 2002; Sweeten, 2006). These results reinforce and mirror other, smaller scale, investigations of students involved within school discipline that have found they miss instructional time and opportunities to learn, fall behind academically, and form negative attitudes or perceptions concerning schools and the school personnel (Jimerson, Anderson, & Whipple, 2002; Skiba, Arredondo, & Rausch, 2014).

School-to-Prison Pipeline

The **school-to-prison pipeline** is not typically a direct referral from school discipline to the juvenile court judge. Nevertheless, there are hundreds of thousands of middle and high school students nationwide who are at significant risk for delinquency adjudication and juvenile court supervision as their problems begin within school discipline protocols. Punitive school environments have counterintuitively made schools less cohesive across the student body and for many have made learning more difficult. These environments have set the stage for a punitive response in many schools to nonviolent misbehaving incidents, disruptions of school routines, and truancy, among other acts that use to be handled informally. Within zero tolerance policies, however, students' involvement with a strict discipline protocol can quickly escalate to school removal and exclusions. The presence of school police officers has many times redirected this response away from the schools to the courts, with officers handling many noncriminal student problems. Across the nation's school districts, there is compelling evidence of the existence of a "school-to-prison pipeline" for many vulnerable and at-risk students.

School-to-Prison Pipeline: Metaphor used to describe the increasing contact students have with the juvenile and adult criminal justice systems as a result of school zero tolerance policies and other factors.

RESEARCH: WHAT WORKS?

PUNITIVE POLICIES DO NOT TYPICALLY IMPROVE SCHOOL SAFETY

Millions of students nationwide are impacted annually by zero tolerance policies, and hundreds of thousands of middle and high school students are caught every year within strict discipline and school exclusion policies through out-of-school suspensions, arrests by school resource officers, and expulsion, increasing their risk for juvenile court involvement (U.S. Department of Education, 2014a). Counterintuitively for many policy makers, schools that have increased their student exclusionary discipline, hoping that the suspension and expulsion of problem students will improve school environments, have often found the opposite to be true: School and student body cohesion has become more fragile, satisfaction with the school and its governance structures has decreased, and the academic achievement of nonsuspended students is harmed. Additionally, increasing school suspensions has been found to increase student misbehavior and recidivism for both those students removed from school but who return and for those nonoffending students who remain in the classroom. There is little evidence showing the effectiveness of harsh punishments in deterring future student misbehavior in schools (American Psychological Association, 2008; Justice Policy Institute, 2011; Losen, Hewitt, & Toldson, 2014; Perry & Morris, 2014). In a review of the Chicago Public School system, it was not the number of school-based arrests that made the schools safer, rather the type and quality of the relationships the police officers formed with the teachers and students. Officers who intervened early to prevent and resolve student conflict before it became disruptive or violent made students feel safer; not retaining and arresting students led to mistrust and decreased the school climate quality and increased disorder across the classrooms (Steinberg, Allensworth, & Johnson, 2011).

1. Why do you think the threat or implementation of harsh punishment is not typically effective in school discipline?
2. What alternatives to harsh punishment may be effective?

CHAPTER REVIEW

CHAPTER SUMMARY

This chapter presents the historical development of discipline in schools, with a primary discussion of the most recent zero tolerance movement that significantly shifted and increased school discipline in the 1990s. These discipline measures brought about by zero tolerance policies increased student exclusion through school suspensions and expulsions, decreasing the chances for these students to succeed in school and increasing their risk for juvenile court involvement. These changes were brought about because of several factors—school shootings, fear of adolescent "super-predators," and the juvenile justice system's swing toward punishment and away from rehabilitation, among others. Because of these changes, most schools greatly increased security measures within their buildings and the use of police officers on campus. This shift has had for many already at-risk students (minorities, those with disabilities, and those who identify as LGBT) some unintended consequences by impacting the learning environment and increasing what has come to be called the "school-to-prison" pipeline.

KEY TERMS

DISCUSSION QUESTIONS

1. What are the parallels across the juvenile justice system and school districts in how they handle children and adolescents over the past 25 years?

2. Why have schools moved toward the use of zero tolerance policies, and what are the implications?

3. What impact have school shootings had on school policies?

4. Are there groups that are disproportionately impacted by school discipline and, in particular, during the zero tolerance policy era?

5. What is the evidence for and against the use of police in schools? Justify your position with empirical evidence.

6. Does the "school-to-prison pipeline" actually exist? Justify your position with empirical evidence.

7. How do you think schools should handle student truancy problems?

8. Why has the number of student suspensions, expulsions, and school-based arrests increased over the past 20 years?

9. How did the No Child Left Behind (NCLB) Act impact the move toward more punitive school environments?

10. What data collection is important in the future to address some of the school punishment disparities?

11. If you were a school principal, how might you best design your school discipline protocols, and how would you handle truant students? What policies or laws impact your decision-making abilities?

12. If you were a school police officer, what would be the most significant challenges in handling disruptive or disrespectful students? What should your role be on the school campus?

---

https://edge.sagepub.com/mallett

 **Sharpen your skills with SAGE edge!**

SAGE edge for students provides a personalized approach to help you accomplish your coursework in an easy-to-use learning environment. You'll find mobile-friendly eFlashcards and quizzes, as well as videos, web resources, and links to SAGE journal articles to support and expand on the concepts presented in this chapter.

CHAPTER 9

TRAUMA AND DELINQUENCY

▲ Trauma impacts many children and adolescents and can increase their risk for delinquency. Why do you think this is the case?

©iStockphoto.com/Daisy-Daisy

INTRODUCTION

Trauma impacts many children, adolescents, and their families. Some of these traumatic experiences are more readily identified—growing up in poverty, living in unsafe and violent neighborhoods, and being victimized by abuse. Other traumas—including neglect, school bullying, losing family members (by death, prison, or other unexpected reasons), and accidents—however, are less frequently cited as significantly impactful, although they may be just as difficult for young people to handle. These traumas often lead to nefarious difficulties in both the short and the long term. In addition, children's exposure to more than one form of trauma, referred to as "poly-victimization," and traumas experienced over time are of serious concern, increasing the risk for school problems and juvenile court involvement. Although the link is not always direct, for many trauma experiences occur in childhood and others over the child's developmental years, most adolescents who become involved with the juvenile justice system and are adjudicated delinquent have significant traumatic and maltreatment backgrounds. In other words, trauma is cumulative: the greater the number of experiences, the greater the impact on the child's development, academic outcomes, and offending behaviors, among other problems (Greenwald, 2002; Klain, 2014).

This chapter reviews the prevalence and far-reaching impact of trauma experiences that are most common for those adolescents who become involved with the juvenile courts. The traumas that are highlighted for this population include maltreatment victimizations, growing up in violent and poor communities, being targets of bullying and intimidation by peers, and witnessing significant violent acts in homes and neighborhoods. This chapter further explores the link and interplay from maltreatment to delinquency (including crossover (dually involved) youth, those involved with child welfare and juvenile courts simultaneously), the impact that trauma has on school academic performance, and the mental health diagnosis of post-traumatic stress disorder (PTSD).

PREVALENCE OF CHILDHOOD AND ADOLESCENT TRAUMA

The trauma field has identified several categorical definitions of trauma, including acute, chronic, and complex. **Acute trauma** is considered a single traumatic event that is time limited, for example, a dog bite, accident, or natural disaster such as an earthquake or tornado. **Chronic trauma** refers to varied and multiple traumatic events, often occurring over time, including domestic violence in the home as well as living in an unsafe and threatening neighborhood. This type of trauma could also be a long-standing or reoccurring problem such as physical abuse victimization. **Complex trauma** is chronic trauma caused by adults or caregivers of children that is also long term in nature—for example, sexual abuse (Buffington, Pierkhising, & Marsh, 2010).

Child Maltreatment

There are four official, legal categories of **child maltreatment victimization**: physical abuse, sexual abuse, emotional (psychological) abuse, and neglect (including medical),

Crossover Youth (Dually-involved youth): Dynamic between child maltreatment and delinquency, with young people having contact with both systems simultaneously.

Acute Trauma: Single traumatic event that is time limited, for example, a dog bite, accident, or natural disaster such as an earthquake or tornado.

depending on state law definitions. Typically, across the states, the following definitions of these maltreatment types are found: physical abuse being the injuring or death of a child, not by an accident; sexual abuse being any act of sexual contact of any type toward a child; emotional abuse being chronic acts or attitudes by caregivers that interferes with or impedes the psychological or social development of a child; and neglect being inadequate or dangerous child-rearing practices by caregivers. Such maltreatment (chronic or complex trauma) has increasingly been found to evoke serious, long-lasting repercussions for many victims (Buffington et al., 2010). Both one-time and ongoing victimizations can be sufficiently traumatic to induce symptoms and to predispose children to poor young adult trajectories and outcomes (Copeland, Keeler, Angold, & Costello, 2007; National Child Traumatic Stress Network, 2008; Widom, DuMont, & Czaja, 2007).

▲ Child maltreatment includes numerous forms of abuse or neglect, including physically harming a child. Why do you think child abuse happens?

Chronic Trauma: Varied and multiple traumatic events, often occurring over time, including domestic violence in the home as well as living in an unsafe and threatening neighborhood. This type of trauma could also be a long-standing or reoccurring problem such as physical abuse victimization.

Complex Trauma: Chronic trauma caused by adults or caregivers of children (for example, sexual abuse) that is long term in nature.

Child Maltreatment Victimization: Four official, legal categories of child maltreatment: physical abuse, sexual abuse, emotional (psychological) abuse, and neglect (including medical), depending on state law definitions.

National Survey of Children's Exposure to Violence: Most comprehensive nationwide survey of the incidence and prevalence of children's exposure to violence.

National Comorbidity Study: First large-scale national study of mental health in the United States; replicated most recently in 2010 and included findings for the first time on the adolescent population.

Maltreatment (abuse and neglect) reports are provided by the U.S. Department of Health and Human Services' Administration of Children and Families. There is concern by stakeholders that these counts underreport actual victimizations because of narrow state definitions of abuse. Nonetheless, with these official counts, over the past ten years, approximately 680,000 to 1,000,000 children and adolescents nationwide each year have been victims of substantiated maltreatment. This represents approximately 20% of all referrals to children's services that are investigated.

Over the past five years, most maltreatment victims have been neglect cases (75% to 80%; with an additional 2% for medical neglect), followed by physical abuse (17% to 18%), sexual abuse (8% to 9%), and emotional/psychological abuse (6% to 9%), with some significant variation across the states (see Tables 9.1–9.4). Almost 10% of these victims had a reported disability, including learning, behavioral, intellectual, and/or physical. More than 91% of these victims' perpetrators were a parent, either acting alone or with other parental caregivers. Males and females were equally at risk; however, they were disproportionately younger (greater than 60% are younger than 10 years of age, and 24% are less than one year old) and minority (black, American Indian, and Pacific Islander; Administration for Children and Families, 2010, 2017). Why certain minority children are overrepresented in maltreatment victimizations is controversial. Some have identified racial bias of the investigative system as the cause (Sedlak & Broadhurst, 1996), whereas others have found no racial bias but poverty, neighborhood instability, and social context to be explanatory factors (Korbin, Coulton, Chard, Platt-Houston, & Su, 1998; Sedlak & Schultz, 2005).

Broader reviews of maltreatment victimization are available through numerous nationally representative samples of victim self-reports and parental reports for younger children: the National Survey of Children's Exposure to Violence, the National Survey of Adolescents, and the National Comorbidity Study (Finkelhor, Turner, Shattuck, & Hamby, 2013; Kessler et al., 2009; McCart et al., 2011). Additional trauma experience studies have used other (regional and local) school-based populations, although the findings are limited to just these localities (Costello, Erkanli, Fairbank, & Angold, 2002; Drake, Lee, & Johnson-Reid, 2009; Felitta et al., 2008).

When researchers have expanded the definitions of trauma victimizations, a broader, and arguably more accurate, count of maltreatment has been identified (Fergusson,

CASE STUDY

ANGELA'S STORY OF EMOTIONAL/PSYCHOLOGICAL ABUSE

My childhood is filled with many memories. There were the normal memories of playing with my brother and friends, going to the movies, and hanging out at the mall. Most of my memories were of a loud angry household. My most vivid childhood memories were of my mother screaming at me, calling me names, and putting me down. Occasionally, she would spank us. When she did, she would be so angry that she would lose control. When she would get angry with me, she would yell and call me names, purposely being hurtful.

My first such memory was when I was 5 years old. We were getting ready for church and I was unable to find one of my shoes. When I told my mother, she yelled and screamed that I had misplaced the shoe on purpose so that I wouldn't have to go to church. On the way to church, she continued by telling me that I was the devil and I had nothing but evil in me. In the fourth grade, I went to a new school. For the first four or five months, I was picked on and bullied. When I told my mother, her first response was to ask me what I had done to make them pick on me. It was about this time that I began to believe that I was less than, not as good as, other kids. I carried that feeling into adulthood, and still fight with it today.

One day during the summer before seventh grade I was working on a puzzle when a friend called. I asked my mother to ask her if I could call her back later because I was almost finished. She did as I asked, but after she hung up the phone she flew into a rage and told me that I was a bitch and that I would never have any friends. I still carry that with me. As a teenager, I was given the offer to train for the U.S. Swimming Team for the 1988 Olympics. I was excited. This was my dream. My mother declined the offer. When I asked her why, she said she didn't have time to waste with that. These events were not as rare as it would appear. My mother would often yell, scream and put me down. By my early to mid-teens, it was routine. It was part of my day. The only upside to my mother's rages was that she wouldn't speak to me for a few days afterward. The silence was calming. I enjoyed it while I could.

Having said all of that, I loved my mother, and I know she loved me. She made many sacrifices so that my brother and I could have some of the things we wanted, and go on vacations. We would look through all of the catalogs that we got in the mail and pretend that we were shopping at the mall. The problem came when she got angry. She responded to me the way her grandmother responded to her. I have always been disappointed that she never tried to be better than that. I did drugs and drank during junior high and high school. I stopped doing drugs during my late teens, but I started drinking rather heavily. (Goodwin-Slater, 2013, para. 1–4)

Boden, & Horwood, 2008; Saunders & Adams, 2014). One of these national surveys that used expanded maltreatment categories found that more than 18% of the population identified as victims of maltreatment or violent trauma as a child or as an adolescent. Also, sexual victimization was defined to include harassment as well as assaults, and the victimization rate rose to almost 10%, with adolescent girls reporting rates of 18%. Finally, both physical abuse and psychological abuse (without expanded definitions) were reported by almost 12% over the lifetime, and almost 19% for adolescent boys and girls (Finkelhor et al., 2013). Other researchers have also found that reported cases of child maltreatment through law enforcement and the police differ significantly from unreported cases on demographics of the offender and victim and the nature and severity of the abuse, warranting further investigations as to why this is the case (Drake et al., 2009; Hanson et al., 2003).

Physical Assault and Abuse

Physical abuse, as noted, is defined by state law, with many commonalities the states. For example, Ohio defines physical abuse of a child as "evidence of any physical or mental injury or death, inflicted other than by accidental means, or an injury or death which is at variance with the history given of it" (Ohio Revised Code 2151.031(B)). This is a commonly used definition in many

Maltreatment Type of Victims

State	Medical Neglect Percent	Neglect Percent	Other Percent	Physical Abuse Percent	Psychological Maltreatment	Sexual Abuse Percent	Unknown Percent	Total Maltreatment Types
Alabama	0.8	38.7	—	52.1	0.2	17.4	—	109.3
Alaska	2.9	81.8	—	11.4	24.8	5.4	—	126.4
Arizona	—	93.1	—	9.1	0.1	2.9	—	105.2
Arkansas	13.2	55.3	0.1	22.0	1.4	20.7	—	112.6
California	0.2	86.2	0.2	9.0	12.6	5.0	—	113.2
Colorado	1.6	80.3	—	11.5	3.1	10.0	0.3	106.7
Connecticut	3.5	84.8	—	6.8	29.4	5.6	—	130.0
Delaware	0.8	29.6	9.9	18.3	42.8	7.0	—	108.4
District of Columbia	—	84.5	0.3	20.2	—	3.0	—	107.9
Florida	2.5	54.3	46.6	9.7	1.4	5.7	—	120.3
Georgia	3.2	74.7	0.0	10.8	21.3	3.4	—	113.4
Hawaii	1.5	15.5	83.7	10.7	0.8	4.4	—	116.6
Idaho	0.6	76.6	0.9	23.4	—	3.9	—	105.4
Illinois	2.2	69.9	—	21.7	0.1	15.0	—	109.0
Indiana	—	87.5	—	8.4	—	10.1	—	106.0
Iowa	1.0	73.3	11.8	16.9	0.7	6.8	—	110.5
Kansas	2.6	19.0	24.8	23.1	13.9	30.4	—	113.8
Kentucky	2.4	92.2	—	8.3	0.4	4.8	—	108.1
Louisiana	—	85.4	—	15.5	0.5	5.4	0.3	107.0
Maine	—	66.5	—	28.9	32.0	6.9	—	134.3
Maryland	—	59.7	—	22.7	0.3	23.8	—	106.5
Massachusetts	—	94.4	0.0	9.6	0.1	2.3	—	106.4
Michigan	1.8	81.1	0.2	23.8	0.4	3.1	—	110.3
Minnesota	1.2	68.1	—	22.7	0.9	18.2	—	111.2
Mississippi	4.1	75.7	0.3	15.7	12.8	9.9	—	118.4
Missouri	4.1	63.5	—	29.3	8.6	23.4	—	128.9
Montana	0.5	94.0	—	5.7	2.6	3.8	—	106.8
Nebraska	—	85.2	—	12.2	1.1	6.9	—	105.4
Nevada	2.2	73.7	—	33.5	0.8	5.6	—	115.8
New Hampshire	3.9	86.6	—	6.4	0.7	10.7	—	108.3
New Jersey	1.9	79.5	27.0	15.2	0.5	8.8	—	105.8
New Mexico	3.7	82.2	0.6	13.4	23.1	2.7	—	125.2

State	Medical Neglect Percent	Neglect Percent	Other Percent	Physical Abuse Percent	Psychological Maltreatment	Sexual Abuse Percent	Unknown Percent	Total Maltreatment Types
New York	6.2	95.3	—	9.7	0.7	3.0	—	141.9
North Carolina	0.4	54.6	—	22.7	1.1	20.3	1.2	101.0
North Dakota	2.2	74.6	—	12.1	31.6	3.7	—	124.2
Ohio	1.7	44.0	46.5	44.3	3.6	20.4	—	113.9
Oklahoma	1.3	76.6	5.7	16.6	26.8	4.3	—	125.6
Oregon	1.4	55.1	0.5	10.0	2.4	8.0	—	123.4
Pennsylvania	3.3	3.6	—	38.5	1.3	50.4	—	102.7
Puerto Rico	7.7	61.9	1.2	27.1	51.8	2.2	—	151.2
Rhode Island	1.3	56.7	—	13.1	39.6	4.0	—	114.6
South Carolina	2.6	62.6	—	46.6	0.7	5.2	—	118.8
South Dakota	—	89.2	0.0	11.8	2.1	2.7	—	105.8
Tennessee	1.5	67.5	5.3	12.7	3.0	23.6	—	108.4
Texas	2.3	82.0	—	16.5	0.6	9.0	0.0	110.4
Utah	0.3	25.7	0.0	41.1	29.2	21.1	—	122.8
Vermont	2.0	2.4	—	47.9	0.8	51.5	—	104.5
Virginia	2.3	65.7	0.3	30.6	1.1	10.7	—	110.4
Washington	—	79.0	—	20.1	—	9.1	—	108.2
West Virginia	—	45.7	0.3	70.4	56.1	4.1	—	181.5
Wisconsin	4.9	63.9	—	17.6	0.8	22.6	—	104.9
Wyoming	–0.6	79.2	0.3	2.0	19.1	7.1	—	108.4
National	2.2	75.3	6.9	17.2	6.2	8.4	0.0	116.3

Source: U.S. Department of Health & Human Services, Child Maltreatment Report (2015). http://www.acf.hhs.gov/programs/cb/research-data-technology/statistics-research/child-maltreatment.

▼ TABLE 9.2

Victims by Race

State	African-American Rate per 1,000 Children	American Indian or Alaska Native Rate per 1,000 Children	Asian Rate per 1,000 Children	Hispanic Rate per 1,000 Children	Multiple Race Rate per 1,000 Children	Pacific Islander Rate per 1,000 Children	White Rate per 1,000 Children
Alabama	7.9	2.2	0.3	4.1	—	9.3	8.5
Alaska	10.8	42.0	1.6	6.1	11.6	10.6	6.4
Arizona	13.9	6.5	1.0	6.6	7.7	10.2	6.6
Arkansas	12.5	3.3	2.1	6.9	27.8	8.2	13.7
California	20.6	19.4	1.6	8.4	3.4	7.1	6.4
Colorado	16.4	7.1	1.8	9.6	8.3	11.5	6.6

(Continued)

State	African-American Rate per 1,000 Children	American Indian or Alaska Native Rate per 1,000 Children	Asian Rate per 1,000 Children	Hispanic Rate per 1,000 Children	Multiple Race Rate per 1,000 Children	Pacific Islander Rate per 1,000 Children	White Rate per 1,000 Children
Connecticut	16.9	5.0	1.6	12.9	12.7	16.4	5.9
Delaware	14.4	1.9	1.8	6.1	3.9	—	5.3
District of Columbia	12.8	4.6	0.4	7.8	3.0	17.2	0.5
Florida	16.4	6.9	1.1	6.3	13.0	3.7	10.3
Georgia	12.9	2.6	1.3	5.5	12.3	6.4	11.3
Hawaii	5.5	1.5	2.3	0.5	6.9	9.2	5.0
Idaho	3.5	8.8	0.7	2.3	2.4	2.7	3.9
Illinois	22.0	5.4	1.9	7.2	5.9	21.3	8.8
Indiana	26.7	2.6	1.8	13.5	31.1	16.5	15.3
Iowa	27.9	43.9	3.0	11.7	10.7	27.9	9.6
Kansas	4.1	2.5	0.5	1.9	3.0	4.7	2.9
Kentucky	20.7	5.7	1.3	12.6	23.9	7.8	17.0
Louisiana	13.5	3.1	1.2	5.2	9.9	8.2	10.4
Maine	—	—	—	—	—	—	—
Maryland	6.9	1.3	0.8	3.1	2.3	4.6	4.0
Massachusetts	33.9	18.5	4.9	34.7	24.6	14.2	13.6
Michigan	—	—	—	—	—	—	—
Minnesota	8.6	21.8	1.7	4.9	12.0	4.6	2.5
Mississippi	11.1	3.2	1.8	5.8	9.1	4.4	13.0
Missouri	4.8	1.8	0.4	2.3	1.6	1.7	4.1
Montana	18.3	19.8	0.6	6.9	9.0	—	6.8
Nebraska	16.9	34.6	3.1	7.3	11.4	10.4	5.6
Nevada	19.3	8.5	1.1	4.4	9.0	10.3	7.3
New Hampshire	2.9	2.0	0.1	3.4	2.5	—	2.7
New Jersey	11.1	2.5	0.6	5.3	4.4	13.7	3.3
New Mexico	26.6	15.3	3.4	17.9	15.0	25.4	15.2
New York	28.1	19.8	3.7	15.8	15.4	10.5	10.3
North Carolina	4.2	5.7	0.6	2.6	5.2	4.1	3.2
North Dakota	14.6	26.5	3.7	10.1	18.2	16.4	7.3
Ohio	14.6	1.7	0.6	8.2	16.4	4.2	7.2
Oklahoma	17.9	10.4	2.5	15.8	41.5	9.2	11.1
Oregon	25.0	27.5	2.5	7.4	8.4	11.6	11.3
Pennsylvania	—	—	—	—	—	—	—
Puerto Rico	—	—	—	—	—	—	—

State	African-American Rate per 1,000 Children	American Indian or Alaska Native Rate per 1,000 Children	Asian Rate per 1,000 Children	Hispanic Rate per 1,000 Children	Multiple Race Rate per 1,000 Children	Pacific Islander Rate per 1,000 Children	White Rate per 1,000 Children
Rhode Island	23.0	11.3	4.1	17.1	24.3	6.5	11.9
South Carolina	15.9	4.1	1.8	6.8	10.9	5.7	13.0
South Dakota	7.6	15.7	—	5.8	13.6	—	2.5
Tennessee	—	—	—	—	—	—	—
Texas	13.6	4.2	1.1	7.8	13.0	12.4	8.8
Utah	26.5	22.7	5.3	11.7	5.8	13.0	10.0
Vermont	5.9	3.0	0.4	0.3	1.1	27.0	8.0
Virginia	4.2	0.2	0.5	2.8	3.5	12.1	3.1
Washington	5.3	16.3	0.8	3.0	4.5	5.8	3.3
West Virginia	9.9	—	0.4	6.3	20.3	11.6	12.8
Wisconsin	8.9	16.6	1.6	3.7	4.8	6.0	2.9
Wyoming	16.6	10.8	4.6	5.7	3.8	—	7.0
National	14.5	13.8	1.7	8.4	10.4	8.8	8.1

Source: U.S. Department of Health & Human Services, Child Maltreatment Report (2015). http://www.acf.hhs.gov/programs/cb/research-data-technology/statistics-research/child-maltreatment.

▼ TABLE 9.3

Victim Age

State	9 Rate per 1,000 Children	10 Rate per 1,000 Children	11 Rate per 1,000 Children	12 Rate per 1,000 Children	13 Rate per 1,000 Children	14 Rate per 1,000 Children	15 Rate per 1,000 Children	16 Rate per 1,000 Children	17 Rate per 1,000 Children
Alabama	6.0	5.7	5.2	5.8	6.0	7.6	7.4	4.6	3.0
Alaska	14.1	12.5	12.4	10.5	12.5	10.8	9.0	9.5	4.8
Arizona	5.8	4.8	4.5	4.2	4.7	4.6	4.8	4.4	2.9
Arkansas	9.9	9.1	8.9	8.8	11.0	10.7	10.8	8.0	5.5
California	6.8	6.2	5.9	5.8	5.9	5.6	5.6	5.2	3.8
Colorado	7.5	6.6	5.8	6.6	6.6	5.5	5.4	4.1	2.5
Connecticut	7.9	7.7	6.9	7.4	7.3	6.8	7.5	6.5	3.5
Delaware	6.5	6.2	6.8	6.0	5.5	5.4	5.8	4.7	4.5
District of Columbia	10.3	9.7	10.6	12.3	13.0	11.5	10.3	9.6	6.8
Florida	8.9	7.8	7.4	6.9	6.7	6.7	6.1	5.5	3.9
Georgia	9.8	9.1	8.8	8.4	8.1	8.6	8.6	7.7	4.0
Hawaii	4.3	4.7	3.4	4.0	4.2	3.9	4.2	3.2	2.8
Idaho	2.8	2.6	2.9	2.7	2.9	2.4	2.9	2.0	1.5
Illinois	9.5	8.2	7.9	7.5	6.9	6.7	5.7	5.1	3.3
Indiana	14.6	13.3	12.5	12.1	13.0	12.3	12.4	9.2	5.8
Iowa	9.6	9.7	7.4	7.1	7.6	6.9	6.4	5.5	3.4

(Continued)

(Continued)

State	9 Rate per 1,000 Children	10 Rate per 1,000 Children	11 Rate per 1,000 Children	12 Rate per 1,000 Children	13 Rate per 1,000 Children	14 Rate per 1,000 Children	15 Rate per 1,000 Children	16 Rate per 1,000 Children	17 Rate per 1,000 Children
Kansas	3.2	2.8	2.2	2.6	3.2	2.7	2.2	1.7	1.2
Kentucky	16.1	14.6	13.0	13.6	13.6	13.2	11.9	10.8	6.6
Louisiana	9.2	9.0	8.2	8.0	8.1	8.0	8.5	6.2	3.5
Maine	11.8	12.6	10.1	8.2	9.3	6.5	6.6	5.3	2.4
Maryland	4.4	4.0	4.1	4.6	4.3	4.6	4.4	4.2	3.0
Massachusetts	19.6	18.2	16.5	15.2	15.3	13.9	13.5	12.0	7.9
Michigan	12.6	11.4	10.6	10.8	10.5	10.2	10.0	8.3	4.8
Minnesota	3.5	3.1	3.0	3.0	3.1	2.7	2.6	2.1	1.5
Mississippi	11.0	10.2	9.8	10.8	10.3	10.7	10.4	8.9	5.3
Missouri	3.5	3.3	3.6	3.3	3.8	4.3	3.2	3.5	1.4
Montana	6.5	6.6	6.8	5.8	5.9	4.0	4.8	3.5	1.7
Nebraska	6.6	6.6	6.0	5.4	4.9	4.6	5.3	3.5	2.5
Nevada	5.8	6.3	5.1	4.9	4.9	4.2	4.2	3.6	2.3
New Hampshire	2.6	2.4	1.8	1.6	2.0	2.8	2.2	1.4	0.8
New Jersey	4.5	4.3	3.7	3.6	4.0	3.7	3.3	3.0	2.1
New Mexico	17.0	15.2	14.2	14.2	12.2	12.3	11.6	9.5	6.4
New York	15.1	13.8	13.5	13.6	14.1	14.9	15.1	13.6	7.2
North Carolina	3.2	2.8	2.9	3.3	3.0	3.1	2.6	2.1	0.8
North Dakota	8.1	8.8	9.5	6.6	8.3	11.8	8.2	7.0	3.3
Ohio	7.8	6.9	6.5	6.9	6.8	7.0	7.3	5.6	4.0
Oklahoma	13.7	11.0	10.1	9.4	9.4	8.6	7.7	6.1	4.3
Oregon	10.9	9.3	9.6	8.2	9.2	8.0	7.1	6.4	5.0
Pennsylvania	1.3	1.3	1.3	1.5	1.6	1.8	2.0	1.7	1.2
Puerto Rico	7.5	7.5	7.3	6.9	7.9	7.5	7.7	6.5	3.8
Rhode Island	13.2	13.4	10.6	9.9	10.0	8.5	9.6	7.5	5.2
South Carolina	11.4	10.1	9.6	9.8	10.4	9.1	9.0	7.8	2.9
South Dakota	4.8	3.0	3.1	2.9	2.8	3.5	1.5	1.4	1.3
Tennessee	5.5	5.2	5.1	6.2	5.4	5.4	5.1	4.7	3.3
Texas	7.3	6.4	6.0	5.8	5.6	5.5	4.7	4.0	1.9
Utah	8.9	9.2	9.0	8.6	9.5	11.3	12.1	9.9	7.5
Vermont	6.2	7.5	6.5	5.6	7.7	9.7	8.8	6.1	4.8
Virginia	3.0	2.6	2.4	2.4	2.2	2.4	2.4	2.2	1.7
Washington	3.2	3.2	2.6	2.7	3.0	3.0	2.4	2.2	1.7
West Virginia	11.4	11.7	8.9	10.5	10.6	8.1	7.4	7.3	4.0
Wisconsin	3.5	3.4	2.7	2.6	2.8	2.8	2.8	2.1	1.5
Wyoming	9.0	5.1	4.8	5.7	4.7	5.6	5.1	3.2	1.8
National	8.0	7.3	6.8	6.8	6.9	6.8	6.5	5.6	3.5

Source: U.S. Department of Health & Human Services, Child Maltreatment Report (2015). http://www.acf.hhs.gov/programs/cb/research-data-technology/statistics-research/child-maltreatment.

Relationship to Perpetrator

Perpetrator	Victims	Reported Relationships	Reported Relationship Percent
Parent	—	—	—
Father	—	132,738	21.1
Father and Nonparent(s)	—	6,828	1.1
Mother	—	257,409	40.9
Mother and Nonparent(s)	—	43,347	6.9
Mother and Father	—	129,837	20.6
Mother, Father, and Nonparent	—	6,036	1.0
Total Parents	—	576,195	91.6
NONPARENT	—	—	—
Child Daycare Provider	—	2,208	0.4
Foster Parent	—	1,424	0.2
Friend and Neighbor	—	4,254	0.7
Group Home and Residential Facility Staff	—	517	0.1
Legal Guardian	—	1,473	0.2
More Than One Nonparental Perpetrator	—	6,964	1.1
Other Professional	—	1,083	0.2
Partner of Parent (Female)	—	2,032	0.3
Partner of Parent (Male)	—	16,882	2.7
Relative (Female)	—	10,524	1.7
Relative (Male)	—	19,139	3.0
Other	—	17,114	2.7
Total Nonparents	—	83,614	13.3
UNKNOWN	—	—	—
Total Nonparents	—	17,743	2.8
National	629,257	677,552	107.7

Source: U.S. Department of Health & Human Services, Child Maltreatment Report (2015). http://www.acf.hhs.gov/programs/cb/research-data-technology/statistics-research/child-maltreatment.

states. Broader physical assault and abuse definitions include acts of hitting, kicking, beating a child, or events that required medical attention. Correspondingly, in expanded abuse definitions, lifetime prevalence rates of physical assault for adolescents have been found to range from 17% to 71% (Finkelhor et al., 2013; McCart et al., 2011). In addition, some have identified and included threats, harassment, and bullying in identifying as physical abuse, with 29% of adolescents reporting these experiences during their lifetime (Finkelhor, Turner, Ormrod, & Hamby, 2009). Additionally, between 3% and 33% of high school students reported being shot at, and

6% to 16% being attacked with a knife, depending on location of the school (Finkelhor, Ormrod, Turner, & Hamby, 2005; Kilpatrick & Saunders, 1997). Nevertheless, these victimization rates at schools have been decreasing since 2003 (Carlton, 2017).

Once young people become involved with the juvenile justice (and adult criminal) system, the risk for abuse and assault exponentially grows. Juvenile justice detention centers and incarceration facilities are often unsafe places and physically abusive places for youthful offenders. Perpetrators of this violence are both adolescent offenders as well as facility staff members.

Sexual Victimization

Sexual victimization includes sexual assault, rape, sexual harassment, statutory sexual offenses, incest (abuse by family members), and sexual exposure by an adult. When including these offense types beyond the more narrow state child welfare system definitions, many more victims, and in particular adolescents, are identified. Between 8% and 11% of adolescents reported a history of at last one sexual assault (three times more likely for girls); 8% for attempted or completed rape (four times more likely for girls); and between 13% and 23% were victims of any sexual victimization in their lifetime (nearly twice as likely for girls; Finkelhor et al., 2013; McCart et al., 2011). In total, it is estimated that between 8% and 10% of adolescents have been a victim of a sexual assault before the age of 18, with girls being more than three times more likely victims than boys (Saunders & Adams, 2014). What follows is a sad, but typical, story:

> When I was eleven years old, my mom's new boyfriend moved in with us. I thought it would be good for mom cause she had a drinking problem and was depressed, and I thought it would make her feel better having him there. At first he was ok and bought me presents, but then mostly he ignored me. Then after a few months he started doing things that made me nervous, like when I was at home alone with him he'd walk around naked. Then he asked me to touch him—I tried to avoid him all the time, but sometimes I couldn't and I was scared to tell him to stop.

> I didn't know how to tell mom what was happening because I didn't even know what to say.

▲ Physical and sexual abuse is common in both juvenile and adult incarceration facilities. Who do you think is most at risk for this harm?

> One day when I was 13, we were fighting because I said I hated him (mom's boyfriend) and she got angry with me. Then I told her how she doesn't know what he does when she's not around, I said 'he tries to touch me.' At first she said I was making it up and exaggerating. Then she said I shouldn't wear skimpy clothes around the house. It upset me deeply because it seemed like she didn't really care about me and she didn't blame him for what he did, it was like she thought it was my fault. I started staying over at friends' places and avoiding going home. I told my friends I hated mom's boyfriend but was too embarrassed to say I'd been abused by him. Sometimes mom told me I couldn't go out, but often she was too stressed or pissed to notice what I was doing. (Domestic Violence Resource Centre Victoria, 2007, p. 2)

Sexual Victimization in Juvenile Facilities

Sexual abuse and assaults also occur in juvenile justice facilities. An estimated 9.5% of youthful offenders in state-operated and large locally or privately operated juvenile facilities reported experiencing one or more incidents of sexual victimization by another youthful offender or facility staff

PHYSICAL ABUSE IN JUVENILE FACILITIES

On January 10, 2008, five male staff dressed in SWAT gear entered the room of a mentally ill 17-year-old, B.B., at the Indiana Juvenile Correctional Facility in Indianapolis. As part of a facility-wide search for drugs, weapons, and other contraband, the men ordered her to another cell and then instructed B.B. to remove all of her clothes for a strip search. B.B., who had been placed on suicide watch eight times during her three years in custody, refused. As documented on a videotape of the incident, B.B. sat quietly on the floor as the men repeated their demand that she take off her clothing. Then they pounced: Pressing her face to the floor, they handcuffed B.B. and shackled her ankles. Using a seat-belt cutting tool, the men sheared off the girl's clothes, including her bra and underwear. The video ends with B.B. lying on the floor wearing nothing but her socks. According to a Justice Department report, "The only item between her and the dirty floor is a fragment of her torn underwear" (Mendel, 2015, pp. 8–9).

In San Diego, a federal lawsuit was filed in July 2014 to limit the use of pepper spray against youth confined in county detention facilities. Earlier news reports revealed that youth in the detention centers (and some in local juvenile corrections institutions) were subjected to pepper spray 461 times in 2011 and 414 times in 2012, and that custodial staff were "using pepper spray routinely and indiscriminately as a first resort to gain compliance rather than only as a last resort" to quell even minor misbehavior. Despite the pain pepper spray inflicts (intense burning, swelling, redness, occasionally blistering, and exacerbation of allergic reactions) and the serious risk of complications for youth with respiratory or mental health problems, San Diego detention staff used it on youth at risk of suicide; youth with respiratory, cardiovascular and skin problems; and youth being treated with psychotropic medications.

In Arkansas, staff at the Yell County Juvenile Detention Center were ordered in September 2014 to end their practice of restraining youth with an unconventional device, called the WRAP, plus a motorcycle helmet covered in duct tape (covering the face shield) and decorated with a cartoonish, hand-drawn face. Youth restrained in this manner were made to sit upright, sometimes for hours at a time, with their legs immobilized and arms handcuffed behind their backs in near-total darkness. In a letter to Yell County, the director of Arkansas's Division of Youth Services wrote, "The WRAP system has no known therapeutic uses. As modified by the Yell County JDC, the system violates the recommended guidelines of the manufacturers, exposes youth to ridicule and humiliation and presents serious risk of harm to youth in your care." The state also urged three other detention centers to end their use of the WRAP restraint device (Mendel, 2015, pp. 20–21).

· ·

I. Why do you think these incidents happened inside the juvenile facilities?

2. What policies could prevent these abuse incidents from happening?

Source: Mendel (2015)

during their first year of incarceration. The most significant risk factor for being victimized in the facility was whether the young person had a history of prior sexual abuse: 65% of those who had previously been sexually assaulted at another correctional facility were also assaulted at their current one.

In prison culture, even in juvenile detention, after an inmate is raped for the first time, he or she is considered "turned out" and fair game for further abuse. Eighty-one percent of those sexually abused by other inmates were victimized more than once, and 32% more than ten times, with 37% being assaulted by more than one perpetrator. Males (8%) were more likely than females (3%) to report sexual activity with facility staff but less likely than females (2% compared to 9%) to report forced sexual activity with another youthful offender. White youthful offenders were more likely than minority youthful offenders to report sexual victimization by another inmate; black youthful offenders were more often victimized by facility staff than were white or Hispanic youthful offenders. Those incarcerated youthful offenders who identified as LGBT were more than five times more likely to report being victimized by another youthful offender (Beck & Caspar, 2013).

Witnessing Violence/Domestic Violence

Witnessing violent acts is common for many children and adolescents and has serious repercussions for these young people including trauma-induced fears, mental health difficulties, increased

©iStockphoto.com/Aaron-H

▲ Most perpetrators of child abuse are parents or caregivers of their child. Why do you think a parent would abuse their child?

risk for substance use, and delinquent behaviors. Seventy percent of older adolescents reported they had witnessed at least one act of violence in their lifetime, and one third reported witnessing some sort of family violence (Cuevas, Finkelhor, Shattuck, Turner, & Hamby, 2013; Finkelhor et al., 2009). Nearly 40% of adolescents have reported witnessing at least one serious community-based violent act (shooting, stabbing, or robbery, among others) over their lifetime, with boys more likely than girls (McCart et al., 2011; Zinzow et al., 2009).

Domestic violence acts can be either witnessed by a family member, or the family member could be the victim of the threats, assaults, and/or battering. These domestic violence problems—also called intimate partner violence or domestic abuse—include emotional abuse, threatened and actual physical abuse, or sexual violence between adults, both heterosexual and same-sex partners. Between three and ten million children are exposed to domestic violence in the United States annually—encompassing 9% to 10% of the child and adolescent population that witnessed a serious violent act between their parents or caregivers—with most these children being younger than 9 years of age (Sickmund & Puzzanchera, 2015; The National Child Traumatic Stress Network, 2016). What follows is a sad story of violence:

"Mommy's boyfriend hurts her . . . " Five-year-old Michael said these words to his teachers during his first week at school. His teachers were startled. Usually, they listened to students talk about summer vacation–not hear a student tell them that his mother's life was in danger. They contacted Michael's mother, Daphne, to report what her son had said. They discovered Michael was right. His teachers put Daphne in touch with Safe Horizon (a domestic violence shelter agency), and a day later, Daphne showed up at our offices, anxious yet hopeful. As Daphne told us about her life, she told us she was shocked to hear that Michael knew what was happening to her. For two years, her boyfriend had routinely beaten and raped her, yet she never called police. She described a harrowing relationship in which her boyfriend was not afraid to punch and kick her in front of his friends, and he would often force her to have sex with them. Daphne told us that once, during a brutal rape, she screamed so loudly that neighbors called the police. Her boyfriend left before the police came. When they asked her what happened, she lied and told them that she and her boyfriend were just arguing. In spite of such horrific behavior, Daphne's boyfriend was careful never to attack her in front of her child. Still, he often threatened to hurt Michael if she ever told anyone about the abuse. Daphne was terrified of what he might do to her son, so she stayed silent and suffered. (Safe Horizon, n.d.)

Deaths—Violent and Nonviolent

Violent deaths of family members and loved ones can be traumatic to children and adolescents. These types of deaths are caused by different violent events, such as suicides and homicides. In 2013, more than 41,000 people committed suicide and 16,000 people were homicide victims in the United States (Centers for Disease Control and Prevention, 2014b). Greater than 18% of adolescents nationwide have lost a family member (which accounts for 47% of the total) or close friend (53%) to a type of homicide. These homicides included criminal homicide, vehicular

Domestic Violence: Emotional abuse, threatened and actual physical abuse, or sexual violence between adults, both heterosexual and same-sex partners.

Violent Deaths: Deaths caused by different violent events, including accidents, suicides, and homicides.

Violence Exposure by Age and Gender

Boys were more likely to be the victim of assaults; girls were more likely to experience sexual victimization								
	Percentage Exposed to Violence in the Past Year							
	Youth ages 0–17			Age of youth				
Type of Violence	All	Male	Female	0–1	2–5	6–9	10–13	14–17
Assaults and bullying								
Any physical assault	46.3%	50.2%	42.1%	17.9%	46.0%	55.6%	49.8%	46.9%
Assault with injury	10.2	12.7	7.7	0.8	5.6	7.5	13.4	18.8
Assault, no weapon, or injury	36.7	38.9	34.4	17.4	38.6	47.5	37.3	32.4
Bullying	13.2	16.7	12.8	NA	19.1	21.5	10.7	8.0
Teasing or emotional bullying	19.7	20.6	23.5	NA	13.5	30.4	27.8	15.8
Property victimization								
Any property victimization	24.6	28.1	27.0	NA	27.8	30.1	24.8	27.6
Robbery (nonsibling)	4.8	6.4	4.2	NA	7.6	5.1	5.1	3.7
Vandalism (nonsibling)	6.0	7.2	6.2	NA	5.2	6.3	6.7	8.6
Theft (nonsibling)	6.9	7.8	7.8	NA	2.3	5.2	10.4	13.0
Sexual victimization								
Any sexual victimization	6.1	4.8	7.4	NA	0.9	2.0	7.7	16.3
Sexual assault	1.8	1.3	2.3	0.0	0.4	0.8	1.4	5.3
Sexual harassment	2.6	1.4	4.4	NA	0.0	0.2	5.6	5.6
Maltreatment								
Any maltreatment	10.2	9.7	10.6	2.2	8.1	7.8	12.0	16.6
Physical abuse	4.4	4.3	4.4	0.6	3.5	2.7	5.2	7.9
Psychological/emotional	6.4	5.5	8.8	NA	4.5	4.5	7.3	12.1
Witness to violence								
Witness any violence (excludes indirect)	25.3	26.1	24.6	10.5	13.8	13.7	33.0	47.6
Witness family assault	9.8	9.0	10.7	7.6	9.6	6.4	11.0	10.1
Witness assault in community	19.2	20.4	17.9	NA	5.8	8.5	27.0	42.2
Exposure to shooting	5.3	5.4	5.1	1.9	2.2	3.1	7.2	10.2
Maltreatment victimization increased with age: youth ages 14–17 were twice as likely to report maltreatment as were youth ages 2–5.								
NA: Violence type not applicable to age group								

Source: Sickmund & Puzzanchera (2014). *Juvenile Offenders and Victims: 2014 National Report.* National Center for Juvenile Justice.

homicide, and negligent homicide, among others. When this death impacts young children, it may cause what is called "traumatic grief"—whereby the child cannot understand the death and experiences severe grief symptoms that lead to frightening thoughts and images of the deceased (Rheingold, Zinzow, Hawkins, Saunders, & Kilpatrick, 2012).

Nonviolent deaths, which can be by natural causes or accidents, may also be traumatic and difficult situations for children and adolescents, particularly when this entails the death of a family member, parent, or peer. Death is often difficult for young people to understand, and without support, many struggle to adapt to the new situation. Children and adolescents most at risk for nonviolent death trauma experiences include those who were close physically and/or emotionally to the deceased, those with preexisting mental health issues, those with preexisting family difficulties or previous loss experiences, and those with a limited support network (Goodman, 2002).

Poverty

Poverty and living in low-income neighborhoods poses serious difficulties for many families and children. Poverty causes significant stressors within many families. Living in poverty increases the number of trauma experiences that families and children have in trying to meet their regular daily living needs, leading often to a state of ongoing crisis. These difficulties disproportionately impact black and Latino families for they are more than twice as likely as white families to experience poverty in the United States, as well as have other related problems including limited education, unemployment, and lack of health insurance (Collins et al., 2010; Reeves, Rodrigue, & Kneebone,2016).

Children living in poverty, and in particular urban poverty, have high rates of reported trauma experiences (70% to 100%). Often, these experiences include exposure to violent neighborhood crime, drug activity, and family violence. For some children and adolescents, these stressors lead to maladjustments, hyper-anxiety, and mental-health- and trauma-related problems. These trauma difficulties that are ongoing and multidimensional impact many children's development, psychological functioning, academic learning, and skill development. These impairments increase the risk for adolescent substance abuse, school failure, delinquency, and suicide (Collins et al., 2010; Cook, Blaustein, Spinazzola, & van der Kolk, 2003; Macy, Barry, & Noam, 2003).

Bloomberg/Bloomberg/Getty Images

▲ Poverty is a difficult family situation to change and disproportionately impacts people of color. What do you think causes poverty?

Nonviolent Deaths:
Deaths by natural causes or accidents.

Poverty, Violence, and Unsafe Schools

Decades of research have shown the link between poverty and education achievement, whereby poor children are more likely to attend underachieving schools with some of the lower per-pupil school funding. These children can learn as well as nonpoor children; however, they are more prone to school transitions, family joblessness, and increased exposure to violence in the home and community (Books, 2004; Lee & Burkam, 2002). Poor schools in less advantaged neighborhoods also have more crime problems on and around the school campus, impacting the environment, exposing students to violence, and lowering high school graduation rates. Students exposed to violence, those who perpetrate violence (bullying, included), and those who are violence victims are more likely to experience emotional problems, do more poorly in school, and perpetuate the crime problems (Bureau of Justice Statistics, 2014a; Child Trends, 2015b). These school environments can increase fears among students—whereby, in 2013, 18% of students reported carrying a weapon while in school, often for protective needs. High school male students were three times more likely to carry a weapon than female students,

Real Median Household Income by Race and Hispanic Origin, 1967–2016

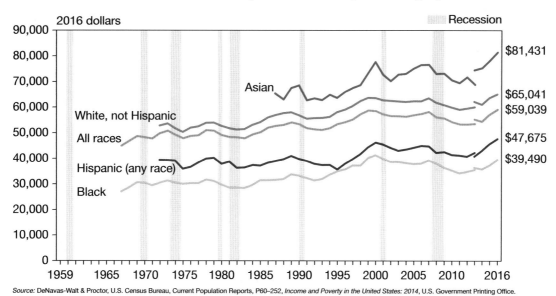

Source: DeNavas-Walt & Proctor, U.S. Census Bureau, Current Population Reports, P60–252, *Income and Poverty in the United States: 2014*, U.S. Government Printing Office.

▼ TABLE 9.6

Income and Earnings Summary Measures by Selected Characteristics 2015 and 2016

(Income in 201+ dollars. Households and people as of March of the following year. For information on confidentiality protection, sampling error, nonsampling error, and definitions, see www2.census.gov/programs-surveys/cpsmar17.pdf)							
		2015			2016		Percentage Change* in Real Median Income (2016 less 2015)
		Median Income (dollars)			Median Income (dollars)		
Characteristic	Number (thousands)	Estimate	Margin of Error¹(±)	Number (thousands)	Estimate	Margin of Error¹(±)	Estimate
HOUSEHOLDS								
All households	125,819	57,230	534	126,224	59,039	717	*3.2	1.56
Type pf Household								
Family households	82,184	73,077	615	82,827	75,062	692	*2.7	1.14
Married couple	60,251	85,696	995	60,804	87,057	695	*1.6	1.36
Female householder, no husband present	15,622	38,275	1,008	15,572	41,027	871	*7.2	3.51
Male householder, no wife present	6,310	56,567	1,615	6,425	58,051	2,172	2.6	4.34
Nonfamily householder	43,635	34,232	786	43,396	35,761	467	*4.5	2.70
Female householder	23,093	29,389	832	22,858	30,572	603	*4.0	3.56
Male householder	20,542	41,278	755	20,539	41,749	701	1.1	2.34

(Continued)

(Continued)

(Income in 201+ dollars. Households and people as of March of the following year. For information on confidentiality protection, sampling error, nonsampling error, and definitions, see www2.census.gov/programs-surveys/cpsmar17.pdf)

| Characteristic | 2015 | | | 2016 | | | Percentage Change* in Real Median Income (2016 less 2015) | |
| | Number (thousands) | Median Income (dollars) | | Number (thousands) | Median Income (dollars) | | | |
		Estimate	Margin of Error[1](±)		Estimate	Margin of Error[1](±)	Estimate	Margin of Error[1](±)
Race[2] and Hispanic Origin of Householder								
White	99,313	60,869	635	99,400	61,858	549	*1.6	1.33
White, not Hispanic	84,445	63,745	903	84,387	65,041	839	*2.0	1.81
Black	16,539	37,364	855	16,733	39,490	1,187	*5.7	3.90
Asian	6,328	78,141	2,826	6,392	81,431	1,917	4.2	4.31
Hispanic (any race)	16,667	45,719	1,024	16,915	47,675	1,113	*4.3	3.45
Age of Householder								
Younger than 65 years	94,820	64,144	832	94,425	66,487	580	*3.7	1.62
15 to 24 years	6,361	36,564	1,350	6,238	41,655	1,145	*13.9	5.11
25 to 34 years	20,047	58,091	1,135	20,109	60,932	802	*4.9	2.55
35 to 44 years	21,222	72,319	970	21,500	74,481	1,834	*3.0	2.81
45 to 54 years	23,294	74,790	1,891	22,808	77,213	1,156	*3.2	3.05
55 to 64 years	23,896	63,596	565	107,192	59,781	691	*3.3	3.04
65 years and older	30,998	39,001	781	31,799	39,823	1,190	*4.9	3.17
Nativity of householder								
Native born	107,081	57,896	565	107,192	59,781	691	*3.3	1.50
Foreign born	18,738	52,956	1,141	19,031	55,559	1,190	*4.9	3.17
Naturalized citizen	9,856	62,766	1,342	10,054	63,894	2,628	1.8	4.58
Not a citizen	8,881	45,708	1,743	8,978	48,066	1,733	5.2	5.63
Region								
Northeast	22,347	62,968	1,359	22,325	64,390	1,806	2.3	3.34
Midwest	27,455	57,803	1,353	27,363	58,305	1,476	0.9	3.23
South	47,822	51,821	630	48,065	53,861	1,160	*3.9	2.36
West	28,195	62,218	957	28,470	64,275	1,708	*3.3	3.04
Residence[3]								
Inside metropolitan statistical areas	107,615	60,007	790	108,215	61,521	535	*2.5	1.60
Inside principal cities	42,615	52,027	654	42,652	54,834	1,187	*5.4	2.65
Outside principle cities	65,000	64,954	964	65,562	66,319	767	*2.1	1.85
Outside metropolitan statistical areas	18,204	45,221	1,562	18,009	45,830	1,013	1.3	3.50

(Income in 201+ dollars. Households and people as of March of the following year. For information on confidentiality protection, sampling error, nonsampling error, and definitions, see www2.census.gov/programs-surveys/cpsmar17.pdf)								
		2015			2016		Percentage Change* in Real Median Income (2016 less 2015)	
		Median Income (dollars)			Median Income (dollars)			
Characteristic	Number (thousands)	Estimate	Margin of Error[1](±)	Number (thousands)	Estimate	Margin of Error[1](±)	Estimate	Margin of Error[1](±)
EARNINGS OF FULL-TIME, YEAR-ROUND WORKERS								
Men with earnings	63,887	51,859	227	64,953	51,640	211	−0.4	0.56
Women with earnings	47,211	41,257	244	48,328	41,554	246	0.7	0.79
Female-to-male earnings ratio	X	0.796	0.0049	X	0.805	0.0052	*1.1	0.85

*An asterisk preceding an estimate indicates change is statistically different from zero at the 90% confidence level.

X Not applicable.

[1]A margin of error is a measure of an estimate's variability. The large the margin of error in relation to the size of the estimate, the less reliable the estimate. This number, when added to and subtracted from the estimate, forms the 90% confidence interval. Margins of error shown in this based on standard errors calculated using replicate weights. For more information, see "Standard Errors and Their Use at <www2.census.gov/library/publications/2017/demo/p60-259sa.pdf>.

[2]Federal surveys give respondents the option of reporting more than one race. Therefore, two basic ways of defining a race group are possible. A group such as Asian may be defined as those who reported Asian and no other race (the race-alone or single-race concept).or as those who reported Asian regardless of whether they also reported another race (the race-alone-or-in-combination concept).This table shows data using the first approach (race alone). The use of the single-race population does not imply that it is the preferred method of presenting or analyzing data. The Census Bureau uses a variety of approaches. Information on people who reported more than one race, such as White and American Indian and Alaska Native or Asian and Black or African American, is available from the 2010 Census through American FactFinder. About 2.9% of people reported more than one race in the 2010 Census. Data for American Indians and Alaska Natives, Native Hawaiians and Other pacific Islanders, and those reporting two or more races are not shown separately.

[3]For information on metropolitan statistical areas and principal cities, see www.gov/programs-survey/metro-micro/about/glossary.html

Note: Inflation-adjusted estimates may differ slightly from other published date due to rounding.

Source: DeNavas-Walt & Proctor, U.S. Census Bureau, Current Population Reports, P60–252, Income and Poverty in the United States: 2014, U.S. Government Printing Office.

▼ FIGURE 9.2

Percentage of Child Poverty by Race and Ethnicity in 2016

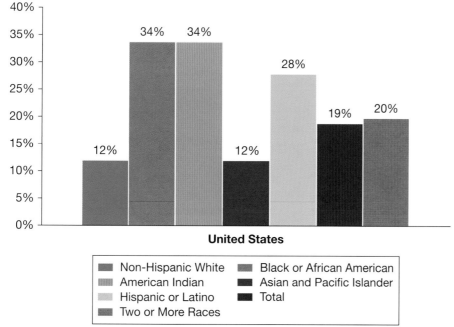

Source: The Annie E. Casey Foundation. Kids Count Data Center. Retrieved from www.aecf.org.

and white students almost twice as likely as minority students (Centers for Disease Control and Prevention, 2014a).

Bullying and Cyberbullying

Bullying includes three major types: physical, social, and verbal; and these victimizations may occur in person and through Internet and social media connections (cyberbullying). Bullying takes many forms, including insults and name-calling, being threatened with harm, being subjected to rumors, physical assaults, forced to do things against your will, purposeful exclusion from activities, and property destruction. **Cyberbullying** also has numerous forms, including hurtful information on the Internet; sharing private information; unwanted contact via e-mail, texting, online gaming, and other social media sites; and purposeful exclusion from an online community (U.S. Department of Education, 2013).

▲ Bullying is a common problem reported by many students, though less bullying is being reported of late. What do you think is causing this improvement?

Bullying is a common experience for children and adolescents, with many of these victimizations occurring on school grounds. National data on bullying across schools were not collected until 2005, when the Department of Education first reported that between 28% and 32% of all students were bullied during the school year. Bullying victims continued to report a high number of experiences, although there has been a decrease to 21% in the 2015 academic reporting year. Female students report higher rates of bullying (23%) compared to male students (19%), as well as more victimizations due to cyberbullying (9% compared to 5% for male students). Younger students—grades sixth through ninth—are more likely to be bullied compared with older students—tenth to twelfth grades, with equal bullying victimization rates across low, middle, and high family incomes (U.S. Department of Education, 2013). The reasons for the recent decline in bullying reports are under investigation, although federal and state efforts have prioritized the problem, including a requirement that public elementary and secondary schools report incidents of harassment based on religion, sexual orientation, gender, race, color, national origin, and disability status (U.S. Department of Education, 2016a).

Students who are victims of bullying do not perform as well academically in school and more often skip class and are truant. In addition, they are at significantly higher risk for using and abusing alcohol and drugs, suffering from depression, and having a higher risk of suicide. Marginalized student populations, including the LGBT community, are most at risk for bullying victimization and these problematic outcomes (Hatzenbuehler & Keyes, 2013; Kowalski & Limber, 2013).

A recent **National School Climate Survey** (2013) found that 55% of LGBT students felt unsafe at school because of their sexual orientation and 38% because of their gender expression. More than 74% of LGBT students reported experiencing harassment (threatened, called names), and 49% were electronically threatened because of their sexual orientation or gender identity, with 17% reporting being physically attacked. It was more likely that minority students were targeted more frequently than white students. A majority (56%) did not report these incidents to school authorities for they doubted an effective outcome and feared a possible worst bullying situation. This lead to greater than 30% of

Bullying (Cyberbullying): Three major types: physical, social, and verbal. These victimizations may occur in person and through Internet and social media connections (cyberbullying).

Cyberbullying: Has numerous forms, including hurtful information on the Internet; sharing private information; unwanted contact via e-mail, texting, online gaming, and other social media sites, as well as purposeful exclusion from an online community.

National School Climate Survey: Series of national surveys of schools identifying the heightened difficulties of the lesbian, gay, bisexual, and transgender (LGBT) population.

Percentage of Students Ages 12–18 Who Reported Being Bullied at School During the School Year, by Type of Bullying and Sex 2015

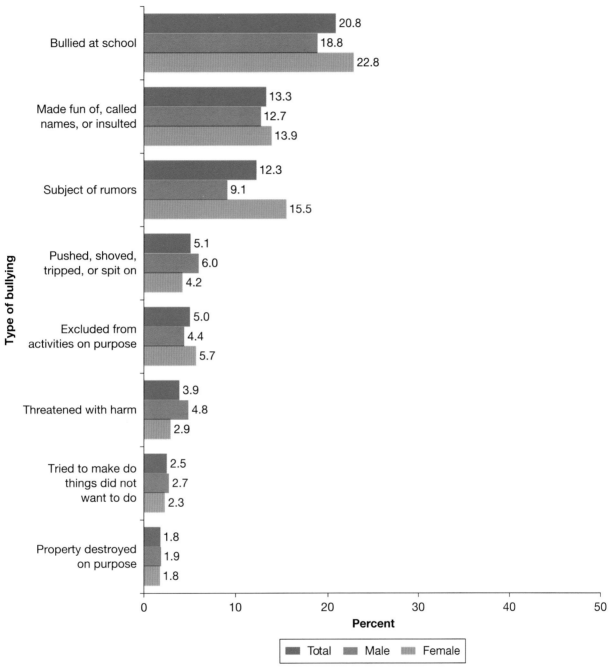

Source: Musu-Gillette, Zhang, Wang, Zhang, and Oudekerk (2017). *Indicators of School Crime and Safety: 2016* (NCES 2017-064/NCJ 250650). National Center for Education Statistics, U.S. Department of Education, and Bureau of Justice Statistics, Office of Justice Programs, U.S. Department of Justice.

LGBT students missing at least one day of school and 10% missing four or more days of school in the past month (Kosciw, Greytak, Palmer, & Boesen, 2014). As discussed, absences from school and truant outcomes greatly increase the risk for school discipline and failure.

And most recently, the first nationwide representative survey of secondary-aged students that asked about their sexuality found this group to be at ongoing risk. The survey identified

Negative Effects of Bullying

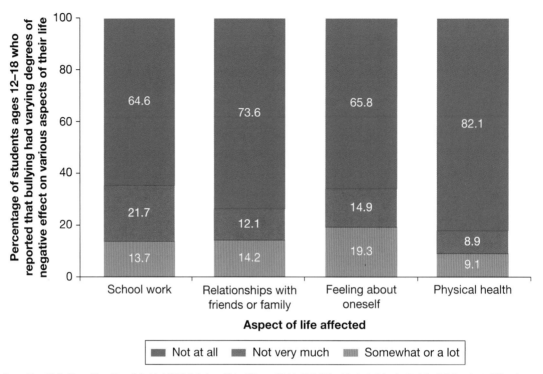

Source: Musu-Gillette, Zhang, Wang, Zhang, & Oudekerk (2017). *Indicators of School Crime and Safety: 2016*. National Center for Education Statistics, U.S. Department of Education, and Bureau of Justice Statistics, Office of Justice Programs, U.S. Department of Justice.

that 8% of high school students self-reported as LGBT as well as the following findings when compared with heterosexual students: They were more than three times more likely to have been raped; they were twice as likely to have been threatened or injured with a weapon on school grounds; and they were four times more likely to have used heroin. More poignantly, more than 40% of LGBT students reported a serious suicide ideation or plan, with 29% who attempted suicide in the prior year (Centers for Disease Control and Prevention, 2016).

Poly-victimization. **Poly-victimization** is the exposure to, and experience of, multiple forms of trauma and/or victimization. Multiple trauma experiences are common for some child and adolescent populations, with up to 20% of those ages 13 to 18 (disproportionately male, black, and older) having experienced more than one type of trauma, and greater than 41% of physical abuse, assault, or sexual abuse victims had also reported additional trauma experiences. More broadly, for all children and adolescents who experienced any direct victimization, more than two thirds reported more than one type. Of concern is that there are a small number (between 6% and 8%) of adolescents reporting exposure from 6 to 15+ different traumatic experiences over their lifetime (Finkelhor et al., 2005; Finkelhor et al., 2013; McCart et al., 2011).

Having certain traumatic experiences exposes the young person to much greater risk for another trauma. A child who was physically assaulted would be five times as likely to have been sexually victimized and more than four times as likely to have been maltreated during a one-year period. And a child who was physically assaulted during his or her lifetime would be more than six times as likely to have been sexually victimized and more than five times as likely to have been maltreated (any type) during his or her lifetime. The greater the number and severity of the trauma experiences, often the greater the impairment for adolescents, including mental health, academic, and behavioral problems. Specifically, poly-victimizations are clearly linked to delinquency and involvement with the juvenile justice system (Finkelhor, 2009; Ford, Elhai, Conner, & Frueh, 2010; Ford, Grasso, Hawke, & Chapman, 2013). In

Poly-Victimization:
Exposure to, and experience of, multiple forms of trauma and/or victimization.

Poly-victimization

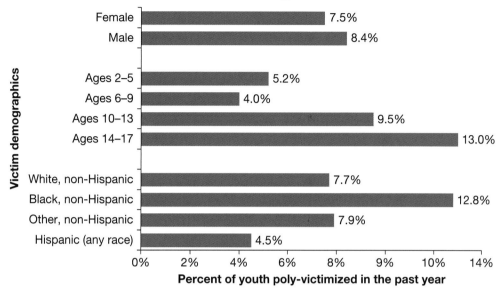

Poly-victimization is the exposure to multiple victimizations from various types of violence or abuse

Victim demographics	Percent
Female	7.5%
Male	8.4%
Ages 2–5	5.2%
Ages 6–9	4.0%
Ages 10–13	9.5%
Ages 14–17	13.0%
White, non-Hispanic	7.7%
Black, non-Hispanic	12.8%
Other, non-Hispanic	7.9%
Hispanic (any race)	4.5%

Percent of youth poly-victimized in the past year

Source: Sickmund & Puzzanchera (2014). *Juvenile Offenders and Victims: 2014 National Report.* National Center for Juvenile Justice.

addition, repeated trauma experiences have been found to double the risk for psychiatric disorders (anxiety, post-traumatic stress disorder, and depression, among others), and this impact lasts for up to three years after the traumas (Copeland et al., 2007; Perkonigg, Kessler, Storz, & Wittchen, 2000).

POST-TRAUMATIC STRESS DISORDER (PTSD)

Many children and adolescents who have experienced trauma, and in particular chronic trauma, will develop symptoms, or partial symptoms, of PTSD (as well as other related anxiety or depression problems). Post-traumatic stress disorder can occur at any age, even for children as young as one or two years old, although there may be a delay of months or years before symptoms can be identified. Different reactions, stressors, and symptoms may vary over time and for children at different developmental stages. Before the age of six, children are more likely to express re-experiencing symptoms through play, and parents or guardians may identify a wide range of emotional and behavioral changes. Older children and adolescents may isolate themselves from family and peers, avoid dating or driving, or judge themselves harshly or as cowards. A diagnosis of PTSD includes a history of trauma(s) event exposure that impacts the person and leads to avoidance, negative reactions, and changes to daily living (American Psychiatric Association, 2013).

Post-Traumatic Stress Disorder Diagnosis

Diagnostic criteria for PTSD includes a history of exposure to a traumatic event(s) that meets specific areas from four symptom categories: intrusion, avoidance, negative alterations in cognitions and mood, and alterations in arousal and reactivity that last at least one month (American Psychiatric Association, 2013).

Hypervigilance and Physiological Impact

One symptom of PTSD, and related trauma difficulties, is a state known as "hypervigilance," which is often defined as "abnormally increased arousal, responsiveness to stimuli, and scanning

THE LIVES OF JUVENILE LIFERS

Some of these more extreme experiences with poly-victimization and complicated trauma histories are found within a group of youthful offenders who have been sentenced to life in prison without any possibility of parole. A national survey of 1,579 "juvenile lifers" (disproportionately male—97%; and minority—60% black, 25% white, and 14% Hispanic) serving this sentence found the following about their child and adolescent years: 79% witnessed violence in their homes, with more than half witnessing violence weekly in their neighborhood; 47% were physically abused (including 80% of females); 21% were sexually abused (including 77% of females); 32% were raised in public housing, with 18% not living with family at the time of arrest (they were homeless or housed in a residential facility); 40% were enrolled in special education programming; and 85% had been suspended or expelled from school during their secondary school-age years. These complicated life histories, maltreatment victimizations, school-related problems and disabilities, and violence exposures have been found to gravely increase the risk for delinquent behaviors, school failure, and involvement in the juvenile justice and adult criminal justice systems (Nellis, 2012).

1. What do you think the connection is from trauma experiences to youthful offending?

2. Are young people who have multiple trauma experiences destined to lead a life of delinquency and crime? Why or why not?

of the environment for threats" (Buffington et al., 2010, p. 3). For children and adolescents, this can look like jumpiness, nervousness, quick to react or startle, high defensiveness, and/or an inability to feel calm or relax. Many highly traumatized young people are in a consistent state of hypervigilance, always worried or fearful of what trauma may impact them next. This "flight-or-fight" response can be debilitating for many, very tiring, and may look like symptoms of other problems: attention-deficit hyperactivity disorder, conduct problems, aggressive behaviors, paranoia, and social interaction or relationship difficulties.

A fight-or-flight response to trauma may also harm or damage a child's brain functioning and development. When traumatic events cause this response, stress hormones (cortisol and adrenaline) are released to prepare the body for either escaping the threat or staying and "fighting" the threat. Although this is an effective response for dealing with an immediate danger, children's and adolescents' bodies are not meant to live in this stressed state for extended periods of time. The hormones released during stressful events can have cumulative, long-term damages on the body. This is potentially harmful for those who are still experiencing sensitive periods of growth and development, and may have significant consequences on brain development. The child or adolescents' brain is adapting to help the individual survive in a traumatic and stress-filled environment. This stress-induced damage can disrupt normal development and lead to emotional, cognitive, and behavioral problems. Potential cognitive impacts include language delays, attentional issues, and memory difficulties. Behavioral issues may include increased aggression, poor social skills, an inability to moderate emotional responses, attachment problems, and an increase in risk-taking behaviors and impulsivity (Substance Abuse and Mental Health Services Administration, 2014b).

PTSD Prevalence

The most recent (2012) nationally representative study, using the American Psychiatric Association's definition of PTSD, of adolescents ages 13 to 18 found 5% met criteria for PTSD during their lifetime, with a higher prevalence rate for girls (8.3%) than for boys (2.3%; Kessler et al., 2012). Higher overall prevalence rates (7% to 11%) have been found in reviews of adolescents living in larger urban areas, with similar gender differences found in these populations (Breslau, Wilcox, Storr, Lucia, & Anthony, 2004).

Young people involved with the juvenile courts are disproportionately impacted by trauma and, subsequently, PTSD symptoms and diagnoses. The further an adolescent penetrates the juvenile justice system, the more likely he or she is to have histories of trauma, multiple systems involvement (child welfare and substance abuse, among others), and severe mental health needs because of these trauma experiences. Studies of PTSD prevalence in juvenile justice–involved youthful offenders are significantly higher than the general adolescent population, ranging from 11% to 50%. The higher rates of PTSD are found within youthful offender detention and incarceration facilities, with more girls diagnosed (25% to 50%) than boys (15% to 30%; Ford, Chapman, Hawke, & Albert, 2007; Kretschmar, Butcher, Flannery, & Singer, 2016). It is more than likely that adolescents involved with the juvenile justice system have had trauma exposure either at home, school, and/or their neighborhood, and that most have developed at least some trauma symptoms (Mueser & Taub, 2008). In one study of youthful offenders being held in the Cook County, Chicago, Detention Center, 92% reported having experienced at least one lifetime trauma event, 84% had two lifetime trauma events, and 57% had six or more lifetime trauma events. Witnessing violence was the most common trauma event reported. Within this group, more than 10% had been diagnosed with PTSD, and 93% had been diagnosed with a comorbid mental health problem (Abram et al., 2013).

RESILIENCY TO TRAUMA EXPERIENCES

Children and adolescents react to trauma experiences in varying ways. Some are highly resilient to such experiences, whereas others are greatly affected and troubled. The term "resilient" has been measured in several ways: the capacity for children and adolescents to thrive in the face of risks and difficulties, avoiding many of the deleterious effects; and the process of, or capacity for, a successful adaption despite the circumstances. However defined, many young people are simply able to withstand the challenge of trauma victimizations and experiences without sustaining harmful long-term consequences (Fergus & Zimmerman, 2004; Masten, Best, & Garmezy, 1990).

The degree of resilience that a young person has depends on a complex interaction of risks factors balanced with protective factors. Protective factors are often considered and measured as the absence of risk factors. When identifying childhood resiliency factors that protect from family dysfunction, poverty, and related difficulties, there is a significant interplay among heritable factors, individual characteristics, and experiences over time. These may include individual cognitive factors such as self-regulation abilities and intelligence, biological factors such as stress and reactivity, interpersonal factors such as peer affiliations, and family-related factors including parenting abilities (Caspi et al., 2002; Collishaw et al., 2007).

Several specific protective factors have been identified that may minimize certain childhood and adolescent trauma risks of impacts. A strong relationship with a positive parent or parental figure may be protection enough for a child to overcome maltreatment experiences. In addition, other factors have been found to protect from maltreatment victimizations: above-average cognitive abilities and learning styles, an internal locus of control, the presence of spirituality, external attributions of blame from traumatic events, and emotional support from others (Heller, Larrieu, D'Imperio, & Boris, 1999; McGee, Wolfe, & Olson, 2001). The school may provide enough of a support system that the dysfunctional and victimizing family system does not greatly impact child development. In some cases, the family environment may provide a stable enough home that even a poor and violent neighborhood will not significantly impede the child's development or school success (Buffington et al., 2010; Fraser, 2004; Hawkens et al., 2000).

The presence of these protections, or other factors yet to be identified, may be the reason for growing evidence that the mental health of a substantial (although still a minority) percentage of maltreated children are relatively unaffected by their adversity (American Bar Association, 2014). Also, children and adolescents who are not maltreated but who are exposed to other trauma experiences (domestic violence and poverty, among others) are still at risk for the development of mental health difficulties, substance abuse problems, learning/academic problems, and subsequent delinquency. Nonetheless, many of these children are also resilient and adapt and develop well into adolescence without significant trouble (Luthar, 2003; National Center for Children in Poverty, 2000).

MALTREATMENT AND ACADEMIC PERFORMANCE

Children and adolescents with maltreatment victimization histories, compared with those without similar histories, are less successful in school. Depending on when the maltreatment occurs, the child's development and school performance may be differentially impacted both in primary as well as in secondary school.

Primary School

For primary school–age students, cognitive and language delays are greater for maltreated children compared with nonmaltreated children from lower socioeconomic backgrounds, and much greater when compared with nonmaltreated children from higher socioeconomic backgrounds (Wiggins, Fenichel, & Mann, 2007). On average, maltreated children enter early primary school grades one-half year behind on academic performance and have poorer academic performance, functioning, and verbal abilities at ages six and eight. These children also have higher absenteeism rates that may be affecting or complicating these delayed education beginnings (Lansford et al., 2002; Leiter, 2007; Perez & Widom, 1994; Smithgall, Gladden, Howard, Goerge, & Courtney, 2004; Zolotor et al., 1999). Experiencing maltreatment at an earlier age may lead to behavior problems and increased placement into special education programs. Children in foster care are more likely to be diagnosed with a special education disability during primary school: between 30% and 50% in some populations. Children in foster care are often behind in grade level and in reading and mathematics ability (Burley & Haplern, 2001; Hyames & de Hames, 2000; Leiter & Johnson, 1997; Scarborough & McCrae, 2009).

Secondary School

For secondary school-age students, maltreatment negatively affects their academic outcomes and social/peer relationships. Older adolescents, particularly those with longer histories of maltreatment victimization, are often three or four grade levels behind in reading abilities and repeat at least one grade significantly more often than nonmaltreated adolescents, making their chances of high school completion much less likely (Coleman, 2004; Slade & Wissow, 2007). Similarly, adolescents who have experienced foster care placement are particularly at risk, with a much higher percentage not completing high school compared with their nonmaltreated peers (Courtney, Roderick, Smithgall, Gladden, & Nagaoka, 2004). Adolescents with maltreatment histories who do not complete high school, those in foster care who are truant or change schools often, and those aging out of the child welfare system are at high risk from involvement in offending activities. Without effective supports or efforts to complete their secondary school education, this group typically finds that the employment and independent living options of its members are limited in young adulthood (Ryan, Herz, Hernandez, & Marshall, 2007).

MALTREATMENT AND DELINQUENCY

Aging Out: When a young person reaches the age of majority (typically 18) in his or her state and is in foster care, he or she "ages out" by legally becoming an adult and no longer is supervised by the child welfare system.

Many of the adolescents involved with the juvenile courts have maltreatment histories; that is, they are past victims of physical, sexual, psychological abuse, or neglect. As discussed earlier in the text, between 26% and 60% of adjudicated delinquent juvenile offenders have been past maltreatment victims (Sedlak & McPherson, 2010). Although maltreatment is a significant risk factor for later juvenile court involvement, it is important to highlight that most children and adolescents who are maltreatment victims never become involved with the juvenile courts. Nevertheless, victims of maltreatment are significantly at risk for involvement in delinquency and to spend time in detention centers and juvenile justice incarceration facilities (Currie & Tekin, 2006; Lemmon, 2006; Yun, Ball, & Lim, 2011). This link from trauma to maltreatment victimizations has been identified for over three decades through studies of mostly male youthful offenders, although research more recently has identified different pathways for female youthful offenders (Maschi, Bradley, & Morgan, 2008). The link from maltreatment to delinquency, however, is complicated.

This connection was first identified in finding that maltreated youthful offenders had a 53% greater chance of being arrested as an adolescent, were much more likely to be arrested a year earlier than did nonmaltreated youthful offenders, and had an increased adult arrest risk rate of 38% (Widom, 1989). The earlier the abuse occurs, the greater the risk for being arrested as adolescents for violent, nonviolent, and status offenses. Additionally, these maltreated adolescents were found more likely to be formally supervised by the juvenile court for more serious offending behaviors than were their nonmaltreated offending peers. All three maltreatment types (physical abuse, sexual abuse, and neglect) have been linked to later antisocial behavior, violent crimes, and court involvement, even in the presence of other risk factors (Lemmon, 2009; Loeber & Farrington, 2001; Smith & Thornberry, 1995; Yun et al., 2011). Repeated maltreatment victimization predicts the initiation, continuation, and severity of delinquent acts and is associated with serious, chronic, and violent offending behaviors as an adolescent and into adulthood (Currie & Tekin, 2010; Verrecchia, Fetzer, Lemmon, & Austin, 2010).

The impact of maltreatment, particularly on younger victims, leads to other problems beyond delinquency. Mental health and substance abuse problems are often outcomes of child and adolescent maltreatment, with the risk exponentially increasing for those with multiple victimizations and victimizations over time. Repeated physical abuse of children often results in depression and post-traumatic stress disorder; sexual abuse is associated with post-traumatic stress disorder and other anxiety difficulties; and neglect often leads to anxiety disorders and related problems (Kilpatrick, Ruggiero, Acierno, Saunders, Resnick, & Best, 2003; Turner, Finkelhor, & Ormrod, 2006). Physical abuse has also been found to lower high school graduation rates for adolescents and to increase chances of being a teen parent for black adolescents. These mental health difficulties, along with the other risks, have been found to exacerbate offending behavior and to make delinquency adjudication more likely (Brezina, 1998; Lansford et al., 2007; Maschi et al., 2008).

Gender Differences

Delinquency pathways and trauma victimization experiences are not the same for adolescent males and females. Girls' delinquency starts earlier than boys,' and certain risk factors have a greater impact on girls—earlier maturation, maltreatment victimization, and anxiety, depression, and post-traumatic stress disorder symptoms (Fontaine, Carbonneau, Vitaro, Barker, & Tremblay, 2009). Juvenile justice–involved girls are also significantly more often victimized by crimes and traumas, in particular extreme and repeated victimizations, than are boys or girls not involved with the juvenile justice system. Acts such as running away from home and other truancy offenses are often related to abuse and trauma being experienced in the home (Sickmund & Puzzanchera, 2014; Zahn et al., 2010).

Evidence to date cannot conclusively find that maltreatment effects for females are greater when compared with those for males in delinquency development, although the impact of abuse and neglect is different. Within delinquent populations, girls are more likely than boys to have been victims of sexual abuse and are equally likely to have experienced physical abuse (Hennessey, Ford, Mahoney, Ko, & Siegfried, 2004; Zahn et al., 2010). The cumulative impact of maltreatment, in addition to other risks often associated with this maltreatment such as substance abuse and school difficulties, may affect girls more negatively than boys, as evidenced by girls' higher rates of PTSD (National Center for Child Traumatic Stress, 2009). It is clear, though, that family conflict has a heightened impact on girls as well as exposure to community violence, which are both risk factors for delinquent activities (Sherman & Balck, 2015).

Dually involved Youth (Crossover Youth): Dynamic between child maltreatment and delinquency, with young people having contact with both systems simultaneously.

POLICY: WHAT'S BEING DONE?

CROSSOVER (DUALLY INVOLVED) YOUTH

Crossover youth, also called dually involved youth, refers to the dynamic between child maltreatment and delinquency, with young people having contact with both systems simultaneously. The challenges for the child welfare agencies, juvenile courts, and those involved can be exponentially more difficult because of the dynamics of trauma, offending behaviors, out-of-home placements, and school problems (Abbott & Barnett, 2015). Although rigorous national epidemiological reviews are missing, one study of this population in Los Angeles may be representative of larger urban areas: 8% of adolescents had at least one arrest before entering the child welfare system; 32% had new child maltreatment victimization referrals after arrest; and 56% were subsequently charged with a second delinquency offense. Many of these young people are at significant risk for out-of-home placement (Huang, Ryan, & Herz, 2012).

In the child welfare system, out-of-home placements occur because the child or adolescent is at risk for continued or ongoing abuse or neglect. These alternative placements may include group homes, foster homes, residential facilities, or with an extended and a nonmaltreatment involved family member (often referred to as "kincare"). In the most recent reporting year (2013), 400,000 children and adolescents younger than 18 years of age were living outside their home due to a children's services placement. These placements have immediate positive outcomes—removal from unsafe homes—but also increase the risk for delinquent peer activities and school transition difficulties (Kolivoski, Shook, Goodkind, & Kim, 2014).

This is particularly true for dually involved adolescents in foster care who have moved homes frequently. These moves, disruptions, and school transitions decrease the family and social connections for the young person and increase the risk for further involvement with the juvenile justice system, as well as difficulties in school (Huang et al., 2012). When placements in group homes or residential care facilities are used, these facilities may not provide certain services and settings to avoid increasing the risk for postdischarge delinquent activities. In addition, when these young people are removed from their homes and held in juvenile justice detention (and, for some, incarceration) facilities, the placement itself is harmful and increases the risk for offending recidivism. Once held in these locked facilities, placement experiences that are traumatic for many adolescents, the chances of a successful transition back to the young person's home, neighborhood, and school become significantly more difficult (Dishion & Dodge, 2005; Petrosino, Turpin-Petrosino, & Guckenburg, 2010).

1. Why do you think young people in foster care are at a significantly higher risk for delinquency involvement?

2. How can being removed from your home due to maltreatment as a child have both positive and negative impacts?

CASE STUDY

JAMES

At school, all the teachers and principals knew was that James was a 14-year-old white male with a history of cursing at others, starting arguments, and not completing his academic work often; and last week he stabbed a classmate in the arm with a pen after they started arguing. James was arrested by the school resource officer and referred to the local juvenile court, as was the school's policy. The juvenile court processed James as a juvenile delinquent and assigned a probation officer. Here is what the school and juvenile court personnel did not know until the probation officer completed the court's investigation: James entered mental health treatment four months ago when he and his mom were in the battered woman's shelter; Mom was with her boyfriend Don for 6 years, and Don nearly killed Mom on

two occasions through strangulation; Don physically abused James for three years; James visits his Dad, who is living with a woman who is an alcoholic; James has nightmares, is afraid to sleep alone, and constantly calls his parents when he is away from them.

1. Would knowing this information have changed the school's response and outcome?

2. What do you think should happen at this point with James?

3. What policies might you change in response to this type of situation?

CHAPTER REVIEW

CHAPTER SUMMARY

This chapter reviewed the multiple types of traumas that impact children and adolescents—maltreatment, poor and unsafe neighborhoods, bullying and cyberbullying, violent deaths, and witnessing violence, among others. The impact of these traumas was explored as to how school learning and success is impacted, as well as to how these traumatic experiences greatly increase the risk for the developing of delinquent behaviors and involvement with the juvenile courts. Most of those under juvenile court supervision have significant trauma histories, experiences that often continue in juvenile justice (and adult) correctional facilities. Many of these young people will develop the mental health problem called "post-traumatic stress disorder (PTSD)" because of these trauma difficulties and their comorbid impact. Nevertheless, many children and adolescents are also resilient to the impact of these problems, something that is important in the treatment of adolescent trauma.

KEY TERMS

acute trauma **187**

aging out **210**

bullying **204**

child maltreatment victimization **187**

chronic trauma **187**

complex trauma **187**

crossover (dually involved) youth **187**

cyberbullying **204**

domestic violence **198**

dually involved youth **212**

National Comorbidity Study **188**

National School Climate Survey **204**

National Survey of Children's Exposure to Violence **188**

nonviolent deaths **200**

poly-victimization **206**

violent deaths **198**

DISCUSSION QUESTIONS

1. What is the link from trauma to school problems? Is it direct? Are all trauma victims destined to end up in trouble?

2. How does trauma impact the risk for adolescents' involvement with the juvenile courts? In other words, what is the link from trauma to delinquency?

3. Which trauma experiences are most detrimental to young people and increase the risk for school failure or delinquent offending behaviors?

4. Why is school bullying a problem, or is it? Who is most at risk for bullying? What types of bullying are most commonly experienced in high school?

5. What is poly-victimization, and which children and adolescents are most at risk for these experiences?

6. Why are so many detained and incarcerated youthful offenders also maltreatment victims?

7. What type of traumas may a child or adolescent experience? Which are more harmful and why?

8. What types of violence exposures are common for children and adolescents? Are any more harmful or damaging than others?

9. Who is most at risk for living in poverty? Why do you think this is the case?

10. Why are official maltreatment reports potentially under-reporting the abuse and neglect victimization rates?

11. What is resiliency? Why do you think some children are more resilient to trauma experiences than others?

12. Are there any gender and/or race differences among trauma victimizations? If so, what are they?

13. What does the term "crossover youth" mean, and what challenges does this group of adolescents pose to the juvenile justice and other youth-caring systems?

https://edge.sagepub.com/mallett

 **SAGE** edge™ **Sharpen your skills with SAGE edge!**

SAGE edge for students provides a personalized approach to help you accomplish your coursework in an easy-to-use learning environment. You'll find mobile-friendly eFlashcards and quizzes, as well as videos, web resources, and links to SAGE journal articles to support and expand on the concepts presented in this chapter.

CHAPTER 10

MENTAL HEALTH DISORDERS, SPECIAL EDUCATION DISABILITIES, AND DELINQUENCY

▲ Mental health difficulties impact numerous children and adolescents. What do you think causes these problems?

©iStockphoto.com/Татьяна Джемилева

INTRODUCTION

This chapter presents additional support for the social disorganization and life-course theoretical frameworks of delinquency by extending the review of trauma and examining the link from mental health disorders and special education disabilities to youthful offending. With most offenders formally involved with juvenile courts diagnosed with at least one, if not more than one, of these difficulties, it is clear that these problems are significant risks for delinquency, detention, and incarceration. First examined are the types and impact of the most prevalent mental health problems for children and adolescents, gender and race identified differences within this population, and links to offending behaviors. Then an overview is provided of the establishment of disability and special education rights for children and adolescents, required school-based services for students with disabilities, and the disproportionate impact these difficulties have within juvenile court populations.

LEARNING OBJECTIVES

1. Identify the most common mental health problems within the child and adolescent population and compare for differences to the juvenile court population

2. Interpret how certain mental health problems increase the risk for delinquency

3. Examine the pathways across child and adolescent mental health problems, trauma, and juvenile court involvement

4. Describe how juvenile justice correctional facilities have become more like psychiatric facilities

5. Appraise the most important disability rights for children and adolescents and their impact on school and education-related services

CHILD AND ADOLESCENT MENTAL HEALTH PROBLEMS

Over the past three decades, there have been significant epidemiological studies of child and adolescent mental health problems in the United States (as well as across several other countries, including Great Britain and Australia and Puerto Rico). Most of these studies have used the American Psychiatric Association's Diagnostic and Statistical Manual of Mental Disorders (current edition is version 5) to define the problems. The DSM (as it is often referred to) is the medical profession's diagnostic criteria and typology for all mental health and substance use disorders identified and treated in the United States (American Psychiatric Association, 2013).

Epidemiology is the study of the extent and type of illnesses within populations as well as of the factors that impact their distribution. These studies may investigate the prevalence, incident, or lifetime rates. Prevalence rates are the number of existing cases in a defined population during a specified time period. Lifetime prevalence rates are the number of existing cases during the person's life. And incidence rates are the number of new cases of a disorder in a defined population during a specified time period of observation—for example, the past 12 months.

Prior to the 1990s, there was limited knowledge of the occurrence of mental health difficulties for this population. Although reviews to date include limited representative national surveys of child and adolescent mental health in the United States, there have been numerous large regional studies, including more than 30,000 observations, from which to extrapolate the prevalence findings (Angold et al., 2002; Costello, Mustillo, Erkanli, Keeler, & Angold, 2003; Costello, Mustillo, Keeler, & Angold, 2004; Costello, Egger, & Angold, 2005; Roberts, Roberts, & Xing, 2007). Investigating these problems is important because most adult mental health difficulties begin in childhood and adolescence. The earlier a mental health problem can be identified, the more effective prevention and intervention programming may be for the young person (Merikangas et al., 2010).

Mental Health Disorder (Psychiatric Disorder): A diagnosis by a mental health professional of a behavioral or mental pattern that may cause suffering or a poor ability to function in life.

Special Education Disability: These disability categories are set forth by the Individuals with Disabilities in Education Act (IDEA).

Diagnostic and Statistical Manual of Mental Disorders (DSM): Psychiatric classification code used in the United States to identify mental health problems and disorders.

Epidemiology (Epidemiological Research): Study of the extent and type of illnesses within populations as well as the factors that impact their distribution.

Prevalence Rates: Number of existing cases in a defined population during a specified time period.

The American Psychiatric Association publishes the DSM, a diagnostic and classification system for mental health problems. Have you heard of this manual or know anything about it?

Lifetime Prevalence Rates: Number of existing cases during a person's life.

Incidence Rates: Number of new cases of a disorder in a defined population during a specified time period of observation—for example, the past 12 months.

Risk Factors: Experiences, traits, or issues that make an outcome (delinquency or mental health problems, for example) more likely.

Behaviorally Based Disorders: Mental health problems and disorders that are externalized; in other words, where acting out or physical violence is involved.

Oppositional Defiant Disorder: Behaviorally based mental health disorder diagnosed for children or adolescents.

Attention-Deficit Hyperactivity Disorder (ADHD): Behaviorally based mental health disorder primarily impacting children and adolescents who have attention problems or hyperactive control issues.

Risk Factors

Child and adolescent risk factors (experiences, traits, or issues that make the outcome more likely) for the development of mental health problems and disorders have been divided into individual, family, and neighborhood categories. Individual factors include the following: gender (type is dependent on mental health diagnoses); age (risk increases during adolescence for most diagnoses, although not all); ethnicity (dependent on mental health diagnoses); poorer overall physical health; lower cognitive function; exposure to illness; increased physical stress over time; substance use and abuse; poor nutrition; and lifetime history of environmental exposures to toxins, stress, infections, and traumatic life events. Family factors include the following: lower parental education, lower economic and social class; poorer employment and work histories; a more extensive psychiatric and medical history; parental history of mental disorders; and poor family functioning and structure. Neighborhood factors include the following: increased number of trauma or violent events; lower income neighborhoods; and poor environmental health (Brauner & Stephens, 2006; Goodman et al., 1998; President's New Freedom Commission Report, 2003).

Prevalence Rates

Results from these reviews and other analyses reveal that most children and adolescents in the United States do not suffer from any mental health symptoms or disorders. It is only between 3% and 20% of children and adolescents that have an identified mental health disorder that impairs their functioning to a moderate or significant degree. Nevertheless, the impact for older children and adolescents, ages 9 to 17, is greater with 21% having a diagnosable mental health or substance abuse issue that causes moderate impairment to their daily living. Unfortunately, when these problems are identified, upward of 75% of this group does not access or receive adequate treatment or services, with greater disparity and fewer services received for minority children and adolescents. For those young people with the most severe symptoms or mental health difficulties, however, most do access and receive community- or school-based services. Reasons for this higher level of access to services are because of the young person's significant impairment, the family's recognition of the problem, comorbidity across other problem areas, and if there was a suicide attempt by the young person. Those who access services through their schools, however, are unlikely to transition to community-based or specialty mental health programming when school services end (DeRigne, Porterfield, & Metz, 2009; Ford, 2008; Gudino, Lau, Yeh, McCabe, & Hough, 2009; Reddy, Newman, De Thomas, & Chun, 2008).

Behaviorally Based Disorders

Within the child and adolescent populations that have had mental health difficulties identified, behaviorally based disorders are some of the most common with between 4% and 14% prevalence rates. This includes lower rates in younger children—more often oppositional defiant disorder (ODD) and attention-deficit hyperactivity disorder (ADHD)—and higher rates for older school-age children—more often conduct disorder (Costello et al., 1996; Nock, Kazdin, Hiripi, & Kessler, 2007). Oppositional defiant disorder, impacting slightly more than 3% of the child and adolescent population, and conduct disorder (CD), impacting 4%, are characterized by persistent violation of age-appropriate societal rules and expected behavioral expectations, as well as persistence of these behaviors for a minimum period of time. Attention-deficit hyperactivity disorder has the opposite prevalence trends, with almost all diagnoses made prior to the age of 12 (prevalence is between 3% and 5%), although for many children the difficulties

IMPORTANT STUDY ON RISKS FOR MENTAL HEALTH PROBLEMS

One of the more informative and rigorous studies of child and adolescent mental health followed a birth cohort of 1,265 children in Great Britain to age 21 and tracked the development of psychopathology and causal links between and among many risk factors. The following risks for adolescent and young adult mental health problems were identified: parental separation and divorce; child abuse; lead exposure and its impact on cognitive abilities; cannabis and other illicit drug abuse; being adopted; family and interfamily violence; and the cumulative impact of adverse family factors (Fergusson & Norwood, 2001). In follow-up reviews that looked at the onset and persistence of mental health problems in these children and adolescents, predictive factors for mental

health problems included physical illness, changes in the number of parents in the home, poor maternal mental health, living in poor communities, special education needs, and instability in the family and home environment (Parry-Langdon, Clements, Fletcher, & Goodman, 2008).

1. If these are risk factors for mental health difficulties, what can practitioners do with this information?

2. Does having these risk factors mean that a young person will develop a mental health problem.

---

continue into the secondary school-age period. All three of these disorders—conduct, oppositional defiant, and attention-deficit hyperactivity disorder—are twice as prevalent for boys than they are for girls (American Psychiatric Association, 2013; Costello, Egger, & Angold, 2005; Debar, Clarke, O'Connor, & Nichols, 2001; Roberts et al., 2007).

Young people with oppositional defiant disorder (ODD) show a pattern of behavior that includes the following: at least four symptoms that occur with at least one individual who is not a sibling; causes significant problems at work, school, or home; and lasts at least six months (American Psychiatric Association, 2013).

These behaviors are seen more often than is typical for the child's peers. For children younger than five years of age, the behavior should happen on most days for a period of at least six months. For individuals five years of age or older, the behavior should occur at least once a week for at least six months. The persistence and frequency of the symptoms should exceed what is normative for an individual's age, gender, and culture.

Young people with conduct disorder show a repetitive and ongoing pattern of behavior in which the basic rights of others and societal rules are violated. This is observed as the young person displays three or more behaviors in the following table over the past 12 months, with at least one behavior within the past six months (American Psychiatric Association, 2013).

These difficulties in the young person's behavior cause clinically significant impairment in social, academic, or work functioning. There are also two subtypes of conduct disorder (Childhood onset Type and Adolescent-Onset Type), and both subtypes can occur in a mild, moderate, or severe form.

Young people with attention-deficit hyperactivity disorder (ADHD) show a persistent pattern of inattention and/or hyperactivity that interferes with their ongoing functioning at home or school. There are two diagnostic types of ADHD—inattention focused (requires six or more of listed symptoms) and hyperactivity or impulsivity focused (also six symptoms required), with differing diagnostic criteria (American Psychiatric Association, 2013).

Anxiety Disorders

Anxiety disorders affect between 2% and 4% of the child and adolescent population with some significantly higher rates in several community-based surveys (median prevalence rate of 8%). These disorders impact both the primary and secondary school-age populations

Conduct Disorder: Behaviorally based mental health disorder diagnosed only for children or adolescents that includes severe acting out of physical aggression.

Anxiety Disorders: Class of mental health problems that includes various diagnoses: separation anxiety, panic disorder, agoraphobia, social phobia, overanxious disorder, and generalized anxiety disorder.

SYBIL'S STORY

A nine-year-old girl named Sybil has been in five different grade schools because of antisocial behavior. Since the age of six, she has frequently initiated physical fights using broken bottles and bricks. In the past year, to the horror of her neighbors, Sybil stole several of their cats, doused them in gasoline and set them on fire. When asked why, she stated that she thought it was "funny" and that she likes "watching what they (the cats) do when they are on fire." Most recently, she threatened to kill her second-grade teacher for preventing her from attending recess. Her family is no longer able to control her violent outbursts and has brought her to a psychiatric inpatient facility, Prentiss Hospital, in a major urban area. This is Sybil's third such hospitalization.

. . .

Sybil was brought to the hospital by her paternal grandmother and her father, who is wheelchair-bound. He has been in and out of jail for drug-related offenses since Sybil's birth and is agitated throughout the interview. Sybil's grandmother tells the story of Sybil's life. At three months of age, she was removed from her mother's custody because of neglect and has only seen her mother twice since then. She seemed to be doing OK until the age of six (records show she has a normal IQ and was doing well in school), but between the ages of six and seven she became increasingly aggressive and exhibited sexually inappropriate behavior. Sybil's performance in school deteriorated rapidly, and she currently has domestic battery charges pending against her in court for hitting her cousin in the face with a brick. Her family appeared relieved but also concerned when they left Sybil at Prentiss Hospital that day, no longer able to cope with a problem they did not fully understand (Hirsch & Sheffield, 2006, para. 1 & 2).

. . . .

1. **Why do you think some young people develop serious mental health problems?**

2. **Do you think these serious difficulties are preventable or treatable?**

Source: Hirsch & Sheffield (2006).

---

equally, although with different diagnoses for each group. Separation anxiety and some related anxiety difficulties are more often found in primary school-age children, whereas panic disorder, agoraphobia, social phobia, overanxious disorder, and generalized anxiety disorder are more often found within secondary school-age adolescents. Girls are slightly more often diagnosed with certain anxiety difficulties, primarily post-traumatic stress disorder and obsessive-compulsive disorders, and are overall at greater risk for any anxiety problems (American Psychiatric Association, 2013; Costello et al., 1996; Kessler et al., 2005; Merikangas, 2005; Rapaport et al., 2000).

One of these difficulties for some young people is generalized anxiety disorder. This is seen by others as excessive worry or anxiety that lasts for more than six months. The young person finds it difficult to control the anxieties and shows at least three symptoms (American Psychiatric Association, 2013).

Depression

Depression: Mental health disorder that includes major depressive disorder and related difficulties. These problems greatly increase the risk for self-harm and suicide.

Depression and related disorders are not common for children younger than 12 years of age, accounting for less than 2% of all cases. Nevertheless, depression rates rise dramatically within the adolescent population and impact between 4% and 5% of this group, greatly increasing the risk for suicide (American Psychiatric Association, 2013; Costello et al., 2002; Simonoff et al., 1997). Depressive disorders, including major depressive disorder, have been found to be more prevalent within white adolescent populations when compared with black adolescent populations as well as more common in female adolescents than in male adolescents (Angold et al., 2002; Gonzalez-Tejera et al., 2005).

Young people who suffer from depression struggle in their daily or weekly functioning, and they are commonly considered to have a major depressive disorder. An adolescent with this

difficulty would be experiencing these troubles most days for at least two weeks and need to have troubles with at least five symptoms (American Psychiatric Association, 2013).

Recent Epidemiology: National Comorbidity Study and National Survey on Drug Use and Health

Because there have been only cumulative and regional epidemiological reviews of child and adolescent mental health in the United States, there is a need for broader and fully representative studies. This is beginning to be addressed for the first time with the completion of the National Comorbidity Survey (Adolescent Supplement) in 2010. This national study was representative of the adolescent population, ages 13 to 18; it surveyed and interviewed 10,123 adolescents and at least one parent or guardian based on DSM diagnostic criteria. The study's design was only cross-sectional and not longitudinal, limiting any follow-up or cohort tracking (this also limits some of the data analyses and potential inferential findings). The sample was evenly split across gender (51% male; 49% female) and fairly evenly split across ages (around 20% per year of age) and ethnicity (66% white, 15% black, 14% Hispanic-American, and 5% other minority groups) (Merikangas et al., 2010). The lifetime diagnostic reported findings are presented in Table 10.1 from the National Comorbidity Survey (Adolescent Supplement) report.

Some of the key study findings include the following: Nearly half of the adolescents reported having met diagnostic criteria for at least one disorder over the lifetime, with 20% of this group reporting symptoms severe enough to impair their daily living; almost 10% reported a behavior disorder; 11% reported any substance use disorders (corresponding to 9% for drug abuse/dependence and 6% for alcohol abuse/dependence, and both less likely in blacks); more than 8% reported being severely impaired by an anxiety disorder; more than 11% reported being similarly impacted by a mood disorder; and 40% who reported one disorder also reported a comorbid second disorder, more often those with a mood disorder (equally likely for males and females). Many of these difficulties began during childhood with symptoms of anxiety emerging at age 6 (median), behavior disorders by age 11, mood disorders by age 13, and substance use disorders by age 15. In reviewing known risk factors, some similar ones to previous research were identified with this population review, including parents with lower levels of education and children of divorced parents (Merikangas et al., 2010).

In comparison with past epidemiological studies of child and adolescent mental health, these findings show a somewhat increased cumulative impact for this population as well as some of the more frequent comorbidity findings. Although the individual diagnostic categories reported were within many prior studies' upper prevalence rate ranges, this increase in mental health diagnoses may be because of the under-identification of past studies due to methodological limitations, the decrease over time of mental health problems stigma and impact on young people and families in admitting to the problems or seeking out services, or that this is the first national representative study completed of the 13- to 18-year-old age group.

The **Substance Abuse and Mental Health Services Administration (SAMSHA)** has been investigating and reporting national drug, alcohol, and behavioral health data across adolescent and adult populations since 2002. In 2014, 9.4% of those aged 12 to 17 were users of illicit drugs, which is a decline from 2002 when 11.6% of this group reported this usage. This includes 7.4% of these adolescents who were users of marijuana (little change since 2002), 2.6% who used nonmedical psychotherapeutic drugs (lower since 2002), 1.7% who used pain relievers (little change since 2011), .7% who used stimulants (an increase since 2008), .6% who used inhalants (a decrease since 2002), .2% who used cocaine or crack (little change since 2002), and .2% who

▲ Depression and related problems impact many teenagers. Who do you think is most at risk?

Substance Abuse and Mental Health Services Administration (SAMSHA): Federal agency charged with improving the quality and availability of prevention, treatment, and rehabilitation services for mental health and substance abuse problems.

Lifetime Prevalence of DSM-IV Disorders by Sex and Age Group and Severe Impairment in the National Comorbidity Survey-Adolescent Supplement

DSM-IV Disorder[a]	DSM-IV Disorders													
	Sex				Age								with Severe Impairment	
	Female		Male		13–14 yr		15–16 yr		17–18 yr		Total			
	%	SE	%	SE	%	SE	%	SE	%	SE	%	SE	%	SE
Mood disorders														
Major depressive disorder or dysthymia	15.9	1.3	7.7	0.8	8.4	1.3	12.6	1.3	15.4	1.4	11.7	0.9	8.7	0.8
Bipolar I or II	3.3	0.4	2.6	0.3	1.9	0.3	3.1	0.3	4.3	0.7	2.9	0.3	2.6	0.2
Any mood disorder	18.3	1.4	10.5	1.1	10.5	1.3	15.5	1.4	18.1	1.6	14.3	1.0	11.2	1.0
Anxiety disorders														
Agoraphobia	3.4	0.4	1.4	0.3	2.5	0.4	2.5	0.4	2.0	0.5	2.4	0.2	2.4[c]	0.2
Generalized anxiety disorder	3.0	0.6	1.5	0.3	1.0	0.3	2.8	0.6	3.0	0.5	2.2	0.3	0.9	0.2
Social phobia	11.2	0.7	7.0	0.5	7.7	0.6	9.7	0.7	10.1	1.0	9.1	0.4	1.3	0.2
Specific phobia	22.1	1.1	16.7	0.9	21.6	1.6	18.3	1.0	17.7	1.3	19.3	0.8	0.6	0.1
Panic disorder	2.6	0.3	2.0	0.3	1.8	0.4	2.3	0.3	3.3	0.7	2.3	0.2	2.3[c]	0.2
Post–traumatic stress disorder	8.0	0.7	2.3	0.4	3.7	0.5	5.1	0.5	7.0	0.8	5.0	0.3	1.5	0.2
Separation anxiety disorder	9.0	0.6	6.3	0.5	7.8	0.6	8.0	0.7	6.7	0.8	7.6	0.3	0.6	0.1
Any anxiety disorder	38.0	1.4	26.1	0.8	31.4	1.9	32.1	0.8	9.0	1.1	8.7	0.6	4.2	0.4
Behavior disorders														
Attention deficit hyperactivity disorder	4.2	0.5	13.0	1.0	8.8	0.9	8.6	0.8	9.0	1.1	8.7	0.6	4.2	0.4
Oppositional defiant disorder (ODD)	11.3	0.9	13.9			1.2	12.6	1.3	13.6	1.4	12.6	0.9	6.5	0.7
Conduct disorder	5.8	1.1	7.9	1.2		1.2	7.5	1.2	9.6	1.3	6.8	0.9	2.2	0.4
Any behavior disorder	15.5	1.2	23.5	1.6	18.2	1.5	19.5	1.7	21.9	1.8	19.6	1.2	9.6	0.8
Substance use disorders														
Alcohol abuse/dependence	5.8	0.5	7.0	0.6	1.3	0.3	6.5	0.6	14.5	1.2	6.4	0.4	—	—
Drug abuse/dependence	8.0	0.8	9.8	0.8	3.7	0.6	9.7	0.9	16.3	1.5	8.9	0.7	—	—
Any substance use disorder	10.2	0.9	12.5	0.8	3.7	0.6	12.2	0.9	22.3	1.6	11.4	0.7	—	—
Other														
Eating disorders	3.8	0.4	1.5	0.3	2.4	0.4	2.8	0.3	3.0	0.4	2.7	0.2	—	—

DSM-IV Disorder[a]	Sex				Age						Total		with Severe Impairment	
	Female		Male		13–14 yr		15–16 yr		17–18 yr					
	%	SE	%	SE	%	SE	%	SE	%	SE	%	SE	%	SE
Any Class[b]	51.0	1.4	48.1	1.6	45.3	2.1	49.3	1.9	56.7	2.7	49.5	1.2	22.2[d]	1.0
1 class	30.3	1.3	30.3	1.3	31.2	1.8	29.4	1.4	30.4	2.3	30.3	0.9	16.2	0.6
2 classes	12.6	0.9	12.1	1.2	9.2	1.0	13.0	1.3	16.5	1.7	12.4	0.9	5.2	0.7
3–4 classes	8.1	1.1	5.7	0.6	5.0	1.1	6.9	0.9	9.9	1.3	6.9	0.7	0.8	0.2

[a]Anxiety, eating, and substance use disorders are based on child interview, whereas mood, behavioral disorders, and disorder classes are based on child interview and parent reports.

[b]Excludes eating disorders.

[c]Rates are identical to total prevalence due to absence of inclusion of assessment of impairment.

[d]Excluding substance use disorder [with substance use disorder; Any class = 27.6(1.0); 1 class = 18.1(0.7); 2 classes = 6.7(0.5); 3–4 classes = 2.9(0.6)].

Source: "Lifetime prevalence of mental disorders in U.S. adolescents: results from the National Comorbidity Survey Replication—Adolescent Supplement (NCS-A)." Merikangas, KR et al. *J Am Acad Child Adolesc Psychiatry*, October, 2010; 49 (10): 980–989.

used heroin. In addition, 7% of adolescents were users of tobacco (of this, 4.9% were cigarette smokers), representing a decline of more than 50% since 2002, whereas 11.5% were current alcohol users, representing a decline of greater than 30% since 2002 (Hedden et al., 2015).

Some of the adolescents who use these substances become addicted, which leads to substance use disorders. Of those ages 12 to 17 in 2014, 5% had an identified or reported substance use disorder. Of these young people, the specific types of substances used that lead to these disorders included both alcohol use disorder (2.7%) and illicit drug use disorders (3.5%). Of those with an illicit drug use disorder, the types were as follows: 2.7% had a marijuana use disorder, .4% had a crack or cocaine use disorder, .2% had a heroin use disorder, and .2% were other types (Hedden et al., 2015).

▼ FIGURE 10.1

Percentage of Past Month Illicit Drug Use Among People Aged 12 or Older, by Age Group, 2002–2014

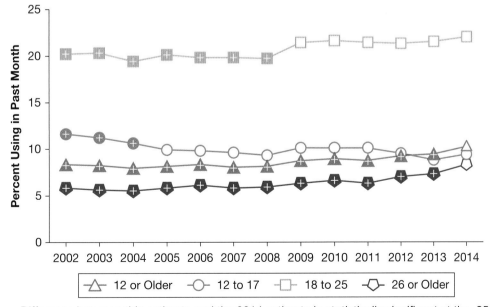

+ Difference between this estimate and the 2014 estimate is statistically significant at the .05 level.

Source: Center for Behavioral Health Statistics and Quality (2015). *Behavioral health trends in the United States: Results from the 2014 National Survey on Drug Use and Health*. Retrieved from http://www.samhsa.gov/data/

Percentage of Substance Use Disorder in the Past Year Among People Aged 12 or Older, by Age Group, 2002–2014

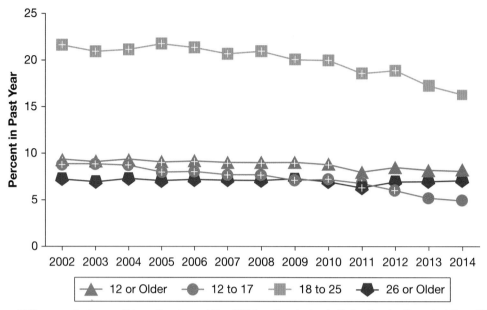

+ Difference between this estimate and the 2014 estimate is statistically significant at the .05 level.

Source: Center for Behavioral Health Statistics and Quality (2015). *Behavioral health trends in the United States: Results from the 2014 National Survey on Drug Use and Health.* Retrieved from http://www.samhsa.gov/data/

A substance use disorder is a problem with alcohol or drugs that causes a young person to have serious problems in school, at home, or at work, and may lead to significant health problems. There is normally evidence of using substances in risky ways, and the use impairs the young person's functioning. There are different criteria depending on the substance type that is being abused, which could be alcohol, cannabis, stimulants, hallucinogens, caffeine, sedatives, tobacco, or opioids. For example, criteria for stimulant use disorder includes a craving for stimulants, failure to control the use when attempted, continued use despite worsening functioning, use of larger amounts over time, developing tolerance for the stimulant, spending a great deal of time to obtain and use stimulants, and withdrawal symptoms that happen when use is decreased or ended (American Psychiatric Association, 2013).

Cumulative and Comorbid Impact

These identified mental health difficulties impair other areas of functioning for children and adolescents. Adolescents with ADHD often have poorer school functioning and performance, their social relationships decrease in quality and quantity, and their long-term prognoses of improving symptom reductions is poor. Although ADHD problems pose more cognitive functioning problems for affected adolescents, the symptoms may appear similar to those of conduct disorder, with functional impairments often exacerbating the behavioral problems (Aronwitz et al., 1994; Barkley, 2002; Romano, Tremblay, Vitaro, Zoccolillo, & Pagani, 2001). Considering that attention-deficit hyperactivity disorder is most commonly identified in younger primary-school children, and many of these symptoms and difficulties last into secondary school, this disorder's comorbidity with other disruptive disorders can pose significant risks for school- and community-related problems. An earlier onset of mental health disorders is associated with an increased risk of having one or more comorbid mental health disorders (Cocozza & Skowyra, 2000; U.S. Surgeon General, 2001).

The comorbidity of mental health disorders, the concurrent prevalence of more than one difficulty, is common for children and adolescents. The coexistence of both a mental health problem and a substance use disorder is referred to as co-occurring disorder. The presence of one mental health disorder may often increase the risk for other mental health problems, making the impact on the child or adolescent more difficult to deal with, and for professionals to address (Angold et al., 2002). Several mental health disorders are often found to be comorbid for the adolescent population: Attention-deficit hyperactivity disorder often co-occurs with conduct disorder; in one review, 30% to 50% of children with an attention-deficit hyperactivity diagnosis also received a conduct disorder diagnosis (Lexcen & Redding, 2000); attention-deficit hyperactivity disorder and anxiety disorders; attention deficit-hyperactivity disorder with depression; and conduct disorder often co-occurs with depression. Anxiety disorders are associated with all of the other major classes of disorders, including mood disorders, eating disorders, and substance use disorders. In addition, adolescents who had reported an episode of depression over the course of a year were twice as likely to have used any illicit drugs during the same year; and a little more than 1% of all adolescents reported having a major depressive episode and a substance use disorder (Costello et al., 2004; Goldstein, Olubadewo, Redding, & Lexcen, 2005; Lofquist, Lugaila, O'Connell, & Feliz, 2012; Merikangas et al., 2010).

From Mental Health Problems to Delinquency

Mental health problems and disorders are linked to later youthful offending behaviors and delinquency adjudication, although it is not clear whether this link is direct or whether these difficulties lead to other risk factors, poor decision-making, or the interaction of various other risks. Many of the risk factors for mental health difficulties and offending behaviors are the same, and risk factors often have multiple impacts and outcomes for adolescents. For example, a dysfunctional or traumatic home life may lead to certain mental health problems—depression or hyperactivity—or to involvement with negative peers and criminal activity. The risk factors that may lead to offending behavior outcomes are multidirectional in that the risk impacts the behavior and the behavior outcomes may further impact the risk. Still, reviews have consistently found that children and adolescents who are involved with mental health services have a significantly higher risk for later juvenile court involvement (Grisso, 2008; Mallett, Stoddard-Dare, & Seck, 2009; Moffitt & Scott, 2008; Rosenblatt, Rosenblatt, & Biggs, 2000; Schubert & Mulvey, 2014).

Several pathways from specific childhood mental health difficulties to juvenile court involvement have been established. Developmental studies have found behavioral and emotional problems to be predictive of later delinquency and substance abuse (Scott & Steinberg, 2010). Early aggressive behaviors have been found predictive of delinquent behaviors and activities, as well as of delinquency over time (Jin & Bae, 2012; Tremblay & LeMarquand, 2001). Attention and hyperactivity problems are linked to later high-risk taking and more violent offending behavior (Elander, Simonoff, Pickles, Holmshaw, & Rutter, 2000; Hawkins et al., 2000). Antisocial behaviors and emotional problems in early childhood are markers for later delinquent activities (Wasserman et al., 2003). In addition, childhood depression and attention-deficit hyperactivity disorder have been found linked to later delinquency, evidenced through physical aggression and stealing behaviors (Moffitt & Scott, 2008; Ryan & Redding, 2004). Depression, however, which is significantly more common in female offenders, has also been identified as an outcome of delinquency in that that these two difficulties may influence each other or have a bidirectional impact (Lalayants & Prince, 2014).

For youthful offenders who are detained or incarcerated, several pathways from earlier mental health problems have been identified. Adolescent mental health and delinquent populations were found to have risk factors for detention or incarceration that included being black or Hispanic American (a potential tie-in with the racial and ethnic disparities problem), having a diagnosis of alcohol problems or conduct disorder in middle school, public health insurance

Co-Occurring Disorder: Coexistence of both a mental health problem and a substance use disorder.

▲ Substance abuse has been a problem for many adolescents and young adults and greatly increases their chance for delinquency. What do you think causes young people to use alcohol or drugs in this way?

coverage, receiving prior mental health services, and reported use or abuse of substances. The questions remain, however, regarding whether drug or other substance use is a predictor of delinquency or whether delinquency predicts use (Brunelle, Brochu, & Cousineau, 2000; Goldstein et al., 2005; Kinscherff, 2012; Scott, Snowden, & Libby, 2002). Adolescents who received mental health system services prior to juvenile court involvement were at risk when compared with peers not involved with the juvenile courts, for drug and/or alcohol abuse and conduct disorder, and to have been a victim of physical abuse (Evans & Vander-Stoep, 1997; Rosenblatt et al., 2000). These two populations, adolescents with mental health problems and those involved in the juvenile justice system, differ little across service delivery systems. In other words, these populations intersect, sharing members, and have similarly identified needs and problems (Kinscherff, 2012; Teplin et al., 2006).

A smaller subset of the adolescent population with mental health problems, between 5% and 10%, develop serious emotional problems that cause substantial impairment in functioning at home, at school, and/or in the community. The mental health diagnoses and issues are normally the more severe: psychotic, bipolar, and other mood disorders. This group with serious emotional difficulties (also referred to as serious emotional disturbance in school settings and by other reporting systems) does not differ significantly in terms of age, ethnicity, or gender from the general child and adolescent population (Kessler et al., 2005; Substance Abuse and Mental Health Services Administration, 2013b). Nevertheless, these severely impaired young people have challenges accessing appropriate mental health services, have significant trouble in school settings, and are at high risk for formal involvement with the juvenile courts (Armstrong, Dedrick, & Greenbaum, 2003; Pastor, Reuben, & Duran, 2012). In fact, this small group of adolescents typically has long histories of multiple mental health disorders that will persist into adulthood and make up an estimated 15% to 20% of the youthful offenders in all juvenile justice detention and incarceration facilities nationwide (Schubert & Mulvey, 2014).

One of the more common diagnoses found within this more severely struggling population is bipolar disorder. This difficulty has periods of what are called "mania" and "depression," symptoms that shift back and forth often for the person. Mania is a distinct period of time where the person is consistently on edge, in a heightened state of awareness or energy, may be irritable and display other symptoms (talks much more, high-risk activities, and agitation, among others) for at least one week. Depression, however, as discussed earlier, is marked by a short-term change (two weeks) of focus: sadness, weight gain, energy loss, thoughts of death or suicide, and poor concentration (American Psychiatric Association, 2013).

MENTAL HEALTH AND TRAUMA

Mental health and trauma problems are inexorably linked. As discussed earlier in the text, these experiences, in particular maltreatment, increase the risk for many children and adolescents to commit offending behaviors, status offenses, and be adjudicated delinquent and juvenile court supervised. Childhood abuse and neglect victimizations that lead to out-of-home placement into

Serious Emotional Difficulties: Designation for young people who have ongoing mental health problems, often more severe and difficult to treat, including psychotic diagnoses, bipolar disorder, and mood disorders.

Serious Emotional Disturbance: Special education (IDEA) diagnosis that means a condition exhibiting over a long period of time and to a marked degree that adversely affects a child's educational performance.

a foster home increase the risk for delinquency and recidivism to delinquency. These trauma experiences often also lead to more severe mental health problems (conduct and other externalizing0type behavior problems, depressive episodes, and PTSD) that are linked to delinquent outcomes, with the highest risk rate for those victimized during adolescence (Barrett, Katsiyannis, Zhang, & Zhang, 2013; Cottle, Lee, & Heilbrun, 2001).

Living in poverty also impacts children and adolescent's mental health, in that a far greater number report these problems: 21% of children in poverty in 2010 had diagnosed mental health disorders, and those not living in poverty reported mental health disorders between 3% and 18% (Stagman & Cooper, 2010). Experiencing poverty, particularly over time, is a dynamic process with some experiences impacting other difficulties (family violence, witnessing violence, substandard housing, unsafe neighborhoods, and family separation, among others) and these interacting further with children and adolescents' coping capacities. Also, poverty during earlier childhood and poverty experienced over time are linked to worsening and progressively harder-to-treat mental health problems for adolescents and young adults (Evans & Cassells, 2013; Yoshikawa, Aber, & Beardslee, 2012).

Bullying and Mental Health

There is significant evidence that children and adolescents who are targets of bullying or cyberbullying suffer from more mental health problems. In particular, bullying victims are at higher risk for using and abusing alcohol or drugs and for suffering from depression. When targeted over time, these children and adolescents are much more likely to report more severe distress and mental health symptoms, including violent behavior and psychotic symptoms, as well as increased suicide risk (Arseneault, Bowes, & Shakoor, 2010; Kowalski & Limber, 2013).

Crossover (Dually Involved) Youth and Mental Health

Young people who are involved simultaneously in the child welfare and juvenile justice systems are identified as "crossover" or "dually involved youth" (discussed in other text chapters). These maltreated and adjudicated delinquent adolescents often struggle with behavioral health problems from childhood through to young adulthood. Reviews of these populations have found 70% to 80% had mental health problems, 40% struggled with drug or alcohol addictions, and almost 20% had co-occurring mental health and drug/alcohol disorders. Many of these young people also struggled with unstable home situations, had academic and behavior problems in school, and suffered difficult transitions into young adulthood. Therefore, their risk for involvement in the adult criminal justice system is significantly greater than that of their peers without this dual system involvement, those peers involved with only one of the child welfare or juvenile justice systems (Herz & Fontaine, 2012; Herz & Ryan, 2008).

JUVENILE INCARCERATION: TODAY'S PSYCHIATRIC ASYLUMS

Up to one in five youthful offenders being held in locked juvenile justice system facilities suffers from persistent and serious mental health problems—typically mood disorders that are intertwined with their offending behaviors. Nevertheless, beyond these more severe cases, many adolescents being detained or incarcerated suffer from mental health difficulties, both prior to their placement as well as in dealing with the difficulties and traumas of being incarcerated (Cauffman, 2004; Mendel, 2012; Schubert & Mulvey, 2014). The high prevalence of serious emotional problems, mental health symptoms, and trauma backgrounds, along with the cumulative impact of locked, often punitively focused institutions, makes these settings very difficult for youthful offenders. Complicating this situation is that the juvenile justice system was not designed to handle such a significant mental health population. Detention and incarceration facilities often lack established policies and practices, sufficient mental health staff resources, or adequate training to work with

▲ Most young people who are incarcerated have an identified mental health problem, some mild, but some quite severe. Why do you think they end up in prison and not in mental health facilities?

a youthful offender population with significant mental health problems. A survey of 83 juvenile detention centers nationwide in 2003 found that only 68% of these facilities reported offering the most basic mental health services such as one-on-one counseling, provided by a few licensed mental health providers; little has changed today (Mendel, 2012; Pajer, Kelleher, Gupta, Rolls, & Gardner, 2007).

The mental health diagnoses of incarcerated youthful offenders include behaviorally based disorders (between 30% and 80%), substance use disorders (between 43% and 75%), anxiety disorders (between 26% and 50%), depressive episodes and other mood disorders (between 14% and 30% of the facility populations), post-traumatic stress disorder (up to 33%), attention-deficit hyperactivity disorder (up to 20%), and psychotic disorders (between 5% and 10%; Abram et al., 2013; Grisso, 2008; Schubert & Mulvey, 2014). Many of these adolescents have more than one mental health diagnosis, including a majority who have a co-occurring substance abuse problem. In particular, the combination of certain mental health problems (affective and anxiety disorders) along with substance abuse disorders is associated with delinquency outcomes and recidivism. PTSD is often comorbid with these difficulties and for many caused or exacerbated by the institutionalization process itself (American Civil Liberties Union, 2014; Kinscherff, 2012; Schubert, Mulvey, & Glasheen, 2011).

Gender and Race

Gender and race differences appear across these disorders for the incarcerated juvenile offender population. Females in juvenile detention and incarceration facilities are at higher risk than males for mental health difficulties, with up to two thirds of males and three quarters of females meeting criteria for at least one mental health disorder (Benner, Nelson, Stage, Laederich, & Ralston, 2010; McReynolds et al., 2008; Teplin, Abram, McClelland, Dulcan, & Mericle, 2002). Regarding race, one earlier review of these incarcerated populations may be representative of other facilities where it was found that 82% of white males, compared with 70% of Hispanic males and 65% of black males, met criteria for a mental health or substance use disorder. For females, 86% of white females, compared with 76% of Hispanic females and 71% of black females, met the criteria for a mental health or substance use disorder. Similar patterns were found across gender by race for most substance use disorders, for significantly more male and female white males met criteria for a substance use disorder than did male and female nonwhite males (Teplin et al., 2002).

Other researchers have also found that incarcerated white youthful offenders reported more mental health problems than did minority youthful offenders, with female white youthful offenders most likely to report a problem and black youthful offenders, either gender, least likely to report a problem while in locked juvenile justice facilities (Vaughn, Wallace, David, Fernandes, & Howard, 2008; Wasserman, McReynolds, Ko, Katz, & Carpenter, 2005). There is still a need for further review of these differences and disparities for incarcerated youthful offenders, for some reviews have found that black youthful offenders were more likely than white youthful offenders to have used mental health services prior to incarceration (Kates, Gerber, & Casey, 2014). If this is confirmed in ongoing research, explanations should be found for why black, Hispanic, and Native American adolescent males are less likely than females and white adolescent males to receive mental health treatment once detained or incarcerated. In fact, it is four times more likely that incarcerated white youthful offenders access treatment for serious mental health problems than incarcerated black youthful offenders (Dalton, Evans, Cruise, Feinstein, & Kendrick, 2009; Teplin, Abram, McClelland, Washburn, & Pikus, 2005).

Psychotic Disorders: More severe and debilitating category of mental health disorders.

1846 VIRGINIA "LUNATIC ASYLUM"

Psychiatric asylums in the United States have a long and jaded history for young people (and adults) with varying degrees of pseudo-science, mysticism, and harmful medical procedures (frontal lobotomies, among the most egregious) performed on those who end up in the institutions. Children and adolescents were often housed in asylums with adults, and during many eras of this country's mental health history, these institutions may have housed as many as 1,000 people. Nevertheless, there has always been a class differential in what today we call "mental health care," with those of means or wealth having more tailored or pampered options. As can be seen in this advertisement from an 1846 asylum in Williamsburg, Virginia:

> The Directors of the Virginia Lunatic Asylum, at Williamsburg, would inform the public of the Southern States that, by a recent law of the Legislature, they are empowered to receive insane patients, paying board, from other States. This is the oldest Institution of the kind in the union, having been founded by the Colonial Government in 1769; and is, from its location, best adapted for Southerners, being removed from the piercing cold of the North, and from the enervating heat of the south. Its curative capacity is of the highest order: nine out of ten cases recover, if received within the first six months of the disease. It is easy of access, as steamers daily stop at a wharf not far from the Asylum. The modern treatment, upon the non-restraint system, is in successful operation. The apartments admit of classification of patients according to their state of mind, and also a complete division of the classes of society. The fare is excellent, and the board $4 per week. We have neat bedrooms, a parlor tastefully furnished with curtains, carpet, sofa, centre-table, ottomans, mirrors, books and a piano; airy verandahs for summer retreats; an extensive enclosure of evening rambles; a carriage for morning and evening rides; a reading room furnished with books and newspapers; and moreover various means of amusement. A chaplain resides in the building and preaches to the patients every Sabbath. (Grob, 1994)

1. Is there a class differential today in mental health care?

2. What are psychiatric institutions like today?

Most of today's juvenile justice institutions are infrequently accommodating or rehabilitative in nature. Like the juvenile justice system's historical use of houses of refuge and reform schools, out-of-home placement has remained an outcome for many children and adolescents. Incarceration of delinquent children and adolescents remained a common juvenile court decision throughout the past century, with some ebbs and flows as to its efficacy and impact. Although this trend of detaining or incarcerating many youthful offenders expanded through the 1980s and 1990s, incarcerations have decreased over the past decade, in some states by more than half. Nevertheless, today, these facilities have become the placement of last resort for many adolescents suffering from serious trauma backgrounds and mental health problems. In most states and jurisdictions, detention and incarceration facilities have become yesterday's psychiatric asylums: uneasy places with little hope, few rehabilitative efforts, or successful outcomes. They are also long-term placements for many disenfranchised and socially isolated young people (Grob, 1994; Hockenberry, 2014; Krisberg, 2005). The following is a story of a young person who has severe mental health concerns, being held in an Ohio juvenile justice facility:

> The teenager in the padded smock sat in his solitary confinement cell here in this state's most secure juvenile prison and screamed obscenities.

> The youth, Donald, a 16-year-old, his eyes glassy from lack of sleep and a daily regimen of mood stabilizers, was serving a minimum of six months for breaking and entering. Although he had received diagnoses for psychiatric illnesses, including bipolar disorder,

Fagernäs Lunatic Asylum near Kuopio.

Mechanical Curator Collection/Flickr Commons/British Library HMNTS 10290.i.4.

▲ Why do you think today's incarceration facilities have become yesterday's mental health facilities (used to be called "asylums")?

a judge decided that Donald would get better care in the state correctional system than he could get anywhere in his county.

That was two years ago.

Donald's confinement has been repeatedly extended because of his violent outbursts. This year he assaulted a guard here at the prison, the Ohio River Valley Juvenile Correctional Facility, and was charged anew, with assault. His fists and forearms are striped with scars where he gouged himself with pencils and the bones of a bird he caught and dismembered.

As cash-starved states slash mental health programs in communities and schools, they are increasingly relying on the juvenile corrections system to handle a generation of young offenders with psychiatric disorders. (Moore, 2009, para. 1–5)

CASE STUDY

MENTAL HEALTH

Hannah, Age 7, Second Grade, White

Hannah started showing angry and explosive behavior with her teacher in the second grade. Her teacher noticed that her drawings were often "dark" with depictions of dead and injured people. There were no prior concerns with Hannah in her first two years at the school, although her family had reported some mental health problems with some other family members. The school social worker began working with the family and provided information on these types of problems and some tools to help Hannah express herself less destructively. The school also designated a safe person and place for Hannah to go to when she felt out of control. Things improved for two years, but in the fourth grade, Hannah began to act out in school, would run out when upset, and would throw objects at other students; at home she was hurting her younger brother.

Pedro, Age 15, Tenth Grade, Black

Pedro had strict patterns and rituals in elementary school, causing other children to tease and pick on him. He would place his books and things always in the same place and in the same order, an eraser was placed exactly at the desk corner, and his papers were arranged in order. This continued into middle and high school. In high school, Pedro had few friends and did not invite people over often to his house because of the time it took to return his things

back to their place. Pedro experienced anxiety when furniture and things were moved in his classroom and he took a long time to transition from his classrooms. He was easily upset when other students moved his things, which was something they did just to pick on Pedro. He began missing class and school, reporting that he was not feeling well, and he dropped from a strong "A" student to an average "C" student this year.

Jan, Age 14, Ninth Grade, Hispanic

Jan just began the ninth grade in the school, after beginning the school year and the first semester at another school. She was vague about her past but seemed to hint that she had moved a lot and changing schools was not something she had not done before. She spent much of her class time with her head down, resting, staring out the window, or sketching drawings in her notebook. When others were around, she hid her notebook with her other belongings. Although she was not part of the classroom discussions, when she was called on, she always had the right answers. Jan avoided other students and isolated herself, even though she was spending time with Marcia. The two of them stayed to themselves, mostly in the library reading dark literature. Marcia approached the school to share that she was worried about Jan. Jan shared her notebook with Marcia, and there were disturbing statements, drawings, and poems about death and how to die.

David, Age 13, Eighth Grade, White

David started coming to school for the last few weeks wearing the same clothes, not looking very good—glassy eyes, slow speech and activity, and inattentive. He began acting avoidant in school, spending significant time in the restroom on breaks. His reactions to school authorities became either evasive or extreme. For example, when confronted by the principal on whether he was using drugs, David ran out of the school. David did not return and was at risk of being charged with truancy for missing too many days of school. His mother became equally frustrated with David, but she was not able to get him to return to school; she worked full time and left before David was supposed to attend school.

Robert, Age 16, 11th Grade, Black

Robert moved into a new neighborhood with his mother, step-father, and two siblings. The family was known by the local children's services agency because of two past investigations for physical abuse. The allegations were unsubstantiated and determined to be untrue. Robert was identified with a serious emotional disturbance and had an Individualized Education Plan. He was suspended from school for three days for marijuana possession on school grounds. The school police officer referred Robert to the local juvenile court, where diversion services were offered (no delinquency charges were filed). Robert did not follow his diversion services, and the school caught Robert smoking on school grounds and disrupting school activities.

For each young person's situation:

1. What are the most urgent issues that need to be addressed?

2. What intervention steps should be taken first, and who should be involved?

DISABILITIES RIGHTS

Prior to the 1970s, there were few significant federal or state laws that protected the rights of people (children or adults) with disabilities in the United States. Although during the 20th century there was recognition of certain groups and disability needs, few broad legal protections or service implementations were set forth. Some of the earliest recognition was for veterans returning from the two World Wars, those with both physical and mental (shell shock) problems. In the 1940s and 1950s, disabled veterans placed increasing pressure on the government to provide for rehabilitation and vocational training. Workplace and other accommodations, however, were not made available outside of veteran groups. Civilians with disabilities were mostly invisible and often found within institutions (psychiatric asylums, nursing homes, and shelters) until the civil rights era and legislation of the 1960s. This legislation set the stage for other groups to be recognized and to demand equality, leading to the **disability rights movement** of the 1970s.

These changes in federal legislation recognized people with disabilities and afforded greater independence and opportunities in daily living and employment, although public attitudes and acceptance of these differences have taken longer and have required educational efforts. These early laws recognized that people with disabilities were not limited because of their disabilities but through limitations in their environments. The same recognition was true for children, where disability rights and parent advocates mobilized at the local level to address physical and social barriers facing the child and adolescent population with disabilities. This included the movement to remove those younger than the age of 18 from the institutions and asylums and place them into schools where they could be with children without disabilities (Longmire & Umansky, 2000)

The shift from recognition of this population to political and civil rights occurred primarily because of four federal laws: the Rehabilitation Act of 1973 (Section 504); the Americans with Disabilities Act (ADA, 1990); the Civil Rights of Institutionalized Persons Act (CRIPA, 1980); and the Individuals with Disabilities Education Act (IDEA, 1975). What follows are the law sections that specifically pertain to children and adolescents with disabilities and the rights established.

Section 504

Section 504 of the Rehabilitation Act was the first law, and predecessor to the ADA, to state that the exclusion of a person with a disability was discrimination, allowing class status for this group,

Disability Rights Movement: 1970s federal legislation that recognized people with disabilities and afforded independence and opportunities in daily living and employment.

mandating affirmative conduct, and requiring accommodations. The law applied to all recipients of federal funds and to regular education public schools. Thus, this entitles students with disabilities to an education comparable to that provided to students who do not have disabilities. Disabilities, in this federal law, are broadly defined and can be demonstrated by both a record of physical or mental impairment and that this impairment substantially limits one or more major life activities such as walking, seeing, hearing, learning, speaking, working, caring for oneself, and performing manual tasks (Pub. L. No. 93–112, 29 U.S.C. § 701). Students are not required to need services through the IDEA (special education) to be protected.

Americans With Disabilities Act (ADA)

The Americans with Disabilities Act is a broad disability rights law that addresses public accommodations, employment, transportation, telecommunication, and state and local government discrimination. Specifically, Title II of the ADA expanded the rights for those with both physical and mental disabilities to include all activities of state and local governments, including services, programs, and public education, whereby Section 504 only applies to federally funded entities (Pub. L. No. 101–336, 42 U.S.C. § 12101 *et seq*). The ADA does not list specific disabilities or impairments covered, and the courts have been defining these disabilities over the past two plus decades (Western New York Law Center, 2015). Also provided under this law, students are not required to need services through the IDEA (special education) to be protected.

Civil Rights of Institutionalized Persons Act

The Civil Rights of Institutionalized Persons Act does not confer additional rights on those with disabilities but does authorize the U.S. Attorney General (U.S. Department of Justice Civil Rights Division) to investigate conditions of confinement in institutions, including juvenile detention and correctional facilities (Pub. L. No. 96–247, 42 U.S.C. § 1997 et seq). This investigatory tool has been infrequently used across the state institutions (Mears & Aron, 2003; Mendel, 2012).

Individuals With Disabilities Education Act (IDEA)

The most important of these federal laws for children and adolescents is the Individuals with Disabilities Education Act (IDEA) because it protects their education and related rights. The original law, the Education for All Handicapped Children Act (1975), established these rights, whereas subsequent amendments have made important changes and expanded access and disability coverage. In 1990, the Act was renamed the Individuals with Disabilities Education Act and subsequent amendments included the following: Substantial requirements were appended to focus on individual behavioral assessments, transitional planning, and school discipline within Individualized Education Programming (IEP); increased focus was placed on employment and independent living for secondary school-age students. The core IDEA educational right is that all students with certain defined disabilities (12 distinct categories) should receive a free, appropriate, public education (FAPE) in the least restrictive environment (LRE) (Pub. L. No. 101–476, 20 U.S.C. § 1400 et seq). Rights under the previous discrimination laws (Section 504 and the ADA) can be incorporated and included within the rights and services under IDEA (Burrell & Warboys, 2000).

IDEA Disability Categories. The 12 distinct IDEA disability categories include specific learning disabilities (LD), hearing impairments (deafness), visual impairments (blindness), deaf-blindness, developmental delay, speech or language impairments, autism, serious emotional disturbance (SED), orthopedic impairments, traumatic brain injury, multiple disabilities, and other health impairments. To qualify, a child or an adolescent must have at least one of these listed disabilities and need special education and related services "by reason of such impairment" (34 C.F.R. § 300.8(a)(1). Adolescents with two of these disability types—learning and serious emotional disturbance—are commonly found in school discipline protocols and the juvenile justice system.

Individuals with Disabilities Education (IDEA) Disability Categories: Specific learning disabilities (LD), hearing impairments (deafness), visual impairments (blindness), deaf-blindness, developmental delay, speech or language impairments, autism, serious emotional disturbance (SED), orthopedic impairments, traumatic brain injury, multiple disabilities, and other health impairments.

Learning Disabilities and Serious Emotional Disturbance

A learning disability is defined as "a disorder in one or more of the basic psychological processes involved in understanding or in using language, spoken or written, that may manifest itself in an imperfect ability to listen, think, speak, read, write, spell, or do mathematical calculations" (34 C.F.R. § 300.8(a)). It may include related conditions such as brain injury, dyslexia, perceptual disabilities, minimum brain dysfunction, and developmental aphasia; however, it excludes learning problems stemming from environmental, economic, or cultural disadvantage. Learning disabilities vary in impact across children and adolescents, are diagnosed on a continuum from mild to severe, and can appear differently in various academic or nonacademic settings.

A serious emotional disturbance means a condition exhibiting one or more of the following characteristics over a long period of time and to a marked degree that adversely affects a child's educational performance: an inability to learn that cannot be explained by intellectual, sensory, or health factors; an inability to build or maintain satisfactory interpersonal relationships with peers and teachers; inappropriate types of behavior or feelings under normal circumstances; a general pervasive mood of unhappiness or depression; and a tendency to develop physical symptoms or fears associated with personal or school problems (34 CFR 300.8(c)(4–10). Across different states, students with these difficulties, although with the same underlying causes and symptoms, can be diagnosed as behaviorally emotionally handicapped (BEH), severely emotionally disturbed (SED), or behavior disordered (BD) (Mears & Aron, 2003). What is difficult for schools, courts, and community-based providers is that these emotional disturbances are often identified as varying psychiatric mental health disorders: depression, anxiety disorders, attention-deficit hyperactivity disorder, psychotic/affective disorders, and behavior disorders. In other words, students identified under special education as having a serious emotional disturbance would most likely be diagnosed outside the school within the mental health system with one or more of these psychiatric disorders. It is the diagnostic systems that differ, not the young person's difficulties (Kinscherff, 2012).

Identification

All children and adolescents residing in the United States, including those in public and private schools, and those who are homeless and wards of the state, must be identified. Schools must locate and evaluate all children and adolescents with these disabilities and determine which are receiving special education services (the child find obligation) (34 C.F.R. § 300.111). Often, states have additional policies and regulations in place to designate who may refer students for special education evaluation.

To determine eligibility for special education services, states must first notify parents or guardians, obtain their consent to evaluate, use several validated assessment measures administered by knowledgeable personnel, and provide for reevaluation (34 C.F.R. § 300.111). State policies and regulations normally set notice, consent, evaluation, and reevaluation time limits. A reevaluation must occur at least every three years, although not more frequently than every year, until age 21, and may be requested by the child's or adolescent's parents or teachers at any time (34 C.F.R. § 300.303).

Individualized Education Plan

If the evaluation determines that the student is in need of special education services, school districts are required to have an Individualized Education Plan (IEP) in effect at the beginning of each academic year for each student with an identified disability. No more than 30 calendar days may pass between the determination that a student needs disability services and an IEP development meeting. The IEP team meeting must include the child's parents or guardians; at least one regular education teacher of the child; at least one special education teacher or service provider, if appropriate, of the child; an individual who can interpret the evaluation results (e.g., school psychologist,

> **Individualized Education Plan (IEP):** Specialized education plan that provides appropriate learning and school-environment accommodations for identified students.

MANDATORY IEP PROVISIONS

- A statement of present educational performance identifying how the student's disability affects involvement and/or progress in the general school curriculum.
- A statement of the special education and related services to be provided to the student.
- A statement of what program modifications or supports are to be provided for the student so that they can be involved in the general curriculum (including extracurricular activities), can be educated with other students with and without disabilities, and may advance toward annual goal attainment.
- A statement of the degree, if any, that the student will not participate with students who do not have disabilities in the regular classroom and extracurricular/nonacademic activities.

- A statement of modifications to state- or district-wide achievement or standardized testing or a statement as to why this testing is not appropriate and alternatives to measuring progress.
- A projected service initiation date (and projected modifications) and the anticipated location, frequency, and duration of services (and modifications).
- A statement of annual measurable goals that includes short-term objectives regarding the student's engagement and progress toward general curriculum involvement, as well as progress toward meeting the student's other disability-related educational needs. This includes a statement of how the student's annual goals will be measured and how the student will meet these goals by the end of the academic year.

MANDATORY IEP PROVISIONS IMPORTANT FOR SECONDARY SCHOOL-AGED STUDENTS

- Numerous services may be most helpful to high school students who qualify for IEP provisions, such as follows:
- Special education services include instruction in the classroom, home, hospitals, and institutions, including juvenile justice correctional facilities.
- A statement of needed transition services for the student's (age 14 and older) course of studies, for example, vocational services.
- For students age 16 and older, this statement should also include, if appropriate, the inter-agency responsibility for linkages to these other supportive programs.
- These services, with a focus on specific results, include vocational training (and supported employment),

postsecondary education, specific adult services, independent living, adult continuing education, and community participation.

....

1. **Why might these provisions for secondary school-age students be helpful in preventing delinquency?**

2. **Is there any stigma or prejudice experienced by students who have a special education disability?**

speech/language pathologist, or remedial reading teacher); a qualified public school district representative; the child, if appropriate; and others, with parental consent, who have knowledge/ expertise regarding the child—may include service providers, probation officers, institutional staff, or those with specialized knowledge. Parents and guardians must be notified in advance and agree to a convenient time and place for the IEP team meeting. In addition, parents and guardians must be notified of their consenting rights regarding others present (34 C.F.R. § 300.321–323).

The team, when developing the IEP, considers the student's present level of educational performance, special education needs, services to be delivered, objectives to be met, timelines for completion, and progress assessment (34 C.F.R. § 300.324). All IEPs must include certain provisions (see Special Interest Policy Section). The implementation of the IEP must occur "as soon as possible" after the initial IEP team meeting. It must be reviewed by the team at least once per year and revised as needed per progress made, reevaluation results, and student needs (34 C.F.R. § 300.43).

Due Process Protections

There are some protections in school discipline protocols provided to students with special education disabilities. Nevertheless, as discussed in earlier chapters, this student group is disproportionately disciplined and suspended when compared with nondisabled peers, showing these due process rights do not preclude suspensions and expulsions from schools because of certain acts or violations (U.S. Department of Education, 2014a).

Students with special education disabilities may be suspended for up to ten days for actions for which a student without a disability would be suspended for up to ten days. Furthermore, a student with a disability may be removed to an interim, 45-day alternative educational setting for carrying or possessing a weapon to school or school function, selling or soliciting the sale of controlled substances, or knowingly possessing or using illegal drugs (states may impose additional qualifying offenses). This alternative placement may also be for other actions or behaviors that are substantially likely to result in injury to the student or others in the school. Disciplinary removal for more than ten days, counted cumulatively for repeat suspensions, requires the school district to review the student's functional behavioral assessment and behavioral implementation plan or, if there is not one in place, to mandate an IEP review to devise a plan. These procedural safeguards also apply to students who have been identified by the school, in writing, as in need of a disability assessment, whether or not a formal referral and evaluation have been initiated (34 C.F.R. § 300.530).

Parents and guardians are guaranteed additional rights under IDEA. Parents and guardians may review all records, participate in all meetings, and initiate due process proceedings, as well as dispute mediation concerning the identification, evaluation, and educational placement of their children. If the student is a ward of the state, a surrogate parent is assigned to protect the student's educational rights. Due process hearings conducted by the state are available through parent or guardian initiation, whereby the officer (not employed by the state) conducts the hearing, and the parents/guardians, who have the right to legal counsel and to other individuals with specialized knowledge of their child's disability, present evidence, confront, cross-examine, and compel witness attendance. In addition to due process and civil remedies, states have in place a compliance procedure for IDEA violations. During any due process proceedings, the student will maintain his or her current educational placement, commonly referred to as the "stay put rule" (34 C.F.R. § 300.501–537).

Prevalence in School Populations

Students with special education disabilities are not common in the overall school population, accounting for fewer than 9% (8.4) of school-aged children and adolescents in 2012 (ages 6 to 21), a percentage that has remained steady since 2005. The most prevalent disability of students was specific learning disabilities (40.1%), followed by speech and language impairment (18.2%), other health impairments (13.2%), autism (7.6%), intellectual disabilities (7.3%), and serious emotional disturbance (6.3%). Across the school student population, specific learning disabilities impacted 3.4% of all students (twice as common for secondary school-age students compared with primary school-age students); speech and language impairments, 1.5% of all students; other health impairments, 1.1% of all students; autism, .7% of all students; intellectual disabilities, .6% of all students; and serious emotional disturbances, .5% of all students (U.S. Department of Education, 2014a).

Black, American Indian, and Pacific Islander students, ages 6 to 21, are disproportionately identified and receive IDEA services for any special education disability, whereas white and Asian students are less likely to be identified with a disability. Certain minority groups are also at higher risk for learning disabilities than white students: Hispanics are 17% more likely; blacks are 43% more likely; and American Indians are 80% more likely. In addition, black students are 25% more likely than white students to be identified and receive services for a serious emotional disturbance disability. Students with serious emotional disturbances, compared with all other disability types, are twice as likely to be removed from school due to weapon or drug possession charges and nearly four times more likely to be suspended or expelled from school. Nearly one in five of these suspended or expelled students was placed in an alternative education setting in 2012. Students with specific learning disabilities are also at much greater risk for both school removal and out-of-school suspension (U.S. Department of Education, 2014a).

Prevalence in Juvenile Court Populations

The prevalence of adolescents with special education disabilities is much higher in juvenile court populations. The two most common special education disability types identified within juvenile justice system populations are specific learning disabilities and serious emotional disturbances, impacting up to 25% of adjudicated delinquent youthful offenders (Advancement Project et al., 2011; Burrell & Warboys, 2000). These disability rates increase as youthful offenders further penetrate the juvenile justice system, with between 28% and 43% of detained and incarcerated youthful offenders having been identified with a special education disability. Among incarcerated youthful offenders with special education disabilities, 48% have been identified with a serious emotional disturbance, 39% with a specific learning disability, 10% with a developmental delay, and 3% with other health impairments. The prevalence rates of these disabilities within juvenile court and incarcerated populations have not changed significantly over time (Kvarfordt, Purcell, & Shannon, 2005; Quinn, Rutherford, Leone, Osher, & Poirier, 2005; Rozalski, Deignan, & Engel, 2008; Rutherford, Nelson, & Wolford, 1985; Wang, Blomberg, & Li, 2005; White & Loeber, 2008). The following story on Billy is not atypical of this population of young people:

> Billy was removed from his home and placed into a foster home at the age of four because of severe neglect. He began to show difficult behaviors and emotional outbursts during his first year in the foster home, as his biological parents lost their custodial rights and the local children's services agency was granted legal custody. Due to his behavior problems, Billy was moved several times to different therapeutic foster homes as he began primary school. He was identified by the 2nd grade to have some significant learning and mental health difficulties, and was found in need of special education services for learning disabilities. In addition, Billy struggled with significant cognitive and developmental delays. Billy needed academic and classroom-based accommodations to learn grade appropriate academic material. Because of Billy's needs, his difficulty dealing with past traumas, and lack of adequate supports in the child welfare system, he changed foster homes a total of 11 times before he was 15 years of age. These transitions continually challenged Billy, as he changed schools often. He was ultimately removed from his home school and placed in an alternative school because of aggressive and inappropriate behaviors; the alternative school did not provide the same level of accommodations for Billy. Although he tried to succeed at the alternative school, Billy made friends with peers who committed offending and delinquent activities. He was arrested, brought under juvenile court supervision, spent time in detention facilities, and continued to recidivate in and out of the juvenile justice system. He was arrested again numerous times as he turned 18 years of age. Billy spent more time in adult jails and prisons, did not complete high school, and had much difficulty finding stable housing or employment when not incarcerated.

From Learning Disabilities to Delinquency. Students with learning disabilities are one of two disability groups (the other being those with serious emotional disturbances) that are most at risk to become involved with school discipline protocols and the juvenile justice system. Some of this heightened risk can be explained by common risk factors identified for both developing learning disabilities and for youthful offending behaviors. These common risks include living in poverty, male gender, poor family functioning, being adopted, and lower education levels of family members. Primary school-aged students with learning disabilities are at high risk to fall significantly behind in reading and writing skills, deficiencies that are often not improved on in secondary school and that may lead to other education-related problems (Altarac & Saroha, 2007; Jenkins & O'Connor, 2002; Shaywitz et al., 1999). It is known that students who underachieve in the classroom, those who are behind in reading and writing abilities, and those who are placed into remedial classrooms are at higher risk for secondary school failure and school dropout, deviant peer friendships, and serious offending behaviors (Jenkins & O'Connor, 2002; Mears & Aron, 2003).

More broadly, students with unidentified learning disabilities may be disproportionately represented among those who are suspended, expelled, and/or drop out of high school. Students identified with learning disabilities, as well as those students not identified but with similar problems, are at two to three times greater risk of being involved in offending activities and delinquency adjudication, to commit more serious offenses, to reoffend, and to be involved with the courts at younger ages (Developmental Services Group, Inc., 2017; Matta-Oshima, Huang, Johnson-Reid, & Drake, 2010; Morris, Schoenfield, Bade-White, Joshi, & Morris, 2006; Wang et al., 2005). More specifically to school discipline protocols, students with learning disabilities are at a significantly increased risk of being arrested while in school as well as within one year after leaving or graduating from school (Doren, Bullis, & Benz, 1996; Wagner, Newman, Cameto, Levine, & Garza, 2006). And with this group comprising the largest number of students with a special education disability nationwide, further investigations are important to determine why these are the outcomes.

Why the Learning Disability Disparity?

Why are students with learning disabilities at significantly higher risk for offending behaviors and formal juvenile court involvement? There are three competing hypotheses, including school failure, susceptibility, and differential treatment. Depending on further research and results, which may vary across juvenile court jurisdictions, addressing the problem may require different remedial and long-term changes.

School Failure Hypothesis. The school failure hypothesis suggests that school failure for students with learning disabilities is a precipitating step that leads eventually to juvenile court involvement. Intermediary steps may include rejection by peers, lower self-worth because of academic difficulties, and school dropout, leading to increased engagement with delinquent peers and activities. What is not clear, though, is whether the disabilities themselves are the reason for school failure or whether there are other factors, such as family structure or functioning, negative peers, poor neighborhoods, emotional difficulties, and similar problems that may influence this outcome. This situation is complicated in that risk factors for school dropout include family difficulties, low-income status, negative peers, grade retention, low parent educational status, school transitions, and urban school location, among others (Bridgeland, DiIulio, & Morrison, 2006; Cruise, Evans, & Pickens, 2010; Hammond, Linton, Smink, & Drew, 2007; Morris & Morris, 2006). Although no one risk factor is paramount in a student's decision to drop out of school, combinations of difficulties increase the risk. In addition, students who drop out of school do not make this decision in haste but over a period of time, making the cumulative impact of these risks more harmful (Rumberger, 2004; Schargel, 2004).

Susceptibility Hypothesis. The susceptibility hypothesis proposes that students with learning disabilities have cognitive, neurological, and intellectual difficulties that contribute to delinquent behaviors. Thus, in addition to their learning disabilities, students may also be afflicted with low social skills, impulsivity, suggestibility, and a lower ability to predict the consequences of their behaviors. In particular, influence from negative peers and an inability to understand the outcomes of negative decisions may play a key role in delinquency activity involvement (Scott & Steinberg, 2008).

School Failure Hypothesis: Hypothesis that suggests school failure for students with learning disabilities is a precipitating step that leads to juvenile court involvement.

Susceptibility Hypothesis: Hypothesis that proposes that students with learning disabilities have cognitive, neurological, and intellectual difficulties that contribute to delinquent behaviors.

Differential Treatment Hypothesis. The **differential treatment hypothesis** suggests that whereas students with learning disabilities are no more involved with delinquent activities than their nondisabled peers, they are more likely to be identified by school personnel, arrested, and formally involved with the juvenile courts. This explanation places the responsibility for this disparity on school, police, and juvenile court personnel reactions to working with students with learning disabilities. For example, school personnel may be more aware of these students because of their disability status, and if the student acts out in disruptive ways, they may be more likely to take punitive action and refer them to the police and courts; whose personnel in turn may repeat this pattern (U.S. Department of Education, 2014a).

CASE STUDY

SPECIAL EDUCATION

❝ I get my high school diploma in a month and I'm outta here a couple months after. I can't read. How am I gonna get a job so I don't violate [parole]? I been here for a long time. I don't wanna come back."

Thomas, one of my teenaged clients, shared his concerns as he sat across from me in the secure facility's interview room. He had been charged and adjudicated accordingly several times over the previous four years. Fifteen months before this meeting, Thomas had been placed in the custody of the state's juvenile justice agency for a period of not more than two years. As his attorney, I was equally concerned about Thomas's ability to meet the post-release conditions. We both knew those conditions would require that he find employment, but he knew he would not be able to read or fill out a job application, let alone find a job that would not require him to be able to read at some level.

Thomas and I spoke at length about the situation. With his permission, I contacted the state's designated disability rights protection and advocacy agency. Within days of our meeting, I asked for an educational evaluation, which was conducted soon thereafter. The educational evaluation indicated that Thomas had a specific learning disability that affected his reading proficiency; he was therefore eligible for special education services. Thomas began receiving intensive tutoring and, within weeks, told me that he had begun to read a "real" book—a "chapter book."

The story of Thomas's success is not one of great legal prowess or even knowledgeable advocacy; in many ways it is one of happenstance and luck. Luckily, Thomas was part of a post-disposition pilot program. The program made it possible for him to meet regularly with me after he had been adjudicated delinquent and committed to the secure juvenile facility. Despite being a new member of the bar and, essentially, a legal neophyte, I had no option but to question the system and get Thomas the help he needed. I found it mind-blowing that Thomas had participated in numerous hearings prior to every one of his adjudications and subsequent dispositions, yet no one in the courtroom had ever realized that he was unable to read. Thomas had read and signed more than one plea agreement over the years. Though Thomas had never volunteered information about his disability with anyone in the juvenile justice system, based on my conversations with him, it was clear that no one had asked him whether he could read. (Geis, 2014, pp. 870–871)

1. **How might this situation have been avoided for Thomas?**

2. **What might have been done to prevent him from falling into the juvenile justice system?**

3. **What do you think may have been the reason Thomas was not identified with a learning disability in primary school?**

Source: Geis, Lisa, An IEP for the Juvenile Justice System: Incorporating Special Education Law Throughout the Delinquency Process (July 1, 2014). *University of Memphis Law Review,* Vol. 44, No. 1, 2014. Available at SSRN: https://ssrn.com/abstract=2473609.

CHAPTER REVIEW

CHAPTER SUMMARY

This chapter summarizes the most prevalent mental health problems and disorders for children and adolescents in the United States, and it shows how these difficulties are linked to delinquency and involvement with the juvenile courts. Problems across behavioral issues, such as anxiety, depression, and substance abuse, for young people are identified, with attention paid to some of the severe mental health problems that are most common in juvenile correctional facility populations. The juvenile justice system has become for many families and adolescents the last alternative for accessing mental health services. In addition, this chapter reviewed the development of disability rights for young people, culminating with the Individuals with Disabilities Education Act (IDEA) and the establishment of "special education" services. These federally mandated services address many behavioral, emotional, and learning problems for students and guarantee education planning to meet their educational and related needs. Nevertheless, there are disproportionate numbers of students with emotional and learning problems that end up involved with the juvenile courts.

KEY TERMS

DISCUSSION QUESTIONS

1. What are the common risk factors for mental health problems, special education disabilities, and youthful offending and delinquency? Why and how do these childhood and adolescent difficulties interact, often leading to poor outcomes?

2. What are the most common mental health problems for children and adolescents in the general population and in the juvenile justice system? What differences are there between these groups? What is the difference among incident, lifetime, and prevalence rates?

3. Why are adolescents with mental health difficulties more likely to be involved in the juvenile courts? Or are they? Justify your position through research findings.

4. What is the relationship between trauma and mental health problems?

5. What is the relationship between mental health problems and delinquency?

6. Are there pathways from mental health problems to school difficulties? If so, what might be some preventative or intervention steps that families, schools, and juvenile courts (when involved) could take?

7. What comorbidity problems are there for students with special education disabilities?

8. Why might students with special education disabilities be at higher risk for juvenile court involvement and delinquency adjudication?

9. Why have today's juvenile justice facilities become the psychiatric asylums of past generations?

10. What protections are provided for students with special education disabilities who are involved with school discipline protocols?

11. What are the more important IEP provisions for secondary school-age students, and why are these important?

12. Why is the IDEA a more useful federal law protecting students than Section 504 or the Americans With Disabilities Act?

---

https://edge.sagepub.com/mallett

 **Sharpen your skills with SAGE edge!**

SAGE edge for students provides a personalized approach to help you accomplish your coursework in an easy-to-use learning environment. You'll find mobile-friendly eFlashcards and quizzes, as well as videos, web resources, and links to SAGE journal articles to support and expand on the concepts presented in this chapter.

SOLUTIONS TO DELINQUENCY

CHAPTER 11

EVIDENCE-BASED DELINQUENCY RISK PREVENTION

▲ Delinquency prevention efforts can be effective across most locations—neighborhoods, schools, and at home. What do you think works to prevent delinquency?

©iStockphoto.com/omgimages

INTRODUCTION

The ecological/psychosocial model, as reviewed in earlier chapters, uses a multidimensional approach in understanding offending behaviors, delinquency, and/or school exclusion outcomes. Through the use of a classification approach, individual, family, peer, school, and community risk and protective factors are identified and strategically analyzed for assessment and treatment purposes. The model also takes into account the developmental stage of the child and how the age of onset of problems (delinquency, trauma, mental health, and others) as well as the cumulative impact of multiple difficulties impacts these risks. Thus, this model investigates the life course of the young person in relation to the people and events that are impactful along the way (Howell, 2009; Loeber & Farrington, 2001). Many of the evidence-based programs and interventions reviewed in this chapter that address child and adolescent maltreatment, trauma (addressed in Chapter 9), mental health (addressed in Chapter 10), and related problems use this multidimensional and/or developmental approach. Decreasing the impact of these child and adolescent problems also decreases significant risk factors for delinquency.

Many difficulties linked to delinquency are rooted in earlier childhood, making it critical to investigate across a multi-developmental time period. In reviewing key risk prevention and intervention programming for children and adolescents, this chapter differentiates between childhood and adolescent life stages. Nevertheless, preventing delinquency, school discipline problems, and/or juvenile court involvement is challenging because of the number of interactive risks and reasons for these outcomes and the wide-ranging impact some problems may cause. The difficulties encountered first in childhood (considered preteen years, birth to 12) may very well continue into adolescence (considered the teenage years) and may be complicated because of the comorbidity of other risks experienced (Thornberry, 2005).

Several epidemiological studies, however, have found that the earlier the problems are identified during childhood, the better the chance that harm can be minimized and poor outcomes averted. By addressing some of the key delinquency risk factors, preventative efforts may divert the young person from delinquency, school problems, or juvenile court outcomes. As the etiology of the problems is identified and understood, more effective delinquency and school discipline prevention policy and programming can be, and has been, used by stakeholders (Child Welfare Information Gateway, 2011). In reviewing what is known to be effective, this chapter first reviews the evidence on prevention and intervention programs for maltreatment victims and trauma assessment and treatment, mental health disorders, and substance abuse problems for the young person and his or her family.

MALTREATMENT VICTIMIZATION

Profound efforts have been focused on designing and evaluating interventions and methods for the treatment of childhood maltreatment. It is hoped that by circumventing maltreatment and its nefarious impact on children and adolescents, the pathway from victimization to delinquency can be minimized. To do so, it is important that early identification of maltreatment be made and that effective trauma programming be used.

AP Photo/The Morning Call, Don Fisher

▲ Nurse–Family Partnerships are effective at decreasing maltreatment and improving child outcomes. Do you think they also help prevent delinquency?

Early Identification and Assessment

Several assessment and decision-making instruments and models have been developed to assist the child welfare and other youth-caring systems in identifying those families most at risk of child maltreatment. Parents and guardians are often the focus because they comprise more than 90% of abuse and neglect perpetrators (Administration for Children and Families, 2015). The following three instruments/models have been found effective in identifying at-risk families.

First, the family assessment approach is designed to be used with families without maltreatment substantiation but who otherwise pose high risks for maltreatment in the future. This assessment approach uses family and community resources in devising a strengths-focused plan on eliminating conditions that place a child at risk at home. Second, the **structured decision-making (SDM) model** is a set of assessment tools that identifies key decision points within each child protection agency case and provides intervention directives. Areas of assessment in the SDM model include response priority, safety, risk factors (individual, family, school, and community), and family strengths and needs. Similarly, the third, the CIVITAS/CCCC Core Assessment focuses on the same domains as the SDM model, including medical needs, family, social areas, life history of traumatic events, emotional difficulties, and academic/cognitive challenges, and provides risk and intervention directives (Children's Research Center, 1999; Siegel & Loman, 2006; Wagner & Bell, 1998; Wiebush, Freitag, & Baird, 2001).

PREVENTION

Home Visiting Programs

Home visiting programs, delivered through multiple methods and with various professional providers, share common intervention goals. These goals include providing parents with education, information, access to other services, support, and instruction on parenting practices. They also share a common perspective of achieving long-term benefits for child development through the alteration of parental practices even if it may not directly prevent child maltreatment. Such in-home programs, often delivered by nurses, social workers, or related paraprofessional staff, may focus on one primary role or service or may offer more complete family support services. In some cases, the home visitor is focused on being a source of support, whereas in other cases, the paraprofessional may serve as a source of information and referral or role model to the parents (Brooks-Gunn, Berlin, & Fuligi, 2000; Sweet & Appelbaum, 2004).

There are three primary types of home visiting programs, each with a leading program model and service delivery: the Nurse–Family Partnership (Olds et al., 1997), Healthy Families America (Harding, Galano, Martin, Huntington, & Schellenbach, 2006), and Early Head Start (Howard & Brooks-Gunn, 2009). The Nurse–Family Partnership connects each low-income, first-time mother with a registered nurse prenatally up to two years of the child's age, teaching health behaviors to the parents and developmentally appropriate skills to the child. Healthy Families America employs trained paraprofessionals to provide services to parents from the prenatal period up to five years of the child's age with parenting skills, child development to disadvantaged mothers, and other maltreatment prevention efforts. Early Head Start,

Structured Decision-Making (SDM) Model: Set of assessment tools that identifies key decision points within child protection agency cases and provides intervention directives.

Home Visiting Programs: Often delivered by nurses or related paraprofessional staff, may focus on one primary role or service, or may offer more complete family support services to parents in their home.

JENNIFER'S STORY AND THE NURSE–FAMILY PARTNERSHIP

Jennifer found out that she was pregnant at age 18. She was excited but apprehensive about the road ahead. During her first visit at a local health clinic, she felt overwhelmed. "I was in a big room and there were several people talking to me about all of the options I had," Jennifer said. "It wasn't until they handed me a brochure about Nurse–Family Partnership that I knew what I wanted to do next." When Jennifer signed up for Nurse–Family Partnership in Greenville, South Carolina, she was paired with nurse home visitor Lisa, who guided her through pregnancy and early motherhood. "The visits were wonderful," Jennifer said. "Before Jayden was born, Lisa taught me everything from what I should eat, to what labor was going to be like, to performing CPR, to sleeping practices—everything."

Jennifer earned her GED while pregnant with Jayden, and after he was born, Nurse–Family Partnership helped her learn time management because she began working and also continuing her education. Nurse–Family Partnership also helped her through the emotional changes that came when she and Jayden's father, Matthew, separated after Jayden was born. Jennifer had no family living close to her, but she said she never felt alone during that difficult time. "It was just amazing that someone from Nurse–Family Partnership was always there for me," Jennifer said. "I was never alone because I could always call Lisa for support or answers, whether good or bad. She was always there waiting to help me whenever I needed it." Lisa helped Jennifer find ways to achieve economic self-sufficiency, one of the key goals of the Nurse–Family Partnership program. For Jennifer, her heart's desire was to finish her education and pursue a career in healthcare. (Nurse–Family Partnership, 2016, p. 2, video: *Jennifer's Story*).

1. Why do you think the Nurse–Family Partnership is effective?

2. Have you or a family member been involved with the program? If so, what was your experience like?

Source: Nurse–Family Partnership, 2016, First Time Mom's, Jennifer's Story. Reprinted with permission from Nurse–Family Partnership, www.nursefamilypartnership.org

a federally funded program, provides both in-home parent training and center-based early care and education for children, using paraprofessionals and teachers.

These home-visiting programs have a profound impact on reducing several child maltreatment risk factors by improving the home environment, parenting, and child development. Except for a few reviews of the Nurse–Family Partnership model, however, a direct decrease in reported child maltreatment incidents has not been established (Mikton & Butchart, 2009; Olds, 2007). The Nurse–Family Partnership results in healthier births and medical outcomes and has shown significant returns on investment: For every dollar invested in the program, a $3 benefit resulting from the reduction in future costs of maltreatment victimization efforts has been estimated (Aos et al., 2011). In addition to these three models of home-visiting programs, there are two additional programs that have been found effective in addressing the risk for future child maltreatment. These programs are designed similarly to the Nurse–Family Partnership. First, the ChildFirst program provides assessment, consultation, and intervention services with a care coordinator. Second, the Project 12-Ways/Safecare program provides parent training in specific risk areas with specialized staff (U.S. Department of Health and Human Services, 2012). It is important to note that to be effective in reducing maltreatment risk, home-visiting programs must design and deliver an individualized program for each case.

Parent Training/Education Programs

Parents who maltreat their children often lack certain parenting abilities, child-rearing knowledge, or the psychological makeup to be positive caregivers, but many can improve with intervention and mediation. Children's service agencies often use education and training programs when trying to prevent abuse or neglect or when supervising parents and their children. These programs share core foundation curriculum planning that is based on the idea that child maltreatment can be reduced if parents modify their attitudes on child rearing, improve skills in taking care of their children, and rely less on coercive parental techniques. In addition to these foundational foci, the programs may also offer anger management, stress control, emotional management, and psycho-educational mental health services to parents because provision of such interventions has been found to decrease neglectful parental behaviors (Barth, 2009; Lundahl, Nimer, & Parson, 2006; Sanders, Cann, & Markie-Dadds, 2003).

Evidence of the effectiveness of training and education programs for parents is mixed because of the lack of longer term follow up and the lower number of programs evaluated, although several programs have shown reductions in child maltreatment incident rates. In one **meta-analysis study** of 23 programs, measuring a wide variety of outcome variables, an impact on reported attitude and child-rearing behaviors by the parents was identified immediately after parent training and education program completion (Klevens & Whittaker, 2007). In other broad reviews, moderate impacts of parent training programs was found on decreasing maltreatment and improving child-rearing skills (Piquero, Farrington, Welsh, Tremblay, & Jennings, 2009). When programs try to address a wide array of maltreatment risk factors, however, the impact on maltreatment reduction is often diluted or negligible. In other words, program should focus more narrowly on maltreatment risks if the effort is to be successful (Lundahl et al., 2006).

From these parent training and education programs, several effective components have been identified: early intervention, clearly articulated model or program, strong theory base, culturally sensitive interventions with multiple components (e.g., group work, individual sessions, and office-based and in-home programming), and longer duration with follow-up (Moran, Ghate, & van der Merwe, 2004; Thomas & Zimmer-Gembeck, 2011). Several programs offer a variety of intervention techniques and have shown effectiveness with reducing maltreatment risk.

The Family Connections program works with at-risk parents and grandparents to prevent child maltreatment through in-home training and service provider coordination (DePanfilis, Dubowitz, & Kunz, 2008). The Triple P (Positive Parenting Program), based on social learning theory, incorporates various intervention techniques and five levels of intervention: a media campaign to inform and identify parents, specific topic training, childhood development and behavior problem programming, serious child behavior and mental health problem programming, and family dysfunction focus and work (Daro & Dodge, 2009; Sanders et al., 2003). Parent–Child Interaction Therapy, also based on social learning theory, teaches and coaches parenting behavior-management techniques to regulate parents' own emotions, maintain limits in parenting, and work with disruptive children (Timmer, Urquiza, Zebell, & McGrath, 2005). The Incredible Years Program uses specific behavioral techniques and sequential learning steps in different settings with parents and children to improve strength-based skill building (Wulczyn, Webb, & Haskins, 2007). Two of these programs—Triple P and Incredible Years—also have shown cost/benefit impacts: The Triple P was found to return between $4 and $10 dollars for every dollar invested, and the Incredible Years Program was found to return $4 dollars for every dollar invested (Aos et al., 2011).

Family/Parent Support Groups

Family and **parent support groups** have gained increased recognition in the prevention and treatment of child maltreatment. There are different variations of family/parent support groups, and they address several key risk factors for neglect and physical abuse. Family support groups provide formal peer-supported and facilitator-led programming, and they typically meet on a regular, often weekly, basis. These groups also help the formation of informal networks among parents and family members involved that help strengthen and carry on the preventative efforts that begun within the program. These formal and informal groups

Meta-analysis Study: Subset of other systematic research studies that combines the results and produces a cumulative finding or impact.

Parent Support Group: Parent or family support groups that provide formal peer-supported and facilitator-led programming, and typically meet on a regular, often weekly, basis.

attempt to improve communication within the families, as well as in parent–child interactions, and to reduce related negative behaviors, such as aggression or fighting (Falconer, Haskett, McDaniels, Dirkes, & Siegel, 2008; Stagner & Lansing, 2009; Thomas, Leicht, Hughes, Madigan, & Dowel, 2003).

Some of these programs are affiliated with childcare centers, such as Head Start (Early Head Start), and show promise in improving parents' attitudes and behaviors in interactions with their children. In particular, the Strengthening Families Initiative builds on existing childcare centers and early intervention programs to help families avoid contact with the child welfare system. Several evaluations have found that group-based parental support and education programs were more effective for some families than were home-visiting services. Others show some encouraging evidence that indicates that parental functioning improves in highly structured group settings. Groups modeled on the Alcohol Anonymous 12-step model (Parents Anonymous groups) showed improvement by all parents, especially with those parents who were at high risk for child maltreatment. Although the evidence is encouraging, ongoing and rigorous reviews are needed to ascertain the overall effectiveness of these widely used preventative and intervention groups (Daro & McCurdy, 2007; Kaminski, Valle, Filene, & Boyle, 2008: Polinsky, Pion-Berlin, Williams, Long, & Wolf, 2010).

Public Education and Information

Public awareness activities may be important in promoting positive parenting and decreasing maltreatment victimizations, especially in terms of encouraging the reporting of child maltreatments. Through the use of a variety of media outlets, such as public service announcements, press releases, information brochures, and television/radio documentaries, some program efforts not only promote positive parenting and improve child safety but also share protocols for reporting suspected victimizations. Examples of these efforts include the prevention of shaken baby syndrome, the Stop It Now Program, and the Prevent Child Abuse America efforts (Kaufman, 2010; Thomas et al., 2003).

Child Sexual Abuse

Substantiated cases of sexual abuse of children have decreased over the past two decades, but it is unclear why it has decreased. Some possible explanations included improved public recognition and awareness of the problem, the impact of federal and state laws mandating how to manage known sex offenders, and the impact of education and intervention strategies. The challenge in continuing this decreasing abuse trend is because of the lack of clear evidence of the effectiveness of these interventions or the combined or cumulative impact of these interventions (Finkelhor, Turner, Ormond, & Hamby, 2009; LaFond, 2005).

Public concern and media attention of child sexual abuse have prompted legislation in state houses and Congress alike, including increased sexual offender registration, community notification of sexual offender residences, residency restrictions around children and schools, longer criminal sentences, and civil commitments that also lengthen incarceration sentences. Yet evidence is insufficient to fully gauge such legislation's impact, although some of these enforcement and supervision strategies seem to be counterproductive and illogical. For instance, requiring residency restrictions for a convicted sex offender only targets a small percentage of offenders. Considering that many abusers are probably never caught or identified, and when identified, most of them are a family member or family friend, these efforts may even provide a false sense of security to the public (Bolen, 2001; Duwe & Donnay, 2008; Loving, Singer, & Maguire, 2008; Prescott & Rockoff, 2008).

Other efforts to reduce sexual abuse of children have included treatment of offenders, both adults and juveniles, as well as education and training programs for children to increase their awareness and self-protection against predation. At this point, mental health treatment has been shown to have significant impact with juvenile offenders but only some limited impact

Head Start (Early Head Start): Program of the U.S. Department of Health and Human Services that provides comprehensive early childhood education, health, nutrition, and parent involvement services to low-income children and their families. Early Head Start is for children ages 0 to 3.

Sexual Offender Registration: Federal and state law requirements that youthful and adult offenders convicted of certain sex crimes must be registered (name, address) in their localities.

SUBSTANCE ABUSE AND DEPENDENCE: PARENTS

Parental substance abuse is common among young people who are victims of maltreatment. Between 11% and 24% of investigated and substantiated maltreatment cases, primarily neglect, stem from parents' substance abuse (Administration for Children and Families, 2015). This is understandable because parents and caregivers with substance abuse problems often experience other risk factors for perpetrating maltreatment, including housing instability, domestic violence, and/or mental health problems (Marsh, Ryan, Choi, & Testa, 2006).

Two concerns challenge the child welfare system regarding parental substance abuse and dependence. First, not many parents are accurately identified as substance abusing or dependent; and, second, when the problem is identified, treatment often is unsuccessful. Improved integration of treatment with child welfare involvement is essential for children at risk for maltreatment and, in particular, to prevent maltreatment recurrence. Once these improvements occur, effective substance abuse treatments and relapse prevention effort should be closely monitored during children's services supervision (Drake, Johnson-Reid, & Sapokaite, 2006; Guo, Barth, & Gibbons, 2006).

An effective approach to treat parental substance abuse requires family involvement. One intervention for families with adolescents, the Strengthening Families Program, has been found to have a significant impact on decreasing parents' alcohol and drug use and their subsequent risk for child neglect. This program uses cognitive-behavioral, social learning, and family systems interventions and involves the whole family with parent and adolescent skills training. Such program components and interventions revolve around retraining interactions among family members and developing new coping skills, which have been found effective across many similarly situated family strengthening programs. For example, Functional Family Therapy and the Focus on Families Program directly address the parents' problems and relapse concerns, as well as the negative impact and influence that substance abuse is having on the family members (Ferrer-Wreder, Stattin, Lorente, Tubman, & Adamson, 2003; Kaminski et al., 2008; Kumpfer, Whiteside, Greene, & Allen, 2010).

1. How difficult do you think it is for someone to end an addiction to drugs or alcohol?

2. Do you know of someone who has struggled with addiction? What was their experience?

with adult offenders. It should be noted that one third of all identified sexual offenders are juveniles, often delinquent adolescents who are developmentally immature in these actions or exploring behaviors inappropriately with other teenagers or children (Finkelhor, 2009; Hunter, 2009). This may explain why the treatment outcomes appear to be much more effective with the juvenile sexual offender population and why most youthful sexual abuse offenders do not recidivate. Alternatively, education and training programs for children, which aim to increase their awareness and protective reactions, have demonstrated success and warrant continued utilization, although it is unclear whether actual future victimization (and not just awareness) is decreased (Zwi, 2007).

Interventions for Maltreatment Victims

For those children and adolescents supervised by child protection agencies, a variety of measures or interventions are offered during the supervision time period. These include the initial safety measures and decision-making required to keep the child safe from further victimization, and if maltreatment impact is apparent, specific programming measures are also initiated to alleviate the effects of maltreatment. Interventions vary according to the victimization type or maltreatment effects and may include individual or family counseling with a wide array of intervention techniques, such as play, behavioral, or psychodynamic therapies (Stagner & Lansing, 2009). These interventions are aimed at short-term intervention and stabilization of crisis situations and are important in addressing the difficulties such as childhood traumatic stress reactions, attention and focus problems, school issues, and other related childhood concerns. In particular, finding safe environments for the victims to reside and recover from trauma is paramount, but additional opportunities for children to recover from the trauma are often necessary (Koball et al., 2011).

Elements of effective programs for children and adolescents with maltreatment victimization who are also at risk for delinquency involvement have been identified. These include the following: thorough individualized assessment; addressing the context of the child and family functioning as a whole; provision of parental supports and parenting education; a focus on improving the parent–child interaction; involving a multimodal intervention approach; utilization of community resources; emphasis on behavior skills development; and a focus on long-term outcomes, including follow-up and relapse prevention. More specifically, when focused on protective factors for maltreatment victims, effective treatment for recovery has been identified across numerous areas. For the individual, for instance, this includes having a sense of purpose, a positive self-control of emotions and cognitions, increased problem-solving skills, positive peer relationships, and involvement in positive activities. For parents, on the other hand, effective treatment needs to be focused on improving parenting competencies and well-being. Finally, for the family as a whole, effective treatment includes a positive and stable living and school environment (Child Welfare Information Center, 2015; Wiig, Spatz-Widom, & Tuell, 2003).

▲ Parental substance abuse is often the cause of childhood neglect. Why do you think it is difficult for some parents to stop using or abusing alcohol or drugs?

Trauma Assessment

Identifying trauma experiences, which also includes maltreatment victimization, can be difficult. The type of trauma or stress, developmental stage (age), cognitive and emotional capacities, and levels of resiliency are all factors that impact the emergence of trauma symptoms and, for some, the experience with post-traumatic stress disorder (PTSD). Fortunately, several assessment measures can be used to identify trauma experiences, PTSD, and related problems. Some of these measures rely on self-reports by the young person, caregivers, and/or teachers and are considered more preliminary methods of identification, whereas others involve professional and clinical personnel to interview and assess the child or adolescent. Some of these measures use the PTSD definition from the American Psychiatric Association's *Diagnostic and Statistical Manual of Mental Disorders* (DSM, 2013), and others expand this definition to include additional trauma symptoms.

Trauma-Informed Care

Over the past decade, a proliferation of program development has occurred on what is commonly called **trauma-informed care**. Trauma can be an outcome of numerous different types of adverse experiences, including poverty, witnessing violence, witnessing violent death, domestic violence, bullying, and maltreatment victimization, among others. Significant advances in treatment for childhood trauma have been made, including some programs and interventions with strong or growing empirical support. Most of these programs range in treatment time from 4 to 36 sessions or weeks and take place in the community family setting. Table 11.1 includes several trauma treatment programs; the last two on the table are specifically designed for use in schools (Duke University School of Medicine, 2015; The National Child Traumatic Stress Network, 2015).

One of the effective interventions is Trauma-focused Coping in Schools (also known as MMTT). This program uses a skills-based and peer-mediated group design to help with trauma and related difficulties for children (fourth grade through high school). The curriculum

Treatment Foster Care: More intense and structured foster care setting that is designed for children and adolescents with more serious adjustment difficulties within their home, school, and community environments.

Trauma-Informed Care: Treatment framework that involves understanding, recognizing, and responding to the effects (psychological, social, and biological) of all types of trauma.

TREATMENT FOSTER CARE

Treatment foster care is a more intense and structured foster care setting that is designed for children and adolescents with serious adjustment difficulties. One type of treatment foster care is the Multidimensional Treatment Foster Care program, a foster family-based intervention that provides young people with programs that are designed to improve behavioral and school outcomes, decrease mental health and behavioral difficulties, and avoid placement recidivism to residential care and/or juvenile court facilities. This program was designed specifically to address the problems of those at high risk for residential, out-of-home care through a long-term, intensely supervised foster home placement using close supervision and predictable environments. The foster care parents are carefully trained and supervised and are the primary providers of support and treatment. The foster homes use behavior management systems, a therapeutic and highly structured environment, and coordinated efforts across other youth-caring systems, including schools, mental health agencies, and others as needed. Most often the young people placed into these foster homes are maltreatment victims who also experience severe mental health and/or antisocial behavioral problems, thereby increasing their risk for juvenile court involvement (Chamberlain, 2003; Chamberlain, Leve, & DeGarmo, 2007).

Treatment foster care is less costly than comparable residential facility placements, juvenile court detention, or incarceration facility placements, and it may be most effective with the 12- to 18-year-old age group in improving positive behaviors and psychological adjustments from maltreatment. Evidence indicates that treatment foster care is significantly effective for crossover/dually involved youthful offenders in decreasing their violent activities, felony convictions, and incarceration. The intense collaboration between child welfare, juvenile courts, and community-based treatment providers has been identified as a key to decreasing delinquency and recidivism (Hahn, Bilukha, Lowy, Crosby, & Fullilove, 2005; Hahn et al., 2004; MacDonald & Turner, 2007). In several evaluations, treatment foster care resulted in between $5 and $14 in taxpayer savings for every dollar spent on the program (Aos et al., 2011).

I. How is treatment foster care different from a foster care home?

2. Do you have any friends or acquaintances who have been in foster care? If so, what were their experiences like?

▼ TABLE 11.1

Effective Trauma Treatment Programs

Alternatives for Families: A cognitive behavioral therapy	Ages 5 to 17; 20 sessions; most appropriate for physical abuse or excessive physical punishment victims
Trauma-focused cognitive behavioral therapy	Ages 3 to 21; for sexual abuse, domestic violence, traumatic grief, and complex traumas experiences
Parent–child integrative therapy	Ages 2 to 12; for physical, sexual, or emotional abuse victims
Child and Family Traumatic Stress Intervention	Ages 7 to 18; 4 sessions; for a wide range of trauma victims including poly-victimizations typically in early or acute stage
Integrative Treatment of Complex Trauma for Adolescents	ages 12 to 21; for a wide range of traumas
Trauma Affect Regulation: Guide for Education and Therapy	Ages 10 and older; for complex and poly-victimization traumas
Trauma and Grief Component Therapy for Adolescents	Ages 12 to 20; for interpersonal violence and traumatic loss
Attachment, Self-Regulation, and Competence: A Comprehensive Framework for Intervention With Complexly Traumatized Youth	Ages 2 to 21, for complex traumas
Trauma-Focused Coping in Schools (MMTT)	Ages 6 to 18; used in a classroom setting; a skills-based approach to address single incident trauma and PTSD symptoms; group setting with 6–8 participants
Cognitive Behavioral Intervention for Trauma in Schools	Ages 10 to 15; addresses community and other violence, most appropriate with ethnic minority students; uses a skills-based group setting with 6–8 participants

is based on cognitive-behavioral techniques focused on teaching coping skills around anger, grief, and anxiety. The intervention is most helpful when started at least one month after the traumatic event (fire, suicide, homicide, or other violence exposure), and it typically includes 14 group sessions with six to eight children per group, held weekly during classroom time (Jaycox, Morse, Tanielian, & Stein, 2006).

MENTAL HEALTH PROBLEMS

If a child or adolescent is not sufficiently resilient to the difficulties, or when trauma is not addressed, he or she may experience certain mental health problems. Some of these mental health problems, such as attention-deficit hyperactivity disorder (ADHD) and anxiety disorder, will not dissipate on their own over time, thus causing harm to the young person and his or her family. Effective child and adolescent interventions and programs for dealing with mental health problems have been developed and are available for use across community-based agencies, as well as other settings, including schools and the juvenile justice system.

Children

Attention-Deficit Hyperactivity Disorder (ADHD). ADHD is characterized by symptoms of hyperactivity, inattention, and/or impulsivity that impair in several areas, including at home, at school, or in the community. More specifically, symptoms include child disorganization, impulsivity, hyperactivity, and attention problems. Several intervention modalities have been identified as useful or effective in treating or managing these symptoms. Psychosocial interventions include classroom-based behavior modification, social skills training, and cognitive-behavioral skills training, as well as home-based/parent training, with varying degrees of success. More specifically, behaviorally focused efforts aim to help a child change targeted behaviors and may include organizing tasks, completing school work, or managing and monitoring his or her own behaviors or emotions. Medication has also been widely prescribed to address the difficult symptoms of ADHD, including antidepressants and stimulants, but also more powerful psychiatric drugs, including **neuroleptics and adrenergic agonists**.

Medications do not cure ADHD, but they control the symptoms, and in some reviews, they show short-term effectiveness in up to 75% of cases, although these medications should be closely monitored for impact and side effects (Brown & LaRosa, 2002; Connor, 2002). Often the use of medications conjointly with behavioral therapy, counseling, and/or academic supports may be most effective. This combination of interventions may be important because medication alone does not significantly improve upward of 30% of children's ADHD symptoms nor does it impact many children's long-term symptoms (Connors et al., 2001; MTA Cooperative Group, 1999).

Anxiety Disorders. Many children respond to several interventions that help decrease or manage their anxiety symptoms and disorders, although other children are unresponsive and struggle with these problems into adolescence, even after intervention. Studies that examined a range of interventions found two with the greatest impact: **cognitive-behavioral therapy** and pharmacotherapy (medications), although the evidence is stronger for the former and thus should be used as an initial treatment (Muris & Broeren, 2009; Podell & Kendall, 2011; Walkup et al., 2008). When children do not respond well to the initial efforts by cognitive-behavioral therapy, then pharmacotherapy, in particular using **Selective Serotonin Reuptake Inhibitors (SSRIs)**, can be recommended in addition to cognitive-behavioral therapy. It should be cautioned, however, that even though this combination of interventions improves the symptoms in the short term, there are side effects and tolerance buildup, often in reaction to the pharmacotherapy regimen (American Academy of Child and Adolescent Psychiatry, 1997; RUPP Anxiety Group, 2001).

Neuroleptics and Adrenergic Agonists: Class of stimulant drugs.

Cognitive-Behavioral Therapy: Type of psychotherapy in which negative patterns of thought about the self and the world are challenged to alter unwanted behavior patterns or treat mood disorders such as depression.

Selective Serotonin Reuptake Inhibitors: One of the commonly prescribed drugs for treating depression and other related problems.

Effective behavioral and cognitive-behavioral therapies typically include components of different programming alternatives, including exposure therapy (systematic desensitization), cognitive restructuring, psycho-education on anxiety and its effects, contingent reinforcement, and modeling. Through the use of these components, children learn to recognize anxious feelings and reactions to anxiety, develop a coping mechanism for anxiety-inducing situations, clarify thoughts in anxious situations, and reinforce these new skills and behaviors (Amaya-Jackson & DeRosa, 2007; Kendall & Suveg, 2006; Suveg, Kendall, Comer, & Robin, 2006).

Behaviorally Based Disorders (Conduct and Oppositional Defiant Disorders).

▲ Many children and adolescents have acting out times at home, school, or in their communities. What differentiates normal development from more serious mental health concerns?

Programs and interventions for dealing with *behaviorally based disorders* target both parents and children. Parent management training, also called "parent training" and "family training," has been found effective in working with children who have behaviorally based and/or aggression problems, and it particularly demonstrates short-term improvements in the development of prosocial behaviors and in minimizing maladaptive behaviors. Parent management training involves teaching parents how to respond consistently and more positively to their children while changing maladaptive interaction habits within the relationship that lead to continued aggressive or antisocial behaviors. In doing so, this training, based on social learning theory, uses operant conditioning procedures to reduce these problem areas. It is important to provide interventions as early as possible because it may help prevent further or escalated behavioral problems. (Bernazzani & Tremblay, 2006; Farrington & Welsh, 2003; Froehlick, Doepfner, & Lehmkuhl, 2002; Piquero et al., 2009).

A related parent management training program type, sometimes called "behavioral parent training," is also based in social learning theory but has a stronger focus on behavioral management. In this, the emphasis is on the importance of observing and modeling the behaviors and attitudes of others to help the child with behavior problems. The programs teach broad behavioral principles for producing and reinforcing positive child behaviors that can be adapted in the home environment through the use of rehearsing and coaching (Dretzke et al., 2004). Reviews of these programs have found that they are high quality and effective in decreasing children's behavior problems (Barlow & Parsons, 2002). Several meta-analyses further supported these findings, with results showing the effectiveness of behavioral parent training programs in several specific areas: working with children with conduct disorders (Gould & Richardson, 2006); improving overall child and parent functioning levels, in particular with older children (ages 9 to 11; Serketich & Dumas, 1996); decreasing classroom disruptions (Wilson, Lipsey, & Derzon, 2003); and modifying behavior problems (Maughan, Christiansen, Jenson, Olympia, & Clark, 2005).

Because children with behaviorally based disorders and problems often struggle in the home, school environments, and community, programs or interventions addressing multiple locations/environments may be necessary. Interventions that focus on behavioral and cognitive-behavioral orientation treatment when working with children with behavioral problems and emotional disturbances have been found to have positive impacts (Beard & Sugai, 2004; Robinson & Rapport, 2002). Interventions include behavioral therapy, individualized therapy, social skills training, medication, and art/play therapy, with the social skills training and a behavioral approach to daily living (token economy model) being two of the more common (Reddy, DeThomas, Newman, & Chun, 2008).

The Promoting Alternative Thinking Strategies (PATHS) Curriculum is an effective school-based program that decreases aggressive behaviors and improves social problem solving through teaching children developmentally based lessons and instructions on emotional literacy and ability to identify feelings, self-control, interpersonal problem-solving skills, and positive peer relations. Sessions take place two to three times a week in elementary classrooms, led by teachers, to connect cognitive understandings to the daily life situations that children face (Child Trends, 2011; Greenberg, Kusché, & Mihalic, 2006). This is one of numerous programs that have the therapeutic goal of improving self-control. These interventions focus on increasing skills for friendship and social skills, social problem-solving abilities, and understanding and communicating emotions. These can take place in multiple settings—school, home, or community—and involve the child, family, and/or peers. A thorough review of 34 programs found these efforts that attempt to improve self-control among children were an effective intervention in reducing problem behaviors and delinquency risks for those younger than the age of ten (Piquero, Jennings, & Farrington, 2010).

Adolescents

Attention-Deficit Hyperactivity Disorder. Although most children with ADHD continue to have symptoms into adolescence, some are not identified or diagnosed until this later developmental stage. Late identification is more common among adolescents with attention problems (difficulties in organizing, completing school work, processing information, and focusing on tasks) than it is among adolescents with disruptive problems (impatience and violating social norms). Adolescents with ADHD many times have added difficulties as academic and social expectations rise in secondary school. Effective interventions used by these young people include behaviorally focused strategies and medication (Barkley, 2002).

Behaviorally focused strategies have been found helpful when they use clear standards, completion of specific tasks, positive reinforcement, easily understandable instructions, and any follow-up supervision in both the home and school environments (Howe, 2009). Behavior modification techniques show some signs of positive impact for many adolescents with ADHD symptoms, although this appears to be less effective compared with the use of stimulant medication alone. The combination of behavior modification techniques and stimulant medication has generally seen better short-term outcomes than either of the treatments alone. Nevertheless, as was noted also for children, there can be resistance to these stimulant medications, decreasing their symptom-reduction impact over time (American Academy of Child and Adolescent Psychiatry, 1997; Fabiano, Pelham, Ghangy, Coles, & Wheeler-Cox, 2000; Jensen et al., 2001).

Behaviorally Based Disorders (Conduct and Oppositional Defiant Disorders). Cognitive-based parent training, focused on teaching practical skills to caregivers to address conflict and interpersonal problems and improve communication, has been found effective. Cognitive-behavioral treatment interventions more broadly used with both adolescents and their families have demonstrated effectiveness in reducing aggressive and antisocial behaviors (Little, 2005). Additionally, these interventions improve positive behavioral and other psychological outcomes. Cognitive-behavioral interventions are designed to identify cognitions—thoughts, expressions, perceptions—and to then alter cognitions that are negative or detrimental to reduce maladaptive or dysfunctional thinking, attitudes, or behaviors. Such approaches may include teaching social skills, parenting skills, problem-solving skills, anger management, and related efforts (Andreassen, Armelius, Egeland, & Ogden, 2006; Connor, 2002; Farrington, 2002; Lipsey & Landenberger, 2006; Turner, MacDonald, & Dennis, 2007).

Other programs and interventions that also use some cognitive-behavioral components have demonstrated positive effects on adolescent conduct disorder symptoms, including

Functional Family Therapy (FFT) and **Multisystemic Therapy (MST)**. Both of these therapies use a framework of modifying individual behaviors and cognitions (family is focused on in FFT and multiple systems are focused on in MST), with an emphasis on the larger family or system groups as the focal area requiring change rather than only on the adolescent. MST is designed for adolescents to deal with severe psychological and behavioral problems through short-term (4 to 6 months), multifaceted (using techniques from structural family therapy and cognitive-behavioral therapy), and home- and community-based interventions. Research has shown that MST reduces offending and delinquency recidivism significantly, with an almost 4-to-1 return on investment (Aos et al., 2011; Henggeler, Schoenwald, Rowland, & Cunningham, 2002; Sexton & Alexander, 2000). Nevertheless, a thorough review of the available research on MST found it to be only as effective as other comparable interventions for adolescents with emotional or behavioral problems, requiring further research to determine whether MST outperforms less expensive alternatives (Little, Popa, & Forsythe, 2005).

FFT, a short-term program that targets the family, is designed to motivate the adolescent and family members to change adolescent behaviors and family member's reactions to these behaviors. Interventions with 11- to 18-year-old adolescents with behavioral disorders lasts from 8 to 30 hours through various engagement and treatment phases, depending on the level of problem severity. FFT has been found to significantly decrease delinquency offending as well as out-of-home placement due to family instability or delinquency involvement (Alexander et al., 2007; Howell, 2009).

Schools can also have an impact on decreasing aggressive behaviors. Many adolescents report troubles dealing with violence, bullying, and related problems within their schools, leading most school districts to offer some sort of preventative programming (Gottfredson et al., 2000). Most of these programs use social processing and cognitive-behavioral techniques to inform and educate students on improving problem-solving skills, identifying consequences to their plans, identifying aggression, and response options. These preventative and intervention programs are offered in both a universal format—to all students in a classroom—or on a selective, individualized basis—students who are identified as having aggression or violence problems. Both social skill development formats, universal and selective programming, have been found to significantly decrease adolescent aggressive and disruptive behaviors, and that the affect for some adolescents was long term (Wilson & Lipsey, 2006a, 2006b).

Depression and Suicide Prevention. Numerous approaches have been used to decrease the symptoms and impact of adolescent depression and related disorders, including various individual and group therapeutic modalities, **psychopharmacology**, and public education, among others. Although some of these approaches, primarily psychopharmacology, are important in stabilizing the most serious depressive symptoms including suicidal ideation and behaviors, others do not appear to be effective in achieving symptom reduction goals, including therapy, **psychotherapy**, and **psychoanalysis** (March et al., 2004).

A smaller set of interventions may be helpful for some adolescents with significant depression problems. Interventions that are more likely to be effective include cognitive-behavioral approaches attuned to adolescent development focused on peer-to-peer social activities, problem-solving abilities, new thinking patterns, psycho-education for parents and adolescents, and mood and emotion regulation. Nevertheless, little long-term follow-up research has been completed, so whether or not lasting effects can be achieved though these approaches is not yet known. In addition, when working with adolescents with multiple or comorbid problems that significantly complicate treatment planning and coordination efforts, care should be taken because, once again, only a few long-term intervention outcomes targeting this population of adolescents are known (Clark et al., 1993; Curry & Wells, 2005; Horowitz & Garber, 2006).

Several risk factors correlate with suicidal behaviors, although having suicidal risk factors does not always lead to suicidal tendencies. Risk factors include depression and other related

---

Functional Family Therapy (FFT): Intervention that attempts to modify individual behaviors and cognitions, with an emphasis on the larger family or groups as the focal area needing change rather than only on the adolescent.

Multisystemic Therapy (MST): MST is designed for adolescents with severe psychological and behavioral problems through short-term (four to six months), multifaceted, and home- and community-based interventions.

Psychopharmacology: Branch of psychology concerned with the effects of drugs on the mind and behavior.

Psychotherapy: Treatment of mental disorders by psychological rather than by medical means.

Psychoanalysis: System of psychological theory and therapy that aims to treat mental disorders by investigating the interaction of conscious and unconscious elements in the mind and bringing repressed fears and conflicts into the conscious mind.

EFFECTIVE SUICIDE PREVENTION

The National Registry of Evidence-Based Programs, supported by the National Institute of Mental Health, highlights effective adolescent suicide prevention programs. These include the following: CARE (Care, Assess, Respond, and Empower), a high-school based program using motivational counseling and social support; CAST (Coping and Support Training), a 12-week program focused on life skills and social support delivered by teachers in a group setting; Emergency Department Means Restriction Education, an adult caregiver program that helps to minimize access to adolescent suicidal risks at home (e.g., firearms and prescription drugs); Lifelines Curriculum, a school-wide prevention program that focuses on available resources and decreasing the stigma of suicidal behaviors; and Reconnecting Youth: A Peer Group Approach to Building Life Skills, a school-based prevention program that teaches skills to build resiliency against suicide risk factors, substance abuse, or emotional problems.

The Blueprints for Healthy Youth Development, supported by the Annie E. Casey Foundation and located at the Center for the Study and Prevention of Violence at the University of Colorado, is a registry of evidence-based programs focused on positive child and adolescent outcomes and on delinquency prevention. These programs are family-, school-, and community-based and focus on both prevention programming and targeted interventions for those young people at risk for negative outcomes.

1. How does a program or intervention become designated as "evidenced-based?"

2. In reviewing the Blueprints website, with which programs are you familiar?

mental health problems, a prior suicide attempt, a family history of suicide or family violence, firearms in the house, and incarceration. When working with adolescents, several suicidal behavior signs or symptoms can be identified, thus allowing immediate and concerted preventative actions. These signs include feelings of hopelessness or worthlessness, a decline in or lack of family or social activity participation, changes in sleeping or eating patterns, feelings of rage or need for revenge, consistent exhaustion, low concentration abilities at home and/or school, regular or frequent crying, lack of self-care, and reckless or impulsive behaviors (Centers for Disease Control and Prevention, 2015; National Institute of Mental Health, 2011).

Of concern among adolescents is the effect of comorbid problems that increase the risk for suicidal behavior. As the number of risk factors increases, the risk for suicidal behavior among adolescents also increases, although this is further complicated by the impact of other mental health or substance abuse problems. Depression, disruptive behavior disorders (conduct and oppositional defiant), and substance abuse are strongly linked to increased suicide risk. Nevertheless, anxiety disorders have not been established as contributing to such risk (Conner & Goldston, 2007; Shaffer et al., 1996).

Substance Abuse Prevention. Substance abuse prevention programs should target the enhancement of protective factors and the reduction of risk factors and focus on all types of drug abuse. These programs should also be designed to be appropriate and effective for the intended adolescent population. Risk factors correlated with adolescent substance abuse include early aggressive behavior, lack of parental supervision, substance use by a caregiver, drug availability, the association with deviant peers, the lack of caring adult relationships, the experience with traumatic life events, mental health difficulties, academic failure, poor social skills, and poverty (Hawkens et al., 2000; National Institute on Drug Abuse, 2003).

Families play a key part in reducing the risk of substance abuse, which can be further strengthened through improving parent's skills in handling these problems, education, and increased involvement among family members. Parental skills training can improve rule-setting, monitoring, and consistent disciplinary actions. Drug education and information can improve family discussions about substance abuse, and specific family-focused interventions can improve parenting behaviors (Spoth, Redmond, & Shin, 2001). Schools can also play an

National Registry of Evidence-Based Programs: Searchable online database from the National Institutes of Mental Health of research-based and effective mental health and substance abuse interventions.

roger askew/Alamy Stock Photo

▲ Families have the greatest impact on their children's social and educational outcomes. What do you think makes a family best equipped for effective parenting?

important preventative role by improving academic skills, such as study habits, self-efficacy, as well as social skills, such as peer relationships and drug resistance skills. School programs should focus on key transition periods during adolescence from middle to high school when alcohol and drug experimentation is common. Communities can also have an impact on family members at risk for substance abuse through the use of consistent messages about the risks for and problems of substance use by targeting populations in various different settings, such as home, schools, and faith-based centers (Dishion, Kavanaugh, Schneiger, Nelson, & Kaufman, 2002).

These efforts, and the use of evidence-based preventative efforts, can be cost-effective, saving more dollars in adolescent and family treatment compared with the costs of later treatment involving serious substance abuse problems. Cost-effective programs include the Midwestern Prevention Project (MPP); the Strengthening Families Program: For Parents and Youth 10–14; Guiding Good Choices; and the Skills, Opportunity, and Recognition (SOAR) Program (Aos et al., 2011; Pentz, Mihalic, & Grotpeter, 2006).

Preventing substance use is easier and less costly than providing substance use treatment by preventing the development of substance abuse and addiction, along with their many associated problems, including overdose death, and reducing the costs and difficulties in recovery from substance dependence. Many efforts are pursued by stakeholders in preventing substance use and abuse, and several programs have been found to have a significant impact in prevention substance abuse. Such programs are offered in three formats: (1) universal, to all young people within a certain environment; (2) selective, to families at high risk for substance abuse; and (3) indicated, to certain adolescents who are identified as high risk for substance abuse (Eggert, Thompson, Herting, & Randall, 2001).

Universal programs with significant preventative impact include the Caring School Community Program, PATHS, Classroom-Centered Intervention, SOAR Program, Guiding Good Choices, Life Skills Training, Project Alert, Project STAR, Positive Family Support Program, Project Towards No Drug Abuse, and the Strengthening Families Program: For Parents and Youth 10 to 14. Effective selective programs include Focus on Families, Strengthening Families Program, and Coping Power. Although effective, indicated programs include Project Towards No Drug Abuse and Reconnecting Youth (Koball et al., 2011; National Institute of Drug Abuse, 2015; Sussman, Rohrbach, & Mihalic, 2004; U.S. Department of Education, 2001).

Substance Abuse Treatment. Among adolescents ages 12 to 17, no more than 5% have been estimated to be in need of substance abuse treatment; however, at most, only one in ten of these young people in need of treatment actually access services. Reasons identified for this chasm between identification and treatment services include concerns that interventions do not work for this population because of the high drop-out rates and substance abuse recidivism (Austin, Macgowan, & Wagner, 2005; Substance Abuse and Mental Health Services Administration, 2014b). In recent years, however, several programs have been found effective in treating adolescents. For instance, family-based therapies have shown promise, with recommendations for additional investigations to identify the specific techniques that are most successful (Kowalski, Lindstrom, Rasmussen, Filger, & Jorgensen, 2011; Rowe & Liddle, 2006). Components of family-based therapies found to be effective include comprehensive interventions, parent support, and individualized adolescent and family care. These multicomponent programs target the risk factors and triggers that lead the young person to abuse substances (Hogue & Liddle, 2009; Waldron & Turner, 2008).

MIDWEST PREVENTION PROJECT

The Midwestern Prevention Project (MPP) is a comprehensive, community-based program intended to prevent or reduce early substance use (alcohol, tobacco, and marijuana) during adolescence. The program focuses on how peer and social pressures influence drug use and teaches assertiveness skills to help minimize these influences. The focus of the program is during middle school, when young people are most often subject to peer influence and delinquency. The program itself is offered in sixth- and seventh-grade classrooms, although it is also a multipronged effort. These efforts are spread across the school (modeling, role-playing, and group discussion), family (parent education and organization), community (organization and training), and mass media (anti-drug messaging) (National Institute of Justice, 2012).

1. **Why do you think this program may be effective with middle-schoolers?**

2. **What experiences did you have with prevention programs during middle or high school?**

Cognitive-behavioral therapy is one of the most reviewed and researched interventions for adolescent substance use and abuse and has shown promising outcomes. Related to this type of therapy, but requiring the inclusion of all family members, is Multidimensional Family Therapy (MDFT), which targets family communications, social competence, and parental involvement with their children across home, community, and school environments (Becker & Curry, 2008; Filges, Knudsen, Swendsen, Kowalski, & Benjaminsen, 2015).

A related intervention is Motivational Interviewing (MI), although it is designed more to move individuals toward addressing their risk factors for substance abuse than actually treating the substance abuse itself. This intervention is based on the philosophy that young people want their substance use behavior to end but are just not able to act on this willingness. Motivational Interviewing is a psychological intervention that tries to enhance an adolescent's motivation to change and to decrease his or her ambivalence to change. Despite popular use of this intervention with adolescents, the empirical evidence for this intervention indicates that it is ineffective as a stand-alone program. When used in conjunction with cognitive-behavioral therapy, in particular when addressing cannabis abuse, however, the empirical evidence indicates that this intervention is significantly effective in decreasing abuse (National Institute on Drug Abuse, 2014; Smedslund et al., 2011).

When adolescents with substance abuse problems pose a safety risk to themselves or require a more intense intervention, a residential treatment setting may be required. Unfortunately, however, there are only few outcome evaluations of the residential treatment for adolescents. These few evaluation studies show improvements in substance dependency and addiction for many residents while at the facility and a significantly smaller number after release. To be effective and to maintain the reduction in adolescent substance use and dependency after residential facility placement, however, running the treatment program as designed is important (Morral, McCaffrey, & Ridgeway, 2004; Vaughn & Howard, 2004; Winters, Botzet, & Fahnhorst, 2011).

Mentoring Programs. Mentoring programs are one of the most common interventions used in working with at-risk adolescents across many areas: delinquency, antisocial behavior, substance abuse, aggression, and school failure, among others. The programs usually have a narrow focus on the outcomes at which the efforts are being directed. Nonetheless, the general format of this program involves a nonfamily member adult taking on a mentoring role that is designed to grow into a long-term relationship between the young person and the mentor. The mentoring programs' goals are focused on minimizing risk factors that lead to problems by using the mentor's skills, abilities,

Mentoring Programs: Programs that are focused on minimizing child and adolescent problem risk factors by using adult mentors who spend time with the young person, sharing skills, abilities, and experiences.

▲ There are many effective therapeutic approaches to helping troubled teens. What do you think works?

experiences, and knowledge that may assist the mentee, providing guidance and advocacy, and sometimes taking on a quasi-parental or guardian role (Jekielek, Moore, & Hair, 2002). Research has shown that there is significant comorbidity across the problem areas that mentoring programs try to address. For example, adolescents with aggression or delinquency problems are often involved with substance use or abuse. Hence, it is possible that mentoring programs may directly or indirectly having positive influences on adolescent substance abuse problems (Dubois & Karcher, 2005; Rhodes, 2002).

Many reviews of mentoring programs have been completed, with generally positive outcomes, although the impact is moderate at best. These reviews have found decreases in adolescent delinquent activities, improved school performance, lower levels of aggression, and other related improvements (DuBois, Holloway, Valentine, & Cooper, 2002; Lipsey & Wilson, 1998). The most effective mentoring programs are those that provide the following: training and ongoing mentor supervision, expectations of more time involved with the mentee, program-sponsored activities, parental support and involvement, and supplemental services (Herrera, Grossman, Kauh, Feldman, McMaken, & Jucovy, 2007; Jolliffe & Farrington, 2007; Tolan, Henry, Schoeny, & Bass, 2008). Moving forward, it is important that mentoring programs thoroughly document their protocols and design and conduct rigorous evaluations to justify the number of programs that are already in place.

CASE STUDY

JACK

Eight years after Jack lost his father in the terrorist attacks on New York City on September 11, 2001, he ran in the Tunnel to Towers race with his Big Brother Matt, holding a flag high in honor of his father's memory.

Their story begins a few years ago, when Jack's mother, Denise, was worried that her two sons—Michael, who was 3 years old when his father died, and Jack, who was only 6 months old—would not have a strong male role model in their lives. Once the two boys were old enough, the New York City Fire Department, where their father was a 10-year veteran, approached Denise to see if she would be interested in working with Big Brothers Big Sisters to find Big Brothers for the two boys. Since they did not have close family members to fill the void, Denise began to investigate.

When Jack grew old enough in September 2007, Big Brothers Big Sisters match specialist Patty paired him with Matt, a New York City fire fighter. Jack remembers their first meeting: "I was kind of nervous because I didn't know who I was going to get or what he would be like. But right away I knew Matt was a nice guy. He smiled and started to laugh. We took a bunch of pictures together—funny, regular, and happy—and Patty gave them to us both to take home."

Nonetheless, Denise was reluctant to leave her son alone with a person she had only just met. Patty continually checked in with the family. When she would talk to Jack, she would ask questions to make sure the match remained positive and rewarding.

Matt also immediately recognized and respected Denise's reservations and took steps to make her feel more comfortable as Jack and he got to know each other. "If

Matt takes Jack to a New York Mets game, he sends me cell phone pictures of Jack with cotton candy all over his face, laughing and enjoying himself," Denise explains. "And when they are done with their outing, Matt texts me saying they are on their way home."

Although Jack is in third grade, he plays on a fourth grade soccer team. Matt arrives early at their house, helps Jack with his shin guards and cleats, gets him warmed up, and then they spend quality time together as they drive to the game. Additionally, Matt and Jack always talk on Tuesday nights. Jack rushes home from school on Tuesday afternoons and exclaims "I'm going to get my phone call tonight!" Denise says that Jack is able to talk with Matt about things that he needs to chat about with another male—a brother, a friend—"not stuff you want to share with your mommy," laughs Denise.

Matt uses these opportunities to teach Jack manners, academics and life lessons. Firstly, Matt teaches "PATYs" or "Please and Thank You's," which has taught Jack to be more respectful to and appreciative of his mother. Denise also remembers that she was having trouble teaching Jack how to use quotation marks. Matt suggested she show Jack newspaper stories quoting his favorite athletes, and Jack quickly picked up the lesson.

"You can't replace a dad," Denise says, "but it's really important to have a guy in your life that is there just for you. That is something that Big Brothers Big Sisters gave back to my family. Matt is not going to be his dad, and Jack knows that. But no matter what, Matt is Jack's one outlet."

In honor of the 343 NYC firefighters who lost their lives during the 9/11 terrorist attacks, the Tunnel to Towers run begins in Brooklyn, passes through the Brooklyn Battery Tunnel and finishes at Ground Zero in Manhattan. This past year, Jack—now 9 years old—ran by his Big Brother's side, carrying a flag together. "It was pouring rain, but when Matt held the flag it was really nice because it had my dad's picture on it," recalls Jack.

Denise reflects on her family's relationship with Big Brothers Big Sisters: "Jack and Matt are a perfect fit. They like the same things and have as much energy as each other, from the soccer field to the basketball court to the playground. Matt loves it all as much as Jack. They hit if off at every aspect. Jack really looks up to him and helps him realize his potential."

She continues, "I'd love for my kids to be able to give back one day from the experience they've had. If you do feel it in your heart, you should become a part of Big Brothers Big Sisters, as a donor or volunteer. My children and I know how lucky we are to have Big Brothers Big Sisters as part of our lives." (Big Brothers Big Sisters of America, 2016, para. 1–11)

1. **Why do you think mentoring is often helpful for young people?**

2. **Were you ever a mentor or mentee? If so, what was that experience like for you?**

Source: Reprinted with permission from Big Brothers Big Sisters of America.

Tutoring Programs. There is strong evidence that several school-based learning/tutoring programs help students who are behind in academic performance or at risk of failing a grade—both risk factors for school discipline protocols and youthful offending behaviors. The first program area is the classroom setting and interactions between teachers and children, when teachers gain knowledge of how to offer effective instruction that can ameliorate several of these risks (National Institute of Child Health and Human Development, 2003). An example of an effective in-class literacy intervention is Read 180 with widely implemented successful results. This program combines individual and small-group, face-to-face, instruction along with computer-based intervention to improve reading abilities (Institute of Education Services, 2009).

Programs that are offered during nonschool hours—after school and summer—have also shown success in improving reading and learning results, with several important components found necessary in the interventions: quality staffing, access to and sustained child or adolescent participation, and strong partnerships with families, schools, and related community stakeholders (Harvard Family Research Project, 2010). An example is the Reading Recovery tutoring model that has been found effective in improving participants' alphabet identifying skills and reading literacy skills. This model uses certified teachers and takes place during the school day. It is designed for the lowest 20% achieving first-grade students and offered normally between 12 and 20 weeks, although discontinued when the student consistently reads at the grade-level average (Lauer et al., 2006).

Children may also benefit from nonteacher driven or taught tutoring programs. Some of these tutoring models are similar to the mentoring programs discussed earlier. These tutoring programs may be structured highly or minimally and may use professional or volunteer tutors. An overview of nonprofessional volunteer tutor programs (all studies had a comparison group with a one-month tutoring duration minimum) for school-aged children (K-8) found positive impacts on reading and language outcomes—specifically oral fluency, overall reading, writing, and letter and word identification improved. There were no significant differences between volunteer tutor type, grade level, or program focus (Ritter, Denny, Albin, Barnett, & Blankenship, 2007). In addition, a meta-analysis of 29 tutoring programs that included both adult nonprofessional and adult trained-professional volunteers demonstrated that these programs were effective at improving reading abilities among elementary school children (Elbaum, Vaughn, Hughes, & Moody, 2000).

CASE STUDY

IN THE FOLLOWING TWO STORIES

1. **What would you do to help the young person, and what rehabilitative pathways do you think may be best for the family?**

2. **What are the possible barriers or obstacles to rehabilitation that you can think of?**

Stephanie. A 9-year-old child is suspected of parental neglect, but the child protective agency case was lacking enough evidence to substantiate the claim. The school teacher and social worker who referred the investigation to the agency are still worried about the fourth-grade student because of an increase in school absences over the past six months, a decrease in homework completion, and an increase in inattention and hyperactivity while in class. In addition, the parents of the child have become more difficult to reach and less involved with the school activities and communications.

Julio. A 14-year-old young man has shared that his home and neighborhood are stressful. He talks about how his parents often fight about money and related problems and how his dad has a real temper. He worries about potential violence in the home. In addition, his friends have been running around the neighborhood trying to start fights with other boys, something he has been caught up in but does not know how to avoid because of not wanting to be left out or ostracized. He has been missing more school days lately because he just cannot get his thoughts together and has been feeling very sad and distraught for the past few months.

CHAPTER REVIEW

CHAPTER SUMMARY

This chapter reviewed the evidence on what works in delinquency prevention and related intervention efforts. In so doing, many effective options were identified for treating some of the key delinquency and juvenile court involvement risk factors—maltreatment, mental health disorders, substance abuse problems, and other related difficulties. In addition, the burgeoning field of trauma-informed care was examined, identifying key assessment and intervention options. Finally, with the proliferation of mentoring and tutoring programs used for young people in need, evidence as to how best to use and implement these programs was analyzed. Overall, the juvenile court and school stakeholders have many effective programs to use in helping those disproportionately impacted by delinquency or school-related risks.

KEY TERMS

cognitive-behavioral therapy **249**

Head Start (Early Head Start) **245**

Functional Family Therapy (FFT) **252**

home visiting programs **242**

mentoring programs **255**

meta-analysis study **244**

Multisystemic Therapy (MST) **252**

National Registry of Evidence-Based Programs **253**

neuroleptics and adrenergic agonists **249**

parent support groups **244**

psychoanalysis **252**

psychopharmacology **252**

psychotherapy **252**

Selective Serotonin Reuptake Inhibitors (SSRIs) **249**

sexual offender registration **245**

Structured Decision-Making (SDM) model **242**

trauma-informed care **247**

treatment foster care **247**

DISCUSSION QUESTIONS

1. What are the advantages or disadvantages to addressing delinquency and school-related discipline problems through an ecological/psychological model?

2. What are some commonly used components of effective prevention and intervention strategies for child maltreatment? Why are these efforts successful?

3. Why is earlier identification and prevention efforts for trauma- and mental health-related problems important? Or, is there a case to make that you should wait until the problems and symptoms are more pronounced?

4. Parent education classes that are based on a weekly psycho-educational approach are required in most cases involving child protective agencies for parents who were found to have neglected their children. Unfortunately, however, these classes are found to be ineffective, neither helpful nor harmful. So, (a) why do you think these parent education classes are still so commonly used across child protective agencies and required for completion in parent case plans? (b) What would you recommend as alternative interventions to decrease parental neglect recidivism?

5. How does trauma or trauma-related victimization lead to mental health problems for young people? What can be done to minimize the impact of trauma on children?

6. What are some of the effective interventions for adolescents with behaviorally based mental health problems? What are the common components of such interventions? Why do you think these interventions work?

7. Why do you think that difficulties in childhood (e.g., trauma or maltreatment) lead to other problems in adolescence (e.g., depression and suicide or delinquency)?

8. Can suicide be prevented for adolescents? If so, how?

9. With such a proliferation of mentoring programs used across problems experienced among adolescents (school academics, truancy, delinquency, substance use, and trauma, among others), what are the findings based on empirical studies on these programs? How would you design a mentoring program?

---

https://edge.sagepub.com/mallett

$SAGE edge™ **Sharpen your skills with SAGE edge!**

SAGE edge for students provides a personalized approach to help you accomplish your coursework in an easy-to-use learning environment. You'll find mobile-friendly eFlashcards and quizzes, as well as videos, web resources, and links to SAGE journal articles to support and expand on the concepts presented in this chapter.

CHAPTER 12

SCHOOL SAFETY AND INCLUSION POLICIES

▲ Schools have a dynamic impact on young people. What do you think makes a school a safe and effective learning environment?
©iStockphoto.com/Rawpixel

INTRODUCTION

Schools prioritize the provision of safe learning environments for all students, for without such environments, there can be little effective education and learning. Stakeholders agree that effective teaching and learning is best achieved in classrooms that minimize fears and safety problems and build positive school climates. Zero tolerance and related school discipline policies have focused on removing the most difficult and persistently disruptive students to improve the learning environment and on spreading the deterrence message that violence and misbehaviors will not be tolerated. Several studies have found that this punitive paradigm within schools has been harmful to students most at risk as well as to the classroom and school climates. Thus, a shift toward rehabilitative and inclusive school policies has been happening across many school districts over the past decade. Although this movement is not universal because many states and school districts still use a zero tolerance framework, there is a growing consensus that inclusion and rehabilitative approaches are better than a punitive approach based on zero tolerance.

Thus, most of the outcomes of interest—improved school safety, student accountability, positive learning outcomes, and efficient school management—are top priorities for school administrators and teachers. Today, there is enough evidence that can guide school district policies and practices to meet these outcomes. This chapter explores and presents the following: how school districts can move away from zero tolerance

policies, the development of inclusive school student codes of conduct, how to increase positive and rehabilitative classroom and school programming, positive student and family engagements, how to implement truancy policies and school dropout prevention, and how effectively school resource officers can be incorporated on school campuses. These changes will decrease the reliance on the juvenile justice system and help to diminish what has come to be called the "school-to-prison pipeline."

LEARNING OBJECTIVES

1. Demonstrate how schools can more effectively use rehabilitative approaches to discipline and move away from zero tolerance policies

2. Identify inclusive student management and discipline protocols

3. Evaluate and identify evidence-based interventions for school personnel and truancy prevention protocols

4. Recognize how and why many state policies are starting to shift toward school inclusion policies and away from a zero tolerance philosophy

5. Understand how state and national policies drive local school district rules and regulations

6. Explicate existing state and national data, and understand today's discipline and school removal trends

STUDENTS, CLASSROOMS, AND SCHOOLS

Improving classroom safety and student behavioral outcomes revolves around creating school climates that emphasize positive staff and student relationships and incorporate preventative programming. These classroom and school environmental themes are core elements for many effective programs and interventions, as well as for school policies focused on student inclusion and minimizing discipline protocols when unnecessary or when students are not safety risks (Muschert & Peguero, 2010).

MOVING AWAY FROM ZERO TOLERANCE POLICIES

Moving away from zero tolerance policies is not simple or easy. It took years for school policies and practices to develop, including state laws that called for this approach; it will take time to turn back this approach. Important stakeholders, including the U.S. Attorney General's Office, the American Academy of Pediatrics, and the American Psychological Association, among others, have recommended student discipline dispensation be determined on a case-by-case basis, looking at the mitigating circumstances around the problems, and using developmentally appropriate and rehabilitative-focused interventions (American Academy of Pediatrics, Council on School Health,

Inclusive School Policies: School policies that minimize students from being out-of-school suspended or expelled; often entails the use of rehabilitative programming and graduated sanctions.

▲ Many students have difficulties at school, either with teachers or peers. What do you think works in making schools successful for struggling students?

2013; American Psychological Association, 2006; Kang-Brown, Trone, Fratello, & Daftary-Kapur, 2013). In schools, these policies are laid out in student codes of conduct.

Student Codes of Conduct

School district **student codes of conduct** outline behaviors that are expected as well as behaviors that are not permitted. They reflect and incorporate state mandates, district rules, and school-based administration's expectations and, for some districts, the expectations of parents and parent groups. Behaviors that are not permitted under the code of conduct may include minor or less serious behaviors such as tardiness, cell phone and other technology use, foul language, and related code violations. In addition, the code of conduct typically covers minor or more serious behaviors that may also be considered a status offense, delinquency, or crime, including truancy, assault, fighting, drug activity, and weapon possession, among others. Some of the most serious violations—certain drug and weapons possession on campus—are driven by federal law based on the 1994 Drug-Free School Act and subsequent amendments that requires immediate student removal from school. The student code of conduct normally indicates the disciplinary action that is to be taken by school personnel for certain violations and is provided in writing to students and families. Discipline-focused codes that rely on punishments for students' infractions, with limited discussion of the school learning environment, are often the outcome of zero tolerance policies (Kupchik, 2010; Morgan, Salmon, Plotkin, & Cohen, 2014).

A school district's code of conduct is important in setting the priorities around building the learning environment and improving school safety. In doing so, the code should convey firm, clear, and consistent rules; provide certain punishments for misbehaving and rule breaking; be sure these punishments are equitable; and effectively communicate these rules to students, families, and school staff. Contrary to the purpose of the zero-tolerance policy approach, student codes of conduct are most effective when they focus on rehabilitation of the students and incorporate graduated responses and not automatic discipline measures in determining the appropriate disciplinary measure, and when they do not remove students from school for minor misbehaviors, attendance problems, or disruptions (Arum, 2003; Gottfredson, Gottfredson, Payne, & Gottfredson, 2005).

Metropolitan Nashville Public School District. In the 2014–2015 academic year, the Metropolitan Nashville Public School District (MNPSD) changed from a zero-tolerance focused student code of conduct (synonymous with an exclusive, or reliance on suspension and expulsions, policy) to one that incorporates an inclusive (keep students in class and school policy). This recent shift was driven by the district's review of its school exclusionary policies that showed the disparate impact on many at-risk student groups and the increasing evidence that indicates that school inclusion improves learning and school climate. The district's revised student code of conduct illustrates how to balance safety, accountability, and rehabilitative discipline.

The MNPSD introduces the student code of conduct by acknowledging the following school climate priorities: positive relationships with all stakeholders (parents and guardians, students, teachers, and school staff); training and resources for teachings and students to resolve conflicts peacefully and respectfully, with suspensions only as a disciplinary measure

Student Codes of Conduct: Written policies by school districts that outline behaviors that are expected as well as behaviors that the districts have determined are not permitted.

of last resort; supports for students who are experiencing emotional crisis, trauma, or serious challenges in their homes and communities; using academic and extracurricular activities for students that have behavioral and academic needs; effective communication among schools, parents, and communities; clean and well-maintained environments that demonstrate school pride and focus on learning; and an environment where students and staff feel physically and emotionally safe (Metropolitan Nashville Public School District, 2016, p. 2).

Discipline Protocols

The MNPSD school discipline philosophy is based on the promotion of positive relationships among students and between students and school personnel. To do so, several classroom strategies have been incorporated, including the program to foster social and emotional skills (via the Daily Rap, a dialogue circle for students, led by teachers and staff), morning classroom meetings focused on building community and resolving conflicts, and student advisories whereby students meet in small groups with an adult adviser regularly to talk about character development. The school also offers a variety of rehabilitative interventions that are used prior to and/or alongside disciplinary actions, if needed.

These interventions are focused on eliminating misbehaviors that lead to disciplinary action or on building social and emotional skills that help build community. The following interventions have strong empirical validity in achieving these goals: conferences with the students, parents/guardians, and school personnel; parent outreach; community service (for example, cleaning up a public space or volunteering at a senior center); conflict resolution (reviewed later in the chapter); functional behavioral assessment and planning (a corrective action plan that uses positive behavioral approaches to address inappropriate or disruptive student behavior); mentoring programs; peer mediation; referrals to appropriate community-based agencies for services (mental health, substance use, after-school programming, tutoring, and leadership development, among others); restorative justice strategies (reviewed later in the chapter); and student support teams, depending on the needs, may include teacher, parent(s), school administrator, social worker, nursing, psychologists, and external school representatives, among others.

The school expects students to demonstrate respect for themselves and others. When students are disruptive or inappropriate, school staff is expected to respond appropriately and consistently. The Discipline Table describes five types of behavior, increasing in seriousness from a Type 1 Behavior to a Type 5 Behavior. The discipline plan also contains five possible responses to inappropriate behavior (Levels A through E), whereby each behavior is assigned to one or more of these levels of intervention and response. A Level A response includes the student, teacher, parent, and school staff as needed in intervening to address the problems. A Level B response includes the same team and a school administrator and provides additional interventions as appropriate; an in-school suspension of up to three days is possible. A Level C response includes an out-of-school suspension option of up to three days only if additional services or interventions fail to mitigate the student behavior. A Level D response is the same as a Level C one, but the in-school suspension may be up to five days after an administrative intervention behavior plan is completed. A Level E response is the same as a Level D, except that the administrator may expel a student if necessary. Expulsion is mandatory by state and federal law for certain offenses. For other offenses, it is a measure of last resort after considering the following: the seriousness; harm caused; student willingness to repair the harm; if an intentional act; and student's age, health, disability, decision-making ability, and prior discipline history (see Table 12.1).

Graduated Responses

This framework provides a **graduated response system (graduated sanction)** as the interventions used are to be progressive. If a behavior has two or more levels of response, then the

Graduated Response Systems (Graduated Sanctions): Policies and practices that work through steps or levels, starting with a minimal intervention or consequence and allowing the young person (or student) to avoid further repercussions.

MNPSD Graduated Responses

	Response	Out-of-school suspension possible	Expulsion possible
Type 1 Behaviors			
Tardy to school or class	A	No	No
Cutting class	A	No	No
Noncompliance with a reasonable request	A	No	No
Agitating other students	A	No	No
Profane or indecent language	A	No	No
Unauthorized possession of medication	A	No	No
Possession of fireworks	A	No	No
Type 2 Behaviors			
Repeated violations of a pattern of Type 1 behaviors, with evidence of implemented interventions	A,B	No	No
Dress code violation	A,B	No	No
Possession of use of tobacco products	A,B	No	No
Electronic devices: Improper use of cell phone, internet or electronic devises	A,B	No	No
Disruption of the school environment	A,B	No	No
Inappropriate physical contact/horseplay	A,B	No	No
Inappropriate sexual conduct	A,B	No	No
Trespassing on school grounds	A,B	No	No
Gambling	A,B	No	No
Possession of counterfeit money	A,B	No	No
Drug paraphernalia	A,B	No	No
Type 3 Behaviors			
Repeated violations of a pattern of Type 2 behaviors, with evidence of implemented interventions	A,B,C	Yes	No
Profane or indecent language toward authority figure	A,B,C	Yes	No
Leaving school grounds	A,B,C	Yes	No
Noncompliance with an administrative directive	A,B,C	Yes	No
Vandalism under $500	A,B,C	Yes	No
Theft under $500	A,B,C	Yes	No
Falsifying school records	A,B,C	Yes	No
Inappropriate sexual behavior	A,B,C	Yes	No
Gang: Display or possession of symbols or paraphernalia	B,C	Yes	No
Gang recruitment	B,C	Yes	No
Fleeing drug or weapon search	B,C	Yes	No
Fighting	B,C	Yes	No
Alcohol or drug-like substance: Use or possession, under the influence	B,C	Yes	No

	Response	Out-of-school suspension possible	Expulsion possible
Threats—Class 1	B,C	Yes	No
Possession of a nonlethal firearm or replica of lethal firearm	B,C,D–only if actual risk of harm to others	Yes	No
Vandalism over $500	B,C,D	Yes	No
Theft over $500	B,C,D	Yes	No
Possession of other weapons	B,C,D	Yes	No
Type 4 Behaviors			
Repeated violations of a pattern of Type 3 behaviors, with evidence of implemented interventions	C,D,E	Yes	No
Assault of a student	C,D,E	Yes	Yes, if premeditated and an ongoing risk to others
Under the influence of illegal drugs	C,D,E	Yes	Yes
Threats—Class 2	C,D,E	Yes	Yes
Bomb threat	C,D,E	Yes	Yes
Bullying and cyberbullying	C,D,E	Yes	Yes, if ongoing and after interventions
Harassment based on race, color, or national origin; religions or creed, gender, gender identity, or sexual orientation; or disability	C,D,E	Yes	Yes
Sexual harassment	C,D,E	Yes	Yes
Assault of teacher or staff	C,D,E	Yes	Yes
Extreme disruption of the school environment	C,D,E	Yes	Yes, only if actual risk of harm
Group fighting	C,D,E	Yes	Yes
Gang fighting	C,D,E	Yes	Yes
Gang intimidation	C,D,E	Yes	Yes
Off-campus behavior: felony charge or act against a student that threatens the safety of the school	C,D,E	Yes	Yes
Sexual assault	C,D,E	Yes	Yes
Robbery	C,D,E	Yes	Yes
Reckless endangerment	C,D,E	Yes	Yes
Aggravated assault of student	C,D,E	Yes	Yes
Type 5 Behaviors			
Rape	E	Yes	Yes
Attempted homicide or homicide	E	Yes	Yes
Threat by electronic transmission	E	Yes	Yes, mandatory
Drugs: use, possession, or distribution	E	No	Yes, mandatory
Aggravated assault of teacher or staff	E	No	Yes, mandatory
Explosives	E	No	Yes, mandatory
Firearm—handgun, shotgun, or rifle	E	No	Yes, mandatory

Source: Reprinted with permission from the Metropolitan Nashville Public School District.

lowest level of intervention is generally used first. If a higher level response is chosen, then the school personnel must consider mitigating information: the student's age, health, disability, decision-making abilities, and discipline history; the student's willingness to repair the harm; the seriousness of the act; the harm caused, or the potential to cause, including any injuries; the extent of disruption to the learning environment; and whether the act was intentional (Metropolitan Nashville Public Schools, 2016, p. 23). This district-wide policy provides administrators and teachers discipline response flexibility and the ability to assess each situation within its own context, reviewing mitigating information, history, and possible explanations for the code violations.

Effective Policies

The MNPSD code of conduct example highlights several important components for the students, families, and school personnel. These components include the following: outlining and effectively communicating a process to establish and reinforce positive student behaviors and expectations; describing supportive student strategies; explaining the appropriate response to student misconduct; a tiered range of increasingly strong interventions before suspension or expulsion for minor offenses; limiting expulsions to extreme cases; and providing due process protections for students. In other words, codes of conduct are most effective when they define expectations for appropriate behavior for the entire school community; responding to misbehavior in a tailored way to the offense severity and the students' and victims' needs, with the inclusion goal of keeping the student in school; and ensuring that disciplinary measures are consistently and properly applied (American Academy of Pediatrics, Council on School Health, 2013; Morgan et al., 2014).

The school's student code of conduct is an important document from which to build a rehabilitative discipline system; thus, it should set the framework for appropriate, reasonable, and graduated responses. This document and its implementation can set the foundation for the safety paradigm of the school, one that is primarily democratic, inclusive, and within a positive psychosocial design. The positive environments outlined by such a system decrease student misbehaviors because they allow the student to have some input into school policies and students come to believe the rules and codes are fair. In addition, positive student behavior is rewarded, behavioral problem-solving skills and interventions are provided, and communal support and values are shared across students, teachers, and staff. Rules are vital but insufficient on their own, and they may alienate students from school personnel through lack of understanding why rules must be followed. It is important how they are enforced, implemented, and integrated with rehabilitative interventions that build a sense of school community and cooperation (Gregory, Bell, & Pollock, 2014; Kupchik, 2010; U.S. Department of Education, 2000).

REHABILITATIVE AND SUPPORTIVE INTERVENTIONS

Within communal and supportive school environments, several preventative and intervening programs have been used effectively to improve student behaviors, classroom environments, and overall school safety. In addition to a revised school code of conduct, themes across these prevention and intervention programs include a focus on increasing student engagement and relationship building among teachers, students, and families, and using problem solving and prevention work to improve student and school outcomes (Losen, Hewitt, & Toldson, 2014).

School Engagement and Connectedness

Effective school programming prioritizes student and family engagement. Feeling connected to school is one of the most important protective factors for students at risk for academic failure, behavior problems, and dropping out. Interventions that increase school connectedness are often more successful at preventing these harmful outcomes than those that target specific problem areas—truancy or acting out in the classroom, for example. Students who are more connected

and engaged with their schools generally believe and experience that their parents and teachers support them; they themselves have a larger commitment to school (e.g., participating in extracurricular activities); and they have a supportive and positive peer network. Such students also believe in the importance of a positive school environment, which includes rehabilitative discipline policies, classroom management practices focused on maintaining students in the classroom, and school programming options (National Council of Juvenile and Family Court Judges, 2016a).

▲ A teacher and the classroom environment sets the stage for student success. What were your experiences in middle and high school classes?

Recognizing and then integrating students' perspectives, understanding students' difficulties or challenges, and understanding what other mitigating impacts may be responsible for the problems they are facing can provide more informed and effective decision-making by school personnel. When students have input and involvement and are provided autonomy, overall engagement with the school is typically increased (Gregory et al., 2014; Hafen et al., 2010). When students and families are more connected and engaged with the school, discipline problems decrease and, correspondingly, safety outcomes in school increase (American Psychological Association, 2006; Kohli, 2012; Steinberg, Allensworth, & Johnson, 2013).

Schools are responsive to threats of violence (such as bomb threats, bringing weapons to school, etc.) made by students. Typically, school removal and prosecution have been the consequences for student threats. Through engaging a student who has made threats against school personnel or students, a more recent shift in safety assessment is to move away from automatic school removal policies. One of the empirically supported alternatives to immediate removal is the Virginia Threat Assessment Guidelines, used across schools in Virginia. Threat assessment across schools is a process of evaluating the threat and the circumstances surrounding the threat to uncover any facts or evidence that indicate the threat is likely to be carried out. It is most concerned about students who pose a threat (more indirect postings, such as a student posting on social media how they are upset at the school or school personnel) and not those who make a threat (a student who states they have a plan to bring weapons to school, for example). In Virginia, threat assessment teams are trained in each school, led by the school administrator, and follow a seven-step process: (1) Evaluate the threat. (2) Determine whether the threat is transient or substantive: (3) if transient, respond within current rehabilitative alternatives; (4) if substantive, determine whether the threat is serious or very serious; (5) if serious, respond to protect, and if very serious, take immediate precautions. (6) Consult with law enforcement, and (7) implement a safety plan (Cornell, 2007; O'Toole, 2000). The use of this system was associated with a 19% reduction in long-term suspensions and with an 8% reduction in expulsions of Virginia school students, with greater reductions in schools that had used the guidelines for longer periods of time (Cornell, Shin, Ciolfi, & Sanncken, 2013).

Social-Emotional Learning.

Social-emotional learning is primarily a classroom-focused paradigm, although it can be a stand-alone program component or a school-wide curriculum. This management approach includes not only the quality instruction planning but also a focus on the behavioral needs of the students, monitoring of student engagement, and developing skills to avoid escalating conflicts. These programming efforts incorporate teaching students to be better to themselves and to others and emotional development interventions aimed at aiding students' acquisition of knowledge, attitude improvement, and skill building to recognize and manage their

Social-Emotional Learning: Primarily a classroom-focused approach that includes quality instruction planning and a focus on the behavioral needs of the students, monitoring of student engagement, and skills application to avoid escalating conflicts.

emotions, establish positive relationships, and make responsible decisions (Durlak & Weissberg, 2007; Osher, Bear, Sprague, & Doyle, 2010).

These programs have had significant impact on building social and emotional skills, reducing aggression and behavior problems, improving academic performance for all grade levels and ethnic groups, and in many cases, improving student tolerance and decreasing out-of-school suspensions. Components of many of these programs found to be effective include mentoring, role-playing, group discussion, and family involvement through extracurricular activities or parent training (Berkowitz & Bier, 2005; Payton et al., 2008; Person, Moiduddin, Hague-Angus, & Malone, 2009).

Three of the programs that are effective include Positive Action, Too Good for Violence, and Connect with Kids. These programs are student centered, with Positive Action programming that focuses on improving learning and encourages cooperation among young people. These efforts are founded on the positive steps students take for themselves and others and have been found to increase academic achievement and significantly decrease problem classroom behaviors. The Too Good for Violence program, as a second example, uses developmentally appropriate activities, typically during a scheduled classroom session, and is a student-driven format that improves social skills through appropriate goal setting, responsible decision-making, managing emotions, communicating effectively, bonding with pro-social peers, and resisting negative influences. When used more broadly in schools, this learning-centered approach may include support teams and planning centers, and it has been found to decrease student behavior problems and safety incidents by more than half, improve attendance rates, and lower out-of-school suspensions district-wide by 60% (Losen et al., 2014; Skiba, Arredondo, & Rausch, 2014; Social and Character Development Research Consortium, 2010; What Works Clearinghouse, 2006a, 2006b).

Positive Behavioral Protocols

Positive behavioral protocol programs are used as targeted interventions for students with behavioral or related difficulties within the classroom or school. Typically, these programs use student (or other) leaders to engage students in daily or weekly social skill-building exercises, including interactive activities designed for improving anger management, conflict resolution, and social skills. Alternative formats include small-group and one-on-one intervention sessions, and family members are often involved for education and learning purposes because the young person may have similar or related difficulties at home (Child Trends, 2007a).

Two of the effective programs are Reconnecting Youth and Cognitive-Behavioral Training Program for Behaviorally Disordered Adolescents. Reconnecting Youth is for high school students dealing with aggression, depression, or substance abuse problems and is a daily, semester-long class that promotes school connectedness, involves parents in planning if necessary, and helps with crisis management. The Cognitive-Behavioral Training Program is for young people with self-control problems that lead to aggression or violence and consists of 12 individual sessions that help students develop problem-solving strategies to minimize harmful outcomes (Child Trends, 2007b; Eggert, Thompson, Herting, & Nicholas, 1994, 1995).

Restorative Practices. **Restorative practices** are student-focused interventions that attempt to change the perspective of students who have caused problems, are disruptive, or have violated school rules or policies. These practices with a focus on accountability are appropriate for those situations when the student is primarily responsible for the disruptions or unsafe school behaviors. This approach uses a constructive collaborative approach involving all willing stakeholders with a focus on repairing the harm to victims, while helping the young person decrease future problems. These practices help to build and improve school climate by increasing student understanding of the rules and trust in the rule enforcement, thus requiring a school philosophy to shift and embrace this foundation at all implementation levels (Bazemore, 2001; Macready, 2009). In

Positive Behavioral Protocol Programs: Targeted interventions for students with behavioral, control, or related school difficulties that use student or other leaders to engage students in daily or weekly social skill-building exercises.

Restorative Practices: Student-focused interventions that try to change the perspective of young people who have caused problems, are disruptive, or have violated school policies, community expectations, or laws.

THE DENVER PUBLIC SCHOOLS

Since 2006, the Denver Public Schools incorporated restorative practices in one each at elementary, middle, and high schools. These three schools did the following: actively adapted classrooms that taught students social, emotional, and conflict resolution skills; involved teachers, service providers, and community members in policy and protocol development; provided professional development to teachers and staff on new discipline protocols and the use of restorative practices; and reallocated funding to hire a full-time restorative practices coordinator for each school. The results have been positive, including the high school with the highest increase in graduation rates of all schools across the district, and the elementary and middle schools moving from being "on watch or probation" to schools that meet district academic and behavior outcome expectations (Anyon, 2016).

1. Why do you think restorative practices have become more widely used in schools?

2. Why do you think restorative practices are found to be effective in reducing conflict?

other words, restorative practice is not just the utilization of behavior modification techniques or a focus on conflict resolution, but it is a school community-wide effort (Calhoun & Daniels, 2008).

Restorative practices take numerous forms, including peer juries that bring together a student who has broken a school code violation with trained student jurors, peer mediation that brings two or more students together for conflict resolution with trained student mediators, and peace circles that allow student dialogue and collective decision-making. Broader school-wide applications of these restorative practices typically incorporate four fundamental values: (1) opportunities for involved parties to meet and discuss the problem and harm; (2) offenders' attempts to repair the harm caused; (3) restoring the victims and offenders to be whole and return to contributing school community members; and (4) inclusion of those with a stake in the problem to participate in its resolution. When implementing school-based practices, the classroom efforts may involve morning meetings to resolve conflicts, student circles, and mediation to build trust and cooperation. School-wide efforts may include assemblies to bring the student body together, and parents and interested citizens may offer their time and volunteer mentoring services.

The following six questions are a sample restorative-practice questions for the person responsible for the incident where a problem or incident occurred: "What happened?," "What were you thinking at the time?," "What have you thought about since?," "Who has been affected/harmed by what you have done?," "In what ways?," and "What do you think you need to do to make things right?." The following four questions are a sample questions for those harmed by other's actions: "What did you think when you realized what had happened?," "What impact has this incident had on you and others?," "What has been the hardest thing for you?," and "What do you think needs to happen to make things right?."

Many school districts have implemented restorative practices, including Baltimore Public Schools, Boston Public Schools, Chicago Public Schools, Cleveland Metropolitan School District, Denver Public Schools, Madison Public Schools, Minneapolis Public Schools, New Orleans, New York City Public Schools, and Oakland Public Schools, among others (Advancement Project, 2014; National Center for Mental Health Promotion and Youth Violence Prevention, 2009). Recent national reviews and numerous school district studies of restorative justice practices have found reduced suspension and expulsion rates, decreased referrals for discipline measures, improved academic achievement, and stronger relationship building across the school, with particular improvements, in some reviews, for African American students (González, 2015; Latimer, Dowden, & Muise, 2005; Losen et al., 2014; Skiba et al., 2014).

School-Wide Positive Behavior Interventions and Supports Model

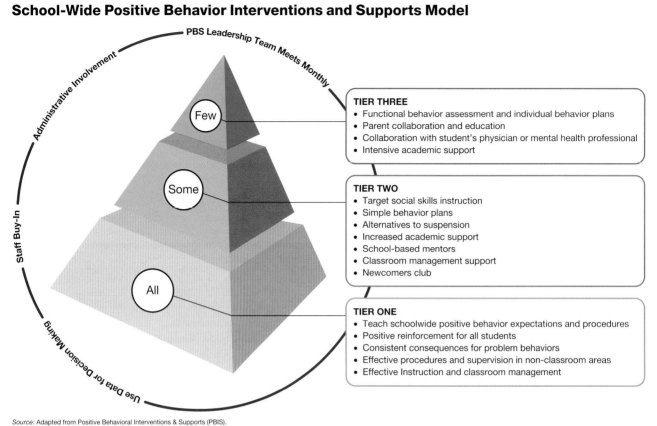

TIER THREE
- Functional behavior assessment and individual behavior plans
- Parent collaboration and education
- Collaboration with student's physician or mental health professional
- Intensive academic support

TIER TWO
- Target social skills instruction
- Simple behavior plans
- Alternatives to suspension
- Increased academic support
- School-based mentors
- Classroom management support
- Newcomers club

TIER ONE
- Teach schoolwide positive behavior expectations and procedures
- Positive reinforcement for all students
- Consistent consequences for problem behaviors
- Effective procedures and supervision in non-classroom areas
- Effective Instruction and classroom management

Source: Adapted from Positive Behavioral Interventions & Supports (PBIS).

School-Wide Positive Behavior Interventions and Supports

One of the strongest empirically supported school-based programs that use a relationship-based philosophy and focus on increasing student connectedness is the **School-Wide Positive Behavior Interventions and Supports (SWPBIS)**, which is used in more than 16,000 schools nationwide (see Figure 12.1). SWBPIS incorporates a three-tiered approach across the classroom and school. The primary tier addresses prevention by teaching behavioral expectations, rewarding positive behavior, providing a continuum of consequences for students, and collecting data for decision-making. The secondary tier is for at-risk students and targets those students for interventions to help with behavioral problems. Finally, the tertiary tier is for students with serious behavior problems and includes more intense individualized interventions with family and community partners. This comprehensive and proactive approach assumes that actively teaching new expectations changes students' behaviors, while requiring the school personnel to define and teach a set of positive expectations for students, acknowledge and reward the behaviors, systematically supervise students throughout the day, and implement a fair and consistent continuum of corrective consequences (Sprague, Vincent, Tobin, & CHiXapkaid, 2013; Sugai & Horner, 2010).

SWPBIS has led to reductions in problem behavior and out-of-class referrals and to improved academic outcomes, including student and teacher school safety perceptions. In addition, these interventions and supports are found to be effective across grade levels and sustainable over time (Bradshaw, Koth, Bevans, Ialongo, & Leaf, 2008; Bradshaw, Mitchell, & Leaf, 2010; Horner et al., 2009; Muscott et al., 2004). Nevertheless, additional research is necessary to determine whether this program model can have long-term effects in addressing the disproportionate impact of school disciplinary measures on certain

School-Wide Positive Behavior Interventions and Supports (SWPBIS): Systematic approach for implementing proactive school-wide discipline to improve school climate and prevent student problem behaviors across school settings.

student populations, although realigning student codes of conduct with the SWPBIS protocols may prove particularly helpful in keeping students in school and improving academic outcomes (Fenning et al., 2013; Sprague, Vincent, Tobin, & CHiXapkaid, 2013). In addition, using SWPBIS in conjunction with other classroom management techniques like social-emotional learning has been found to improve classroom and student behavior outcomes (Osher et al., 2010).

Identifying Mental Health Problems. Many students experience home-, community-, or school-based traumas. Some of these traumatic events may lead to mental health problems, which are difficulties that increase the risk for learning problems and school discipline. Schools can improve prevention efforts through the identification of these mental health problems. Although schools would not normally provide mental health prevention or programming, students can be referred or linked to community-based providers of mental health services. There are several valid and fairly easy-to-use tools for school personnel to screen children and adolescents for mental health problems (Dennis, Feeney, Stevens, & Bedoya, 2006; Kamphaus & Reynolds, 2007; Psychological Assessment Resources, 2014; SASSI Institute, 2014).

Professional Development/Cultural Competency

Conflict resolution is an important in-classroom starting point to improve safety and learning outcomes. It revolves around several principles, including supportive teacher/student relationships, academic rigor, and culturally responsive interactions and teachings. These principles, and supported interventions and programs, identify the cause of the conflicts, recognize the impact of culture and cultural differences, use problem-solving approaches to discipline decisions, incorporate students and families into the decisions and resolutions, and reintegrate students back into the classroom after conflict resolution (Gregory et al., 2014; Osher, Coggshall, Colombi, Woodruff, Francois, & Osher, 2012).

Culturally responsive teaching entails reflecting back to the students their identities and cultures and improving student-to-school connectedness, thus improving academic outcomes (Sleeter, 2011; Toomey & Russell, 2011). Effective strategies of this teaching include the following: the incorporation of classroom, library material, and school-wide events across the range of ethnic, cultural, gender, and sexual identities of the students; the use of self-reflection by teachers to identify implicit or unfair biases; the use of discussion and book groups across diverse topics; and professional development programs to help teachers self-assess, including several programs that are considered high quality, such as Effective Communication, the Double-Check Program, and Connection to Curriculum (Gregory et al., 2014; Kang & Banaji, 2006; Schultz, 2008; Sharma, 2008).

Culturally Responsive Teaching: Practice of reflecting back to the student his or her identities and cultures and improving school connections, with the goal of improving social and academic outcomes.

▼ TABLE 12.2

Screening Tools for Mental Health/Trauma

Behavioral and Emotional Screening System (BESS): screening for behavioral and emotional strengths and weaknesses; preschool to high school ages, completed by students, parents, and teachers
Adolescent Substance Abuse Subtle Screening Instrument (SASSI-3): screening for substance abuse and substance use disorders; ages 12 to 17
Global Appraisal of Individual Need–Short Screen (GAIN-SS): screening for substance use disorders and mental health problems
Trauma Symptom Checklist for Children (TSCC): measures severity of post-traumatic stress and related psychological symptomatology (anxiety, depression, anger, dissociation) in ages 8 to 16 who have experienced traumatic events, such as physical or sexual abuse, major loss, or natural disasters

THE RESPONDER MODEL

The state of Connecticut and Summit County, Ohio, have created school-based programs for students with mental health problems to minimize their involvement in discipline procedures. The program goals are to link middle school students (grades 5 to 8) to needed treatment and services, keep students in school, and reduce referrals to the juvenile courts. Referrals to the program include students who are disruptive in classroom and/or school settings or who have ongoing attendance/truancy problems. The "responders" are community-based mental health providers who work with the school personnel to help identify mental health problems and to link students with treatment and case management services. School personnel are trained in mental health problem identification and with ongoing behavior assessment.

Recent reviews of the outcomes of this program have been positive. In Connecticut, schools with the program have decreased referrals to juvenile courts between 19% and 92%, depending on location. In Summit County, Ohio, between 55% and 68% of the participants, who had already been disciplined by the school and referred to juvenile court, received no additional charges during their first year of involvement with the program (Models for Change, 2013; Skowyra & Teodosio, 2014).

. . . .

I. **The Responder Model takes a rehabilitative approach to mental health problems. Do you think this would work across most schools and student populations? Why or why not?**

2. **How do mental health problems impact school performance?**

It is increasingly recognized that values or implicit biases can be addressed and interventions can reduce this possible cause for disparate impact (Wald, 2014). More research within the schools is necessary, however, to determine the specific steps to take in addressing implicit bias and its potential impact, increasing teachers and administrators' knowledge of other culture's behavioral norms, and employing appropriate behavior management strategies that are take into account cultural differences, such as clothing attire choices (Majd, Marksamer, & Reyes, 2009; Monroe, 2005; Rudd, 2014; Staats, 2014).

Supportive relationships are ones that entail trust and can prevent conflict. Trust can be built through various "getting to know you" instructional activities, working with students' strengths, and professional development programs. One of the effective programs is My Teaching Partner (MTP), the pairing of a coach and a teacher for an academic year, focusing on restorative practices, cultural competency trainings, and understanding and working with the actual student experiences (Schiff, 2013; Singleton & Linton, 2006). Evaluations of this program have found significant reductions in student office referrals and an elimination of racially disproportionate discipline in the classroom at some schools (Gregory, Allen, Mikami, Halen, & Pianta, 2012). Programs similar to MTP that bring a proactive and a preventative approach to the classroom and use the setting as a broad approach to impact the students have also been found effective. Teachers' universal classroom management practices have a significant, positive effect on decreasing problem behavior in both primary and secondary school grade classrooms, and these improvements help establish the context for effective teaching/learning (Oliver, Wehby, & Reschly, 2011).

Professional development focuses on improving the school climate, which in turn improves outcomes across most measures, especially among those students disproportionately impacted by school discipline procedures. Quality professional development requires ongoing training and reinforcement on teacher and administrator behavior management and skill development. In particular, key topics should include building strong learning communities in the classroom, establishing behavior norms and expectations and reinforcing these throughout the classroom and school, understanding the impact of trauma on learning, using trauma-informed care

approaches, understanding child and adolescent development, using early warning and screening assessments, collaborating with families, and making informed decisions based on available data related to intervention strategies (Grisso, 2008; Morgan et al., 2014).

TRUANCY PREVENTION

Chronic absenteeism is defined as missing more than 10% of school during an academic year. In recent academic years, 7% of fourth graders, 6% of eighth graders, and 8% of twelfth graders missed five or more days of school in a given month, with greater numbers of absent students in poorer and urban school districts and with greater numbers of absences among students with disabilities (Chen, Culhane, Metraux, Park, & Venable, 2016). Truancy is the habitual, unexcused absence from school that exceeds the number allowed under state law and is the most common status offense. Chronic absenteeism and truancy are both associated with poor academic achievement, increased school suspensions and expulsions, substance use and abuse, dropping out, and delinquency adjudication (Levin & Cohen, 2014).

Truancy prevention is best addressed on multiple fronts by parents and schools. Parents are the first line of defense against their children missing school, but schools play an important role in supporting the efforts by parents. Communication of the school truancy and attendance rules is an important first step, so that families are aware of what is allowed (excused) or not allowed (unexcused). Beyond this, parents should be aware of changes in their children's friendships, attitudes toward school or homework, and behavior. Parents should seek help when necessary and know that there are parenting education programs that increase skills in working with their children. In addition, parents should have consistent expectations and be involved with the school. In turn, schools can focus on increasing student engagement and connectedness as well as on improving school climate and safety for all students through, for instance, conflict resolution, rehabilitative discipline, and anti-bullying programming (National Council of Juvenile and Family Court Judges, 2016b).

National stakeholders have developed recommendations when working to reduce truancy among students. These include the following: understand emerging knowledge on adolescent developmental issues; investigate and treat trauma; engage and involve the family; understand gender differences and developmental pathways; redirect those with disabilities back toward school rehabilitative services; train first responders on diversion; and use graduated responses and meaningful incentives for attendance problems (Baker, Sigmon, & Nugent, 2001; Coalition for Juvenile Justice, 2013).

There is considerable evidence that truancy prevention works. Both collaborative (multimodal) and stand-alone programs have been found to reduce truancy, with community-, school-, and juvenile court-based interventions (Maynard, McCrea, Pigott, & Kelly, 2012). Collaborative approaches may have a more profound impact because students who miss many school days and those who are truant have been found to have a myriad of difficulties in their lives that collaborative approaches focus on. These may include school problems, bullying victimization, poor-to-failing grades, troubled family situations, mental health difficulties, and/or substance use problems (Dembo et al., 2011).

SCHOOL DROPOUT

Interventions that can lower the risk of school dropout have posed challenges because of the multiple factors that contribute to a decision to discontinue education. Risk factors for

▲ Effective teaching and learning happens best in classrooms that are inclusive of all students and that focus on positive changes. Did you have this experience in classrooms?

CASE STUDY

TYUNIQUE'S STORY

Intersectionality (describing systems of oppression and how they overlap for subgroups within oppressed groups) is important because we need to recognize what's going on in all communities and not just for a specific community. It is important for people in the lesbian community to be educated about the trans community, and the gay community to be educated about the asexual community. There is a major disconnect between every community within the queer community. As a youth who still has to move through the world into adulthood, allies in communities not specific to my own will be vital to my growth and exposure.

My school has an extremely strict assimilation culture. Every morning, we enter the building and remove all evidence of individuality. We wear the same uniform and follow the rules, so it is pretty easy to notice if someone steps out of line. Our students go through their whole middle and high school years following the same rules, and then they go off to college. They go to college and they don't fit in or they cannot function because they have spent the last couple of years of their lives being told what to do. They drop out, get kicked out, or fail out.

This year I started a program where students from different campuses of my school district could go to another campus and observe the school's culture. They take note of different teaching styles, language, and

workloads. They then have conversations with teachers, deans, and students about their findings. This prompts the students to dig into ideas about school policy that they may have never thought about. This opens doors to more conversations with students and staff members, and those conversations lead to ways to change our school's policy. This will ultimately dismantle the school-to-prison pipeline.

Intersectionality is the beginning of a new appreciation and understanding for each other's thoughts. The LGBTQ community simply asks for respect and acknowledgment. Educating others about our community who are not part of our community is the first in a long list of steps toward building healthy relationships. (Advancement Project, Equality Federation Institute, & Gay Straight Alliance Network, 2016, p. 7)

1. **What are your experiences with subgroups within the LGBT community?**

2. **Did your high school support or recognize the LGBT community?**

Source: Advancement Project, Equality Federation Institute, & Gay Straight Alliance Network (2016). *Power in partnerships: Building connections at the intersections of racial justice and LGBTQ movements to end the school-to-prison pipeline.* Advancement Project, Washington, DC. Reprinted with permission.

dropout include family difficulties, poverty, negative peers, grade retention, low parental educational status, changing schools often, living in urban areas, and unidentified learning problems (Hammond, Linton, Smink, & Drew, 2007). Although no single risk factor is paramount in a student's decision to drop out of school, the comorbidity of difficulties makes this outcome more likely. The decision to dropout is often a process and not a one-event situation because students who drop out of school often consider doing so over a period of time (Rumberger, 2004).

Programs that are student centered and address multiple risk factors in a strategic, long-term manner show the greatest impact on decreasing school dropout rates. These programs often combine skill-building, family outreach, academic support, and community-based supports. Students tend to be more successful in school academics and graduation rates when their parents or caregivers are involved (Harvard Family Research Project, 2010; Hill & Tyson, 2009; Lehr, Johnson, Bremer, Cosio, & Thompson, 2004).

Although few programs offer a full range of intervention components, some effective programs that address several risk factors and problem areas include the Adolescents Transition Program, Big Brothers/Big Sisters, Families & Schools Together (FAST), the Midwestern Prevention Project (Project STAR), Schools & Families Educating Children (SAFE Children), Strengthening Families Program, Job Corp, and Jobs for America's Graduates (Martin & Halberin, 2006; Schochet, Burghardt, & McConnell, 2008; Wilson, Tanner-Smith, Lipsey, Steinka-Fry, & Morrison, 2011).

LGBT STUDENTS: SCHOOL SAFETY AND INCLUSION

Advocates and experts across the country have identified several successful strategies to improve school climates for students who identify as LGBT. These efforts can be used in tandem with other positive and inclusive policies discussed in this chapter, and they can help to improve the environment for all students. These programs and steps may include the following: offer a gay-straight alliance club as a regular school club activity; enforce dress codes among all students equally and empower students to express themselves; use gender-inclusive language for school events and community-wide communications; include anti-bullying policies that specifically protect this student population, including gender identity and expression; evaluate the effectiveness of anti-bullying programming; and train and educate teachers and staff about this population (Teaching Tolerance, 2013).

1. Did your school experience include any of these types of LGBT groups or supports?

2. Which of these efforts do you think might be more effective? Why do you think this?

SCHOOL DISTRICTS

Data Collection

The school district is responsible for implementing and setting policies for all schools in the district, although as discussed earlier, state and federal regulations dictate some discipline requirements for drug and weapon possession. Data-based decision-making has not been the norm at the school district level. One way to make effective district policy decisions moving forward is to use school data to inform practice. School districts can best do this by publically reporting annual data on the following: number of students suspended and expelled; reasons for these out-of-school discipline outcomes; days of lost student instruction; on-campus arrests; referrals to juvenile courts; reasons for referrals; and bullying data. Although making this data available to review via grade level, ethnicity, gender, disability, and poverty status—a proxy could be those who access free or reduced lunch plans. School districts, with many already leading the way, could then incorporate the data to inform policy and practice around school discipline decisions, student codes of conduct, resource allocation, implemented program effectiveness, and identified school-level disparities (Losen et al., 2014; Morgan et al., 2014).

School Police: School-Justice Partnerships

School districts should be cautious in their use of school resource officers, although the case for using these officers is much stronger to make for schools with serious crime problems. Having school resource officers provides feelings of safety and increased positive views of police across school personnel and some student groups, leading to increases in crime reporting by students. Nevertheless, it has more consistently been found that their presence reinforces zero tolerance policies and increases campus arrest rates and referrals to the juvenile courts (Kupchik, 2010; Martinez, 2009; Theriot, 2009). If these harmful discipline outcomes continue to be found, moving away from the presence of police officers in schools will require significant reform efforts. These reform efforts include reviewing current school–police partnership models; collecting and assessing data on need for officers in schools to maintain safety while minimizing arrests and juvenile justice system referral; having policies that clearly define the officers' role and engagement in nonemergency situations; and training school personnel on appropriate use of officers (Finn, Townsend, Shively, & Rich, 2005).

Schools and classrooms are most helpful when they are responsive or aware of cultural differences. Was this your experience growing up and going to school?

If school districts determine that the use of school resource officers is warranted because of serious crime and safety concerns or other data-driven reasons, then it is important that the districts adhere to certain guidelines. These guidelines include the following: Recruit and select officers who want and like to work with children and adolescents; hire officers who are committed to maintaining safety while minimizing student involvement with the juvenile courts; provide extensive training to educate on adolescent development, school policies, mental health, trauma, and working with students in a school setting; monitor officers through ongoing evaluation; and establish **memoranda of understanding (MOUs) or memoranda of agreement (MOAs)** between the police department and the school district.

Memoranda of Understanding. A memoranda of understanding (MOU) is a multilateral agreement among key stakeholders—the police force and school district—that expresses a common vision for the partnership, although this agreement is not legally binding. When developing a comprehensive MOU, the following is important to be included: formalization of the key partnership elements; clarification of party roles, responsibilities, and chain of command among police and school personnel; allocation of funds or resources; agreement on protocols for the use of graduated sanctions; and review of the agreement regularly by using data and stakeholder feedback (Majd et al., 2009; U.S. Department of Justice, 2013).

Alternative Education/Reintegration

When schools exclude (expulsion or alternative education) students, it is important that reentry back into the classroom be handled with careful planning and with the focus on the reduction of student recidivism. Forty-two state laws allow or encourage the use of alternative educational placements for students, leading to 64% of school districts having at least one alternative school or program. Hundreds of thousands of students are placed into alternative programing annually, which may include alternative schools with separate facilities, charter schools, or community-based schools. Students usually stay on average between one and six months in alternative programs (Carver & Lewis, 2010; U.S. Department of Education, 2014a).

Alternative education placements are more likely to be used on students in urban districts with high minority enrolments and in districts with high poverty concentrations. These programs are disproportionately used on students of color, those with disabilities, and those with mental health problems (Chlang & Gill, 2010; Kim, Losen, & Hewitt, 2010; Ruiz de Velasco et al., 2008). Not all alternative school placements are effective and, for some school environments, may even exacerbate the difficulties for many students because of how alternative programs are organized and because of the high concentration of young people with difficult problems (Dishon, Dodge, & Lansford, 2006). In addition, after being placed in alternative school programs, many students become increasingly alienated from their home school. Some school districts may have limited resources or efforts focused on reintegration and reconnecting these students back with classmates, teachers, and administrators.

Schools can better serve students who have been removed by developing an individualized reintegration plan that connects them and their families to necessary support services. These

To see an example of Advancement Project Guidelines, visit the study site at edge.sagepub.com/mallett

Memoranda of Understanding (MOUs) or Memoranda of Agreement (MOAs): Multilateral agreement among key stakeholders (typically the police force and school district) that expresses a common vision for the partnership.

services can include advocacy and mentoring programs, along with school-based transition centers that collaborate with community-based providers, such as mental health, juvenile court, child welfare, family support, and health professionals. These centers help manage the student problems that are identified and make the transition back to school more successful. These efforts are often led by a transition coordinator, a school staff member responsible for all reentering students. The coordinator works with the home schools and other youth-caring systems to ensure re-enrollment happens as quickly as possible, especially for those returning from juvenile justice facilities. Many school districts offer effective programming for these students and in their return to their home school, including Montgomery County, Maryland; Hillsborough County, Florida; and Orange County, California (Gregory et al., 2014; Majd et al., 2009; Morgan et al., 2014).

STATE POLICIES

State legislatures, along with Congress, are key stakeholders establishing and perpetuating zero tolerance policies at schools and at times direct the utilization of inflexible discipline regulations that have led to harsh and disparate student outcomes. Nevertheless, these policy stakeholders are also the solution to many of the unintended problems these policies have wrought. Numerous states, and subsequent local school districts, have taken steps to ameliorate and discontinue zero tolerance policies through the enactment of new laws. More broadly, states can take several proactive and important steps toward addressing disparities of the use of school discipline and the exclusion of many students from education.

Data Collection

An important step that state departments of education have taken to better identify discipline and disproportionate impact problems is requiring, collecting, and disseminating data across all school districts, including charter and alternative education schools. Data are collected on student offenses, suspension and expulsion frequency, bullying, and the extent of disproportionate impact on at-risk student groups (The Center for Civil Rights Remedies, 2013). To do so, a common definition of disciplinary terms must be used across schools. This database would be in addition, although complimentary, to already required data collections, including the Office for Civil Rights' (CRDC) biennial report on school discipline; the Individuals with Disabilities Education Act's report on long-term suspension and expulsion data for those with disabilities and any racially disparities within this student disability group; and the Safe and Drug Free Schools and Communities Title IV, Part A Act's requirement to report annual truancy rates and violent- and drug-related offenses that result in out-of-school removal (Elementary and Secondary Education Act, 20 U.S.C. § 4112, 2013; Individuals with Disabilities Education Act, 20 U.S.C. § 1412(a)(22), 2013). Several information-sharing resources are available to school districts, police departments, and juvenile courts in managing and adhering to federal laws when collecting, using, and sharing student data across youth-caring systems. Two in particular are the Navigating Information Sharing (NIS) Toolkit (National Center for Mental Health Promotion and Youth Violence Prevention, 2009) and the Models for Change Information Sharing Toolkit (MacArthur Foundation, 2015).

State Law Changes

State legislatures can also review or amend current laws to move away from strict discipline policies. Depending on the state, there are five areas of focus on these laws. The first is to

CLAYTON COUNTY, GEORGIA

Under Georgia law, the chief judge of each county Superior Court can establish a Student Attendance Protocol Committee to ensure coordination between stakeholders involved in compulsory attendance issues and to help reduce the number of unexcused absences from county schools. In 2010, using this state law and his inherent convening authority as leverage, the Honorable Steven Teske, Presiding Judge of the Juvenile Court of Clayton County, GA, developed a court-wide Truancy Intervention and Other Status Youth Protocol.

The protocol mandates that county schools cannot petition a chronically absent student to court until [the following has occurred]: the student has first been referred to a multi-disciplinary child study team; the child study team has conducted an assessment and evaluation of the child to determine the underlying causes of his/her truant behavior; and the child study team has developed an individualized treatment plan for the child. Under the protocol a petition for truancy can only be filed if the child or parent refuses to cooperate or a court order is necessary to access services that cannot otherwise be accessed voluntarily. Under no circumstances can the student be detained as punishment for not attending school. (Coalition for Juvenile Justice, 2014, p. 2)

I. **Could this approach work in your school district and community?**

2. **What do you think the outcomes have been for Clayton County, GA?**

Source: "Clayton County, Georgia's Approach to Diverting Truant Youth Away from the Court System," in CJJ Emerging Issues Policy Brief, *Addressing truancy and other status offenses*, by Lisa Pilnik. Coalition for Juvenile Justice (2014). Washington, DC. Reprinted with permission.

define clearly school disciplinary terms used in policies and codes of conduct (such as "disruptive behavior," "inappropriate behavior," "violent offense," "disorderly conduct," "disturbing the peace," "serious risk," and "zero tolerance," among others), so that these are not overly broad and encompass too many students. The second is to encourage school districts to replace rigid disciplinary strategies with graduated systems of discipline, having consequences on par with the seriousness of the student offense through an array of disciplinary alternatives. The third is to require school resource officers, if used, to have sufficient training to work with the adolescent population. The fourth is to require sufficient training for teachers and school administrators concerning behavior management and culturally sensitive pedagogy. Finally, the fifth is to shift funding from security management toward effective school programming to minimize out-of-school discipline outcomes (American Psychological Association, 2008; Losen et al., 2014).

Since 2012, numerous states have changed laws related to school discipline. California has provided school district superintendents and school principals the discretion to use alternative interventions in lieu of suspension or expulsions; prohibited public schools from refusing to readmit a student because they were involved with the juvenile courts; and provided flexibility to schools to not automatically refer a truant student to the juvenile justice system. Colorado has minimized the referral of students with minor misbehaviors to the juvenile courts if the difficulties are typical of the students' developmental stage; used prevention strategies such as restorative justice, counseling, peer mediation, and other rehabilitative approaches; and collected data on school-based arrests and referrals based on the students' age, gender, school, ethnicity, and offense. Washington has developed standard definitions for discretionary actions and data collection methods for school discipline across school districts; limited expulsion to the most serious cases and allowed short-term suspension to only 10 days in an academic year; and required any removed student to have a "reengagement" plan coordinated with the family, having the student return to their home school as soon as possible (Morgan et al., 2014, pp. 74–75).

NATIONAL POLICIES

There are numerous areas in which federal laws and rules have led to the creation of policies that are focused on control and punishment in the nation's schools. These same laws and legislatures, however, now have the opportunity to change the course toward rehabilitative and positive school climates for all students. Leadership across research and funding opportunities can, and in some areas, has shifted a tide in policy toward the rehabilitative school model (Mediratta, 2012).

Data Collection

Federal laws could be amended to strengthen data collection and reporting. Federal law currently requires states to report graduation rates and enrollment numbers annually as well as disaggregated and comparative to nondisabled students' discipline data for students with special education disabilities (IDEA, 20 U.S.C. § 1418(1)). These laws could be expanded to require discipline data on all students, not just those covered under IDEA, and include the LGBT student community. It should be noted that the U.S. Department of Education's Office of Civil Rights has begun collecting important discipline data for every two years. It would be more informative if this data were collected annually.

Funding

The U.S. Department of Justice and the U.S. Department of Education could provide additional funding across important areas. These include an increase in the availability of federal funds to replace exclusionary discipline methods with proven and effective alternatives; fund strategies for comprehensive local stakeholder collaborations including the schools, police, juvenile courts, and youth-caring systems to investigate the problems and find solutions; improve national data collection and research on effective practices that local school districts and juvenile courts could implement; and determine whether federal funding for K–12 schools can help address disparate local and state-wide school district funding (Advancement Project, Alliance for Educational Justice, & Gay Straight Alliance Network, 2012; National Juvenile Justice and Delinquency Prevention Coalition, 2013; Torres & Stefkovich, 2009).

In one area, progress has recently been made by a collaboration of 20 federal agencies (Justice, Education, Health and Human Services, Homeland Security, and Treasury, among others) awarding significant grant dollars to school districts and research organizations through the Comprehensive School Safety Initiative. The focus of the Initiative is three-fold: (1) to continue to build a large-scale research effort at the national level identifying empirically sound strategies to increase school safety nationwide; (2) to convene stakeholders to identify evidence-based practices and policies; and (3) to conduct innovative research and evaluate pilot projects within school districts (National Institute of Justice, 2014).

Over the past 20 years, nearly $1 billion in federal money across numerous agencies has been invested in hiring police to work as school resource officers, with more than 17,000 employed annually in nearly half of all elementary, middle, and high schools (Justice Policy Institute, 2011; Thurae & Wald, 2010). Considering the limited and controversial evidence to date on the effectiveness of the use of school resource officers in schools, and the emerging evidence of some unintended negative consequences to at-risk students by having officers in schools, it would be policy wise to slow the proliferation of funding for this effort until definitive impact is known. The Comprehensive School Safety Initiative and research funding is a step in this direction in helping to clarify the benefits and costs of these types of efforts within the nation's schools.

CASE STUDY

LOCAL SCHOOL DISTRICT RESEARCH

You are asked to do some research in answering the following questions. What are the laws and regulations in your state and local school district for the following: (1) school climate and discipline policies; (2) truancy and referrals to the juvenile justice system; and (3) student code of conduct definitions of "misbehaving," "school disturbance," and other low-level offenses. In addition, what data are collected by your school district around school discipline and bullying? With this information:

I. Write a short report on the school district's current state of affairs regarding school discipline and potential impact on at-risk students.

2. Prioritize any recommendations or policy changes that should be pursued by the school administrators and/or local juvenile court judges.

CHAPTER REVIEW

CHAPTER SUMMARY

This chapter presented how school districts and states have begun to shift away from zero tolerance policies and implement more effective student inclusion practices in recent years. Through the reformation of student codes of conduct and the use of graduated sanctions and responses to student misbehaving, schools improve both their learning culture and safety outcomes. By reforming through rehabilitative classroom and school-wide interventions, moreover, schools can minimize the use of police officers and referrals to the juvenile courts. To be effective, school must establish agreements across stakeholders—police, school district, and youth-caring systems—as to how to best coordinate efforts.

KEY TERMS

culturally responsive teaching **271**

graduated response systems (graduated sanctions) **263**

inclusive school policies **261**

memoranda of understanding (MOUs) and memoranda of agreement (MOAs) **276**

positive behavioral protocol programs **268**

restorative practices **268**

School-Wide Positive Behavior Interventions and Supports (SWPBIS) **270**

social-emotional learning **267**

student codes of conduct **262**

DISCUSSION QUESTIONS

1. If you were a school superintendent of your local school district, how best would you balance safety, discipline, and learning for all students? In other words, what policies around codes of conduct, use of school resource officers, classroom efforts, and coordination with the local juvenile court would you recommend in the schools and why?

2. What are the key rehabilitative components of an effective school district student code of conduct?

3. How would you handle the issue of school resource officers? How do you think different constituencies—parents, students, teachers, and principals—might respond to having school resource officers on campus?

4. What school discipline and school climate data would you collect if you were a school principal, and how would you use the data?

5. How does the Responder Model work? How might this be implemented (or not) in your community?

6. Can you be a teacher, principal, police officer, or social worker and be race neutral in your work? Do you believe explicit or implicit bias exists? Why or why not?

7. How can truancy and school absenteeism be reduced? Develop an outline for a school plan to address these problems.

8. What is a school-justice partnership memorandum of understanding? Why is this a useful or important agreement for schools, students, and parents?

9. If you were the chief of the local juvenile court's probation department, how would you work with your local schools? What policies and priorities should the juvenile court pursue with the schools?

---

https://edge.sagepub.com/mallett

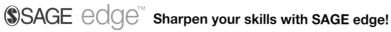 **Sharpen your skills with SAGE edge!**

SAGE edge for students provides a personalized approach to help you accomplish your coursework in an easy-to-use learning environment. You'll find mobile-friendly eFlashcards and quizzes, as well as videos, web resources, and links to SAGE journal articles to support and expand on the concepts presented in this chapter.

CHAPTER 13

REHABILITATION OF LOW-LEVEL YOUTHFUL OFFENDERS

▲ Most young people who get involved with juvenile offending discontinue with diversion programming. Why do you think this is the case?

©iStockphoto.com/Magaiza

INTRODUCTION

Children and adolescents are involved with the juvenile courts for many reasons—home difficulties, violence, school problems, peer troubles, offending activities, and status offenses, among others. Many of the young people who have police contact, especially those formally involved with the juvenile justice system, have experienced traumas, family dysfunction, poverty, and other related delinquency risks. Even with these challenges, the good news is that a significant majority (almost 80%) of adolescents who are arrested one time will never be arrested a second time. Thus, having most adolescents avoid formal involvement with the juvenile justice system is an appropriate policy (Mulvey, 2011; Puzzanchera & Robson, 2014).

Nevertheless, this is not reality across most juvenile courts nationwide, for most young people who are formally adjudicated delinquent and probation-supervised are low-level or status offenders. Once formally involved, it is more likely that the adolescent will continue additional delinquent behaviors in large part because of how the juvenile justice system operates, increasing their risk for ongoing supervision, detention, and/or incarceration. In other words, for many young people, formal juvenile court involvement becomes a vortex, keeping the adolescent involved with the system. For this reason, along with the cost of the juvenile justice system and the poor long-term outcomes for most adolescents formally involved, prevention and diversion are the best alternatives for youthful offenders who don't pose serious self or community safety risks (National Juvenile Justice and Delinquency Prevention Coalition, 2013; Petitclerc, Gatti, Vitaro, & Tremblay, 2013; Petrosino, Turpin-Petrosino, & Guckenburg, 2010).

This chapter reviews important approaches, as well as diversion and preventions efforts and examples, stakeholders can use to help young people at risk for juvenile justice system involvement. Significant research-based knowledge recommends early intervention efforts aimed at both minimizing risks and offending behaviors and subsequent contact with the juvenile courts. In doing so, first reviewed are important principles for minimizing adolescent involvement with the juvenile justice system; second, what works in delinquency prevention; third, diversion efforts both pre- and post-formal involvement with the courts, including risk and needs assessment; and, fourth, effective community-based corrections efforts for adjudicated delinquent youthful offenders, with a focus on graduated probation supervision.

EFFECTIVE FRAMEWORK

National stakeholders—the Office of Juvenile Justice and Delinquency Prevention, **Bureau of Justice Assistance** (both part of the U.S. Department of Justice), MacArthur Foundation, **The Council of State Governments**, and the **National Reentry Resource Center**—relying on research evidence and policy experts across the country, have identified important principles to improve the juvenile justice system. The focus on achieving these goals includes leveraging existing resources and evidence of what works, reducing recidivism, and improving related outcomes for young people involved with the courts (Seigle, Walsh, & Weber, 2014). These recommendations help to frame this chapter's focus on low-level and first-time offenders, as well as the next chapter's focus on more serious and chronic youthful offenders.

Bureau of Justice Assistance: Office of the U.S. Department of Justice and a component of the Office of Justice Programs that funds justice programming and directs federal initiatives.

The Council of State Governments: Nonpartisan, nonprofit organization that serves all three branches of state government with policy research reviews.

Principles for the Juvenile Justice System

Principle 1: Base supervision, service, and resource-allocation on the results of validated risk and needs assessment.

> Minimize juvenile justice system supervision and services for young people who are at a low risk of offending.

> Maximize the impact and value of system resources by prioritizing services for young people most likely to reoffend and by minimizing the use of confinement.

> Use validated assessments to identify the primary causes of a young person's delinquent behaviors and focus system interventions and resources on addressing these causes.

> Use specialized validated screenings and assessments to identify those young people with mental health and substance use treatment needs and match them to services, minimizing juvenile justice intervention when appropriate.

Principle 2: Adopt and effectively implement programs and services demonstrated to reduce recidivism and improve other (related) adolescent outcomes, and use data to evaluate system performance and direct system improvement.

> Eliminate the use of programs and practices that do not reduce recidivism or improve other key adolescent outcomes.

> Support and fund services shown to reduce recidivism and improve other adolescent outcomes.

> Evaluate recidivism and other adolescent outcomes, and use this data to guide policy, practice, and resource allocation.

Principle 3: Employ a coordinated approach across service systems (mental health, disability, schools, for example) to address young people's needs.

> Partner the juvenile justice system with other key service systems (mental health, disability, and schools, among others) in which young people are or should be involved in order to assess and effectively address their needs.

Principle 4: Tailor system policies, programs, and supervision to reflect the distinct developmental needs of adolescents.

> Engage families and other supportive adults in major system decisions and processes.

> Employ a developmentally appropriate approach to system supervision by focusing resources on promoting positive behavior change and using a graduated response to violations.

> Hold young people accountable for their actions in ways that address the harm caused to victims and communities and that support positive behavior change.

> Promote young people's respect for and compliance with the law by engaging them in system decisions and processes and by addressing system bias and the disparate treatment of youth of color and other groups that are disproportionately represented in the juvenile justice system. (Seigle et al., 2014, pp. iii–iv)

By pursuing and implementing these planning steps, many local jurisdictions have successfully reduced youthful offender involvement with the juvenile justice system as well as have prevented first-time offenders from being adjudicated delinquent. Through coordinated

National Reentry Resource Center: Organization that provides education, training, and technical assistance to states, tribes, territories, local governments, service providers, nonprofit organizations, and corrections institutions working on prisoner reentry.

efforts across the courts, schools, and treatment providers, fewer young people have become involved formally with the juvenile justice system.

DELINQUENCY PREVENTION

Investments in effective delinquency prevention programs decrease the risk that young people will become involved with the juvenile courts. Over the past 20 years as delinquency risk models have been researched and developed, interventions have been designed to address these risks and consistently reduce the likelihood that delinquency will occur. As reviewed in Chapter 6, delinquency risks are both static and dynamic. Static risks are difficult to change, so delinquency prevention addresses dynamic risks, focused on parenting quality, school issues, adolescent skills deficits such as anger management, and peer associations, among other problem areas. Delinquency prevention can be effective across different program approaches and at various childhood and adolescent developmental stages. There is strong evidence supporting certain strategies and a few dozen highly effective programs and interventions.

Delinquency prevention strategies include the following: parent training, increasing parent skills in managing behaviors and emotions as well as increasing parent and adolescent life skills; preschool enrollment; child and adolescent behavior modification; and the use of peer supports. In addition, specific programs that also prevent delinquency include the Nurse-Family Partnership for young moms, mentoring programs based on the Big Brothers/Big Sisters of America model, Homebuilders, and Multi-dimensional Treatment Foster Care for those young people involved in the child welfare system and in need of a highly structured out-of-home placement. In addition, two programs often found used in juvenile courts include Functional Family Therapy (FFT) and Multisystemic Therapy (MST; Blueprints for Healthy Youth Development, 2016; Greenwood, 2008).

Interventions

The Office of Juvenile Justice and Delinquency Prevention supports and highlights delinquency prevention programs in its Model Programs Guide. The programs with the strongest preventative impact can be found in Table 13.1 (Office of Juvenile Justice and Delinquency Prevention, 2016). Several of these programs [Big Brothers/Big Sisters of America, Families and Schools Together (FAST), Functional Family Therapy, Midwestern Prevention Project, Multisystemic Therapy, School-Wide Positive Behavioral Interventions and Supports (SWPBIS), and Trauma-Focused Cognitive Behavioral Therapy (TF-CBT)] have been discussed in earlier chapters on mental health, substance use, school difficulties, and trauma. Several other programs will be further described and explained next.

▼ TABLE 13.1

Effective Delinquency Prevention Programs

Adolescent Diversion Project	Midwestern Prevention Project
Aggression Replacement Training	Multidimensional Family Therapy
Big Brothers/Big Sisters of America	Multisystemic Therapy (MST)
Cognitive Behavioral Intervention for Trauma in Schools	Parent–Child Interaction Therapy (PCIT)
Families and Schools Together (FAST)	Positive Action
Functional Family Therapy (FFT)	Promoting Alternative Thinking Strategies (PATHS)
Homebuilders	School-Wide Positive Behavioral Interventions and Supports (SWPBIS)
Life Skills Training	Trauma-Focused Cognitive Behavioral Therapy (TF-CBT)

Promoting Alternative Thinking Strategies (PATHS)

PATHS is a comprehensive program for promoting emotional and social competencies and for reducing aggression and behavior problems of elementary school-aged children, while supporting the educational process in the classroom. The curriculum is used by educators and counselors in a multiyear, universal prevention model, and it is developed for use in the elementary school-aged classroom with several special needs student groups—those with deafness, hearing impairment, learning disabilities, and emotional disturbances. The program plan is to initiate the curriculum at the entrance to schooling and to continue through the fifth grade, being taught three times per week for a minimum of 20–30 minutes per day.

The curriculum provides teachers with systematic, developmentally based lessons, materials, and instructions for teaching their students emotional literacy, self-control, social competence, positive peer relations, and interpersonal problem-solving skills. These skills are developed by improving specific competencies: identifying and labeling, expressing, and managing feelings; understanding the difference between feelings and behaviors; delaying gratification; controlling impulses; reducing stress; improving self-talk; reading and interpreting social cues; understanding the perspectives of others; using steps for problem-solving and decision-making; and improving self-awareness, as well as verbal and nonverbal communication skills. Activities are also included for use with parents to help support improvements in the home, as well as in school (Office of Juvenile Justice and Delinquency Prevention, 2016).

Homebuilders

The Homebuilders program provides in-home crisis intervention, counseling, and life skills education for families who have children at imminent risk of placement to state-funded care. This family preservation program's goal is to prevent the unnecessary out-of-home placement of children through home-based efforts, teaching families new problem-solving skills to divert future crises. Referrals to Homebuilders are normally through public agencies—child protective agencies (CPS) and juvenile courts—for children and adolescents (birth to 17 years) who are in imminent risk of being placed into foster, group, or institutional care. The program's goal is to remove the risk of harm to the child, instead of removing the child, and is accomplished through the use of small caseloads, high program intensity, and 24-hour a day service. For juvenile court-involved adolescents, the program keeps the young person in the community while helping with court compliance, school-related issues, and rehabilitative-focused activities and counseling (Office of Juvenile Justice and Delinquency Prevention, 2016).

Schools are important, and for many young people vital, in delinquency prevention. As discussed in Chapter 12, school success is a strong protective factor in avoiding offending behaviors or school discipline protocols. Many students' troubles begin at home, but the school's structure, design, programs, and policies can also be strongly supportive of students and help minimize offending behaviors. In addition, schools can, and many have, taken proactive steps to offer student supports around mental health needs, behavioral or self-control, trauma-related difficulties, and other troubles that are known to impact academic abilities.

One approach that has some important and effective outcomes is the Turnaround for Children organization that tries to transform high-poverty schools in Washington, DC; Newark, NJ; and New York, NY. The program focuses on trauma, chronic failure, and related problems by integrating mental health care and needed behavioral supports for students (and families). Mental health approaches include early problem identification and assessment, psychiatric care, and ongoing treatment when needed. There is significant integration of the mental health care with the school personnel and other collaborative needs (Morgan, Salomon, Plotkin, & Cohen, 2014).

DIVERSION

Diversion has come to mean several different things for youthful offenders, including nonarrest and release back to the community, addressing the identified problems through rehabilitative means, and any attempt to divert from the juvenile justice system (Griffin & Torbet, 2000). Other terms are used across the states to denote diversion efforts or programming. These include informal processing, adjustment, probation adjustment, deferred prosecution, civil citation, or consent decree. State diversion laws typically define various procedures, including eligibility criteria (the offense type, age of youthful offender, and any prior diversion outcomes, among others), the program's purpose, offender accountability, and the voluntary nature of participation. Diversionary programming may be offered by a juvenile court, referred to as formal diversion, or prior to any juvenile court involvement through using community-based alternatives, referred to as caution or warning programs (Models for Change Juvenile Diversion Workgroup, 2011).

Diversion is an option for many first-time or low-level youthful offenders, particularly for those involved with school-based arrests and referrals or those who commit status offense, to the juvenile courts because most of this population does not pose any serious threat of reoffending. Beyond this, many of these young people may be effectively assisted through the identification and treatment of related problems, such as substance use, school failure, or mental health concerns (Coalition for Juvenile Justice, 2013). The goals of different diversion programs may vary, but they all focus on minimizing young people's involvement with the juvenile courts. The themes for diversion programs thus revolve around reducing contact and offending recidivism, providing services, avoiding labeling the young person, and reducing costs to the juvenile justice system (Models for Change Juvenile Diversion Workgroup, 2011; Wilson & Hoge, 2012).

Police and Youthful Offenders

Options for police when making a decision on a youthful offense include the following: questioning, warning, and community release; taking the adolescent to the police station and recording the offense; a referral to a diversion program; issuing a citation and making a formal referral to the juvenile court; or taking the adolescent to a detention center or group home. Many factors are influential at this decision-making point, including the youthful offender's profile (age, gender, or offending history, among others), the police officer's perspectives on the crime and community, departmental policies, specific offense and circumstances, and any community pressures (Lawrence & Hemmens, 2008).

> **Low-Level Youthful Offenders:** First-time, misdemeanor-offending, or status-offending young people.

CASE STUDY

FLORIDA CIVIL CITATION ALTERNATIVE PROGRAM

A civil citation is an alternative to arrest that allows first-time misdemeanants in the state of Florida to participate in intervention services in lieu of formal processing through the juvenile justice system. Florida Statute 985.12 requires the establishment of civil citation opportunities for all non-serious, first-time misdemeanors. The local chief circuit judge, state attorney, public defender, and head of each law enforcement agency determine how civil citation will operate in the community, including which offenses are eligible for civil citation. . . . When a youth receives a civil citation he or she undergoes a needs assessment to inform the development of an intervention plan. Typically youth participate in community service and may receive some sort of intervention programming. Both the youth and parent(s) or guardian(s) must commit to the program. Youth who successfully complete mandated programming will not have a criminal history record. Those who do not complete the programming are referred to the state attorney for processing on the original charge. (Morgan et al., 2014, p. 291)

1. Would this type of program work in your state or community?

2. What would the impact of this type of program be for young people most at risk for school troubles?

If the officer determines that questioning and community release is not appropriate, then two diversion alternatives are available—caution or warning programs and formal juvenile justice system diversion programs. Referrals to either diversion type can occur before or after a formal charge is brought against the young person for the offending act. Precharge referrals normally involve police apprehension and immediate diversion of the young person, either by caution/warning and release or by referral to an intervention program.

Caution or Warning Programs

Caution or warning (diversion) programs are the least restrictive of diversion program options because they divert the young person away from the juvenile justice system with no further action taken by the police. Beyond this formal caution or warning to refrain or discontinue the activities, police involvement typically ends at this point and the young person is free to go. The target population for warning programs are normally first-time misdemeanor and status offenders—curfew violations, alcohol use, and similar type concerns.

Formal Diversion Programs

Formal diversion programs usually require the young person to take certain corrective steps, typically an admission of guilt and an agreement to participate in programming that is suitable. Services may be provided within the program or through a community-based provider for therapeutic or treatment needs, or they could be just oversight and surveillance of the adolescent. The target population is first-time or low-level offenders, as well as higher risk juvenile offenders with mental health or substance abuse problems. Successful completion of the formal diversion agreement will normally discontinue the juvenile justice system's involvement, with no further requirements or actions taken. Diversion interventions can include a broad array of options, for example, community service, restorative justice programs, individual or family treatment or counseling, skills building programs (anger management, peer relations, among others), drug courts, or teen courts. In one recent meta-analytic review of 73 diversion programs, it was found that both caution and intervention alternatives, in particular, those that focused on assessing the risk and needs level of those entering the programs, were significantly more effective at reducing recidivism than traditional formal processing (Wilson & Hoge, 2013). Several program examples may be instructive.

The Multidisciplinary Team (MDT) Home Run Program of San Bernardino County, California, is a case management intervention designed to identify the youthful offender's difficulties and to provide intense family and individual treatment. The treatment planning process includes the family, school personnel, and other relevant individuals in the adolescent's life. This strength-based and goal-oriented program targets first-time youthful offenders who are 17 or younger and at risk for more serious criminal activity. The case management team includes the probation officer (when formally involved with the juvenile court), public health nurse, licensed therapist, social service practitioner, school personnel, and volunteers who coordinate, as necessary, interventions such as restitution, restorative justice, community service, counseling, and group therapy (Office of Juvenile Justice and Delinquency Prevention, 2016).

The Lancaster County, Pennsylvania, Youth Aid Panels were established to prevent young people from becoming more involved in delinquency and poor decision-making, and to make the youthful offender accountable for his or her actions through services to the victim and/or the community. The program is overseen by local law enforcement and the Lancaster County District Attorney's Office. To be eligible, the young person must be between the ages of 10 and 18, charged with committing a nonviolent offense, and must admit to the charge; then, diversion occurs at the young person's initial contact with law enforcement. The Youth

Caution or Warning (Diversion) Programs: Least restrictive alternative that diverts a young person out of the juvenile justice system with no further action taken by the police.

Formal Diversion Programs: Typically involve some conditions for the young person, an admission of guilt, and an agreement to participate in programming that is suitable. Services may be provided within the program or through a community-based provider for therapeutic or treatment needs, or could be just oversight and surveillance of the adolescent.

16 STEPS FOR PLANNING A DIVERSION PROGRAM (MODELS FOR CHANGE)

Key national stakeholders and advocates for young people at risk for involvement with the juvenile justice system have produced the Juvenile Diversion Guidebook. This working document is supported by evidence to date around what works, what does not, and how to implement effective diversion programs for adolescents. The Guidebook describes a 16-step process to follow to maximize the impact of diversion and minimize formally delinquency adjudication. These steps are organized into six categories: purpose, oversight, intake criteria, operation policies, legal protections, and quality. This approach asks some of the most important questions in designing an effective diversion program, particularly around intake criteria and legal impact (Models for Change Juvenile Diversion Workgroup, 2011, pp. 19–21).

PURPOSE

1. Objectives
   a. What will be the primary objectives of the diversion program?
   b. In your community, what stakeholders from the juvenile justice public/private youth-caring services systems will be involved to provide input and support in shaping the development of your diversion program?

2. Referral Decision Points
   a. At what point or points will referral decisions be made?
   b. Who will be responsible for making the decision to divert youthful offenders?

3. Extent of Intervention
   a. What degree of intervention(s) will the program utilize?
   b. Will the program provide the young person with a written contract (either formal or informal)?

OVERSIGHT

4. Operations
   a. What agency or entity will establish and maintain the program policies, provide staffing, and take responsibility for program outcomes?
   b. Will an advisory board or panel be developed to oversee the development of policies and procedures for the diversion program?
   c. How will the engagement and buy-in of stakeholders be obtained?

5. Funding
   a. How will the diversion program be funded?
   b. Are secure funding streams currently in place that can help to sustain the program in the future?
   c. Has the possibility of using other local, state, or federal resources to help support the diversion program or key aspects of the program been explored?

INTAKE CRITERIA

6. Referral and Eligibility
   a. Which young people will be eligible for diversion?
   b. What offense will be accepted for diversion?
   c. Are there any offenses that might make a young person ineligible and will there be options for discretion?

7. Screening and Assessment
   a. Will any screening and/or assessment methods/tools be used to determine a young person's eligibility, and if so, how will these tools be chosen and who will administer them?
   b. For what purposes will screening and assessment be used?
   c. Are there any protocols in place to deal with the sensitive nature of information collected and how, if at all, it can be shared among child serving agencies?

OPERATION POLICIES

8. Participant Requirements
   a. What obligations and conditions will the program require for the young person's participation and successful completion?
   b. How will requirements focus on the young person's strengths, address mental health needs, satisfy victim concerns, and involve community efforts?

9. Services
   a. What services will be provided for the young person while participating in the diversion program?
   b. Will the diversion program need to perform an inventory of community services, and if so, who will be responsible for this effort?
   c. Will the diversion program encourage or require the young person's family to participate in services?

(Continued)

(Continued)

d. Are there any agreements in place or Memoranda of Understanding (MOU) among the program and community service providers that will better facilitate services to the young people?

10. Incentives

a. Will the diversion program use any incentives to motivate young people and/or caretakers throughout the diversion process? If so, what forms of incentives will be used?

b. Is the use of incentives economically feasible for the diversion program, and what funding sources will support incentives?

c. Will the court agree to dropping charges against the young person or expunging records once the youth successfully completes the terms of diversion?

11. Consequences of Failure to Comply

a. Will there be any negative consequences for young people who fail to comply with the diversion program's requirements? If so, what will these sanctions be?

b. Will the young person ultimately be formally processed for failing to comply with diversion?

12. Program Completion/Exit Criteria

a. How will the diversion program monitor success or failure during program participation?

b. How will successful program completion be defined, and will there be established exit criteria?

LEGAL PROTECTIONS

13. Information Use

a. What will be the conditions/guidelines for the use of information obtained during the young person's participation in the diversion program?

b. How will policies concerning the collection and use of information be clearly established and conveyed to young person and caretakers prior to participation in diversion?

14. Legal Counsel

a. What role will defense counsel play? Are there local policy provisions in place or statutory guidelines that establish the role of counsel?

b. Will the diversion program make counsel available to young people and their family?

QUALITY

15. Program Integrity

a. Are there clear policies and procedures that will be put into manual form for program personnel to maintain program quality and fidelity?

b. How will training be developed and delivered for diversion program personnel?

c. How will information be collected and in what formats?

d. Will the program conduct a process evaluation?

16. Outcome Evaluation

a. What kind of record keeping and data collection will be used to provide periodic evaluations of the diversion program and monitor achievement of goals and objectives?

b. What young person and program outcomes will be used to measure success?

- -

1. **How difficult would it be to set up a diversion program following these guidelines? In other words, what is helpful about the guidelines?**

2. **Why does diversion work for many low-level youthful offenders?**

Source: © Center for Juvenile Justice Reform, National Center for Mental Health and Juvenile Justice, National Juvenile Defender Center, National Youth Screening and Assessment Project, and Robert F. Kennedy Children's Action Corps, March 2011.

Aid Panel is composed of citizens of varying ages, professions, ethnicities, and socioeconomic groups who review the young person's case and determine a resolution for both the victim and the offender, using the input of the offender and his or her family and resulting in some form of restitution to the victim. Diversion contracts may require writing of an essay, performing community service, attending an educational class, or providing a verbal or written apology letter to the victim, among other alternatives. Not completing the contract might result in sanctions ranging from a warning to unsuccessful program discharge and the filing of a formal petition with the juvenile court (Models for Change Juvenile Diversion Workgroup, 2011, p. 50).

Evidence-Based Community Alternatives

Most youthful offenders who are in contact with the juvenile justice system have histories or current problems with trauma, mental health, substance use, school issues, or a combination of these difficulties. As reviewed in Chapters 11 and 12, there are many evidence-based treatments, programs, and protocols available to this population, such as cognitive-behavior therapy, mentoring programs, tutoring, family- and parent-focused therapy, psychosocial interventions, and trauma treatment. When diverting young people from the juvenile justice system, or when diverting them with formal programs, the use of these effective options is important to lower youthful offender recidivism. Addressing some of the key risk factors of status offenses and delinquent behaviors can help minimize contact with the juvenile courts, as well as adjudication and supervision. Many of these programs require the involvement and commitment of the family.

For example, the Project Back-on-Track is an after-school diversion program designed for low- and mid-level youthful offenders—domestic violence, assault, drug, and property offenses, among others—to divert from further juvenile court involvement. This multifaceted program curriculum involves the youthful offender and family for four weeks, with the provision of individual and group therapy, parent support groups, community service projects, psycho-educational sessions, and adolescent empathy-building sessions. The adolescents participate in 32 hours of programming (two hours per day, four days per week), and the parents participate in 15 hours (Myers et al., 2000; Office of Juvenile Justice and Delinquency Prevention, 2016).

Other efforts also focus on the risk and impact that mental health difficulties have on young people who become involved with the police and juvenile justice system. Knowing that most young people who become formally involved with the juvenile courts have at least one diagnosable mental health problem, this may be a priority to address first along with the offending behavior. Unfortunately, law enforcement officers have become the default response to young people with serious mental health problems. These are situations most officers are not trained or prepared for to respond.

Because of this deficiency, and borrowing from the adult criminal justice system and success with **Crisis Intervention Teams (CITs)**, some states have developed these teams for youthful offenders. The CIT model trains police officers in response techniques that are appropriate for people suffering from mental health symptoms or problems. Training includes learning about mental illness, its impact, what community-based resources are available, adolescent development, and how best to respond to young people in need. The programs are used in districts and areas of nine states: Colorado, Connecticut, Illinois, Louisiana, Michigan, Ohio, Pennsylvania, Texas, and Washington. Michigan, however, has gone further and implemented strategies for state-wide adoption of CIT teams. These teams have helped decrease emergency healthcare needs, law enforcement responses, and officer injuries in working with these populations (National Center for Mental Health and Juvenile Justice, 2012, 2013).

The TeamChild Program has operated since 1995 across seven counties in Washington State. TeamChild attorneys provide free legal advocacy and community education, along with other staff members, including, at times, social workers, to help justice system-involved young people (ages 12 to 18, at any stage of the juvenile justice process) secure education, housing, vocational, healthcare, mental health, and other identified needs. The

Crisis Intervention Teams (CITs): Police officer model that trains in response techniques that are appropriate for people suffering from mental health symptoms or problems.

Personality Profile Assessment

▲ There are many effective screening and assessment tools used in the youth-caring systems to identify concerns or problems. What problems might be looked for?

team works closely with the school districts and educates court personnel on nonjustice-related areas that affect the young person's decision-making, academic limitations, and related problem areas. Over time, TeamChild participants have been almost four times less likely than comparable youthful offenders without TeamChild Program assistance to come into contact with the juvenile justice system six months postdischarge (Models for Change Juvenile Diversion Workgroup, 2011; Washington State Institute for Public Policy, 2007).

With an increased rate of girls entering the juvenile justice system over the past 15 years, diversion and prevention are increasingly important. The Girls Circle Program is a strengths-based group that works with girls, ages 9 to 18, through the integration of cultural differences, resiliency practices, and skills training to assist in reducing offending behaviors. The program consists of an 8- to 12-session curriculum, normally held weekly, led by a facilitator who follows a 6-step format of gender-specific themes, motivational interviewing techniques, and identified improvement areas—coping with stress, sexuality, drugs or alcohol, decision-making, relationships, and trust, among other topics. Long-term follow-up reviews of program participants found significant improvements in alcohol abuse and use, attachment to school, self-harming behavior, social support, and self-efficacy (Irvine, 2005; Office of Juvenile Justice and Delinquency Prevention, 2016).

A broad, state-wide approach to using alternatives to school removal and juvenile justice involvement for disruptive or troubled young people has been ongoing in Florida. The Florida Civil Citation Alternative Program encourages the use of alternatives to student school removal through the use of civil citations, teen court, restorative justice, and other rehabilitative options.

ASSESSMENT

Early identification of delinquency risks and difficulties, along with prevention and rehabilitative efforts, can desist many youthful offending acts. Nevertheless, many juvenile courts do not use, or correctly apply, empirically supported structured screening or assessment tools, sometimes relying more on practice wisdom or intuition of whether the young person poses a community safety risk or is amenable to rehabilitative juvenile justice system alternatives. With such a large number of youthful offenders troubled by mental health, substance use, and trauma difficulties, it is helpful for diversion programs and juvenile courts to incorporate the use of appropriate assessment measures. Once identified, subsequent rehabilitative and treatment alternatives can be recommended and coordinated with other youth-caring systems (Vincent, Guy, & Grisso, 2012).

Screening: Brief process used to identify problems that are in need of further attention or assessment.

Assessments (Risk Assessments): Thorough investigation of the identified risks or problem areas for young people and their families.

Screening is a brief process used to identify problems that are in need of further attention or assessment. Youthful offenders may benefit from screenings for mental health, trauma, and related problems and may, in fact, require more thorough assessment. Screening efforts can occur at any point during the juvenile justice process, but they are likely best performed as soon as a young person is involved. Screening may initially identify problems related to mental health, substance use, family troubles, school difficulties, trauma, and other related or comorbid difficulties, allowing for further informed review. Assessments (risk assessments) are more thorough investigations of the identified risks or problem areas for young people and their families. This clinical method develops a coherent view of the risk or offending outcomes through the construction of a theory or explanation of why the event happens by gathering information from the individual, family, and school personnel, among others. Screening and assessment tools and instruments are of two types: for risk of offending or recidivism and for specific delinquency risk factors such as mental health, trauma, and substance use (Chapin & Griffin, 2005; Mulvey & Iselin, 2008).

Offending Risk Assessment

Risk assessments in the juvenile justice system most often measure the risk of reoffending or rearrest as the outcome of interest. In determining a young person's overall risk of recidivism, these assessment measures commonly include offending history, substance use/abuse, peer delinquency, family problems, and school-related problems, among others areas and do so through interviews or self-reporting or standardized rating scales. Effective risk assessment tools include risk, protective, and responsivity factors in the determination of offending or recidivism. Risk and protective factors are important in determining risk for delinquency (see Figure 13.1), although responsivity factors are those areas that can be changed by the young person and his or her family—individual motivation level, parental involvement, and compliance are influential, for example (Schwalbe, 2008).

Two of the more commonly used and standardized—established empirical reliability and validity—measures include the Youth Level of Service/Case Management Inventory (YLS-CMI) and the Structured Assessment of Violence Risk for Youth (SAVRY). The Y-LSI is a 42-item checklist with eight subscales, including offense history, family circumstances/parenting, education, peer relations, substance abuse, leisure/recreation, personality/behavior,

▼ FIGURE 13.1

Types of Factors Commonly Found in Risk Assessment Tools

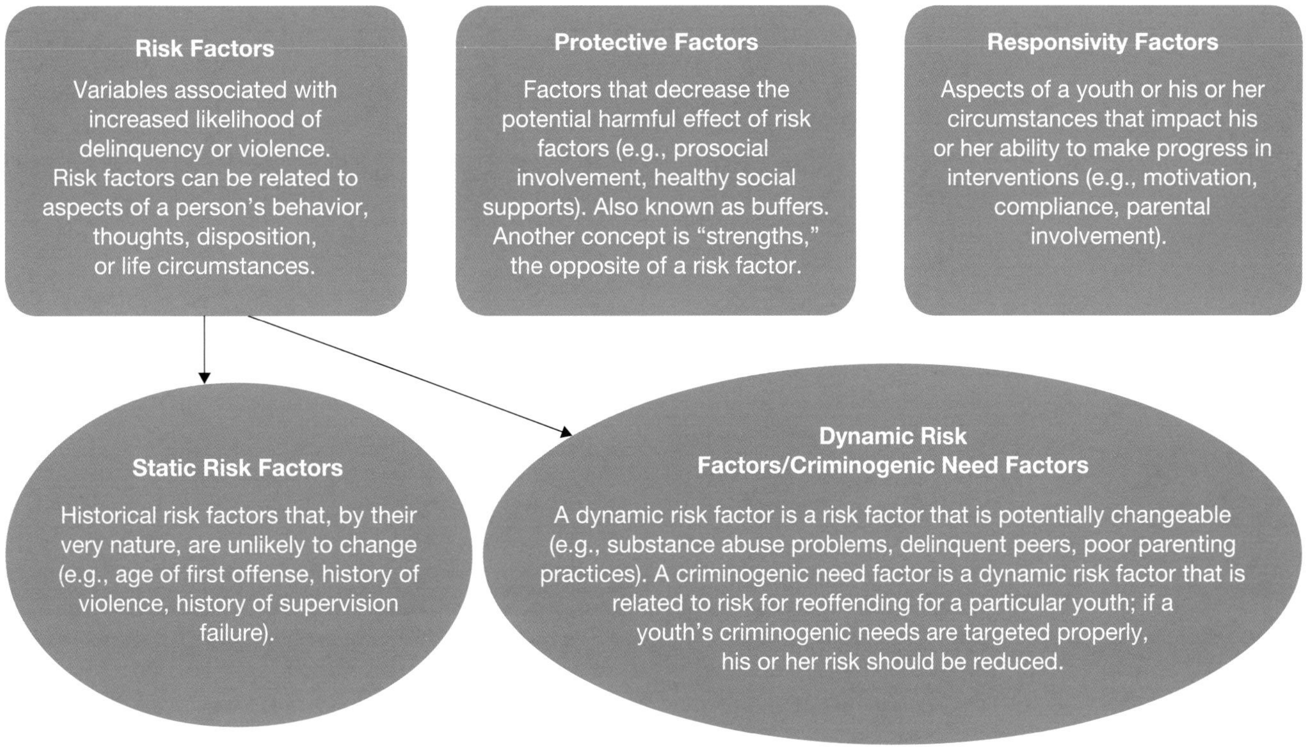

Risk Factors

Variables associated with increased likelihood of delinquency or violence. Risk factors can be related to aspects of a person's behavior, thoughts, disposition, or life circumstances.

Protective Factors

Factors that decrease the potential harmful effect of risk factors (e.g., prosocial involvement, healthy social supports). Also known as buffers. Another concept is "strengths," the opposite of a risk factor.

Responsivity Factors

Aspects of a youth or his or her circumstances that impact his or her ability to make progress in interventions (e.g., motivation, compliance, parental involvement).

Static Risk Factors

Historical risk factors that, by their very nature, are unlikely to change (e.g., age of first offense, history of violence, history of supervision failure).

Dynamic Risk Factors/Criminogenic Need Factors

A dynamic risk factor is a risk factor that is potentially changeable (e.g., substance abuse problems, delinquent peers, poor parenting practices). A criminogenic need factor is a dynamic risk factor that is related to risk for reoffending for a particular youth; if a youth's criminogenic needs are targeted properly, his or her risk should be reduced.

Source: Vincent, G.M., Guy, L.S., & Grisso, T. (2012). *Risk assessment in juvenile justice: A guidebook for implementation.* Models for Change: Systems Reform in Juvenile Justice, MacArthur Foundation, Chicago, IL. Reprinted with permission.

and attitudes/orientation (Schmidt, Hoge, & Gomes, 2005). The SAVRY is composed of 24 items across three risk areas (historical, social/contextual, and individual/clinical) as well as protective areas, and it is based on the structured professional judgment model (see Table 13.2; Borum, Bartel, & Forth, 2002; Gammelgard, Koivisto, Eronen, & Kaltiala-Heino, 2015).

These screening tools are used both to predict future risk of offending or violence and to identify specific problem areas that may be intertwined with the young person's offending behaviors. These tools identify risk factors, focused on dynamic risks that can be addressed, as well as responsivity factors. Such standardized screening tools can assist in identifying risk for offending and other potential problems.

Several practice-related guidelines are best incorporated and integrated when juvenile justice personnel use risk offending and related assessments. These include the following: The assessment tool should be used and implemented properly; child and adolescent development should be considered in the use of an assessment tool or subsequent case management planning, for most adolescent behaviors can be changed and risk levels can be lowered; most youthful offenders are at low risk for reoffending, showing that diversion is effective for many; high risk levels do not mean that detention or incarceration must happen, but they may be needed at times to protect public safety; and services and case planning should be individualized based on a comprehensive assessment of the young person's situation, including level of risk.

Beyond this framework, a research-supported risk assessment approach is important. For example, the risk–need–responsivity (RNR) incorporates four principles: The highest risk offenders should receive the most intensive monitoring and services—lower risk, lower monitoring and services; risks for reoffending should be the focus of response, addressing those areas that are most able to be changed (negative peers, lack of social ties, antisocial attitude, poor academic performance, and parenting practices, among others); other factors also need to be addressed, including mental health and motivation levels; and discretion by juvenile

▼ TABLE 13.2

SAVRY Risk and Protective Areas

Historical Risks	Individual/Clinical Risks
History of violence	Negative attitudes
History of nonviolent offending	Risk taking/impulsivity
Early initiation of violence	Substance use difficulties
Past supervision/intervention failures	Anger management problems
History of self-harm or suicide attempts	Psychopathic traits
Exposure to violence in the home	Attention deficit/hyperactivity difficulties
Childhood history of maltreatment	Poor compliance
Parental/caregiver criminality	Low interest/commitment to school
Early caregiver disruption	
Poor school achievement	
Social/Contextual Risks	**Protective Factors**
Peer delinquency	Prosocial involvement
Peer rejection	Strong social support
Poor parental management	Strong attachments and bonds
Lack of person/social support	Positive attitude toward intervention and authority
Community disorganization	Strong commitment to school
	Resilient personality traits

justice and other professionals should be allowed, balancing treatment or placement decisions on both risk/needs and professional judgment (Lipsey, 2009):

> Screening and assessment methods should be tied to a particular *decision-point*, or a point in the juvenile justice decision-making process. The decision point will have a large impact on the resources and amount of information available to conduct the assessment. Moreover, different decision points are associated with different assessment questions. At *intake*, for example, the question may be whether the youth is appropriate for diversion from the juvenile justice system. At detention, the primary question is whether the youth needs secure pretrial detention to prevent recidivism or failure to appear in court. With respect to *judicial processing*, the question might be in regard to waiver to adult court or transfer back to juvenile court. At *disposition*, several questions are relevant, including the appropriate placement (community or custody), security level, and subsequent treatment or service plans for the youth. Disposition decisions require the court to consider both the most appropriate sanctions and interventions with the best potential for reducing the likelihood of delinquent behaviors in the future. Community re-entry or *aftercare* planning can benefit from risk assessment to determine the essential level of monitoring and interventions for the youth while in the community. (Vincent et al., 2012, p. 64)

Assessment for Mental Health, Trauma, Substance Use, and Related Problems. Over the past decade, screenings for mental health, trauma, substance use, and other related delinquency risk factors have become somewhat commonplace in the juvenile justice system. With the expanded use of valid screenings and assessments, a focus on diverting young people away from the juvenile courts and toward treatment, and recognition that the juvenile courts are not the most appropriate place to address many of these problems, has taken place. Before deciding which screening or assessment tools to use, for offending risk as well as mental health, trauma, or related concerns, juvenile justice system personnel should ask some important questions (see Table 13.3; Office of Juvenile Justice and Delinquency Prevention, 2009).

As reviewed, mental health screening is a brief process that can be administered by non-professional staff using a standardized tool, often used as a triage assessment to identify a potentially serious mental health problem or suicide risk. It provides an immediate response and can address immediate needs (suicide risk, medication, and other high-risk issues), and identifies young people who require additional attention. The results from screenings, however, should not be presumed to describe a young person's mental or emotional condition beyond two to four weeks (Vincent, 2011). Quick initial screenings can identify young people who are in need for further diagnostic assessments by trained clinicians.

There are several commonly used screening tools in the juvenile justice system and mental health field: the Massachusetts Youth Screening Instrument (MAYSI-2), a 52-item standardized instrument with seven subscales used to identify mental health problems (Grisso & Barnum, 2006); the Child and Adolescent Functional Assessment Scale (CAFAS), assesses the degree of impairment with emotional, behavioral, or substance use symptoms (Hodges, 2005); and the Global Appraisal of Individual Needs Short Screener (GAIN-SS), with four subscales for internal, behavioral, and substance use disorders, as well as crime/violence risk (Dennis, Feeney, Stevens, & Bedoya 2006; Skowyra & Cocozza, 2007).

To see an example of the Texas MAYSI Protocol screening tool, visit the study site at edge.sagepub.com/mallett

If significant clinical needs are identified, a thorough professional assessment may be the next step. Two of the more rigorously validated assessment tools include the Behavioral and Emotional Screen System (BESS) and the Diagnostic Interview Schedule for Children Version 4 (DISC-R). Both require a longer time investment because they include reports from young people, parents, or guardians and, for the BESS, from teachers as well. The BESS is used to identify behavioral and emotional strengths and weaknesses for adolescents through secondary school ages and can screen for a variety of behavioral and emotional disorders that

▼ FIGURE 13.2

Santa Clara County (CA) Juvenile Probation Department, Detention Risk Assessment Instrument

SANTA CLARA COUNTY (CA) JUVENILE PROBATION DEPARTMENT DETENTION RISK ASSESSMENT INSTRUMENT

Name: _____   File No._____   DOB _____

Admit Date: _____   Admit time:_____   Ethnicity_____   Sex: M F

Primary referral offense: _____

A. OFFENSE (Score only the most serious instant offense) *DESCRIBE AND CITE CODE SEC. IF KNOWN*

WIC Section 707 (b) offenses	10
Sale of narcotics/drugs	10
Possession of firearm	10
Assaultive felonies against persons including sex felonies	7
Domestic violence offenses (see guidelines)	7
Possession of narcotics/drugs for sale	6
Felony property crimes including auto	5
Felony possession of narcotics/drugs	3
Other felony not covered above	4
Misdemeanors excluding no-time misdemeanors	3
Infractions, no-time misdemeanors or noncriminal probation violations	0 A. ____ *OFFENSE POINTS*

B. PRIOR OFFENSE HISTORY (Score only one of the following)

Felony petition or serious person misdemeanor petition pending	6
Current felony wardship	5
Prior felony adjudication within the last 36 months	3
Documented escape from secure custody, last 18 months.	5
Documented court FTA within the last 12 months	1 B. ____ *HISTORY POINTS*

C. AGGRAVATING FACTORS (Add all that apply, up to 3 points)

Multiple offenses are alleged for this referral	1
Crime or behavior alleged was particularly severe or violent	1
Confirmed runaway history or minor has no known community ties	1
Minor is under the influence of drugs/alcohol at arrest	1 C. ____ *AGGRAVATION POINTS*

D. MITIGATING FACTORS (Subtract all that apply, up to 3 points)

Involvement in offense was remote, indirect or otherwise mitigated	1
Parent or relative is able to assume immediate responsibility for minor	1
No arrests or citations within the last year	1
Minor demonstrates stability in school or employment	1 D. ____ *MITIGATION POINTS*

TOTAL RISK SCORE (A + B + C–D)

DECISION SCALE: *0–6 RELEASE, 7–9 RESTRICTED RELEASE, 10+ DETAIN*

SPECIAL DETENTION CASES (Check as applicable)

_____ WIC 625.3 mandatory detention (14 or older charged w/707 (b) or felony with use of firearm)

_____ Bench or arrest warrant, minor not authorized for release by probation officer

_____ Placement return or failure—non-secure option not available

_____ Pre-disposition community release (CRP) or electronic monitoring (EM) failure

_____ Inter-county transfer, minor not authorized for release by probation officer

DETENTION OVERRIDE

_____ Parent, guardian or responsible relative cannot be located

_____ Parent, guardian or responsible relative refuses to take custody of minor

_____ Youth refuses to return home

_____ Other. Minor is detained because_____

RELEASE OVERRIDE

_____ The minor is released because: _____

OVERRIDE APPROVAL *(Supervisor signature required):* Approved by: _____ *Supervisor*

RISK INSTRUMENT COMPLETED BY:_____, Probation Officer

The Santa Clara County Juvenile Probation Detention Risk Assessment shown in Figure 13.2 is an example of a focused and helpful decision-making tool for the juvenile court, and these question areas are commonly found across other detention-risk tools.

1. What seems to be the important detention (and delinquency) risk factors being identified by this tool?

2. How do you know a risk assessment tool is appropriate or accurate to use?

Source: Santa Clara Juvenile Court Probation Department, CA.

▼ TABLE 13.3

Important Assessment Questions

Questions to Consider	Importance of these Questions
What do we want to accomplish? What are the decisions we want to make? Do we want to do an initial screening or an assessment? Are we trying to find an instrument to do an initial screening to decide who might need further assessment, or are we doing an assessment to determine who needs treatment or follow-up care?	This helps stakeholders identify which young people are most at risk, what problems are most often of concern, and localizes the decision-making.
Are we interested in assessing a single factor or a host of factors? Are we interested in screening for either substance abuse or suicide risk or for multiple mental health risks, such as psychosocial functioning across a variety of contexts?	This helps stakeholders determine what comorbid problems some of their young people are dealing with—mental health, trauma, and substance use, among others. Different assessment tools provide different foci.
Who do we want to assess—every child referred or a certain subgroup? Are we going to administer this instrument to every referred child or just those who meet certain criteria or are flagged by a screening tool?	This is important in determining the scope of the problem and what resources the court or community have (who can do assessments, location, timing).
What will be the source of the information—information in the case file or a personal interview? If an interview, with whom? How accessible are the parties being interviewed, particularly if we are not interviewing the young person who is central to the case?	Stakeholders have to determine where, when, and who is available to provide important assessment information.
Who will administer the instrument? Will administration involve many staff within the system? Will it involve general intake staff, case supervision staff, or specialists? What kinds of special training will these staff need? Will administration be contracted outside to a special vendor?	Important to assess current staff and resources to determine how and when assessments can occur.
Has the instrument we are considering actually been used in a juvenile justice population? Has it been used on girls? How well does the instrument work for various racial and ethnic populations? Is the instrument culturally appropriate for the types of clients we serve? Has the instrument been normed or validated? If so, on what population? Was the sample representative?	An instrument has to match the local community's demographics to be most useful or valid.
What are the costs of purchasing or using the instrument? Is it in the public domain, or must it be purchased? What are the startup or per-use costs? What are the costs associated with training existing staff or hiring trained staff?	Costs and training are often key barriers to using effective assessments as designed and needed.

Source: OJJDP (2010).

can lead to adjustment problems. The DISC-R is a comprehensive, structured interview that assesses for over three dozen child and adolescent mental health disorders (Kamphaus & Reynolds, 2011; Shaffer, Lucas, & Fisher, 2011). Because of the increased suicidal behavior risks for youthful offenders involved with the juvenile justice system, the use of the Suicidal Ideation Questionnaire (SIQ) may be important. The SIQ is a 25-item, self-report screening instrument used to assess suicidal ideation in adolescents (Reynolds, 1988).

Substance use and abuse are not only risk factors for delinquency but also chargeable offenses for adolescents. Therefore, it is important to know whether offenders have or are at risk of developing these problems. Several reliable screening tools are available that are appropriate to use with the youthful offender population, including the Adolescent Substance Abuse Subtle Screening Instrument (SASSI-3), the Michigan Alcohol Screening Test–Adolescent Version (MAST), and as discussed earlier, the Global Appraisal of Individual Need–Short Screen (GAIN-SS). The SASSI-3 is a psychological screening measure that can identify adolescents with chemical dependency, substance abuse, and substance use disorders. The MAST is a 25-item structured screening tool that can be used to detect an alcohol problem. The GAIN-SS can be used to quickly and accurately identify young people who may need a more thorough assessment for substance use disorders.

Girl Delinquency

There are gender differences in delinquency risk and juvenile justice outcomes for girls. These differences have been found across individual traits (biological and developmental), families (dysfunction, supervision), peer choices, and school issues. Because girls' pathways to delinquency are not the same as boys,' some specific program components are important when working with or diverting girls from the juvenile justice system (Chesney-Lind & Shelden, 2014). These efforts include the use of appropriately reliable and valid assessments, the building of a therapeutic and healthy alliance, using gender-responsive cognitive-behavioral approaches, and recognizing subsets (race, culture) within girl populations involved with the juvenile courts (Matthews & Hubbard, 2009).

Working with girls and delinquency necessitates some unique intervention recommendations. These include the following: identifying and addressing physical maltreatment, including sexual abuse and assault that are more common for girls than for boys in the juvenile justice system; improving parental supervision of girls and family functioning, focused on effective

▼ FIGURE 13.3
Critical Intervention Points

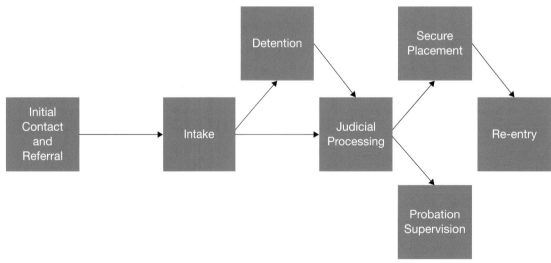

Source: Skowyra & Cocozza (2007).

parenting practices and discontinued use of harsh or inconsistent discipline; identifying and addressing mental health problems, particularly anxiety, depression, and post-traumatic stress disorders, all more common in girls; addressing comorbid difficulties with trauma and mental health; improving school success and connectedness; and addressing truancy problems and running away, status offenses that disproportionately impact girls (Hawkins, Graham, Williams, & Zahn, 2009; Zahn et al., 2010).

Net-widening Effect of Diversion

Formal diversion programs may have an unintended and harmful outcome—bringing more young people into the juvenile courts. This phenomenon is called the **net-widening effect (diversion)** and occurs when diversion programs that involve sanctions for young people who do not meet expectations are then drawn into the juvenile justice system. Many of these young people would not ordinarily be involved with the juvenile courts if not for the unsuccessful completion of a formal diversion program. There is evidence that the use of formal diversion and early intervention programs, when compared with informal diversion or no involvement with the juvenile justice system, has had this widening impact. This may include, for example, status offenders (curfew violations or alcohol possession) and first-time misdemeanor offenders who are referred by the courts to complete certain educational programming but fail to do so. These unintended outcomes shift resources toward those who are least likely to reoffend or recidivate, and away from those more serious or high-risk youthful offenders who need additional intervention and supervision services (Ohio Juvenile Justice Alliance, 2015; Winder & Denious, 2013).

▲ Girl delinquency has been more recently recognized as a growing concern in the juvenile courts. Why do you think this is the case?

COMMUNITY-BASED CORRECTIONS

Ineffective Programs

Knowing what works, and what does not, in the juvenile justice system requires research and data to track the impact of programs and policies on youthful offenders' outcomes. Through the evaluation process, many commonly used interventions and juvenile court decisions for youthful offenders have been found to be ineffective, or worse, harmful. These include curfew laws (ineffective), boot camps, and other disciplinary-focused programs (ineffective and harmful), prison visitation programs (ineffective), Scared Straight and other "shock therapy" programs (harmful), self-help or self-esteem programs (ineffective), restrictive out-of-home mental health residential placements (ineffective after leaving the facility), and large and overcrowded correctional facilities (harmful).

Effective Programs

There are challenges when using evaluation to inform juvenile justice stakeholders. Some of these include the following: Addressing particular behaviors or offending problems is often just the beginning of the work that needs to be accomplished to resolve the young person's problems; implementing rehabilitative programs within punitively focused policies decreases their effectiveness; and expanding the use of evidence-based programs to a larger, system-wide scale has not been accomplished. With that said, some effective programs prevent and reduce youthful offending outcomes. It is choosing and implementing them correctly that poses difficulties to the juvenile justice system. Otherwise, it is well recognized that when youthful offenders end their juvenile

Net-Widening Effect (Diversion): Phenomenon that occurs when diversion programs that involve sanctions on young people who do not meet expectations are then drawn into the juvenile justice system and supervised.

GIRLS AND RUNNING AWAY

A frequent adage you'll hear is that "Girls are different from boys." The old age applies just as importantly for boys and girls who get into trouble at school and for those who end up involved with the juvenile courts. Boys and girls have different risk factors and pathways to delinquency, and stakeholders are only recently recognizing how to address these differences and provide divergent prevention and intervention measures. For example, girls are more likely to be exposed to family violence and are much more likely than boys to run away from home. This is often so that girls can get to a safer place and to avoid harm in their home. Nevertheless, the act of running away poses its own risks: poor peer choices, substance use, higher risk for sexual victimization, and disconnection from school. These situations often lead to police and juvenile court involvement and, for some, detention or incarceration. These placements are most often harmful.

Addressing girls and running away is a complicated endeavor, but to be effective, it needs to be comprehensive. In so doing the following is recommended: assessments that are developmentally appropriate and focused on reasons and social contexts for running away; outreach and family involvement, including readily available and appropriate social services; respite care (homes, nonsecure shelters, etc.) to provide housing alternative for girls that does not include juvenile justice facilities; and services that include counseling, parent education, and other necessary education or vocational skills (Sherman & Balck, 2015).

1. **Why would detention or incarceration facilities be inappropriate placements for girls who run away?**

2. **Do you know of friends or others who have run away from home? What were the reasons or the outcomes?**

Source: Sherman & Balck (2015).

court supervision they tend to revert back to previous offending or delinquent-type behaviors if their skills, attitudes, or support systems have not significantly changed (Lipsey, Howell, Kelly, Chapman, & Carver, 2010; Seigle et al., 2014)

Specific programs and interventions can reduce youthful offender recidivism and related problems. Many of these are used by the juvenile courts when young people are formally involved and under supervision. These programs and interventions (see Table 13.4) have been thoroughly researched (Greenwood, 2008; Office of Juvenile Justice and Delinquency Prevention, 2016; National Council of Juvenile and Family Court Judges, 2016d) with cost–benefit analysis provided by the Washington State Institute for Public Policy (Washington State Institute for Public Policy, 2016).

Aggression Replacement Training and Juvenile Drug Courts

Cost–Benefit Analysis: Systematic approach to estimating the strengths and weaknesses of alternatives; often a monetary approach finding the costs for programs and comparing with short- and long-term outcomes.

Juvenile Drug Courts: Courts that are different than other juvenile dockets, whereby youthful offenders are diverted to work in tandem with community-based service providers under supervision of the juvenile court judge.

Some of these effective delinquency interventions have been reviewed in earlier parts of the text (FFT, cognitive behavioral therapies, MST, and MTFC); it is useful to look more closely at several other programs and rehabilitative approaches. Aggression Replacement Training (ART) is appropriate for youthful offenders who are at high risk for continued offending activities and have problems with aggression or lack skills in pro-social abilities or functioning. The program builds the young person's capacities through techniques to more appropriately manage anger and find positive alternatives in interacting with peers and adults. This work is completed both individually and in group settings (8–10 adolescents) over a 10-week, 30-hour intervention, and is administered by either juvenile court staff or trained, community-based providers (Washington State Institute for Public Policy, 2016).

Juvenile drug courts selectively divert youthful offenders from the regular juvenile court dockets to work in tandem with community-based service providers, thereby having the judge oversee the therapeutic treatment of the adolescent and family, while maintaining adjudication authority. Juvenile drug courts look to be best suited for youthful offenders who

META-ANALYSIS

One of the most extensive reviews of juvenile justice program evaluation findings included 548 published and unpublished studies of youthful offenders ages 12 to 21 (from 1958 to 2002). This *meta-analysis* included these 548 studies that measured at least one delinquency or recidivism outcome and compared to a control group of similarly situated youthful offenders who did not receive the program intervention. A meta-analysis is a statistical approach that combines the results from numerous studies to determine cumulative impact and that identifies the following components that were effective in reducing recidivism: an assessment of delinquency or reoffending risk; therapeutic approaches and philosophies, as compared to control or punishment; and a variety of intervention techniques including family involvement, behavioral and cognitive behavioral techniques, a focus on improving academics and social skills, mentoring, and positive peer-focus and choices. Four significant implications from this review for juvenile court practice were identified: targeting high-risk cases and providing the most effective programs possible; using programs that take a therapeutic approach to changing behavior and focusing on constructive personal development; using programs with the strongest research-based evidence that matches the juvenile court's population; and implementing, monitoring, and evaluating the programs correctly (Lipsey, 2009).

- -

1. Are there themes in the four significant implications from the meta-analysis?

2. Why do you think that a rehabilitative approach is found more effective than a punitive approach in delinquency prevention?

▼ TABLE 13.4

Effective Delinquency Prevention Program

Effective Programs or Interventions for Community-Based Corrections	Impact (percent chance the program benefit will exceed the cost)	Benefit to Cost Ratio ($ benefit gained for each $1 spent on the program)
Functional Family Therapy (FFT)	99%	$31.24
Family-Based Therapies	98%	$20.56
Cognitive-Behavioral Therapy	94%	$28.56
Aggression Replacement Training (ART)	91%	$7.78
Coordination of Services	95%	$15.20
Victim Offender Mediation	78%	$4.65
Therapeutic Communities (Substance Abuse)	76%	$2.51
Multisystemic Therapy (MST)	75%	$1.74
Multidimensional Treatment Foster Care (MTFC)	61%	$1.70
Juvenile Drug Court	57%	$1.53
Brief Strategic Family Therapy (substance abuse)	n/a	

▲ Juvenile drug courts have been increasingly used to monitor drug treatment for youthful offenders. Why do you think this diversion effort helps many young people?

are at a moderate-to-high risk for both delinquency and continued substance abuse, are between the ages of 14 and 17, have a history of juvenile court involvement, and have prior treatments for substance abuse (Thomas, Schiller, & Lucero, 2013). More effective drug courts focus on five areas in the supervision of the youthful offender: providing immediate intervention treatment, providing skills to lead to substance and delinquency discontinuation, improving home and school levels of functioning, strengthening families, and promoting accountability for the young person and treatment providers (National Council of Juvenile and Family Court Judges, 2014)

In achieving these implementation goals, several areas are pivotal for juvenile drug courts: planning collaboratively across all members (judge, prosecutor, defense attorney, probation/case manager, treatment provider, and coordinator); needing to operate as a collaborative team; establishing clearly defined eligibility criteria and target population of youthful offenders; having a judge that believes in the model and rehabilitative approach; providing comprehensive treatment planning, a strengths-based focus, and goal-oriented sanctions and incentives for the young person and his or her family; establishing strong community provider partnerships; and integrating cultural and gender-specific interventions (Kinscherff & Cocozza, 2011; National Council of Juvenile and Family Court Judges, 2014). Although outcomes have been positive for established juvenile drug courts, not following known and effective court and case planning may be the reason some drug courts have a more limited impact on decreasing delinquency and substance abuse (Mitchell, Wilson, Eggers, & MacKenzie, 2012).

Probation Supervision

Probation supervision is the most common outcome for adjudicated delinquent youthful offenders. Supervision that focuses on authority and control by the probation officer, and contact that is limited and relies on enforcing probation conditions (court-ordered list of changes or activities/programs the youthful offender must complete), are typically ineffective because of this controlling and punitive-focused approach (Bonta, Rugge, Scott, Bourgon, & Yessine, 2008). Probation departments that have more successful outcomes have adjusted the officer's role, changed the expectations of supervision, and incorporated graduated sanctions with a focus on positive and incremental youthful offender changes.

Probation officers can more effectively work with youthful offenders when they have smaller caseloads that allow for more time together with the young person, his or her family, and other important support people. In addition, it is best when the supervision takes place in the home and community settings, the officer is trained in evidence-based practices, and ongoing risk assessments are incorporated into a monitored case plan. It is important to hold young people accountable for their offending actions and to address the harm caused to victims and communities, focused on positive behavior changes. This approach requires youthful offenders to take responsibility for their wrongdoing and may include a variety of rehabilitative alternatives—community service, restitution, victim and/or family conferences, and mediation (Thomas, Torbet, & Deal, 2011; Seigle et al., 2014).

Graduated Response Model

Graduated response model supervision uses a continuum of interventions in working with youthful offenders. The response choices are based on assessment of risk and on the young person's progress or noncompliance, and they take a step-by-step approach to making supervision decisions. Through having clear expectations and effective programming available, the youthful offender can both understand what to do but be allowed to make mistakes without immediate serious repercussions, violation of court order charges, or detention/incarceration (Latessa, 2012).

The National Council of Juvenile and Family Court Judges (NCJFCJ) has developed a model juvenile court graduated sanctions protocol for probation supervision and secure confinement. This continuum of disposition options is available to both judges and probation officers and provides services as well as safety and accountability for the youthful offender (National Council of Juvenile and Family Court Judges, 2016d).

▲ Probation officers are commonly used for young people who are adjudicated delinquent. What approaches do you think probation officers should take when working with their probationers?

Level 1: Immediate Sanctions. Level 1 immediate sanctions are targeted for lower level, less serious offenders and use preventative interventions to secure needed services. These immediate sanctions divert from formal court involvement and target disruptive behaviors, truancy and other status offenses, and low-level delinquent acts such as trespassing or vandalism. Program services may include school-based services, truancy prevention, community-based mental health or substance abuse services, restitution, mentoring, parenting and family support, and/or crisis intervention.

Level 2: Intermediate Sanctions. Level 2 intermediate sanctions are for the young person who continues to offend after immediate interventions and for those who have committed more serious felony offenses. This involves formal adjudication and supervision by the court and may include day treatment, electronic monitoring, and/or alternative school placement. Program services may include probation or more intensive services, family involvement and counseling, community-based mental health or substance abuse services, mentoring, parenting classes, interpersonal skills training, and/or other individual therapies.

Orange County, California, for example, has developed its youthful offender probation supervision through a comprehensive three-tier system, using graduated sanctions, in conjunction with a parallel system of intervention and supervision options to develop the 8% Early Intervention Program. The 8% Program was developed because the juvenile court found that a small percentage of more serious youthful offenders accounted for a significant amount of juvenile court resources, although many of these adolescents could be diverted from recidivist outcomes. Youthful offenders in this high-risk 8% group, those most at risk for ongoing offending, are referred to an intensive, community-based program—the Early Intervention Youth and Family Resource Center. The medium-risk group (typically around 25% of the court probation population) members are probation supervised and linked to community-based programs, including, as needed, in-home family services, health screenings, substance abuse and mental health treatment, and educational services. The low-risk group (typically around 70% of the court probation population) receives diversion and delinquency prevention programming (Lipsey et al., 2010; National Council of Juvenile and Family Court Judges, 2016d).

Level 3: Community Confinement. Level 3 services are for those youthful offenders who continue to offend despite prior immediate or intermediate sanctions. The focus is on those who commit more serious property or person crimes and are at moderate-to-high risk to continue. Depending on the home environment situation, several options are available: day treatment or after-school programming, alternative school placement, substance abuse and mental health treatment (both community-based and residential), in-home family services, and additional therapeutic interventions (Multisystemic Therapy and Functional Family Therapy, among others).

Level 4: Secure Confinement. Level 4 services are for those youthful offenders who are more serious and chronic offenders and who have failed at community-based supervision and services and continue to offend. The youthful offenders are at high risk for recidivism, have significant treatment needs, and pose community safety concerns. Placement options include detention, state facility incarceration, and residential treatment centers for mental health or substance abuse problems. These alternatives and impact, along with how best to design juvenile justice facilities, are reviewed in Chapter 14.

▼ TABLE 13.5

Missouri Risk and Offense Case Classification Matrix

Offense	Group 1 Offenses	Group 2 Offenses	Group 3 Offenses
Risk Level	Status Offenses Municipal Ordinances/Infractions	Class A, B, and C Misdemeanors/ Class C and D Felonies	A* and B Felonies
Low Risk	A. Warn and Counsel B. Restitution C. Community Service D. Court Fees and Assessments E. Supervision	A. Warn and Counsel B. Restitution C. Community Service D+. Court Fees and Assessments E. Supervision	B+. Restitution C+. Community Service D+. Court Fees and Assessments E. Supervision F. Day Treatment G. Intensive Supervision H. Court Residential Placement I. Commitment to DYS
Moderate Risk	A. Warn and Counsel B. Restitution C. Community Service D. Court Fees and Assessments E. Supervision	A. Warn and Counsel B. Restitution C+. Community Service D+. Court Fees and Assessment E. Supervision F. Day Treatment	B+. Restitution C+. Community Service D+. Court Fees and Assessments E. Supervision F. Day Treatment G. Intensive Supervision H. Court Residential Placement I. Commitment to DYS
High Risk	A. Warn and Counsel B. Restitution C. Community Service D. Court Fees and Assessments E. Supervision	B+. Restitution C+. Community Service D+. Court Fees and Assessments E. Supervision F. Day Treatment G. Intensive Supervision H. Court Residential Placement I. Commitment to DYS	H. Court Residential Placement I. Commitment to DYS

*Mandatory certification hearings are required by statute for all Class A Felonies. In the event the juvenile is not certified, the juvenile officer should refer to this column of the matrix for classification purposes.

+ This symbol indicates options that should never be used as a sole option for youths who score in the cell but only in conjunction with other options.

Crossover Youth

The Center for Juvenile Justice Reform and the Robert F. Kennedy Children's Action Corps have developed approaches to prevent young people involved with either the juvenile courts or the child welfare system from "crossing over" to the other. The focus is on decreasing "dual status" youthful offenders, those with delinquency involvement and open child welfare agency cases. There are several practice recommendations for local communities to pursue in improving outcomes for these populations: coordinating court hearings and using one judge—the one-family, one-judge model—for all legal and child welfare matters; sharing information and data across the agency and court; a coordinated case plan and supervision using effective and informed interventions and services; and engagement and involvement of the family in decisions and planning. This **Crossover Youth Practice Model** is implemented in more than 90 jurisdictions, and initial results have found improved outcomes in child welfare, school, mental health, and lower confinement and reoffending rates (Herz et al., 2012; Thomas, 2015).

Crossover Youth Practice Model: Program established by The Center for Juvenile Justice Reform and the Robert F. Kennedy Children's Action Corps that has developed approaches to prevent young people involved with either the juvenile courts or the child welfare system from "crossing over" to the other.

CHAPTER REVIEW

CHAPTER SUMMARY

This chapter reviewed how low-level and status-offending young people are best diverted from formal juvenile court supervision. Effective diversion efforts were highlighted, as well as how the juvenile justice system can use caution/warning programs and, when justified, formal diversion interventions. Most youthful offenders who do not pose community safety risks are best served through these efforts. When brought under supervision or adjudicated delinquent, treating many of the risk factors—mental health, substance use, and family conflicts, among others—that lead to juvenile court involvement is often the best strategy, and some model programs were highlighted. Most of these effective programs use evidence-based interventions and graduated sanctions in minimizing further or long-term juvenile court involvement for the low-level youthful offender.

KEY TERMS

assessments (risk assessments) **292**

Bureau of Justice Assistance **283**

caution or warning (diversion) programs **288**

cost–benefit analysis **300**

Crisis Intervention Teams (CITs) **291**

Crossover Youth Practice Model **305**

formal diversion programs **288**

juvenile drug courts **300**

low-level youthful offenders **287**

National Reentry Resource Center **283**

net-widening effect (diversion) **299**

screening **292**

The Council of State Governments **283**

DISCUSSION QUESTIONS

1. Why might a focus on diversion, as compared with formal juvenile court involvement or delinquency adjudication, be important for most low-level, status, and first-time offenders?

2. If you were a probation department supervisor, what policies would you develop for informal diversion? In other words, which young people would be diverted away and which young people should come under formal diversion services with the juvenile court? Justify your policies and decisions with research evidence.

3. What does evidence-based practice mean, and why do certain delinquency prevention efforts work?

4. What options does a police officer have when dealing with a youthful offender, and what factors might impact his or her decision?

5. What are the differences between risk and needs assessments? How are they best used and by whom in the juvenile justice system? What about gender and cultural assessment implications?

6. What are the concerns about the net-widening effect of diversion? If this is the case, what can be done to address the problem?

7. What is a meta-analysis study, and what research-to-practice implications does this type of evaluation offer? What are the key findings of some meta-analytic studies on juvenile court involvement and programming?

8. Why have some local communities and states more readily adopted rehabilitative and reform efforts within their juvenile justice system? What issues or factors might have influenced these stakeholders in moving away from the last generation's "tough-on-crime" approach to its juvenile courts and, in particular, with low-level offenders?

9. How would you work with or address someone who believes that "nothing works" when dealing with youthful offenders and that they should just be prosecuted and dealt with harshly?

10. How do graduated sanctions work within probation supervision? How are these protocols similar or different than graduated sanctions used in school's codes of conduct and discipline protocols (see the earlier text example of the Nashville Public School District, Chapter 12)?

---

https://edge.sagepub.com/mallett

$SAGE edge™ **Sharpen your skills with SAGE edge!**

SAGE edge for students provides a personalized approach to help you accomplish your coursework in an easy-to-use learning environment. You'll find mobile-friendly eFlashcards and quizzes, as well as videos, web resources, and links to SAGE journal articles to support and expand on the concepts presented in this chapter.

CHAPTER 14

REHABILITATION OF SERIOUS AND CHRONIC YOUTHFUL OFFENDERS

▲ Serious youthful offenders often spend time in detention or incarceration facilities. Do you think this is an approach the juvenile courts should continue to use?

The Washington Post/Getty Images

INTRODUCTION

A dolescents who become mired in offending behaviors and with the juvenile courts over time are the most difficult to divert from ongoing troubles. The youthful offenders who are involved with the juvenile justice system at earlier ages and are adjudicated delinquent in their early adolescence, and those placed outside of their home into detention and incarceration facilities, are at greatest risk for ongoing felony convictions and recidivism. As discussed in Chapter 7, two types of delinquent offenders have been identified—adolescence-limited and life-course-persistent. It is this latter group that tends to continue committing offending behaviors into adulthood (Moffitt, 1993). Also, this group is often referred to as serious and chronic youthful offenders and for some includes gang involvement or membership (Furdello & Puzzanchera, 2015).

This chapter is focused on how to effectively work with and rehabilitate many of these more serious and entrenched adolescents within the juvenile justice system. In so doing, the following is addressed: using a developmentally appropriate framework in working with this population, including appropriate and necessary legal representation, juvenile competency standards, and in decisions to transfer a youthful offender to the adult criminal justice system; detention reform; incorporating a rehabilitative model within juvenile justice incarceration facilities, with an emphasis on education; focusing on reentry and return to the youthful offenders' communities; effective gang prevention efforts; and racial and ethnic disparities.

JUVENILE JUSTICE: A DEVELOPMENTAL FRAMEWORK

Most serious and chronic youthful offenders become involved at early ages with the juvenile or adult courts. The juvenile justice system is most effective when its stakeholders' (judges, magistrates, probation officers, and administrators) decision-making and resources are guided by what is most appropriate for adolescents. Because adolescents are not young adults, their needs are different, their learning ongoing, they are impulsive and risk taking, and they have a limited ability to comprehend long-term consequences. Accounting for and acknowledging these adolescent developmental differences is important in reducing serious and chronic youthful offending and recidivism (Bonnie, Johnson, Chemers, & Schuck, 2013).

Access to Counsel

In *re Gault* (1967), the Supreme Court ruled that youthful offenders facing delinquency proceedings must be afforded the **right to legal counsel**, along with other due process rights. Even though the right to counsel is guaranteed, often youthful offenders or parents waive this right, something allowed in most states. Some other states, however, require proof of indigence before providing a court-appointed attorney. Ten states—Georgia, Illinois, Iowa, Kentucky, Michigan, Mississippi, New York, North Carolina, Pennsylvania, and Wisconsin—prohibit or limit the waiver of counsel for youthful offenders, leaving 80% of the country's juvenile court jurisdictions not guaranteeing this right (MacArthur Foundation, 2015). Trends across the states over the past decade, however, have been toward increasing legal representation and limiting youthful offenders' abilities to deny counsel. Although these limitations vary, they include prohibiting the waiver

Serious and Chronic Youthful Offenders: Adolescents who become mired in offending behaviors and/or gangs over time. This group is the most difficult to divert from ongoing troubles.

Right to Legal Counsel: Constitutionally guaranteed right to legal counsel for any individual charged with an offense or crime by the courts.

▲ Youthful offenders are entitled to an attorney during their adjudication process. Why do you think many youthful offenders waive their right to counsel?

based on the young person's age or offense type, meaningful consultation with an attorney before waiver can be decided, having parents be present or consulted, and requiring the waiver to be voluntary and knowing (National Juvenile Defender Center, 2016).

Youthful offenders can be assigned and represented by counsel in three ways: (1) assigned counsel whereby private attorneys are appointed by judges on an ad hoc basis or oversight assignment system; (2) by contract whereby private attorneys, law firms, or nonprofit organizations are used by the local or state entities; or (3) through public defender offices, where public or private nonprofit entities employ full- or part-time attorneys. In many states and jurisdictions, the more common of these three attorney assignment systems is the public defender office; and if funded adequately, salaried and specially trained attorneys can more effectively represent their clients when compared with private attorneys, law firms, or other legal organizations (Gohara, Hardy, & Hewitt, 2005; Majd & Puritz, 2009).

The concern for the young people who waive their right to counsel is that developmentally they are typically unable to appreciate their legal rights or the longer term consequences of their decisions, as well as being susceptible to coercion by adults (Grisso & Schwartz, 2000). For these and other reasons, numerous national stakeholder organizations have developed guidelines for standards of practice in guaranteeing access to counsel and in the representation of youthful offenders. Because of the relative benefits, compared with other alternatives (assigned counsel or by contract), of using public defenders to represent youthful offenders, the **National Juvenile Defender Center** and the **National Legal Aid and Defender Association** have identified ten core principles to guide the public defense delivery system.

These principles are as follows: (1) uphold juveniles' Constitutional rights throughout the delinquency process and recognize the need for competent and diligent representation; (2) recognize that legal representation of children is a specialized area of law; (3) support quality juvenile delinquency representation through personnel and resource parity; (4) use expert and ancillary services to provide quality juvenile defense services; (5) supervise attorneys and staff and monitor work and caseloads; (6) supervise and systematically review juvenile law staff according to national, state, or local guidelines; (7) provide and require comprehensive, ongoing training for all attorneys and support staff; (8) present independent treatment and disposition alternatives to the court; (9) advocate for the educational needs of children; and (10) promote fairness and equity for children (National Legal Defender Center and the National Legal Aid and Defender Association, 2008). In addition, the National Juvenile Defender Center has developed thorough national standards for youthful offender defense practice and policy. These standards cover the role of the attorney from earliest juvenile justice stages to case closure and recognize juvenile defense as a specialized practice, requiring ongoing training, evaluation, and leadership (National Juvenile Defender Center, 2012).

Juvenile Competency

Competency for legal purposes refers to a young person's ability to understand and participate in proceedings—hearings and trials, among others. This understanding should include several areas—the nature of the charges against them, the roles of the people involved in the proceedings, appropriate decision-making, and whether to testify on their own behalf. Historically, these standards have been based on adult competency standards and the *Dusky v. United States* Supreme Court decision (362 U.S. 402, 1960).

The **National Center for Juvenile Justice** has reviewed current state law for determining juvenile competency. This analysis identified the following that are being used: specific

National Juvenile Defender Center: Nonprofit organization dedicated to promoting justice for all children by ensuring excellence in juvenile defense.

National Legal Aid and Defender Association: Nation's largest nonprofit membership organization dedicated to equal justice and legal representation for all.

National Center for Juvenile Justice: Research division of the National Council of Juvenile and Family Court Judges (NCJFCJ). NCJFCJ is the largest organization in the country representing juvenile court judges and magistrates.

AP Photo/Steven Georges, Pool

Juvenile Competency

State	Legal Authority	Factors	Definitions	Dusky Standard	Age as Factor	Procedures	Recent Law	Transfer Procedures
Alabama	■	■		■				
Alaska								
Arizona	■		■	■	■	■		
Arkansas	■	■		■	■			
California	■	■		■		■		
Colorado	■		■	■		■		
Connecticut	■			■	■	■	■	■
Delaware	■	■	■	■		■	■	
Dist. of Columbia	■		■	■		■		■
Florida	■	■		■		■		
Georgia	■	■	■	■	■	■	■	■
Hawaii								
Idaho	■	■		■	■	■	■	
Illinois	■			■				
Indiana	■	■				■		
Iowa	■			■		■		
Kansas	■			■		■		
Kentucky	■			■				■
Louisiana	■	■	■	■		■		■
Maine	■	■		■	■	■	■	■
Maryland	■	■	■	■	■	■		■
Massachusetts	■			■				
Michigan	■	■		■	■	■	■	
Minnesota	■	■		■		■		
Mississippi								

Source: Szymanski, Linda A. 2013. Juvenile Competency Procedures. *JJGPS StateScan*. Pittsburgh, PA: National Center for Juvenile Justice. Reprinted with permission.

laws or the *Dusky* decision, juvenile definitions, factor determination (age and others), and transfer to criminal court procedural rules. Almost all states (the exceptions are Alaska, Hawaii, Mississippi, Oklahoma, Oregon, and Rhode Island) have either new state laws (the 30 listed below) or modified their juvenile competency review standards away from adult only standards.

Nevertheless, over the past decade, 30 states have passed legislation to determine specific juvenile competency and standing trial standards (Szymanski, 2013; see Figure 14.1). Many of these state juvenile competency standards are similar in language to Georgia's, whereby it is statutorily defined as "[i]ncompetent to proceed means lacking sufficient present ability to understand the nature and object of the proceedings, to comprehend his or her own situation in relation to the proceedings and to assist his or her attorney in the preparation and presentation of his or her case in adjudication, disposition, or transfer hearings" (O.C.G.A. 15–11–153, 2010). North Dakota further instructs the need to identify four factors relevant to determine whether evidence at trial should have reasonably raised a doubt about the youthful offender's competence: irrational behavior, demeanor before trial, any prior medical opinions on competency, and any questioning of competency by counsel (Szymanski, 2013).

These modifications are important in differentiating youthful from adult offenders' competency for a variety of reasons. Based on today's understanding of adolescent and young adult development, much of the person, biology, brain chemistry, and other influences mark how adolescents are different. In addition, there can be issues concerning mental health problems, intellectual disabilities (special education status), and cognitive limitations. These differences and potential impairments make adolescents developmentally immature and pose difficulties in managing and understanding complex legal issues. Evidence has convincingly found that adolescents, and in particular those who are 14 years of age or younger, are not equipped to participate or assist in their own trials (MacArthur Foundation, 2006; National Juvenile Justice Network, 2012; Scott & Steinberg, 2008a).

Juvenile Court Jurisdiction and Transfers to Criminal Court

Tens of thousands of youthful offenders are transferred to the adult criminal justice system every year. As discussed earlier in the text, some of these transfers are through automatic laws based on offender age and offense type that do not take into account an adolescent's history, age, maturity, or other rehabilitative concerns. Transfers of adolescents to the adult criminal justice system are controversial because they divide the serious and chronic youthful offender population into

▼ FIGURE 14.1

30 States With Juvenile Competency Laws

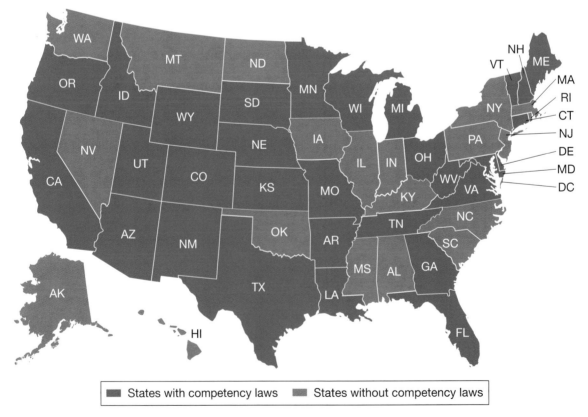

■ States with competency laws   ■ States without competency laws

Source: Data from MacArthur Foundation, 2015, p. 28.

a group determined amenable to rehabilitation and a group less amenable and more appropriate for punishment. Once transferred, the adolescent is treated as an adult with adult sentencing laws and sent to prisons if convicted; institutions that rarely protect the young person or offer educational or rehabilitative programming (Redding, 2010; Sickmund & Puzzanchera, 2014).

Developmentally, few adolescents can cope with the adult criminal justice system or incarceration. Beyond not understanding their legal rights or the legal procedures, they are less able to work with their legal counsel or make knowing and reasonable long-term decisions due to lower maturity and reasoning abilities. Those who work in the adult criminal justice system are not trained to work with this age cohort, often assuming they are adults. When incarcerated, these adolescents are more likely to suffer abuse and trauma, to develop mental health problems, and to have few educational or employment opportunities upon release (MacArthur Foundation, 2015).

▲ Juvenile detention centers are found across most counties. When do you think it is best to place a youthful offender in a center?

DETENTION REFORM

Serious and chronic youthful offenders are likely to be detained and/or incarcerated in either juvenile or adult facilities, and they are most at risk to continue offending patterns into adulthood. Nevertheless, this continued offending outcome is not a fixed pathway for many of these youthful offenders can be deterred or rehabilitated. Detention center efforts can desist youthful offending through various interventions; however, individual lengths of stay vary in length of time and impact (Degue & Widom, 2009; Howell, 2003).

Detention centers are typically used for youthful offenders who are awaiting a court appearance or disposition, and stays are best when short term. They are not designed nor programmed for longer term detainment of this population. The detention of youthful offenders is best limited to those who have committed a serious offense and who pose a clear danger to public safety due to a high risk of their reoffending. Nevertheless, detaining youthful offenders in and of itself does little to improve delinquent behaviors or offending outcomes and, in certain circumstances, causes harm by lowering functioning levels and increasing mental health problems and recidivism risk (Loughran et al., 2009; Winokur et al., 2008). Nevertheless, when detention centers incorporate the identification of youthful offender delinquency risk factors, include subsequent rehabilitative efforts, and move away from a punitive framework, outcomes can be significantly improved (Models for Change, 2011; Sedlak & McPherson, 2010).

With racial and ethnic disparities found across most detention facilities, there are concerns that even rehabilitative approaches within the centers won't address or reduce this problem. The use of certain risk assessment instruments that use past offending or juvenile justice involvement as criteria in determining level of reoffending risk may perpetuate a higher risk for youthful offenders of color. This use would subsequently identify more minority offenders as higher risk and in need of juvenile court supervision because past offending or involvement with the juvenile justice system is counted as additional risk. And minority youthful offenders have a higher level of past offending or involvement. Within detention facilities, beyond risk assessment, it is important to adopt strategies to assist those young people of color. In doing so, it is important to build strong collaborations across families and community stakeholders, as well as to use data collection and analysis to help dispel myths and misperceptions, which more directly address racial and ethnic disparities (Office of Juvenile Justice and Delinquency Prevention, 2009; The Burns Institute, 2015).

JUVENILE DETENTION ALTERNATIVES INITIATIVE (JDAI)

The Annie E. Casey Foundation has taken a leadership role through advocacy and training efforts with the Juvenile Detention Alternatives Initiative (JDAI). JDAI works to decrease the use of detention through collaboration across child welfare, mental health, schools, and social service agencies, builds community-based rehabilitative alternatives, uses standardized assessment instruments to identify those most likely to reoffend, and uses data collection within juvenile courts to direct decision-making. JDAI has also focused on identifying specific strategies to address and reduce the disproportionate detention of youthful offenders of color. Results, depending on length of implementation, have been significant in the more than 300 jurisdictions across 39 states in which the Initiative has been involved. These include the following: the lowering of detention populations and reoffending rates, sometimes by greater than 40% and state incarceration placements by more than 34%; reducing the number of youthful offenders of color in detention; and in some communities evening the odds that youthful offenders of color are detained after arrest (McCarthy, Schiraldi, & Shark, 2016).

These efforts have freed up limited juvenile justice system resources to be used for more productive and cost-effective programming. For example, in Albuquerque, New Mexico, JDAI reduced the detention center population by 44% through reorganization of the juvenile court's resources, as well as by expanding innovated, community-based treatment alternatives. Ultimately, juvenile court staff members in this jurisdiction were reassigned from the two closed secure detention facilities that were no longer needed to front-end delinquency diversion and treatment services (diversion, mental health, and school-based, to name a few), shifting the emphasis to prevention (The Annie E. Casey Foundation, 2009, 2012).

. . . .

1. Why do you think the JDAI approach is effective?

2. Why is it important that the use of detention (and incarceration) be decreased across the juvenile justice system?

INCARCERATION

Many incarcerated youthful offenders do not receive services that may assist in mitigating the influence of prior offending behavior or address problems that may have led to offending (Schubert & Mulvey, 2014). Many, but not all, incarceration facilities use punitive approaches. Nevertheless, recognition is growing that a rehabilitative approach better achieves important public policy goals of decreasing youthful offender recidivism and, subsequently, increasing community safety. There is evidence that incarceration facilities that identify adolescent risk factors and provide treatment services can have a significant impact on decreasing reoffending upon release (Armelius & Andreassen, 2007; Garrido & Morales, 2007; Texas Appleseed, 2011).

Facility Programming

Numerous programming designs shift from a punitive to a rehabilitative paradigm inside incarceration facilities. These include behavior management, individual counseling, skill building (improving anger management skills, for example), group counseling, education, and vocational training. In addition, though, when such rehabilitative interventions are used, they must be well designed, of high quality, and of sufficient duration to have an impact (Hoge, 2001; Lipsey, 2009). Incorporating treatment and rehabilitation for incarcerated youthful offenders is important because the trauma, mental health, and education-related problems of this population are pervasive. As discussed earlier in the text, most of those incarcerated suffer from at least one serious or significant problem; however, many deal with comorbid difficulties while incarcerated (see Table 14.2). Of the serious youthful offenders in these facilities, few receive necessary behavioral health services and even fewer access coordinated care upon release (Schubert & Mulvey, 2014).

Nevertheless, several specific programs and interventions have been found effective, and are used in some more progression facilities: Aggression Replacement Training (ART),

Juvenile Detention Alternatives Initiative (JDAI): Part of the Annie E. Casey Foundation that works to decrease the use of detention through collaboration across child welfare, mental health, schools, and social service agencies, along with data-driven decision-making.

Problems for Incarcerated Serious Youthful Offenders

Problem Type	Incarcerated Youthful Offender Population (%)
Maltreatment victimization	26–60
Special education disabilities (learning disabilities and emotional disturbances)	28–45
Mental health disorders	35–80
Substance abuse	30–70

Source: Schubert & Mulvey (2014). *Behavioral health problems, treatment, and outcomes in serious youthful offenders.* Office of Juvenile Justice and Delinquency Prevention, Office of Justice Programs, U.S. Department of Justice.

cognitive-behavioral therapy, sex offender programming, Functional Family Therapy, and the Family Integrated Transitions Program. Aggression Replacement Training uses certain cognitive-behavioral techniques to identify anger triggers, improve behavioral skills, and increase adolescent pro-social skills; cognitive-behavioral therapy focuses on a step-by-step curriculum to affect change; and the Family Integrated Transitions Program uses a combination of interventions (Multisystemic Therapy, relapse prevention, etc.) to address adolescent mental health and substance abuse problems and to ease transitions back to the community after facility release (Aos, 2004; Greenwood, 2008; Lipsey & Landenberger, 2006; Washington State Institute for Public Policy, 2007).

Missouri is a state that has taken the lead for over two decades in moving away from serious youthful offender incarceration through the use of rehabilitative facilities. The lead state agency, Missouri Division of Youth Services, first closed the larger state incarceration institutions (called "training schools"), divided the state into five regions, and developed a continuum of programs—day treatment, nonsecure group homes, medium-security facilities, and secure-care facilities—within each region. The facilities house only 40–50 young people and are further grouped into family-size units. The facilities' philosophy revolves around strong, supportive peer and adult relationships using the positive youth development approach that becomes the focus of compliance and security and not coercive approaches. Each young person has an individualized treatment planning including restorative justice practices. Families are involved at the inception of placement for therapy, case management, and reentry planning. Recidivism reoffending rates for youthful offenders across the state is 31% annually (a 50% decrease), and only 12% of all serious and chronic youthful offenders are returned to the facilities or committed to an adult prison within three years (a nearly 60% decrease; Bonnie et al., 2013; Mendel, 2011).

California has also made a significant turnaround since 2007. Prior to then, California had some of the highest youthful offender incarceration rates in the country (10,000 youthful offenders in 11 facilities) due to a tough-on-crime juvenile justice approach and a law that allowed county judges to commit youthful offenders to state institutions at no cost to the county. In 2016, there were 700 youthful offenders in three facilities. There were two reasons for this drastic decrease: a 1996 law that required counties to pay part of the correctional facility cost for certain low-level offenders and a 2007 "Juvenile Justice Realignment" law that limits the types of offenders who can be committed to the facilities, as well as provides community-based funding with the state incarceration cost savings. Efforts continue across California to further limit the incarceration of serious and chronic youthful offenders, as well as to decrease some of the transfers of youthful offenders to criminal courts (Little Hoover Commission, 2008; The Annie E. Casey Foundation, 2016).

▲ Juvenile incarceration facilities can be designed to be rehabilitative, focusing on helping the young person upon release. How do you think this can work?

Spencer Weiner/Los Angeles Times via Getty Images

National Youthful Offender Incarceration

Progress has also been made nationwide. Incarceration rates for juvenile justice facilities across the country have been reduced by more than half since 2000. Of those youthful offenders held in larger state correctional facilities (more than 200 beds), placement has decreased more dramatically by 66% between 2001 and 2013. These changes have led to the closure of 970 state juvenile facilities nationwide from 2002 to 2012, a 33% decline (Rovner, 2015).

Larger states have made more dramatic changes in these youthful offender incarcerations. In Alabama, executive and judicial leadership, initiated through the Juvenile Detention Alternatives Initiative, decreased the state incarceration facility population by 46% from 2007 to 2014, thereby reallocating funding to nonresidential, community-based services. In New York, a combination of strong state leadership and litigation around lack of quality conditions and mental healthcare has downsized or closed two dozen juvenile justice incarceration facilities, correspondingly decreasing the population by more than 73%. In addition, the Closer to Home Program in New York City is used to keep serious youthful offenders closer to their homes in small (24 bed) facilities. In Ohio, juvenile institutional placements decreased from 2,200 in 2002 to 700 in 2015, allowing the state to close three of its eight facilities. Within the remaining institutions across Ohio, a culture shift across most facilities has also occurred, moving away from punishment and control to positive development and treatment. And in Texas, strong advocacy efforts by the Texas Criminal Justice Coalition, Texas Appleseed, and Texans Care for Children, and a state reform bill that passed because of abuse by staff that had occurred within the facilities, led to a 63% reduction in the incarcerated youthful offender population, with many of these dollars being reallocated to the juvenile courts to fund diversion programs (McCarthy et al., 2016; National Juvenile Justice Network, 2011; Ohio Department of Youth Services, 2015).

Effective Education in the Detention and Incarceration Facilities

Contact with the juvenile justice system, from arrests to incarceration, has been clearly established to harm student education progress and school outcomes, with only three in ten incarceration facility-released youthful offenders engaged in school or work 12 months after reentry (Aizer & Doyle, 2013; Zajac, Sheidow, & Davis, 2013). Part of the problem is that education within the incarceration facilities is ineffective for most youthful offenders. When a young person is placed in pre-adjudication detention with length of stays that range from a few days to a few months, or a correctional facility where lengths of stay range from 3 to more than 36 months, the obligation to continue education services remains, and it is particularly necessary for those students with special education disabilities and subsequent Individualized Education Plans (Boundy & Karger, 2011; Musgrove & Yudin, 2014).

Coordination between the juvenile courts' detention facilities and schools is impeded by poor school records transfers, instructional communication, and appropriate coursework. Within longer term correctional facilities, the education services and instructional strategies vary widely: The programs are often less rigorous than traditional schools, are not aligned with grade-level standards, often not monitored by state education officials, and many times prerelease planning is not conducted, leading to enrollment barriers and loss of academic credit (Bahena, Cooc, Currie-Rubin, Kuttner, & Ng, 2012; Mears & Travis, 2004).

Educational programming within the institutions is most effective when educational plans are coordinated with home schools, when higher quality teachers are employed, and

Reasoned and Equitable Community and Local Alternatives to the Incarceration of Minors (RECLAIM) Program: This program was designed to divert youthful offenders from the state of Ohio juvenile justice incarceration facilities through funding to local counties for appropriate programs to target delinquency and serious youthful offending.

RECLAIM OHIO

In 1993, the state of Ohio created the *Reasoned and Equitable Community and Local Alternatives to the Incarceration of Minors (RECLAIM) Program*. This program was designed to divert youthful offenders from the Ohio Department of Youth Services state juvenile justice incarceration facilities to keep them in their communities. RECLAIM funding was provided for local counties to make available appropriate programs to target delinquency and serious youthful offending. Thus, this system of funding incentivized the county juvenile courts to develop and use community-based rehabilitative and diversion alternatives by capping the state allocations for incarceration and moving these dollars where they can have the most diversion impact.

The Program expanded as the youthful offender needs were identified. This includes the Behavioral Health and Juvenile Justice Initiative that supports evidence-based community programs for those youthful offenders with mental health and/or substance use impairments. The RECLAIM program has incorporated several effective strategies with successful outcomes: using a validated risk assessment tool is important to identify low-, moderate-, and high-risk youthful offenders; low- and moderate-risk offenders are best diverted from incarceration for the experience makes offending recidivism three times more likely upon release; and high-risk youthful offenders who received community-based RECLAIM services had much lower felony adjudication and incarceration placement rates compared to those without the services. Thus, RECLAIM has saved between $11 and $45 in state incarceration facility costs for every $1 spent while reducing incarceration placements by more than 80% (Latessa, Lovins, & Lux, 2014).

1. What should the state of Ohio do with the cost savings found through the RECLAIM program?

2. Why do you think RECLAIM Ohio is effective?

when correctional and educational staff work together in their efforts throughout the classroom. In addition, schools within these facilities can improve their learning environment and education outcomes by moving away from harsh discipline protocols and incorporating appropriate restorative practices, focusing on social-emotional learning and development, offering flexible and individualized curriculum, incorporating positive behavior protocols to engage students, building social skills, and promoting positive relationship building across students and staff (Karger, Rose, & Boundy, 2012; Osher, Bear, Sprague, & Doyle, 2010). Specific programs that are effective and more fully reviewed in Chapter 12, in both traditional and alternative schools, include School-Wide Positive Behavior Interventions and Supports, a tiered and graduated management approach that focuses on positive steps in managing difficult behaviors, and increased conflict resolution and cultural competency training for teachers and staff (Gregory, Allen, Mikami, Hafen, & Pianta, 2012).

Without continued education and a quick and seamless reentry to their school, the chances for reoffending and school dropout significantly increase. To avoid these outcomes, it is important to designate a transition coordinator in the school to work with the juvenile courts, families, and school staff; develop reenrollment guidelines within the school system; and have returning students reenroll as soon as possible from institutional release (The Sentencing Project, 2012). The U.S. Departments of Education and Justice strongly recommend that formal procedures be established through state legislative statutes. This includes memoranda of understanding and/or practices that ensure successful navigation across youth-caring systems as well as meaningful planning that is focused on reentry of youthful offenders back into their communities and home school (U.S. Department of Education & U.S. Department of Justice, 2014).

▲ It is difficult to transition to and from a school in a locked facility. What do you think would make this an easier process?

Residential Treatment Centers

Residential treatment centers are an alternative to incarceration for youthful offenders with serious emotional, behavioral, and/or substance use problems who are in need of more structure than nonsecured, community-based treatment. These facilities are typically operated within the private mental health or substance abuse youth-caring systems and offer an array of intervention services, behavior management, 24-hour supervision, counseling (individual, group, family), and medication management. Residential treatment centers differ significantly from group homes that are commonly used within the juvenile justice system and that provide daily living care and assistance but infrequent therapeutic treatment services. Many juvenile courts have recognized that they are not equipped to be mental health or substance abuse program providers. Thus, up to one third of these facility referrals come from the juvenile courts (Hockenberry, Wachter, & Sladky, 2016).

Residential treatment centers have an established history of providing mental health treatment; however, although the outcomes are encouraging, there is still a need for improved evaluation designs, including more frequent and rigorous studies with consistent recidivism and functioning measurements. Still some findings for youthful offenders with serious mental health or behavioral problems are positive, for their recidivism rates are significantly improved compared with similarly situation offenders in juvenile justice facilities (Bettman & Jasperson, 2009; Leichtman, Leichtman, Barber, & Neese 2001). In addition, there have been substantial reductions in mental health and substance abuse symptoms, orientation to treatment, and improved family and social functioning for this population (Hooper, Murphy, Devaney, & Hultman, 2000; Lyons, Baerger, Quigley, Erlich, & Griffin, 2001). These positive outcomes have been found associated with increased family involvement, shorter lengths of placement, and involvement with after-care programming. Nevertheless, residential facility placements longer than two years may cause regression in negative symptoms and behaviors (Armelius & Andreassen, 2007; Smith, Duffee, Steinke, Huang, & Larkin, 2008).

REENTRY AND RETURN HOME

More than 38,000 youthful offenders are confined on any given day in juvenile state correctional facilities and an additional 18,000 in detention facilities; almost every one of these young people will return to their homes or communities upon release. Although these placement and confinement numbers have been decreasing significantly since 2002, this still entails a significant number who are facing difficulties and barriers to a successful release (Sickmund & Puzzanchera, 2014). These challenges include reenrolling in school, continuing or accessing mental health or substance abuse treatment, avoiding negative or harmful peers, and finding job-ready training and employment, among others.

Reentry is the process of preparing these youthful offenders to make a successful transition back home from confinement. This process is most successful when planning begins at the early stages of placement and continues with the youthful offender during confinement, post-release, and after-care upon returning home. Families (immediate family members, extended family, and other important adults) should be involved as extensively as is possible, including engagement, treatment, and planning for return home. It is important to collaborate with

Residential Treatment Centers: Alternative to incarceration for youthful offenders with serious emotional, behavioral, and/or substance use problems who are in need of more structure than nonsecured, community-based treatment.

youth-caring systems and providers to determine the best level of supervision in the community, what services are available, and as discussed earlier, strong coordination with the school district and home school. Probation departments are more effective when they use a developmental approach with the adolescents and promote and expand pro-social behaviors and job skills training. In doing so, it is important to take into account the young person's gender, age, and social and functioning abilities (Federal Interagency Reentry Council, 2015).

Reentry grants provided by the U.S. Department of Justice require local communities who receive the funds to establish a task force that effectively coordinates services across mental health agencies, housing, child welfare, schools, victims services, and employment/training options for young people:

> Palm Beach County, Florida, for example, has developed an effective multidisciplinary task force that meets regularly to discuss policies related to court-involved youth. Led by a juvenile court judge, the task force provides an ongoing structure for agencies to collaborate to reform policies and practices in the best interest of youth served across agencies. Through the work of the task force, these agencies have been able to partner with the Palm Beach County School District to ensure a smoother educational transition for youth returning after confinement, and they have modified the county's existing web-based, multiagency, case management data warehouse to enhance communication with service providers. (Seigle et al., 2014, p. 63)

One of the important components of Palm Beach County, Florida, juvenile justice system's efforts is the ongoing assessment of the youthful offender. These standardized assessments identify the level of offending/recidivism risk, as well as the goals and strategies to help with reentry planning. Assessment findings identify treatment needs and are incorporated through the use of evidence-based components including cognitive-behavioral interventions to help develop pro-social skills, family engagement, and permanency planning (Altschuler & Bilchik, 2014). In similar efforts, Pennsylvania has developed a comprehensive after-care model framework for youthful offenders placed into residential facilities. This integrated plan is established early at disposition and directs care throughout the placement. During this time, the following is reviewed by the young person, his or her family, and the probation officer: progress and performance in placement; anticipated postrelease expectations for school, work, and living arrangements; expectations for transition, immediate engagement, and reintegration during all postrelease phases; and activities that need to be completed by the young person. Within this planning phase, there is a broad focus and inclusion of youthful offender accountability, improving skills and competencies (education, employment, leisure time usage), establishing family supports as needed, and linking to community-based services (Torbet, 2008).

GANG MEMBERSHIP AND PREVENTION

Gang membership and activity in communities and schools grew throughout the 1980s and peaked during the mid-1990s. After a precipitous decline through 2004, gang membership has increased across rural, suburban, and urban locations since; however, some declines have been found since 2012. Most of this gang activity has been concentrated in urban areas. Studies have identified that approximately 8% of adolescents report belonging to or having belonged to a gang, with typical length of involvement around one year. These percentages are higher (9% to 32%) for cities with known gang problems. The peak age for joining a gang is 14 and 15 years of age. Some locations and reviews have found gang membership to be disproportionately minority (black, Hispanic/Latino), whereas others have found membership to be fairly even across ethnicity. Historically, boys have outnumbered girls in reported gang membership two to one, yet more recent reports of urban locations have found a fairly even split across gender, with both

boys and girls reporting membership around 8% (Egley, Howell, & Harris, 2014; Esbensen, Peterson, Taylor, & Freng, 2010; Sickmund & Puzzanchera, 2014).

Involvement with gangs or gang activity is typically the result of an accumulation of individual, family, school, and community risk factors or difficulties. The more influential risks are when young people are involved with the juvenile courts and delinquency at earlier ages, have numerous family and caretaking transitions (a result of maltreatment, trauma, and/or poverty, for example), experience school problems and failure, have friends who are delinquent or gang involved, and live in unsafe neighborhoods. In addition, children and adolescents who are delinquent with more serious and violent offending histories are more likely to become gang involved (Howell, 2010).

▲ Youth gangs have been around for decades. What do you think would prevent troubled young people from joining a gang?

Gang prevention or desistance from membership is often difficult. Although many delinquency and offending prevention and intervention efforts, as well as mental health and trauma treatments, for low-level offenders discussed in earlier text chapters are important for this population as well. Research has also found specific gang prevention programs to be effective: The Gang Resistance Education And Training (GREAT) Program is a school-based prevention curriculum where law enforcement officers work with middle school students and their families; the Preventive Treatment Program works with primary school-aged boys from poor communities and improves school performance and behavior, while working with parents to help prevent gang involvement; the Aggression Replacement Training (ART) program works with high school-aged students who are highly aggressive and delinquent (see Chapter 13); CeaseFire Chicago is a violence prevention program using public education campaigns and alternatives to violence; the OJJDP Comprehensive Gang Prevention, Intervention, and Suppression Model is a comprehensive approach to integrating outreach activities and services along with law enforcement surveillance; and the Boys and Girls Clubs Gang Prevention through Targeted Outreach program involves getting gang-involved young people into club activities to offer mentoring, alternative activities, and positive peer support (Esbensen, Osgood, Taylor, Peterson, & Freng, 2001; Esbensen, Peterson, Taylor, & Osgood, 2012; Howell, 2010; Skogan, Hartnett, Bump, & Dubois, 2008).

A second important area in reducing serious and chronic offending is the movement toward and requirement by states to use evidence-based practices and programs across the juvenile justice system and in incarceration facilities. As of 2015, 18 states had laws supporting a commitment to evidence-based programs in juvenile justice, and 28 additional states had lead juvenile justice agency administrative regulations requiring the use of these practices in some ways. In addition, 13 states (Colorado, California, Connecticut, Florida, Illinois, Louisiana, Maryland, Nebraska, New York, Ohio, Pennsylvania, Washington, and West Virginia) have established a support center or collaborative that implements and evaluates evidence-based programming within their juvenile justice systems (Thomas, Hyland, Deal, Wachter, & Zaleski, 2016; see Table 14.3).

Juvenile Justice Geography, Policy, Practice, and Statistics (JJGPS): Research-focused organization and part of the National Center for Juvenile Justice that provides state- and national-level juvenile justice data.

ADDRESSING RACIAL AND ETHNIC DISPARITIES

Many of the preventative and intervention efforts discussed throughout this text have or could effectively decrease the number of young people coming into contact or becoming formally involved and supervised by the juvenile courts. There is no guarantee through these efforts, though, that the disproportionate involvement of adolescents of color (as noted earlier in the text,

JUVENILE JUSTICE GEOGRAPHY, POLICY, PRACTICE, AND STATISTICS

The Juvenile Justice Geography, Policy, Practice, and Statistics (JJGPS) is a research-focused organization that is part of the National Center for Juvenile Justice. The JJGPS has surveyed and analyzed state juvenile justice and correctional facility stakeholders nationwide to document a wide range of topics: juvenile and adult system jurisdictional boundaries, juvenile defense, racial/ethnic fairness, juvenile justice services, and status offense issues, among others. Although this movement in the juvenile justice system and youthful offender detention and incarceration facilities has recognized the broad array of problems and needs of the adolescents involved, not all states require or include important procedures or programs for serious and chronic youthful offenders. One area is risk assessment/mental health screenings for those in the correctional facilities or for those at risk for incarceration. This JJGPS review of required mental health screenings found the following: 26% of states (13 of 50) require screening protocols for youthful offenders placed on probation; nearly 50% of states (24 of 50) require screenings for detention center admissions; and 60% of states (30 of 50) require screenings for those being placed into state-run juvenile corrections facilities. A significant majority of the time the screening tools used are the Massachusetts Youth Screening Instrument (MAYSI-2) and the Global Appraisal of Individual Need–Short Screen (GAIN-SS; Wachter, 2015).

See which states require mental health screenings and the tools that are used on the study site at edge.sagepub.com/mallett

I. **What is the link from mental health problems to serious youthful offending?**

2. **How have juvenile incarceration facilities become today's psychiatric hospitals?**

▼ TABLE 14.3

Evidence-Based Program State Support Centers

California	The Center for Evidence-Based Corrections at the University of California Irvine promotes the research-based policies and practices with empirical research.
Colorado	The Evidence-Based Practices Implementation for Capacity Resource Center within the Colorado Division of Criminal Justice assists agencies serving juvenile (and adult) justice populations to develop, implement, and sustain evidence-based practices.
Connecticut	The Court Support Services Division of the state judicial branch has established the Center for Best Practices to identify, promote, and monitor the use of evidence-based practices throughout the state.
Florida	The Department of Juvenile Justice's Programming and Technical Assistance Unit provides local support for the adoption of evidence-based practices throughout the state.
Illinois	The Illinois Criminal Justice Information Authority evaluates policies, programs, and legislation that address critical issues facing the juvenile justice systems.
Louisiana	The Institute for Public Health and Justice, within the Louisiana State University, is a policy, research, training, and technical assistance organization focused on health policy/practice and the justice system.
Maryland	The Institute for Innovation and Practice at the University of Maryland assists state and local partners in the implementation of evidence-based and promising practices.
Nebraska	The Juvenile Justice Institute (JJI) at the University of Nebraska-Omaha provides research-based information to stakeholders statewide as well as training and technical assistance across the juvenile justice system.
New York	The New York Division of Juvenile Justice Opportunities for Youth is responsible for quality assurance and has developed an evidence-based community initiative portfolio.
Ohio	The Center for Innovative Practices at Case Western Reserve University supports the proliferation of evidence-based programs and practices in juvenile justice.
Pennsylvania	The Evidence-based Prevention and Intervention Support Center at Penn State University supports the dissemination, quality implementation, sustainability, and impact assessment of effective preventions.
Washington	The Washington State Institute for Public Policy at Evergreen State College conducts practical, non-partisan research at the direction of the legislature or its Board of Directors.
West Virginia	The Justice Center for Evidence Based Practice supports research, effective planning/coordination and the use of evidence for informed decisions making.

Source: Wachter, A. (2015). *Mental health screening in juvenile justice services.* Juvenile Justice Geography, Policy, Practice & Statistics; National Center for Juvenile Justice, Pittsburgh, PA. Reprinted with permission.

JURISDICTIONS THAT REDUCED RACIAL AND ETHNIC DISPARITIES

Bernalillo County (including Albuquerque), New Mexico, is the largest county in New Mexico, and it has reduced racial disparities for African American, Hispanic, and Native American youthful offenders among law enforcement referrals to probation and diversions from court. To accomplish this, County stakeholders focused on systems reform, improving data collection and analysis, and increasing community-based services for court-involved young people. As a Juvenile Detention Alternatives Initiative (JDAI) location, another significant focus has been on reducing the number of young people who are detained and in reducing detention recidivism. To help with these efforts, Bernalillo County established a licensed mental health clinic adjacent to its detention facility to serve court-involved youths in the community and increased access to diversion for most youthful offenders coming into contact with the juvenile courts (Spinney et al., 2014).

1. Why do you think that so many young people in county detention centers suffer from significant mental health difficulties?

2. Why is the Juvenile Detention Alternatives Initiative (JDAI) program effective in detention reform?

called "disproportionate minority contact" or DMC) would change, even though the number of youthful offenders coming under probation supervision, detention, and incarceration has been significantly decreasing since 2002. In fact, although nationwide incarceration rates for youthful offenders decreased by half over this time period, the racial disparity between blacks and whites in correctional facilities grew by 15% (Henning, 2013; The Sentencing Project, 2016).

Addressing the disproportionate involvement of young people of color in the juvenile justice system is a multilayered problem. With decision-making points across the spectrum from investigations to arrests to formal supervision, and for some detention and incarceration, the answers are different for each community. This requires local- and state-driven efforts to identify the problems and then to find collaborative ways to address the causes. Two leading national organizations—**The Burns Institute** and Urban America Forward: Civil Rights Roundtable Series (an organization of over 60 civil rights leaders, scholars, and community organizers)—have highlighted policy and practice areas to address DMC and other, broader civil rights concerns. These recommendations and efforts highlight the need to go further than what the Juvenile Justice and Delinquency Prevention Acts (1988 and 2002 reauthorizations) have accomplished in requiring states to identify the racial and ethnic disparities as well as the causes, implement intervention strategies, and evaluate strategy effectiveness. Unfortunately, the Acts requirements do not include the actual reduction of racial and ethnic disparities; this could be addressed in future Congressional reauthorizations (National Resource Council, 2013).

The Urban America Forward's policy and practice framework encapsulates much of what others have recommended in shifting the juvenile justice system away from a punitive paradigm, addressing individual child and adolescent needs in a developmentally appropriate way, and focusing on early intervention (Urban America Forward, 2016). First, there needs to be a decrease in the criminalization of so many children and adolescents by increasing education about structural racism and inherent bias, child development, and the impact of trauma, as well as by increasing diversion programs and removing police officers from schools. Second, investment in local community solutions to youthful law violations needs to take place using developmentally appropriate responses. Third, the prosecution of young people in criminal courts and incarceration with adult offenders needs to end, as well as other extreme sentences. And, fourth, data must be required to understand and improve the decisions local stakeholders are making, and this information needs to be shared with the public in a transparent manner

The Burns Institute:
Leading national nonprofit organization focused on protecting and improving the lives of youthful and adult offenders of color by ensuring fairness and equity throughout the justice system.

(Ridolfi & Benson, 2016). The increasing racial and ethnic disparities in the juvenile justice system remain a serious problem across the country.

CASE STUDY

FROM "CORRECTIONAL VERSUS HOME-LIKE ATMOSPHERE" STORIES

Correctional . . . Picture MJ, a 16-year-old who is on his way to the Elm Tree Correctional Center to begin serving an 18-month sentence. He is shackled and placed in the back of a van with three other teenage boys. He knows one of the guys, with whom he has hung out in his neighborhood, but the uniformed correctional officer tells them to shut up when anybody starts to talk. After about three hours, they arrive at an old and dingy building surrounded by two tall fences topped with razor wire. One big gate opens, they pull the van forward, and before the next gate opens, the one behind them clanks closed. The van doors open, and another officer yells his last name and tells him to get moving. They are directed into a vestibule where the door behind them bangs shut loudly. Then, the door in front of them buzzes and unlocks, and MJ is directed into a small cell. He hears doors clanging, voices yelling, walkie-talkies squawking, somebody barking out orders. After a while, two officers come in. He is told to strip naked and they conduct a detailed search of his body, including body cavities. He is handed an orange jumpsuit, underwear, socks, and slip-on shoes—most of which have obviously been worn by others in the past—and ordered to put them on. He is then led down a long hallway and into a large room with metal tables in the center, bolted down, ringed by a series of metal doors, each with a small window, some of which have faces staring blankly out of them. He doesn't see any youth out of their cells in the common area. He is taken over to one of the doors, the officer unlocks it and tells him to go in, and then the door is locked behind him. His cot has a thin blanket on it, with no sheets or pillow on his plastic mattress, and there is a metal toilet-sink combination in one corner of the room. There is another bunk with another guy on it who was sleeping before he got there. His "cellie" just glares at him.

At the end of his first 24 hours in Elm Tree, MJ has no idea what to expect next. All he knows is that he has never felt so alone and afraid in his life.

. . . *Versus Home-Like Atmosphere* Now, picture DS, also 16 years old, who is on his way to the Back on Track House where he knows he will stay at least through the end of the school year, around six to nine months, depending on his behavior. He is driven about 10 minutes to the house by a guy who calls himself a "counselor" and wears khaki pants and a "Back on Track" polo shirt. DS recognizes the building and the block it's on; it's a former school just around the corner from the barber shop where his uncle works. When they arrive, the counselor walks him to the door and rings a doorbell. He notices a fence much like the one that was there when it was a school, but now there's no way to enter it or exit the school yard from the street. Another staff member opens the door, says hello, and escorts him into what used to be the principal's office, calling him by his first name and saying that he's been expecting him. The two counselors explain the need to pat him down, after which they walk him into a room with "Imani" (the name of the unit) posted in wooden letters on the outside. The room has some sofas and beanbag chairs in the middle, and some desks with computers on the side.

There are three or four guys there who immediately introduce themselves to him. One of them, RM, comes over and says he is to be DS's "buddy" to help him get settled and learn the ropes. With staff always within seeing and hearing range, RM takes DS down a short hallway with bedrooms on either side. The doors are open and he can see inside. Each has two beds; he can see people's clothes and some family pictures on the walls. They get to his room and he meets his roommate, who tells him not to look so scared, that this place could actually help him if he works the program. He points to a poster on the wall that lists what is expected of every resident; he, his roommate, and his "buddy" go over the house rules while staff look on, chiming in occasionally. They show him where the bathrooms are, down the hall, and tell him to wash up for dinner. In the dining room, he sits next to his roommate at one of the wooden tables, along with eight or nine other guys and a counselor. The food is passed around family style, and there is a moment of silence so people can pray if they want to (but they don't have to) before everyone starts eating. He is told that this room doubles as a place where kids' families come and visit, which is allowed most evenings and is required with counseling staff twice a month. (McCarthy et al., 2016, pp. 8–9)

1. **How does DS's experience differ from MJ's?**

2. **Which approach is more helpful for incarcerated youthful offenders, and why; justify your answer with research evidence.**

3. **If you were to design a correctional (detention or incarceration) facility, what programming and planning would you prioritize and why?**

Source: McCarthy, Schiraldi, & Shark (2016). "The Future of Youth Justice: A Community-Based Alternative to the Youth Prison Model." *New Thinking in Community Corrections Bulletin.* U.S. Department of Justice, National Institute of Justice.

CHAPTER REVIEW

CHAPTER SUMMARY

This chapter presented the important strategies and approaches to working with serious and chronic youthful offenders—those young people most at risk for detention, incarceration, and other poor long-term outcomes. In so doing, the problems with access to legal counsel and determining juvenile competency for trials and other court matters were explored, finding some progress and reforms that are developmentally appropriate being made at the state level. There has also been more recent, although not nationwide, changes made in moving incarceration facilities toward a rehabilitative model by addressing the risks and difficulties (family, mental health, trauma, etc.) youthful offenders bring to the facilities. Models of success were highlighted, showing that even chronic offenders, if provided the appropriate supports, can succeed in reentering their communities from an out-of-home placement. Nevertheless, it is important to prioritize addressing the pervasive problem of racial and ethnic disparities throughout the juvenile justice system and in using data-driven results to make policy and practice decisions.

KEY TERMS

Juvenile Detention Alternatives Initiative (JDAI) **314**

Juvenile Justice Geography, Policy, Practice, and Statistics (JJGPS) **321**

National Center for Juvenile Justice **310**

National Juvenile Defender Center **310**

National Legal Aid and Defender Association **310**

Reasoned and Equitable Community and Local Alternatives to the Incarceration of Minors (RECLAIM) Program **316**

residential treatment centers **318**

right to legal counsel **309**

serious and chronic youthful offenders **309**

The Burns Institute **322**

DISCUSSION QUESTIONS

1. What does approaching juvenile justice within a developmental adolescent framework mean? Is this the approach that should be taken? Justify your position with research evidence.

2. What does juvenile competency mean? Why have states moved away from using adult competency standards, and what has supported this approach? Are youthful offenders different from adult offenders; if so, how?

3. What is the impact of detention and incarceration on youthful offenders? What has worked in lowering detention and incarceration rates while maintaining community safety?

4. If you were a director of your local juvenile detention center and the facility had serious problems with managing the youthful offenders, keeping them safe, and with high recidivism rates, what would you do to address these problems over the next 24 months? Cover all areas of concern, education needs, mental health concerns, gender differences, racial and ethnic disparities, and reentry.

5. Now answer the same scenario in Question 4, but this time you are the director of your state's youthful offender incarceration facilities. These facilities have the same problems across the state.

6. How best can education outcomes be improved for youthful offenders in correctional facilities?

7. How can residential treatment centers be of use with serious and chronic youthful offenders?

8. Is gang membership a problem for the juvenile justice system? Justify your answer. If it is, what approaches are best in addressing the problem?

9. Go to the National Center for Juvenile Justice's JJGPS website (www.jjgps.org) and choose one of their major topic areas—jurisdictional boundaries, juvenile defense, racial/ethnic fairness, juvenile justice services, status offense issues, and systems integration. Next, write a summary of one of these areas' subtopics (for example, courtroom shackling under Juvenile Defense, or coordination under Systems Integration) that you believe is (a) most difficult to address, and (b) propose how to fix the problem based on evidence to date.

---

https://edge.sagepub.com/mallett

 **Sharpen your skills with SAGE edge!**

SAGE edge for students provides a personalized approach to help you accomplish your coursework in an easy-to-use learning environment. You'll find mobile-friendly eFlashcards and quizzes, as well as videos, web resources, and links to SAGE journal articles to support and expand on the concepts presented in this chapter.

GLOSSARY

Acute Trauma: Single traumatic event that is time limited, for example, a dog bite, accident, or natural disaster such as an earthquake or tornado.

Adolescence: Formative developmental stage that changes the young person rapidly and dramatically, but also in major social contexts, including within the family, in peer groups, and at school.

Adolescence-Limited Offenders: Phenomenon that most adolescents will discontinue delinquent and criminal activity on their own by age 16.

Adjudges: Jurist makes a decision; also, adjudicates.

Adjudicatory Hearing: Hearing in which the purpose is making a judicial ruling such as a judgment or decree. It is sometimes used in juvenile criminal cases as another term for a trial.

Aggravating Circumstances: Factors that increase the severity or culpability of a criminal act, including, but not limited to, heinousness of the crime, lack of remorse, and prior conviction of another crime.

Aging Out: When a young person reaches the age of majority (typically 18) in his or her state and is in foster care, he or she "ages out" by legally becoming an adult and no longer is supervised by the child welfare system.

A.L.I.C.E. (Action, Lockdown, Inform, Counter, Evacuate): Series of trainings for students on what to do during an active shooter situation.

Almshouses: Colonial-era, locked, one-room buildings that housed many types of people with many different problems, including troubled or orphaned children.

Alternative Education Program: Separate school, or part of a school building, where students are removed to because they were unsuccessful academically or behaviorally in their original classroom.

Anxiety Disorders: Class of mental health problems that includes various diagnoses: separation anxiety, panic disorder, agoraphobia, social phobia, overanxious disorder, and generalized anxiety disorder.

Assessments (Risk Assessments): Thorough investigation of the identified risks or problem areas for young people and their families.

Attention-Deficit Hyperactivity Disorder (ADHD): Behaviorally based mental health disorder primarily impacting children and adolescents who have attention problems or hyperactive control issues.

Attorney General: Principal legal officer who represents a country or a state in legal proceedings and provides legal advice to the government.

Behaviorally Based Disorders: Mental health problems and disorders that are externalized; in other words, where acting out or physical violence is involved.

Bullying (Cyberbullying): Three major types: physical, social, and verbal. These victimizations may occur in person and through Internet and social media connections (cyberbullying).

Bureau of Justice Assistance: Office of the U.S. Department of Justice and a component of the Office of Justice Programs that funds justice programming and directs federal initiatives.

Caution or Warning (Diversion) Programs: Least restrictive alternative that diverts a young person out of the juvenile justice system with no further action taken by the police.

Census Data: Data collected from everyone in the population of interest (e.g., all juveniles who are incarcerated).

Child Maltreatment Victimization: Four official, legal categories of child maltreatment: physical abuse, sexual abuse, emotional (psychological) abuse, and neglect (including medical), depending on state law definitions.

Child-Saving Movement: A 19th century movement that influenced the development of the juvenile courts and focused on the prevention of delinquency through education and training of young people.

Child Welfare System: U.S. government agency responsible for investigating child abuse and neglect allegations; also known as children's protective services (CPS).

Chronic Trauma: Varied and multiple traumatic events, often occurring over time, including domestic violence in the home as well as living in an unsafe and threatening neighborhood. This type of trauma could also be a long-standing or reoccurring problem such as physical abuse victimization.

Civil Courts: Courts dealing with noncriminal cases.

Codified: Arranging laws or rules into a systematic code; for example, state laws are codified.

Cognitive-Behavioral Therapy: Type of psychotherapy in which negative patterns of thought about the self and the world are challenged to alter unwanted behavior patterns or treat mood disorders such as depression.

Columbine High School Shooting: 1999 school shooting at Columbine High School in Colorado that remains one of the deadliest mass shootings in the United States and the deadliest high school shooting.

Comorbid (Comorbidity): Simultaneous presence of two problems (difficulties, diseases) in one person—for example, post-traumatic stress disorder (PTSD) and physical abuse for a child.

Competency: Mental capacity of an individual to participate in legal proceedings or transactions, and the mental condition a person must have to be responsible for his or her decisions or acts.

Complaint: First document filed with the court (actually with the County Clerk or Clerk of the Court) by a person or entity claiming legal rights against another. The party filing the complaint is usually called the "plaintiff" and the party against whom the complaint is filed is called the "defendant."

Complex Trauma: Chronic trauma caused by adults or caregivers of children (for example, sexual abuse) that is long term in nature.

Conduct Disorder: Behaviorally based mental health disorder diagnosed only for children or adolescents that includes severe acting out of physical aggression.

Confidentiality: Process of keeping juvenile court records and proceedings private.

Consent Decree: An agreement or settlement that resolves a dispute between two parties without admission of guilt (in a criminal case) or liability (in a civil case).

Control Variable: A characteristic (e.g., gender) that is held constant in statistical analysis to examine a relationship between two main variables (the independent and dependent variables).

Co-occurring Disorder: Coexistence of both a mental health problem and a substance use disorder.

Corporal Punishment: Disciplinary action that is physical in nature and delivered by teachers or school administrators as punishment for some type of student misbehavior.

Cost–Benefit Analysis: Systematic approach to estimating the strengths and weaknesses of alternatives; often a monetary approach finding the costs for programs and comparing with short- and long-term outcomes.

Crack Cocaine Epidemic: 1980s surge in the use of crack cocaine nationwide, but with the greatest impact in urban environments. This lead to increases in large city crime rates and influenced the shift toward a "tough-on-crime" approach.

Criminal Courts: Courts dealing with personal and property criminal cases.

Criminal Homicide: Killing of one person by another; often, first degree homicide is the most serious, requiring preplanning of the murder.

Crisis Intervention Teams (CITs): Police officer model that trains in response techniques that are appropriate for people suffering from mental health symptoms or problems.

Crossover Youth (Dually-involved youth): Dynamic between child maltreatment and delinquency, with young people having contact with both systems simultaneously.

Crossover Youth Practice Model: Program established by The Center for Juvenile Justice Reform and the Robert F. Kennedy Children's Action Corps that has developed approaches to prevent young people involved with either the juvenile courts or the child welfare system from "crossing over" to the other.

Culturally Responsive Teaching: Practice of reflecting back to the student his or her identities and cultures and improving school connections, with the goal of improving social and academic outcomes.

Cyberbullying: Has numerous forms, including hurtful information on the Internet; sharing private information; unwanted contact via e-mail, texting, online gaming, and other social media sites, as well as purposeful exclusion from an online community.

Delinquency (Delinquent): Ongoing committing of criminal acts or offenses by a young person, normally younger than 18 years of age.

Delinquency Adjudication: Juvenile court order that finds the minor delinquent and places the young person under state (and typically probation) supervision.

Depression: Mental health disorder that includes major depressive disorder and related difficulties. These problems greatly increase the risk for self-harm and suicide.

Detention Center: County-run facility that houses low-level, status, or other youthful offenders, typically for short periods of time.

Deterrence: Act of discouraging an action by instilling doubt or fear of the consequences.

Developmentally Delayed (Developmental Disability): Description of individuals who are cognitively impaired or limited in some related ways; term used in earlier times was "mentally retarded."

Diagnostic and Statistical Manual of Mental Disorders (DSM): Psychiatric classification code used in the United States to identify mental health problems and disorders.

Differential Treatment Hypothesis: Hypothesis that suggests that even though students with learning disabilities are no more involved with delinquent activities than their nondisabled peers, they are more likely to be identified by school personnel, arrested, and formally involved with the juvenile courts.

Disability Rights Movement: 1970s federal legislation that recognized people with disabilities and afforded independence and opportunities in daily living and employment.

Disposition (Hearing): A legally binding decision by a judge or magistrate.

Disproportionate Minority Confinement (Racial and Ethnic Disparities): Phrase that represents the disproportionate number of youthful offenders of color who are placed into juvenile (and adult) correctional facilities.

Disproportionate Minority Contact (Racial and Ethnic Disparities): Phrase that represents the disproportionate number of youthful offenders of color who come into contact with the juvenile justice (and adult) system.

Diversion: Definitions include nonarrest and release of a youthful offender back to the community, addressing the identified problems through rehabilitative means, and any attempt to divert from the juvenile justice system.

Domestic Violence: Emotional abuse, threatened and actual physical abuse, or sexual violence between adults, both heterosexual and same-sex partners.

Dually involved Youth (Crossover Youth): Dynamic between child maltreatment and delinquency, with young people having contact with both systems simultaneously.

Dynamic Risk Factors: Risk factors for individuals that are changeable, for example, parenting quality, school issues, adolescent skills deficits, and peer associations.

Ecological/Psychosocial Model: Multidimensional classification approach, identifying risks as the young person relates and interacts with family, peers, school, and community/neighborhood.

Empirical Validity: Describes how closely an idea corresponds to empirical data (what we observe).

Epidemiology (Epidemiological Research): Study of the extent and type of illnesses within populations as well as the factors that impact their distribution.

Etiology: Cause, or set of causes, for a certain outcome.

Explicit Bias: Attitudes and beliefs one has about a person or group on a conscious level.

Expulsion: Decision by the school that the student is removed for a period of time and not allowed back on campus.

Evidence-based interventions: Research-based (empirical) programs that have been found effective at their stated goals (for example, delinquency prevention and truancy reduction).

Evidence-Based Practices: Research-based (empirical) programs that have been found effective at their stated goals (for example, delinquency prevention and truancy reduction).

Federal Juvenile Delinquency Act: The first federal law established to handle those younger than the age of 18 who committed federal offenses.

Forced Sterilization: Programs or government policies that mandated the surgical sterilization, preventing individuals the ability to have children.

Formal Diversion Programs: Typically involve some conditions for the young person, an admission of guilt, and an agreement to participate in programming that is suitable. Services may be provided within the program or through a community-based provider for therapeutic or treatment needs, or could be just oversight and surveillance of the adolescent.

Forcible Rape: Sexual assault of another person against his or her will.

Free Will: Acting on one's own discretion, not believing in fate.

Functional Family Therapy (FFT): Intervention that attempts to modify individual behaviors and cognitions, with an emphasis on the larger family or groups as the focal area needing change rather than only on the adolescent.

Functionalism: An idea that things that exist in society (e.g., crime, as argued by Durkheim in the previous chapter) exist because they serve a function in society.

Gerald (Jerry) Gault: Fifteen-year-old from Arizona who was prosecuted and incarcerated for six years for prank phone calls. Upon consideration, this landmark U.S. Supreme Court established Constitutional due process rights for youthful offenders in 1967 including notice of charges, a detention hearing, a complaint at the hearing, sworn testimony, records of proceedings, and a right to appeal the judicial decision.

Goss v. Lopez: 1975 Supreme Court decision that found a public school must conduct a hearing before subjecting a student to suspension. Also, a suspension without a hearing was found to violate the Due Process Clause of the U.S. Constitution's Fourteenth Amendment.

Graduated Response Systems (Graduated Sanctions): Policies and practices that work through steps or levels, starting with a minimal intervention or consequence and allowing the young person (or student) to avoid further repercussions.

Gun-Free Schools Act: Passed in 1994, a federal law that encouraged states to take a tough on crime approach to their schools by introducing "zero tolerance policies."

Head Start (Early Head Start): Program of the U.S. Department of Health and Human Services that provides comprehensive early childhood education, health, nutrition, and parent involvement services to low-income children and their families. Early Head Start is for children ages 0 to 3.

Home Visiting Programs: Often delivered by nurses or related paraprofessional staff, may focus on one primary role or service, or may offer more complete family support services to parents in their home.

Houses of Refuge: Facilities built in the 1800s and established in major cities to help control troubled, wayward, or orphaned children.

Implicit Bias: Bias in judgment and/or behavior that results from subtle cognitive processes.

Incarceration Facilities: State-run correctional facilities that house youthful offenders, typically for longer periods of time.

Incidence Rates: Number of new cases of a disorder in a defined population during a specified time period of observation—for example, the past 12 months.

Inclusive School Policies: School policies that minimize students from being out-of-school suspended or expelled; often entails the use of rehabilitative programming and graduated sanctions.

Individuals with Disabilities Education (IDEA) Disability Categories: Specific learning disabilities (LD), hearing impairments (deafness), visual impairments (blindness), deaf-blindness, developmental delay, speech or language impairments, autism, serious emotional disturbance (SED), orthopedic impairments, traumatic brain injury, multiple disabilities, and other health impairments.

Individualized Education Plan (IEP): Specialized education plan that provides appropriate learning and school-environment accommodations for identified students.

In loco parentis: A philosophical and legal doctrine that is part of the juvenile justice framework and means "in place of the parents."

In-School Suspension: Suspension (typically 1 to 3 days) from the regular classroom whereby the student is to remain and complete academic work in a supervised school room.

Jury Trial: Legal proceeding in which a jury makes a decision or findings of fact, which then directs the actions of a judge.

Juvenile (Juvenile Offenders): Term used commonly in the juvenile justice system for adolescents (persons younger than 18 years of age) involved with the courts.

Juvenile Death Penalty: Practice of sentencing to death those who committed their crime (homicide in all cases) when younger than 18 years of age. This was allowed from 1976 until 2005 when the U.S. Supreme Court found in *Roper v. Simmons* the juvenile sentence to violate the Constitutions' Eighth Amendment forbidding cruel and unusual punishment.

Juvenile Detention Alternatives Initiative (JDAI): Part of the Annie E. Casey Foundation that works to decrease the use of detention through collaboration across child welfare, mental health, schools, and social service agencies, along with data-driven decision-making.

Juvenile Drug Courts: Courts that are different than other juvenile dockets, whereby youthful offenders are diverted to work in tandem with community-based service providers under supervision of the juvenile court judge.

Juvenile Justice and Delinquency Prevention Act: Federal law, originally passed in 1974, providing funds to states that follow a series of federal protections, known as the "core protections," on the care and treatment of youthful offenders in the justice system.

Juvenile Justice Geography, Policy, Practice, and Statistics (JJGPS): Research-focused organization and part of the National Center for Juvenile Justice that provides state- and national-level juvenile justice data.

Kincare Placements: When a child is removed from a parent's or guardian's home because of maltreatment concerns and placed with a related family member.

Learning Disability: Disorder in one or more of the basic psychological processes involved in understanding or in using language, spoken or written, that may manifest itself in an imperfect ability to listen, think, speak, read, write, spell, or do mathematical calculations.

Life-Course-Persistent Offenders: Name category for adolescents (fewer than 5% of all youthful offenders) who continue criminal activity into adulthood.

Life Sentence Without the Possibility of Parole (LWOP): Sentence that requires the offender to serve the rest of his or her life in prison (state or federal) without the chance of being released.

Lifetime Prevalence Rates: Number of existing cases during a person's life.

Longitudinal Studies: Cohort studies that follow over time a group of similar individuals who differ with respect to certain factors under study, to determine how these factors affect rates of a certain outcome.

Low-Level Youthful Offenders: First-time, misdemeanor-offending, or status-offending young people.

MacArthur Foundation (Models for Change Initiative): Leading national organization that has led juvenile justice reform from punishment toward a rehabilitative approach.

Memoranda of Understanding (MOUs) or Memoranda of Agreement (MOAs): Multilateral agreement among key stakeholders (typically the police force and school district) that expresses a common vision for the partnership.

Mental Health Disorder (Psychiatric Disorder): Diagnosis by a mental health professional of a behavioral or mental pattern that may cause suffering or a poor ability to function in life. In the United States, diagnosis is through the use of the Diagnostic and Statistical Manual of Mental Disorders (DSM).

Mentoring Programs: Programs that are focused on minimizing child and adolescent problem risk factors by using adult mentors who spend time with the young person, sharing skills, abilities, and experiences.

Meta-analysis Study: Subset of other systematic research studies that combines the results and produces a cumulative finding or impact.

Miranda Warning: A right-to-silence warning given by police to criminal suspects in police custody before they are interrogated.

Mitigating Circumstances: Situations and factors that lead to an event. For example, bullying that preceded a student from hitting another student.

Multisystemic Therapy (MST): MST is designed for adolescents with severe psychological and behavioral problems through short-term (four to six months), multifaceted, and home- and community-based interventions.

National Center for Juvenile Justice: Research division of the National Council of Juvenile and Family Court Judges (NCJFCJ). NCJFCJ is the largest organization in the country representing juvenile court judges and magistrates.

National Comorbidity Study: First large-scale national study of mental health in the United States; replicated most recently in 2010 and included findings for the first time on the adolescent population.

National Juvenile Defender Center: Nonprofit organization dedicated to promoting justice for all children by ensuring excellence in juvenile defense.

National Legal Aid and Defender Association: Nation's largest nonprofit membership organization dedicated to equal justice and legal representation for all.

National Reentry Resource Center: Organization that provides education, training, and technical assistance to states, tribes, territories, local governments, service providers, nonprofit organizations, and corrections institutions working on prisoner reentry.

National Registry of Evidence-Based Programs: Searchable online database from the National Institutes of Mental Health of research-based and effective mental health and substance abuse interventions.

National School Climate Survey: Series of national surveys of schools identifying the heightened difficulties of the lesbian, gay, bisexual, and transgender (LGBT) population.

National Survey of Children's Exposure to Violence: Most comprehensive nationwide survey of the incidence and prevalence of children's exposure to violence.

Net-Widening Effect (Diversion): Phenomenon that occurs when diversion programs that involve sanctions on young people who do not meet expectations are then drawn into the juvenile justice system and supervised.

Neuroleptics and Adrenergic Agonists: Class of stimulant drugs.

No Child Left Behind (NCLB) Law: 2001 law (expired in 2016) that set standards across the nation's public schools that required all students to be tested across certain academic areas in all primary and secondary grades. School districts were required to take disciplinary and administrative actions based on results.

Nonviolent Deaths: Deaths by natural causes or accidents.

Office of Juvenile Justice and Delinquency Prevention: Office of the U.S. Department of Justice and a component of the Office of Justice Programs that funds juvenile justice programming and directs federal initiatives.

Oppositional Defiant Disorder: Behaviorally based mental health disorder diagnosed for children or adolescents.

Out-of-Home Placement: Placement of a youthful offender to a shelter home, residential facility, detention center, or incarceration facility. For child welfare purposes, the placement into a kincare, foster, or adoptive home.

Out-of-School Suspension: Suspension from school where the student is not allowed back on the campus until the suspension ends.

Paradigm: A distinct set of thoughts; a school of thoughts.

Parens patriae: Philosophical and legal doctrine ("parent of the country") that becomes a guiding juvenile justice principal with the state acting as benevolent legal parent to a child.

Parent Support Groups: Parent or family support groups that provide formal peer-supported and facilitator-led programming, and typically meet on a regular, often weekly, basis.

Patriarchy: A cultural context where men hold power over every aspect of society.

Placing Out: Failed 19th century practice for impoverished, troubled, or orphaned children whereby more than 50,000 children from mostly urban East Coast cities boarded trains and were sent to western states to be adopted by farm families.

Plea Bargain: Arrangement between a prosecutor and a defendant whereby the defendant pleads guilty to a lesser charge in the expectation of leniency.

Poly-victimization: Exposure to, and experience of, multiple forms of trauma and/or victimization.

Positive Behavioral Protocol Programs: Targeted interventions for students with behavioral, control, or related school difficulties that use student or other leaders to engage students in daily or weekly social skill-building exercises.

Poverty: U.S. Government considers a person to be living in poverty if household income is below a certain income threshold. These poverty guidelines are available through the Department of Health and Human Services and are revised annually.

Pretrial Holding: Placement of a youthful offender in a detention center prior to adjudication or judicial decision.

Prevalence Rates: Number of existing cases in a defined population during a specified time period.

Probation Officers: Juvenile court employees that supervise youthful offenders who have been adjudicated delinquent.

Property Offenses (Crimes): Offenses that are committed only on property, not against persons, for example, burglary or motor vehicle theft.

Protective Factors: Protective factors may be the absence of certain delinquency risk factors. Or, protective factors may be an external or internal influence that decreases the impact of risk factors or influences a more positive outcome.

Psychiatric Asylum: Hospital for mentally incompetent people; the use of the term *asylum* comes from the earlier 20th century.

Psychoanalysis: System of psychological theory and therapy that aims to treat mental disorders by investigating the interaction of conscious and unconscious elements in the mind and bringing repressed fears and conflicts into the conscious mind.

Psychopharmacology: Branch of psychology concerned with the effects of drugs on the mind and behavior.

Psychosocial Maturity: Ability to respond appropriately to the environment. For adolescents, this refers to peers, family, school, and other environments.

Psychotherapy: Treatment of mental disorders by psychological rather than by medical means.

Psychotic Disorders: More severe and debilitating category of mental health disorders.

Racial and Ethnic Disparities (Disproportionate Minority Contact): Phrase that represents the disproportionate number of youthful offenders of color who come into contact with the juvenile justice (and adult) system.

Racial profiling: The use of race or ethnicity as grounds for suspecting someone of having committed an offense.

Reasoned and Equitable Community and Local Alternatives to the Incarceration of Minors (RECLAIM) Program: This program was designed to divert youthful offenders from the state of Ohio juvenile justice incarceration facilities through funding to local counties for appropriate programs to target delinquency and serious youthful offending.

Recidivism: Repeating of criminal behavior, including offending, detention, or incarceration placement.

Re-entry: Process of returning from an incarceration facility back to a home community.

Reform Schools: 19th century movement and reaction to ineffective houses of refuge consisting of homes designed as small, rural, cottage-like facilities run by parental figures who educated and cared for the children and adolescents.

Residential Placement: Placement of a young person into a shelter home or mental health or substance abuse treatment facility.

Residential Treatment Centers: Alternative to incarceration for youthful offenders with serious emotional, behavioral, and/or substance use problems who are in need of more structure than nonsecured, community-based treatment.

Resiliency: Measured and defined in several ways: the capacity for children and adolescents to thrive in the face of risks and difficulties, and a capacity for successful adaption despite the circumstances.

Restorative Practices: Student-focused interventions that try to change the perspective of young people who have caused problems, are disruptive, or have violated school policies, community expectations, or laws.

Right to Bail: Release of an arrested or imprisoned accused person when a specified amount of security is deposited or pledged (as cash or property) to ensure the accused's appearance in court.

Right to Legal Counsel: Constitutionally guaranteed right to legal counsel for any individual charged with an offense or crime by the courts.

Risk Factors: Experiences, traits, or issues that make an outcome (delinquency or mental health problems, for example) more likely.

Rules of Law: Restriction of the arbitrary use of power by restricting it by established laws.

Sandy Hook Elementary School Shooting: 2012 school shooting in Connecticut where Adam Lanza shot and killed 20 children and 6 adult staff members. This remains the most deadly school shooting in U.S. history.

School Code of Conduct: Document that spells out school policies, rules, and consequences for students and families.

School Failure Hypothesis: Hypothesis that suggests school failure for students with learning disabilities is a precipitating step that leads to juvenile court involvement.

School Management: Philosophy or framework that guides school policies on conduct and discipline.

School Resource Officers: Police officers that work on school campuses.

School-to-Prison Pipeline: Metaphor used to describe the increasing contact students have with the juvenile and adult criminal justice systems as a result of school zero tolerance policies and other factors.

School-Wide Positive Behavior Interventions and Supports (SWPBIS): Systematic approach for implementing proactive school-wide discipline to improve school climate and prevent student problem behaviors across school settings.

Screening: Brief process used to identify problems that are in need of further attention or assessment.

Segregated (Segregation): To separate or divide (people, activities, or institutions) along racial, sexual, or religious lines.

Selective Serotonin Reuptake Inhibitors: One of the commonly prescribed drugs for treating depression and other related problems.

Serious and Chronic Youthful Offenders: Adolescents who become mired in offending behaviors and/or gangs over time. This group is the most difficult to divert from ongoing troubles.

Serious Emotional Difficulties: Designation for young people who have ongoing mental health problems, often more severe and difficult to treat, including psychotic diagnoses, bipolar disorder, and mood disorders.

Serious Emotional Disturbance: Special education (IDEA) diagnosis that means a condition exhibiting over a long period of time and to a marked degree that adversely affects a child's educational performance.

Sexual Offender Registration: Federal and state law requirements that youthful and adult offenders convicted of certain sex crimes must be registered (name, address) in their localities.

Social-Emotional Learning: Primarily a classroom-focused approach that includes quality instruction planning and a focus on the behavioral needs of the students, monitoring of student engagement, and skills application to avoid escalating conflicts.

Solitary Confinement: Holding of an incarcerated young person (from hours to months) in an isolated locked room with no contact with other offenders, and most of the time with little-to-no staff contact.

Special Education: Form of learning provided to students with exceptional needs, such as students with learning disabilities or behavioral challenges. These disability categories are set forth by the Individuals with Disabilities in Education Act (IDEA).

Special Education Disability: These disability categories are set forth by the Individuals with Disabilities in Education Act (IDEA).

Standard Juvenile Court Act: A federal act that was originally issued in 1925 concerning the handling of children under the care of the court.

Static Risk Factors: Risk factors for individuals that are difficult to change.

Status Offense: The committing of acts that are illicit for only those younger than the age of 18 (truancy, liquor law violation, curfew violation, ungovernability, and running away).

Stereotyping: Unfair belief that all people or things with a particular characteristic are the same.

Structured Decision-Making (SDM) Model: Set of assessment tools that identifies key decision points within child protection agency cases and provides intervention directives.

Student Codes of Conduct: Written policies by school districts that outline behaviors that are expected as well as behaviors that the districts have determined are not permitted.

Substance Abuse and Mental Health Services Administration (SAMSHA): Federal agency charged with improving the quality and availability of prevention, treatment, and rehabilitation services for mental health and substance abuse problems.

Superpredator: 1990s phrase used to describe a fictional class of impulsive, brutal, and remorseless adolescents who committed serious violent crimes.

Susceptibility Hypothesis: Hypothesis that proposes that students with learning disabilities have cognitive, neurological, and intellectual difficulties that contribute to delinquent behaviors.

The Annie E. Casey Foundation: Leading national organization that has led juvenile justice reform since the 1980s from punishment toward a rehabilitative approach, including the Juvenile Detention Alternatives Initiative.

The Burns Institute: Leading national nonprofit organization focused on protecting and improving the lives of youthful and adult offenders of color by ensuring fairness and equity throughout the justice system.

The Civil Rights Project in Los Angeles: Organization with a mission to create a new generation of research in social science and law on the critical issues of civil rights and equal opportunity for racial and ethnic groups in the United States.

The Council of State Governments: Nonpartisan, nonprofit organization that serves all three branches of state government with policy research reviews.

Transfer and Waiver Criteria Laws: State laws that allow the transfer of youthful offenders to adult criminal courts based on certain age and offense criteria.

Trauma: Acute trauma is considered a single traumatic event that is time limited, for example, a dog bite, accident, or natural disaster such as an earthquake or tornado.

Trauma-Informed Care: Treatment framework that involves understanding, recognizing, and responding to the effects (psychological, social, and biological) of all types of trauma.

Treatment Foster Care: More intense and structured foster care setting that is designed for children and adolescents with more serious adjustment difficulties within their home, school, and community environments.

Truancy: Act of staying away from school without good cause.

Unformed Character Development: Trait of adolescence whereby ongoing social, cognitive, and psychological development continues.

Ungovernability: When a young person is deemed incapable of being monitored, controlled, or subdued.

U.S. Supreme Court: Highest federal court in the United States that decides cases on Constitutional issues and has jurisdiction over all other courts.

Victimless crimes: Crimes that do not involve a victim because everyone who is involved consents to the law-breaking behavior.

Violations of a Court Order: Technical violation for not adhering to a judge's order, not a criminal violation or a new offense.

Violent Offenses (Crimes): Crimes that are often against persons and felonies (homicide, rape, robbery).

Violent Crime Control and Law Enforcement Act: Passed in 1994, the largest crime bill in federal history that focused on punishment for crimes and a "tough on crime" approach to adult and juvenile justice.

Violent Deaths: Deaths caused by different violent events, including accidents, suicides, and homicides.

Youthful Offenders: Those under the age of majority (typically 18 years of age) who come under juvenile court supervision.

Zero Tolerance Policies: School district policies that mandate predetermined consequences or punishments for specific offenses that are intended to be applied regardless of the seriousness of the behavior, mitigating circumstances, or situational context.

REFERENCES

Abbott, S., & Barnett, E. (2015). *The crossover practice model.* Washington, DC: Center for Juvenile Justice Reform, Georgetown University.

Abram, K.M., Choe, J.Y., Washburn, J.J., Teplin, L.A., King, D.C., Dulcan, M.K., & Bassett, E.D. (2014). *Suicidal thoughts and behaviors among detained youth.* Washington, DC: Office of Juvenile Justice and Delinquency Prevention, Office of Justice Programs, U.S. Department of Justice.

Abram, K.M., Teplin, L.A., King, D.C., Longworth, L.S., Emanuel, K.M., Romero, E.G, McClelland, G.M., Dulcan, M.K., Washburn, J.J., Welty, L.J., & Olson, N.D. (2013). *PTSD, trauma, and comorbid psychiatric disorders in detained youth.* Washington, DC: Office of Juvenile Justice and Delinquency Prevention, Office of Justice Programs, U.S. Department of Justice.

Addington, L.A. (2009). Cops and cameras: Public school security as a policy response to Columbine. *American Behavioral Scientist*, 52, 1424–1446.

Addington, L.A. (2014). Surveillance and security approaches across public school levels. In G.W. Muschert, S. Henry, N.L. Bracy, & A.A. Peguero (Eds.), *Responding to school violence: Confronting the Columbine Effect* (pp. 71–88). Boulder, CO: Lynne Rienner.

Adler, F. (1975). *Sisters in crime: The rise of the new female criminal.* New York, NY: McGraw-Hill.

Administration for Children and Families. (2008). *Adolescents involved with child welfare: A transition to adulthood.* Washington, DC: U.S. Department of Health and Human Services.

Administration for Children and Families. (2010). *Child maltreatment 2009.* Washington, DC: U.S. Department of Health and Human Services.

Administration for Children and Families. (2015). *Child maltreatment 2014.* Washington, DC: U.S. Department of Health and Human Services.

Administration for Children and Families. (2017). *Child maltreatment 2015.* Washington, DC: U.S. Department of Health and Human Services.

Advancement Project. (2005). *Education on lockdown: The schoolhouse to jailhouse track.* Washington, DC: Author.

Advancement Project. (2014). *Restorative practices: Fostering healthy relationships & promoting positive discipline in schools: A guide for educators.* Washington, DC: Author.

Advancement Project, Alliance for Educational Justice, & Gay Straight Alliance Network. (2012). *Two wrongs don't make a right: Why zero tolerance is not the solution to bullying.* Washington, DC: Advancement Project.

Advancement Project, Education Law Center—PA, FairTest, The Forum for Education, and Democracy, Juvenile Law Center, NAACP Legal Defense and Educational Fund, Inc. (2011). *Federal policy, ESEA reauthorization, and the school-to-prison pipeline.* Washington, DC: Advancement Project.

Advancement Project, Education Law Center—PA, FairTest, The Forum for Education and Democracy, Juvenile Law Center, NAACP Legal Defense and Educational Fund, Inc. (2011). *Federal policy, ESEA reauthorization, and the school-to-prison pipeline.* Washington, DC: Advancement Project, Education Law Center.

Advancement Project, Equality Federation Institute, & Gay Straight Alliance Network. (2016). *Power in partnerships: Building connections at the intersections of racial justice and LGBTG movements to end the school-to-prison pipeline.* Washington, DC: Advancement Project.

Agnew, R. (1985). A revised strain theory of delinquency. *Social Forces*, 64, 151–167.

Agnew, R. (1992). Foundation for a general strain theory of crime and delinquency. *Criminology*, 30, 47–87.

Agnew, R. (2001). Building on the foundation of general strain theory: Specifying the types of strain most likely to lead to crime and delinquency. *Journal of Research in Crime and Delinquency*, 38, 319–361.

Agnew, R. (2007). *Pressured into crime: An overview of general strain theory.* Los Angeles, CA: Roxbury.

Agnew, R. (2012). Reflection on a revised strain theory of delinquency. *Social Forces*, 91, 33–38.

Aichorn, A. (1984). *Wayward youth.* Evanston, IL: Northwestern University Press. (Originally published in 1925)

Aizer, A., & Doyle, J. (2013). *Juvenile incarceration, human capital and future crime: Evidence from randomly-assigned judges* (NBER Working Paper 19102). Cambridge, MA: National Bureau of Economic Research.

Akers, R.L. (1973). *Deviant behavior: A social learning approach.* Los Angeles, CA: Wadsworth.

Akers, R.L., & Jensen, G.F. (2008). The empirical status of social learning theory of crime and deviance: The past, present, and future. In F.T. Cullen, J.P. Wright, & K.R. Blevins (Eds.), *Taking stock: The status of criminological theory: Advances in criminological theory* (Vol. 15, pp. 37–76). New Brunswick, NJ: Transaction.

Akers, R.L., & Sellers, C.S. (2009). *Criminological theories: Introduction, evaluation, and application.* New York, NY: Oxford University Press.

Alexander, J., Barton, C., Gordon, D., Grotpeter, J., Hansson, K., Harrison, R., Mears, S., Mihalic, S., Parsons, B., Pugh, C., Schulman, S., Waldron, H., & Sexton, T. (2007). In D.S. Elliott (Ed.), *Functional family therapy: Blueprints for violence prevention, book three* (Blueprints for Violence Prevention Series). Boulder: Center for the Study and Prevention of Violence, Institute of Behavioral Science, University of Colorado.

Allen, F.A. (1964). *The borderland of criminal justice.* Chicago, IL: The University of Chicago Press.

Altarac, M., & Saroha, E. (2007). Lifetime prevalence of learning disability among US children. *Pediatrics*, 119, 577–584.

Altschuler, D., & Bilchik, S. (2014). *Critical elements of juvenile reentry in research and practice.* Austin, TX: Justice Center, Council of State Governments.

Amaya-Jackson, L., & DeRosa, R.R. (2007). Treatment considerations for clinicians in applying evidence-based practice to complex presentations in child trauma. *Journal of Traumatic Stress*, 20, 379–390.

American Academy of Child and Adolescent Psychiatry. (1997). Practice parameters for the assessment and treatment of children, adolescents, and adults with attention deficit/hyperactivity disorder. *Journal of the American Academy of Child and Adolescent Psychiatry*, 36, 85S–121S.

American Academy of Pediatrics, Council on School Health. (2013). Out-of-school suspension and expulsion. *Pediatrics*, 131, 1000–1007.

American Bar Association. (2014). *ABA policy on trauma-informed advocacy for children and youth.* Washington, DC: Author.

American Civil Liberties Union. (2014). *Alone & afraid: Children held in solitary confinement and isolation in juvenile detention and correctional facilities.* New York, NY: Author.

American Psychiatric Association. (2013). *Diagnostic and statistical manual of mental disorders* (5th ed). Washington, DC: Author.

American Psychological Association. (2006). *Are zero tolerance policies effective in the schools? An evidentiary review and recommendations.* Washington, DC: American Psychological Association Zero Tolerance Policy Task Force.

American Psychological Association. (2012). *Facing the school dropout dilemma.* Washington, DC: Author.

American Psychological Association (Zero Tolerance Task Force). (2008). Are zero tolerance policies effective in the school? *American Psychologist*, 63, 852–862.

Anderson, E. (1990). *Streetwise: Race, class, and change in an urban community.* Chicago, IL: The University of Chicago Press.

Anderson, E. (2000). *Code of the street: Decency, violence, and the moral life of the inner city.* New York, NY: W.W. Norton.

Andreassen, T.H., Armelius, B., Egelund, T., & Ogden T. (2006). *Cognitive-behavioural treatment for antisocial behavior in youth in residential treatment (protocol).* Oslo, Norway: Cochrane Database of Systematic Reviews.

Angold, A., Erkanli, A., Farmer, E.M., Fairbank, J.A., Burns, B.J., Keeler, G., & Costello, J. (2002). Psychiatric disorder, impairment, and service use in rural African American and white youth. *Archives of General Psychiatry*, 59, 893–901.

Anyon, Y. (2016). *Taking restorative practices school-wide: Insights from three schools in Denver.* Denver, CO: Denver School-Based Restorative Practices Partnership.

Aos, S. (2004). *Washington State's family integrated transitions program for juvenile offenders: Outcome evaluation and benefit-cost analysis.* Olympia: Washington State Institute for Public Policy.

Aos, S., Lee, S., Drake, E., Pennucci, A., Klima, T., Miller, M., Anderson, L., Mayfield, J., & Burley, M. (2011). *Return on investment: Evidence-based options to improve statewide outcomes.* Olympia: Washington State Institute for Public Policy.

Armelius, B.A., & Andreassen, T.H. (2007). *Cognitive-behavioural treatment for antisocial behavior in youth in residential treatment.* Oslo, Norway: The Campbell Collaboration.

Armstrong, K.H., Dedrick, R.F., & Greenbaum, P.E. (2003). Factors associated with community adjustment of young adults with serious emotional disturbances: A longitudinal analysis. *Journal of Emotional and Behavioral Disorders*, 11, 66–76.

Aronwitz, B., Liebowitz, M.R., Hollander, E., Fazzini, E., Durlach-Misteli, C., Frenkel, M., Mosovich, S., Garfinkel, R., Saoud, J., & DelBene, D. (1994). Neuropsychiatric and neuropsychological findings in conduct disorder and attention-deficit hyperactivity disorder. *Journal of Neuropsychiatry & Clinical Neurosciences*, 6, 245–249.

Arseneault, L., Bowes, L., & Shakoor, S. (2010). Bullying victimization in youths with mental health problems: 'Much ado about nothing'? *Psychological Medicine*, 40, 717–729.

Arum, R. (2003). *Judging school discipline: The crisis of moral authority.* Cambridge, MA: Harvard University Press.

Austin, A.M., Macgowan, M.J., & Wagner, E.E. (2005). Effective family-based interventions for Adolescents with Substance use Problems: A systematic review. *Research on Social Work Practice*, 15, 67–83.

Austin, J., Johnson, K.D., & Weitzer, R. (2005). *Alternatives to the secure detention and confinement of juvenile offenders.* Washington, DC: Office of Juvenile Justice and Delinquency Prevention, U.S. Department of Justice.

Bahena, S., Cooc, N., Currie-Rubin, R., Kuttner, P., & Ng, M. (2012). *Disrupting the school-to-prison pipeline.* Cambridge, MA: Harvard Educational Review.

Baird, C., Healy, T., Johnson, K., Bogie, A., Dankert, E.W., & Scharenbroch, C. (2013). *A comparison of risk assessment instruments in juvenile justice.* Madison, WI: National Council on Crime and Delinquency.

Baker, R., Sigmon, J.N., & Nugent, M.E. (2001). *Truancy reduction: Keeping students in school.* Washington, DC: Office of Justice Programs, Office of Juvenile Justice and Delinquency Prevention, U.S. Department of Justice.

Balfanz, R., Byrnes, V., & Fox, J. (2015). Sent home and put off-track: The antecedents, disproportionalities, and consequences of being suspended in the ninth grade. In D.J. Losen (Ed.), *Closing the school discipline gap: Research for policymakers.* New York, NY: Teachers College Press.

Balfanz, R., & Letgers, N. (2004). Locating the dropout crisis: Which schools produce the nation's dropouts? In G. Orfield (Ed.), *Dropouts in America: Confronting the graduation rate crisis.* Cambridge, MA: Harvard Education Press.

Bandura, A. (1977). *Social learning theory.* Englewood Cliffs, NJ: Prentice Hall.

Barkley, R.A. (2002). Major life activity and health outcomes associated with attention-deficit/hyperactivity disorder. *Journal of Clinical Psychiatry*, 63, 10–15.

Barlow, J., & Parsons, J. (2002). *Group-based parent-training programmes for improving emotional and behavioural adjustment in 0–3 year old children* (Vol. 1). Oslo, Norway: The Campbell Collaboration.

Barnert, E.S., Dudovitz, R., Nelson, B.B., Coker, T.R., Biely, C., Li, N., & Chung, P.J. (2017). How does incarcerating young people affect their adult health outcomes? *Pediatrics*, 139. doi:10.1542/peds.2016–2624

Barnes, J.C., Wright, J.P., Boutwell, B.B., Schwartz, J.A., Connolly, E.J., Nedelec, J.L., & Beaver, K.M. (2014). Demonstrating the validity of twin research in criminology. *Criminology*, 52, 588–626.

Barrett, D.E., Katsiyannis, A., Zhang, D., & Zhang, D. (2013). Delinquency and recidivism: A multicohort matched-control study of the role of early adverse experiences, mental health problems, and disabilities. *Journal of Emotional and Behavioral Disorders*, 22, 3–15.

Barth, R.B. (2009). Preventing child abuse and neglect with parent training: Evidence and opportunities. *The Future of Children*, 19, 95–118.

Baumer, E., Lauritsen, J.L., Rosenfeld, R., & Wright, R. (1998). The influence of crack cocaine on robbery, burglary, and homicide rates: A cross-city longitudinal analysis. *Journal of Research in Crime and Delinquency*, 35, 316–340.

Bazemore, G. (2001). Young people, trouble, and crime: Restorative justice as a normative theory of informal social control and social support. *Youth & Society*, 33, 199–226.

Bazemore, G., Leip, L., & Stinchcomb, J.B. (2004). Boundary changes and the nexus between formal and informal social control: Truancy intervention as a case study in criminal justice expansionism. *Notre Dame Journal of Law, Ethics, & Public Policy*, 18, 521–570.

Beard, K.Y., & Sugai, G. (2004). First step to success: An early intervention for elementary children at risk for antisocial behavior. *Behavioral Disorders*, 29, 396–409.

Beccaria, C. (1986). *On crimes and punishments.* Boston, MA: Hackett Classics. (Originally published in 1764.)

Beck, A.J., Cantor, D., Hartge, J., & Smith, T. (2013). *Sexual victimization in juvenile facilities report by youth, 2012.* Washington, DC: U.S. Department of Justice, Office of Justice Programs, Bureau of Justice Statistics.

Beck, A.J., & Caspar, M.F. (2013). *Sexual victimization in prisons and jails reported by inmates, 2011–2012*. Washington, DC: U.S. Department of Justice, Office of Justice Programs, Bureau of Justice Statistics.

Becker, H. (1963). Becoming a marijuana user. *The American Journal of Sociology*, 59: 235–242.

Becker, S.J., & Curry, J.F. (2008). Outpatient interventions for adolescent substance abuse: A quality of evidence review. *Journal of Consulting and Clinical Psychology*, 76, 531–543.

Bellair, P.E., & Kowalski, B.R. (2011). Low-skill employment opportunity and African American-white difference in recidivism. *Journal of Research in Crime and Delinquency*, 48, 176–208.

Bender, K. (2009). Why do some maltreated youth become juvenile offenders? A call for further investigation and adaption of youth services. *Children Youth Services Review*, 32, 466–473.

Benner, G.J., Nelson, J.R., Stage, S.A., Laederich, M., & Ralston, N.C. (2010). Sex differences on MAYSI-2 mental health symptoms of juvenile detainees: Impact on status offenses and delinquency. *The Journal of Behavior Analysis of Offender and Victim Treatment and Prevention*, 2, 37–50.

Bennett, W.J., DiIulio, J.J., & Walters, J.P. (1996). *Body count*. New York, NY: Simon & Schuster.

Bentham, J. (1789). An introduction to the principles of morals and legislation. *Behavioral Sciences and the Law*, 16, 303–318.

Berkowitz, M.W., & Bier, M.C. (2005). *What works in charter education: A research driven guide for educators*. Washington, DC: Charter Education Partnership.

Berman, M.E., & Coccaro, E.F. (1998). Neurobiologic correlates of violence: Relevance to criminal responsibility. *Behavioral Sciences & the Law*, 16, 303–318.

Bernard, T.J., & Kurlychek, M.C. (2010). *The cycle of juvenile justice* (2nd ed.). New York, NY: Oxford University Press.

Bernazzani, O., & Tremblay, R.E. (2006). Early parent training. In B.C. Welsh & D.P. Farrington (Eds.), *Preventing crime: What works for children, offenders, victims, and places* (pp. 2–21). Dordrecht, the Netherlands: Springer.

Bettman, J.E., & Jasperson, R.A. (2009). Adolescents in residential and inpatient treatment: A review of the outcome literature. *Child Youth Care Forum*, 38, 161–183.

Bhati, A.S., & Piquero, A.R. (2007). Estimating the impact of incarceration on subsequent offending trajectories: Deterrent, criminogenic, or null effect? *The Journal of Criminal Law and Criminology*, 98, 207–254.

Big Brothers Big Sisters of America. (2016). *Carrying the flag together*. Retrieved from http://www.bbbs.org/site/apps/nlnet/content2.aspx?c=9iILI3NGKhK6F&b=6195821&ct=8399741&notoc=1

Binder, A., Geis, G., & Bruce, D. (1988). *Juvenile delinquency: Historical, cultural, legal perspectives*. New York, NY: Macmillan.

Birkland, T.A., & Lawrence, R. (2009). Media framing after Columbine. *American Behavioral Scientist*, 52, 1426–1446.

Bishop, D.M. (2006). The role of race and ethnicity in juvenile justice processing. In D.F. Hawkins & K. Kempf-Leonard (Eds.), *Our children, their children: Confronting racial and ethnic differences in American juvenile justice* (pp. 23–82). Chicago, IL: The University of Chicago Press.

Bishop, D.M., Lanza-Kaduce, L., & Frazier, C.E. (1998). Juvenile justice under attack: An analysis of the causes and impact of recent reforms. *University of Florida Journal of Law and Public Policy*, 10, 129–156.

Black Organizing Project. (2013). *From report card to criminal record*. Oakland: Black Organizing Project, Public Counsel, and the ACLU of Northern California.

Blueprints for Healthy Youth Development. (2016). *Blueprints programs: Healthy youth development*. Boulder: Center for the Study and Prevention of Violence, Institute of Behavioral Science, University of Colorado.

Blumstein, A. (1995). Violence by young people: Why the deadly nexus? *National Institute of Justice Journal*, 229, 2–9.

Boden, J.M., Horwood, L.J., & Fergusson, D.M. (2007). Exposure to childhood sexual and physical abuse and subsequent educational achievement outcomes. *Child Abuse and Neglect*, 10, 1101–1114.

Bolen, M. (2001). *Child sexual abuse: Its scope and our failure*. New York, NY: Kluwer Academic/Plenum.

Bonger, W. (1970). *Criminality and economic conditions*. Indianapolis: Indiana University Press. (Originally published in 1905.)

Bonnie, R.J., Johnson, R.L., Chemers, B., & Schuck, J. (2013). *Reforming juvenile justice: A developmental approach*. Washington, DC: National Academies Press.

Bonta, J., Rugge, T., Scott, T.L., Bourgon, G., & Yessine, A.K. (2008). Exploring the black box of community supervision. *Journal of Offender Rehabilitation*, 47, 248–270.

Books, S. (2004). *Poverty and schooling in the U.S.: Contexts and consequences*. Mahwah, NJ: Lawrence Erlbaum.

Booth, A., & Osgood, D.W. (1993). The influence of testosterone on deviance in adulthood: Assessing and explaining the relationship. *Criminology*, 31, 93–117.

Borum, R., Bartel, P., and Forth, A. (2002). *Manual for the structured assessment for violence risk in youth (SAVRY)* (Consultation version). Tampa: Florida Mental Health Institute, University of South Florida.

Bouchard, T., Lykken, D.T., McGue, M., Segal, N.L., & Tellegen, A. (1990). Sources of human psychological differences: The Minnesota study of twins reared apart. *Science*, 250, 223–250.

Boundy, K.B., & Karger, J. (2011). The right to a quality education for children and youth in the juvenile justice system. In F. Sherman & F. Jacobs (Eds.), *Juvenile justice: Advancing research, policy, and practice* (pp. 286–309). Hoboken, NJ: Wiley.

Bracy, N.L. (2010). Circumventing the law: Students' rights in schools-with police. *Journal of Contemporary Criminal Justice*.

Bradshaw, C.P., Mitchell, M.M., & Leaf, P.J. (2010). Examining the effects of schoolwide positive behavioral interventions and supports on student outcomes. *Journal of Positive Behavior Interventions*, 12, 133–148.

Bradshaw, C.P., Koth, C.W., Bevans, K.B., Ialongo, N., & Leaf, P.J. (2008). The impact of school-wide Positive Behavioral Interventions and Supports (PBIS) on the organizational health of elementary schools. *School Psychology Quarterly*, 23, 462–473.

Brady, K.P. (2002). Weapons of choice: Zero tolerance school discipline policies and the limitations of student procedural due process. *Children's Legal Rights Journal*, 22, 2–10.

Brauner, C.B., & Stephens, C.B. (2006). Estimating the prevalence of early childhood serious emotional/behavioral disorders: Challenges and recommendations. *Public Health Report*, 121, 303–310.

Bremner, R., Barnard, J., Hareven, T.K., & Mennell, R.M. (1970). *Children and youth in America: A documentary history* (Vol. 1). Cambridge, MA: Harvard University Press.

Breslau, N., Wilcox, H.C., Storr, C.L., Lucia, V.C., & Anthony, J.C. (2004). Trauma exposure and posttraumatic stress disorder: A study of youths in urban America. *Journal of Urban Health*, 81, 530–544.

Brezina, T. (1998). Adolescent maltreatment and delinquency: The question of intervening processes. *Journal of Research in Crime and Delinquency*, 35, 71–99.

Briar, S., & Pilliavin, I. (1965). Delinquency, situational inducements, and commitment to conformity. *Social Problems*, 13, 35–45.

Bridgeland, J.M., DiIulio, J.J., & Morrison, K.B. (2006). *The silent epidemic: Perspectives of high school dropouts*. Washington, DC: Civic Enterprises, LLC.

Brooks-Gunn, J., Berlin, L.J., & Fuligni, A.S. (2000). Early childhood intervention programs: What about the family? In J.P. Shonkoff &

S.J. Meisels (Eds.), *Handbook on early childhood intervention* (2nd ed., pp. 549–588). New York, NY: Cambridge University.

Brown, R.T., & LaRosa, A. (2002). Recent developments in the pharmacotherapy of attention-deficit/hyperactivity disorder (ADHD). *Professional Psychology—Research and Practice*, 33, 591–595.

Bruinius, H. (2006). *Better for all the world: The secret history of forced sterilization and America's quest for racial purity*. New York, NY: Random House.

Brunelle, N., Brochu, S., & Cousineau, M. (2000). Drug-crime relations among drug-consuming juvenile delinquents: A tripartite model. *Contemporary Drug Problems*, 27, 835–867.

Buffington, K., Pierkhising, C.B., & Marsh, S. (2010). *Ten things every juvenile court judge should know about trauma and delinquency*. Reno, NV: National Council of Juvenile and Family Court Judges.

Burdge, H., Licona, A.C., & Hyemingway, Z.T. (2014). *Youth of color: Discipline disparities, school push-out, and the school-to-prison pipeline*. San Francisco, CA: Gay-Straight Alliance Network and Tucson, AZ: Crossroads Collaborative at the University of Arizona.

Bureau of Justice Statistics. (2014a). *Indicators of school crime and safety: 2014*. Washington, DC: U.S. Department of Justice.

Bureau of Justice Statistics. (2014b). *National crime victimization survey: Technical documentation*. Washington, DC: Bureau of Justice Statistics, U.S. Department of Justice.

Bureau of Labor Statistics. (n.d.). *National longitudinal surveys: A program of the U.S. Bureau of Labor Statistics*. Washington, DC: National Longitudinal Surveys, Bureau of Labor Statistics.

Burgess-Proctor, A. (2006). Intersections of race, class, gender, and crime: Future directions for feminist criminology. *Feminist Criminology*, 1, 27–47.

Burley, M., & Halpern, M. (2001). *Educational attainment of foster youth: Achievement and graduation outcomes for children in state care* (Document No. 01–11–3901). Olympia: Washington State Institute for Public Policy.

Burrell, S., & Stacy, R.F. (2011). *Collateral consequences of juvenile delinquency proceedings in California: A handbook for juvenile law professionals*. Los Angeles, CA: Pacific Juvenile Public Defender Center.

Burrell, S., & Warboys, L. (2000). *Special education and the juvenile justice system*. Washington, DC: Office of Juvenile Justice and Delinquency Prevention, Office of Justice Programs, U.S. Department of Justice.

Bursik, R. (1988). Social disorganization and theories of crime and delinquency: Problems and prospects. *Criminology*, 26, 519–551.

Burt, C.H., & Simons, R.L. (2014). Pulling back the curtain on heritability studies: Biosocial criminology in the postgenomic era. *Criminology*, 52, 223–262.

Burwick, A., Oddo, V., Durso, L., Friend, D., & Gates, G. (2014). *Identifying and serving LGBTQ youth: Case studies of runaway and homeless youth program grantees*. Washington, DC: Office of Justice Programs, Bureau of Justice Statistics, U.S. Department of Justice.

Butrymowicz, S., & Mader, J. (2014, Oct. 16). Pipeline to prison: How the juvenile justice system fails special education students. *The Heckinger Report*. pp. 1–3. Retrieved from http://hechingerreport.org/pipeline-prison-juvenile-justice-system-fails-special-education-students/

Butts, J.A. (2000). *Can we do without juvenile justice?* Washington, DC: The Urban Institute.

Butts, J.A., & Travis, J. (2002). *The rise and fall of American youth violence: 1980–2000*. Washington, DC: Urban Institute, Justice Policy Center.

Caldwell, R.G. (1961). The juvenile court: Its development and some major problems. *Journal of Criminal Law, Criminology, and Police Science*, 51, 493–511.

Calhoun, A., & Daniels, G. (2008). Accountability in school responses to harmful incidents. *Journal of School Violence*, 7, 21–47.

Campaign for Youth Justice. (2017). *Raising the bar: State trends in keeping youth out of adult courts (2015–2017)*. Washington, DC: Author.

Carlton, M.P. (2017). *Summary of school statistics*. Washington, DC: National Institute of Justice, Office of Justice Programs, U.S. Department of Justice.

Carter, P.L., Fine, M., & Russell, S. (2014). *Discipline disparities overview* (Discipline Disparities: A Research-to-Practice Collaborative). Bloomington, IN: The Equity Project at Indiana University, Center for Evaluation and Education Policy.

Carver, P.R., & Lewis, L. (2010). *Alternative schools and programs for public school students at risk of educational failure: 2007–2008*. Washington, DC: U.S. Department of Education, National Center for Education Statistics.

Caspi, A., McClay, J., Moffitt, T.E., Mill, J., Martin, J., Craig, I.W., Taylor, A., & Poulton, R. (2002). Role of genotype in the cycle of violence in maltreated children. *Science*, 297, 851–854.

Cauffman, E. (2004). A statewide screening of mental health symptoms among juvenile offenders in detention. *Journal of the American Academy of Child & Adolescent Psychiatry*, 43, 430–439.

Center for American Progress. (2017). *Unjust: LGBTQ youth incarcerated in the juvenile justice system*. Washington, DC: Center for American Progress, Movement, Advancement Project, and Youth First.

Centers for Disease Control and Prevention. (2009). *Suicide prevention: Youth suicide*. National Atlanta, GA: Center for Injury Prevention and Control, Division of Violence Prevention.

Centers for Disease Control and Prevention. (2013). *2010, US suicide injury deaths and rates per 100,000*. Atlanta, GA: Author.

Centers for Disease Control and Prevention. (2014a). *1991–2013 high school youth risk behavior survey data*. Atlanta, GA: Author.

Centers for Disease Control and Prevention. (2014b). *Fatal injury reports, 1999–2014*. Atlanta, GA: Author.

Centers for Disease Control and Prevention. (2015). *Suicide risk and prevention factors*. Atlanta, GA: Author.

Centers for Disease Control and Prevention. (2016). *Sexual identify, sex of sexual contacts, and health-related behaviors among students in grades 9–12—United States and selected sites, 2015*. Atlanta, GA: Author.

Centers for Disease Control and Prevention. (n.d.). *Youth Risk Behavior Surveillance System (YRBSS) overview*. Washington, DC: U.S. Department of Health and Human Services.

Chamberlain, P. (2003). *Treating chronic juvenile offenders: Advances made through the Oregon multidimensional treatment foster care model*. Washington, DC: American Psychological Association.

Chamberlain, P., Leve, L., & DeGarmo, D. (2007). Multidimensional treatment foster care for girls in the juvenile justice system: Two year follow-up of a randomized clinical trial. *Journal of Consulting and Clinical Psychology*, 75, 187–193.

Chapin, D.A., & Griffin, P.A. (2005). Juvenile diversion. In K. Heilbrun, N.E. Goldstein, & R.E. Redding (Eds.), *Juvenile delinquency: Prevention, assessment, and intervention* (pp. 161–178). New York, NY: Oxford University Press.

Chassin, L. (2008). Juvenile justice and substance abuse. *The Future of Children*, 18, 165–184.

Chen, C., Culhane, D.P., Metraux, S., Park, J.M., & Venable, J.C. (2016). The heterogeneity of truancy among urban middle school students: A latent class growth analysis. *Journal of Child and Family Studies*, 25, 1066–1075.

Chesney-Lind, M. (1986). Women and crime: The female offender. *Signs*, 12, 78–101.

Chesney-Lind, M. (1999). Girls, gangs, and violence: Reinventing the liberated female crook. In M. Chesney-Lind & J. Hagedorn (Eds.), *Female gangs in America: Essays on girls, gangs and gender* (pp. 295–310). Chicago, IL: Lakeview Press.

Chesney-Lind, M. (2006). Patriarchy, crime, and justice: Feminist criminology in an era of backlash. *Feminist Criminology*, 1, 6–26.

Chesney-Lind, M., & Irwin, K. (2008). *Beyond bad girls: Gender, violence and hype*. New York, NY: Routledge.

Chesney-Lind, M., & Pasko, L. (2004). *The female offender: Girls, women and crime*. Thousand Oaks, CA: Sage.

Chesney-Lind, M., & Rodriguez, N. (1983). Women under lock and key: A view from the inside. *The Prison Journal*, 63, 47–65.

Chesney-Lind, M., & Shelden, R.G. (2014). *Girls, delinquency, and juvenile justice* (4th ed.). Malden, MA: Wadsworth.

Child Trends. (2007a). *Cognitive-behavioral training program for behaviorally disordered adolescents*. Washington, DC: LINKS Database.

Child Trends. (2007b). *Reconnecting youth*. Washington, DC: LINKS Database.

Child Trends. (2011). *Promoting alternative thinking strategies (PATHS)*. Washington, DC: Author.

Child Trends. (2015a). *High school dropout rates: Indicators on children and youth*. Washington, DC: Author.

Child Trends. (2015b). *Indicators on children and youth*. Washington, DC: Author.

Child Welfare Information Center. (2015). *Promoting protective factors for victims of child abuse and neglect: A guide for practitioners*. Washington, DC: Administration for Children and Families, U.S. Department of Health and Human Services.

Child Welfare Information Gateway. (2011). *Child maltreatment prevention: Past, present, and future*. Washington, DC: Administration on Children, Youth, and Families Children's Bureau, Administration for Children and Families, U.S. Department of Health and Human Services.

Child Welfare Information Gateway (2013). *How the child welfare system works*. Washington, DC: Administration on Children, Youth, and Families Children's Bureau, Administration for Children and Families, U.S. Department of Health and Human Services. Accessed at https://www.childwelfare.gov/pubpdfs/cpswork.pdf

Children's Defense Fund. (1975). *School suspensions: Are they helping children?* Cambridge, MA: Washington Research Project.

Children's Defense Fund (2012). *Portrait of inequality*, 2012. Washington, DC.

Children's Defense Fund. (2014). *The state of America's children*. Washington, DC: Author.

Children's Research Center. (1999). *A new approach to child protective services: Structured decision making*. Madison, WI: National Council on Crime and Delinquency, Children's Research Center.

Chlang, H., & Gill, B. (2010). *The impacts of Philadelphia's accelerated schools on academic progress and graduation*. Cambridge, MA: Mathematica Policy Research, Inc.

Clark, H., Boyde, L., Redditt, C., Foster-Johnson, L., Hardy, D., Kuhns, J., Lee, G., & Stewart, E. (1993). An individualized system of care for foster children with behavioral and emotional disturbances: Preliminary findings. In K. Kutash, C. Liberton, A. Algarin, & R. Friedman (Eds.), 5th *annual research conference proceedings for a system of care for children's mental health* (pp. 365–370). Tampa: University of South Florida, Florida Mental Health Institute, Research and Training Center for Children's Mental Health.

Cloward, R.A. (1959). Illegitimate means, anomie, and deviant behavior. *American Sociological Review*, 24, 164–176.

Cloward, R.A., & Ohlin, L.E. (1960). *Delinquency and opportunity: A theory of delinquent gangs*. New York, NY: Free Press.

Coalition for Juvenile Justice. (1998). *A celebration or a wake: The juvenile court after 100 years*. Washington, DC: Author.

Coalition for Juvenile Justice. (2013). *National standards for the care of youth charged with status offenses*. Washington, DC: Author.

Coalition for Juvenile Justice. (2014). *Addressing truancy and other status offenses*. Washington, DC: Author.

Cochran, J.K., Chamlin, M.B., & Seth, M. (1994). Deterrence or brutalization—An impact assessment of Oklahoma return to capital punishment. *Criminology*, 32, 107–134.

Cocozza, J., & Skowyra, K. (2000). Youth with mental health disorders: Issues and emerging responses. *Juvenile Justice Journal*, 7, 3–13.

Cohen, A.K. (1955). *Delinquent boys: The culture of the gang*. New York, NY: Free Press.

Cohen, L., & Felson, M. (1979). Social change and crime rate trends: A routine activity approach. *American Sociological Review*, 44, 588–608.

Cohen, M.A., & Piquero, A.R. (2009). New evidence of the monetary value of saving a high risk youth. *Journal of Quantitative Criminology*, 25, 25–49.

Cohen, S., & Ratner, L. (Eds.). (1970). *The development of an American culture*. Englewood Cliffs, NJ: Prentice Hall.

Coie, J.D., & Miller-Johnson, S. (2001). Peer factors and interventions. In R. Loeber & D.P. Farrington (Eds.), *Child delinquents: Development, intervention, and service needs* (pp. 191–209). Thousand Oaks, CA: Sage.

Coleman, M.S. (2004). *Children left behind: The educational status and needs of youth living in foster care in Ohio*. Washington, DC: National Center for Research and Data, The Child Welfare League of America.

Collins, K., Connors, K., Donohue, A., Gardner, S., Goldblatt, E., Hayward, A., Kiser, L., Strieder, F., & Thompson, E. (2010). *Understanding the impact of trauma and urban poverty on family systems: Risks, resilience, and interventions*. Baltimore, MD: Family Informed Trauma Treatment Center.

Collishaw, S., Pickles, A., Messer, J., Rutter, M., Shearer, C., & Maughan, B. (2007). Resilience to adult psychopathology following childhood maltreatment: Evidence from a community sample. *Child Abuse & Neglect*, 31, 211–229.

Community Strategy Center. (2013). *Black, brown and over-policed in LA schools*. Los Angeles, CA: Community Rights Campaign of the Labor/Community Strategy Center.

Comte, A. (2001). *A system of positive polity*. New York, NY: Bloomsbury Academic. (Originally published in 1851.)

Conner, K.R., & Goldston, D.B. (2007). Rates of suicide among males increase steadily from age 11 to 21: Developmental framework and outline for prevention. *Aggression and Violent Behavior*, 12, 193–207.

Connor. D.F. (2002). *Aggression and antisocial behaviour in children and adolescents: Research and treatment*. New York, NY: The Guilford Press.

Connors, C.K., Epstein, J.N., March, J.S., Angold, A., Wells, K.C., & Klaric, J. (2001). Multimodal treatment of ADHD in the MTA: An alternative outcome analysis. *Journal of the American Academy of Child and Adolescent Psychiatry*, 40, 159–167.

Cook, A., Blaustein, M., Spinazzola, J., & van der Kolk, B. (2003). *Complex trauma in children and adolescents* (White paper). Washington, DC: National Child Traumatic Stress Network Complex.

Copeland, W.E., Keeler, G., Angold, A., & Costello, E.J. (2007). Traumatic events and posttraumatic stress in childhood. *Archives of General Psychiatry*, 64, 577–584.

Cornell, D.G. (2006). *School violence: Fears versus facts*. Mahwah, NJ: Lawrence Erlbaum Associates.

Cornell, D.G. (2007). *The Virginia model for student threat assessment*. Paper presented at Confronting Violence in Our Schools: Planning Response, and Recovery—A PERI Symposium, University of Virginia.

Cornell, D.G., Shin, C., Ciolfi, A., & Sancken, K. (2013). *Prevention v. punishment: Threat assessment, school suspensions, and racial disparities*. Charlottesville: Legal Aid Justice Center and University of Virginia.

Cornish, D., & Clarke R. (1986). *The reasoning criminal: Rational choice perspectives on offending*. New York, NY: Springer-Verlag.

Costello, E.J., Angold, A., Burns, B., Stangl, D., Tween, D.L., Erkanli, A., & Worthman, C.M. (1996). The Great Smoky Mountains study of youth: Goals, design, methods, and the prevalence of DSM-III-R Disorders. *Archives of General Psychiatry*, 43, 1129–1136.

Costello, E.J., Egger, H.L., & Angold, A. (2005). The developmental epidemiology of anxiety disorders: Phenomenology, prevalence, and comorbidity. *Child and Adolescent Psychiatric Clinics of North America*, 14, 631–648.

Costello, E.J., Erkanli, A., Fairbank, J.A., & Angold, A. (2002). The prevalence of potentially traumatic events in childhood and adolescence. *Journal of Traumatic Stress*, 15, 99–112.

Costello, E.J., Mustillo, S., Erkanli, A., Keeler, G., & Angold, A. (2003). Prevalence and development of psychiatric disorders in childhood and adolescence. *Archives of General Psychiatry*, 60, 837–844.

Costello, E.J., Mustillo, S., Keeler, G., & Angold, A. (2004). Prevalence of psychiatric disorders in children and adolescents. In B. Levine, J. Petrila, & K. Hennessey (Eds.), *Mental health services: A public health perspective* (pp. 111–128). New York, NY: Oxford University Press.

Costello, E.J., Pine, D.S., Hammen, C., March, J.S., Plotsky, P., Weissman, M.M., Biederman, J., Goldsmith, H.H., Kaufman, J., Lewinsohn, P.M., Heelander, M., Hoagwood, K., Koretz, D.S., Nelson, C.A., & Leckman, J.F. (2002). Development and natural history of mood disorders. *Biological Psychiatry*, 52, 529–542.

Cottle, C.C., Lee, R.J., & Heilbrun, K. (2001). The prediction of criminal recidivism in juveniles: A meta-analysis. *Criminal Justice and Behavior*, 28, 367–394.

Council of Juvenile Correctional Administrators. (2009). *CJCA yearbook: A national perspective on juvenile corrections*. Braintree, MA: Author.

Courtney, M.E., Roderick, M., Smithgall, C., Gladden, R.M., & Nagaoka, J. (2004). *The educational status of foster children*. Chicago, IL: Chapin Hall Center for Children.

Cremin, L. (1988). *American eduction: The metropolitan experience 1876–1980*. New York, NY: Harper & Row.

Croysdale, A., Drerup, A., Bewsey, K., & Hoffman, N. (2008). Correlates of victimization in a juvenile justice population. *Journal of Aggression, Maltreatment & Trauma*, 17, 103–117.

Cruise, K.R., Evans, L.J., & Pickens, I.B. (2010). Integrating mental health and special education needs into comprehensive service planning for juvenile offenders in long-term custody settings. *Learning and Individual Differences*, 21, 30–40.

C-Span. (1996, January 28). Mrs. Clinton Campaign Speech. *C-Span Interview*. Retrieved from https://www.youtube.com/watch?v=j0uCrA7ePno

Cuevas, C.A., Finkelhor, D., Shattuck, A., Turner, H., & Hamby, S. (2013). *Children's exposure to violence and the intersection between delinquency and victimization*. Washington, DC: Office of Juvenile Justice and Delinquency Prevention, Office of Justice Programs, U.S. Department of Justice.

Currie, J., & Tekin, E. (2006). *Does child abuse cause crime?* Atlanta: Andrew Young School of Public Policy, Research Paper Studies, Georgia State University.

Currie, J., & Tekin, E. (2010). Understanding the cycle: Childhood maltreatment and future crime. *Journal of Human Resources*, 47, 509–549.

Curry, J.F., & Wells, K.C. (2005). Striving for effectiveness in the treatment of adolescent depression: Cognitive behavior therapy for multisite community intervention. *Cognitive and Behavioral Practice*, 12, 177–185.

Dahlberg, R.L. (2012). *Arrested futures: The criminalization of school discipline in Massachusetts' three largest school districts*. New York, NY: American Civil Liberties Union and Boston, MA: Citizens for Juvenile Justice.

Dalton, R.F., Evans, L.J., Cruise, K.R., Feinstein, R.A., & Kendrick, R.F. (2009). Race differences in mental health service access in a secure male juvenile justice facility. *Journal of Offender Rehabilitation*, 48, 194–209.

Daly, K., & Chesney-Lind, M. (2004). Feminism and criminology. In P.J. Shram & B. Koons-Witt (Eds.), *Gendered (in)justice: Theory and practice in feminist criminology* (pp. 9–48). Chicago, IL: Waveland Press.

Darensbourg, A., Perez, E., & Blake, J.J. (2010). Overrepresentation of African American males in exclusionary discipline: The role of school-based mental health professionals in dismantling the school to prison pipeline. *Journal of African American Males in Education*, 1, 196–211.

Daro, D., & Dodge, K.A. (2009). Creating community responsibility for child protection: Possibilities and challenges. *The Future of Children*, 29, 67–93.

Daro, D., & McCurdy, K. (2007). Interventions to prevent maltreatment. In L. Doll, S. Bonzo, D. Sleet, J. Mercy, & E.N. Haas (Eds.), *The handbook of injury and violence prevention* (pp. 137–155). New York, NY: Springer.

Darwin, C. (1998). *On the origin of species*. Nashville, TN: WordsWorth Classics. (Originally published in 1859.)

Debar, L.L., Clarke, G.N., O'Connor, E., & Nichols, G. (2001). Treated prevalence, incidence, and pharmacotherapy of child and adolescent mood disorders in an HMO. *Mental Health Services Research*, 3, 73–89.

Degue, S., & Widom, C.S. (2009). Does out-of-home placement mediate the relationship between child maltreatment and adult criminality? *Child Maltreatment*, 14, 344–355.

DeMatteo, D., & Marczyk, G. (2005). Risk factors, protective factors, and the prevention of antisocial behavior among juveniles. In K. Heilbrun, N.E. Sevin Goldstein, & R.E. Redding (Eds.), *Juvenile delinquency: Prevention, assessment, and intervention* (pp. 19–44). New York, NY: Oxford University Press.

Dembo, R., Briones-Robinson, R., Barrett, K., Winters, K.C., Schmeider, J., Ungaro, R.A., Karas, L., Belenko, S., & Gulledge, L. (2011). Mental health, substance use, and delinquency among truant youth in a brief intervention project: A longitudinal study. *Journal of Emotional and Behavioral Disorders*, 21, 176–192.

Dembo, R., Wothky, W., Shemwell, M., Pacheco, K., Seeberger, W., Rollie, M., Smeidler, J., & Livingston, S. (2000). A structural model of the influence of family problems and child abuse factors on serious delinquency among youths processed at a juvenile assessment center. *Journal of Child and Adolescent Substance Abuse*, 10, 17–31.

Dennis, M.L., Feeney, T., Stevens, L.H., & Bedoya, L. (2006). *Global appraisal of individual needs–short screener (GAIN-SS): Administration and scoring manual for the GAIN-SS version 2.0.1*. Bloomington, IL: Chestnut Health Systems.

Dennis, M.L., Feeney, T., Stevens, L.H., & Bedoya, L. (2008). *Global appraisal of individual needs—short screener: Administration and scoring manual*. Normal, IL: Chestnut Health Systems.

Denver Public Schools. (2014). *Parent student policy handbook*. Denver: Author.

DePanfilis, D., Dubowitz, H., & Kunz, J. (2008). Assessing the cost-effectiveness of family connections. *Child Abuse & Neglect*, 32, 335–351.

DeRigne, L., Porterfield, S., & Metz, S. (2009). The influence of health insurance on parent's reports of children's unmet mental health needs. *Maternal and Child Health Journal*, 13, 176–186.

Development Services Group, Inc. (2010). *Diversion programs, literature review*. Washington, DC: Office of Juvenile Justice and Delinquency Prevention, Bureau of Justice Affairs, U.S. Department of Justice.

Development Services Group, Inc. (2015). *Status offenders, literature review*. Washington, DC: Office of Juvenile Justice and Delinquency Prevention, Bureau of Justice Affairs, U.S. Department of Justice.

Developmental Services Group, Inc. (2017). *Youths with intellectual and developmental disabilities in the juvenile justice system: Literature review*. Washington, DC: Office of Juvenile Justice and Delinquency Prevention, Bureau of Justice Affairs, U.S. Department of Justice.

Devine, J. (1996). *Maximum security: The culture of violence in inner-city schools*. Chicago, IL: The University of Chicago Press.

Dishion, T.J., & Dodge, K.A. (2005). Peer contagion in interventions for children and adolescents: Moving towards an understanding of the ecology and dynamics of change. *Journal of Abnormal Child Psychology*, 33, 395–400.

Dishon, T.J., Dodge, K., & Lansford, J.E. (Eds.). (2006). *Deviant peer influences in programs for youth: Problems and solutions*. New York, NY: Guilford Press.

Dishion, T.J., Kavanagh, K., Schneiger, A.K.J., Nelson, S., & Kaufman, N. (2002). Preventing early adolescent substance use: A family centered strategy for the public middle school. *Prevention Science*, 3, 191–202.

Dmitrieva, J., Monahan, K.C., Cauffman, E., & Steinberg, L. (2012). Arrested development: The effects of incarceration on the development of psychosocial maturity. *Development and Psychopathology*, 24, 1073–1090.

Dodge, K.A., Dishion, T.J., & Landsford, J.E. (2006). *Deviant peer influences in programs for youth*. New York, NY: Guilford Press.

Domestic Violence Resource Centre Victoria, (2007). *Bursting the bubble*. Victoria, Australia: Author.

Dong, M., Anda, R.F., Felitti, V.J., Dube, S.R., Williamson, D.F., Thompson, T.J., Loo, C.M., & Giles, W.H. (2004). The interrelatedness of multiple forms of childhood abuse, neglect, and household dysfunction. *Child Abuse and Neglect*, 28, 771–784.

Doren, B., Bullis, M., & Benz, M.R. (1996). Predicting the arrest status of adolescents with disabilities in transition. *The Journal of Special Education*, 29, 363–380.

Drake, B., & Zuravin, S. (1998). Bias in child maltreatment reporting. *American Journal of Orthopsychiatry*, 68, 295–304.

Drake, B., Johnson-Reid, M., & Sapokaite, L. (2006). Reporting of child maltreatment: Does participation in other public sector services moderate the likelihood of a second maltreatment report? *Child Abuse & Neglect*, 30, 1201–1226.

Drake, B., Lee, S.M., & Johnson-Reid, M. (2009). Race and child maltreatment reporting: Are blacks overrepresented? *Youth Services Review*, 31, 261–272.

Dretzke, J., Frew, E., Davenport, C., Barlow, J., Stewart-Brown, S., Sandercock, J., Bayliss, S., Raftery, J., Hyde, C., & Taylor, R. (2004). *The effectiveness and cost effectiveness of parent-training/education programmes for the treatment of conduct disorder, including oppositional defiant disorder in children*. Birmingham, UK: West Midlands Health Technology Assessment Collaboration, Department of Public Health and Epidemiology, University of Birmingham.

Drizin, S.A., & Leo, R.A. (2004). The problem of false confessions in the post-DNA world. *North Carolina Law Review*, 82, 891–912.

DuBois, D.L., Holloway, B.E., Valentine, J.C., & Cooper, H.M. (2002). Effectiveness of mentoring programs for youth: A meta-analytic review. *American Journal of Community Psychology*, 30, 157–197.

DuBois, D.L., & Karcher, J.J. (2005). Youth mentoring: Theory, research, and practice. In D.L. DuBois and J.J. Karcher (Eds.), *Handbook of youth mentoring* (pp. 2–12). Thousand Oaks, CA: Sage.

Duke University School of Medicine. (2015). *Duke evidence-based practice implementation center*. Durham, NC: Duke University Press.

Durkheim, E. (1966). *Suicide: A study in sociology*. Boston, MA: Free Press. (Originally published in 1897.)

Durkheim, E. (1982). *The rules of sociological method*. New York, NY: Free Press. (Originally published in 1895.)

Durkheim, E. (2014). *The division of labor in society*. Boston, MA: Free Press. (Originally published in 1893.)

Durlak, J.A., & Weissberg, R.P. (2007). *The impact of after-school programs that promote personal and social skills*. Chicago, IL: Collaborative for Academic, Social, and Emotional Learning.

Durlak, J.A. (1998). Common risk and protective factors in successful prevention programs. *American Journal of Orthopsychiatry*, 19, 512–520.

Durose, M.R., Cooper, A.D., & Snyder, H.N. (2014). *Recidivism of prisoners released in 30 states in 2005: Patterns from 2005 to 2010*. Washington, DC: Bureau of Justice Statistics, Office of Justice Programs, U.S. Department of Justice.

Duster, T. (1970). *The legislation of morality: Law, drugs, and moral judgement*. Detroit, MI: Free Press.

Duwe, G., & Donnay, W. (2008). The impact of Megan's Law on sex offender recidivism: The Minnesota experience. *Criminology*, 46, 411–446.

Easteal, P.W. (1991). Women and crime: Premenstrual issues. In *Trends and Issues in Crime and Criminal Justice* (No. 31). Sydney: Australian Institute of Criminology.

Eggert, L.L., Thompson, E.A., Herting, J.R., & Nicholas, L.J. (1994). Preventing adolescent drug abuse and high school dropout through an intensive social network development program. *American Journal of Health Promotion*, 8, 202–215.

Eggert, L.L., Thompson, E.A., Herting, J.R., & Nicholas, L.J. (1995). Reducing suicide potential among high-risk youth: Tests of a school-based prevention program. *Suicide & Life-Threatening Behavior*, 25, 276–296.

Eggert, L.L., Thompson, E.A., Herting, J.R., & Randall, B.P. (2001). Reconnecting youth to prevent drug abuse, school dropout, and suicidal behaviors among high-risk youth. In E. Wagner & H.B. Waldron (Eds.), *Innovations in adolescent substance abuse intervention* (pp. 51–84). Oxford, England: Elsevier Science.

Egley, A., Howell, J.C., & Harris, M. (2014). *Highlight of the 2012 national youth gang survey*. Washington, DC: Office of Juvenile Justice and Delinquency Prevention, Office of Justice Programs, U.S. Department of Justice.

Elander, J., Siminoff, E., Pickles, A., Holmshaw, J., & Rutter, M. (2000). A longitudinal study of adolescent and adult conviction rates among children referred to child psychiatric services for behavioural or emotional problems. *Criminal Behaviour and Mental Health*, 10, 40–59.

Elbaum, B., Vaughn, S., Hughes, M.T., & Moody, S.W. (2000). How effective are one-to-one tutoring programs in reading for elementary students at risk for reading failure? A meta-analysis of the intervention research. *Journal of Educational Psychology*, 92, 605–619.

Elliott, D.S., & Ageton, S.S. (1980). Reconciling race and class differences in self-reported and official estimates of delinquency. *American Sociological Review*, 45, 95–110.

Elliott, D.S., Huizinga, D., & Ageton, S.S. (1985). *Explaining delinquency and drug use*. Beverly Hills, CA: Sage.

Erlanger, H. (1974). The empirical status of the subculture of violence thesis. *Social Problems*, 22, 280–292.

Esbensen, F.A., & Huizinga, D. (1993). Gangs, drugs, and delinquency in a survey of urban youth. *Criminology*, 31, 565–589.

Esbensen, F.A., Osgood, D.W., Taylor, T.J., Peterson, D., & Freng, A. (2001). How great is G.R.E.A.T.? Results from a longitudinal quasi-experimental design. *Criminology & Public Policy*, 1, 87–118.

Esbensen, F.A., Peterson, D., Taylor, T.J., & Freng, A. (2010). *Youth violence: Sex and race differences in offending, victimization, and gang membership*. Philadelphia, PA: Temple University Press.

Esbensen, F.A., Peterson, D., Taylor, T.J., & Osgood, D.W. (2012). Results from a multisite evaluation of the G.R.E.A.T. Program. *Justice Quarterly*, 29(1), 125–151.

Estrada, R., & Marksamer, J. (2006). Lesbian, gay, bisexual and transgender young people in state custody: Making the child welfare and juvenile justice systems safe for youth through litigation, advocacy and education. *Temple Law Review*, 79, 415–438.

Eterno, J.A., & Silberman, E.B. (2012). *The crime numbers game: Management by manipulation*. New York, NY: CRC Press.

Evans, C.C., & Vander-Stoep, A. (1997). Risk factors for juvenile justice system referral among children in a public mental health system. *The Journal of Mental Health Administration*, 24, 443–455.

Evans, G.W., & Cassells, R.C. (2013). Childhood poverty, cumulative risk exposure, and mental health in emerging adults. *Clinical Psychological Science*, 2, 287–296.

Eysenck, H. J. (1964). *Crime and personality.* New York, NY: Routldge & Kegan Paul Ltd.

Fabelo, T., Thompson, M.D., Plotkin, M., Carmichael, D., Marchbanks, M.P. III, & Booth, E.A. (2011). *Breaking schools' rules: A statewide study of how school discipline relates to students' success and juvenile justice involvement.* College Station: Council of State Governments Justice Center, Public Research Policy Research Institute of Texas A&M University.

Fabiano, G.A., Pelham, W.E., Ghangy, E.M., Coles, E.K., & Wheeler-Cox, T. (2000). *A meta-analysis of behavioral and combined treatments for ADHD.* Washington, DC: American Psychological Association.

Fagan, J. (2000). Contexts of choice by adolescents in criminal events. In T. Grisso & R. Schwartz (Eds.), *Youth on trial.* Chicago, IL: The University of Chicago Press.

Fagan, J. (2008). Juvenile crime and criminal justice: Resolving border disputes. *The Future of Children*, 18, 81–118.

Fagan, J., & Wilkinson, D. (1998). Guns, youth violence, and social identity. In M. Tonry & M.H. Moore (Eds.), *Youth violence* (pp. 106–138). Chicago, IL: Chicago University Press.

Falconer, M.K., Haskett, M.E., McDaniels, L., Dirkes, T., & Siegel, E.C. (2008). Evaluation of support groups for child abuse prevention: Outcomes of four state evaluations. *Social Work with Groups*, 31, 165–182.

Farber, H.B. (2004). The role of the parent/guardian in juvenile custodial interrogations: Friends or foe. *American Criminal Law Review*, 41, 1277–1312.

Farrington, D.P. (1997). Early prediction of violent and nonviolent youthful offending. *European Journal on Criminal Policy and Research*, 5, 51–66.

Farrington, D.P. (2002). Developmental criminology and risk-focused prevention. In M. Maguire, R. Morgan, & R. Reiner (Eds.), *The Oxford Handbook of Criminology* (pp. 657–701). Oxford, England: Oxford University Press.

Farrington, D.P., & Welsh, B.C. (2003). Family-based prevention of offending: A meta-analysis. *Australian and New Zealand Journal of Criminology*, 36, 127–151.

Farrington, D.B., & West, D.J. (1981). The Cambridge study in delinquent development. In Mednick, S.A. & Baert, A.E. (Eds) *Prospective longitudinal research: An empirical basis for the prevention of psychosocial disorders,* Oxford: Oxford University Press (pp. 137–145).

Federal Bureau of Investigation. (2016a). *National incident-based reporting system: Methodology.* Washington, DC: Author.

Federal Bureau of Investigation. (2016b). *Uniform crime report, crime in the United States.* Washington, DC: Author.

Federal Interagency Reentry Council. (2015). *Juvenile reentry.* Washington, DC: Author.

Feieman, J., Lindell, K.U., & Eaddy, N. (2017). *Unlocking youth: Legal strategies to end solitary confinement in juvenile facilities.* Washington, DC: Juvenile Law Center.

Feld, B. (1999). *Bad kids, race, and the establishment of the juvenile courts.* New York: Oxford University Press.

Feld, B.C. (2009). Violent girls or relabeled status offenders? An alternative interpretation of the data. *Crime & Delinquency*, 55, 241–165.

Feld, B.C. (2013). Real interrogation: What actually happens when cops question kids. *Law & Society Review*, 47, 1–36.

Felitta, V.J., Anda, R.F., Nordenberg, D., Williamson, D.F., Spitz, A.M., Edwards, V., Koss, M.P., & Marks, J.S. (2008). The relationships of adult health status to childhood abuse and household dysfunction. *American Journal of Preventive Medicine*, 14, 245–258.

Fenning, P., Pigott, T., Engler, E., Bradshaw, K., Gamboney, E., Grunewald, S., & McGrath-Kato, M. (2013). *A mixed methods approach examining disproportionality in school discipline.* Paper presented at the Closing the School Discipline Gap: Research to Practice Conference, Washington, DC.

Fergus, S., & Zimmerman, M.A. (2004). Adolescent resilience: A framework for understanding healthy development in the face of risk. *Annual Review of Public Health*, 26, 399–419.

Ferguson, A.A. (2000). *Bad boys: Public schools in the making of black masculinity.* Ann Arbor: The University of Michigan Press.

Fergusson, D.M., Boden, J.M., & Horwood, L.J. (2008). Exposure to childhood sexual and physical abuse and adjustment in early adulthood. *Child Abuse and Neglect*, 32, 707–619.

Fergusson, D.M., & Norwood, U. (2001). The Christchurch health and development study: Review of findings on child and adolescent mental health. *Australia and New Zealand Journal of Psychiatry*. 35, 287–296.

Ferrer-Wreder, L., Stattin, H., Lorente, C.C., Tubman, J., & Adamson, L. (2003). *Prevention and youth development programs: Across borders.* New York, NY: Kluwer/Plenum Academic.

Filges, T., Knudsen, A., Swendsen, M., Kowalski, K., Benjaminsen, L., & Jorgensen, A. (2015). *Cognitive-behavioral therapies or young people in outpatient for non-opiod drug use: A systematic review.* Oslo, Norway: The Campbell Library, The Campbell Collaboration.

Finkelhor, D. (2009). The prevention of childhood sexual abuse. *The Future of Children*, 19, 169–194.

Finkelhor, D., Ormrod, R.K., & Turner, H.A. (2009). Lifetime assessment of poly-victimization in a national sample of children and youth. *Child Abuse and Neglect*, 33, 403–411.

Finkelhor, D., Ormrod, R.K., Turner, H.A., & Hamby, S.L. (2005). The victimization of children and youth: A comprehensive, national survey. *Child Maltreatment*, 10, 5–25.

Finkelhor, D., Turner, H., Ormrod, R.K., & Hamby, S.L. (2009). Violence, abuse, and crime exposure in a national sample of children and youth. *Pediatrics*, 124, 1411–1423.

Finkelhor, D., Turner, H., Shattuck, A., & Hamby, S.L. (2013). Violence, abuse, and crime exposure in a national sample of children and youth: An update. *JAMA Pediatrics*, 167, 614–621.

Finn, P., Townsend, M., Shively, M., & Rich, T. (2005). *A guide to developing, maintaining, and succeeding with your school resource officer program.* Washington, DC: Office of Community Oriented Policing Services, U.S. Department of Justice.

Flavin, J. (2001). Feminism for the mainstream criminologist: An invitation. *Journal of Criminal Justice*, 29, 271–285.

Florida Department of Juvenile Justice. (2010). *2010 Legislative & General Budget Report.* Tallahassee: Author.

Fontaine, N., Barbonneau, R., Vitaro, F., Barker, E.D., & Tremblay, R.E. (2009). Research review: A critical review of studies on the developmental trajectories of antisocial behavior in females. *Journal of Child Psychology and Psychiatry*, 50, 363–385.

Ford, D.F., Chapman, J.F., Hawke, J., & Albert, D. (2007). *Trauma among youth in the juvenile justice system: Critical issues and new directions.* Delmar, NY: National Center for Mental Health and Juvenile Justice.

Ford, J.D., Elhai, J.D., Connor, D.F., & Frueh, B.C. (2010). Poly-victimization and risk of posttraumatic, depressive, and substance use disorders and involvement in delinquency in a national sample of adolescents. *Journal of Adolescent Health*, 46, 542–552.

Ford, J.D., Grasso, D.J., Hawke, J., & Chapman, J.F. (2013). Poly-victimization among juvenile justice–involved youths. *Child Abuse & Neglect*, 37, 788–800.

Ford, T. (2008). Practitioner review: How can epidemiology help us plan and deliver effective child and adolescent mental health services? *Journal of Child Psychology and Psychiatry*, 49, 900–914.

Fox, J. A. (1996). *Trends in juvenile justice: A report to the United States attorney general on current and future rates of juvenile offending.* Washington, DC: U.S. Department of Justice, Bureau of Justice Studies.

Fraser, M.W. (Ed.). (2004). *Risk and resilience in childhood: An ecological perspective* (2nd ed.). Washington, DC: NASW Press.

Fredlanger, K. (1947). *The psychoanalytic approach to juvenile delinquency.* London, England: Routledge.

Froehlick, J., Doepfner, M., & Lehmkuhl, G. (2002). Effects of combined cognitive behavioural treatment with parent management training in ADHD. *Behavioural and Cognitive Psychotherapy*, 30, 111–115.

Fry, R., & Taylor, P. (2012). *The rise of residential segregation by income.* Washington, DC: Pew Research Center.

Fuentes, A. (2012, September 5). The truancy trap. *The Atlantic.* Retrieved from https://www.theatlantic.com/national/archive/2012/09/the-truancy-trap/261937/

Fuentes, A. (2014). The schoolhouse as jailhouse. In A.J. Nocella II, P. Parmar, & D. Stovall (Eds.), *From education to incarceration: Dismantling the school-to-prison pipeline.* New York, NY: Peter Lang.

Furdello, J., & Puzzanchera, C. (2015). *Delinquency cases in juvenile court, 2013.* Washington, DC: Office of Juvenile Justice and Delinquency Prevention, Office of Justice Programs, U.S. Department of Justice.

Gagnon, J.C., & Leone, P.E. (2002). Alternative strategies for school violence prevention. *New Directions for Youth Development*, 92, 101–125.

Gallagher, C., & Dobrin, A. (2006). Facility-level characteristics associated with serious suicide attempts and deaths from suicide in juvenile justice residential facilities. *Suicide and Life Threatening Behavior*, 36, 363–375.

Gammelgard, M., Koivisto, A.M., Eronen, M., & Kaltiala-Heino, R. (2015). Predictive validity of the structured assessment of violence in youth: A 4-year follow up. *Criminal Behavior and Mental Health*, 25, 192–206.

Garland, A.F., Hough, R.L., McCabe, K.M., Yeh, M., Wood, P.A., & Aarons, G. (2001). Prevalence of psychiatric disorders in youths across five sectors of care. *Journal of the American Academy of Child and Adolescent Psychiatry*, 49, 409–426.

Garofalo, R. (1885). *Criminologia: Studio sul delitto, sulle sue cause e sui mezzi di repression.* Torino, Italy: Fratelli Bocca.

Garrido, V., & Morales, L.A. (2007). *Serious (violent and chronic) juvenile offenders: A systematic review of treatment effectiveness in secure corrections.* Philadelphia, PA: The Campbell Collaboration Reviews of Intervention and Policy Evaluations (CT-RIPE), Campbell Collaboration.

Geis, L.M. (2014). An IEP for the juvenile justice system: Incorporating special education law throughout the delinquency process. *University of Memphis Law Review*, 44, 869–919.

Gibbons, D.C. (1979). *The criminological enterprise: Theories and perspectives.* Upper Saddle River, NJ: Prentice Hall.

Giedd, J.N. (2004). Structural magnetic resonance imaging of the adolescent brain. *Annals of the New York Academy of Science*, 83, 1021.

Goddard, H. (1912). *The Kallikak family: A study in the heredity of feeble-mindedness.* New York, NY: Macmillan.

Goddard, H. (1915). *The criminal imbecile: An analysis of three remarkable murder cases.* New York, NY: Macmillan.

Goffman, A. (2014). *On the run: Fugitive life in American city.* Chicago, IL: The University of Chicago Press.

Gohara, M.S., Hardy, J.S., & Hewitt, D.T. (2005). The disparate impact of an under-funding patchwork indigent defense system on Mississippi's African Americans: The civil rights case for establishing a statewide, fully funded public defender system. *Howard Law Journal*, 49, 81–95.

Golding, W. (1959). *Lord of the flies.* London, England: Faber & Faber.

Goldstein, N., Olubadewo, O., Redding, R., & Lexcen, F. (2005). Mental health disorders: The neglected risk factor in juvenile delinquency. In K. Heilbrum (Ed.), *Juvenile delinquency: Prevention, assessment and intervention* (pp. 85–110). New York, NY: Oxford University Press.

Golinelli, D., & Minton, T. (2014). *Prison and jail inmates at midyear.* Washington, DC: Office of Justice Programs, Bureau of Justice Statistics, U.S. Department of Justice.

González, T. (2015). Socializing schools: Addressing racial disparities in discipline through restorative justice. In D.J. Losen (Ed.), *Closing the school discipline gap: Research for policymakers.* New York, NY: Teachers College Press.

Gonzalez-Tejera, G., Canino, G., Ramirez, R., Chavez, L., Shrout, P., Bird, H., Bravo, M., Martinez-Taboas, A., Ribera, J., & Bauemeister, J. (2005). Examining minor and major depression in adolescents. *Journal of Child Psychology and Psychiatry*, 46, 888–899.

Goodman, R.F. (2002). *Caring for kids after trauma and death: A guide for parents and professionals.* New York: The Institute for Trauma and Stress, The New York University Child Study Center.

Goodman, S.H., Hoven, C.W., Narrow, W.E., Cohen, P., Fielding, B., Alegria, M., Leaf, P.J., Kandel, D., Horwitz, S.M., Bravo, M., Moore, R., & Dulcan, M.K. (1998). Measurement of risk for mental disorders and competence in a psychiatric epidemiologic community survey: The National Institute of Mental Health Methods for the Epidemiology of Child and Adolescent Mental Disorders (MECA) Study. *Social Psychiatry and Psychiatric Epidemiology*, 33, 162–173.

Goodwin-Slater, A. (2013). Child abuse: A survivor's story. *American Psychological Association.* Retrieved from http://www.apa.org/pi/about/newsletter/2013/04/child-abuse.aspx

Gottfredson, G.D., Gottfredson, D.C., Czeh, E.R., Cantor, D., Crosse, S., & Hantman, I. (2000). *National study of delinquency prevention in schools* (Final report). Ellicott City, MD: Gottfredson Associates.

Gottfredson, G.D., Gottfredson, D.C., Payne, A.A., & Gottfredson, N.C. (2005). School climate predictors of school disorder: Results from a national study of delinquency prevention in schools. *Journal of Research in Crime and Delinquency*, 42, 412–444.

Gottfredson, M., & Hirschi, T. (1990). *A general theory of crime.* Stanford, CA: Stanford University Press.

Gould, N.G., & Richardson, J. (2006). Parent-training/education programmes in management of children with conduct disorders: Developing an integrated evidence-based perspective for health and social care. *Journal of Children's Services*, 1, 47–60.

Graham, P.A. (1974). *Community and class in American education, 1865–1918.* New York, NY: Wiley.

Graham, S., & Lowry, B.S. (2004). Priming unconscious racial stereotypes about adolescent offenders. *Law and Human Behavior*, 28, 483–504.

Graham, T., & Corcoran, K. (2003). Mental health screening results for Native American and Euro-American youth in Oregon juvenile justice settings. *Psychological Reports*, 92, 1053–1061h.

Grasmick, G.H., & Green, D. E. (1980). Legal punishment, social disapproval and internalization as inhibitors of illegal behavior. *Journal of Criminal Law and Criminology*, 71, 325–335.

Gray, D., Achilles, J., Keller, T., Tate, D., Haggard, L., Rolfs, R., Cazier, C., Workman, J., & McMahon, W. (2002). Utah youth suicide study, phase 1: Government agency contact before death. *Journal of the American Academy of Child and Adolescent Psychiatry*, 41, 427–434.

Greenberg, M.T., Kusché, C., & Mihalic, S.F. (2006). *Promoting alternative thinking strategies (PATHS): Blueprints for violence prevention, book ten* (Blueprints for Violence Prevention Series, D.S. Elliott, Series Ed.). Boulder: Center for the Study and Prevention of Violence, Institute of Behavioral Science, University of Colorado.

Greenwald, R. (2002). *Trauma and juvenile delinquency: Theory, research, and interventions*. Binghamton, NH: The Haworth Press.

Greenwood, P. (2008). Prevention and intervention programs for juvenile offenders. *The Future of Children*, 18, 185–210.

Gregory, A., Allen, J.P., Mikami, A.Y., Hafen, A., & Pianta, R.C. (2012). *The promise of a teacher professional development program in reducing the racial disparity in classroom exclusionary discipline*. Washington, DC: Center for Civil Rights Remedies and the Research-to-Practice Collaborative, National Conference on Race and Gender Disparities in Discipline.

Gregory, A., Bell, J., & Pollock, M. (2014). *How educators can eradicate disparities in school discipline: A briefing paper on school-based interventions*. Bloomington, IN: Discipline Disparities: A Research-to-Practice Collaborative, The Equity Project at Indiana University, Center for Evaluation and Education Policy.

Gregory, A., Skiba, R.J., & Noguera, P.A. (2010). The achievement gap and the discipline gap: Two sides of the same coin? *Education Researcher*, 59, 59–68.

Griffin, P. (2008). *Different from adults: An updated analysis of juvenile transfer and blended sentencing laws, with recommendations for reform*. Pittsburgh, PA: National Center for Juvenile Justice.

Griffin, P., Addie, S., Adams, B., & Firestine, K. (2011). *Trying juveniles as adults: An analysis of state transfer laws and reporting*. Washington, DC: Office of Juvenile Justice and Delinquency Prevention, Office of Justice Programs, U.S. Department of Justice.

Griffin, P., & Torbet, P. (Eds.). (2000). *Desktop guide to good juvenile probation practice*. Washington, DC: Office of Juvenile Justice and Delinquency Prevention, National Center for Juvenile Justice.

Grisso, T. (1980). Juvenile's capacities to waive Miranda rights: An empirical analysis. *California Law Review*, 68, 1134–1166.

Grisso, T. (2008). Adolescent offenders with mental disorders. *The Future of Children*, 18, 143–162.

Grisso, T., & Barnum, R. (2006). *Massachusetts Youth Screening Instrument—Version 2: User's manual and technical report*. Sarasota, FL: Professional Resource Press.

Grisso, T., & Schwartz, R.G. (Eds.). (2000). *Youth on trial: A developmental perspective on juvenile justice*. Chicago, IL: The University of Chicago Press.

Grob, G.N. (1994). *The mad among us: A history of care of America's mentally ill*. New York, NY: Free Press.

Grob, G.N. (2008). *Mental institutions in America: Social policy to 1875*. Piscataway, NJ: Transaction.

Gudino, O.G., Lau, A.S., Yeh, M., McCabe, K.M., & Hough, R.L. (2009). Understanding racial/ethnic disparities in youth mental health services: Do disparities vary by problem type? *Journal of Emotional and Behavioral Disorders*, 17, 3–16.

Guerry, A. (2002). *Essay on the moral statistics of France*. New York, NY: Edwin Mellen Press. (Originally published in 1833)

Guo, S., Barth, R.P., & Gibbons, C. (2006). Propensity score matching strategies for evaluating substance abuse services for child welfare clients. *Children and Youth Services Review*, 28, 357–383.

Hafen, C.A., Allen, J.P., Mikami, A.Y., Gregory, A., Hamre, B., & Pianta, R.C. (2010). The pivotal role of adolescent autonomy in secondary classrooms. *Journal of Youth and Adolescence*, 41, 245–255.

Hagan, J. (1993). The social embeddedness of crime and unemployment. *Criminology*, 31, 465–491.

Hahn, R.A., Bilukha, O., Lowy, J., Crosby, A., & Fullilove, M.T. (2005). The effectiveness of therapeutic foster care for the prevention of violence: A systematic review. *American Journal of Preventative Medicine*, 28, 72–90.

Hahn, R.A., Lowy, J., Bilukha, O., Snyder, S., Briss, P., Crosby, A., Fullilove, M.T., Tuma, F., Moscici, E.K., Liberman, A., Schofield, A., & Corso, P.S. (2004). Therapeutic foster care for the prevention of violence. *Morbidity and Mortality Weekly Report*, 53, 1–8.

Hammond, C., Linton, D., Smink, J., & Drew, S. (2007). *Dropout risk factors and exemplary programs: A technical report*. Clemson, SC: National Dropout Prevention Center/Network.

Hanson, R.F., Kievet, L.S., Saunders, B.E., Smith, D.W., Kilpatrick, D.G., Resnick, H.S., & Ruggiero, K.J. (2003). Correlates of adolescent reports of sexual assault: Findings from the National Survey of Adolescents. *Child Maltreatment*, 9, 62–77.

Harding, K., Galano, J., Martin, J., Huntington, L., & Schellenbach, C. (2006). Healthy Families America effectiveness: A comprehensive review of outcomes. *Journal of Prevention and Intervention in the Community*, 34, 149–179.

Harry, B., & Klingner, J. (2006). *Why are so many minority students in special education: Understanding race and disability in schools*. New York, NY: Teachers College Press.

Harvard Family Research Project. (2010). *Family engagement as a systemic, sustained, and integrated strategy to promote student achievement*. Cambridge, MA: Harvard Graduate School of Education.

Hatzenbuehler, M.L., & Keyes, K.M. (2013). Inclusive anti-bulling policies and reduced risk of suicide attempts in lesbian and gay youth. *Journal of Adolescent Health*, 53, 21–26.

Hawes, J. (1971). *Children in urban society: Juvenile delinquency in nineteenth century America*. New York, NY: Oxford University Press.

Hawkens, J.D., Herrenkohl, T.I., Farrington, D.P., Brewer, D., Catalano, R.F., Harachi, T.W., & Cothern, L. (2000). *Predictors of youth violence*. Washington, DC: Office of Juvenile Justice and Delinquency Prevention, Office of Justice Programs, U.S. Department of Justice.

Hawkens, J.D., Herrenkohl, T.I., Farrington, D.P., Brewer, D., Catalano, R.F., & Harachi, T.W. (1998). A review of predictors of youth violence. In R. Loeber & T.P. Farrington (Eds.), *Serious and violent juvenile offenders: Risk factors and successful interventions* (pp. 106–146). Thousand Oaks, CA: Sage.

Hawkens, J.D., Herrenkohl, T.I., Farrington, D.P., Brewer, D., Catalano, R.F., Harachi, T.W., & Cothern, L. (2000). *Predictors of youth violence*. Washington, DC: Office of Juvenile Justice and Delinquency Prevention, Office of Justice Programs, U.S. Department of Justice.

Hawkins, S.R., Graham, P.W., Williams, J., & Zahn, M.A. (2009). *Resilient girls—Factors that protect against delinquency*. Washington, DC: Office of Juvenile Justice and Delinquency Prevention, Office of Justice Programs, U.S. Department of Justice.

Hayes, L. (2009). *Characteristics of juvenile suicide in confinement*. Washington, DC: Office of Juvenile Justice and Delinquency Prevention, Office of Justice Programs, U.S. Department of Justice.

Haynie, D.L., Giordano, P.C., Manning, W.D., & Longmore, M.A. (2005). Adolescent romantic relationships and delinquency involvement. *Criminology*, 43, 177–210.

Hedden, S.L., Kenner, J., Lipari, R., Medley, G., Tice, P., Copello, E.A., Kroutil, L.A., & Hunter, D. (2015). *Behavioral health trends in the United States: Results from the 2014 national survey on drug use and health*. Washington, DC: Substance Abuse and Mental Health Services Administration, U.S. Department of Health and Human Services.

Heilbrun, K. (1997). Prediction versus management models relevant to risk assessment: The importance of legal decision-making context. *Law and Human Behavior*, 21, 347–359.

Heitzeg, N.A. (2014). Criminalizing education: Zero tolerance policies, police in the hallways, and the school to prison pipeline. In A.J. Nocella II, P. Parmar, & D. Stovall (Eds.), *From education to incarceration: Dismantling the school-to-prison pipeline* (pp. 11–46). New York, NY: Peter Lang.

Heller, S.S., Larrieu, J.A., D'Imperio, R., & Boris, N.W. (1999). Research on resilience to child maltreatment: Empirical considerations. *Child Abuse & Neglect*, 23, 321–338.

Henggeler, S.W., Schoenwald, S.K., Rowland, M.D., & Cunningham, P.B. (2002). *Serious emotional disturbance in children and adolescents: Multisystemic therapy.* New York, NY: Guilford Press.

Hennessey, M., Ford, J.D., Mahoney, K., Ko, S.J., & Siegfried, C.B. (2004). *Trauma among girls in the juvenile justice system.* Los Angeles, CA: National Child Traumatic Stress Network.

Henning, K.N. (2013). Criminalizing normal adolescent behavior in communities of color: The role of prosecutors in juvenile justice reform. *Cornell Law Review*, 98, 412–465.

Herrera, C., Grossman, J.B., Kauh, T.J., Feldman, A.F., McMaken, J., & Jucovy, L.Z. (2007). *Big brothers big sisters school-based mentoring impact study.* Philadelphia, PA: Public/Private Ventures.

Herrnstein, R., & Murray, C. (1994). *The bell curve: Intelligence and class structure in American life.* New York, NY: Simon & Schuster.

Herz, D.C., & Fontaine, A. (2012). *Preliminary results for the crossover youth practice model.* Washington, DC: Georgetown University McCourt School of Public Policy, Center for Juvenile Justice Reform.

Herz, D.C., Lee, P., Lutz, L., Stewart, M., Tuell, J., & Wiig, J. (2012). *Addressing the needs of multi-system youth: Strengthening the connection between child welfare and juvenile justice.* Washington, DC: Center for Juvenile Justice Reform and Robert F. Kennedy Children's Action Corps, Georgetown University.

Herz, D.C., & Ryan, J.P. (2008). Exploring the characteristics and outcomes of 241.1 youth crossing over from dependency to delinquency in Los Angeles County. *Center for Families, Children, and the Courts Research Update*, 1–13.

Hill, N.E., & Tyson, D. (2009). Parental involvement in middle school: A meta-analytic assessment of the strategies that promote achievement. *Developmental Psychology*, 45, 740–763.

Hill, R.B. (2005). The role of race in parental reunification. In D. Derezotes, J. Poertner, & M.F. Testa (Eds.), *Race matters in child welfare: The overrepresentation of African American children in the system* (pp. 187–200). Washington, DC: Child Welfare League of America.

Himmelstein, K.E.W., & Bruckner, H. (2011). Criminal-justice and school sanctions against nonheterosexual youth: A national longitudinal study. *Pediatrics*, 127, 49–57.

Hindelang, M.J., Hirschi, T., & Weis, J.G. (1981). *Measuring delinquency.* Beverly Hills, CA: Sage.

Hirsch, S., & Sheffield, R. (2006, October). Coping with a child's conduct disorder. *Virtual Mentor, American Medical Association.* Retrieved from http://journalofethics.ama-assn.org/2006/10/ccas3–0610.html

Hirschfield, P.J. (2008). Preparing for prison? The criminalization of school discipline in the USA. *Theoretical Criminology*, 12, 79–101.

Hirschfield, P.J. (2010). School surveillance in America: Disparate and unequal. In T. Monahan & R.D. Torres (Eds.), *Schools under surveillance: Cultures of control in public education* (pp. 38–54). New Brunswick, NJ: Rutgers University Press.

Hirschfield, P.J., & Piquero, A.R. (2010). Normalization and legitimization: Modeling stigmatizing attitudes toward ex-offenders. *Criminology*, 48, 27–55.

Hirschi, T. (1969). *Causes of delinquency.* Berkeley: University of California Press.

Hirschi, T. (1979). Separate and unequal is better. *Journal of Research in Crime and Delinquency*, 16, 34–38.

Hobbes, T. (1982). *Leviathan.* London, England: Penguin Classics. (Originally published In 1651.)

Hockenberry, S. (2014). *Juveniles in residential placement, 2011.* Washington, DC: Office of Juvenile Justice and Delinquency Prevention, Office of Justice Programs.

Hockenberry, S., & Puzzanchera, C. (2014a). *Delinquency cases waived to criminal court, 2011.* Washington, DC: Office of Juvenile Justice and Delinquency Prevention, Bureau of Justice Affairs, U.S. Department of Justice.

Hockenberry, S., & Puzzanchera, C. (2014b). *Juvenile court statistics, 2011.* Washington, DC: Office of Juvenile Justice and Delinquency Prevention, Office of Justice Programs, U.S. Department of Justice.

Hockenberry, S., & Puzzanchera, C. (2015). *Juvenile court statistics 2013.* Washington, DC: National Center for Juvenile Justice, Office of Juvenile Justice and Delinquency Prevention.

Hockenberry, S., Wachter, A., & Sladky, A. (2016). *Juvenile residential facility census, 2014: Selected findings.* Washington, DC: Office of Juvenile Justice and Delinquency Prevention, Office of Justice Programs, U.S. Department of Justice.

Hodges, K. (2005). Child and adolescent functional assessment scale. In T. Grisso, G. Vincent, & D. Seagrave (Eds.), *Mental health screening and assessment in juvenile justice* (pp. 123–151). New York, NY: Guilford Press.

Hoffman, J.P., Erickson, L.D., & Spence, K.R. (2013). Modeling the association between academic achievement and delinquency. *Criminology*, 51, 629–660.

Hoge, R.D. (2001). *The juvenile offender: Theory, research and applications.* Norwell, MA: Kluwer Plenum.

Hogue, A., & Liddle, H.S. (2009). Family-based treatment for adolescent substance abuse: Controlled trials and new horizons in services research. *Journal of Family Therapy*, 31, 126–154.

Holsinger, K., & Holsinger, A. (2005). Differential pathways to violence and self-injurious behavior: African American and white girls in the juvenile justice system. *Journal of Research in Crime and Delinquency*, 42, 211–242.

Holzer, H., Schanzenbach, D.W., Duncan, G.G., & Ludwig, J. (2007). *The economic costs of poverty: Subsequent effects of children growing up poor.* Washington, DC: Center for American Progress.

Hooper, S.R., Murphy, J., Devaney, A., & Hultman, T. (2000). Ecological outcomes of adolescents in a psychoeducational residential treatment facility. *The American Journal of Orthopsychiatry*, 70, 491–500.

Horner, R.H., Sugai, G., Smolkowski, K., Todd, A., Nakasato, J., & Esperanza, J. (2009). A randomized control trial of school-wide positive behavior support in elementary schools. *Journal of Positive Behavioral Interventions*, 11, 133–144.

Horowitz, J.L., & Garber, J. (2006). The prevention of depressive symptoms in children and adolescents: A meta-analytic review. *Journal of Consulting and Clinical Psychology*, 24, 401–415.

Howard, K.S., & Brooks-Gunn, K. (2009). The role of home-visiting programs in preventing child abuse and neglect. *The Future of Children*, 19, 119–146.

Howe, D. (2009). ADHD and its comorbidity: An example of gene-environment interaction and its implications for child and family social work. *Child & Family Social Work*, 15, 265–275.

Howell, J.C. (2003). *Preventing & reducing juvenile delinquency: A comprehensive framework.* Thousand Oaks, CA: Sage.

Howell, J.C. (2009). *Preventing & reducing juvenile delinquency: A comprehensive framework* (2nd ed.). Thousand Oaks, CA: Sage.

Howell, J.C. (2010). *Gang prevention: An overview of research and programs.* Washington, DC: Office of Juvenile Justice and Delinquency Prevention, Office of Justice Programs, U.S. Department of Justice.

Howell, J.C., Feld, B.C., Mears, D.P., Farrington, D.P., Loeber, R., & Petechuk, D. (2013). *Bulletin 5: Youth offenders and an effective response in the juvenile and adult court systems: What happens, what should happen, and what we need to know.* Washington, DC: U.S. Department of Justice.

Huang, H., Ryan, J.P., & Herz, D. (2012). The journey of dually-involved youth: The description and prediction of rereporting and recidivism. *Children and Youth Services Review*, 34, 254–260.

Human Rights Watch. (2005). *The rest of their lives: Life without parole for child offenders in the United States.* New York, NY: Author.

Human Rights Watch. (2009). *Hatred in the hallways: Violence and discrimination against lesbian, gay, bisexual, and transgender students in U.S. schools*. New York, NY: Author.

Human Rights Watch & American Civil Liberties Union. (2012). *Growing up locked down: Youth in solitary confinement in jails and prisons across the United States*. New York, NY: Author.

Hunt, J., & Moodie-Mills, A.C. (2012). *The unfair criminalization of gay and transgender youth: An overview of the experiences of LGBT youth in the juvenile justice system*. Washington, DC: Center for American Progress.

Hunter, J.A. (2009). *Juvenile sex offenders: A cognitive-behavioral treatment program*. New York, NY: Oxford University Press.

Hyames, S., & de Hames, M.V. (2000). *Educational experiences and achievement of children and youth in the care of the department receiving services from Chicago public schools*. Urbana-Champaign: Children and Family Resource Center, University of Illinois.

Hyman, I.A., & McDowell, E. (1979). *Corporal punishment in American education*. Philadelphia, PA: Temple University Press.

Insley, A.C. (2001). Suspending and expelling children from educational opportunity: Time to reevaluate zero tolerance policies. *American University Law Review*, 50, 1039–1073.

Institute of Education Services. (2009). *Intervention: Read 180*. Washington, DC: What Works Clearinghouse, U.S. Department of Education.

International Association of Chiefs of Police. (2012). *Reducing risks: An executive's guide to effective juvenile interview and interrogation*, Washington, DC: Office of Juvenile Justice and Delinquency Prevention. Retrieved from http://www.theiacp.org/Portals/0/pdfs/ReducingRisksAnExecutiveGuidetoEffectiveJuvenileInterviewandInterrogation.pdf

Irvine, A. (2005). *Girls circle: Summary of outcomes for girls in the juvenile justice system*. Santa Cruz, CA: Ceres Policy Research.

Irvine, A. (2010). "We've had three of them": Addressing the invisibility of lesbian, gay, bisexual, and gender nonconforming youths in the juvenile justice system. *Columbia Journal of Gender and Law*, 18, 675–701.

Irvine, A., Wilber, S., & Canfield, A. (2017). *Lesbian, gay, bisexual, questioning, and/or gender nonconforming and transgender girls and boys in the California juvenile justice system: A practice guide*. Oakland, CA: Impact Justice & the National Center for Lesbian Rights.

Jaycox, L.H., Morse, L.K., Tanielian, T., & Stein, B.D. (2006). *How schools can help students recover from traumatic experiences: A tool kit for supporting long-term recovery*. Arlington, VA: Rand Corporation.

Jeffrey, C.R. (1965). Criminal behavior and learning theory. *The Journal of Criminal Law and Criminology*, 56, 294–300.

Jeffrey, C.R. (1971). *Crime prevention through environmental design*. Beverly Hills, CA: Sage.

Jekielek, S.M., Moore, K.A., & Hair, E.C. (2002). *Mentoring: A promising strategy for youth development* (Research brief). Washington, DC: Child Trends.

Jenkins, J.R., & O'Connor, R.E. (2002). Early identification and intervention for young children with reading/learning disabilities. In R. Bradley, L. Danielson, & D.P. Hallahan (Eds.), *Identification of learning disabilities* (pp. 99–161), Mahwah, NJ: LEA.

Jensen, A. (1969). How much can we boost IQ and scholastic achievement. *Harvard Education Review*, 39, 1–123.

Jensen, P.S., Hinshaw, S.P., Swanson, J.M., Greenhill, L.L., Conners, K.C., Arnold, E.L., Abikoff, H.B., Elliott, G., Hechtman, L., Hoza, B., March, J.S., Newcorn, J.G., Severe, J.B., Vitiello, B., Wells, K., & Wigal, T. (2001). Findings from the NIMH multimodal treatment study of ADHD (MTA): Implications and applications for primary care providers. *Journal of Developmental & Behavioral Pediatrics*, 22, 60–73.

Jimerson, S.R., Anderson, G.E., & Whipple, A.D. (2002). Winning the battle and losing the way: Examining the relation between grade retention and dropping out of high school. *Psychology in the Schools*, 39, 441–457.

Jin, H.M., & Bae, S.W. (2012). A meta-analysis on the variables related with juvenile delinquency. *Journal of Adolescent Welfare*, 14, 47–59.

Johnson, C. (2016, April 18). Solitary confinement is what destroyed my son, grieving mom says. *NPR Politics*. Retrieved from https://www.npr.org/2016/04/18/474397998/solitary-confinement-is-what-destroyed-my-son-grieving-mom-says

Johnston, L.D., O'Malley, P.M., & Bachman, J.G. (1996). *National survey results on drug use from the Monitoring the Future study, 1975–1995*. Rockville, MD: U.S. Department of Health and Human Services.

Jolliffe, D., & Farrington, D.P. (2007). *A rapid evidence assessment of the impact of mentoring on re-offending: A summary* (Cambridge University Online Report). Cambridge, England: Cambridge University Press.

Jones, M.A., & Krisberg, B. (1994). *Images and reality: Juvenile crime, youth violence, and public policy*. Washington, DC: National Council on Crime and Delinquency.

Jones, V. (1996). Classroom management. In J. Sikula, T. Buttery, & E. Guiton (Eds.), *Handbook of research on teacher education*. New York, NY: Macmillan.

Joseph, J. (2001). Is crime in the genes? A critical review of twin and adoption studies of criminality and antisocial behavior. *The Journal of Mind and Behavior*, 22, 179–218.

Justice Policy Institute. (2009). *The costs of confinement: Why good juvenile justice policies make good fiscal sense*. Washington, DC: Author.

Justice Policy Institute. (2011). *Education under arrest: The case against police in schools*. Washington, DC: Author.

Kahn, D. (2016, April 26). Troubled no more, youths bring stories of their resilience to probation professionals. *Juvenile Justice Information Exchange*. Retrieved from http://jjie.org/troubled-no-more-youths-bring-the-story-of-their-resilience-to-probation-professionals/234395

Kaminski, J.W., Valle, L.A., Filene, J.H., & Boyle, C.L. (2008). A meta-analysis review of components associated with parent training program effectiveness. *Journal of Abnormal Psychology*, 36, 567–589.

Kamphaus, R.W., & Reynolds, C.R. (2007). *BASC-2: Behavioral and emotional screening system*. Toronto, CA: Pearson.

Kamphaus, R., & Reynolds, C.R. (2011). *Behavioral and emotional screening system (BESS)*. Circle Pines, MN: American Guidance Service.

Kang, K., & Banaji, M.R. (2006). Fair measures: A behavioral realist revision of affirmative action. *California Law Review*, 94, 1063–1085.

Kang-Brown, J., Trone, J., Fratello, J. & Daftary-Kapur, T. (2013). *A generation later: What we've learned about zero tolerance in schools*. New York, NY: Vera Institute of Justice, Center on Youth Justice.

Karger, J., Rose, D., & Boundy, K. (2012). Applying universal design for learning to the education of youth in detention and correctional facilities. In S. Bahena, N. Cooc, R. Currie-Rubin, P. Kuttner, & M. Ng (Eds.), *Disrupting the school-to-prison pipeline* (pp. 119–140). Cambridge, MA: Harvard Educational Review.

Kates, E., Gerber, E.B., & Casey, S. (2014). Prior service utilization in detained youth with mental health needs. *Administration and Policy in Mental Health*, 41, 86–92.

Katz, J. (1988). *Seductions of crime: Moral and sensual attractions in doing evil*. New York, NY: Basic Books.

Katz, M.B. (1975). *Class, bureaucracy, and schools: The illusion of educational change in America*. New York, NY: Praeger.

Kaufman, K.L. (2010). *The prevention of sexual violence: The practitioner's sourcebook*. Holyoke, MA: NEARI Press.

Kempf-Leonard, K. (2007). Minority youths and juvenile justice: Disproportionate minority contact after nearly 20 years of reform efforts. *Youth Violence and Juvenile Justice*, 5, 71–87.

Kendall, P.C., & Suveg, C. (2006). Treating anxiety disorders in youth. In P.C. Kendall (Ed.), *Child and adolescent therapy: Cognitive-behavioral procedures* (3rd ed.). New York, NY: Guilford Press.

Kessler, R.C., Avenvoll, S., Costello, E.J., Georgiades, K., Green, J.G., Gruber, M.J., He, J.P., Koretz, D., McLaughlin, K.A., Petukhova, M., Sampson, N.A., & Zaslavsky, A.M. (2012). Prevalence, persistence, and sociodemographic correlates of DSM-IV disorders in the National Comorbidity Survey Replication Adolescent Supplement. *Archives of General Psychiatry*, 69, 372–380.

Kessler, R.C., Avenvoll, S., Costello, E.J., Green, J.G., Gruber, M.J., Heeringa, S., Merikangas, K.R., Pennell, B.E., Sampson, N.A., & Zaslavsky, A.M. (2009). Design and field procedures in the U.S. National Comorbidity Survey Replication Adolescent Supplement (NCS-A). *International Journal of Methods in Psychiatric Research*, 18, 69–83.

Kessler, R.C., Berglund, P., Demler, O., Jin, R., Merikangas, K.R., & Walters, E.E. (2005). Lifetime prevalence and age-of-onset distributions of DSM-IV Disorders in the national comorbidity survey replication. *Archives of General Psychiatry*, 62, 593–602.

Kilpatrick, D.G., Ruggiero, K.J., Acierno, R., Saunders, B.E., Resnick, H.S., & Best, C.L. (2003). Violence and risk of PTSD, major depression, substance abuse/dependence, and comorbidity: Results from the national survey of adolescents. *Journal of Consulting and Clinical Psychiatry*, 71, 692–700.

Kilpatrick, D.G., & Saunders, B.E. (1997). *Prevalence and consequences of child victimization: Results from the National Survey of Adolescents* (Final report). Washington, DC: U.S. Department of Justice,

Kim, K.Y., Losen, D.J., & Hewitt, D.T. (2010). *The school-to-prison pipeline: Structuring legal reform*. New York: New York University Press.

Kinscherff, R. (2012). *A primer for mental health practitioners working with youth involved in the juvenile justice system*. Washington, DC: Technical Assistance Partnership for Child and Family Mental Health.

Kinscherff, R., & Cocozza, J.J. (2011). *Developing effective polices for addressing the needs of court-involved youth with co-occurring disorders - Advancing juvenile drug court treatment courts: Policy and program briefs*. Delmar, NY: National Center for Mental Health and Juvenile Justice and the National Council of Juvenile and Family Court Judges.

Kirwan Institute. (2014). *State of the science: Implicit bias review 2014*. Columbus, OH: Kirwan Institute for the Study of Race and Ethnicity, The Ohio State University.

Klain, E. (2014). Understanding trauma and its impact on child clients. *Child Law Practice*, 33. Retrieved from https://www.americanbar.org/groups/child_law/what_we_do/projects/child-and-adolescent-health/polyvictimization/understanding-trauma-and-its-impact-on-child-clients.html

Klehr, D.G. (2009). Addressing the unintended consequences of No Child Left Behind and zero tolerance: Better strategies for safe schools and successful students. *Georgetown Journal on Poverty, Law, & Policy*, 16, 585–597.

Klevens, J., & Whittaker, D.J. (2007). Primary prevention of child physical abuse and neglect: Gaps and promising directions. *Child Maltreatment*, 12, 364–377.

Koball, H., Dion, R., Gothro, A., Bardo, M., Dworsky, A., Lansing, J., Stagner, M., Korom-Djakovic, D., Herrera, C., & Manning, A.E. (2011). *Synthesis of research and resources to support at-risk youth* (OPRE Report #2011–22). Washington, DC: Office of Planning, Research and Evaluation, Administration for Children and Families, U.S. Department of Health and Human Services.

Kohli, R. (2012). Racial pedagogy of the oppressed: Critical interracial dialogue for teachers of color. *Equity & Excellence in Education*, 45, 181–196.

Kolivoski, K.M., Shook, J.J., Goodkind, S., & Kim, K.H. (2014). Developmental trajectories and predictors of juvenile detention, placement, and jail among youth with out-of-home child welfare placement. *Journal of the Society for Social Work and Research*, 5, 137–160.

Korbin, J.E., Coultin, C.J., Chard, S., Platt-Houston, C., & Su, M. (1998). Impoverishment and child maltreatment in African American and European American neighborhoods. *Development and Psychopathology*, 10, 215–233.

Kosciw, J.G., Greytak, E.A., Diaz, E.M., & Bartkiewicz, M.J. (2010). *The 2009 national school climate survey: The experience of lesbian, gay, bisexual, and transgender youth in our nation's schools*. New York, NY: Gay, Lesbian, and Straight Education Network.

Kosciw, J.G., Greytak, E.A., Palmer, N.A., & Boesen, M.J. (2014). *The 2013 national school climate survey: The experiences of lesbian, gay, bisexual and transgender youth in our nation's schools*. New York, NY: Gay, Lesbian, & Straight Education Network.

Kowalski, K., Lindstrom, M., Rasmussen, P.S., Filges, T., & Jorgensen, A.K. (2011). *Title registration for a review proposal: Functional family therapy (FFT) for young people in treatment for illicit non-opiad drug use*. Oslo, Norway: The Campbell Collaboration.

Kowalski, R.M., & Limber, S.P. (2013). Psychological, physical, and academic correlates of cyberbullying and traditional bullying. *Journal of Adolescent Health*, 53, 13–20.

Kracke, D., & Hahn, H. (2008). The nature and extent of childhood exposure to violence: What we know, why we don't know more, and why it matters. *Journal of Emotional Abuse*, 8, 24–49.

Kraner, N.J., Barrowclough, N.D., Wang, N., Weiss, C., & Fisch, J.M. (2015). *51-jurisdiction survey of juvenile solitary confinement rules in juvenile justice systems*. New York, NY: Lowenstein Center for the Public Interest.

Kretschmar, J.M., Butcher, F., Flannery, D.J., & Singer, M.I. (2016). Diverting juvenile justice–involved youth with behavioral health issues from detention: Preliminary findings from Ohio's Behavioral Health Juvenile Justice (BHJJ) Initiative. *Criminal Justice Policy Review*, 27, 302–325.

Krisberg, B. (2005). *Juvenile justice: Redeeming our children*. Thousand Oaks, CA: Sage.

Kumpfer, K.L., Whiteside, H.O., Greene, J.A., & Allen, K.C. (2010). Effectiveness outcomes of four age versions of the strengthening families program in statewide field sites. *Group Dynamics: Theory, Research, and Practice*, 14, 211–229.

Kupchik, A. (2010). *Homeroom security: School discipline in an age of fear*. New York, NY: New York University Press.

Kupchik, A., & Bracy, N.L. (2009). To protect, serve, and mentor: Police officers in public schools. In T. Monahan and R.D. Torres (Eds.), *Schools under surveillance: Cultures of control in public education* (pp. 21–37). New Brunswick, NJ: Rutgers University Press.

Kupchik, A., & Monahan, T. (2006). The new American school: Preparation for post-industrial discipline. *British Journal of Sociology of Education*, 27, 617–632.

Kvarfordt, C.L., Purcell, P., & Shannon, P. (2005). Youth with learning disabilities in the juvenile justice system: A training needs assessment of detention and court services personnel. *Child & Youth Care*, 34, 27–42.

LaFond, J.Q. (2005). *Preventing sexual violence: How society should cope with sex offenders*. Washington, DC: American Psychological Association Press.

Lalayants, M., & Prince, J.D. (2014). Delinquency, depression, and substance use disorder among child welfare-involved adolescent females. *Child Abuse and Neglect*, 38, 797–807.

Lansford, J., Dodge, K.A., Pettit, G.S., Bates, J.E., Crozier, J., & Kaplow, J. (2002). Maltreatment on psychological, behavioral, and academic problems in adolescence. *Archives of Pediatric and Adolescent Medicine*, 156, 824–830.

Lansford, J., Miller-Johnson, S., Berlin, L.J., Dodge, K.A., Bates, J.E., & Pettit, G.S. (2007). Early physical abuse and later violent delinquency: A prospective longitudinal study. *Child Maltreatment*, 12, 233–245.

Larson, K., & Grisso, T. (2012). *Developing statutes for competence to stand trial in juvenile delinquency proceedings: A guide for lawmakers*. Baltimore, MD: Models for Change, The Annie E. Casey Foundation.

Lash, J. (2012, Apr. 20). Beyond the horrible, the reality of sexual assault in youth detention. *Juvenile Justice Information Exchange*. Retrieved from http://jjie.org/2012/04/20/beyond-horrible-reality-of-sexual-assault-youth-detention/

Latessa, E. (2012). *Effective practices in community supervision (EPICS)*. Cincinnati, OH: University of Cincinnati, School of Criminal Justice.

Latessa, E., Lovins, B., & Lux, J. (2014). *Evaluation of Ohio's RECLAIM Programs*. Cincinnati, OH: Center for Criminal Justice Research, School of Criminal Justice.

Latimer, J., Dowden, C., & Muise, D. (2005). The effectiveness of restorative justice practices: A meta-analysis. *Prison Journal*, 85, 127–144.

Laub, J.H. (1983). Urbanism, race, and crime. *Journal of Research in Crime and Delinquency*, 20, 283–298.

Laub, J.H., & Sampson, R.J. (2003). *Shared beginnings, divergent lives*. Cambridge, MA: Harvard University Press.

Lauer, P., Akiba, A.M., Wilkerson, S.B., Apthorp, H.S., Snow, D., & Martin-Glenn, M.L. (2006). Out-of-school time programs: A meta-analysis of effects for at-risk students. *Review of Educational Research*, 76, 275–313.

Lawrence, R.G. (2007). *School crime and juvenile justice* (2nd ed.). New York, NY: Oxford University Press.

Lawrence, R.G., & Hemmens, C. (2008). *Juvenile justice: A text/reader*. Thousand Oaks, CA: Sage.

Lee, V.E., & Burkam, D.T. (2002). *Inequality at the starting gate: Social background differences in achievement as children begin school*. Washington, DC: Economic Policy Institute.

Lehr, C.A., Johnson, D.R., Bremer, C.D., Cosio, S., & Thompson, M. (2004). *Essential tools. Increasing rates of school completion: Moving from policy and research to practice*. Minneapolis: National Center on Secondary Education and Transition, College of Education and Human Development, University of Minnesota.

Leichtman, M., Leichtman, M.L., Barber, C.C., & Neese, D.T. (2001). Effectiveness of intensive short-term residential treatment with severely disturbed adolescents. *American Journal of Orthopsychiatry*, 71, 227–235.

Leiter, J. (2007). School performance trajectories after the advent of reported maltreatment. *Children and Youth Services Review*, 29, 363–382.

Leiter, J., & Johnson, M.C. (1997). Child maltreatment and school performance declines: An event-history analysis. *American Educational Research Journal*, 34, 563–589.

Lemert, E. M. (1972). *Human deviance, social problems, and social control*. Upper Saddle River, NJ: Prentice Hall.

Lemmon, J.H. (2006). The effects of maltreatment recurrence and child welfare services on dimensions of delinquency. *Criminal Justice Review*, 31, 5–32.

Lemmon, J.H. (2009). How child maltreatment affects dimensions of juvenile delinquency in a cohort of low-income urban males. *Justice Quarterly*, 16, 357–376.

Leone, P.E., & Weinberg, L. (2010). *Addressing the unmet educational needs of children and youth in the juvenile justice and child welfare systems*. Washington, DC: Center for Juvenile Justice Reform, Georgetown University.

Lerman, P. (2002). Twentieth century developments in America's institutional systems for youth in trouble. In M.K. Rosenheim (Ed.), *A century of juvenile justice* (pp. 74–110). Chicago, IL: The University of Chicago Press.

Levin, M., & Cohen, D. (2014). *Kids doing time for what's not a crime: The over-incarceration of status offenders*. Austin: Texas Public Policy Foundation.

Levinson, J. (2007). Forgotten racial equality: Implicit bias, decision making, and misremembering. *Duke Law Review*, 12, 307–350.

Levy-Pounds, N. (2014). Warehousing, imprisoning, and labelling youth "minorities." In A.J. Nocella II, P. Parmar, & D. Stovall (Eds.), *From education to incarceration: Dismantling the school-to-prison pipeline* (pp. 131–144). New York, NY: Peter Lang.

Lexcen, F., & Redding, R.E. (2000). Mental health needs of juvenile offenders. *Juvenile Correctional Mental Health Report*, 3, 1, 2, 8–16.

Liazos, A. (1974). Class oppression: The functions of juvenile justice. *Critical Sociology*, 5, 2–24.

Lipsey, M.W. (2009). The primary factors that characterize effective interventions with juvenile offenders. *Victims & Offenders*, 4, 124–147.

Lipsey, M.W., & Derzon, J.H. (1998). Predictors of violent or serious delinquency in adolescence and early adulthood: A synthesis of longitudinal research. In R. Loeber & D.P. Farrington (Eds.), *Serious and violent juvenile offenders: Risk factors and successful interventions*. Thousand Oaks, CA: Sage.

Lipsey, M.W., Howell, J.C., Kelly, M.R., Chapman, G., & Carver, D. (2010). *Improving the effectiveness of juvenile justice programs: A new perspective on evidence-based practice*. Washington, DC: Center for Juvenile Justice Reform, Georgetown University.

Lipsey, M.W., & Landenberger, N.A. (2006). *Cognitive-behavioural programs for juvenile and adult offenders: A meta-analysis of controlled intervention studies*. Oslo, Norway: The Campbell Library, The Campbell Collaboration.

Lipsey, M.W., & Wilson, D.B. (1998). Effective intervention for serious juvenile offenders: A synthesis of research. In R. Loeber & D. Farrington (Eds.), *Serious and violent juvenile offenders: Risk factors and successful interventions* (313–341). Thousand Oaks, CA: Sage.

Little, G.L. (2005). Meta-analysis of moral reconation therapy(r): Recidivism results from probation and parole implementations. *Cognitive-Behavioral Treatment Review*, 10, 4–6.

Little Hoover Commission. (2008). *Juvenile justice reform: Realigning responsibilities*. Sacramento: State of California.

Little, J.H., Popa, M., & Forsythe, B. (2005). *Multisystemic therapy for social, emotional, and behavioral problems in youth aged 10–17*. Oslo, Norway: The Campbell Collaboration.

Loeber, R., & Farrington, D.P. (2001). Executive summary. In R. Loeber & D.P. Farrington (Eds.), *Child delinquents: Development, intervention, and service needs* (pp. xix–xxxi). Thousand Oaks, CA: Sage.

Loeber, R., & Farrington, D.P. (2008). *From juvenile offending to young adult offending* (IJ-CX-K-42). Washington, DC: National Institute of Justice, Office of Justice Programs, U.S. Department of Justice.

Loeber, R., Farrington, D.P., & Petechuk, D. (2003). *Child delinquency: Early intervention and prevention*. Washington, DC: Juvenile Justice Bulletin, Office of Juvenile Justice and Delinquency Prevention, U.S. Department of Justice.

Loeber, R., Farrington, D.P., Stouthamer-Loeber, M., & White H.R. (2008). *Violence and serious theft: Development and prediction from childhood to adulthood*. New York, NY: Routledge.

Lofquist, D., Lugaila, T., O'Connell, M., & Feliz, S., (2012). *Households and families: 2010, Census Briefs*. Washington, DC: U.S. Census Bureau, U.S. Department of Commerce.

Lombroso, C. (2006). *Criminal man*. Durham, NC: Duke University Press. (Originally published in 1876.)

Longmire, P.K., & Umansky, L. (2000). *The new disability history: American perspectives*. New York: New York University Press.

Losen, D.L. (2012). Sound discipline policy for successful schools: How redressing racial disparities can make a positive impact for all. In

S. Bahena, N. Cooc, R. Currie-Rubin, P. Kuttner, & M. Ng (Eds.), *Disrupting the school-to-prison pipeline*. Cambridge, MA: Harvard Educational Review.

Losen, D.L., & Gillespie, J. (2012). *Opportunities suspended: The disparate impact of disciplinary exclusion from school*. Los Angeles, CA: The Civil Rights Project at UCLA.

Losen, D.L., & Martinez, T. (2013). *Out of school & off track: The overuse of suspensions in American middle and high schools*. Los Angeles, CA: The Civil Rights Project at UCLA.

Losen, D.L., & Skiba, R.J. (2010). *Suspended education: Urban middle schools in crisis*. Los Angeles: The Civil Rights Project at UCLA and the Southern Poverty Law Center.

Losen, D.L., Hewitt, D., & Toldson, I. (2014). *Eliminating excessive and unfair discipline in schools: Policy recommendations for reducing disparities*. Bloomington, IN: Discipline Disparities: A Research-to-Practice Collaborative. The Equity Project at Indiana University, Center for Evaluation and Education Policy.

Loughran, T., Mulvey, E., Schubert, C., Fagan, J., Piquero, A., & Losoyo, S. (2009). Estimating a dose-response relationship between length of stay and future recidivism in serious juvenile offenders. *Criminology*, 47, 699–740.

Loving, R., Singer, J.K., & Maguire, M. (2008). *Homelessness among registered sex offenders in California: The numbers, the risks, and the response* (pp. 1–44). Sacramento: California Sex Offender Management Board, California State University.

Lu, Y.E., Landsverk, J., Ellis-MacLeod, E., Newton, R., Ganger, W., & Johnson, E. (2004). Race, ethnicity and case outcomes in child protective services. *Children and Youth Services Review*, 26, 447–461.

Lundahl, B.W., Nimer, J., & Parson, B. (2006). Preventing child abuse: A meta-analysis of parent training programs. *Research on Social Work Practice*, 16, 251–262.

Luthar, S.S. (Ed.). (2003). *Resilience and vulnerability: Adaption in the context of childhood adversities*. Cambridge, England: Cambridge University Press.

Lyons, J., Baerger, D., Quigley, P., Erlich, J., & Griffin, E. (2001). Mental health service needs of juvenile offenders: A comparison of detention, incarceration, and treatment settings. *Children's Services: Social Policy, Research, and Practice*, 4, 69–85.

MacArthur Foundation. (2006). *Issue brief 1: Adolescent legal competence in court*. Chicago, IL: Author.

MacArthur Foundation. (2012). *Juvenile justice and mental health: A collaborative approach* (Models for Change: Systems Reform in Juvenile Justice). Chicago, IL: Author.

MacArthur Foundation. (2015). *Juvenile justice in a developmental framework: A 2015 status report*. Chicago, IL: Juvenile Justice Report.

MacDonald, G.M., & Turner, W. (2007). Treatment foster care for improving outcomes in children and young people. *Campbell Systematic Reviews*, 9, 1–67.

Macready, T. (2009). Learning social responsibility in schools: A restorative practice. *Educational Psychology in Practice*, 25, 211–220.

Macy, R.D., Barry, S., & Noam, G.G. (2003). Threat and trauma: An overview. In R.D. Macy, S. Barry, & G.G. Noam (Eds.), *New directions for youth development: Youth facing threat and terror: Supporting preparedness and resilience* (pp. 11–28). San Francisco, CA: Jossey-Bass.

Majd, K. (2011). Students of the mass incarceration nation. *Howard Law Journal*, 54, 343–394.

Majd, K., Marksamer, J., & Reyes, C. (2009). *Hidden justice: Lesbian, gay, bisexual and transgender youth in juvenile courts*. San Francisco, CA: National Center for Lesbian Rights.

Majd, K., & Puritz, P. (2009). The cost of justice: How low-income youth continue to pay the price of failing indigent defense systems. *Georgetown Journal on Poverty Law & Policy*, 16, 543–583.

Mallett, C. (2009). Disparate juvenile court outcomes for disabled delinquent youth: A social work call to action. *Child and Adolescent Social Work Journal*, 26, 197–207.

Mallett, C. (2011). *Seven things juvenile courts should know about learning disabilities*. Reno, NV: National Council of Juvenile and Family Court Judges.

Mallett, C., Stoddard-Dare, P., & Seck, M. (2009). Predicting juvenile delinquency: The nexus of child maltreatment, depression, and bipolar disorder. *Criminal Behaviour and Mental Health*, 19, 235–246.

Malloy, L.C., Shulman, E.P., & Cauffman, E. (2013). Interrogations, confessions, and guilty pleas among serious adolescent offenders. *Law and Human Behavior*, 38, 1–13.

March, J., Silva, S., Petrycki, S., Curry, J., Wells, K., Fairbank, J., Burns, B., Domino, M., McNulty, S., Vitiello, B., & Severe, J. (2004). Treatment for adolescents with depression study (TADS) team. Fluoxetin, cognitive-behavioral therapy, and their combination for adolescents with depression: Treatment for adolescents with depression study (TADS) randomized controlled trial. *Journal of the American Medical Association*, 292, 807–820.

Marchbanks, M.P. III, Blake, J., Booth, E., Carmichael, A., Seibert, A.L., & Fabelo, T. (2015). The economic effects of exclusionary discipline on grade retention and high school dropout. In D.J. Losen (Ed.), *Closing the school discipline gap: Research for policymakers*. New York, NY: Teachers College Press.

Marchblanks, M.P., Blake, J.J., Smith, D., Seibert, A.L., Carmichael, D., & Fabelo, T. (2014). More than a drop in the bucket: The social and economic costs of dropouts and grade retentions associated with exclusionary discipline. *Journal of Applied Research on Children*, 5, 17–31.

Margolin, G., & Gordis, E.B. (2000). The effect of family and community violence on children. *Annual Review of Psychology*, 51, 445–479.

Marrus, E., & Rosenberg, M. (2005). After *Roper v. Simmons*: Keeping kids out of adult criminal court. *San Diego Law Review*, 42, 1151–1176.

Marsh, J., Ryan, J., Choi, S., & Testa, M. (2006). Integrated services for families with multiple problems: Obstacles to family reunification. *Children and Youth Services Review*, 28, 1074–1087.

Martin, N., & Halperin, S. (2006). *Whatever it takes: How twelve communities are reconnecting out-of-school youth*. Washington, DC: American Youth Policy Forum.

Martinez, S. (2009). A system gone berserk: How are zero-tolerance policies really affecting schools? *Preventing School Failure*, 53, 153–157.

Martinson, R. (1974). What works? Questions and answers about prison reform. *The Public Interest*, 35, 22–54.

Marx, G.T. (1981). Ironies of social control: Authorities as contributors to deviance through escalation, nonenforcement and covert facilitation. *Social Problems*, 28, 221–246.

Maschi, T., Bradley, C.A., & Morgen, K. (2008). Unraveling the link between trauma and delinquency. *Youth Violence and Juvenile Justice*, 6, 136–157.

Masten, A.S., Best, K.M., & Garmezy, N. (1990). Resilience and development: Contributions from the study of children who overcome adversity. *Development and Psychopathology*, 2, 425–444.

Matta-Oshima, K.M., Huang, J., Johnson-Reid, M., & Drake, B. (2010). Children with disabilities in poor households: Association with juvenile and adult offending. *Social Work Research*, 34, 102–113.

Matthews, B., & Hubbard, D.J. (2009). Moving ahead: Five essential elements for working effectively with girls. *Journal of Criminal Justice*, 36, 494–502.

Matza, D. (1964). *Delinquency and drift: From the research program of the Center for the Study of Law and Society, University of California, Berkeley*. Berkeley: University of California Press.

Maughan, D.R., Christiansen, E., Jenson, W.R., Olympia, D., & Clark, E. (2005). Behavioral parent training as a treatment for externalizing behaviors and disruptive behavior disorders: A meta-analysis. *School Psychology Review*, 34, 267–286.

Maxson, C.L., & Klein, M. (1995). Investigating gang structures. *Journal of Gang Research*, 3, 33–40.

Mayer, M.J., & Leone, P.E. (1999). A structural analysis of school violence and disruption: Implications for creating safer schools. *Education and Treatment of Children*, 22, 333–356.

Maynard, B.R., McCrea, K.T., Pigott, T.D., & Kelly, M.S. (2012). *Indicated truancy interventions: Effects on school attendance among chronic truant students*. Oslo, Norway: The Campbell Collaboration.

McCart, M.R., Zajac, K., Danielson, C.K., Strachan, M., Ruggiero, K.J., Smith, D.W., Saunders, B.E., & Kilpatrick, D.G. (2011). Interpersonal victimization, posttraumatic stress disorder, and change in adolescent substance use prevalence over a ten-year period in 1995 and 2005. *Journal of Clinical Child and Adolescent Psychology*, 40, 136–143.

McCarthy, B., Felmlee, D., & Hagan, J. (2004). Girl friends are better: Gender, friends, and crime among school and street youth. *Criminology*, 42, 805–836.

McCarthy, P., Schiraldi, V., & Shark, M. (2016). *The future of youth justice: A community-based alternative to the youth prison model*. Washington, DC: New Thinking in Community Corrections Bulletin, National Institute of Justice, U.S. Department of Justice.

McCurdy, J. (2014). Targets for arrest. In A.J. Nocella II, P. Parmar, & D. Stovall (Eds.), *From education to incarceration: Dismantling the school-to-prison pipeline* (pp. 86–101). New York, NY: Peter Lang.

McGee, R., Wolfe, D., & Olson, J. (2001). Multiple maltreatment, attribution of blame, and adjustment among adolescents. *Development and Psychopathology*, 13, 827–846.

McIntosh, K., Ty, S.V., & Miller, L.D. (2014). Effects of school-wide positive behavioral interventions and supports on internalizing problems: Current evidence and future directions. *Journal of Positive Behavior Interventions*, 16, 209–218.

McLoughlin, C.S., & Noltemeyer, A.L. (2010). Research into factors contributing to discipline use and disproportionality in major urban schools. *Current Issues in Education*, 13, 1–20.

McNulty-Eitle, T., & Eitle, D.J. (2004). Inequality, segregation, and the overrepresentation of African Americans in school suspension. *Sociological Perspectives*, 47, 269–287.

McReynolds, L.S., Wasserman, G.A., DeComo, R.E., John, R., Keating, J.M., & Nolen, S. (2008). Psychiatric disorder in a juvenile assessment center. *Crime & Delinquency*, 54, 313–334.

Mears, D.P., & Aron, L. (2003). *Addressing the needs of youth with disabilities in the juvenile justice system: The current state of knowledge*. Washington, DC: The Urban Institute.

Mears, D.P., & Travis, J. (2004). *The dimensions, pathways, and consequences of youth reentry* (Youth Reentry Roundtable Series). Washington, DC: Urban Institute.

Mechanic, D. (2008). *Mental health and social policy: Beyond managed care* (5th ed.). Boston, MA: Allyn & Bacon.

Mediratta, K. (2012). Grassroots organizing and the school-to-prison pipeline: The emerging national movement to roll back zero tolerance discipline policies in the U.S. public schools. In S. Bahena, N. Cooc, R. Currie-Rubin, P. Kuttner, & M. Ng (Eds.), *Disrupting the school-to-prison pipeline*. Cambridge, MA: Harvard Educational Review.

Memory, J. (1989). Juvenile suicides in secure detention facilities: Correction of published rates. *Death Studies*, 13, 455–463.

Mendel, R.A. (2011). *No place for kids: The case for reducing juvenile incarceration*. Baltimore, MD: The Annie E. Casey Foundation.

Mendel, R.A. (2014). *Juvenile detention alternatives initiative progress report: 2014*. Baltimore, MD: The Annie E. Casey Foundation.

Mendel, R.A. (2015). *Maltreatment of youth in U.S. juvenile corrections facilities*. Baltimore, MD: The Annie E. Casey Foundation.

Mennel, R. (1973). *Thorns and thistles*. Hanover: The University of New Hampshire Press.

Merikangas, K.R. (2005). Vulnerability factors for anxiety disorders in children and adolescents. *Child and Adolescent Psychiatric Clinics of North America*, 14, 649–679.

Merikangas, K.R., He, J., Burstein, M., Swanson, S.A., Venevoli, S., Cui, L., Berjet, C., Georgiades, K., & Swendsen, J. (2010). Lifetime prevalence of mental disorders in US adolescents: Results from the National Comorbidity Study—adolescent supplement (NCS-A). *Journal of the American Academy of Child and Adolescent Psychiatry*, 49, 980–989.

Merrell, K.W., & Walker, H.M. (2004). Deconstructing a definition: Social maladjustment versus emotional disturbance and moving the EBD field forward. *Psychology in the Schools*, 41, 899–910.

Merton, R.K. (1938). Social structure and anomie. *American Sociological Review*, 3, 672–682.

Messner, S.F., & Rosenfeld, R. (1994). *Crime in the American dream*. Belmont, CA: Wadsworth.

Metropolitan Nashville Public School District. (2016). *Student parent handbook: 2015–2016*. Nashville, TN: Author.

Mikton, C., & Butchart, A. (2009). Child maltreatment prevention: A systematic review of reviews. *Bulletin of the World Health Organization*, 87, 353–361.

Miller, W.B. (1958). Lower class culture as a generating milieu of gang delinquency. *Journal of Social Issues*, 14, 5–19.

Miller, J.L., & Anderson, A.B. (1986). Updating the deterrence doctrine. *Journal of Criminal Law and Criminology*, 77, 418–438.

Mischel, W., Shoda, Y., & Rodriguez, M.I. (1989). Delay of gratification in children. *Science*, 26, 933–938.

Mitchell, O., Wilson, D.B., Eggers, A., & MacKenzie, D.L. (2012). *Drug courts' effects on criminal offending for juveniles and adults*. Oslo, Norway: The Campbell Collaboration.

Mitchum, P., & Moodie-Mills, A.C. (2014). *Beyond bullying: How hostile school climate perpetuates the school-to-prison pipeline for LBGT youth*. Washington, DC: Center for American Progress.

Models for Change. (2011). *Does mental health screening fulfill its promise?* Chicago, IL: The John D. and Catherine T. MacArthur Foundation.

Models for Change. (2013). *Schools torn to treatment, not punishment, for children with mental health needs*. Chicago, IL: The John D. and Catherine T. MacArthur Foundation.

Models for Change Juvenile Diversion Workgroup. (2011). *Juvenile diversion guidebook*. Washington, DC: Author.

Moffitt, T.E. (1993). Adolescence limited and life course persistent antisocial behavior: A developmental taxonomy. *Psychological Review*, 100, 674–701.

Moffitt, T.E., & Scott, S. (2008). Conduct disorders of childhood & adolescence. In M. Rutter (Ed.), *Child psychiatry* (ch. 35). London, England: Wiley-Blackwell.

Monahan, J., & Steadman, H. (1983). Crime and mental disorders: An epidemiological approach. In N. Morris & M. Tonry (Eds.), *Crime and justice: An annual review of research* (pp. 145–189). Chicago, IL: The University of Chicago Press.

Monahan, J., Steadman, H.J., Silver, E., Appelbaum, P.S., Robbins, P.C., Mulvey, E.P., Roth, L., & Silver E. (2001). *Rethinking risk assessment: The MacArthur study of mental disorder and violence*. New York, NY: Oxford University Press.

Monroe, C.R. (2005). Why are "bad boys" always black? Causes of disproportionality in school discipline and recommendations for change. *The Clearing House: A Journal of Educational Strategies, Issues, and Ideas*, 79, 45–50.

Moore, S. (2009, August 9). Mentally ill offenders stretch the limits of juvenile justice. *New York Times*. Retrieved from http://www.nytimes.com/2009/08/10/us/10juvenile.html

Moran, P., Ghate, D., & van der Merwe, A. (2004). *What works in parenting support: A review of the international evidence*. London, England: Policy Research Bureau, Department for Education and Skills.

Morgan, E., Salomon, N., Plotkin, M., & Cohen, R. (2014). *The school discipline consensus report: Strategies from the field to keep students engaged in school and out of the juvenile justice system*. Washington, DC: The Council of State Governments Justice Center.

Morral, A., McCaffrey, D., & Ridgeway, G. (2004). Effectiveness of community-based treatment for substance-abusing dependents: 12-month outcomes of youths entering Phoenix Academy or alternative probation dispositions. *Psychology of Addictive Behaviors*, 18, 257–268.

Morris, K.A., & Morris, R.J. (2006). Disability and juvenile delinquency: Issues and trends. *Disability & Society*, 21, 613–627.

Morris, K.A., Schoenfield, G., Bade-White, P., Joshi, D., & Morris, R.J. (2006). Disability and juvenile delinquency. In R.J. Morris (Ed.), *Disability research and policy* (pp. 141–161). Mahway, NJ: Lawrence Erlbaum.

MTA Cooperative Group. (1999). A 14-month randomized clinical trial of treatment strategies for attention-deficit hyperactivity disorder. *Archives of General Psychiatry*, 56, 1073–1086.

Mueser, K.T., & Taub, J. (2008). Trauma and PTSD among adolescents with severe emotional disorders involved in multiple service systems. *Psychiatric Services*, 59, 627–634.

Mulvey, E.P. (2011). *Highlights from pathways to desistance: A longitudinal study of serious adolescent offenders*. Washington, DC: Office of Juvenile Justice and Delinquency Prevention, Office of Justice Programs, U.S. Department of Justice.

Mulvey, E.P., & Iselin, A.R. (2008). Improving professional judgments of risk and amenability in juvenile justice. *The Future of Children*, 18, 35–58.

Mulvey, E.P., & Shubert, C.A. (2012). *Transfer of juveniles to adult court: Effects of a policy in one court*. Washington, DC: Office of Juvenile Justice and Delinquency Prevention, Office of Justice Programs, U.S. Department of Justice.

Murdock, T.B., & Bolch, M.B. (2005). Risk and protective factors for poor school adjustment in lesbian, gay, and bisexual (LBG) high school youth: Variable and person-centered analyses. *Psychology in the Schools*, 42, 159–172.

Muris, P., & Broeren, S. (2009). Twenty-five years of research on childhood anxiety disorders: Publication trends between 1982 and 2006 and a selective review of the literature. *Journal of Child and Families Studies*, 18, 388–395.

Muschert, G.W. (2009). Frame-changing in the media coverage of a school shooting: The rise of Columbine as a national concern. *Social Science Journal*, 46, 164–170.

Muschert, G.W., & Peguero, A.A. (2010). The Columbine effect and school antiviolence policy. *Research in Social Problems and Public Policy*, 17, 117–148.

Muscott, H.S., Mann, E., Benjamin, T.B., Gately, S., Bell, K.E., & Muscott, A.J. (2004). Positive behavioral interventions and supports in New Hampshire: Preliminary results of a statewide system for implementing schoolwide discipline practices. *Education and Treatment of Children*, 27, 453–475.

Musgrove, M., & Yudin, M.K. (2014). *An open letter to juvenile justice correctional facilities*. Washington, DC: Office of Special Education and Rehabilitative Services, U.S. Department of Education.

Myers, W.C., Burton, P.R., Sanders, P.D., Donat, K.M., Cheney, J., Fitzpatrick, T., & Monaco, L. (2000). Project back-on-track at 1 year: A delinquency treatment program for early-career juvenile offenders. *Journal of American Child and Adolescent Psychiatry*, 39, 1127–1134.

Na, C., & Gottfredson, D. (2011). Police officers in schools: Effects on school crime and the processing of offending behaviors. *Justice Quarterly*, 30, 1–32.

NAACP. (2005). *Interrupting the school to prison pipeline*. Washington, DC: Author.

Naffine, M. (1996). *Feminism & criminology*. Philadelphia, PA: Temple University Press.

National Center for Child Traumatic Stress. (2009). *Child sexual abuse: Coping with the emotional stress of the legal system*. Los Angeles, CA: UCLA.

National Center for Children in Poverty. (2000). *Promoting resilience: Helping young children and parents affected by substance abuse, domestic violence, and depression in the context of welfare reform*. New York, NY: Author.

National Center for Mental Health and Juvenile Justice. (2012). *Law enforcement-based diversion*. Chicago, IL: Models for Change, Systems Reform in Juvenile Justice, MacArthur Foundation.

National Center for Mental Health and Juvenile Justice. (2013). *Improving diversion policies and programs for justice-involved youth with co-occurring mental and substance use disorders*. Chicago, IL: Models for Change, Systems Reform in Juvenile Justice, MacArthur Foundation.

National Center for Mental Health Promotion and Youth Violence Prevention. (2009). *An introduction to restorative justice*. Washington, DC: Substance Abuse and Mental Health Services Administration, U.S. Department of Health and Human Services.

National Center for Youth Law. (2008). *The incarceration of status offenders under the valid court order exception to the Juvenile Justice and Delinquency Prevention Act*. Washington, DC: First National Conference on Homeless Youth and the Law.

National Child Traumatic Stress Network (NCTSN). (2008). *Child welfare trauma training tool kit: Comprehensive guide* (2nd ed.). Los Angeles, CA: National Center for Child Traumatic Stress.

National Conference of State Legislatures. (2015). *Trends in juvenile justice state legislation: 2011–2015*. Washington, DC: Author.

National Council of Juvenile and Family Court Judges. (2014). *Practical tips to help juvenile drug court teams implement the 16 strategies in practice*. Reno, NV: Author.

National Council of Juvenile and Family Court Judges. (2016a). *Disproportionately rates for children of color in foster care (FY 2014)*. Reno, NV: National Council of Juvenile and Family Court Judges.

National Council of Juvenile and Family Court Judges. (2016b). *Introduction to chronic absenteeism and truancy*. Reno, NV: School-Justice Partnership, National Council of Juvenile and Family Court Judges.

National Council of Juvenile and Family Court Judges. (2016c). *Introduction to school engagement and connectedness*. Reno, NV: School-Justice Partnership, National Council of Juvenile and Family Court Judges.

National Council of Juvenile and Family Court Judges. (2016d). *Juvenile graduated sanctions e-tool: Effective program services and models associated with the five graduated sanction and intervention levels for juvenile justice*. Reno, NV: National Council of Juvenile and Family Court Judges.

National Council on Crime and Delinquency. (2007). *And justice for some: Differential treatment of youth of color in the justice system*. Oakland, CA: Author.

National Council on Crime and Delinquency. (2014). *NCCD compares juvenile justice risk assessment instruments: A summary of the OJJDP-funded study*. Oakland, CA: Author.

National Council on Disability. (2003). *Addressing the needs of youth with disabilities in the juvenile justice system: The current status of evidence-based research*. Washington, DC: Author.

National Healthcare for the Homeless Council. (2012). *Criminal justice, homelessness, and health: 2012 policy statement.* Nashville, TN: Author.

National Institute of Child Health and Human Development. (2003). Social functioning in first grade: Prediction from home, child care and concurrent school experience. *Child Development, 74,* 1639–1662.

National Institute of Justice. (2012). *Crime solutions, Midwest Prevention Project.* Retrieved from https://www.crimesolutions.gov/ProgramDetails.aspx?ID=247

National Institute of Justice. (2014). *Comprehensive School Safety Initiative (CSSI) funding awards.* Washington, DC: Office of Justice Programs, U.S. Department of Justice.

National Institute of Mental Health. (2011). *Suicide: A major, preventable mental health problem.* Washington, DC: National Institutes of Health, U.S. Department of Health and Human Services.

National Institute on Drug Abuse. (2003). *Preventing drug use among children and adolescents: A research-based guide for parents, educators, and community leaders* (2nd ed.). Washington, DC: National Institutes of Health, U.S. Department of Health and Human Services.

National Institute on Drug Abuse. (2014). *Principles of adolescent substance use disorder treatment: A research-based guide.* Bethesda, MD: National Institute of Health.

National Juvenile Defender Center. (2016). *Juvenile waiver of counsel.* Washington, DC: Author.

National Juvenile Justice and Delinquency Prevention Coalition. (2013). *Promoting safe communities: Recommendations for the 113th Congress.* Washington, DC: Author.

National Juvenile Justice Network. (2011). *Bringing youth home: A national movement to increase public safety, rehabilitate youth, and save money.* Washington, DC: Author.

National Juvenile Justice Network. (2012). *Competency to stand trial in juvenile court: Recommendations for policymakers.* Washington, DC: Author.

National Legal Defender Center and the National Legal Aid, and Defender Association. (2008). *Ten core principles for providing quality delinquency representation through public defense delivery systems.* Washington, DC: Author.

National Low Income Housing Coalition. (2013). *Out of reach, 2013.* Washington, DC: Author.

National Resource Council. (2013). *Reforming juvenile justice: A developmental approach.* Washington, DC: The National Academies Press.

Neelum, A. (2011). *State trends: Legislative changes from 2005 to 2010 removing youth from the adult criminal justice system.* Washington, DC: Campaign for Youth Justice.

Nellis, A. (2012). *The lives of juvenile lifers: Findings from a national survey.* Washington, DC: The Sentencing Project.

Nellis, A. (2016). *A return to justice: Rethinking our approach to juveniles in the system.* Lanham, MD: Rowman & Littlefield.

New Freedom Commission. (2003). *The President's New Freedom Commission on Mental Health.* Rockville, MD: Author. Retrieved from http://govinfo.library.unt.edu/mentalhealthcommission/reports/FinalReport/downloads/FinalReport.pdf

New York State Archives. (1989). *The greatest reform school in the world: A guide to the records of the New York State House of Refuge.* Albany: New York State Education Department, Cultural Education Center.

Nicholson-Crotty, S., Birchmeier, Z., & Valentine, D. (2009). Exploring the impact of school discipline on racial disproportion in the juvenile justice system. *Social Science Quarterly, 90,* 1003–1018.

Nock, M.K., Kazdin, A.E., Hiripi, E., & Kessler, R.C. (2007). Lifetime prevalence, correlates, and persistence of oppositional defiant disorder: Results from the national comorbidity survey replication. *Journal of Child Psychology and Psychiatry, 48,* 703–713.

Nolan, K. (2011). *Police in the hallways: Discipline in an urban high school.* Minneapolis: University of Minnesota Press.

Noltemeyer, A., & McLoughlin, C.S. (2010). Patterns of exclusionary discipline by school typology, ethnicity, and their interactions. *Perspectives on Urban Education, 7,* 27–40.

Nurse–Family Partnership. (2016). *Jennifer's story* (Video). Retrieved from http://www.nursefamilypartnership.org/First-Time-Moms/Stories-from-moms

Nye, F.I. (1958). *Family relationships and delinquent behavior.* Hoboken, NJ: Wiley.

O'Toole, M.E. (2000). *The school shooter: A threat assessment perspective.* Quantico, VA: National Center for the Analysis of Violent Crime, Federal Bureau of Investigation.

Office of Juvenile Justice and Delinquency Prevention. (2009). *Reducing disproportionate minority contact: Preparation at the local level.* Washington, DC: Office of Justice Programs, U.S. Department of Justice.

Office of Juvenile Justice and Delinquency Prevention. (2013). *Statistical briefing book.* Washington, DC: Bureau of Justice Affairs, U.S. Department of Justice. Retrieved from https://www.ojjdp.gov/ojstatbb/

Office of Juvenile Justice and Delinquency Prevention. (2014a). *Annual report 2014.* Washington, DC: Office of Justice Programs, U.S. Department of Justice.

Office of Juvenile Justice and Delinquency Prevention. (2014b). *Statistical briefing book.* Washington, DC: Bureau of Justice Affairs, U.S. Department of Justice. Retrieved from https://www.ojjdp.gov/ojstatbb/

Office of Juvenile Justice and Delinquency Prevention. (2015a). *Easy access to the census of juveniles in residential placement.* Washington, DC: Office of Justice Programs, U.S. Department of Justice.

Office of Juvenile Justice and Delinquency Prevention. (2015b). *Statistical briefing book.* Washington, DC: Bureau of Justice Affairs, U.S. Department of Justice. Retrieved from https://www.ojjdp.gov/ojstatbb/

Office of Juvenile Justice and Delinquency Prevention. (2016). *Model programs guide.* Washington, DC: Office of Justice Programs, U.S. Department of Justice.

Office of Juvenile Justice and Delinquency Prevention. (2017, August 7). *Easy access to FBI arrest statistics: 1994–2014.* Washington, DC: Bureau of Justice Affairs, U.S. Department of Justice. Retrieved from https://www.ojjdp.gov/ojstatbb/ezaucr/asp/ucr_display.asp

Office of Juvenile Justice and Delinquency Prevention. (n.d.). *Statistical briefing book* (Online. Case flow diagram). Washington, DC: Bureau of Justice Affairs, U.S. Department of Justice. Retrieved from http://www.ojjdp.gov/ojstatbb/structure_process/qa04206.asp?qaDate=2011 (released on August 05, 2013).

Ohio Department of Youth Services. (2015). *Ohio Department of Youth Services fiscal year 2015 annual report.* Columbus: Author.

Ohio Juvenile Justice Alliance. (2015). *What is diversion?* Columbus: Juvenile Diversion Fact Sheet Series, Ohio Juvenile Justice Alliance.

Olds, D.L. (2007). Preventing crime with prenatal and infancy support of parents: The nurse-family partnership. *Victims & Offenders, 2,* 205–225.

Oliver, R.M., Wehby, J.H., & Reschly, D.J. (2011). *Teacher classroom management practices: Effects on disruptive or aggressive student behavior.* Oslo, Norway: The Campbell Collaboration.

Orfield, G. (2009). *Reviving the goal of an integrated society.* Los Angeles, CA: Civil Rights Project.

Orfield, G., Kucsera, J., & Siegel-Hawley, G, (2012). *E Pluribus . . . separation: Deepening double segregation for more students.* Los Angeles: UCLA Civil Rights Project.

Osgood, D.W., Johnston, L.D., O'Malley, P.M., & Bachman, J.G. (1988). The generality of deviance in late adolescence and early adulthood. *American Sociological Review, 53,* 81–93.

Osher, D., Bear, G.G., Sprague, J.R., & Doyle, W. (2010). How can we improve school discipline? *Educational Researcher, 39,* 48–58.

Osher, D., Coggshall, J., Colombi, G., Wodruff, D., Francois, S., & Osher, T. (2012). Building school and teacher capacity to eliminate the school-to-prison pipeline. *Teacher Education and Special Education: The Journal of the Teacher Education Division of the Council for Exceptional Children, 35,* 284–295.

Ousey, G.C., & Augustine, M.C. (2001). Young guns: Examining alternative explanations of juvenile firearm homicide rates. *Criminology, 39,* 938–956.

Pajer, K.A., Kelleher, K., Gupta, R.A., Rolls, J., & Gardner, W. (2007). Psychiatric and medical health care policies in juvenile detention facilities. *Journal of the American Academy of Child Adolescent Psychiatry, 46,* 1660–1667.

Park, R., & Burgess, E. (1925). *The city.* Chicago, IL: The University of Chicago Press.

Parry-Langdon, N., Clements, A., Fletcher, D., & Goodman, R. (2008). *Three years on: Survey of the development and emotional well-being of children and young people.* Newport, England: Office for National Statistics.

Pasko, L., & Chesney-Lind, M. (2010). Under lock and key: Trauma, marginalization, and girls' juvenile justice involvement. *Justice Research and Policy, 12,* 25–49.

Pastor, P.N., Reuben, C.A., & Duran, C.R. (2012). *Identifying emotional and behavioral problems in children aged 4–17 years: United States, 2001–2007.* Washington, DC: National Health Statistics Reports, U.S. Department of Health and Human Services.

Paternoster, R. (1987). The deterrent effect of the perceived certainty and severity of punishment: A review of the evidence and issues. *Justice Quarterly, 4,* 173–217.

Payne, A.A. (2012). Communal school organization effects on school disorder: Interactions with school structure. *Deviant Behavior, 33,* 507–524.

Payne, A.A., Gottfredson, D.C., & Gottfredson, G.D. (2008). Schools as communities: The relationships among communal school organization, students bonding, and school disorder. *Criminology, 41,* 749–777.

Payne, A.A., & Welch, K. (2010). Racial threat and punitive school discipline. *Social Problems, 25,* 26–39.

Payton, J., Weissberg, R.P., Durlak, J.A., Dymnicki, A.B., Taylor, R.D., Schellinger, K.B., & Pachan, M. (2008). *The positive impact of social and emotional learning for kindergarten to eighth-grade students: Findings from three scientific reviews.* Chicago, IL: Collaborative for Academic, Social, and Emotional Learning.

Pentz, M.A., Mihalic, S.F., & Grotpeter, J.K. (2006). *The midwestern prevention project: Blueprints for violence prevention, book two* (Blueprints for Violence Prevention Series, D.S. Elliott, Series Ed.). Boulder: Center for the Study and Prevention of Violence, Institute of Behavioral Science, University of Colorado.

Perez, C., & Widom, C.S. (1994). Childhood victimization and long term intellectual and academic outcomes. *Child Abuse & Neglect, 18,* 617–633.

Perkinson, H. (1968). *The imperfect panacea: American faith in education, 1865–1965.* New York, NY: Random House.

Perkonigg, A., KIessler, R.C., Storz, S., & Wittchen, H.U. (2000). Traumatic events and post-traumatic stress disorder in the community: Prevalence, risk factors and comorbidity. *Acta Pscyhiatrica Scandainavica, 101,* 46–59.

Perry, B.L., & Morris, E.W. (2014). Suspending progress: Collateral consequences of exclusionary punishment in public schools. *American Sociological Review, 79,* 1067–1087.

Person, A.E., Moiduddin, E., Hague-Angus, M., & Malone, L.M. (2009). *Survey of outcomes measurement in research on character education programs.* Washington, DC: National Center for Educational Evaluations and Regional Assistance, Institute of Education Sciences, U.S. Department of Education.

Petitclerc, A., Gatti, U., Vitaro, F., & Tremblay, R.E. (2013). Effects of juvenile court exposure on crime in young adulthood. *Journal of Child Psychology and Psychiatry, 54,* 291–297.

Petrosino, A., Turpin-Petrosino, C., & Guckenburg, S. (2010). *Formal system processing on juveniles: Effects on delinquency.* Oslo, Norway: The Campbell Collaboration.

Petteruti, A. (2011). *"Education under arrest": The case against police in schools.* Washington, DC: Justice Policy Institute.

Petteruti, A., & Walsh, N. (2008). *Jailing communities: The impact of jail expansion and effective public safety strategies.* Washington, DC: Justice Policy Institute.

Pew Center on the States. (2011). *State of recidivism: The revolving door of America's prisons.* Washington, DC: The Pew Charitable Trusts.

Pillmann, F., Rohde, A., Ullrich, S., Draba, S., Sannemuller, U., & Marneros, A. (1999). Violence, criminal behavior, and the EEG: Significance of left hemispheric focal abnormalities. *The Journal of Neuropsychiatry and Clinical Neurosciences, 11,* 454–457.

Pinard, M. (2006). The logistical and ethical difficulties of informing juveniles about the collateral consequences of adjudication. *Nevada Law Journal, 6,* 1111–1129.

Piquero, A.R. (2008). Disproportionate minority contact. *The Future of Children, 18,* 59–79.

Piquero, A.R., Farrington, D., & Blumstein, A. (2003). The criminal career paradigm. In M. Tonry & N. Morris (Eds.), *Crime and justice: An annual review of research 30.* Chicago, IL: The University of Chicago Press.

Piquero, A.R., Farrington, D.P., Welsh, B.C., Tremblay, R., & Jennings, W.C. (2009). Effects of early family/parent training programs on antisocial behavior and delinquency. *Journal of Experimental Criminology, 5,* 83–120.

Piquero, A.R., Jennings, W.G., & Farrington, D.P. (2010). *Self-control interventions for children under age 10 for improving self-control and delinquency and problem behaviors.* Oslo, Norway: The Campbell Library, The Campbell Collaboration.

Platt, A. (1969). *The child savers.* Chicago, IL: The University of Chicago Press.

Platt, A. (2009). *The child savers: The intervention of delinquency.* New Brunswick, NJ: Rutgers University Press.

Podell, J.L., & Kendall, P.C. (2011). Mothers and fathers in family cognitive-behavioral therapy for anxious youth. *Journal of Child and Family Studies, 20,* 182–195.

Pogarsky, G., Lizotte, A.J., & Thornberry, T.P. (2003). The delinquency of children born to young mothers: Results from the Rochester youth development study. *Criminology, 41,* 1249–1286.

Polinsky, M.L., Pion-Berlin, L., Williams, S., Long, T., & Wolf, A.M. (2010). Preventing child abuse and neglect: A national evaluation of parents anonymous groups. *Child Welfare, 89,* 43–62.

Potter, H. (2006). An argument for "black feminist criminology": Understanding African American women's experiences with intimate partner abuse using an integrated approach. *Feminist Criminology, 1,* 106–124.

Prescott, J.J., & Rockoff, J.E. (2008). *Do sex offender registration and notification laws affect criminal behavior?* Cambridge, MA: National Bureau of Economic Research, Columbia University.

President's Commission on Law Enforcement and Administration of Justice. (1967). *Task force report: Corrections.* Washington, DC: U.S. Government Printing Office.

President's New Freedom Commission on Mental Health. (2003). *Final report to the President.* Washington, DC: Commission on Mental Health.

Psychological Assessment Resources. (2014). *Trauma symptom checklist for children (TSCC).* Lutz, FL: Author.

Putnin̦s, A.L. (2005). Correlates and predictors of self-reported suicide attempts among incarcerated youths. *International Journal of Offender Therapy and Comparative Criminology, 49,* 143–157.

Puzzanchera, C. (2011). *Juvenile arrests, 2011.* Washington, DC: Office of Juvenile Justice and Delinquency Prevention, Office of Justice Programs, U.S. Department of Justice.

Puzzanchera, C., & Hockenberry, S. (2010). *Juvenile court statistics, 2010*. Pittsburgh, PA: National Center for Juvenile Justice.

Puzzanchera, C., & Robson, C. (2014). *Delinquency cases in juvenile court, 2010*. Washington, DC: Office of Juvenile Justice and Delinquency Prevention, Office of Justice Programs, U.S. Department of Justice.

Quinn, M.M., Rutherford, R.B., Leone, P.E., Osher, D.M., & Poirier, J.M. (2005). Youth with disabilities in juvenile corrections: A national survey. *Exceptional Children*, 71, 339–345.

Quinney, R. (1974). *Critique of the legal order: Crime control in capitalist society*. Los Angeles, CA: Transaction.

Raine, A. (1993). *The psychopathology of crime: Criminal behavior as a clinical disorder*. San Diego, CA: Academic Press.

Rapaport, J.L., Inoff-Germain, G., Weissman, M.M., Greenwald, S., Narrow, W.E., Jensen, P.S., Lahey, B.B., & Ganino, G. (2000). Childhood obsessive-compulsive disorder in the NIMH MECA study: Parent versus child identification of cases. Methods for the epidemiology of child and adolescent mental disorders. *Journal of Anxiety Disorders*, 14, 535–548.

Rausch, M.K., & Skiba, R.J. (2004). *Unplanned outcomes: Suspensions and expulsions in Indiana*. Bloomington, IN: Center for Evaluation and Education Policy.

Reckless, W.C. (1967). *The crime problem*. New York, NY: Appleton-Century-Crofts.

Redding, R.E. (1997). Juveniles transferred to criminal court: Leal reform proposals based on social science research. *Utah Law Review*, 709–797.

Redding, R.E. (2010). *Juvenile transfer laws: An effective deterrent to delinquency?* Washington, DC: Office of Juvenile Justice and Delinquency Prevention, Office of Justice Programs, U.S. Department of Justice.

Reddy, L.A., De Thomas, C.A., Newman, E., & Chun, V. (2008). School-based prevention and intervention programs for children with emotional disturbance: A review of treatment components and methodology. *Psychology in the Schools*, 46, 132–153.

Reddy, L.A., Newman, E., De Thomas, C.A., & Chun, V. (2008). Effectiveness of school-based prevention and intervention programs for children and adolescents with emotional disturbance: A meta-analysis. *Journal of School Psychology*, 47, 77–99.

Redlick, A.D. (2010). The susceptibility of juveniles to false confessions and false guilty plea. *Rutgers Law Review* 62, 943–957.

Reeves, R., Rodrigue, E., & Kneebone, E. (2016). *Five evils: Multidimensional poverty and race in America*. Washington, DC: The Brookings Institute.

Reiss, A.J. (1951). Delinquency as the failure of personal and social controls. *American Sociological Review*, 16, 196–207.

Reynolds, W. (1988). *Manual for the suicidal ideation questionnaire*. Odessa, FL: Psychological Assessment Resources.

Rheingold, A.A., Zinzow, H., Hawkins, A., Saunders, B.E., & Kilpatrick, D.G. (2012). Prevalence and mental health outcomes of homicide survivors in a representative US sample of adolescents: Data from the 2005 National Survey of Adolescents. *Journal of Child Psychology and Psychiatry*, 53, 687–694.

Rice, J.M. (1893). *The public school system of the United States*. Stanford, CA: Forum.

Rich-Shae, A.M., & Fox, J.A. (2014). *Zero-tolerance policies*. In G.W. Muschert, S. Henry, N.L. Bracy, & A.A. Peguero (Eds.), *Responding to school violence: Confronting the Columbine effect* (pp. 89–104). Boulder, CO: Lynne Rienner.

Ridolfi, L., & Benson, T. (2016). *Decriminalizing childhood for youth of color* [Civil Rights Roundtable Series, M. Keels (Ed.)]. Chicago, IL: Urban America Forward.

Ritter, G., Denny, G., Albin, G., Barnett, J., & Blankenship, V. (2007). *The effectiveness of volunteer tutoring programs: A systematic review*.

Oslo, Norway: Campbell Systematic Reviews, The Campbell Collaboration.

Robers, S., Zhang, J., & Truman, J. (2012). *Indicators of school crime and safety: 2011*. Washington, DC: National Center for Education Statistics, Institute of Education Services.

Roberts, A.R. (2004). Treating juveniles in institutional and open settings. In A.R. Roberts (Ed.), *Juvenile justice sourcebook: Past, present, and future* (pp. 129–146). New York, NY: Oxford University Press.

Roberts, R.E., Roberts, C.R., & Xing, Y. (2007). Rates of DSM-IV psychiatric disorders among adolescents in a large metropolitan area. *Journal of Psychiatric Research*, 41, 959–967.

Robinson, K.E., & Rapport, L.J. (2002). Outcomes of a school-based mental health program for youth with serious emotional disorders. *Psychology in the Schools*, 39, 661–675.

Roch, C.H., Pitts, D.W., & Navarro, I. (2010). Representative bureaucracy and policy tools: Ethnicity, student discipline, and representation in public schools. *Administration & Society*, 42, 38–65.

Rocha, R.R., & Hawes, D.P. (2009). Racial diversity, representative bureaucracy, and equity in multiracial school districts. *Social Science Quarterly*, 90, 326–344.

Rogers, R., Blackwood, H.L., Fiduccia, C.E., Steadham, J.A., & Drogin, E.Y. (2012). Juvenile Miranda warnings: Perfunctory rituals or procedural safeguards? *Criminal Justice and Behavior*, 39, 229–249.

Rogers, R., Hazelwood, L.L., Sewell, K.W., Harrison, K.S., & Shuman, D.W. (2008). The language of Miranda warnings in American jurisdiction: A replication and vocabulary analysis. *Law and Human Behavior*, 32, 124–136.

Romano, E., Tremblay, R.E., Vitaro, F., Zoccolillo, M., & Pagani, L. (2001). Prevalence of psychiatric diagnoses and the role of perceived impairment: Findings from an adolescent community sample. *Journal of Child Psychology and Psychiatry*, 42, 451–461.

Rosado, L.M. (2005). Training mental health and juvenile justice professionals in juvenile forensic assessment. In K. Heilbrun, M.E. Sevin-Goldstein, & R.E. Redding (Eds.), *Juvenile delinquency: Prevention, assessment, and intervention* (pp. 310–322). New York, NY: Oxford University Press.

Rosenblatt, J.A., Rosenblatt, A.R., & Biggs, E.E. (2000). Criminal behavior and emotional disorder: Comparing youth served by the mental health and juvenile justice systems. *The Journal of Behavioral Health Services & Research*, 27, 227–237.

Rothman, D. (1971). *The discovery of the asylum*. Boston, MA: Little, Brown.

Rovner, J. (2015). *Declines in youth commitments and facilities in the 21st century*. Washington, DC: The Sentencing Project.

Rowe, C.I., & Liddle, H.A. (2006). Treating adolescent substance abuse: State of the science. In H.A. Liddle & C.L. Rowe (Eds.), *Adolescent substance abuse—research and clinical advances* (pp. 1–21). New York, NY: Cambridge University Press.

Rozalski, M., Deignan, M., & Engel, S. (2008). The world of juvenile justice according to the numbers. *Reading and Writing Quarterly: Overcoming Learning Difficulties*, 24, 143–147.

Rudd, T. (2014). *Racial disproportionality in school discipline*. Columbus: Kirwan Institute for the Study of Race and Ethnicity, The Ohio State University.

Ruddy, S.A., Bauer, L., Neiman, S., Hryczaniuk, C.A., Thomas, T.L., & Parmer, R.J. (2010). *2007–08 school survey on crime and safety (SSOCS): Survey documentation for restricted-use data file uses*. Washington, DC: U.S. Department of Education.

Ruiz de Velasco, J., Austin, G., Dixon, D., Johnson, J., McLaughlin, M., & Perez, L. (2008). *Alternative education options: A descriptive study of California continuation high schools*. San Francisco, CA: WestEd.

Rumberger, R.W. (2004). Why students drop out of school. In G. Orfield (Ed.), *Dropouts in America: Confronting the graduation rate crisis*. Cambridge, MA: Harvard Education Press.

Rumberger, R.W., & Losen, D.J. (2016). *The high cost of harsh discipline and its disparate impact.* Los Angeles, CA: The Center for Civil Rights Remedies at the Civil Rights Project.

RUPP Anxiety Study Group. (2001). Fluvoxamine for the treatment of anxiety disorders in children and adolescents. *The New England Journal of Medicine*, 344, 1279–1285.

Russell, S.T., Kostroski, O., Horn, S., & Saewyc, E. (2010). Social policy report: Safe schools policy for LGBTQ students. *Center for Research in Child Development*, 24, 1–24.

Rutherford, R.B., Nelson, C.M., & Wolford, B.I. (1985). Special education in the most restrictive environment: Correctional/special education. *Journal of Special Education*, 19, 59–71.

Ryan, E.P., & Redding, R.E. (2004). Mood disorders in juvenile offenders. *Psychiatric Services*, 55, 1397–1407.

Ryan, J.E. (2004). The perverse incentives of the No Child Left Behind Act. *New York University Law Review*, 79, 932–945.

Ryan, J.P., Herz, D., Hernandez, P., & Marshall, J. (2007). Child maltreatment and juvenile delinquency: Investigating child welfare bias in juvenile justice processing. *Children and Youth Services Review*, 27, 227–249.

Safe Horizon. (n.d.). Michael's story (Blog post). Retrieved March 21, 2017, from http://www.safehorizon.org/page/michaels-story-when-a-child-witnesses-domestic-violence-212.html

Salsich, A., & Trone, J. (2013). *From courts to communities: The right response to truancy, running away, and other status offenses.* New York, NY: Vera Institute of Justice.

Sampson, R.J. (1985). Structural sources of variation in race-age-specific rate of offending across major U.S. cities. *Criminology*, 23, 647–673.

Sampson, R.J. Raudenbush, S.W., & Earls, F. (1997). Neighborhoods and violent crime: A multilevel study of collective efficacy. *Science*, 277(5328): 918–24.

Sampson, R.J., & Laub, J. (1993). *Crime in the making: Pathways and turning points through life.* Cambridge, MA: Harvard University Press.

Sanborn, J.B., & Salerno, A.W. (2005). *The juvenile justice system: Law and process.* Los Angeles, CA: Roxbury.

Sanders, M.R., Cann, W., & Markie-Dadds, C. (2003). The triple p-positive programme: A universal population-level approach to the prevention of child abuse. *Child Abuse Review*, 12, 155–171.

SASSI Institute. (2014). *Adolescent substance abuse subtle screening instrument.* Springville, IN: Author.

Savage, T.A., & Schanding, G.T. (2013). Creating and maintaining safe and responsive schools for lesbian, gay, transgender, and queer youths: Introduction to the special issue. *Journal of School Violence*, 12, 1–6.

Saunders, B.E., & Adams, Z.W. (2014). Epidemiology of traumatic experiences in childhood. *Child and Adolescent Psychiatric Clinics of North America*, 23, 167–184.

Scalia, J. (1997). *Juvenile delinquents in the federal criminal justice system.* Washington, DC: Bureau of Justice Statistics.

Scarborough, A., & McCrae, J. (2009). School-age special education outcomes of infants and toddlers investigated for maltreatment. *Children and Youth Services Review*, 32, 80–88.

Scarpitti, F.R., & Stephenson, R.M. (1968). A study of probation effectiveness. *Journal of Criminal Law, Criminology, and Police Science*, 3, 361–369.

Schargel, F.P. (2004). Who drops out and why. In J. Smink & F.P. Schargel (Eds.), *Helping students graduate: A strategic approach to dropout prevention.* Larchmont, NY: Eye on Education.

Schiff, M. (2013). *Dignity, disparity and desistance: Effective restorative justice strategies to plug the "school-to-prison pipeline.* Paper presented at the Closing the School Discipline Gap: Research to Practice Conference, Washington, DC.

Schmidt, F., Hoge, R., & Gomes, L. (2005). Reliability and validity analysis of the youth level of service/case management inventory. *Criminal Justice and Behavior*, 32, 329–344.

Schochet, P., Burghardt, J., & McConnell, S. (2008). Does job corps work? Impact findings from the national job corps study. *American Economic Review*, 98, 1864–1886.

Schubert, C.A., & Mulvey, E.P. (2014). *Behavioral health problems, treatment, and outcomes in serious youthful offenders.* Washington, DC: Office of Juvenile Justice and Delinquency Prevention, Office of Justice Programs, U.S. Department of Justice.

Schubert, C.A., Mulvey, E.P., & Glasheen, C. (2011). The influence of mental health and substance use problems and criminogenic risk on outcomes in serious juvenile offenders. *The Journal of the American Academy of Child and Adolescent Psychiatry*, 50, 925–937.

Schultz, K. (2008). Interrogating students' silences. In M. Pollock (Ed.), *Everyday antiracism: Getting real about race in school* (pp. 217–221). New York, NY: The New Press.

Schwalbe, C.S. (2008). A meta-analysis of juvenile justice risk assessment instruments: Predictive validity by gender. *Criminal Justice and Behavior*, 35, 1367–1381.

Schwartz, D., & Gorman, A. (2003). Community violence exposure and children's academic performance. *Journal of Educational Psychology*, 95, 163–173.

Schwartz, R.G. (2001). Juvenile justice and positive youth development. In P.L. Benson & K.J. Pittman (Eds.), *Trends In youth development: Visions, realities and challenges* (pp. 231–267). Boston, MA: Kluwer Academic.

Scott, E.S., & Grisso, T. (1997). The evolution of adolescence: A developmental perspective on juvenile justice reform. *Journal of Criminal Law & Criminology*, 88, 137–189.

Scott, E.S., & Steinberg, L. (2008a). Adolescent development and the regulation of youth crime. *The Future of Children*, 18, 18–33.

Scott, E.S., & Steinberg, L. (2008b). *Rethinking juvenile justice.* Boston, MA: Harvard University Press.

Scott, E.S., & Steinberg, L. (2010). *Rethinking juvenile justice.* Cambridge, MA: Harvard University Press.

Scott, M., Snowden, L., & Libby, A.M. (2002). From mental health to juvenile justice: What factors predict this transition? *Journal of Child and Family Studies*, 11, 299–311.

Sedlak, A.J., & Broadhurst, D. (1996). *Executive summary of the third national incidence study of child abuse and neglect.* Washington, DC: National Center on Child Abuse and Neglect, Administration for Children, Youth, and Families, Administration for Children and Families, U.S. Department of Health and Human Services.

Sedlak, A.J., & McPherson, K. (2010). *Survey of youth in residential placement: Youth's needs and services* (SYRP Report). Rockville, MD: Westat.

Sedlak, A.J., & Schultz, D. (2005). Racial differences in child protective services investigations of abused and neglected children. In D.M. Derezoes, J. Poertner, & M.F. Testa (Eds.), *Race matters in child welfare: The overrepresentation of African American children in the system* (97–124). Washington, DC: Child Welfare League of America.

Seigle, E., Walsh, N., & Weber, J. (2014). *Core principles for reducing recidivism and improving other outcomes for youth in the juvenile justice system.* New York, NY: The Council on State Governments.

Sellin, T. (1931). The basis of a crime index. *Journal of Criminal Law and Criminology*, 22, 335–356.

Sellin, T. (1938). Culture conflict and crime. *American Journal of Sociology*, 44, 97–103.

Serketich, W.J., & Dumas, J.E. (1996). The effectiveness of behavioural parent training to modify antisocial behavior in children: A meta-analysis. *Behaviour Therapy*, 27, 171–186.

Sexton, T., & Alexander, J. (2000). *Functional family therapy.* Washington, DC: Juvenile Justice Bulletin, Office of Juvenile Justice and Delinquency Prevention, U.S. Department of Justice.

Shaffer, D., Gould, M.S., Fisher, L.A., Trautman, P., Moreau, D., Kleinman, M., & Flory, M. (1996). Psychiatric diagnosis in child and adolescent suicide. *Archives of General Psychiatry*, 53, 339–348.

Shaffer, D., Lucas, C., & Fisher, P. (2011). *Diagnostic interview schedule for children version four*. New York, NY: DISC Development Group.

Sharma, S. (2008). Teacher representations of cultural differences through film. In M. Pollock (Ed.), *Everyday antiracism: Getting real about race in school* (pp. 186–190). New York, NY: The New Press.

Sharp, S.F., & Hefley, K. (2004). *This is a man's world . . . or at least that's how it looks in the journals*. Paper presented at the annual meeting of the American Society of Criminology, Nashville, TN.

Shaw, C. (1929). *Delinquency areas*. Chicago, IL: The University of Chicago Press.

Shaw, C., & McKay, H.D. (1931). Social factors in juvenile delinquency. In *Report on the Cause of Crime, vol. 2, National Commission on Law Observance and Enforcement* (Report no. 13). Washington, DC: U.S. Government Printing Office.

Shaw, C., & McKay, H.D. (1942). *Juvenile delinquency and urban areas*. Chicago, IL: The University of Chicago Press.

Shaywitz, S.E., Fletcher, J.M., Holahan, J.M., Schneider, A.E., Marchone, K.E., Stuebing, K.K., Francis, D.J., Pugh, K.R., & Shaywitz, B.A. (1999). Persistence of dyslexia: The Connecticut longitudinal study at adolescence. *Pediatrics*, 104, 1351–1359.

Shear, M. (2016). Obama bans solitary confinement of juveniles in federal prisons. *The New York Times*, A12.

Shepherd, R.E. (1999). Film at eleven: The news media and juvenile crime. *Quinnipiac Law Review*, 18, 687–700.

Shepherd, R.E. (2008). Plea bargaining in juvenile court. *Criminal Justice*, 23(3). Retrieved from https://www.americanbar.org/content/dam/aba/publishing/criminal_justice_section_newsletter/crimjust_cjmag_23_3_shepherd.authcheckdam.pdf

Sheridan, W.H. (1969). *Legislative guide for drafting family and juvenile court acts*. Washington, DC: U.S. Department of Health, Education, and Welfare, Social and Rehabilitation Service, Children's Bureau.

Sherman, F.T., & Balck, A. (2015). *Gender injustice: System-level juvenile justice reforms for girls*. Portland, OR: The National Crittenton Foundation and the National Women's Law Center.

Sherman, L.W., Smith, D.A., Schmidt, J.D., & Rogan, D.P. (1992). Crime, punishment, and stake in conformity: Legal and informal control of domestic violence. *American Sociological Review*, 57, 680–690.

Sherman, R. (1994). Juvenile judges say: Time to get tough. *National Law Journal*, 1–16.

Shollenberg, T.O. (2015). Racial disparities in school suspension and subsequent outcomes: Evidence from the National Longitudinal Survey of Youth, 1997. In D.J. Losen (Ed.), *Closing the school discipline gap: Research for policymakers*. New York, NY: Teachers College Press.

Short, J.F., & Nye, F.I. (1958). Extent of unrecorded juvenile delinquency: Tentative conclusions. *Journal of Criminal Law and Criminology*, 49, 296–302.

Sickmund, M. (2003). *Juveniles in court*. Washington, DC: Office of Juvenile Justice and Delinquency Prevention, Bureau of Justice Affairs, U.S. Department of Justice.

Sickmund, M., & Puzzanchera, C. (2014). *Juvenile offenders and victims: 2014 national report*. Pittsburgh, PA: National Center for Juvenile Justice.

Sickmund, M., Sladky, T.J., & Wang, W. (2014). *Easy access to juvenile court statistics: 1985–2011*. Pittsburgh, PA: National Center for Juvenile Justice.

Siegel, G.L., & Loman, T. (2006). *Extended follow-up study of Minnesota's family assessment response: Final report*. St. Louis, MO: Institute of Applied Research.

Simons, R.J. (1975). *Women and crime*. Lexington, KY: Lexington Books.

Simonoff, E., Pickles, A., Meyer, J.M., Silberg, J.L., Maes, H.H., Loeber, R., Rutter, M., Hewitt, J.K., & Eaves, L.J. (1997). The Virginia twin study of adolescent behavioral development. Influences of age, sex, and impairment on rates of disorder. *Archives of General Psychiatry*, 54, 801–808.

Singleton, G.E., & Linton, C. (2006). *Courageous conversations about race: A field guide for achieving equity in schools*. Thousand Oaks, CA: Corwin Press.

Sipe, P. (2012). Newjack: Teaching in a failing middle school. In S. Bahena, N. Cooc, R. Currie-Rubin, P. Kuttner, & M. Ng (Eds.), *Disrupting the school-to-prison pipeline* (pp. 32–41). Cambridge, MA: Harvard Educational Review.

Skiba, R.J., Arredondo, M.I., & Rausch, M.K. (2014). *New and developing research on disparities in discipline*. Bloomington, IN: Discipline Disparities: A Research-to-Practice Collaborative. The Equity Project at Indiana University, Center for Evaluation and Education Policy.

Skiba, R.J., Michael, R.S., Nardo, A.C., & Peterson, R.L. (2002). The color of discipline: Sources of racial and gender disproportionality in school punishment. *The Urban Review*, 34, 317–342.

Skiba, R.J., Reynolds, C.R., Graham, S., Sheras, P., Conoley, J.C., & Garcia-Vasquez, E. (2006). *Are zero tolerance policies effective in the schools? An evidentiary review and recommendations*. Washington, DC: American Psychological Association Zero Tolerance Task Force.

Skiba, R.J., Shure, L., & Williams, N. (2012). *Racial and ethnic disproportionality in suspension and expulsion*. In A.L. Noltemeyer & C.S. McLoughlin (Eds.), *Disproportionality in education and special education* (pp. 89–118). Springfield, IL: Charles C. Thomas.

Skiba, R.J., & Williams, N.T. (2014). *Are black kids worse? Myths and facts about racial differences in behavior* (Discipline Disparities: A Research-to-Practice Collaborative). Bloomington, IN: The Equity Project at Indiana University, Center for Evaluation and Education Policy.

Skogan, W.G., Hartnett, S.M., Bump, N., & Dubois, J. (2008). *Evaluation of CeaseFire—Chicago*. Chicago, IL: Northwestern University Press.

Skowyra, K.R., & Cocozza, J.J. (2007). *Mental health screening within juvenile justice: The next frontier*. Delmar, NY: National Center for Mental Health and Juvenile Justice.

Skowyra, K.R., & Teodosio, L. (2014). *Trends in state courts 2014: Special issue, juvenile justice and elder issues*. Williamsburg, VA: National Center for States Courts.

Slade, E.P., & Wissow, L.S. (2007). The influence of childhood maltreatment on adolescents' academic performance. *Economics of Education Review*, 26, 604–614.

Sleeter, C.E. (2011). *The academic and social value of ethnic studies: A research review*. Washington, DC: National Education Association.

Smedslund, G., Berg, R.C., Hammerstrøm, K.T., Steiro, A., Leiknes, K.A., Dahl, H.M., & Karlsen, M. (2011). *Motivational interviewing for substance abuse: A systematic review*. Oslo, Norway: The Campbell Library, The Campbell Collaboration.

Smith, B.D., Duffee, D.E., Steinke, C.M., Huang, Y., & Larkin, H. (2008). Outcomes in residential treatment for youth: The role of early engagement. *Children and Youth Services Review*, 30, 1425–1436.

Smith, C.A., & Thornberry, T.O. (1995). The relationship between childhood maltreatment and adolescent involvement in delinquency. *Criminology*, 33, 451–481.

Smith, C.A., Ireland, T.O., & Thornberry, T.P. (2005). Adolescent maltreatment and adolescent involvement in delinquency. *Child Abuse and Neglect*, 29, 1099–1119.

Smithgall, C., Gladden, R.M., Howard, E., Goerge, R., & Courtney, M.E. (2004). *Education experiences of children in out-of-home care.* Chicago, IL: Chapin Hall Center for Children.

Snyder, H.N., & Sickmund, M. (2006). *Juvenile offenders and victims: 2006 national report.* Washington, DC: Office of Juvenile Justice and Delinquency Prevention, Office of Justice Programs, U.S. Department of Justice.

Social and Character Development Research Consortium. (2010). *Efficacy of school-wide programs to promote social and character development and reduce problem behavior in elementary school children.* Washington, DC: National Center for Education Research, Institute of Education Sciences, U.S. Department of Education.

Sojoyner, D.M. (2014). Changing the lens: Moving away from the school to prison pipeline. In A.J. Nocella II, P. Parmar, & D. Stovall (Eds.), *From education to incarceration: Dismantling the school-to-prison pipeline* (pp. 54–66). New York, NY: Peter Lang.

Soler, M., Schoenberg, D., & Schindler, M. (2009). Juvenile justice: Lessons for a new era. *Georgetown Journal of Poverty Law and Policy, 26,* 483–541.

Somerville, L.H., & Casey, B. (2010). Developmental neurobiology of cognitive control and motivational systems. *Current Opinion in Neurobiology, 20,* 236–241.

Spinney, E., Cohen, M., Feyerherm, W., Stephenson, R., Yeide, M., & Hopps. M. (2014). *Case studies of nine jurisdictions that reduced disproportionate minority contact in their juvenile justice systems.* Bethesda, MD: Development Services Group.

Spoth, R.L., Redmond, C., & Shin, C. (2001). Randomized trial of brief family interventions for general populations: Adolescent substance use outcomes four years following baseline. *Journal of Consulting and Clinical Psychology, 69,* 627–642.

Sprague, J.R., Vincent, C.G., Tobin, T.J., & CHiXapkaid. (2013). Preventing disciplinary exclusions of students from American Indian/Alaska Native backgrounds. *Family Court Review, 51,* 452–459.

Staats, C. (2014). *Implicit racial bias and school discipline disparities.* Columbus: Kirwan Institute for the Study of Race and Ethnicity, The Ohio State University.

Stagman, S., & Cooper, J.L. (2010). *Children's mental health: What every policymaker should know.* New York, NY: National Center for Children in Poverty, Columbia University.

Stagner, M.W., & Lansing, J. (2009). Progress toward a prevention perspective. *The Future of Children, 29,* 19–38.

Steeves, V., & Marx, G.T. (2014). Safe schools initiatives and the shifting climate of trust. In G.W. Muschert, S. Henry, N.L. Bracy, & A.A. Peguero (Eds.), *Responding to school violence: Confronting the Columbine effect* (pp. 105–124). Boulder, CO: Lynne Rienner.

Steinberg, L. (2014a). *Age of opportunity: Lessons from the new science of adolescence.* Boston, MA: Houghton Mifflin Harcourt.

Steinberg, L. (2014b). Should the science of adolescent brain development inform public policy? *Court Review, 50,* 70–77.

Steinberg, L., Dahl, R., Keating, D., Kupfer, D.J., & Masten, A.S. (2006). The study of development psychopathology in adolescence: Integrating affective neuroscience with the study of context. In D. Cicchetti & D.J. Cohen (Eds.), *Developmental Psychopathology* (2nd ed., pp. 710–741). Hoboken, NJ: Wiley.

Steinberg, M.P., Allensworth, E.M., & Johnson, D.W. (2011). *Student and teacher safety in Chicago public schools: The roles of community context and school social organization.* Chicago, IL: University of Chicago, Consortium on Chicago School Research, Urban Education Institute.

Steinberg, M.P., Allensworth, E., & Johnson, D.W. (2013). *What conditions jeopardize and support safety in urban schools? The influence of community characteristics, school composition and school organizational practices on student and teacher reports of safety in Chicago.* Paper presented at the Closing the School Discipline Gap: Research to Practice conference, Washington, DC.

Stewart, A., Livingston, M., & Dennison, S. (2008). Transitions and turning points: Examining the links between child maltreatment and juvenile offending. *Child Abuse and Neglect, 32,* 51–66.

Stinchcomb, J. B., Bazemore, G., & Riestenberg, N. (2006). Beyond zero tolerance: Restoring justice in secondary schools. *Youth Violence and Juvenile Justice, 4.* doi: 10.101177/1541204006286287

Stretesky, P.B., & Lynch, M.J. (2004). The relationship between lead and crime. *Journal of Health and Social Behavior, 45,* 214–229.

Substance Abuse and Mental Health Services Administration. (2013a). *Mental health, United States, 2012.* Washington, DC: Center for Mental Health Services, U.S. Department of Health and Human Services.

Substance Abuse and Mental Health Services Administration. (2013b). *National survey on drug use and health.* Washington, DC: Center for Mental Health Services, U.S. Department of Health and Human Services.

Substance Abuse and Mental Health Services Administration. (2014a). *Results from the 2013 national survey on drug use and health: Summary of national findings.* Washington, DC: Office of Applied Studies, U.S. Department of Health and Human Services.

Substance Abuse and Mental Health Services Administration. (2014b). *SAMSHA's concept of trauma and guidance for a trauma-informed approach.* Washington, DC: Office of Planning, Policy, and Innovation, U.S. Department of Health and Human Services.

Sugai, G., & Horner, R. (2010). School-wide positive behavior support: Establishing a continuum of evidence-based practices. *Journal of Evidence-Based Practices for Schools, 11,* 62–83.

Suh, S., & Suh, J. (2007). Risk factors and levels of risk for high school dropouts. *Professional School Counseling, 10,* 297–306.

Sulok, M.M. (2007). Extended jurisdiction juvenile prosecution: To resolve or not to revoke. *Loyola University Chicago Law Review, 215,* 270–295.

Sum, A., Khatiwada, I., McLaughlin, J., & Palma, S. (2009). *The consequences of dropping out of high school: Joblessness and jailing for high school dropouts and the high cost to taxpayers.* Boston, MA: Center for Labor Market Studies, Northeastern University.

Summers, A., Wood, S., & Donovan, J. (2013). *Disproportionality rates for children of color in foster care* (Technical Assistance Bulletin). Reno, NV: National Council of Juvenile and Families Court Judges.

Sussman, S., Rohrbach, L., & Mihalic, S. (2004). *Project towards no drug abuse: Blueprints for violence prevention, book twelve* (Blueprints for Violence Prevention Series, D.S. Elliott, Series Ed.). Boulder: Center for the Study and Prevention of Violence, Institute of Behavioral Science, University of Colorado.

Sutherland, E.H., & Cressy, D.R. (1966). *Principles of criminology* (7th ed.). Chicago, IL: J.B. Lippincott.

Sutherland, E.H., Cressey, D.R., & Luckenbill, D.F. (1992). *Principles of criminology* (11th ed.). New York, NY: General Hall, Division of Rowman & Littlefield.

Suveg, C., Kendall, P.C., Comer, J.S., & Robin, J. (2006). Emotion-focused cognitive-behavioral therapy for anxious youth: A multiple baseline evaluation. *Journal of Contemporary Psychotherapy, 36,* 77–85.

Sweet, M.A., & Appelbaum, M.I. (2004). Is home visiting an effective strategy? A meta-analysis of home visiting programs for families with young children. *Child Development, 75,* 1435–1456.

Sweeten, G. (2006). Who will graduate? Disruption of high school education by arrest and court involvement. *Justice Quarterly, 23,* 462–473.

Sykes, G.M., & Matza, D. (1957). Techniques of neutralization: A theory of delinquency. *American Sociological Review, 22,* 664–670.

Szalavitz, M. (2012, August 17). My brain made me do it: Psychopaths and free will. *Time*. Retrieved from http://healthland.time.com/2012/08/17/my-brain-made-me-do-it-psychopaths-and-free-will/

Szymanski, L.A. (2013). *Juvenile competency procedures*. Pittsburgh, PA: National Center for Juvenile Justice.

Tannenbaum, F. (1938). *Crime and the community*. New York, NY: Columbia University Press.

Teaching Tolerance. (2013). *Creating an LGBT-inclusive school environment*. Montgomery, AL: Teaching Tolerance, The Southern Poverty Law Center.

Tepfer, J.A., Nirider, L.H., & Tricarico, L. (2010). Arresting development: Convictions of innocent youth. *Rutgers Law Review*, 62, 887–941.

Teplin, L., Abram, K., McClelland, G., Dulcan, M., & Mericle, A., (2002). Psychiatric disorders in youth in juvenile detention. *Archives of General Psychiatry*, 59, 1133–1143.

Teplin, L., Abram, K., McClelland, G., Mericle, A., Dulcan, M., & Washburn, D. (2006). *Psychiatric disorders of youth in detention*. Washington, DC: Office of Justice Programs, Office of Juvenile Justice and Delinquency Prevention, U.S. Department of Justice.

Teplin, L., Abram, K., McClelland, G., Washburn, J., & Pikus, A. (2005). Detecting mental disorder in juvenile detainees: Who receives services? *American Journal of Public Health*, 95, 1773–1780.

Texas Appleseed. (2011). *Thinking outside the cell: Alternatives to incarceration for youth with mental illness*. Austin: Disability Rights Texas National Center for Youth Law.

The Annie E. Casey Foundation. (2009). *Two decades of JDAI: A progress report. From demonstration project to national standard*. Baltimore, MD: Author.

The Annie E. Casey Foundation. (2012). *Expanding JDAI's focus to reduce commitments and placements*. Baltimore, MD: Author.

The Annie E. Casey Foundation. (2016). *A shared experience: The devastating toll of parental incarceration on kids, families and communities*. Baltimore, MD: Author.

The Burns Institute. (2015). *Stemming the rising tide: Racial and ethnic disparities in youth incarceration & strategies for change*. Oakland, CA: Author.

The Center for Civil Rights Remedies. (2013). *A summary of new research, closing the school discipline gap: Research to practice*. Washington, DC: Author.

The Council of State Governments Justice Center. (2015). *Reducing recidivism and improving other outcomes for young adults in the juvenile and adult criminal justice systems*. Austin, TX: Author.

The Equity Project at Indiana University. (2014). *Discipline disparities series: Key findings*. Bloomington, IN: Discipline Disparities: A Research-to-Practice Collaborative. The Equity Project at Indiana University, Center for Evaluation and Education Policy.

The National Child Traumatic Stress Network. (2015). *National child traumatic stress network empirically supported treatments and promising practices*. Los Angeles, CA: UCLA.

The National Child Traumatic Stress Network. (2016). *Types of traumatic stress*. Los Angeles, CA: UCLA.

The School District of Philadelphia. (2010). *2009–2010 Student Code of Conduct*. Philadelphia, PA: Author.

The Sentencing Project. (2012). *Youth re-entry*. Washington, DC: Author.

The Sentencing Project. (2015). *Trends in U.S. corrections*. Washington, DC: Author.

The Sentencing Project. (2016). *Racial disparities in youth commitments and arrests*. Washington, DC: Author.

The White House. (2016, Jan. 25). *Fact sheet: Department of Justice review of solitary confinement*. Washington, DC: Office of the Press Secretary, The White House.

Theriot, M.T. (2009). School resource officers and the criminalization of student behavior. *Journal of Criminal Justice*, 37, 280–287.

Thomas, D. (2015). *When systems collaborate: How three jurisdictions improved their handling of dual-status cases*. Pittsburgh, PA: National Center for Juvenile Justice.

Thomas, D., Hyland, N., Deal, T., Wachter, A., & Zaleski, S. (2016). *Evidence-based policies, programs, and practices in juvenile justice: Three states achieving high standards through state support centers*. Pittsburgh, PA: National Center for Juvenile Justice.

Thomas, D., Leicht, C., Hughes, C., Madigan, A., & Dowell, K. (2003). *Emerging practices in the prevention of child abuse and neglect*. Washington, DC: U.S. Department of Health and Human Services.

Thomas, D., Schiller, W.L., & Lucero, L.R. (2013). *The right youth for your drug court*. Reno, NV: National Council of Juvenile and Family Court Judges.

Thomas, D., Torbet, P., & Deal, T. (2011). *Implementing effective case management strategies: A guide for probation administrators*. Pittsburgh, PA: National Center for Juvenile Justice.

Thomas, R., & Zimmer-Gembeck, M.J. (2011). Accumulating evidence for parent-child interaction therapy in the prevention of child maltreatment. *Child Development*, 82, 177–192.

Thomas, W.I., & Znaniechi, F. (1927). *The Polish peasant in Europe and America*. New York, NY: Knopf.

Thompson, M., Ho, C., & Kingree, J. (2007). Prospective associations between delinquency and suicidal behaviors in a nationally representative sample. *Journal of Adolescent Health*, 40, 232–237.

Thornberry, T.P. (1987). Toward an interactional theory of delinquency. *Criminology*, 25, 863–891.

Thornberry, T.P. (2005). Explaining multiple patterns of offending across the life course and across generations. *The ANNALS of the American Academy of Political and Social Science*, 602, 156–195.

Thornberry, T.P., & Krohn, M.D. (2000). The self-report method for measuring delinquency and crime. In D. Duffee (Ed.), *Criminal justice 2000* (pp. 33–84). Washington, DC: The National Institute of Justice, U.S. Department of Justice.

Thurae, L., & Wald, J. (2010). Controlling partners: When law enforcement meets discipline in public schools. *New York Law School Law Review*, 54, 977–1020.

Tibbetts, S.G., & Hemmens, C. (2010). *Criminological theory/a text/reader*. Thousand Oaks, CA: Sage.

Timmer, S.G., Urquiza, A.J., Zebell, N.M., & McGrath, J.M. (2005). Parent-child interaction therapy: Application to maltreating parent-child dyads. *Child Abuse and Neglect*, 29, 825–842.

Toby, J. (1957). Social disorganization and stake in conformity: Complementary factors in the predatory behavior of hoodlums. *Journal of Criminal Law and Criminology*, 48, 12–18.

Tolan, P., Henry, D., Schoeny, M., & Bass, A. (2008). *Mentoring interventions to affect juvenile delinquency and associated problems*. Oslo, Norway: Campbell Systematic Reviews, The Campbell Collaboration.

Tolou-Shams, M., Brown, L.K., Gordon, G., Fernandez, I. & SHIELD study group. (2007). Arrest history as an indicator of adolescent/young adult substance use and HIV risk. *Drug and Alcohol Dependence*, 88: 87–90. PMID 17092660.

Toomey, R.B., & Russell, S.T. (2011). Gay-straight alliances, social justice involvement, and school victimization of lesbian, gay, bisexual, and queer youth: Implications for school well-being and plans to vote. *Youth & Society*, 20, 1–23.

Toomey, R.B., Ryan, C., Diaz, R.M., & Russell, S.T. (2011). High school gay-straight alliances (GSAs) and young adult well-being: An examination of GSA presence, participation, and perceived effectiveness. *Applied Developmental Science*, 15, 175–185.

Torbet, P. (2008). *Building Pennsylvania's compressive aftercare model: Probation case management essentials for youth in placement*. Pittsburgh, PA: National Center for Juvenile Justice.

Torres, M., & Stefkovich, J.A. (2008). Demographics and police involvement: Implications for student civil liberties and just leadership. *Education Administration Quarterly, 45,* 450–473.

Tracy, P.E., Kempf-Leonard, K., & Abramoske-James, S. (2009). Gender differences in delinquency and juvenile justice processing: Evidence from national data. *Crime & Delinquency, 55,* 171–215.

Tremblay, R.E., & LeMarquand, D. (2001). Individual risk and protective factors. In R. Loeber & D.P. Farrington (Eds.), *Child delinquents: Development, intervention, and service needs* (pp. 137–164), Thousand Oaks, CA: Sage.

Trulson, C.R., Haerle, D.R., DeLisi, M., & Marquart, J.W. (2011). Blended sentencing, early release, and recidivism of violent institutionalized delinquents. *The Prison Journal, 91,* 255–278.

Truman, J.L., & Langton, L. (2015). *Criminal victimization, 2014.* Washington, DC: U.S. Bureau of Justice Statistics, U.S. Department of Justice.

Truman, J.L., & Morgan, R.E. (2016). *Criminal victimization, 2015.* Washington, DC: U.S. Bureau of Justice Statistics, U.S. Department of Justice. Retrieved from https://www.bjs.gov/content/pub/pdf/cv15.pdf

Turk, A. (1969). *Criminality and legal order.* Chicago, IL: Rand McNally.

Turner, H.A., Finkelhor, D., & Ormrod, R. (2006). The effect of lifetime victimization on the mental health of children and adolescents. *Social Science & Medicine, 62,* 13–27.

Turner, W., MacDonald, G.M., & Dennis J.A. (2007). *Cognitive-behavioural training interventions for assisting foster carers in the management of difficult behaviour.* Oslo, Norway: Cochrane Library, The CampbellCollaboration.

U.S. Census Bureau. (2014). *2014 national population projections.* Washington, DC: U.S. Department of Commerce.

U.S. Department of Education. (2000). *21st annual report to congress on the implementation of the individuals with disabilities education act.* Washington, DC: Author.

U.S. Department of Education. (2001). *Safe, disciplined, and drug-free schools programs.* Washington, DC: Office of Special Education Research and Improvement, Office of Reform Assistance and Dissemination.

U.S. Department of Education. (2012). *31st annual report to Congress on the implementation of the Individuals with Disabilities Education Act, 2009.* Washington, DC: Office of Special Education and Rehabilitative Services, Office of Special Education Programs.

U.S. Department of Education. (2013b). *Digest of education statistics, 2012* (NCES 2014–015, ch. 2). Washington, DC: National Center for Education Statistics.

U.S. Department of Education. (2013c). *Student reports of bullying and cyberbullying: From the 2011 school crime supplement to the national crime victimization survey.* Washington, DC: Author.

U.S. Department of Education. (2014a). *36th annual report to Congress on the implementation of the Individuals with Disabilities Education Act, 2012.* Washington, DC: Office of Special Education and Rehabilitative Services, Office of Special Education Programs.

U.S. Department of Education. (2014b). *Appendix 1: U.S. Department of Education: Director of federal school climate and discipline resources.* Washington DC: Author.

U.S. Department of Education. (2014c). *Civil rights data collection, data snapshot: School discipline, Issue brief No. 1.* Washington, DC: Office of Civil Rights.

U.S. Department of Education. (2014d). *Guiding principles: A resource guide for improving school climate and discipline.* Washington, DC: Author.

U.S. Department of Education. (2014e). *Indicators of school crime and safety, 2014.* Washington, DC: National Center for Education Statistics, Institute of Education Services.

U.S. Department of Education (2016a). *2013–2014 civil rights data collection: A first look.* Washington, DC: Office of Civil Rights.

U.S. Department of Education (2016b). *Indicators of school crime and safety.* Washington, DC: National Center for Education Statistics.

U.S. Department of Education & U.S. Department of Justice. (2014). *Guiding principles for providing high-quality education in juvenile justice secure care settings.* Washington, DC: Author.

U.S. Department of Health and Human Services. (2001). *Youth violence: A report of the surgeon general.* Washington, DC: U.S. Government Printing Office.

U.S. Department of Health and Human Services. (2012). *Home visiting evidence of effectiveness.* Washington, DC: Author.

U.S. Department of Health and Human Services. (2013a). *Child maltreatment 2012.* Washington, DC: U.S. Government Printing Office.

U.S. Department of Health and Human Services. (2013b). *How the child welfare system works.* Washington, DC: Administration for Children and Families, Children's Bureau.

U.S. Department of Health and Human Services. (2014a). *Child maltreatment 2013.* Washington, DC: U.S. Government Printing Office.

U.S. Department of Health and Human Services. (2014b). *Information on poverty and income statistics: A summary of current 2013 current population survey data.* Washington, DC: U.S. Government Printing Office.

U.S. Department of Justice. (2012). *Disproportionate minority contact technical assistance manual* (4th ed.). Washington, DC: Office of Juvenile Justice and Delinquency Prevention, Office of Justice Programs, U.S. Department of Justice.

U.S. Department of Justice. (2013). *Memorandum of understanding for FY 2013 school-based partnerships.* Washington, DC: Office of Community Oriented Policing Services.

U.S. Department of Justice (2014). *Changing lives: Prevention and intervention to reduce serious offending.* Washington, DC: Office of Juvenile Justice and Delinquency Prevention, Office of Justice Programs, U.S. Department of Justice.

U.S. Department of Labor, Children's Bureau. (1922). *Proceedings of the conference on juvenile-court standards* [Bureau Publication No. 97], Washington, DC: Author.

U.S. Government Accountability Office. (2007). *African American children in foster care: Additional HHS assistance needed to help states reduce the proportion in care.* Washington, DC: Author.

U.S. Surgeon General. (2001). *Report on the surgeon general's conference on children's mental health.* Washington, DC: U.S. Department of Health and Human Services.

Uggen, C. (2000). Work as a turning point in the life course of criminals: A duration model of age, employment, and recidivism. *American Sociological Review, 65,* 529–546.

Urban America Forward. (2016). *Urban America Forward: Civil rights roundtable series.* Chicago, IL: Center for the Study of Race, Politics, and Culture, University of Chicago.

Urban, W., & Wagoner, J.L. (2009). *American education: A history* (4th ed.). New York, NY: Routledge.

Vanderhaar, J.E., Petrosko, J.M., & Munoz, M. (2015). Reconsidering the alternatives: The relationship between suspension, disciplinary alternative school placement, subsequent juvenile detention, and the salience of race. In D.J. Losen (Ed.), *Closing the school discipline gap: Research for policymakers.* New York, NY: Teachers College Press.

Vaughn, M.G., & Howard, M.O. (2004). Adolescent substance abuse treatment: A synthesis of controlled evaluation. *Research on Social Work Practice, 14,* 325–335.

Vaughn, M.G., Wallace, J.M., Davis, L.E., Fernandes, G.T., & Howard, M.O. (2008). Variations in mental health problems, substance use, and delinquency between African American and Caucasian juvenile offenders: Implications for reentry services. *International Journal of Offender Therapy and Comparative Criminology*, 53, 311–329.

Verrecchia, P.J., Fetzer, M.D., Lemmon, J.H., & Austin, T.L. (2010). An examination of direct and indirect effects of maltreatment dimensions and other ecological risk on persistent youth offending. *Criminal Justice Review*, 35, 220–243.

Vincent, G.M. (2011). *Screening and assessment in juvenile justice settings: Identifying mental health needs and risk of reoffending.* Washington, DC: Technical Assistance Partnership for Child and Family Mental Health.

Vincent, G.M., Guy, L.S., & Grisso, T. (2012). *Risk assessment in juvenile justice: A guidebook for implementation.* Chicago, IL: Models for Change, Systems Reform in Juvenile Justice, MacArthur Foundation.

Vold, G. (1958). *Theoretical criminology.* New York, NY: Oxford University Press.

Vold, G.B., Bernard T.J., & Snipes, J.B. (1998). *Theoretical criminology* (4th ed.). New York, NY: Oxford University Press.

Wachter, A. (2015). *Mental health screening in juvenile justice services.* Pittsburgh, PA: Juvenile Justice Geography, Policy, Practice & Statistics; National Center for Juvenile Justice.

Wagner, D., & Bell, P. (1998). *The use of risk assessment to evaluate the impact of intensive protective service intervention I: A practice setting.* Madison, WI: National Council on Crime and Delinquency, Children's Research Center.

Wagner, M., Kutash, K., Duchnowski, A.J., Epstein, M.H., & Sumi, W.C. (2005). The children and youth we serve: A national picture of the characteristics of students with emotional disturbances receiving special education. *Journal of Emotional and Behavioral Disorders*, 13, 79–96.

Wagner, M., Newman, L., Cameto, R., Levine, P., & Garza, N. (2006). *An overview of findings from wave 2 of the National Longitudinal Transition Study–2 (NLTS2).* Menlo Park, CA: SRI International.

Wald, J.W. (2014). *Can "de-biasing" strategies help to reduce racial disparities in school discipline?* Cambridge, MA: Institute for Race & Justice, Harvard Law School.

Waldron, H.B., & Turner, C.W. (2008). Evidence-based psychosocial treatments for adolescent substance abuse. *Journal of Clinical Child and Adolescent Psychology*, 37, 238–261.

Walker, S., Spohn, C., & DeLone, M. (2012). *The color of justice: Race, ethnicity and crime in America* (6th ed.). Belmont, CA: Wadsworth.

Walkup, J., Albano, A.M., Piacentini, J., Birmaher, B., Compton, S., Sherrill, J., Ginsburg, G., Rynn, M., McCracken, J., Waslick, B., Iyengar, S., March, J., & Kendall, P. (2008). Cognitive behavioral therapy, sertraline, or a combination in childhood anxiety. *New England Journal of Medicine*, 359, 2753–2766.

Walsh, A. (1995). Genetic and cytogenetic intersex anomalies: Can they help us to understand gender differences in deviant behavior? *International Journal of Offender Therapy and Comparative Criminology*, 39, 151–166.

Wang, X., Blomberg, T.G., & Li, S.D. (2005). Comparison of the educational deficiencies of delinquent and nondelinquent students. *Evaluation Review: A Journal of Applied Social Research*, 29, 291–312.

Ward, G. (2012). *The black child-savers: Racial democracy and juvenile justice.* Chicago, IL: The University of Chicago Press.

Warr, M. (1996). Organization and instigation in delinquent groups. *Criminology*, 34, 11–37.

Warr, M. (2002). *Companions in crime: The social aspects of criminal conduct.* New York, NY: Cambridge University Press.

Washington State Institute for Public Policy. (2007). *Evidence-based juvenile offender programs: Program description, quality assurance, and cost.* Olympia, WA: Author.

Wasserman, G.A., Keenan, K., Tremblay, R.E., Cole, J.D., Herrenkohl, T.I., Loeber, R., & Petechuk, D. (2003). *Risk and protective factors of child delinquency.* Washington, DC: Office of Juvenile Justice and Delinquency Prevention, U.S. Department of Justice.

Wasserman, G.A., McReynolds, L.S., Ko, S., Katz, L., & Carpenter, J. (2005). Gender differences in psychiatric disorders at juvenile probation intake. *American Journal of Public Health*, 95, 131–137.

Welch, K., & Payne, A.A. (2010). Racial threat and punitive school discipline. *Social Problems*, 47, 25–48.

Welsh, B.C., Loeber, R., Stevens, B., Stouthamer-Loeber, M., Cohen, M.A., & Farrington, D.P. (2008). Costs of juvenile crime in urban areas: A longitudinal perspective. *Youth Violence and Juvenile Justice*, 6, 3–27.

Western New York Law Center. (2015). *Selected Supreme Court ADA/504 cases.* Buffalo, NY: Author.

What Works Clearinghouse. (2006a). *Connect with kids.* Washington, DC: Institute of Education Statistics, U.S. Department of Education.

What Works Clearinghouse. (2006b). *Too good for violence.* Washington, DC: Institute of Education Statistics, U.S. Department of Education.

White, N.A., & Loeber, R. (2008). Bullying and special education as predictors of serious delinquency. *Journal of Research in Crime and Delinquency*, 45, 380–397.

Widom, C.S. (1989). Child abuse, neglect, and violent criminal behavior. *Criminology*, 27, 251–271.

Widom, C.S., DuMont, K., & Czaja, S.J. (2007). A prospective investigation of major depressive disorder and comorbidity in abused and neglected children grown up. *Archives of General Psychiatry*, 64, 49–56.

Wiebush, R., Freitag, R., & Baird, C. (2001). *Preventing delinquency through improved child protection services.* Washington, DC: Office of Juvenile Justice and Delinquency Prevention, Office of Justice Programs, U.S. Department of Justice.

Wiggins, C., Fenichel, E., & Mann, T. (2007). *Developmental problems of maltreated children and early intervention options for maltreated children.* Washington, DC: U.S. Department of Health and Human Services, Child Protective Services Project.

Wiig, J., Spatz-Widom, C., & Tuell, J.A. (2003). *Understanding child maltreatment & delinquency: From research to effective program, practice, and systematic solutions.* Washington, DC: Child Welfare League of America.

Williams. N. (2018, January 28). Behind bars: Four teens in prison tell their stories. *LA Youth.* Retrieved from http://www.layouth.com/behind-bars-four-teens-in-prison-tell-their-stories/

Wilson, B.D., Cooper, K., Kastanis, A., & Nezhad, S. (2014). *Sexual and gender minority youth in foster care: Assessing disproportionality and disparities in Los Angeles.* Los Angeles, CA: The Williams Institute, UCLA School of Law.

Wilson, H.A., & Hoge, R.D. (2012). The effect of youth diversion programs on recidivism: A meta-analytic review. *Criminal Justice and Behavior*, 40, 497–518.

Wilson, S.J., & Lipsey, M.W. (2006a). *The effects of school-based social information processing interventions on aggressive behavior, Part I: Universal programs.* Oslo, Norway: Campbell Systematic Reviews, The Campbell Collaboration.

Wilson, S.J., & Lipsey, M.W. (2006b). *The effects of school-based social information processing interventions on aggressive behavior, Part II: Selected/indicated pull-out programs.* Oslo, Norway: Campbell Systematic Reviews, The Campbell Collaboration.

Wilson, S.J., Lipsey, M.W., & Derzon, J.H. (2003). The effects of school-based intervention programs on aggressive behavior: A meta-analysis. *Journal of Consulting and Clinical Psychology*, 71, 136–149.

Wilson, S.J., Tanner-Smith, E., Lipsey, M.W., Steinka-Fry, K., & Morrison, J. (2011). *Dropout prevention and intervention programs: Effects on school completion and dropout among school-aged children and youth.* Oslo, Norway: The Campbell Collaboration.

Wilson, W.J. (1987). *The truly disadvantaged: The inner city, the underclass, and public policy.* Chicago, IL: The University of Chicago Press.

Wilson, W.J. (1997). *When work disappears: The world of the new urban poor.* New York, NY: Vintage Books.

Winder, C., & Denious, J. (2013). *Statewide evaluation of juvenile diversion programming: Literature review.* Denver: Colorado Division of Criminal Justice.

Winokur, K.P., Smith, A., Bontrager, S.R., & Blankenship, J.L. (2008). Juvenile recidivism and length of stay. *Journal of Criminal Justice, 36,* 126–137.

Winters, K.C., Botzet, A.M., & Fahnhorst, T. (2011). Advances in adolescent substance abuse treatment. *Current Psychiatry Reports, 13,* 416–421.

Witkin, H.A., Goodenough, D.R., & Hirschorn, K. (1977). XYY men: Are they criminally aggressive? *Sciences, 17,* 10–13.

Wolff, N., Blitz, C., Shi, J., Siegel, J., & Bachman, R. (2007). Physical violence inside prisons: Rates of victimization. *Criminal Justice and Behavior, 34,* 588–599.

Wolfgang, M.E., & Ferracuti, F. (1967). *The subculture of violence: Toward an integrated theory in criminology.* London, England: Tavistock.

Wolfgang, M.E., Figlio, R.M., & Sellin, T. (1972). *Delinquency in a birth cohort.* Chicago, IL: The University of Chicago Press.

Wolfgang, M.E., Thornberry, T.P., & Figlio, R.M. (1987). *From boy to man, from delinquency to crime.* Chicago, IL: The University of Chicago Press.

Wulczyn, F., Webb, M., & Haskins, R. (Eds.). (2007). *Child protection: Using research to improve policy and practice.* Washington, DC: Brookings Institution Press.

Yoshikawa, H., Aber, J.L., & Beardslee, W. R. (2012). The effects of poverty on the mental. emotional, and behavioral health of children and youth: Implications for prevention. *American Psychologist, 67*(4): 272–284> PMID31883341.

Yun, I., Ball, J.D., & Lim, H. (2011). Disentangling the relationship between child maltreatment and violent delinquency: Using a nationally representative sample. *Journal of Interpersonal Violence, 26,* 88–110.

Zahn, M.A., Agnew, R., Fishbein, D., Miller, S., Winn, D., Dakoff, G., Kruttschnitt, C., Giordano, P., Gottfredson, D.C., Payne, A.A., Feld, B.C., & Chesney-Lind, M. (2010). *Girls study group: Causes and correlates of girls' delinquency.* Washington, DC: Office of Juvenile Justice and Delinquency Prevention, Office of Justice Programs, U.S. Department of Justice.

Zahn, M.A., Hawkins, S.R., Chiancone, J., & Whitworth, A. (2008). *The girls study group: Charting the way to delinquency prevention for girls.* Washington, DC: Office of Juvenile Justice and Delinquency Prevention, Office of Justice Programs, U.S. Department of Justice.

Zajac, K., Sheidow, A.J., & Davis. M. (2013). *Transition age youth with mental health challenges in the juvenile justice system.* Washington, DC: Technical Assistance Partnership for Child and Family Mental Health, Substance Abuse and Mental Health Services Administration, U.S. Department of Health and Human Services.

Zhang, L. (1997). Informal reactions and delinquency. *Criminal Justice and Behavior, 24,* 129–150.

Zimring, F. (1998). *American youth violence.* New York, NY: Oxford University Press.

Zimring, F. (2005). *American juvenile justice.* Oxford, England: Oxford University Press.

Zinzow, H.M., Ruggiero, K.J., Resnick, H., Hanson, R., Smith, D., Saunders, B., & Kilpatrick, D. (2009). Prevalence and mental health correlates of witnessed parental and community violence in a national sample of adolescents. *Journal of Child Psychology and Psychiatry, 50,* 441–450.

Zolotor, A., Kotch, J., Dufort, V., Winsor, J., Catellier, C., & Bou-Saada, I. (1999). School performance in a longitudinal cohort of children at risk of maltreatment. *Maternal and Child Health Journal, 3,* 19–27.

Zwi, K.J. (2007). School-based education programs for the prevention of child sexual abuse. *Cochrane Database for Systematic Reviews, 2,* 1–44.

INDEX

Note: Page numbers in *italics* refer to figures and tables.